THE
APPROACHING
STORM

ALSO BY NEIL LANCTOT

Campy: The Two Lives of Roy Campanella
Negro League Baseball
Fair Dealing and Clean Playing

THE
APPROACHING
STORM

ROOSEVELT, WILSON, ADDAMS,
AND THEIR CLASH OVER
AMERICA'S FUTURE

Neil Lanctot

RIVERHEAD BOOKS NEW YORK 2021

RIVERHEAD BOOKS
An imprint of Penguin Random House LLC
penguinrandomhouse.com

Library of Congress Cataloging-in-Publication Data
Names: Lanctot, Neil, 1966– author.
Title: The approaching storm : Roosevelt, Wilson,
Addams, and their clash
over America's future / Neil Lanctot.
Other titles: Roosevelt, Wilson, Addams,
and their clash over America's future
Description: New York : Riverhead Books, 2021. |
Includes bibliographical references and index. |
Identifiers: LCCN 2021025544 (print) |
LCCN 2021025545 (ebook) | ISBN 9780735210592
(hardcover) | ISBN 9780735210615 (ebook)
Subjects: LCSH: United States—Politics and
government—1913–1921. |
Wilson, Woodrow, 1856–1924. | Roosevelt,
Theodore, 1858–1919—Influence. | Addams, Jane,
1860–1935—Influence. | Progressivism (United States
politics) | World War, 1914–1918—United States. | United
States—Foreign relations—1913–1921. | Neutrality—United
States—History—20th century. | Peace movements—
United States—History—20th century. | Presidents—
United States—Election—1916.
Classification: LCC E780 .L36 2021 (print) |
LCC E780 (ebook) | DDC 973.91/30922—dc23
LC record available at https://lccn.loc.gov/2021025544
LC ebook record available at https://lccn.loc.gov/2021025545

Printed in the United States of America
1   3   5   7   9   10   8   6   4   2

Book design by Amanda Dewey

In memory of my mother,
Claire Lanctot

CONTENTS

THE
APPROACHING
STORM

THE ROUGH RIDER, THE REFORMER, AND THE SCHOLAR

ummer 1912 in Chicago. A national convention unlike America had ever witnessed. In just three August days, a new political party—the Progressive—began to take shape thanks to the ten thousand earnest, yet determined, men and women eager to transform the nation's political landscape.

The excitement at the Coliseum that week was inescapable, punctuated by lusty and heartfelt renditions of the old favorites "Onward Christian Soldiers" and "The Battle Hymn of the Republic." "This convention," remarked one correspondent, "has had the appearance of a great religious revival." Cynics like the Baltimore journalist H. L. Mencken later scoffed at such "quasi-religious monkey-shines," but the impassioned fervor of the true believers could not be denied. "The men in the press," noted one reporter, "looked on in amazement. They were not accustomed to anything like this . . . for the simple reason that nothing like this had happened within the memory of any political manager alive."

The new party was the logical culmination of the broad-based liberal reform movement—known by its followers as "progressivism"—that had swept the nation since the 1890s in response to the changes wrought in America by frightening new technologies, a rising tide of new immigrants, and the discomforting growth of superpowerful mega-corporations. A passionate desire for reform bound the great mass of progressive men and women together, but they did not always support the same causes. Housing standards, child labor, regulation of big business, the referendum, minimum wage, and maximum hours were just some of the many reforms under the broad progressive umbrella. And their message seemed to be resonating with much of the nation. "Four-fifths of the whole country is radically progressive," the Democratic leader William Jennings Bryan had insisted a few weeks earlier.

The excited delegates waited impatiently for the third and final day of the convention when the new party would officially nominate its first candidate, former president Theodore Roosevelt. That Wednesday afternoon, August 7, the convention chairman, Albert Beveridge, called upon "America's most eminent and beloved woman" to deliver one of the speeches seconding Colonel Roosevelt's nomination. No further introduction was necessary. When Jane Addams, the noted social worker, reformer, and occasional presidential adviser, stood up and made her way to the platform, a "gracious figure in white," the crowd erupted for ten minutes. "Not even the Colonel got much more rousing cheers," later wrote the journalist William Allen White.

As only the second woman ever to second a nomination, the fifty-one-year-old Addams made the most of her time on stage. Her speech, many an observer noted approvingly, was "brief . . . and to the point."

"I arise on behalf of Illinois to second the nomination of Colonel Roosevelt, stirred by that splendid platform upon which this party stands," she began. This unprecedented platform called for "real industrial reforms" to address the previously neglected rights of children, women, and workers. "In the United States we are unaccountably slow in reducing a movement to political action," she continued. "But we have here crystallized into a political cause the aims and hopes of all who have seen the suffering of the masses and know something of their needs." Roosevelt, she explained, was "one of the few men in our public life who has been responsive to the social appeal and who has caught the significance of the modern movement. Because of that, because the program will require a leader of invincible courage, of open mind, of democratic sympathies, one endowed with power to interpret the common man and to identify himself with the common lot, I heartily second the nomination."

No sooner had she finished than a female conventioneer pressed a yellow

"Votes for Women" banner into her hands. Addams soon found herself in the midst of a makeshift demonstration for woman's suffrage, a cause long near and dear to her but only recently embraced by Roosevelt and the new party's platform. "I was so excited," one suffragist enthused, "that I wanted to jump over the railing of the balcony and join in the procession. . . . It was grand. It marks the beginning of the end of our fight for suffrage."

The man of the hour, of course, was Roosevelt. Now fifty-three and out of the White House for three years, the man they called "TR" was taking the political risk of his life. Dissatisfied with the policies of his handpicked Republican successor, William Howard Taft, he had attempted to secure the nomination for himself in 1912 and won nine of the primaries in the twelve states that had adopted the new process, but found his candidacy effectively blocked by reactionary party regulars at the convention. In the six weeks that followed the Republican gathering, Roosevelt and his followers had laid the groundwork for a new organization, informally known as the "Bull Moose" party, after a typically colorful comment by TR that he was feeling "fine! Just like a bull moose!"

The Roosevelt seconded by Addams that afternoon was not the same man nominated and elected by the Republicans in 1904. As president, he was unmistakably sympathetic to, but not a fanatical disciple of, progressivism. After leaving office, he had watched the reform impulse continue to escalate while his own political fortunes drifted. That he began to shift further to the left was not surprising. Roosevelt, one reformer noted approvingly after a visit earlier that year, was now "just as radical as we want him." (TR considered himself a "sane radical.") And the new party's platform was a testament to the "new" Roosevelt. "A minimum wage, old-age pensions, child labor, equal suffrage, protection of women in the industries, and all the other things that I have devoted my life to working for and urging will be in the platform of this new party," Addams excitedly told a reporter, although she was well aware of TR's shortcomings. The refusal of the party to seat black delegates from the South profoundly disturbed her, as did a platform plank calling for the construction of two battleships a year. "There are many of the Roosevelt views with which I do not agree," she admitted. "I overlook these things because of the program of social work subscribed to by this Convention."

With the formalities completed and his nomination secured, Roosevelt appeared before the convention for a brief acceptance speech. He had delivered a longer address the day before (dubbed his "Confession of Faith") that had electrified the convention, although more conservative observers, such as a *New York Times* reporter, believed it reeked of "frankly Socialistic doctrine." The frenzied crowd, exhausted from three days of cheers, songs, frantic waving of bandannas, and constant shouting of the Bull Moose call—"Moo-oo, Moo-oo"—waited for TR to speak.

"Of course, I accept," he said. "I have been president and I have seen much of life. . . . I count this the greatest honor of my life, to be called to lead this movement in the interest of all the American people."

Eight hundred miles away, at Sea Girt, New Jersey, another recent convert to progressivism was also accepting the nomination of his party that afternoon. New Jersey governor Woodrow Wilson, a former academic and onetime president of Princeton University, had captured the Democratic nomination in July after a bruising fight on the Baltimore convention floor requiring forty-six ballots. Like Roosevelt, the fifty-five-year-old Wilson had been swept up in the recent tidal wave of reform, shedding his more conventional attitudes over the past five years.

"I am *not* conservative," he insisted to a friend in 1911, "I am a radical." Wilson had compiled an impressive reform record in his eighteen months at the helm of the Garden State, shepherding through a legislative program calling for the regulation of utilities, state primaries, workman's compensation, and a crackdown on dirty politics through the passage of a Corrupt Practices Act.

The Sea Girt event was a bit of staged pageantry where Democratic honchos made a pilgrimage to the "Little White House," the traditional summer home of New Jersey governors, to formally tender the nomination to Wilson. The normally sleepy shore community was overrun by six thousand curiosity seekers who viewed the ceremony as an excuse for a summer excursion. Some arrived, one reporter wrote, "in farm wagons, with big tin horns and luncheon baskets," while the more affluent types pulled up in the automobiles that were now a common part of the American landscape. Vendors made a killing that afternoon, hawking popcorn, peanuts, sandwiches, balloons, pink lemonade, and Wilson badges.

Wilson was out of his comfort zone that day. The Democrats insisted that after accepting the nomination, he must read or recite from memory a prepared address from the veranda, which was torture for a skilled stump speaker who preferred to speak extemporaneously or from notes. "Oh, I wish I didn't have to read this," he quipped to the crowd, "it would be so much more interesting if I didn't have to." Nevertheless, he plowed through his message in about an hour, only occasionally abandoning the script for a quick aside. Americans, he told the audience, "have come to a critical turning point in their moral and political development." It was now *a new age*. The tonic of such a time is very exhilarating. It requires self-restraint not to attempt too much, and yet it would be cowardly to attempt too little." To the delight of the crowd, he spoke of a nation where monopolies could be stopped, workers protected, and currency reformed. "There is no indispensable man," he insisted. "The Government will not collapse and go to pieces if any one of the gentlemen who are seeking to be entrusted with its guidance should be left at home." The subtle jab at TR was not lost on the audience. "Third term!" yelled a wag or two.

In the span of a few hours, three giants of the age—Jane Addams, Theodore Roosevelt, and Woodrow Wilson—had placed themselves squarely in the forefront of a movement that seemed likely to permanently change the direction of America regardless of the result in November. Progressivism was in, they believed, and reform was here to stay.

Born within four years of one another before the outbreak of the Civil War, they had come of age at a time that now seemed impossibly quaint and backward in the new era of the early twentieth century. Over the prior four decades, each had gradually shed much of the parochialism and conservatism surrounding them in youth to embrace a new understanding of America's responsibilities toward its citizens and other nations.

Addams grew up solidly Midwestern, the daughter of John Huy Addams, a prosperous northern Illinois banker and miller who also served in the state legislature, knew Abraham Lincoln (who called him "double-d'd Addams"), and opposed slavery. Her mother died when she was two, and John Addams remarried several years later, to Anna Haldeman. Jane

Addams would trace her own interest in social justice to an early childhood exposure to poverty, when she accompanied her father to a business appointment in a downtrodden community and was puzzled its inhabitants lived "in such horrid little houses so close together." A quiet bookish girl who suffered from "curved spine" from spinal tuberculosis and considered herself "ugly," Addams found that her opportunities were severely restricted by the predominant Victorian view that women belonged in the home and should not bother themselves with silliness such as voting or pursuing a profession. Still, her father had always encouraged her intellectual pursuits, paying her five or ten cents as a young girl when she was able to summarize wordy tomes such as Washington Irving's *Life of George Washington* or Plutarch's *Lives*. Eventually, she passed the admissions test to one of the new women's colleges, Smith, only to be told by her father that he preferred that she attend Rockford Seminary, a single-sex institution closer to home, then known as the "Mount Holyoke of the West."

It was at Rockford where Addams began to fully understand and push against the limitations society imposed upon her as a woman. She and another student prodded the administration to allow them to complete the requirements for a bachelor's degree, rather than the certificate normally offered, and were among the first to earn a B.A. when Rockford finally became a college. As a senior, soon to be named valedictorian, she was even allowed to compete against college men as Rockford's representative in an interstate oratorical contest, finishing fifth in a field of nine (one of her opponents that day was William Jennings Bryan, also destined for bigger and better things).

Her mere pursuit of higher education set her apart from the vast majority of the American women of her time, as did her acceptance into the Woman's Medical College of Philadelphia in 1881. But within a year recurring spinal problems and emotional strain following the death of her father forced her to withdraw. Medical treatment and a long recuperative European jaunt followed, although her future path remained frustratingly unclear. "I was absolutely at sea so far as any moral purpose was concerned," she later wrote, "clinging only to the desire to live in a really living world and refusing to be content with a shadowy intellectual or aesthetic reflection of it." She knew only that she wanted something beyond the traditional roles for women. It was not until a second trip to Europe and a visit to Toynbee Hall in the East End of London that she realized her calling. At Toynbee, she witnessed the beginnings of what would soon be known as the settlement house movement, where dedicated men and women lived among the urban poor while providing much needed social services.

In 1889, Addams and a friend, Ellen Gates Starr, opened the second settlement house in America, Hull-House, on South Halsted Street in Chicago. Most family and friends had already advised her against undertaking such a ridiculous proposition. Within a year, the once decrepit mansion was bustling with a variety of activities, including a kindergarten, library, cooking classes, and discussion groups, all designed to brighten and enrich the bleak lives of the neighborhood residents, many of them recent immigrants. And with every day, Addams's eyes opened to the realities of the urban poor, the "little Italian bride of fifteen" beaten by her husband, the baby born with a cleft palate who died of neglect, the tuberculosis-ridden youth "treated" with whiskey by well-meaning friends.

The success of Hull-House soon drew donations and scores of idealistic followers willing to volunteer their services. "They were not to live in sordid tenements," explained Addams's friend Dr. Alice Hamilton, who would spend more than twenty years there, "but they were to suffer with the rest from the squalor and discomforts of the slums so far as outer things were concerned, and in the knowledge they acquired they would be better equipped to fight against these evils."

Fighting against urban "evils" in Chicago increasingly became part of Addams's mission. During the 1890s, she and other Hull-House workers pushed local officials to tackle growing municipal problems in the Windy City ranging from trash pickup to cocaine marketed to young boys as "happy dust." And larger issues such as imperialism, woman's suffrage, and the relationship between capital and labor began to attract her attention. Some socialists even believed she was one of them but was "too much of a coward to say so" (actually, she was sympathetic but believed the party "went further than I was wanting to go," preferring to work within the system). Slowly, she began to formulate a unique philosophy based on her experiences, given full expression in her 1902 work *Democracy and Social Ethics*, where she argued that a wider range of human interactions would lead to a more fully realized democracy. "We are learning that a standard of social ethics is not attained by traveling a sequestered byway," she wrote, "but by mixing on the thronged and common road where all must turn out for one another, and at least see the size of one another's burdens."

Although the book sold well, few readers paid much attention to the dedication to one "M.R.S." By the time the book appeared, Mary Rozet Smith had occupied a unique place in the life of Jane Addams for several years. She came from privilege, the child of a wealthy Chicago manufacturer, but like Addams wanted more than what a conventional 1890s lifestyle could offer an intelligent young woman. Soon after Hull-House opened, Smith began to volunteer, donated money while encouraging her father to do the same, and ultimately developed a close personal friendship with Addams that evolved into a full-blown partnership. They often traveled together, Smith's stately home on 12 West Walton Place provided a convenient getaway from the hassles of Hull-House, and the content of Addams's surviving letters to Smith reveals the depth of their commitment with references to "Dearest" and "how I long for you all the time." Such language does not in itself confirm that their relationship was sexual, as women of their generation and upbringing often wrote lovey-dovey letters to their friends sprinkled with similar Victorian sentimentality. But it is clear that Smith was the most significant and beloved figure in Addams's personal life, and her "career," as Addams's nephew James Weber Linn later noted, was "primarily concerned in making life easier for Jane Addams."

Addams's life grew more complicated by the early 1900s. Ongoing coverage of Hull-House, her involvement with the burgeoning reform movement, her lectures, and her writings made her into a national if not world celebrity. When Ethel Snowden, an English suffragist, prepared to set sail for the United States in 1908, the radical MP and labor leader John Burns encouraged her to be sure to "see the greatest man in America" while abroad. Theodore Roosevelt? she asked. "I mean Jane Addams. . . . The greatest man in America is a woman." That same year, the *Ladies' Home Journal* ranked her as "the foremost living woman in America today . . . having accomplished most for womankind, and, for that matter, for humankind." But it was not until the publication of *Twenty Years at Hull-House* in 1910 that her permanent legacy was cemented. The autobiography became an immediate classic, sold thousands of copies, and further broadened her already sizable influence, an influence that Roosevelt and the new Progressive party were eager to cultivate.

Like Addams's early years, Roosevelt's reflected a more comfortable upbringing than the average American of the mid-nineteenth century. Anyone who was anyone in Manhattan respected and admired the well-to-do and influential Roosevelts, especially TR's father, Theodore Sr. ("Thee"), long active in local business and society circles. Thee, like John Huy Addams, knew Lincoln and supported the Union cause during the Civil War, although his Southern-born wife, Martha "Mittie" Bulloch, held an unbroken loyalty to Dixieland.

Two forces profoundly shaped young Theodore's early years: his health and his father. Like Addams, Roosevelt struggled with a chronic health condition—asthma in his case—throughout childhood. After years of delicate living, trips to recuperative spas, and various odd treatments, he resolved at age fourteen to shed his old "weakling" self by aggressive exercise and pursuing what he later famously dubbed the "strenuous life." Contrary to his own exaggerated claims, his asthma never fully disappeared, but he successfully mastered and overcame an invalid existence that seemed likely to determine his fate. For the rest of his life, he remained obsessed with physical prowess, risk taking, and "manliness," while disdaining "mollycoddles" who preferred more sedate lifestyles.

Most of all, he aspired to measure up to his father, "the best man I ever knew." Thee, TR later wrote, "combined strength and courage with gentleness, tenderness, and great unselfishness." He was also a gentleman reformer, strongly imbued with the notion of "muscular Christianity," and interested in causes ranging from the suppression of vice to civil service hiring practices. His only flaw, at least in TR's eyes, was his decision, influenced by his Southern wife, to hire substitutes rather than serve in the Union Army during the Civil War. It was a choice that haunted Thee and made his son all the more determined to fight if and when his time came.

The "strenuous life" TR pursued coexisted with a true passion for learning. From an early age, natural history especially fascinated him, so much so that he even considered pursuing it as a career before deciding on law after graduating from Harvard in 1880. But the law, he soon discovered, bored him. He was far more interested in completing his first book, *The Naval War of 1812*, and dipping his toe into the Republican political waters. At twenty-three, he was elected to the New York State Assembly, where he found himself exposed to the rough-and-tumble world of urban politics and problems for the first time. Though TR was still fundamentally an upper-crust elite, the fact-finding trips he took to crowded inner-city tenements slowly raised his consciousness.

Both triumph and tragedy marked the next fifteen years. Professionally, he continued to climb the Republican political ladder while broadening his name recognition from the confines of the Empire State. Six years on the federal Civil Service Commission, followed by a stint as president of the Police Commission in New York earned him plaudits for his increasingly aggressive and energetic approach to reform and snuffing out corruption. His literary reputation also blossomed, culminating with the publication of his popular four-volume *The Winning of the West*. And frequent trips to the Dakota Badlands for hunting and ranch investments further enlarged his once narrow elitist worldview.

But Roosevelt was also devastated by the near simultaneous deaths—just hours apart—of his mother and young wife in 1884, days after giving birth to daughter Alice. Two years later, he married his childhood friend Edith Carow. A son, Theodore III, was born in 1887, followed by four more children (Kermit, Ethel, Archie, Quentin), all of whom grew up at Sagamore Hill, the recently built Roosevelt estate in Oyster Bay, Long Island.

Long an advocate of American sea power and expansionism, TR was delighted to be named assistant secretary of the navy in 1897 as part of the new McKinley administration. When a crisis with Spain flared over its brutal handling of a colonial revolt in Cuba, Roosevelt believed war with Spain was inevitable and did his best to prepare the U.S. fleet. Two months after a mysterious explosion in the Havana harbor sank the battleship *Maine*, which had been sent to safeguard American interests in Cuba, Congress voted to declare war on Spain. For TR, there was no thought of remaining stateside. "I had always felt," he later explained, "that if there were a serious war I wished to be in a position to explain to my children why I did take part in it, and not why I did not take part in it."

His brief combat stint in Cuba as part of First U.S. Volunteer Cavalry, or "Rough Riders," that summer of 1898 made him a legend. Millions thrilled to the dramatic accounts of how TR courageously (some said foolishly) led his troops up Kettle Hill (not San Juan Hill, as was so often written at the time) while under fire during the Battle of San Juan Hill (his critics would claim that the real heroes were African American regular troops who made the charge possible). "Roosevelt, mounted high on horseback, and charging the rifle-pits at a gallop and quite alone," wrote his war correspondent friend Richard Harding Davis, "made you feel that you would like to cheer." The "splendid little war," as John Hay, the American ambassador to Britain, labeled it in a letter to TR, was soon over with Spain crushed, Cuba liberated, and the United States now a colonial power in control of Puerto Rico, the Philippines, and Guam, much to the chagrin of Addams and other anti-imperialists. As for Roosevelt, now a colonel, he returned home that August a hero, soon to be elected governor of New York and then vice president as William McKinley's running mate two years later.

More reactionary elements within the Republican party were glad to see him placed on the shelf for the next four years where he could do no damage. But the assassination of McKinley in September 1901 put TR in the White House at the age of forty-two, the youngest man ever to serve as president.

It was soon obvious that TR was a very different kind of leader, one who believed strongly in a far more active role for the federal government. The Roosevelt "Square Deal" called for an aggressive approach to domestic issues, seen in greater attempts to regulate railroads and big business, mediate labor disputes, protect consumers, and preserve America's natural resources through a program of conservation. In foreign affairs, TR stressed greater international involvement to promote American interests and ensure lasting peace by following his infamous maxim to "speak softly and carry a big stick." He did not hesitate to utilize the big stick—namely, the specter of American sea power—to answer the German blockade of Venezuela; to support the Panamanian revolution against Colombia, which would also allow for the construction of a U.S.-built-and-controlled canal; and to demonstrate the nation's position as a major player on the world stage. But he was just as willing to use diplomacy in helping to end the Russo-Japanese War, a role that won him world praise and the Nobel Peace Prize.

To the American public, TR was not just a politician, but a genuine celebrity whose familiar pince-nez, mustache, and toothy grin were inescapable. For the press, he was a dream subject: a president who not only loved the spotlight but was truly *interesting*. What other commander in chief had ever demonstrated wrestling holds in the White House, advocated a new system of "simplified spelling," or pontificated long and loud about the need for large families? And Roosevelt, unlike nearly every man who has held the office, actually *liked* being president, although after his election in 1904 he announced he would not seek another term, a decision he would come to regret.

In his last years in office, TR's interest in progressive reform continued to grow, much to the discomfort of conservatives and the big business elite. "The very rich people," he wrote to his son Kermit in 1906, "seem to be in a mood to look at me as an anarchist." He assumed that his successor and friend, William Howard Taft, would pursue the same liberal policies after his election in 1908, only to be disillusioned to discover the new president was less a disciple than he realized. Throwing off all restraints, TR now embraced progressivism with a fervor, enthusiastically advocating currency reform, inheritance taxes, a graduated income tax, workman's compensation, and the direct primary, among other reform goodies in his "New Nationalism" speech of August 1910. The battle was now on for the soul of the GOP, culminating in a split at the 1912 Republican convention and TR's jump to the Progressive party.

Unlike Roosevelt and Addams, Thomas Woodrow Wilson spent his entire childhood in the South, first in Virginia and later in Georgia and South Carolina. The region's influence was most apparent later in his less than progressive attitudes toward African Americans and occasionally old-fashioned views toward women. But he would never be completely defined by his Dixieland upbringing. His parents, after all, were both non-Southerners; his father, Joseph Ruggles Wilson, was an Ohio-born Presbyterian minister, and his mother, Janet ("Jessie") Woodrow, was born in England before immigrating to America at age five. Although old enough to remember the Civil War and the slaves provided to his family by the church, Wilson was not obsessed by the "Lost Cause" and would later intentionally shed his Southern accent.

As a child, young Tommy Wilson did not devour books as easily as Roosevelt and Addams; in fact, his reading difficulties throughout his life have led some to speculate whether he may have been dyslexic. Still, he learned the power of language from his father, the "best teacher I ever had," who would require his son to write an account of a recent outing together, read it to him verbatim and then in his "own words," and finally rewrite it based on the more concise conversational version. Such training promised to be invaluable in crafting sermons had he chosen the ministerial path of his father, uncle, and maternal grandfather, a profession that had allowed Tommy and his family to live comfortably. But he was ultimately more attracted to a life of the mind, though his Presbyterian faith remained rock solid.

At sixteen, he entered Davidson College in North Carolina, lasting only a year before returning home to Wilmington, North Carolina, where his father had recently taken a new job. After the false start at Davidson and a year of additional preparation, he entered Princeton, still known as the College of New Jersey, in 1875. The minister's son, while lacking the wealth and social stature of more than a few of his classmates, began to flourish in these novel northern environs. "Father, I have made a discovery," he wrote. "I have found that I have a mind." And politics and government increasingly fascinated him, so much so that he began to dream of a career in public service, one that would allow him to also pursue his passion for writing. But politics, he understood, was a rich man's game, and he lacked the resources of Roosevelt to immediately plunge into the arena. Instead, Wilson decided a career in law would have to suffice, with the hope that it might lead him into elected office later.

At the University of Virginia law school, Wilson soon arrived at the same conclusion that TR was simultaneously reaching roughly four hundred miles to the north at Columbia: that the study of law was deadly dull for

ambitious men far more interested in doing bigger things from a political
and literary standpoint. His stint at Virginia was marked mostly by his
decision to discard "Tommy" in favor of his middle name, Woodrow, and
by an unhappy love affair with his cousin Hattie Woodrow, who rejected
his marriage proposal. Eventually, he passed the Georgia bar exam and
practiced law in Atlanta without much distinction or success.

Like Addams, Wilson was experiencing an existential crisis by 1883.
The legal career that he hoped would be a springboard to political success
had proved unfulfilling. Academia, he finally decided, would be a more
prudent career path, although the life of a college professor would seemingly squelch his political aspirations for good. That fall, he entered Johns
Hopkins to pursue a Ph.D. in history and political science, emotionally
bolstered by his recent engagement to Ellen Louise Axson, an intelligent
and artistic young woman from Rome, Georgia, also the child of a Presbyterian minister. Graduate study did not always suit him; he had little use
for most of his professors, and the heavy reading load was torture for him.
"I have no patience for the tedious toil of what is known as 'research'"
Wilson complained. "I have a passion for interpreting great thoughts to the
world." Not surprisingly, he left Johns Hopkins without completing his
doctoral requirements to take a teaching job at a new woman's college, Bryn
Mawr, in 1885, although he eventually earned the Ph.D. and his disserta-
tion, *Congressional Government*, was good enough to be published to critical
acclaim by Houghton Mifflin that year. For the next five years, he taught
at Bryn Mawr and then Wesleyan, always with a vague disenchantment
about the caliber of his students, male and female. Ellen, meanwhile, gave
birth to three daughters: Margaret in 1886, Jessie in 1887, and Eleanor
("Nell") in 1889.

He wanted to be at Princeton, and in 1890 an offer finally came through.
Over the next twelve years, Wilson became an academic superstar as a
prolific scholar, exceptionally popular lecturer, and public intellectual
whose writings graced the same pages, sometimes the same issues, as Addams and TR in *The Atlantic Monthly* and *The Forum*. His reputation had
grown such that magazines and publishers willingly forked over large sums
for him to produce a biography of George Washington and a five-volume

History of the American People. But the "old longing for public life" never dissipated.

Politics would have to wait. Dissatisfaction with the slow pace of change at Princeton under the current regime led to Reverend Francis Patton's stepping down as president and Wilson's selection as replacement in 1902. George Harvey, the conservative Democratic owner and editor of *Harper's Weekly*, made a mental note as he watched Wilson's inaugural address at Princeton that October. This forty-five-year-old academic, Harvey believed, might be presidential timber someday. For now, Wilson busied himself with bringing Princeton into the twentieth century with expansion of the faculty and curriculum. But his ambitions ultimately grew larger: first, to replace the snobby "eating clubs" with the "Quad plan," where groups of undergraduates would live together; and then to oversee the construction of a new graduate school in a central location on campus. Not only did both initiatives fail, due to his own rigidity and neglect of the preliminary groundwork, but they also destroyed his friendship with his closest male companion, Jack Hibben, who ultimately succeeded Wilson as Princeton president. His Princeton struggles haunted him the rest of his life, even in dreams.

His private life also suffered while at Princeton. The tragic deaths of his wife's brother, sister-in-law, and nephew in an April 1905 accident threw Ellen into a deep depression, one that never quite lifted. A little over a year later, Wilson faced his own calamity: left-sided blindness, the result of arteriosclerosis. Already afflicted with ongoing stomach issues and various other maladies, he was initially told that he would need to minimize all activity permanently, but ultimately rest, a lighter workload, and travel were prescribed, allowing for some subsequent improvement in vision. As part of his recuperation, he journeyed alone to Bermuda in early 1907, where he met a forty-four-year-old American, Mary Hulbert Peck, whose second marriage was in a shambles and would eventually end in divorce. Almost immediately, he was smitten by her vivaciousness, keen intellect, and fondness for poetry. "It is not often that I can have the privilege of meeting anyone whom I can so entirely admire and enjoy," he wrote her. In the years that followed, he exchanged dozens of letters with Peck, who seemed to fill the void vacated by Hibben and Ellen, at least in her current troubled state. Whether their relationship became sexual remains uncertain, but the extremely personal tone of their letters suggests at least an "emotional affair" in today's parlance.

For someone as ambitious as Wilson, the presidency of Princeton would never be enough. As early as 1908, he admitted to Peck that he was "bored." Meanwhile, George Harvey had continued to trumpet the Princeton president as a political possibility, one who would champion the ideals of the sane and safe wing of the Democratic party, although Wilson had begun to move in a different direction. Whether inspired by the struggle over the wealth and prestige of the eating clubs or simply grasping that reform was in the air, a "new" Wilson now began to emerge, fully sympathetic to progressive causes (with the exception of suffrage and racial issues). Harvey, meanwhile, went to work on the New Jersey Democratic political bosses, who finally agreed to Wilson's nomination for governor in 1910 with the belief that he would be a pliable puppet once in office. But Wilson surprised everyone. He not only won the election handily but also defied the Democratic machine by governing the Garden State as a genuine reformer.

That a scholar with less than two years of elected office under his belt would gain the Democratic nomination for president could have happened only in 1912, when the progressive wave was almost uncontrollable in both parties. But some remained dubious. Until recently, Wilson was opposed to the initiative and referendum, showed ambivalence toward industrial regulation, and assessed the powerful agrarian party leader William Jennings Bryan as little more than a dunce. And his name recognition beyond the East Coast was also suspect, at least when compared with the sitting president, Taft, and Roosevelt. But the "schoolmaster," as his detractors labeled him, would prove to be far more skilled as a politician and campaigner than anyone had reason to anticipate.

The 1912 campaign was not the first time that Wilson, Roosevelt, and Addams crossed paths. In the past sixteen years, they had exchanged letters, expressed admiration for one another's work, and at times seemed destined to become close friends.

TR and Wilson had first met in 1896, at a mutual speaking engagement in Baltimore. Despite very different backgrounds and beliefs about "manliness" (Wilson is said to have fired a pistol just once in his life), the two hit it off almost immediately. Roosevelt, Wilson realized, was much more than the militaristic, war-obsessed caricature seen by the public and actually had "a very sane, academic side" that appealed strongly to his professorial sensibilities. TR, meanwhile, deemed Wilson a "perfect trump," delighted in his election as Princeton's president, and invited him for a White House stay in 1903, although Wilson declined because of his father's recent death. While a lifelong Democrat, Wilson found himself succumbing to the lure of TR and his Square Deal. "I believed in Roosevelt," he later told a reporter. "I followed him with enthusiasm. He is the kind of a fellow that arouses your feeling, makes your heart beat, and you feel like getting out and whooping it up for him, and feel enthusiastically enlisted in his cause, and that was the way I felt."

The honeymoon did not last long. As Wilson's political views began to evolve, his attitudes toward TR cooled. In a 1907 *New York Times* article, he not only scoffed at Roosevelt's idea that government intervention could restrain the growing power of the "trusts" but also took a potshot at the President himself. "I have not seen much of Mr. Roosevelt since he became President," he told a reporter, "but I am told that he no sooner thinks than he talks, which is a miracle not wholly in accord with an educational theory of forming an opinion." Privately, he labeled TR "the most dangerous man in public life—all the more dangerous because he was sincere and believed in himself."

Wilson's statements did not go unnoticed by TR. Politically, they no longer shared common ground, even after Wilson moved decisively into the progressive camp. Dr. Wilson, Roosevelt increasingly believed, was an insincere reformer, a hypocrite who until recently had "advocated . . . the outworn doctrines which are responsible for four-fifths of the political troubles of the United States," only to do "an absolute somersault so far as at least half of these doctrines was concerned" when he became governor. That Wilson might block TR's return to the White House intensified his growing feeling against his onetime fond acquaintance, though a grudging respect between the two lingered. TR could not help but admit that Wilson was "able," while

Wilson disclosed to his lady confidant Mary Hulbert Peck that a matchup against TR in 1912 "would make the campaign worthwhile."

But the split was irrevocable, and the bad blood between them would only worsen in the years ahead, especially on Roosevelt's end. Bainbridge Colby, a former Roosevelt man who later switched loyalties to Wilson, believed TR's hostility was driven more by jealousy than ideology. Wilson, Colby argued, was not only a superior speaker and writer but a true scholar—unlike TR, who, while exceptionally well read, was ultimately "still an amateur." For Wilson, TR and his "egotistical" ways were intolerable. "His egotism makes it impossible for his judgment to be safe on anything else," Wilson told a reporter. "His judgment is so warped about the status he occupies in the equation, that it renders him impossible to form any decision of judgment that is reasonable." But as much as they cattily dismissed each other, Roosevelt and Wilson remained permanently linked in both the public's mind and their own private thoughts.

Roosevelt had known Addams for years and long respected her work at Hull-House. They had grown closer during his presidency, when Addams and her reform cadre discovered that TR was actually receptive to the advice of experts such as Addams on labor and immigration issues. At times, she and her fellow social workers grew somewhat embarrassed by their frequent trips to the White House and sheepishly "explained that we came so often because he was the first president who had really known that there was a social question and that we had to make hay while the sun shone."

"There can't be too much hay to suit me," TR boomed. "We'll make all we can."

And he especially appreciated Addams's practical and sensible nature when she came calling, so much so that he planned to give her a cabinet position if a Roosevelt third term materialized. "I have such awful times with reformers of the sensational stamp," he wrote her in 1906, "and yet I so thoroughly believe in reform that I fairly revel in dealing with anyone like you."

But there were limits to his tolerance. Already, he could not abide her writings in support of the pacifist movement and rejection of militarism. When one of her associates came to Washington late in his second administration to discuss immigration, he launched into a tirade. "Jane Addams—don't talk to me about Jane Addams! I have always thought a lot of her, but she has just written a bad book, a very bad book! She is all wrong about peace." After a lecture of several minutes explaining the various fallacies of her reasoning, TR finally calmed down. "But she is a fine woman in every other way. Now that I've got that out of my system, she sent you here, did she? What can I do for you?"

Addams found herself just as exasperated with Roosevelt, whose advocacy of large families showed little awareness of the reality of life for the urban poor. He also was slow to grasp the significance of woman's suffrage, although Addams and others finally converted him "into a zealous instead of a lukewarm adherent of the cause." But like so many others, she could not help but fall under his sway. "She had no illusions regarding T.R.," her nephew later wrote. "She knew him, liked him, and understood him."

Addams had yet to develop a relationship with Wilson, whose primary interests had until recently been academic. Understandably, she saw TR as a far safer horse to back in 1912, rather than an unknown commodity said to have "something of the old Southern chivalric attitude toward women." And Wilson's view that suffrage should be left to the states to decide gave her additional pause.

Ideological differences aside, there was much that bound them together. Even in the limited media landscape of the 1910s, they were all immediately recognizable as three archetypal figures: the Rough Rider, the Reformer, and the Scholar. Of course, everyone knew Roosevelt, whose distinctive image had been seen in thousands of photographs and political cartoons over the previous fifteen years. And Addams, with her "large sad eyes" and sensible schoolmarmish look, which belied her more radical tendencies, virtually dressed the part of the selfless, do-gooder, female saint. For Wilson, his pince-nez glasses, dignified bearing, and prominent lantern jaw screamed academic, although he was the least well-known of the three when the campaign began. "Well, he may be all right, but he ain't good-looking" was the common assessment when crowds got their first look at him.

Their intellects were remarkable. In an era when the mental capability of women was still questioned, Addams's breadth of knowledge on a variety of subjects was formidable. The journalist Ida Tarbell considered her "one of the best read women that I have ever known." But unlike most experts, Addams remained open-minded to other viewpoints. "Her mind had more 'floor space' in it than any other I have known," recalled the feminist author Charlotte Perkins Gilman. "She could set a subject down, unprejudiced, and walk all around it, allowing fairly for every one's point of view."

Although more dogmatic in his views, Roosevelt also enjoyed a prodigious capacity for learning on the hundreds of subjects that caught his fancy. Visitors to the White House were often shocked that TR could converse with them intelligently on even the most esoteric of topics. "He knew the species of Hannibal's elephants through the shape of their ears as shown on the Carthaginian coins of the period," his son Ted later recalled. "He could recite 'The Song of Roland' in the original French. He knew the latest laws adopted in the reorganization of the State government in Illinois. . . . It was never safe to contradict him on any statement, no matter how recent you might feel your information was." TR's mental gymnastics were aided by an almost freakish memory, one that allowed him to recall the names of people he had met once years earlier and the actual snapshot image of the pages of books he read. As a more narrow reader, Wilson could never compete with the parlor tricks of a human encyclopedia like TR. But his cognitive discipline, perhaps honed by years in the publish-or-perish world of academia, was almost otherworldly. To the California congressman William Kent, Wilson was "the most remarkable mental machine I had met. He had the capacity for doing almost anything through sheer mental power."

But they were not stereotypical eggheads without personality or passion. Those who expected "Saint Jane" to be a prim and proper goody two-shoes were often shocked to learn that she could be "full of fun," even willing to share humorous stories of her misguided opium experiments in college after reading Thomas De Quincey's famous addiction memoir, *Confessions of an English Opium Eater*. The same was true of Wilson, whose reputation as a cold unfeeling "thinking machine" who did not like people often preceded him. Around family and friends, he displayed a more outgoing side the public seldom saw. Wilson, the English journalist A. G. Gardiner wrote, "loves a little nonsense now and then, delights in limericks and droll stories, is fond of play and a good song." But the playful side of Wilson often struggled with an inherent rigidity to his behavior. Certain tasks were religiously performed at the same time each day. "One could set the clocks by his comings and goings," his brother-in-law Stockton Axson later observed. He was the "most thoroughly self-disciplined and self-controlled man he had ever known." Not surprisingly, many found the Wilson exterior difficult to penetrate. "I would as soon think of striking him in the face as to slap him on the back or put my arm around his shoulder," one supporter admitted.

While more outgoing than Wilson, Addams betrayed a similar distance at times. The journalist Arthur Gleason was profoundly disillusioned after meeting her in 1906. Addams, he wrote his mother, was "no Florence Nightingale, nor bread-feeding legendary nun," but a "sarcastic" and "cold" female power broker who relished her influence with "politicians" and "millionaires." To her niece Marcet Haldeman-Julius, she seemed "hard and cruel" to her as a child, not a "very auntly person," though their relationship blossomed in adulthood. Her nephew James Weber Linn detected a similar coolness: "Even her closest friends, even the nephews and nieces whom she watched over and 'mothered' . . . sometimes felt her love as a radiation rather than as a direct and individual beam," he wrote. "They adored her, but they felt her sometimes to be a little withdrawn." They also knew enough not to call her "Jane," instead choosing the safe "Sister" Jane "following the custom of the neighbors" or simply "J.A."

Roosevelt, of course, was "Teddy," a character whose irresistible joie de vivre and restless energy could not help but elicit the familiarity lacking with Addams and Wilson. "I never saw him when he did not give me the impression that he was in danger of bursting his clothes with excitement," recalled Ida Tarbell. Such unrestrained behavior was not Wilson's way. "Life," Wilson once mused, "doesn't consist in eternally running to a fire." Nor could Wilson relate to TR's incessant need to dominate the room or pontificate in "a voice that underscores everything but the periods."

In their personal relationships, they all exhibited a certain need for validation. Roosevelt was always convinced he was right ("the undisputed Chief of the Kingdom of Righteousness," *The New Republic* once quipped) and was never shy about "smashing" in vitriolic language those who disagreed with him. "When I am in the midst of a fight I feel like climbing up a man's chest," he once observed. Wilson could be just as intolerant with those who did not share his views and had no patience for those he considered intellectually lacking or who wasted his time with extraneous talk. And both men, when crossed, were known to develop into world-class "haters," capable of holding an intense grudge for years. For Addams, there was a strong longing to be in sync with the public and to enjoy its support. "She was very dependent on a sense of warm comradeship and harmony with the mass of her fellow men," her close friend Alice Hamilton recalled. But when the public turned on her, as it eventually did, it would ultimately bring her "great unhappiness."

During the 1912 campaign, thousands flocked to hear Addams, Wilson, and Roosevelt offer their unique perspectives on what direction modern America should take in the exciting new world of the twentieth century. The outcome of the election was never really in doubt; a divided Republican party ensured that Wilson would win easily. TR could take grim pleasure that he and his hastily established third party outpolled Taft and the regular Republican "burglars" he believed had stolen the nomination from him. Perhaps most impressive, 75 percent of the votes were cast for candidates espousing progressive views: Wilson, Roosevelt, and the socialist Eugene Debs. And the campaign, Addams wrote to TR shortly after the election, had accomplished a great deal by simply publicizing the "social reform measures in which I have been interested for many years, but which have never before become so possible of fulfillment at the present moment. I had never dared hope that within my life-time thousands of people would so eagerly participate in their discussion." The real winner, she sensed, was progressivism, and reformers confidently expected more gains in their social justice agenda in the future.

Wilson, who considered himself a "Progressive with the brakes on," did not always move aggressively enough on social reform legislation in his first eighteen months in office. Still, he had successfully tackled currency reform (Federal Reserve Act) and had turned his attention by the summer of 1914 to consumer protection (a Federal Trade Commission bill) and antitrust measures (Clayton Act), both of which became law in the fall. Addams, meanwhile, continued her active involvement in the suffrage movement during 1913 and 1914 while speaking out in support of nearly every liberal cause of the day, including overly aggressive policing, a minimum wage for women, immigration, "mentally deficient children," and the Leo Frank murder case. In between writing his autobiography and preparing for a South American expedition, the newly "radical" TR also remained dedicated to the movement and his new party, while speaking in favor of woman's suffrage, prison reform, and a garment workers' strike.

That the assassination of an obscure royal named Archduke Franz Ferdinand, the heir to the throne of Austria-Hungary, along with his wife, would force TR, Wilson, and Addams to abandon their current domestic crusades for more international concerns seemed impossible when most Americans learned the news on June 29, 1914. Virtually no one anticipated that a global war was about to unfold, one that might determine the future course of the United States. For Roosevelt, Wilson, and Addams, their lives would never be the same.

Chapter 1

A MORE COMPLICATED WORLD

JULY 1–OCTOBER 4, 1914

*We are a very short-sighted and ignorant people in
international affairs.*

—Theodore Roosevelt, September 1914

A merica had changed dramatically in the two decades before the
archduke's assassination in Sarajevo. The United States was now
the wealthiest nation in the world, and its 100 million citizens
enjoyed a standard of living inconceivable to the older generations, including the now elderly Civil War veterans who still marched each year in
Decoration Day parades. The simpler Currier-and-Ives-postcard lifestyle of
the United States that TR, Addams, and Wilson knew during their
childhoods was gone forever, replaced by a sometimes frightening, sometimes exhilarating modern America that traditionalists strongly resisted at
every turn.

The changes were most apparent in the major cities of the East and
"Middle West," as it was called in those days. There, millions of recent
immigrants from southern and eastern Europe now walked the streets,
many still conversing in their native tongues, a threatening presence to
some natives who questioned their desire to assimilate. And a new strain
of secularism in urban centers was increasingly unavoidable. That May of
1914, the dean of the Yale School of Religion lamented declining church

attendance, "commonplace" divorces, "greed for gain," and, worst of all, the "overemphasis upon and a strained self-consciousness of the matter of sex."

The "new" American woman generated similar controversy, especially concerning her desire to vote. "Women as a class have neither leisure opportunity nor inclination to take up the grave study of governmental problems which should occupy men," scoffed one female antisuffragist. "The present electorate is bad enough . . . and its quality, not its quantity, needs improving." Female smoking was another battleground. The once shocking sight of a woman lighting up in a restaurant or hotel became common, much to the horror of society's moral guardians such as the *Chicago Tribune*'s advice columnist Doris Blake. "No decent man could seriously entertain the hope of finding lovely womanhood and divine motherhood in a female cigarette smoker," she wrote. "A self-respecting, nice, girl would scorn to pollute her lips with the taint of tobacco." The growing prohibitionist movement was just as committed to ensuring that her lips should never taste alcohol either.

To a Frenchwoman visiting America, the "audacity" of young women in New York was especially startling. "They paint too much," she lamented. "A little powder, yes; that I do not mind, but the red, the white, the eye black, it is silly, very silly. . . . Then there are the short skirts. They show their stockings. Their skirts are so short, so very short." But she admired the fast pace of American life. "I like the way you jump and run and hurry about. Every one seems to have hope and ambition."

New entertainment options further accelerated America's social transformation in the second decade of the twentieth century. Cheaper models of the Victrola, introduced just eight years earlier, allowed middle-class families the once unimaginable pleasure of hearing stars like Enrico Caruso and John Philip Sousa in the comfort of their own homes, although they could still journey to the nearest big city to see legends such as Houdini ("The Man Who Breaks All Bonds") and Al Jolson.

The booming motion picture industry was also reshaping the nation's leisure patterns. Religious leaders not only fretted over whether the powerful lure of the "picture show" might thin out their congregations each Sunday but also feared the impact of immoral content. Throughout America, local censorship boards carefully scrutinized films for anything remotely objectionable, although standards differed wildly from community to community. A Pennsylvania censor decided that no on-screen kiss should last longer than thirty-six seconds, while Chicago authorities snipped out scenes showing counterfeiters and "an immoral woman and the ruses she employs to seduce men."

But it was the emergence of the motorcar that truly reflected the new modern America, replacing the sleepy horse-and-buggy pace of yesteryear. By 1914, the automobile was no longer a toy for the rich but a valuable addition to modern living that drastically widened personal and professional horizons for anyone who could afford one (Addams did not own a car and never learned to drive; Roosevelt and Wilson had chauffeurs). Less enthusiastic observers believed the automobile was a sinister force in modern life, especially for young people. "In the last ten years," claimed the president of Brown University, "probably as many students in American colleges have been demoralized by the automobile as by alcohol. The dazzling attractions of a luxury-loving age constitute the greatest possible danger to American education."

Technology, industrialization, and immigration had wrought permanent changes to the American scene. Life was no longer quite so simple nor as orderly as it had once seemed, even a few years earlier, nor would it ever be again. "The world is becoming more complicated every day," Wilson had warned in a July 4 speech. "Therefore, no man ought to be foolish enough to think he understands it." It was about to grow much more complicated than Wilson or any other American ever imagined.

The developments in Sarajevo did not attract more than the usual press attention throughout much of July. The joint funeral and burial, the grieving royal family, and photographs of the assassin were all deemed newsworthy, but few grasped that a world tragedy was about to unfold. Even fewer had even the most basic comprehension of European affairs and alliances or the smoldering jealousies, fears, hatred, and greed pulsating throughout the Continent. Nor did most understand that Germany had been preparing for war, a war that might not only bring new colonies to match the British and French possessions but also neutralize the perceived threat of "encirclement" from the west and especially from the east. "The future lies with Russia, she grows and grows, and lies on us like a nightmare," lamented the German chancellor Theobald von Bethmann Hollweg.

It was not until July 23, when Austria-Hungary issued a harsh ultimatum insisting that Serbia yield to a series of humiliating demands, that the words "European war" began to appear with alarming frequency on the front pages of American newspapers. "War between Austria and Servia would almost certainly embroil all the great European powers and develop into the most colossal struggle in history," *The Washington Post* editorialized, using the then-common spelling for the nation that Austria-Hungary blamed for the assassination. "Apparently the world is on the eve of witnessing a collision destined to set all thrones a-trembling and to abruptly change the course of events throughout Europe."

The *Post* proved remarkably prophetic. Austria-Hungary's July 28 declaration of war on Serbia, encouraged by her ally Germany, set off a chain reaction that entangled Europe's two major alliances. Russia soon began to mobilize its forces in support of its Slavic brothers and sisters in Serbia, prompting Germany to declare war on Russia on August 1. Since France, allied to Russia since 1894, now posed a serious threat, Germany declared war on its hated neighbor two days later.

The German military had long believed a two-front war of this kind could be won by defeating France quickly and then turning their attention to Russia. The main attack on France would come through the north by way of Belgium, thus avoiding the heavily fortified French border (the strategy was a revised version of the Germans' von Schlieffen plan, which had been in the works for close to a decade). But Great Britain was not prepared to permit a violation of Belgium's neutrality. There was also fear of what a German victory over France might mean to national security. After Germany ignored a Whitehall ultimatum to keep its army out of Belgium, the British declared war on August 4. It was exactly what the Germans had dreaded. "If England doesn't go in we are all right," a German officer told an American three days earlier. "If England goes in, I'm afraid it will be very hard for us."

The war immediately resonated throughout America, especially in the diverse immigrant populations of the larger cities. In Philadelphia, "an almost hysterical gathering" of Serbians sang songs of their homeland amid periodic shouts of "'Long Live Servia!' and 'Down with Austria!'" That same day in the City of Brotherly Love, an argument between two men that began over whether Italy would join the war ended in murder. And everywhere, reservists of the warring countries flocked to consulates, hoping to find a way to get across the ocean and into the thick of the fight. In Chicago, already overworked British consular officials also had to contend with well-meaning "experts," who offered not so helpful advice on how to win the war. "All you have to do is build a tunnel under the Atlantic to Austria," one insisted. "Then you can give Austria a bully smash in the eye."

On the other side of the ocean, thousands of American tourists, students, and businessmen in Europe were faced with the daunting prospect of finding passage home. In London, desperate souls besieged the American embassy, including President Wilson's sister Annie Howe, who managed to get out of France, sans luggage, with her daughter and granddaughter. A largely unknown engineer named Herbert Hoover performed yeoman duty assisting his stranded countrymen and -women, including an older lady who "demanded a written guarantee" that her ship would not be torpedoed. Hoover, taken aback, nevertheless promised her she would make it home safely.

Such demanding attitudes were all too common in the first hectic days of the war. A Frenchwoman trying to get home to her family in Philadelphia was shocked by what she encountered at a Paris train station. "People of culture beat one another over the heads with canes, umbrellas and luggage," she marveled. "They pulled and dragged at each other and shrieked in their anxiety to get aboard the only train departing." Tired of waiting to buy a ticket, one pompous American complained long and loud that he was "a man of some consequence in New York. I am president of a bank and director in a trust company." Ultimately, those who were willing to pay scalper's prices for passage or superior accommodations fared best, much to the chagrin of those forced to go home third-class or even in steerage.

Some were in no hurry to leave the Continent. "Most Americans traveling in Germany have not yet come to realize the real gravity of the situation," remarked one journalist who had just left Berlin for The Hague.

"They seem to think the war a kind of play, 'great fun,' and cannot realize that war in Germany is not like war in Mexico." But scenes of French "peasants singing 'The Marseillaise' . . . at 3 o'clock in the morning in some little village buried in the woods" and angry Germans mobbing an unfortunate Russian violinist in a Berlin café could not help but open American eyes to the reality of the nightmare unfolding.

That America might somehow be ensnared had already begun to occur to the pacifist George Herman Borst, who noted that many on his transatlantic steamer had mistaken a tanker for a cruiser: "Is it not then quite easy to see how a German, French or even British ship might mistake a signal or possibly be commanded by a stupid officer and subject an American ship to some indignity? Would such an event warrant plunging a whole nation into war?"

Not everyone regarded the prospect of war as distasteful. Thirsting for adventure, more than a few young Americans were determined to get into battle. "We came over to Europe just for a pleasure trip, but have made up our minds we want to fight for the allies," one college student from North Carolina explained. "France is in the thick of the fight and we want to help her out as best we can. . . . We realize how serious the game is, but are willing, if necessary, to offer our lives for the allies." Some flocked to the French Foreign Legion, avoiding the current ban on service under the flag of any foreign nation, while others signed up to serve as ambulance drivers or in other noncombat capacities.

In London, a twenty-seven-year-old would-be writer named James Norman Hall found himself succumbing to war fever. Back in the spring, he had quit his social worker job in Boston to travel abroad in hopes of finding his literary muse. By the end of July, not only had he accomplished little, but he was also facing returning home with no prospects. The outbreak of war seemed to be an answer to his prayers. He watched young men by the thousands flock to recruiting stations drunk with patriotism and an unshakable belief that war was something glorious and beautiful. Such feelings resonated in Hall, as did a sense that the "adventure" of the thing would be far preferable than returning home with his tail between his legs.

His close friend Roy Cushman back in Boston sensed what was about to happen. "Whatever you do," he wrote Hall in desperation, "keep your head and *don't enlist!* Do you hear, *Don't enlist!*" By the time the letter arrived, it was too late. After changing his mind twice, Hall finally managed to join the British army as a member of the Royal Fusiliers even after informing the recruiting officers that he was an American. "We'll take you," they told him. "You'll just say you are an Englishman, won't you, as a matter of formality." His fellow recruits quickly saw through his disguise and dubbed him Jamie the Yank.

He was sure he had made the right decision, even though he feared telling his parents back in Iowa. "There are really very many reasons . . . why it will be good for me," he wrote Cushman. "I believe that a period of good strenuous military training will be invaluable. . . . And if I do go to the continent and go through the supreme tests and come out with honor which I am determined to do if I come out at all—that satisfaction of knowing that will be certainly a treasure." But Hall could not hide his anxiety over going into combat in the future. "It makes one serious to think that perhaps, just *perhaps* he has something less than a year to live."

His parents could not understand why he would place himself in harm's way. After all, this war was not America's fight, and the United States was protected by two oceans. "The first, most important duty of the United States in this world crisis is to mind its own business," *The Washington Post* recommended. Such advice, however well intended, would prove unrealistic. In the coming months, the United States would be confronted with a series of complex questions not easily answered. Should America take sides in the war or retain her usual neutrality? What course was most appropriate to ensure our national security? How will a country of more than 13 million immigrants respond to a war involving their native countries? How will a global war affect our economy? And exactly what should America's global role be?

Unlike most of their countrymen and -women, Wilson, Roosevelt, and Addams immediately understood the gravity of the situation. This global war, they knew, could very well determine the future course of the United States. Their starkly different responses to the conflict represented their unique visions of what America could and should be.

For Wilson, the drama in Europe could not have arrived at a worse time. Ellen, the love of his life, was not well. Since late 1913, her increasing weakness, a fall in her bedroom, and eating difficulties suggested that something was seriously wrong. She had managed to attend their youngest daughter Eleanor's wedding to the widowed fifty-year-old Treasury Secretary William Gibbs McAdoo in May but had been steadily deteriorating since.

Wilson refused to acknowledge what was happening. His wife, he believed, had a "nervous break down" but he was certain she was fine "organically." Ellen was more discouraged. "The doctor says that, considering how very ill I was, the progress is very rapid, but it seems snail-like indeed to me," she wrote her daughter. Through much of July, Wilson continued to believe that she was "making actual advance from day to day. . . . We are hoping and believing that it is only the weather that holds her back." His dedication and faith never flagged. Some nights he would awaken at three in the morning to keep her company in her bedroom. Meanwhile, the public knew nothing of the First Lady's condition.

By the beginning of August, Wilson knew her condition was likely terminal. "The trouble," he wrote his brother Joseph, "centers in the kidneys." Ellen had Bright's disease, then a general term encompassing a variety of kidney disorders, for which doctors had no effective treatment. Absent family members were called back to Washington, and the press was finally briefed on August 5. That day, Roosevelt wired his rival at the White House. "Very deep sympathy. Earnestly hope reports of Mrs. Wilson's condition are exaggerated." Wilson admitted they were not, "but we have by no means given up hope and the indications are today a little encouraging." Ironically, TR's first wife, Alice, had died of the same ailment thirty years earlier.

At the very moment Wilson was drafting his reply to Roosevelt, Ellen had but a few short hours to live. On the afternoon of August 6, 1914, she drifted into a coma, though not before she managed to tell Cary Grayson, Wilson's physician and friend, to "take good care of Woodrow."

The end came at 5:00 p.m. "Is it all over?" Wilson asked. For a few fleeting moments, his prodigious sense of self-control finally abandoned him. "Oh my God," he sobbed, "what am I to do?" He quickly gained his composure and would not lose it to such a degree again, even in the deepest depths of his grief. "I must not give way," he insisted. He took some solace that she had died "just as the world seems crashing to ruin. She could hardly have stood all that. It would have broken her heart."

After a simple funeral in the White House, the body was transported to Rome, Georgia, for burial. Wilson seldom left the casket during the long train ride from Washington. To friends and family Wilson appeared to have "held up *wonderfully* well," under the circumstances. But Dr. Grayson witnessed Wilson's despair in less guarded moments when he returned to Washington. "A great man with his heart torn out," he described him in a letter to his friend Edith Galt.

To capital gossips such as Ellen Slayden, wife of Texas congressman James Slayden, Ellen's death did not command the typical "effusion and gush that such events usually bring forth in Washington" because of the war. Slayden did not care for the President, whom she had known for decades, but pitied the First Lady. "She never seemed to enjoy the greatness her husband had achieved," she wrote in her journal, "her manner was almost apologetic, her hands limp and cold."

Slayden was certain Wilson would marry again, much to the horror of Eleanor Lansing, the prim and proper suffrage-opposing wife of State Department counselor Robert Lansing, who believed "public opinion would not permit it" as long as he was president. "He is a youngish man," Slayden reminded her, "and we have reason to believe rather leans to the ladies." Finally, they agreed to settle their disagreement with a bet, the winner to receive five pounds of Huyler's candy. "My bet is that he will marry before leaving the White House," Slayden wrote. "I expect to win, but Mrs. L. is so good and romantic that I think she was almost hurt at my levity."

In the final months of Ellen Wilson's life, subtle hints had already emerged that Europe was a potential powder keg ready to explode. Weeks before the Sarajevo assassination, Wilson's adviser and friend Colonel Edward House had traveled to Europe to meet with German and British leaders in the hopes of reaching an agreement that would bring peace and arms reduction among the great powers with the involvement of the United States. The ambitious mission, approved by the President, accomplished nothing. "I find that both England & Germany have one feeling in common and that is fear of one another," House admitted. He was especially disturbed by what he encountered in Berlin in May. "The situation is extraordinary. It is jingoism run stark mad. Unless someone acting for you can bring about a different understanding, there is some day to be an awful cataclysm."

The fifty-six-year-old House occupied a singularly unique position in the Wilson administration. A native Texan, the diminutive, delicate, and reserved House bore little resemblance to the stereotypical boisterous Stetson-wearing, bronco-busting cowboy from the Lone Star State. He had grown up in wealth, the son of a prosperous English immigrant, whose considerable fortune would allow House to pursue his major interest in life: politics. As early as the 1870s, his friendship with the son of an Indiana senator had provided a path into the halls of power in Washington, though he made no attempt to run for elected office. Instead, he relished the role of adviser and kingmaker, playing a crucial role in the election of several Texas governors, including James Hogg, who later conferred upon him the honorary title of Colonel. But Texas was not big enough for the little man who proved to have a considerable ego, one he never seemed to recognize. "I had never been seriously interested in state or local politics except as a means to get into national affairs as early as possible," House explained.

With the Democrats' chances of recapturing the White House minimal in the early years of the twentieth century, House chose to bide his time. It was not until 1911 that he became seriously interested in influencing the choice of the party's nominee in the next election. At first, he backed the New York mayor William Gaynor, whose presidential boom quickly petered out. Later that year, a meeting was arranged in New York between Wilson and House, who had recently moved to the city. Almost immediately, the two men sensed a special connection, bound by their Southern roots, love of poetry, shared health maladies, and world outlook. It was not long before House began to play a significant role in the new Wilson administration.

"Mr. House is my second personality," Wilson later insisted. "He is my independent self. His thoughts and mine are one." Admittedly, House could not compare to Wilson as a great thinker or trenchant writer. But the columnist Walter Lippmann viewed him as an ideal "complement of Wilson," who did not suffer fools or bores gladly, even when politically expedient. "The things which Colonel House did best, meeting men face to face and listening to them patiently and persuading them gradually, Woodrow Wilson could hardly bear to do at all," Lippmann explained.

Best of all, Wilson could detect no ambition in his new acquaintance. "He wants nothing for himself. He will not hold office and is a truly disinterested friend—the most valuable possession a man could have."

Or so Wilson thought. Others perceived House very differently, as a schemer who relished being the President's pal and understood all too well that his current unofficial role gave him far more power than any appointed or elected position might. "It is safe to say that no private citizen was ever so close to a President," one of House's own friends conceded. And he knew how to maintain his favorable position with Wilson. One cabinet member would later claim that House would "go around among all of the President's friends and find out exactly what was in the wind, and especially, if possible, what the President himself was thinking about." Armed with the current scuttlebutt, he would carefully parrot Wilson's views in his next discussion with the President.

Nevertheless, Wilson appeared to rely on House (the "Assistant President," according to one Boston newspaper) a great deal. Not only did the two men keep in regular contact by mail and telephone, but House also often journeyed to the White House from New York to discuss appointments, policy, and ongoing political developments, gleaned from the constant stream of visitors to his Manhattan apartment. Everything was documented nightly in a dictated diary, an enormously valuable record of the times, but one that lacks any sense of self-awareness and presents House as a brilliant visionary whose opinion is seldom if ever proved wrong.

Though his fingers were in many a Wilson administration pie, House's greatest interest was foreign affairs, a field where Wilson's experience and knowledge were unexceptional at best. In his fanciful, anonymously published 1912 novel, *Philip Dru: Administrator*, House had already articulated his vision of a future world where the United States, the United Kingdom, and other major powers would "join hands in a world wide policy of peace and commercial freedom" with "disarmaments to be made to an appreciable degree."

Within weeks following Wilson's inauguration in 1913, House was on his first mission to Europe to meet with British and French officials. That House's activities might be undermining Secretary of State William Jennings Bryan and the American ambassadors in Europe did not appear to bother Wilson, especially when House's flattery came thick and fast. "I have a keen desire for you to become the world figure of your time," he wrote Wilson from London three days after the Sarajevo assassination in the summer of 1914. "Never again can the old order of statesman hold sway, and you are and will continue to be the prophet of a new day."

As global war became inevitable in late July, House was already envisioning a role for himself. "There may be a time soon when your services will be gladly accepted," he wrote Wilson. "It is then I would hope to be of use to you." He was also quick to undercut Bryan's potential involvement. "Please let me suggest that you do not let Mr. Bryan make any overtures to any of the powers involved. They look upon him as purely visionary and it would lessen the weight of your influence if you desired to use it yourself later."

Wilson already understood that America might have a part to play in the great drama unfolding in Europe. Even before the outbreak of war, he recognized that the United States would need to decide "what are we going to do with the influence and power of this great nation." But Wilson's options appeared frustratingly limited. The United States had always avoided "entangling alliances" throughout her history, and the public, he believed, would strongly reject any whiff of American involvement, even with the object to bring the war to a speedy conclusion. Neutrality would have to be declared, but the question remained whether America could ultimately act as a mediator or peacemaker.

At a July 27 press conference as the European situation escalated dangerously, a reporter asked the President "whether the United States is in a position to maintain the peace of Europe at this time." Wilson's answer was not encouraging: "I can only say that the United States has never attempted to interfere in European affairs."

War was alien to him. And unlike Roosevelt, he never possessed the slightest lust for glory on the battlefield. "President Wilson is one of the new generation of Peace Advocates," wrote the radical journalist John Reed in an unpublished profile that summer, "the kind that believes that war is objectionable not primarily because it is bloody or cruel, but because it no longer accomplishes its purposes." In the days before Ellen's death, the President debated whether to offer America's good offices to the combatants "while hoping and praying there may not be any general European war." Even though House believed such a gesture would be premature, Wilson sent a message to the leaders of Germany, Russia, Austria-Hungary, France, and Britain on August 4. "It can, at least," he wrote House, "do no harm." Polite acknowledgments followed, but none of the belligerents was interested, especially when they were convinced the other side was at fault. America's role as a mediator, it was clear, would have to wait.

The devastating one-two punch of the onset of war and Ellen's death that August took a tremendous emotional toll on Wilson. At times, he feared that "a single word would open the flood-gates and I would be lost to all self-control." "Hard work," he hoped, might alleviate his grief, but he found it increasingly difficult to tackle the tasks demanded of him every day. "Every night finds me exhausted,—dead in heart and body, weighted down with a leaden indifference and despair," he wrote to the now-divorced Mary Hulbert (she elected to drop her ex-husband's name and resume using her late first husband's surname). "God helping me, I shall regain command of myself and be fit for my duties again."

The war's economic impact on America also weighed heavily upon him. Spooked by the threat of a global war, the stock market plunged in late July, resulting in the closing of the New York Stock Exchange until December 1914. He also fretted about undue "excitement" among Americans likely to take sides or press for involvement. His fellow citizens, he believed, must maintain the "self-possession" that Wilson prized so highly in himself. In a public statement on August 18, he reiterated that the United States must "exhibit the fine poise of undisturbed judgment, the dignity of self-control, the efficiency of dispassionate action." Such a course, he admitted, might be difficult in a nation of immigrants ready to favor their own native country and "it will be easy to excite passion and difficult to allay it." Still, "the United States must be neutral in fact as well as in name during these days that are to try men's souls. We must be impartial in thought as well as in action."

The words were vintage Wilson: noble, high-minded, but more than a bit unrealistic. The Allies, for example, could easily count on the support of Anglophile WASPs on the Eastern Seaboard who still cherished their English roots. In New York, not one of the seventeen English-language newspapers sided with Germany. But the large German American populations of Milwaukee, Cincinnati, St. Louis, and other Midwestern centers could not help but root for the Fatherland, regardless of its disturbing militaristic tendencies, encouraged by Kaiser Wilhelm. And thousands of first- and second-generation Irish immigrants looked forward to seeing the hated John Bull's nose bloodied in the fight.

Millions of other Americans had no strong feeling one way or the other in the early days of the war. All they knew was that Europe was an ocean away, and its problems paled in comparison to the normal daily pressures of making a living and raising a family in the United States.

But war news, even in the remotest corners of America, was inescapable. Newspapers were soon filled with dispatches and photographs from the front, most of them reflecting a strong pro-Allied slant, since the British had already succeeded in cutting the German cable to the United States. Meanwhile, American press syndicates, newspapers, and magazines began sending their best men across the ocean to cover what looked to be the story of the century. Several, including the celebrated war correspondent Richard Harding Davis, contacted Roosevelt beforehand, hoping that a word or two from an ex-president would weaken the stubborn resistance of military authorities intent on keeping out the press. TR was only too glad to help the man who had helped make him a household word sixteen years earlier.

Davis sailed on the *Lusitania* on August 5. Arriving in Europe, he was disappointed that the Allies had no intention of providing him with credentials to access the front lines. Still, he managed to witness a remarkable yet disturbing development unfold. On the evening of August 27, Davis was riding a slow-moving troop train heading to the German border and then Holland. The train came to a stop at Louvain, Belgium, known for its historic library, university, and town hall. He soon discovered that German military officials, in response to supposed deadly sniper fire from Louvain citizens, had ordered the beautiful old city destroyed, and Davis was on hand to record the grisly deed in all its horrific glory.

"For two hours on Thursday night I was in what for six hundred years had been the city of Louvain," he wrote. "The Germans were burning it, and to hide their work kept us locked in the railroad carriages. But the story was written against the sky, was told to us by German soldiers incoherent with excesses; and we could read it in the faces of women and children being led to concentration camps and of the citizens on their way to be shot."

If Davis's stirring account did not convince Americans of the need for intervention abroad, it succeeded in converting millions to the Allied cause. Additional sensational Allied reports of bayoneted Belgian babies and young girls whipped, tortured, and murdered in a sadistic frenzy convinced previously ambivalent Americans that the "Teutons" were nothing less than savage beasts capable of the most horrific of atrocities. "American and other neutral witnesses . . . now make doubt impossible about some of the most barbarous acts in human annals," Walter Hines Page, the U.S. ambassador in London, informed Secretary of State Bryan. "Man after man and woman after woman tell of very young girls whom they have seen that were violated by German soldiers. They tell of Belgian boys the tendons in whose arms and legs were cut with swords. I am told by two persons who have seen him, of a physician whose hand was cut off while he was dressing a Belgian soldier's wounds."

The Germans, of course, denied the gruesome allegations, as did several American war correspondents upon their return to the United States. After the war, many began to suspect that the worst of the so-called atrocity stories were nothing more than skillful British propaganda. More recent studies suggest that "trigger-happy" German soldiers, anticipating civilian attacks, were in fact guilty of excessive brutality, leading to the deaths of close to six thousand Belgians in 1914.

Wilson understood that the media-driven "rape of Belgium" narrative had complicated the domestic situation and made his ideal neutrality "in thought as well as in action" considerably more difficult. He himself could not help but betray his own disgust with the German actions in Belgium. "I found him as unsympathetic with the German attitude as is the balance of America," House wrote in his diary on August 30 after a conversation with Wilson at Harlakenden, the President's summer home in Cornish, New Hampshire. "He goes even further than I in his condemnation of Germany's part in this war, and almost allows his feelings to include the German people as a whole rather than the leaders alone. He said German philosophy was essentially selfish and lacking in spirituality."

But such statements did not mean that Wilson was prepared to publicly denounce the violence in Belgium or, for that matter, pass judgment on Germany's own claims of Allied brutality and use of prohibited dumdum bullets, which expanded on impact. Instead, he fretted over what the current struggle would mean for civilization in general. Wilson, House noted, "thought the war would throw the world back three or four centuries."

The war notwithstanding, his beloved Ellen remained foremost in his thoughts. During House's two days in New Hampshire, Wilson "showed me photographs of her, read poems written about her, and talked of her as freely as if she were alive." The President continued to doubt his fitness for the task ahead and "looked forward to the next two years and a half with dread." Alarmed by Wilson's comment that "he felt like a machine that had run down, and there was nothing left in him worth while," House did his best to encourage him by reminding him "of the great work there was to do for humanity in the readjustment of the wreckage that would come from the European war."

The pressures surrounding Wilson seemed to mount every day. He could not ignore the nation's 8 million first- and second-generation German Americans, who increasingly believed that his administration, along with most of the country, was unfairly against the Fatherland, a perception difficult for the President to dispel in view of the overwhelming negative press. Such attitudes baffled German Americans, who were accustomed to being praised as the "ideal" immigrant group. "About Germans there has never been a misgiving," *Life* magazine admitted that September. "They have always been welcomed as a strengthening stock." As for Germany itself, American attitudes prior to the war were mostly positive. "German baths were good; so were German razors," *Life* noted in a subsequent editorial. "The Germans were the best chemists, and made excellent toys. We knew them as efficient people; traded with them extensively; welcomed them here as visitors or settlers." The German American press did its best to combat what they considered to be negative propaganda, as did a new American publication, *The Fatherland*, under the leadership of the distinguished poet George Sylvester Viereck, a friend of Roosevelt whose highly partial writings would soon prove him to be "more German than the Kaiser."

A clamor of voices within his own administration, each with his own agenda, would prove just as difficult for Wilson to control, especially the pacifist tendencies of Secretary of State William Jennings Bryan. As a three-time presidential candidate and influential power within the Democratic party, the fifty-four-year-old Nebraskan had been rewarded with a place in Wilson's cabinet, although many doubted the still popular "Great Commoner's" forte was foreign affairs. Critics quickly pounced on the prohibitionist Bryan's insistence on serving grape juice rather than alcohol at diplomatic dinners and other functions, his periodic departures from Washington for lucrative speaking engagements on the Chautauqua circuit on such topics as "The Prince of Peace," and his idealistic, Christianity-infused approach to diplomacy. "He has the simplicity of a son of the plains," the British writer A. G. Gardiner noted. "There is a certain crudity in Mr. Bryan's mind." (Roosevelt believed Bryan had the "temperament best fitted to make a success as 'barker' for a patent medicine.") Others dismissed him as the punch line to a cruel joke: "What are the three funniest words in the language?" Answer: "William Jennings Bryan."

Wilson not only accepted Bryan's limitations and idiosyncrasies but also had endorsed Bryan's "cooling-off" treaties. These pacts, negotiated with thirty different countries, required both parties to refrain from war for one year while potentially explosive disputes were arbitrated (signers received a plowshare paperweight made from melted-down swords, taken from the biblical reference "They shall beat their swords into plowshares"). That such agreements might not be workable in the current crisis did not appear to occur to Bryan. "*Love* is the only foundation upon which permanent peace can rest; peace is promoted, therefore, by anything which promotes good will," he told a Philadelphia audience.

Bryan's views horrified House. "He talked as innocently as my little grandchild," House wrote in his diary after a meeting with the secretary of state. "He spoke with great feeling and I fear he may give trouble." "Trouble," of course, meant interference with House's own diplomatic schemes. Already, the Colonel was laying the groundwork for another European mission. "If the President would send me over alone or with a small commission and permit me to go to The Hague and get in personal touch with each of the warring nations," he mused that September, "something might be done to bring about a basis for peace."

In the meantime, House put out feelers to both sides' ambassadors to America. He did not get very far with the high-strung British diplomat Cecil Spring Rice. "He said to forgive Germany now and to make peace was similar to forgiving a bully and making peace with him after he had knocked you down and trampled upon you pretty much to his satisfaction," wrote House. Nor did Spring Rice want any part of House's proposed tête-à-tête with the mustachioed German ambassador Count Johann von Bernstorff, who had agreed to such a meeting.

Bernstorff, unlike his superiors in Berlin, appeared strangely inclined toward some kind of settlement, even in the early heady days of German victories. He was a career diplomat, known for his considerable charm, his genuine interest in American ways and institutions, and his New York–born wife. But he already sensed the reality of the situation, especially after the French and British halted the German advance at the Battle of the Marne in early September. Germany, he realized, would have a difficult time winning the war even under the best of circumstances. And if America joined the Allies, the odds of success would shrink considerably, although most German officials perceived the world's largest neutral nation as less relevant militarily than, say, Denmark or Holland. His mission, as Bernstorff now saw it, was to keep the United States neutral if at all possible, limit her assistance to Germany's enemies, and encourage any move for peace, even if he had to overstep his own instructions from home. The German ambassador, House noted, "believes that unless peace is brought about soon, the war will be a long drawn out affair . . . and that if either side is markedly successful, public opinion would not permit peace proposals, short of almost complete annihilation."

The daily anxiety and urgency Bernstorff experienced were not shared by Wilson, at least in House's eyes. The President, he believed, did not fully grasp the "importance of this European crisis" and did "not seem to have a proper sense of proportion as between domestic and foreign affairs." Nor did Wilson appear especially inclined toward discussion of war-related national security issues at present. But he understood all too well what the war meant and that his own decisions, if not made with the strictest of impartiality, might tilt the balance in favor of one side or the other and destroy any potential for a lasting peace in the future. And while he did not dash cold water on House's various machinations, the President realistically believed "there is nothing that we can as yet do or even attempt." For now, a "deadlock in Europe" seemed the most ideal outcome, one that would not only "show to them the futility of employing force in the attempt to resolve their differences," but also prevent one side from "enforcing its will upon the others" in the peace settlement and setting the stage for "further calamities."

And Wilson, perhaps more than House, understood that he would have to proceed carefully in a nation whose citizens strongly disdained militarism of any kind (especially immigrants subjected to it in their homelands) and even feared that the Boy Scouts were "training the boys of America to be soldiers." The enthusiastic response to his call for a "Peace Sunday" on October 4 suggested that the President had correctly divined the public's current mood. That day, millions of Americans, Wilson among them, flocked to their local churches and synagogues to "pray for peace in Europe" (there had been some controversy about a few newspapers trying to direct the prayers for an Allied victory).

In Washington, where Wilson appeared at the Central Presbyterian Church, the reporter Arthur Sears Henning noted that "such a day of church going has not been observed in many a year. The churches were crowded to capacity and in many the peace prayers were repeated at several services." The faithful were hoping for a miracle: a quick end to the war, which would spare America.

Although she had supported TR in the 1912 election, Addams as a good pacifist could not help but be pleased that Wilson was in charge during the current crisis. Perhaps Wilson was not as social reform oriented as Roosevelt, but he was surely less likely to lead the nation down a militaristic path. As a progressive, the President would also understand that peace could be approached like any other social problem that Addams and her followers had tackled: by gathering facts, proposing recommendations, and then acting appropriately. If state, local, and federal governments could be persuaded to act rationally, then why not foreign nations?

At the eve of the war's outbreak, the pacifist (or "pacificist," TR's favored derogatory term) movement had been growing steadily in the United States for several decades. The major players included the American Peace Society, the World Peace Foundation, and Andrew Carnegie's pet project: the Carnegie Endowment for International Peace (Carnegie had tried to get TR involved, without success). Once perceived as a fringe group of quacks who objected to war solely as an affront to "Christian brotherhood," the pacifist movement had shifted its emphasis to the development of formal entities designed to resolve disputes peacefully. Its hopes were raised by the Hague Conventions of 1899 and 1907, two unprecedented attempts at international cooperation attended by representatives of twenty-six and forty-four countries, respectively. Signatories not only agreed to more humane rules governing the conduct of war but also the creation of a Permanent Court of Arbitration where squabbling nations could voluntarily submit their disagreements. Such ideas were now so mainstream that prewar peace societies counted conservative Republicans William Howard Taft and Elihu Root as members, along with Democratic luminaries Bryan, Robert Lansing, and Wilson himself, a onetime member of the American Peace Society.

Pacifism had been one of Addams's core beliefs for nearly two decades, the product of multiple influences, including her father and the work of Tolstoy, whom she met with in Moscow in 1896 (TR later scorned him as a "sexual and moral pervert"). Her experiences among the mélange of ethnicities at Hull-House further crystallized her vision. If nineteen different groups could live together in a sort of harmonious internationalism in the same Chicago neighborhood, then why couldn't nations do so as well? "When a South Italian Catholic," she explained, "is forced by the very exigencies of the situation to make friends with an Austrian Jew, representing another nationality and another religion, both of which cut into his most cherished prejudices, he finds it harder to utilize them a second time, and gradually loses them."

Pacifism, then, was Addams's response to conflict, which she perceived as the true enemy of progress among both nations and individuals. "It had nothing to do with compromise or what people mean by 'peace at any price,'" her friend and fellow peace advocate Emily Balch later wrote. "It was a state of mind, a method of dealing with contentious problems of all sorts. It was a deep part of herself, at once her philosophy and her life." The Spanish-American War of 1898 proved to be a defining moment in her maturing philosophy. Unlike TR, the imperialism, the war play of children, what Addams called the "gilt and lace and tinsel," and the subsequent occupation of the Philippines disgusted her. "The troubles of our unrighteous war," she wrote to Mary Rozet Smith, "will never come to an end."

Addams increasingly came to view militarism in its obvious and more subtle forms as the antithesis to the causes she so cherished. In *Newer Ideals of Peace*, the book TR so detested, she argued that archaic militaristic values, necessary in the distant past to ensure survival, unfortunately continued to persist in the modern city. "We may admire much that is admirable in this past life of courageous warfare, while at the same time we accord it no right to dominate the present, which has traveled out of its reach into a land of new desires." The current urban problems faced by immigrants, organized labor, children, and women, especially the continued denial of suffrage, all were a product of what Addams called the "old virtues" of war. Yet she was encouraged by the emergence of opposing values—namely, a "newer humanitarianism" and a "rising concern for human welfare"—that would hopefully undermine the old militarism and lead to peace, one not defined as "an absence of war, but the unfolding of worldwide processes making for the nurture of human life."

The coming of a global war had been a cruel blow to Addams and other pacifists who believed that the tide had been turning toward peace. "Nobody who was not a mature person in the summer of 1914 can realize now how remote, how unbelievable, a European war then seemed," her friend Alice Hamilton later wrote. "Believing as we did then in the slow but sure progress of the human race, we looked forward to nothing worse than sporadic outbursts in such unknown regions as the Balkans or South America, never in the highly civilized countries of the Europe which we knew so well."

For Addams, the moment of truth came in early August at her Hulls Cove, Maine, summer home (purchased jointly with Mary Smith). She was shocked to discover that nearby Bar Harbor, the vacation playground of the well-to-do, had abruptly become the unexpected new home of the *Kronprinzessin Cecilie*, a German ocean liner laden with passengers and $13 million worth of gold and silver; it had turned around and fled back to America after learning of the outbreak of war. The peculiar sight of the massive ship anchored in Frenchman's Bay, Addams recalled, "was the first fantastic impression of that strange summer when we were so incredibly required to adjust our minds to a changed world."

Adjustment, of course, did not mean abandoning her cause. But Addams and other pacifists of the social reform stripe were disappointed by the timid response of the established American peace organizations who feared appearing "ridiculous" and seemed unwilling to advocate anything stronger than prayers. "We must wait patiently until we reach peace thru the exhaustion of one or the other parties," Andrew Carnegie explained to Secretary of State Bryan. "Then is the time to go with the healing bandages in our possession."

Veteran pacifists such as the elderly Fannie Garrison Villard, a "Tolstoyan" and the daughter of famed abolitionist William Lloyd Garrison, were not surprised. "They are weak and ineffectual because they are compromisers," Villard told a gathering. "They assert in one breath that war is wrong and wicked, and then with perfect equanimity and amazing inconsistency they say a recourse to war is sometimes justifiable."

Villard, like Addams herself, believed that women, as nurturers of human life, could and should take a leading role in the peace movement. Days after the war began, she and other New York–based women activists began to organize an unprecedented "peace parade," entirely feminine in nature.

The plan received mixed responses from some of Addams's closest New York colleagues such as Lillian Wald, the founder of the Henry Street Settlement on the Lower East Side, the city's counterpart to Hull-House. "I feel that the proposed parade is a feeble protest to make against the awful tragedy of this war," Wald said. "But since it is the only protest open to women I shall help all I can." The suffrage leader Carrie Chapman Catt was even less enthusiastic: "If anybody thinks . . . that 1,000 or 2,000 or 10,000 women marching down Fifth av. are going to have the slightest effect on the situation in Europe it is because they don't know the situation. . . . We might achieve something practical if we could join together in great numbers and induce the women of the neutral countries of Europe to work with us for peace. But I dare to stand here as a prophet and say that no power can stop this mighty war."

Addams, an invitee but a nonparticipant, may very well have shared Catt's doubts or at least did not feel enthusiastic enough to travel nearly five hundred miles from Maine to march.

Except for its female composition, the entire scheme was a fairly conservative strategy, at least in contrast to the old Populist party firebrand Mary Elizabeth Lease, who instead proposed that the women should "[s]tarve the armies out! . . . march to the docks and forbid the exportation of foodstuffs." And once the President issued a proclamation against "unneutral" behavior, more than a few ladies began to get cold feet about any kind of protest. Nervously, they contacted the White House to determine whether the administration would "object" to such a parade. The committee was relieved when Wilson gave his blessing, after being assured of "safeguards . . . that there shall be no grouping by nationalities, and no public speaking connected with it."

Could such a genteel demonstration accomplish much? The chairman, Alice Carpenter, thought so. "A public protest against wrong may not right that wrong," she admitted, "but collective action not only crystallizes sentiment, but emphasizes the need of constructive and preventive measures." She and other committee members did their best to make the parade a success, passing out thousands of handbills throughout the city, plastering department store restrooms with posters, and even providing local theaters

Women marching down Fifth Avenue in New York peace parade, August 29, 1914.
(Library of Congress, LC-B2-3207-11)

with "great slides" to be shown between films urging patrons to "Join the Monster March Down Fifth Avenue."

Saturday, August 29, was parade day. Overcast weather limited the actual turnout to somewhere between one and three thousand. But the twenty thousand spectators present could not help but be affected as they watched waves of serious women, clad all in black or in white with a black armband, silently marching down Fifth Avenue, accompanied by "muffled drums," mostly played by a group of young Boy Scouts (the lack of female drummers forced the organizers to break their no-male rule). They came from all walks of life: well-known luminaries like Wald, Villard, and Charlotte Perkins Gilman, elderly widows of Civil War veterans, socialists, poor African American women from Hell's Kitchen, even the suffragette wife of Wilson's nephew. Only a single banner was seen in the entire parade—a dove with the word "Peace"—which was carried by Carpenter.

The parade accomplished its purpose: local and national press coverage. The next step, the organizers hoped, was a genuine movement, something different from the stodgy pacifist groups, few of which had even bothered to send female representatives to the parade. "I am filled with a burning desire to have the women of the United States found a society for peace among nations," Fannie Villard remarked afterward. "The time has come for founding an organization totally different from the existing peace societies. . . . And to whom better should we turn for aid than to women, now coming into their own, socially, economically, and politically?"

If there were to be a women's peace movement, Addams seemed to be the ideal choice as leader. Fannie Villard may have had more impressive pacifist credentials, but no one in America approached the stature of Addams, possibly the most famous and respected woman in the nation, someone who was even touted by her admirers as a more than fit occupant for the White House. But such a prominent role, Addams knew, would likely invite criticism from those who already believed that the lady who "taught the world the art of being kind" (as she had been introduced at a recent speaking engagement) should limit her activities to Hull-House and stay out of the suffrage movement and politics. It would also ultimately mean more radical positions than she normally embraced. "My temperament and habit had always kept me rather in the middle of the road," she later admitted, "in politics as well as in social reform I had been for 'the best possible.'" But she would soon find herself "pushed far towards the left on the subject of war."

For now, she was not yet ready to take that step. Like others, she grappled with how to respond. Paul Kellogg, the editor of the leading social work journal *The Survey*, which counted Addams as one of its associate editors, envisioned that September a "gathering of the first men and women of the United States" who would issue a ringing American "message which would breathe the spirit of democracy . . . enunciate a world policy" and "set forth a social conception for the reconstruction of Europe." Since the old-line pacifists had nothing to offer, he suggested that "those who deal with the social fabric" should take the lead, with Addams spearheading the effort and lending her name to the invitation.

As a progressive who had seen similar meetings evolve into successful reform campaigns, Addams found the idea appealing, especially since she had already been considering a "plan of getting joint action by social workers and the peace people." On September 29, she presided over a daylong gathering at Lillian Wald's Henry Street Settlement; it was attended by about twenty men and women, mostly of the reformer stamp, although Thomas Edison received an invite, as did Louis Brandeis (Kellogg at one point had considered asking TR, whom he believed "would bring vigor" but apparently thought better of it). Beyond plans to issue a future statement, nothing tangible resulted initially from the first meeting of what became known as the "Henry Street group," which subsequently evolved into the American Union against Militarism (an AUAM committee, the Civil Liberties Bureau, later became the ACLU). Still, the meeting proved to be transformative. It placed Addams and her reform cohorts, normally experts in the fields of social work, "labor conditions . . . sanitation, or immigration," in the forefront of the American peace movement.

Addams understood all too well that peace could not be separated from the causes near and dear to her. During her suffrage speeches that fall, she attempted to link the war to women's disfranchisement. Women in the belligerent countries had no say in any of the decisions leading to war, she reminded a Boston audience: "Women, if they were in control, would not hesitate to send their country into a war of self-preservation . . . but . . . they would not permit an insane outburst like the present European conflict." Men, she argued, were to blame for war. "It is the result of being in arms and ready to fight. Men do not like to see weapons rust: they would rather try them out now and then."

Too often the menfolk present preferred to engage in silly suffrage debates with her rather than discuss the causes of war. What if women didn't vote as their husbands did? "Won't that mean friction in the home?" one old coot asked in Kansas City. "Not if the woman knows how to hold her tongue at the right moment," Addams responded. "There is always the secret ballot for the timid." Wouldn't women voting result in more divorces? No, she patiently explained. The state of Wyoming already allowed women to vote yet had the "lowest divorce rate" in the country. One joker tried to trap her with a question about a potential foreign invasion of America. Would "all the old maids and widows go to the front?" Years of public speaking had taught her how to dispense with would-be comedians and hecklers. "Voting is not a question of fighting," she replied. "If it were, every man of 60 years should be disfranchised."

Whether audiences would continue to be receptive to discussions of any reform with an unprecedented war raging remained to be seen. At the Henry Street meeting, she and others present despaired over the impact on progressivism. The hopes of a new socially conscious America, which seemed within reach during the heady 1912 campaign just two years before, now seemed unlikely to materialize anytime soon. The war, Addams observed, "will set us back." Campaigns for the "various woman's movements" and "old age pensions" seemed irrelevant when hundreds, if not thousands, of young men were dying daily. "It will be years before these things are taken up again," she told a reporter. "The whole social fabric is tortured and twisted."

Her words betrayed a certain inescapable sadness, one that would only intensify when she returned to Chicago and watched groups of young Italian and Bulgarian men march off to war. Her sister Alice's cancer recurrence and need for treatment only added to her gloom, although not enough to cancel her speaking tour. But Addams could not help but be encouraged that the war had injected a much needed jolt into the peace movement. "The affairs in Europe are most depressing and most disgusting," David Starr Jordan, the former president of Stanford University and a leading pacifist, wrote to his brother that fall. "They are, however, creating hundreds of workers for peace where there was one before."

Like Addams, Roosevelt experienced a profound sense of helplessness with the outset of the "frightful tragedy," albeit for far different reasons. Not only was he not in charge during the most significant world event in a millennium, but men whom he frankly despised were calling the shots.

His feelings toward Wilson had only intensified since the last election. He had once conceded the "adroitness" of the President, but the administration's plan to offer Colombia an apology and $25 million compensation for the loss of Panama (and the Canal Zone, the site of one of TR's greatest achievements) enraged him.

Somehow, he managed to set aside his contempt to stop at the White House in late May during a trip to Washington to discuss his recent expedition to Brazil and his discovery of the "River of Doubt." To everyone's surprise, the two men apparently had a pleasant chat, as the press reported that "all controversial topics were avoided."

Wilson and Secretary of State Bryan were, Roosevelt was certain, foreign policy incompetents under the best of circumstances. The President, he snorted, was just a "college professor who has never had anything but an academic interest in foreign affairs," and Bryan was a dolt "who knows nothing but ward politics and crack-brained economics." In the current crisis, such rank amateurs were likely to do real damage. TR would increasingly come to believe that there was at least a slim chance that war might have been averted had he been in the White House. The failed last-minute attempt of Edward Grey, the British foreign secretary, to pursue mediation through a conference might have succeeded with more time—time, Roosevelt believed, that bold American action might have bought. This would have ideally involved a "direct demand for a conference, because of our own interests in preventing the invasion of Belgium. We are one of the signatories to the Hague Conventions, and that not only gives us a right to concern ourselves in such matters, but lays an obligation upon us to do so." At the same time, American ambassadors across Europe would be instructed to inform their host governments "the very grave concern felt by the United States over the situation . . . because of our own obligations." The potential of an American monkey wrench tossed suddenly into the works might have given Germany reason to pause, at least momentarily. "We certainly could have supplied those few days if Washington had cared to do so, or had known how," TR later lamented. "Cleveland would have done it, or McKinley. I should have felt myself a criminal, if I had been President, and had not done so."

But he was not president. And his influence with the people seemed to be at an all-time low. The split with the regular Republicans, his move to the left, the 1912 electoral defeat, and what TR called a "ceaseless campaign of lying and slander against me" had knocked him far from his once enviable political position. "A very large number of ordinary decent men are convinced that I am a bad man or else a thoroughly wild and unsafe man," he wrote a friend that summer. "I believe my usefulness in public life is about at an end."

Some of his political enemies seemed eager to hasten the process. One of them, the reactionary New York Republican boss William Barnes, slapped TR with a $50,000 libel lawsuit for a recent speech he gave suggesting that the "bipartisan boss rule" of Barnes and Tammany Democrat Charles Murphy controlled a "State Government" that was "rotten throughout."

In the past, no one would have doubted his ability to withstand such political blows. But TR, while only fifty-five, was not the same TR of even two years earlier. The Brazilian expedition, an adventure he knew he could never attempt again, had nearly killed him and left him with a permanent fever, treated with quinine, that would wax and wane for the rest of his life. Well-wishers advised he try a variety of remedies—olive oil, "grape fruit tonic," and "modern eating" habits—but he seemed resigned to his deterioration. "I am an old man," he told friends and family. "But I have had a remarkable run for my money."

A long rest or perhaps a trip abroad might have alleviated at least some of his political and health woes. But 1914 was a national election year, and for the moment he still believed in the Bull Moose party. "I am in every fiber of my body a radical," he insisted. "I very emphatically believe that there is . . . altogether too great inequality of reward in our industrial life, altogether too much of giving enormous bonuses to men who are not entitled to be rewarded for anything and altogether too little thought of the fact that many men are compelled to spend their lives in working hard under such conditions that they really get no reward whatever." Such words could not help but hearten Addams and other progressives who had supported him two years before.

He realized that the Progressives' performance in the 1914 midterm elections would very likely determine whether it would follow the Republican party's example five decades earlier of remarkable exponential growth or, like so many other third parties, fade into irrelevance. At times, the entire fate of the party seemed to rest on his shoulders. ("You are the Progressive party," his journalist friend John Callan O'Laughlin told him.) The obligations were inescapable. There were requests, admittedly silly, that he run for governor of New York (perhaps against his fifth cousin Franklin Delano Roosevelt, now Wilson's assistant secretary of the Navy and himself eager to climb the political ladder). Others were already strategizing for another TR presidential bid in 1916, which would hopefully result in the final "destruction of the Republican party." Each day hundreds of letters poured in demanding his attention, some of them trivial—like those earnestly requesting the cash assistance the writers believed TR had promised any mother who bore eight sons—but many more from Progressives begging him to speak on their behalf that fall. With his voice nearly shot from the fever, he knew that was impossible. Still, he planned to do all he could in the upcoming campaign, even if the odds were against most of the Progressive candidates. "I do not feel that I can go back on my friends," he explained.

Roosevelt was doubtful that his endorsement would sway many votes in November. But even at the nadir of his political influence, more than a few Americans remained receptive to his voice. They hoped that the Nobel Prize winner who had helped bring a war to a close just nine years earlier could somehow work his magic again. "You are the only man that can stop that terrible slaughter," one correspondent gushed. "The world would welcome your assistance in these hours of gloom," another insisted. Others begged him to use his "great influence" with Kaiser Wilhelm. Even Wilson found himself on the receiving end of such letters, urging him to press TR into diplomatic service or "see Mr. Roosevelt and have a good heart to heart talk with him about this fearful war situation."

TR was not about to discuss foreign policy with Wilson or send any telegrams to the kaiser. He did, however, sense that Americans were interested in what he had to say about the war. "Colonel, please speak out," pleaded one correspondent. "The Nation is waiting in breathless silence for some word from you. . . . Let the Nation hear from you."

As a former president, Roosevelt had no shortage of offers to write for publication, although he was no longer a regular contributor to his usual outlet, *The Outlook*. The Wheeler Syndicate, a press service whose decision to send Richard Harding Davis to cover the war had paid off handsomely, was especially persistent. TR, the syndicate informed his secretary John McGrath, could "set his own price" for a series of articles.

What TR might say was not entirely clear, at least initially. George Sylvester Viereck was confident he would be "on the side of the Teuton as against the Russians" and even sent the former president an ode Viereck had recently penned to the kaiser. And Roosevelt, who had spent time in

Germany as a teenager and was of partial German descent, had always found a great deal to admire about the German people, especially what he described as their "capacity for hard work" and "sense of duty." Like others, he was shocked by the vitriolic anti-German reaction in America in the early days of the war, such as stories of Maine women shouting "they wished the German people had ceased to exist and that the German Emperor would be made to die" and New York crowds cheering news that "the Germans were being slaughtered like rats."

His sympathy for the German people did not extend to its leaders. In the four decades since unification, Germany had grown into a first-rate world power with global ambitions as sizable as its military. TR had long viewed "Prussianized Germany" warily. "For the last forty-three years Germany has spread out everywhere," he observed, "and has menaced every nation where she thought it was to her advantage to do so." Roosevelt himself had witnessed such behavior in his first presidential term, when Germany appeared ready to use unpaid debts as an excuse to involve herself in Venezuela, only to agree to arbitration when TR promised to uphold the Monroe Doctrine with force.

Roosevelt believed that his stand had earned him the respect of the kaiser, whose bluster, "impulsiveness," and militaristic ways often drew comparisons to TR. "Both roared for doughty armies, eternally prepared—for the theory that the way to prevent war is to make all conceivable enemies think twice, thrice, ten times," wrote H. L. Mencken. "Both dreamed of gigantic navies, with battleships as long as Brooklyn Bridge." And Wilhelm did his best to curry favor with TR, hoping the American might be of use to him, although Roosevelt was hardly fooled.

"I do admire him," he told one friend, "very much as I do a grizzly bear." In 1910, the two men finally met during Roosevelt's European trip, although the encounter was somewhat disappointing to TR, who hoped for a more wide-ranging conversation. "He knows armies, and that is all," he would later grumble. More concerning was the kaiser's "curious mixture of admiration and resentment" toward the United Kingdom, notwithstanding a peculiar comment he made to TR: "I ADORE ENGLAND!" That the two countries might clash in the future was already apparent to Roosevelt. "I do not believe that Germany consciously and of set purpose proposes to herself the idea of a conquest of England, but Germany has the arrogance of a very strong power," he wrote a friend after the visit. "If she had a navy as strong as that of England, I do not believe that she would intend to use it for the destruction of England; but I do believe that incidents would be very likely to occur which might make her so use it."

TR also detected a curious undercurrent of anti-Americanism during his stay. His reception, he admitted, was polite enough, although far less animated than others he encountered in Europe. Germany's government, military, and business elite viewed America with thinly veiled disgust and more than a trace of envy. They were frustrated, TR believed, that the upstart United States, "entirely unorganized," not only should challenge Germany for industrial supremacy but should also be militarily "wholly independent and slightly defiant" because of "our Navy and our ocean protected position." By the end of the trip, he was convinced that "the Germans did not like me, and did not like my country."

TR's ties to the Allies were far stronger. Jean-Jules Jusserand and Cecil Spring Rice, the current French and British ambassadors in Washington, were both old friends of Roosevelt's (Spring Rice had been the best man at TR's second wedding) and kept in steady contact. On the other side of the Atlantic, there was no shortage of Roosevelt admirers eager to keep him abreast of the latest war developments, with a decidedly pro-Allied slant and a dash of Wilson bashing. Arthur Lee, a Conservative MP who had known TR since the Rough Rider days, filled him in on the patriotic mood in Britain, the admirable performance of Winston Churchill as First Lord of the Admiralty, and tidbits about the massive Russian army mostly composed of "'16th century' peasants who genuinely believe . . . that they are engaged in a Holy War." Letters from Rudyard Kipling, meanwhile, suggested that the war might last three years, while warning TR of the dangers of a German victory and the need for Americans to "arm steadily . . . at once by land and by sea." Kipling and other British correspondents also offered disturbing accounts of Belgians, one of whom had supposedly "witnessed the awful sight of a pregnant woman being ripped open by German barbarians in the guise of Soldiers. The child was taken from her & hoisted upon a bayonet!!!" Such stories did not sway TR one way or another, especially when several American war correspondents questioned their validity. As a historian, he also realized that his own country had been guilty of unspeakable crimes against Native Americans.

Much to the disappointment of his British friends, he could not, or would not yet, offer public support of the Allies. As much as he despised Wilson and his foreign policy, Roosevelt did not disagree with American neutrality, at least in the early weeks of the war. "What is needed from public men in this country now is a position of real impartiality in this terrible contest," TR insisted in a letter in late August. "That is the position I am trying to take." Instead, he emphasized the lesson to be learned from the invasion of Belgium: treaties were worthless without force behind them. In his first lengthy piece on the war, published in the August 22 *Outlook*, he not only suggested that Belgium's unfortunate plight was inevitable but refused to assess blame for "the violation or disregard of these treaties. . . . When giants are engaged in a death wrestle . . . they are certain to trample on whoever gets in the way of either of the huge, straining combatants, *unless it is dangerous to do so.*"

The article denounced neither Germany nor Wilson, whom TR noted "very properly has offered his services as mediator." In his next *Outlook* piece, in the September 23 edition, he again refused to take sides. While he deeply sympathized with Belgium, Germany had behaved no differently from other countries facing similar "national life or death" struggles. "It is certainly eminently desirable that we should remain entirely neutral," he wrote. "Nothing but urgent need would warrant breaking our neutrality and taking sides one way or the other." As for Wilson, "all of us, without regard to party differences, must stand ready loyally to support the Administration." These were words that Roosevelt would come to regret, so much so that many of them would be edited out of a compilation of his war articles issued a few months later. Years later, he would even demand his neutrality views from the early days of the war be purged from New York high school textbooks.

After his views on Germany and America's responsibility to Belgium shifted in a far different direction, TR claimed that he had deliberately pulled his punches to give Wilson a fair chance to "formulate his policy with regard to all the international questions involved," in the hope that the President would eventually do the right thing. He would also claim he had been "misled" by the administration's statements that "there was no obligation on our part at the Hague Conventions requiring any protest from us." A more plausible explanation is that Roosevelt, like so many others, was himself not entirely sure about how America should proceed in the early weeks of the war. And for the time being, he sensed that it would be wise not to attack Wilson, a recent widower, nor was it advisable from a political protocol standpoint. "An ex-President must be exceedingly careful in a crisis like this how he hampers his successor in office who actually has to deal with the situation," he admitted. A friend, the historian Albert Bushnell Hart, praised TR for his apparent "support of the administration . . . what you would have had a right to expect under like circumstances." Still, TR confided to Spring Rice that "it has been very hard for me to keep myself in."

If Roosevelt's vision of America's role in the war had not yet fully crystallized in the early fall, he was certain of one thing: the uselessness of any peace movement at present. "The prayers appointed by President Wilson, the peace parades, the protests against war, the use of peace postage stamps, and the like," TR believed, "amount to precisely and exactly nothing." And he held nothing but contempt for pacifists such as the "blue-rumped ape Bernard Shaw" and others of his ilk. Yet Roosevelt insisted that he believed in peace as much as they did. Peace, along with arbitration of disputes and disarmament, could be achieved only when the "armed strength" of America and other superpowers acted in concert to "work for international justice."

Most Americans were not interested in such responsibilities, preferring to play the part of uninterested bystander. And more than a few saw TR as an out-of-touch warmonger. In Chicago, a Roosevelt supporter was appalled by the public attacks on him during the October 4 Peace Sunday services. While Addams urged a "revolt against war" before an enthusiastic crowd, Roosevelt was described by another speaker as "an arrogant man going up and down the country whose desire was to gratify the fighting spirit and an instigator desirous of involving this country in war." Such reports could not help but dishearten TR. "The kaleidoscope has been shaken," he admitted, "my influence has very nearly gone."

Chapter 2

A WAR WITH WHICH WE HAVE NOTHING TO DO

OCTOBER 5–DECEMBER 31, 1914

*I pray God night and day that the United States will
prevent Europe from committing suicide.*

—Rosika Schwimmer, December 1914

Roosevelt well understood that most Americans recoiled at the thought of involving the United States in any European conflict. But the emotional impact of the war was already apparent throughout the nation. Many could not help but deeply empathize with the unfortunates caught in the crossfire. Belgian relief became the *cause du jour* that fall. It seemed that one could not take three steps in any direction without being prodded to dig deep and relieve the suffering. Even schoolchildren were asked to "adopt a certain number of Belgian children" and come up with three pennies a day for their support. A seventeen-year-old boy sent TR the $275 raised by a "War Relief Club" formed with a group of his friends, assuming that Roosevelt would send the funds "where they will do most good." TR advised the youngster to forward it to J.P. Morgan & Company "for the American Ambulance Hospital" in Paris, where his daughter Ethel and her surgeon-husband, Dr. Richard Derby, were currently volunteering their services.

But alongside the do-gooding charitable impulse there existed a certain voyeuristic fascination with the titanic struggle in Europe. In Chicago and other cities, war news and extra editions sent newspaper circulation sky-rocketing. In New York, the *Sun* published an eight-page "war illustrated" each Sunday, balanced by an eight-page alternative of "timely features of general interest" for individuals sick of "war pictures and war articles." And any writer able to get even remotely near one of the armies was guaranteed readers, much to the chagrin of veteran war correspondents such as Frederick Palmer. "The most desperate journalistic faking ever known appears in the form of war-correspondence," he noted. "Men sitting in the cafés of Calais were writing as if they were at the front. There is no competing with that kind of thing."

But the most accurate accounts came not from the journalists but from the letters of Americans currently serving, like James Norman Hall, whose brief stint as part of British War Secretary Lord Kitchener's new volunteer army had already exposed him to the realities of military life. His fellow soldiers, he soon realized, were not the "flower of the nation" touted by the English press. A good many were poorly educated (some officers were unable to spell "sanitary"). Others were "downright London toughs," including some ex-cons. "God pity King George if it's ever up to any of you to save him," a drill sergeant roared in disgust. Yet in the weeks spent training in Colchester in Essex, Folkestone on the English Channel, and then nearby Sandling, Hall could not help but forge a bond with the men in his regiment. Together, they were being asked to do what seemed to be impossible: become soldiers in three months, all for the princely sum of seven shillings per week, or $1.75. From 6:30 a.m. to nightfall, they drilled, marched (sometimes up to twenty-two miles at a time), practiced bayonet charges, and took rifle practice, all while coping with a steady onslaught of rain and mud. "Our beds are wet, our clothes are wet, in fact everything is damp but our spirits," he wrote in one letter. "I, being an American, have the good name of all Americans to uphold. I pretend that I don't mind this miserable way of living in the least."

In the rare moments he had to himself, Hall increasingly began to consider what the war was all about and what it might mean to America. The "love of adventure" that had motivated his enlistment had been replaced by unquestioning devotion to the Allied cause, further strengthened by the "pitiful sights" of Belgian refugees. "If Germany is victorious in this war,

Heaven help the U.S.A," he wrote his mother. "The Allies are really fighting our battles for us. For this reason more than for any other I would not, for any consideration be otherwise than here at this time." He doubted the war would be over anytime soon, though he kept such pessimistic thoughts from his already fearful parents. "How in Heaven's name is the thing to be settled in the end! What a stupendous task awaits the statesmen who shall undertake it!"

Hall had yet to experience combat, but he already realized that this was a very different war. An officer from his unit transferred to France was killed within a week. "The daily list of casualties makes one sick at heart," he admitted. "Scores of men in my battalion alone had lost brothers and cousins and friends. And still the slaughter goes on!" Other Americans such as the Bostonian William Robinson, who signed up in London a few weeks after Hall, could attest to the unprecedented brutality. In his first chaotic months in the British army that fall, he witnessed a series of disturbing incidents that showed him there was nothing glorious about war. He saw panic-stricken Belgian civilians desperately trying to dodge German shells. "The roads were littered with dead and dying, wounded horses screaming their horrible scream and kicking. The din was terrible." He observed several Belgians collaborating with the Germans, including a teenage sniper paid six francs for every officer picked off—all of them were later arrested and summarily executed by the English. And he came to understand all too well the human meat grinder that was the Western Front. "I saw one regiment go into action for the first time," he wrote later. "I watched them go up singing and shouting, and in high spirits generally. There were over eleven hundred strong going into action, but two days later they came out, and there were only twenty three of them to answer the last roll call."

Robinson had already spent time in the trenches, a critical component of the fighting on both sides. The Harvard-educated poet Alan Seeger, who had enlisted in the French Foreign Legion, vividly described trench life in a December article in the *New York Sun*. "For the poor common soldier it is anything but romantic," he wrote. "His role is simply to dig himself a hole in the ground and to keep hidden in it as tightly as possible. . . . Exposed to all the dangers of war, but with none of its enthusiasms or splendid *élan*, he is condemned to sit like an animal in its burrow." And the unprecedented "terrific and incessant shell fire," the journalist Henry Beach Needham wrote TR, was almost unbearable.

Such dire descriptions did not discourage Roosevelt, who expected his four boys to participate in "any war during their lifetime" and was delighted to learn from Rudyard Kipling that his only son, John, age seventeen, was now in the British army. (The unfortunate young Kipling would be killed in action less than a year later.)

To many Americans, then, the Great War resembled a horrible automobile wreck from which they could not turn their heads. In New York, the newly arrived British suffragist Emmeline Pethick-Lawrence was startled by the hundreds of columns of war news each day. The people, she wrote her husband, "cannot think of anything else." In fact, she wondered whether America might be "more obsessed by the war than England."

Pethick-Lawrence was very much the "modern woman" detested by social conservatives in England and America. Like Addams, she began her career in the settlement movement, but she was also a socialist and a feminist who upon marriage chose to combine her surname with that of her new husband, Frederick Lawrence (who did the same). The Pethick-Lawrences had once been major players in the militant Women's Social and Political Union's fight for suffrage in Britain, withstanding jail time and force-feedings, but their discomfort with extreme tactics such as arson and vandalism resulted in their ouster in 1912 by the WSPU's leaders, Emmeline Pankhurst and her daughter Christabel. Recently, Pethick-Lawrence and her husband helped to organize a more mainstream pressure group, the United Suffragists, who unlike the WSPU refused to set aside their suffrage efforts during the current crisis. The war, she believed, was inextricably tied to the suffrage moment. "When suffrage gets a firm hold on the world," she insisted, "there will be no more war. The mothers of the world will not permit the continuance of a world's social system which allows war."

The Women's Political Union, headed by Harriot Stanton Blatch, the daughter of Elizabeth Cady Stanton, had invited Pethick-Lawrence to speak in America on the subject of women and war at a suffrage gathering at Carnegie Hall in late October. Her message would be simple. The position of women during wartime, she believed, had unfortunately changed little over the centuries. "It is for her to sacrifice her loved ones, it is true, and to remain at home and anxiously await their return." Yet no one seemed to notice or care very much about the devastating economic impact on war widows who had no voice in the governments that unleashed such calamities. Women, then, should not only be granted "full democracy," but the "whole . . . movement must be turned to the destruction of this monster, war." Pethick-Lawrence was certain that a new day was coming: "the nineteenth century is in ruins . . . the twentieth century is emerging, and it must come with women on its wings."

She arrived in New York on October 26 after a seven-day transatlantic crossing worsened by seasickness and a bout of tonsillitis. The press was immediately charmed by her "sweetly gracious" manner. "Far from being anything that suggests a militant," wrote one reporter, "she is womanliness itself." Whether her appearance would draw more than a few curious suffragists remained questionable, especially since her estranged comrade-in-arms Christabel Pankhurst had just given a rather warlike pro-Allies talk before a "half full" Carnegie Hall a few days earlier. But New Yorkers proved eager to hear her words and those of Olive Schreiner, a South African writer, who sent a special message promising to support any attempt of the "women of America" to "start an International Woman's Peace Society." The enthusiastic crowd poured more than $45,000 into the coffers of the Women's Political Union that night, leading Pethick-Lawrence to sense that something was happening. "I begin to see the possibility of a new movement taking shape," she wrote her husband the next day. "All I know is this—I am not wanted in England. I may be wanted here."

Americans, she believed, could be reached. Following her talk in New York, she addressed gatherings in Boston and Washington while spearheading the organization of new women's peace groups in each city. The hopes of the Women's Peace March appeared to be coming true. In the meantime, she began to articulate a specific platform calling for woman's suffrage and full citizenship, "democratic control" of diplomacy, government ownership of munitions factories, a ban on munitions exports, and a female representative such as Jane Addams at the next Hague Conference. "I want the people of the United States to realize that the only effective weapon against militarism in the world to-day is—well, I do not like to call it 'Feminism,'" Pethick-Lawrence wrote. "I dislike the word. I will call it the Women's Movement."

She found herself falling in love with the lively, irrepressible nature of many Americans. "This is an amazing country," she wrote a friend. "There are more amazing people to the square mile then ever I dreamed possible!" At the same time, she became aware of a "strangely conservative + reactionary" strain, even in New York. "In some ways," she concluded, "America is 50 years behind social thought in England."

Not surprisingly, TR was apparently uninterested in meeting with her, despite the efforts of a mutual acquaintance, and later scoffed at her "brain of three-guinea-pig power," the same choice insult he once used to describe Bryan's intellect. And there were aspects of American life Pethick-Lawrence found distasteful: the "perpetual noise of the street," the "ear piercing voices" of the women, and "how horribly expensive everything is."

Pethick-Lawrence's reception in the East came to the attention of Addams, who sent her "very kind letters" and arranged for her to come to Chicago in November. The two women had already met at a conference in 1913, and husband Frederick had visited Hull-House years earlier. "I find Hull-House a delightful place to be in," Pethick-Lawrence wrote Frederick after arrival. "There are no servants while you are at breakfast. Your bed gets magically made (you see nobody. I believe there is a woman who comes in for a few hours) and that is all. A man puts the food on the table. Everything is informal, yet everything is orderly." And adding to the convivial atmosphere was the presence of another rabble-rousing foreign suffragist and pacifist in the next room: a Hungarian force of nature named Rosika Schwimmer.

Short, plump, with thick dark hair and glasses, Schwimmer was a woman ahead of her time. A militant feminist and a hard-core atheist, she exhibited none of the docile Victorian feminine traits still embedded in the consciousness of many an American and European woman. She smoked, took an occasional drink, and rejected both corsets and brassieres in favor

Rosika Schwimmer, 1914.
(Library of Congress, LC-H261-4302)

of "bright, loose-fitting dresses." And her persona was big as life—brash, passionate, and sometimes loud—or, as one American suffrage leader perceived her, "all force and fire, alive from her feet to her fingertips."

Schwimmer had grown up in Budapest, the oldest child of Jewish middle-class parents whose own nonconformist notions rubbed off on their exceptionally bright, if a bit sickly, daughter. Still, she was frustrated by the restrictions imposed on her sex. "I found that there was very little place for a girl in the world," she later told a reporter. "The hands of everybody seemed to be raised against a girl who wanted to do anything that wasn't strictly conventional." At eighteen, family financial setbacks forced her to find employment. She took a stab at teaching, bookkeeping, and secretarial work before finally finding her true calling: organizing female office workers and then as a prominent feminist activist in Hungary. Suffrage soon became her primary focus, and the international movement was more than glad to benefit from her trenchant pen, fluency in several languages, and compelling stage presence. "She talks to the people as though she were conversing with them," an observer noted. "Everything has so much substance that both the smartest and the most stupid are enraptured." Audiences especially appreciated Schwimmer's stinging and all-too-truthful observations about men (her own marriage lasted only two years), so much so that she was labeled the "comedienne" of the suffrage set.

By the summer of 1914, she had relocated to London, where she was working as the press secretary for the International Woman Suffrage Alliance. As a Hungarian and keen observer of foreign affairs, she understood far earlier than most what the assassination in Sarajevo might mean. Even during the prior winter while in Russia, she sensed that a war might be on the horizon. Somehow, she managed to see cabinet member and future prime minister David Lloyd George, who considered her July 9 warnings "alarmist," although his mind would change just a few short weeks later. When Great Britain entered the war on August 4, her initial reaction was far from passive. That night, she took pen in hand and feverishly worked out a plan to stop the conflict. America, through Wilson or Bryan, must spearhead a conference of neutrals whose job would be to "send offers of mediation daily" until the belligerents found one to their liking and agreed to a "settlement of the conflict by arbitration." Such a strategy, she believed, might have an actual chance to succeed since both sides would be the *recipients* of arbitration offers rather than proposing peace terms themselves and potentially appearing weak.

She was horrified by the war fever, the same that had swept James Norman Hall into the service of the king and country. "We must not let them die," she thought. "We must not let them kill each other, destroy civilisation, we must not let them." But any hope to jump-start her plan in London disappeared when Britain declared war on Austria-Hungary. Now considered an enemy alien and unable to travel beyond five miles from her home without a permit, she would need to leave the country immediately. America seemed the best option, especially since Carrie Chapman Catt, the current president of the IWSA and Schwimmer's mentor, had already invited her to come to New York to assist in a suffrage campaign and do some paid lecturing.

For now, Schwimmer desperately needed money, both for her passage to the States and to publicize her peace scheme. She sold her typewriter and other belongings, pawned her family jewels, and reached out to her contacts in Europe and America for encouragement and assistance. "I looked always forward to come over to your States," she wrote Addams, "but I never dreamt that I will have to go under such terrible circumstances." She even tried to interest Andrew Carnegie, only to receive a tepid reply from his secretary ("Idiots!!" she scribbled on the letter). The British pacifist Keir Hardie warned her to expect such responses from the mainstream peace movement. "You will find the so called Peace people the most helpless and inefficient crowd on the face of the earth," he wrote. "If you are going to see President Wilson, Bryan and others that may be of some use but otherwise you will be wasting your time."

To her credit, the indefatigable Schwimmer somehow managed to gain an audience with the President shortly after she arrived in America in September, thanks to Catt's connections and a White House culture far more open to visitors than it is today. Schwimmer was annoyed that Catt would not be accompanying her, but Catt thought it might be for the best: "The President is an Anti-Suffragist, and I might even antagonize him," she told her European friend. "You know Mr. Wilson has written a History of the United States without mentioning any women in it."

Wilson, already bombarded with schemes of all kinds by this point, listened politely to Schwimmer's plan, now touted as a message from the women of thirteen different nations, although she spun the conversation far more positively. "The President was deeply interested in the peace plea," she told reporters. "He said he would lose no opportunity in taking practical steps to end war, and that he was praying night and day for the possibility of peace in Europe."

But Wilson's comments at a press conference a few days later were far less charitable. Without singling out Schwimmer, he stressed that his own efforts "may be blocked by all this talk of things that are impossible and unwise, and in themselves unworkable. . . . We may make it impossible . . . to do the right thing by constantly saying that she [the United States] thinks of silly things to do."

There was nothing left for Schwimmer to do but hit the lecture circuit, where in the pre-radio/television world a well-known and skilled speaker could still make good money (Christabel Pankhurst was getting $300 a talk—the equivalent of about $7,500 today—much to Schwimmer's chagrin). She was not used to lecturing in English; in fact, she joked how she once mistakenly told an audience at a suffrage convention last year to "see the undertaker" if they were interested in taking a mountain excursion. Catt wanted her to stress suffrage and became increasingly annoyed with her lengthy pacifist discourses and impractical spending on telegrams. It was not surprising that Catt began to notice more than a trace of fanaticism and perhaps martyrdom in her Hungarian friend.

"I wonder if she is a little mad over all this world's madness," Catt wrote a European suffragist. "Her plans for peace are impractical." Such criticisms, if Schwimmer knew of them, had little effect: she concluded every speech by imploring her audience to pressure Wilson into action.

Like Pethick-Lawrence, it was inevitable that Schwimmer would make a pilgrimage to Hull-House. Addams had met Schwimmer a year earlier in Budapest at a suffrage conference, where she had witnessed her theatrical nature firsthand. To emphasize that the women's rights movement should not be class-based, Schwimmer paraded a "group of Hungarian peasant women wearing farm clothes." Such attention-grabbing demonstrations were not Addams's way. Nor was she especially enthusiastic about the women's appeal Schwimmer had taken to Wilson. "I have signed it reluctantly," she wrote Paul Kellogg, "simply because I don't like to damp any plan which is so widespread, but it doesn't seem very feasible." Still, Addams invited Schwimmer to stay at Hull-House in November and perhaps intentionally placed Pethick-Lawrence in the next room.

Pethick-Lawrence respected Schwimmer's abilities as an organizer and publicist. But like others, she found it difficult to get past the Hungarian's occasionally haughty, high-strung, tactless, and overly dogmatic nature, or what Schwimmer herself described as her "unfortunate temperament." "She is embittered, savage + impatient with any measures short of *immediate intervention*," Pethick-Lawrence wrote her husband. Not surprisingly, Schwimmer was less than enthusiastic about Pethick-Lawrence's proposals designed to prevent future war rather than stop the current one. Still, the two women, representing opposing sides in the conflict, began to make joint lecture appearances. "We are working hand in hand," Pethick-Lawrence told a reporter. "While the men of the world are at war, the women are united for peace."

Their stay at Hull-House (which Schwimmer dismissively likened to a convent) seemed to confirm for both that America and its women could in fact be instrumental in bringing peace to Europe. "I have the impression that the work in Chicago may result in a strong popular move to press your government into a conventional action," Schwimmer wrote Catt in late November. Her goal, she told Catt, was "moving people into action." The two Europeans had given the sleepy American peace movement a much needed jolt, one that Addams would soon find difficult to ignore.

The peace issue was not one Wilson could easily dismiss. In one ear, there was the ultimate pacifist Bryan, prodding him to "urge mediation" on the belligerents; in the other was Colonel House preaching delay, with House conveniently permitted to "keep the matter in my hands and advise him what was being done."

While self-serving, House's strategy appeared more realistic in the fall of 1914. Even the mere prospect of American mediation, arising from a casual conversation between Bernstorff and former Roosevelt cabinet official Oscar Straus, was quickly rejected by the major players that September. Bryan got nowhere with French ambassador Jules Jusserand, who scoffed at any "return to the status quo." "I replied to him," he told his superiors, "that we would accept it when the Germans, in order to re-establish it, could give us back the lives of our dead ones." Spring Rice, meanwhile, reminded House how the Lincoln administration responded to Britain's offer of mediation during the Civil War: in other words, it would be best for America to butt out. And Bernstorff discovered that Berlin was unwilling to pursue any strategy that might be seen as a "sign of weakness," even though he well understood that any show of interest in mediation might soften American attitudes toward Germany. It would not be the last time that the German leaders dismissed Bernstorff's warnings about the "power of public opinion" in the United States (or what some Germans called "Dollarica"), which had only been further inflamed by the then shocking news of zeppelins dropping bombs on civilian populations.

Wilson himself was disturbed by the bombings and their effect on a "real neutrality of public opinion." Reports of movie audiences cheering scenes of the armies of both sides also concerned him, although the Universal production company had begun to address potential partisanship complaints by inserting disclaimers such as: "A GENTLE REMINDER. The Millions who enjoy Universal Moving Pictures are again reminded [of] President Wilson's plea for strict neutrality. Forget the horrors of war. Don't take sides. Appreciate the glories of Peace." Such sentiments were consistent with Wilson's belief that American emotions and passions must be checked at all times, lest they carry the nation needlessly into war. It was not surprising, much to House's chagrin, that Wilson felt no obligation to be truthful when reporters badgered him about foreign policy. But as much as the President wished it to be so, strict American impartiality in the great contest unfolding would not guarantee peace.

As the wealthiest nation in the world, the United States was now a commercial juggernaut, and very much part of what one economist called the "new interdependence of nations." As a neutral, America was theoretically able to trade with both sides and with other neutrals; in fact, the 1909 Declaration of London had attempted to formally define international neutrality rights by classifying cargoes as *absolute contraband* (strictly for military purposes, such as munitions) and *conditional contraband* (useful in both nonmilitary and military settings, such as food or clothing). Warring nations, of course, would have the right to confiscate absolute contraband carried by a neutral ship, but conditional contraband could be seized only if bound for the port of a belligerent, and other materials on the so-called free list (e.g., paper, soap, glass, cotton) would not be subject to seizure. The Declaration of London had never been formally ratified, but the Wilson administration hoped that the United Kingdom would abide by its principles once the war began.

Almost immediately, British officials decided it would be folly to follow this policy and neuter its most effective weapon: the powerful Royal Navy. They not only expanded the absolute contraband list to include commodities such as copper, petroleum, and rubber, but began stopping American ships bound for neutral ports, citing the doctrine of "continuous voyage," whereby the final destination of a cargo was the determining factor. The

British, then, believed that they had every right to intercept an American vessel bound for Copenhagen if they believed it carried contraband, absolute or conditional (including food), that might eventually find its way into German hands (unfortunately for American officials, the Lincoln administration had employed the same argument during the Civil War to prevent contraband from reaching the Confederacy through Nassau and other nearby neutral ports). According to a letter to the *New York Evening Post*, even a ship bound for neutral Spain not containing contraband of any kind might require a "sworn statement before the British consul in New York" that the goods would not be reshipped to Germany or its allies. "Are the United States a vassal state?" the letter writer complained.

This policy guaranteed American conflict with the Allies, as did the extension of the British blockade of Germany in early November to the whole of the North Sea, which was now mined and declared a "war zone." Under international law, blockading neutral ports was illegal; nevertheless, any American ship headed for a Dutch or Scandinavian destination was now subject to being stopped, diverted into a British port, sometimes for long periods of time (up to forty days), searched for contraband, and then escorted safely around the mines to its final destination. "Great Britain," one State Department official later recalled, "threw all conventions, treaties, precedents, rules, etc. to the windows, taking the position that this war was different from any that the world had ever experienced."

But was it? Wilson was not entirely convinced that current conditions permitted such blatant interference with American trade. A response was certainly warranted, but how far should he go? Should he insist that Britain follow the Declaration of London, even if the North Sea was not an important area for American trade? The President held more than a few aces up his sleeve—namely, the threat of an embargo of the Allies, which might compel the British, who recognized the importance of American exports, especially munitions, to back off. It would also convince an already dubious Germany that Wilson was truly neutral and might be trusted as a peace mediator at some future date. The economic impact and potential political ramifications would be steep (America traded far more with the Allies than the Central Powers), so steep that the administration chose not to push Britain very hard at the moment and rejected possible cooperation in a protest with Norway, Sweden, and Denmark. It was a decision that likely affected the entire trajectory of the war.

The British breathed a sigh of relief. Unless Wilson had a change of heart, they need not fear America flexing its muscle to threaten the success of the blockade now or perhaps ever. Still, as Foreign Secretary Edward Grey recognized, Great Britain would still need to maintain a delicate balancing act between pacifying the United States as best as possible and maintaining the strongest possible blockade of Germany.

As a student of history, Wilson wondered whether British maritime policy might drag America unnecessarily into another European war, just as it had a century earlier. Chatting with House one day, he began reading an excerpt out loud from his *History of the American People* about the War of 1812 and how "Madison was compelled to go to war despite the fact that he was a peace-loving man, and desired to do everything in his power to prevent it, but popular feeling made it impossible." "Madison and I are the only two Princeton men that have become President," he told House. "The circumstances of the war of 1812 and now run parallel. I sincerely hope they will not go further."

Wilson unfortunately was not at his best as he made such momentous policy decisions. The pain of his wife's death had not abated. In a dark moment, he confided to House that "he was broken in spirit . . . and was not fit to be President because he did not think straight any longer, and had no heart in the things he was doing." To escape his grief, he tried desperately to focus his thoughts on anything but himself while throwing himself into his duties. "There is nothing but the work for me," he insisted. "I fight to keep going."

Besides the situation in Europe, domestic affairs such as the yearlong Colorado coal strike, midterm elections, and the signing of the Federal Trade Commission and Clayton Antitrust Acts kept him busy, much to the annoyance of House, who continued to believe such matters should be put on the back burner. Not surprisingly, his typical presidential day was packed with activity from morning to night. After breakfast at eight, he dictated letters to his secretary and reviewed papers. By ten, he was in his office seeing "visitors and delegations of all sorts" until lunch. In the afternoon, he saw a few more visitors before heading out for his daily golf game

(Wilson told a friend that his "chief real interest is GOLF," although his failure to tip did not win him many friends among the caddies). Returning to the White House, he bathed and dressed for dinner while squeezing in additional paperwork. After dinner, more meetings awaited him "on pending business or foreign affairs" or there might be "papers to prepare on questions which only I ought to formulate." By bedtime, Wilson was exhausted, "so tired I cannot think."

But the emotions that he strove so hard to suppress could not always be controlled. One November day, a group of African American leaders headed by the Boston editor William Monroe Trotter called upon Wilson to address the increasing segregation in government departments, namely black employees now placed "at separate tables, in eating, and in toilets." He did not mince words with the President. "Have you a 'new freedom' for white Americans," he asked, "and a new slavery for your 'Afro-American fellow citizens' God forbid."

Wilson was not used to being spoken to that way, let alone by a black man. Still, he maintained his composure enough to give the standard Southern argument that his "colleagues" (much of the cabinet) believed that separating the races was best to avoid "friction." Certainly, this was not meant as "degradation." "If you think," he insisted, "that you are being humiliated, you will believe it. If you take it as a humiliation, which it is not intended as, and sow the seed of that impression all over the country, why the consequences will be very serious."

Wilson, while not a rabid race baiter, simply could not transcend the racist views of his Southern youth (the Library of Congress was about to contact him about an overdue copy of Joel Chandler Harris's *Uncle Remus*). And Trotter, to his credit, tried to educate him on the harm of segregation. "It creates in the minds of others that there is something the matter with us—that we are not their equals, that we are not their brothers, that we are so different that we cannot work at a desk beside them," he explained. "We are sorely disappointed that you take the position that segregation itself is not wrong, is not injurious, is not rightly offensive to you." This was too much for Wilson. His vaunted self-control finally snapped. "If this organization wishes to approach me again, it must choose another spokesman," he barked. "Your tone, sir, offends me. You are an American citizen, as fully an American citizen as I am, but you are the only American citizen that has ever come into this office who has talked to me with a tone with a passion that was evident." After a few more exchanges, the appearance of Secret Service men signaled to Trotter and his group that the conversation had come to an end.

The irritability, the loss of temper, the argumentativeness all suggested that Wilson was not himself (some suffragists claimed he had been equally petulant during one of their White House meetings). "I want to run away, to escape something," he admitted. Nothing seemingly could lift his mood, even though his daughters, his brother-in-law Stockton Axson, and his cousin Helen Bones, who lived at the White House, did their best. And his normal disdain for Washington, "a hideously empty place, a desolately lonely place" only added to his gloom. With Ellen gone, it was not surprising that Wilson, whose fondness for feminine company was legendary, reached out for a surrogate of sorts. He poured out his heart in frequent correspondence to his old confidant, the "lady of wit and understanding," Mary Hulbert. "I long for the time when I may be released and allowed an individual life and daily fortune again," he confessed to her in November. At times his words seemed to be written by a smitten lover. "If I could see you your irrepressible vivacity would, I think, draw something out of me," he gushed in one letter.

If letters to Hulbert provided a distraction from Wilson's day-to-day depression, Colonel House was his closest male companion, their bond growing even stronger. "The President is a peculiar man, in as much as he does not care for many people," House mused in his diary. "He never seems to want to discuss things with anyone, as far as I know, excepting me." Such an arrangement could not help but please House, whose dual role as friend and adviser apparently superseded any cabinet member's influence, including the uber-ambitious Treasury Secretary William Gibbs McAdoo, who already believed his father-in-law's delicate health would preclude a second term.

Physically, Wilson appeared fine, McAdoo's allusion to claims of his "hardening of the arteries" notwithstanding. But House could not help but be concerned about the President's state of mind. During a visit to New York one November evening, Wilson had attracted a crowd as he walked with House. When they returned to House's residence, Wilson talked of his grief "and he could not help wishing when we were out tonight that someone would kill him." It was not the first time House had heard such alarming words. "He spoke of not wanting to live longer, and of not being fit to do the work he had in mind," House recorded in his diary. "He said he had himself so disciplined that he knew perfectly well that unless someone killed him, he would go on to the end doing the best he could."

The disturbing conversation likely unnerved House far more than the matter-of-fact account in his diary indicates. The nation was facing a major challenge, and the President was on the verge of a breakdown.

Most of the American public, unaware of the President's current mental state, seemed confident in Wilson's leadership at the moment, much to the chagrin of Roosevelt. The true measure, TR knew, would be the November midterm election, which would not only determine the fate of the Progressive party but likely his own political future. Regardless of the result, he had already decided there would be no return to the Republican party. "Both old parties today," he insisted, "are reactionary."

The demands placed upon him were immense. Every Progressive candidate from every two-bit tank town expected TR to speak on their behalf. If that wasn't possible, then a public letter endorsing their candidacy would do, as long as he stayed clear of any talk of the war or attacks on Wilson that might create more Republican voters than Progressive. Since many of the requesters had supported Roosevelt two years earlier, he found it difficult to say no. From Maine to Kansas, he dutifully preached the Bull Moose gospel, but the incessant politicking, "as if he were a candidate for township supervisor," was somewhat of a comedown for a former president. He also sensed that the more he spoke, the less newsworthy his words became. "I use myself up to no purpose," he grumbled. And the speeches, he came to believe, "did not do one particle of good."

But everyone undoubtedly wanted to see Teddy, still a genuine American folk hero whose larger-than-life status was unmatched by any other politician of his time. Certainly, neither Wilson nor Taft nor even Bryan attracted such fanatical devotion. That October, a Pennsylvania congressman told TR of a "young man who has his room practically papered with your pictures on photographs, china, banners, and badges. He has a library of every book you have written or has been written about you." Such idolatry was hardly uncommon and encouraged more than a few down-on-their-luck Americans to turn to a man five years out of office for help. "It is a habit of mind with me," one New York actress confessed, "to think of him as above ordinary humanity—a sort of beneficent Superman, to whom one's thoughts, in time of trouble turn instinctively, with full faith in his power to do—oh, almost anything!"

The crowds were happy to get a glimpse of Roosevelt in the flesh, perhaps even vote for him again in the future should the opportunity arise, but on election day their interest in the other Progressive candidates proved to be marginal. Nationally, the party polled only half as many votes as TR received in 1912, winning only six congressional seats. More disturbing was the strong showing of the Republicans, who gained sixty-six seats in the House of Representatives, although the Democrats retained majorities in both houses, much to the relief of House and Wilson.

Although Roosevelt was disappointed, he was not surprised by the outcome. The two-party system was too ingrained, he glumly noted, with the "average American in his party affiliations . . . largely influenced by a feeling quite as unreasoning as that which makes the average fan depressed or exultant over the victory of a professional baseball team." He also sensed that the voters were "tired of reformers" and had tuned out their message. "The American public," he griped afterward, "has a mind about four inches long." And the currently stagnant economy had also played a significant role. "If men have not enough to eat, they are entirely uninterested in social justice; they want a job," he noted.

If the Progressive party was now clearly a shell, was the movement so cherished by Addams and other reformers now dead? TR didn't think so. The "cause is exactly as good as ever" and one that he promised never to abandon, but their timing was off. In fact, he correctly predicted that "there is not an idea championed by the Progressive party two years ago which will not be generally accepted twenty-five or thirty years hence." But the reluctance to support the Progressive ticket, even among liberals, revealed an uncomfortable reality that he found difficult to accept. As much as TR scoffed that Wilson was no progressive but a "wonderful dialectician" with "no definitive purpose at all," many voters, impressed by the legislative achievements of the current administration, now saw Wilson and Bryan as a potentially more effective vehicle for continued reform. The radical wing (or "lunatic fringe," as Roosevelt dubbed them) of the Progressives had never fully trusted the former president's commitment to the cause, but even more mainstream followers questioned his continued willingness to grant such a huge party role to the wealthy financier George Perkins, aka the Dough Moose. "The people of this country," one Progressive explained to TR, "cannot understand how Perkins—former partner of J. P. Morgan, one of the organizing partners of the steel trust and of the Harvester trust—can be taking an unselfish interest in leading the organization of a new political party."

Of course, Roosevelt understood that without Perkins's money, there might not be a party at all. But that mattered little to him at the moment. Two years after its formation, the Bull Moose party likely had no future and had become an albatross around his neck. He had tired of its obligations and its limitations on what he could and could not say. With the election over, he could now speak freely "and do just what I damned please."

What that might be was hardly clear to anyone, let alone to TR himself. His announcement that he was now a "private citizen of the privatest sort, and I haven't a thing to say about anything" raised eyebrows, including those of his estranged friend Taft, who guffawed when reading the comments. From a political perspective, it might be best to keep mum for the present. As Perkins reminded Roosevelt, the war was likely to create "enormous changes in political and economic questions" and "no man is wise enough or far-sighted enough to see how these questions are going to shape themselves and affect political parties." But his enemies were certain he was now a dead man politically. "On no spot in the United States can Roosevelt place his finger and say: 'Here the people are with me,'" *The Philadelphia Inquirer*, a loyal GOP organ, smugly editorialized. Old Guard Republicans could now rest easy, no longer fearing another destructive Roosevelt run in 1916 and potential Progressive control of the party. Rumors surfaced that an embarrassed TR would go abroad "for a good long period," news that House hopefully reported to Wilson.

Roosevelt had no intention of riding off into the sunset. Even in the midst of a grueling campaign, the "hideous disaster" in Europe and America's role therein had remained foremost in his thoughts. Somehow, he found time during his hectic speaking schedule to complete five weekly newspaper articles before the election for the Wheeler Syndicate; the series, titled "What America Should Learn from the War," reached an estimated 15 million readers each Sunday. What he hoped to achieve was to educate the "good people, who are busy people and not able to devote much time to thoughts about international affairs" and who were "often confused by men whose business it is to know better."

Like a stern schoolmaster, TR did his best to drill simple, yet important, lessons into the minds of his hapless pupils. The much touted arbitration treaties were no solution to war. "Great military empires in the old world," he wrote, "will pay not one moment's heed to the most solemn and binding treaty if it is to their interest to break it," and the United States would probably do the same. The peace movement, "loquacious but impotent," was just as worthless, fixated on peace for peace's sake and "too timid even to say that they want the Peace to be a righteous one." He was not a warmonger, he insisted, "but if I must choose between Righteousness and Peace I choose Righteousness." A premature peace during the Civil War, he reminded his readers, would have left slavery intact. And those who believed this was the "last great war" were sadly mistaken; in fact, some sort of instrument was needed to prevent a repeat of such a disaster. He hearkened back to an idea he had proposed several years earlier: "an agreement among the great powers, in which each should pledge itself not only to abide by the decisions of a common tribunal but to back with force the decision of that common tribunal." Thus, this "international police force" would fulfill the same duties as a municipal police force, but on a global scale. "Such a scheme is for the immediate future Utopian," he admitted, but "it certainly will not be Utopian for the remote future."

As far as the war itself, the upcoming election had forced Roosevelt to choose his words exceedingly carefully. He insisted that he was "not criticizing nor taking sides," adding that "[t]here are plenty of instances of violations of treaties to be credited to almost all of the nations engaged on one side or the other." He could not help but admire Germany's "powerful forward movement of the first six weeks of the war" and one might even argue that the German invasion of Belgium was justifiable "from the standpoint of the preservation of her national life," just as one might also believe that Belgium "has been terribly wronged." And the kaiser was no "devil, merely bent on gratifying a wicked thirst for bloodshed"; in fact, the overwhelming defeat of Germany would be a disaster for the world, just as the "destruction of Russia . . . would be a most frightful calamity."

Once the midterm election was over, TR no longer felt the need for discretion. He had increasingly come to believe that Germany was not only the "villain," but that the Wilson administration had utterly failed to live up to its international obligations by failing to protest the Belgian invasion in August. The change of heart had come gradually. Back in September, Roosevelt had met in Cleveland with a group of Belgian commissioners sent over by King Albert to present evidence of German atrocities to Wilson, who promised nothing except that such matters would be addressed after the war. TR's meeting, in French, went well on both sides, although Roosevelt still believed that "there is a tendency to exaggerate such outrages." But it was his own daughter Ethel's letters from Paris detailing the pitiful sights of brutalized Belgian refugees that finally erased all doubts. It also provided him with a convenient issue with which to club Wilson.

His first postelection syndicated article demonstrated that the gloves were completely off. He could no longer refrain from criticism of the "spiritless and selfish neutrality" of "Messrs. Wilson and Bryan." Nor could he agree that "our sole concern should be to keep ourselves at peace, at any cost, and not to help other powers that are oppressed, and not to protect against wrongdoing." If the Hague Conventions meant anything, then the "invasion and subjugation" of a neutral state such as Belgium demanded an American response (actually, the Hague agreements had numerous loopholes, such that the United States was not required to do anything). The response did not necessarily have to be military, although Roosevelt's detractors may have believed he was advocating such a stance. "The extent to which the action should go may properly be a subject for discussion," he explained. "But that there should be some action is beyond discussion."

That he clearly indicted Germany for the first time was a politically dangerous move, likely to inflame thousands of German American voters.

"I have a very genuine respect and admiration for the Germans, and I alienate them with great reluctance," he privately admitted. The die, however, was cast. As much as TR tried to explain that he was not anti-German, was part-German himself, and would condemn any nation guilty of international wrongdoing, he was soon swamped by a sea of angry letters from both home and abroad. A wounded Prussian officer who had been to America several years earlier informed Roosevelt that there had been no atrocities and "our men behaved simply splendidly," except for perhaps "some rascals." Others were eager to see the former president in person to explain the German position. His old friend George Viereck arranged a meeting at Sagamore Hill in November with Bernhard Dernburg, a banker and former member of the kaiser's cabinet now in America handling German propaganda efforts. Viereck was surprised to see TR clearly suffering from the lingering effects of tropical fever, but his mind was very much intact. Not only did he remember meeting Dernburg in Berlin several years earlier and the book he had presented him, but he then engaged in a lengthy "intellectual wrestling match" that lasted until nearly midnight. "Neither man had convinced the other," Viereck later wrote. Afterward, Viereck mentioned that Roosevelt was "losing many of his old-time supporters," including Viereck himself in the very near future. That was of no concern, TR responded. "I know that I am finding myself increasingly out of touch with the majority of my fellow citizens."

Such a realization could not help but darken his mood, even though outwardly he insisted that everything was fine. "I am happy as possible," he wrote his daughter-in-law Belle. He was content to "walk and row" with his wife, Edith. "I am really glad that it has become my duty to stay quietly at Sagamore Hill and loaf and invite my soul." But the decisive rejection from the public, "just at the very time when he most wanted it," one friend recalled, was devastating. The masses, he believed, had simply stopped listening to him or were certain that he was a saber rattler eager to risk American lives unnecessarily in contrast to the White House's current more civilized occupant. He doubted his ongoing war series would make much of an impression; in fact, the average reader was probably more interested in his Brazilian adventures, which were being simultaneously serialized by another syndicate. "The dreadful thing," he lamented, "is that the people don't seem to care." And modern America, "very self-absorbed," and its increasingly materialistic nature were at least partially to blame. "I wish to heavens that this country would wake up to the hideous damage, moral and physical caused by the deification of mere industrialism, of softness, and of self-indulgence," he wrote a British friend.

His frustration surfaced in growing bitterness of his attacks on Wilson. Privately, Roosevelt denounced the President as a "timid man physically . . . shifty and rather unscrupulous . . . entirely cold-blooded and selfish" and eager to "gain great glory as the righteous peacemaker." That "our educated men" and British Foreign Secretary Edward Grey did not share his views baffled him. Publicly, he blasted the administration's current do-nothing policy in Mexico, now in the midst of a civil war, which he argued had left American citizens and Catholics vulnerable to terroristic acts by both sides. "The action of the President and Mr. Bryan," TR wrote, "has been such as to make this country partly responsible for the frightful wrongs that have been committed."

Whether such venomous language achieved anything was questionable. To some observers, Roosevelt was hitting the President "below the belt." But Wilson was not especially concerned. "The very extravagance and un-restrained ill feeling of what he is now writing serve to nullify any influence that his utterances could have," he wrote an associate a few days after TR's last and most vicious syndicated article appeared. "He cannot possibly in his present situation or temper cause any embarrassment which need give us a second thought." It was a shame, Wilson thought, that Roosevelt "should have so forgotten the dignity and responsibility of a man placed as he is who might exercise so great an influence for good if he only saw and chose the way." Even Progressive allies such as Kansas editor William Allen White advised TR to back off for the moment in his Wilson bashing. Write about anything else, say, "modern tendencies in architecture" or "national moving picture censorship. . . . Friend Bryan and friend Wilson will not last long at their present rate and I think you will be a lot stronger if you do not have their blood on your hands."

Roosevelt claimed such a strategy was impossible: much of his income now came from writing, and political commentary of this sort paid the bills. And he had no shortage of offers to write by the end of 1914. The

Wheeler Syndicate wanted more articles, and even the notorious TR-hater William Randolph Hearst came calling. But the monthly *Metropolitan Magazine* won the TR stakes with a whopping $25,000 a year contract (about $650,000 today) for fifty thousand words. That TR would be employed by a magazine with a decided radical slant puzzled more than a few of his followers, who warned that it was filled with "Socialist propaganda."

Never an ideological purist about where his writings appeared, Roosevelt brushed aside such concerns. After all, *The New York Times*, "one of my most bitter opponents" that "represents the extreme capitalistic feeling," had carried his syndicated war articles.

The *Metropolitan* deal would hopefully help to fill the inescapable void he felt being on the sidelines while the greatest of all wars was under way. And the money, TR noted, "guarantees me against any unfavorable result from the libel suit," which he thought was more than likely because of the "mania" against him in New York. It would also allow him a healthy cash flow until all his children were out of college. The youngest, Quentin, was now at Groton and writing for the school newspaper. Older brother Archie was an unenthusiastic Harvard student whose slovenly ways ("there are moments when he looks as if he came out of a scrap basket," TR admitted) occasionally concerned his father. His other children were married and out on their own but never far from TR and Edith's thoughts. They were disturbed to find Ethel ailing and requiring surgery when she and her husband, Richard Derby, returned from their stint at the American Ambulance Hospital in Paris. "She ought never to have been taken abroad," Roosevelt insisted. "I am no friend to have women traipsing around to take part in what ought to be men's jobs." They also fretted about the safety of Kermit and his wife, Belle, during their recent voyage to Buenos Aires, where Kermit was now working for a branch of the National City Bank. Ted, their oldest son, meanwhile, had already considered enlisting in the British forces at the outset of the war but decided to stay in his current position as an investment banker. And vivacious daughter Alice was now somewhat settled as the wife of Nick Longworth, an Ohio Republican recently returned to Congress, although the marriage would soon turn sour.

As 1914 wound down, TR appeared ambivalent about his future. On the one hand, he considered himself "no longer fit, physically or in any other way, to continue to lead an active life"; on the other, he still fantasized about leading "a division of my Rough Riders trying to do what I could for the Belgians!" But a different path would soon present itself, one that would propel him into the next act of his political life. American military preparedness, an issue he had harped on in his syndicated articles, was about to become a national concern, with Roosevelt its spokesman.

National defense had long been a Roosevelt obsession, but one that had seldom gained much traction with the American public. "Of all the nations of the world," he grumbled, "we are the one that combines the greatest amount of wealth with the smallest ability to defend that wealth." But with a global war in full swing, he would find a more receptive audience to his views. The press had fanned the flames early on by reprinting a Prussian officer's hypothetical invasion plan of the United States published in Berlin thirteen years earlier. No one, TR believed, should be surprised that such plans existed. "I myself have seen the plans of at least two empires now involved in war to capture our great cities and hold them for ransom because our standing army is too weak to protect them," he informed a Princeton audience. Between the lines, it was clear that the "two empires" were Germany and Japan, nations that Roosevelt privately believed might form a troublesome alliance "if Germany comes out even a little ahead in the present war."

Were such fears of invasion rational? He and close friends such as General Leonard Wood thought so. Like Roosevelt, the previously obscure military physician had been propelled to fame thanks to his involvement with the Rough Riders during the Spanish-American War two decades earlier. By 1910, Wood had become Army Chief of Staff, though his relationship with Wilson was uneasy at best, and the General had no interest in continuing in the position when his four-year term ended in April 1914. Now commanding the army's Eastern Department at Governors Island in New York, Wood began beating the preparedness drum and was not averse to scare tactics. "Modern wars come like the avalanche and not like the glacier," he warned. And the U.S. army was dangerously small. "A Regular Army slightly in excess of 100,000, reinforced by 108,000 state militia, is in no sense prepared to battle with any first-class power on the globe," he explained.

For some, it was not difficult to dismiss Wood's comments as the hysterical ravings of an overexcited military man long convinced of the inadequacy of America's defenses. Liberals such as *New York Evening Post* editor Oswald Garrison Villard, son of Fannie Villard of the recent woman's march and grandson of William Lloyd Garrison, informed Wilson that he thought Wood "one of the most dangerous men in the country today." Wilson, who never trusted Wood or his penchant for "intrigue" and insubordination, was inclined to agree. But he could not entirely ignore Wood and TR's preparedness cries, especially when the issue threatened to become an annoyance to the administration that fall, thanks to a pudgy, Republican congressman from Massachusetts named August Peabody Gardner.

Gussie Gardner was a quintessential polo-playing, Harvard-attending, upper-crust New England Yankee whose background was not dissimilar from that of his more powerful father-in-law, TR's old friend Senator Henry Cabot Lodge. His wife, Constance, was as conservative as her Old Guard Republican father. The Washington know-it-all Ellen Slayden characterized her fellow congressional wife as "a leading antisuffragist, a violent antipacifist, and an incessant smoker. I believe I would rather have a man's right to *vote* than his privilege of *smoking*." At the war's outset, the Lodges and Gardners were in London, but Gardner was soon pressed into service to rescue stranded relatives in France, including twelve-year-old Henry Cabot Lodge Jr., the future running mate of Richard Nixon in 1960. When Gardner, who had served during the Spanish-American War, returned to the States in late September, he was convinced of two things: first, Germany was the bogeyman in the current crisis; and second, the United States must strengthen its defenses.

Perhaps emboldened by TR's recent articles, Gardner went public with his views on October 16 by introducing a House resolution to create a nine-member commission to investigate America's military and naval capabilities. "The belief held by the country that we can create an Army and Navy when the need arises is wrong from beginning to end," he explained. The issue, the congressman believed, was political. "Every voter in this land has been taught to believe that at any minute we can create an army and a navy fit to face the world, and we do not like to tell them otherwise."

To his credit, Gardner was not simply taking a cheap shot at Wilson, admitting that "the blame for our insecurity falls on Republicans and Democrats alike." In fact, administration officials such as Assistant Secretary of the Navy Franklin Roosevelt were preparedness supporters, so much so that FDR discreetly provided Gardner with juicy evidence of the navy's deficiencies. And FDR himself was not shy about voicing his opinion publicly in the weeks that followed, although he was careful to avoid any "talk about the present war," per Wilson's strongly stated preference. "We are from 30,000 to 50,000 men short of the needs of the Navy," FDR announced. "The question is . . . whether we are willing today to conclude that the human race has reached the point where we can leave our homes and nation totally unprepared against attack. If we have, then why have any army or navy? If we have not reached that point, then let us prepare."

Franklin Roosevelt, of course, was not a particularly influential voice in the Wilson administration. But someone who was—Colonel House—also saw the need for some movement toward preparedness. House had even met with General Wood to discuss the Swiss system of universal military training for all young men, an idea long favored by TR. In early November, House began pushing Wilson to do something about the army and "make the country too powerful for any nations to think of attacking us." Wilson, who likely thought House had been reading too much TR lately, was not especially enthusiastic, although he did accept the notion of a "large reserve force." ("But not a large army.") House sighed. "The President does not seem to fully grasp the importance of such matters."

Wilson was hardly clueless; he simply believed the pros would be outweighed by the cons. Politically, preparedness did not make much sense at the moment. The big business/Anglophilic East Coast would back a defense buildup, but the rest of the country would be unenthusiastic or openly hostile. Much of the South, the Midwest, and the West Coast believed that America was not Europe, did not want or need a large military, and recoiled at the thought of a draft. And, so their thinking went, with two oceans protecting us, why burden our people with the expense and high taxes sure to follow? More important, the President was certain that any move toward preparedness would undo all the groundwork he had laid to keep American citizens cool, calm, and collected in the current crisis. Not only would an aggressive call for preparedness "shock the country" and perhaps lead it down the path of war, but it would also undermine America's own position as a potential peacemaker, especially since its leading advocate, Gardner, had already described Germany's intentions as "unholy." It would also play into the hands of Wilson's political rival TR, who would certainly take credit for such a move.

Almost immediately the President went to work to squelch preparedness talk. First, he informed Gardner that he was not interested in considering any special commission except perhaps as a "mental exercise." Without Wilson's support, the Gardner resolution would get nowhere in Congress. "It may be easy enough to chloroform my resolution," a defiant Gardner insisted, "and it may not be difficult to chloroform me; but all the anesthetics in the world can never lull to sleep the demand of an alarmed public sentiment that the truth must be revealed." But Wilson proceeded to do just that. He decided he would address the issue head-on in his annual message to Congress on December 8, which he would read in person, something he had done since first taking office, breaking a hundred-year precedent. "Wouldn't Teddy have been glad to think of that," he chortled at the time. "I put one over on Teddy."

In the course of his speech, Wilson first questioned the notion of "being prepared." If that meant "ready upon brief notice to put a nation in the field," then "we are not ready to do that; and we shall never be in time of peace so long as we retain our present political principles and institutions." As far as defending the nation against any attack, "we have always found means to do that, and shall find them whenever it is necessary without calling our people away from their necessary tasks to render compulsory military service in times of peace. . . . We shall not turn America into a military camp. We will not ask our young men to spend the best years of their lives making soldiers of themselves." He was not against preparation per se, but it should take the form of a "citizenry trained and accustomed to arms" and the bolstering of the National Guard. Going beyond this would not only undermine the national "self-possession" that he deemed so essential but would also show "that we had been thrown off our balance by *a war with which we have nothing to do*, whose causes can not touch us, whose very existence affords us opportunities of friendship and disinterested service." Of course, national security would not be neglected now or in the future, but "we shall not alter our attitude toward it because some amongst us are nervous and excited." That the "nervous and excited" comment referred to Gardner was obvious to everyone present, especially since Wilson had been intentionally looking in his direction during the preparedness part of his speech. The House, per one press report, "rocked with applause and laughter," while Gardner's "naturally florid face flushed a deeper red."

The speech more than satisfied cabinet pacifists such as Bryan and Secretary of the Navy Josephus Daniels, a North Carolina newspaperman whose limited knowledge of nautical affairs and passive preparedness attitudes frustrated his subordinate FDR. Daniels, his predecessor George von L. Meyer raged, seemed more interested in making "red school houses out of the battle ships!" and persistently asking sailors "are you happy and do you get enough to eat?"

Meanwhile, TR was apoplectic. The smooth-talking Wilson had tricked the nation once again, with a speech that was nothing less than "an elaborate argument against preparedness, excellently calculated to puzzle our people and to keep them from trying to get ready." (Years later, he would insist that it was "more responsible than any one thing for the wrong attitude of this country toward preparedness.") More than ever, TR was convinced that "Messrs. Wilson and Bryan" were the "very worst men we have ever had in their positions." Such venomous criticism did not especially concern the President. "Partisan tactics," he wrote a friend a few days later, "only excite my contempt, and not a lively enough contempt to make me unhappy."

But the genie was out of the bottle. In the days that followed, administration officials such as Daniels and FDR testified before Congress about the current state of the navy, while Secretary of War Lindley Garrison, one of the few cabinet officials TR thought competent and who also disdained the "Bryan yellow crowd," issued a report that challenged Wilson's placid view of the nation's military capabilities. Military training for college students began to attract support, especially at Harvard, where it was spear-headed by TR's son Archie. And two newly formed preparedness organizations, the American Defense League and the more formidable National Security League, began to make noise, advocating among other things target practice in high schools and colleges and an education campaign to offset the "harm . . . done to the country by the peace societies."

The growing preparedness talk that December disturbed Addams. "The enormity of the war has driven the sane view of militarism from the public mind," she lamented. To Addams, no need existed for a costly military or naval buildup, which would ultimately amount to a "tax of militarism." And preparedness, regardless of TR's beliefs, was not the way to prevent war. Germany, after all, was "the best prepared country in the world," and England also had an "enormous army and navy." (Roosevelt's inevitable reply to such "foolish" arguments was to cite the feeble status of his favorite whipping boy—China—"entirely peaceful and is unable to defend herself.") Besides, changes were sure to come after the war. She, like TR, envisioned the existence of some sort of future global organization, perhaps with an international navy, that would allow America and other countries to reduce, not increase, their defense spending. "Why should the United States build up a great army at this time when we are on the eve of a readjustment of militarism?" she asked. "It seems absurd."

Addams was still wrestling with the dilemma of how best to channel her activism in the midst of war. It would not be through the Progressive party, although George Perkins asked her to delay her resignation from the executive board. The party's poor showing in the midterm elections and TR's recent utterances likely convinced her that its usefulness to her was at an end. Continued suffrage work always called to her, even if her speeches during the campaign had failed to bear much fruit. Five of seven states rejected votes for women, a result she believed partly related to the war. "The war has set suffrage back both in America and in Europe," she explained. "War is man's business. It invariably throws into prominence man's power and force. Women are not taken into the counsels. Their share of the burden is not so apparent as man's, and therefore is deprecated." And Hull-House and its doings, especially unemployment relief that winter, still provided more than enough opportunities to keep her busy.

Peace remained foremost in Addams's mind. To her, the Henry Street meeting in New York back in September following the women's peace parade suggested the direction that such a movement ought to take, a broad-based effort and one that would involve economists, "'social workers' and others representing the new point of view—the saving of life by all sorts of social devices." The newly organized Chicago-based Emergency Peace Federation, which she took charge of as chairman in the days following Wilson's address, included not only the usual pacifist suspects but also socialists, union officials, playground and recreational workers, and teachers. But how far should she go with any peace activism at the moment remained uncertain, especially when any high-profile efforts were likely to offend at least some segment of her usual supporters, perhaps even the philanthropists so essential to Hull-House. Already, the local press was less than sympathetic. And her own health was not the best at the moment. Headaches plagued her, so much so that she was required to stay in bed an extra hour each morning.

The enthusiastic reception received by Schwimmer and Pethick-Lawrence on their American tours had intensified the pressure on Addams to do more. The Emergency Peace Federation's "Program for Constructive Peace" had heavily incorporated both Pethick-Lawrence's and Schwimmer's ideas, and Pethick-Lawrence had already organized women's peace groups in several cities with a plan for a January conference in Washington. Addams found herself unable to ignore the growing and insistent demand for something bigger: a national women's peace meeting. "There is great eagerness for some sort of expression," she admitted, "and while I do not wish it to lead to a foolish demonstration it does seem a pity not to give definite form to so much zeal!"

Her misgivings were considerable. She had successfully worked with both men and women in the past and saw no reason to change now, regardless of the success of the single-sex peace march back in August. And she was dubious that a potentially "large and ill assorted assemblage" of women brought together "merely because they are eager for Peace" and "who do not know each other well" could accomplish much beyond a "good deal of emotionalism." The participation of Pethick-Lawrence and Schwimmer also had to be considered, especially since their presence, as one friend reminded Addams, unfortunately suggested the "necessity of foreign women being used to awake American women to their duty."

Both of the visiting European pacifists came with more than their share of baggage. Pethick-Lawrence's perceived "arrogance" rubbed some American ladies the wrong way, as did her former association with the militant suffrage movement in England. Schwimmer's unbridled passion for peace, bordering on obsession, presented greater difficulties to Addams. She had already witnessed Schwimmer's unfortunate tendency to stretch the truth, first by prematurely claiming back in November that Addams was organizing a "woman's mass meeting" and then with a fanciful public statement (which she later denied) that Addams, Bryan, and others would soon go to Europe as part of an "arbitration committee." Nor could she ignore Schwimmer's overly sensitive, sometimes tearful reactions in the face of any criticism or disagreement. A less charitable observer, the young pacifist Louis Lochner, deemed her "evidently unstrung and nothing short of hysterical."

Not surprisingly, Schwimmer sulked when Addams expressed reservations about a national women's peace meeting. "I am sorry not to be as enthusiastic as Madame Schwimmer wants us to be," Addams wrote Carrie Chapman Catt, "but I am sure you understand that it is not that I am languid in the cause of peace."

Catt, who favored the meeting provided it did not affect her cherished suffrage cause, did her best to sway Addams. The established peace organizations have "little use for women," so why not a new female-driven movement? And Addams, as the most respected woman in America, not only was the ideal person to take charge, but would represent a much needed break from the stodgy old-line pacifists, both male and female. Finally, Addams relented. "At the invitation of Mrs. Catt," she wrote in a December 28 form letter, "I am uniting with her to call together a number of women's organizations to meet in Washington January 10th to consider the organization of a National Peace Committee of Women." The letter went out to virtually any women's organization worth its salt in Progressive-era America, conservative, liberal, or otherwise, along with the women's divisions of the existing peace organizations, some of whom were likely to be annoyed by "outsiders . . . taking their work out of their hands."

What could such a meeting accomplish? Addams believed in the power of public opinion. Draw enough attention to an issue, and politicians would be forced to act. A decade or more of progressive legislative successes under her belt convinced her that this was undoubtedly true. A massive gathering of women might very well create the necessary momentum to force some sort of action from Congress or the President, whom she and other reformers believed was one of them, especially after his recent comments on preparedness.

Whether Wilson would pay much attention remained questionable. As the year wound down, his mental state was still not the best, the loss of Ellen as shattering as it had been in August. "I do not know yet how to carry this grief that has come to me," he wrote a friend. "It has weakened me at the very sources of my life." He continued to find Mary Hulbert and her various problems a welcome diversion, one that allowed him to play the role of courtly Southern gentleman rescuing a damsel in distress. Hulbert was now living in Boston in dire straits after her dopey son had squandered all of their money, a fact that she did not attempt to hide from Wilson. "You were *right* to tell me everything, and to tell me at once," he reassured her. The President of the United States then took the time from his extremely busy schedule to send five separate letters to Boston acquaintances asking them to help find his lady friend a job of some kind, perhaps in interior decorating. "I would put real pleasures in her way if I could," he wrote.

If Wilson was unlikely to be especially receptive at the moment, his secretary of state Bryan was a more obvious administration ally, and Addams did her best to have Schwimmer see him in Washington. The Great Commoner believed more than ever that something must be done now, "when the cup of sorrow is overflowing and when new horrors are being added daily." His florid prose notwithstanding, Bryan was not inaccurate in his assessment of the European situation, especially since the recent battles of Ypres (mispronounced by many an American as "wipes" or "wipers") in Belgium on the Western Front and of Łódź in Poland on the Eastern had resulted in staggering losses: at least 350,000 killed, wounded, or missing. To Bryan, it was time for Wilson to make another attempt to bring the combatants to the peace table; nay, it was our "duty, as the leading exponent of Christianity" to do so. "Surely these Christian nations ought to be willing to state to the world the terms upon the acceptance of which they are willing to cease hostilities," he wrote Wilson that December. As a man of devout fundamentalist faith, one that would place him squarely in the center of the famous Scopes "monkey" trial eleven years later, Bryan did not doubt a word he wrote. Even his detractors such as Secretary of War Garrison admitted that Bryan "had a profound and sincere belief in the omnipresence of Providence and His working in the affairs of men." Wilson agreed. "If Bryan had been an evangelist," he once remarked, "he would have been the greatest evangelist the world had ever known."

Colonel House conceded that "something must be done some time, by somebody . . . to initiate a peace movement." The "somebody," however, would not be women or Bryan, at least if House could help it. He had already done his best even before the outbreak of war to make sure that no one in Europe would take the secretary of state seriously, assuring foreign leaders that "they must not judge the President by Bryan." With Bryan effectively rendered irrelevant, House's own foreign policy role in the administration continued to grow. And Wilson, grateful for the close friendship during his current emotional turmoil, did nothing to restrain House. A delighted House happily confided in his diary that Bryan had no idea that Wilson was "working for peace wholly through me. . . . The President had a feeling that I could do more to initiate peace unofficially than anyone could do in an official capacity, for the reason I could talk and be talked to without it being binding upon anyone, and we might in this way arrive at conditions. He has placed this problem squarely up to me."

More significantly, the "President's Ambassador-at-large," as some dubbed House, was about to undertake yet another jaunt to the European capitals in the very near future. TR, after all, had brought peace to Russia and Japan in 1905; the Wilson administration, with a little groundwork laid, could do the same.

Vague communications from both sides had led House to believe peace might be feasible if the Germans would agree to restore Belgium and accept some sort of disarmament plan among the major powers. He reached out to the ambassadors in Washington, only to encounter the same German willingness from Bernstorff (who generally spoke more for himself than Berlin) and Allied hostility from Spring Rice he had already experienced in September. And Spring Rice, whose frequent emotional outbursts led House to question his stability, had a better read of the current situation. The Germans were currently winning the war, occupying much of Belgium and parts of France. Why would they be interested in making peace now? "If the Kaiser should seriously propose peace at this time, he would probably be assassinated," Spring Rice told House. House disagreed. He was certain the German leadership "knew that the war was already a failure and did not dare take the risk involved, provided they could get out of it whole now." It would not be the last time that he would completely misread the intentions of the belligerents.

Wilson was more than willing to overlook House's mistakes, present and future. He did not trust his own ambassadors, Walter Hines Page in London and James Gerard in Berlin. He perceived Page, an old friend and cofounder of the Doubleday, Page publishing company, as far too Anglophilic and Gerard, a Tammany Democrat and former judge, as "a reactionary of the worst sort." And the President was not especially enamored with Bryan (his "oldest son," he privately called him) or his undue concern with trivial patronage matters ("a spoilsman to the core," Wilson believed; Bryan, meanwhile, felt a sense of obligation to those who had supported him in three prior presidential runs). "We both thought he had served his usefulness as Secretary of State," House wrote in December, "and that it would be a good thing for the administration and for the country if he would pleasantly take himself out of the Cabinet." But Bryan would do nothing of the kind, and Wilson, likely fearful of the political blowback from Bryan's huge following, decided not to replace him for now.

On New Year's Eve, the nation learned of a remarkable event on the Western Front: the Christmas truce and startling fraternization between the German and British forces. The American William Robinson witnessed its beginnings on Christmas Eve. "During the evening the Germans started singing, and I heard some of the most beautiful music I ever listened to in my life," he later wrote. "When they had finished we would applaud with all our might, and then we would give them a song in return." Perhaps, many Americans hoped, peace was not so far away after all.

Four days before Christmas, the novelist Willa Cather expressed her desire for the war to end in a letter to her editor. "There will be nothing agreeable in the world until it *is* stopped," she wrote. But she was not confident about the future. "I suppose they will patch up a temporary peace and then, in twenty-five years, beat it again with a new crop of men."

Chapter 3

A STRICT ACCOUNTABILITY

JANUARY 1–MARCH 28, 1915

An accident, it is true, some chance collision, some
blunder by somebody, a bit of arrogance by an
irresponsible officer, may any day seem to bring us
to the verge of war. But even then we shall merely
need to stick by our rights under international law,
and to be calm about it.

—Editorial, *New York Evening Post*, February 1915

I n early January 1915, a strange incident occurred one evening in the German trenches on the Western Front in Lille, France, involving two American war correspondents, Robert Dunn of the *New York Evening Post* and John Reed of the *Metropolitan Magazine*. Handing them both Mausers, a Bavarian officer asked if they might be interested in trying them out.

"It's useless to arraign our feelings the eagerness with which . . . we leaped to do this," Dunn later wrote. "Maybe it was partly in retaliation to the deadly storm whiffing for hours around us . . . or mostly in homage to the brave and patient men of the pit, a deep-reaching instinct of brotherhood to be for a moment, once just like them." Reed, who would deny the incident in a congressional hearing four years later, admitted at the time that "we blasted away carelessly into the darkness." Presumably, the two amateur soldiers hit no one, although there was no way of telling for sure.

Dunn made no attempt to censor the incident in his dispatches home. The two men had simply been swept up in the moment. "As for our good

President and his warnings about neutrality," he wrote, "I will wage anything that if he had been there, he would have made a good third." But
Reed, already a well-known figure for his reporting during the Mexican
revolution, was remorseful, especially when the episode appeared likely to
block his plans to cover the war for *Metropolitan* from the French lines.

As a fellow *Metropolitan* writer, Roosevelt was pulled into the controversy. Dunn, he thought, "ought to be shot at once," but Reed was a different
story. Ideologically, TR and Reed were a universe apart—Reed was a true
radical—but TR believed Reed's story that he "loved France" and that limited
visibility made it virtually impossible for any French soldier to have been
harmed. And Reed, TR explained to the French ambassador Jusserand, "can
write"; his vivid accounts of the French military would be invaluable propaganda for the Allied side. Jusserand was sympathetic to his old friend's arguments but he knew that his superiors in Paris would never permit it and
Reed would probably "be shot if he is caught by the French." But Reed's
concerns that he might also be barred from going to Russia proved un-
founded. His time in Russia during the 1917 revolution later provided the
basis for his greatest literary triumph, *Ten Days That Shook the World*.

The angry reaction to a few shots fired by Dunn and Reed was somewhat
hypocritical, in view of the hundreds of Americans currently serving in the
Allied forces—men such as the Iowan James Norman Hall, recently introduced to the machine gun and "learning the fine art of butchering at the
rate of 350 to 500 per minute," as he described it in a letter home. Like
the rest of Lord Kitchener's "New Army," he was nearing the end of his
training in early 1915, with his final stop a massive military garrison at
Aldershot in Hampshire. Even with 100,000 others to share his plight, Hall
still found close friendships elusive, although many Tommies (the popular
nickname for the common British soldier) were eager to make his acquaintance once they discovered Jamie the Yank had a pocket camera, a gift from
one of his Boston friends. "All the fellows are simply crazy about it and
keep me busy ordering snaps for them," he wrote his mother. The folks in
Iowa also learned of his brushes with celebrity: first with Kitchener himself
in a troop review and then with the royal family at a church service. King
George V, he noted, cut a rather unimpressive figure: "small . . . very ordinary looking and without any of those kingly qualities of physique which

one always associates with monarchs." Queen Mary, "a head taller," seemed likely to "wield the scepter more capably than her husband."

Six months of military life had changed and matured Hall. Combat would be the final part of his transformation. "If I come safely through the strenuous times ahead of us, which I have but little doubt that I shall, the years to come will be greatly enriched by the experience," he wrote his father. He was impatient to fight, especially since he was certain that "some of the greatest battles in all history" were coming that spring. Still, he was happy to escape his increasingly grueling workload, albeit briefly, in the pages of his pocket Shakespeare or an occasional furlough to London, where he eagerly took in performances of *Peter Pan* and *David Copperfield* starring the celebrated actor Sir Herbert Tree in the dual roles of Micawber and Mr. Peggoty. In the British capital, Hall noticed that virtually every young man was in uniform; slackers could expect to be accosted by "white feather" brigades of women who handed them the symbol of cowardice to shame them into enlisting.

Thoughts of home were seldom far from his mind. He missed Iowa winters "when we used to coast all day on Saturday," a sense of humor ("a rarity with Englishmen"), and the typical "hearty American hand clasp." As much as possible, he did his best to follow recent developments in the United States, especially the recent talk of preparedness. "What a wretchedly small army we have," Hall lamented in a letter to his Boston friend Roy Cushman. "If we were forced to raise a great army as England has had to do, we should not have enough officers in all of our standing army to drill recruits to say nothing of going to fight." And America, he believed, was not safe. "We can pooh-pooh at thoughts of danger but the time may very possibly come when we shall have to stand up for our rights," he warned. "Thank Heaven we have a level headed President, who can steer us through safely if the thing is possible."

As the new year began, the levelheaded Mr. Wilson continued to outwardly present himself and his administration as the epitome of impartiality, sometimes to an extreme degree. The press had recently raised a kerfuffle over an incident in which Secretary of the Navy Daniels had reportedly squelched the singing of "It's a Long, Long Way to Tipperary" at a navy function. While visiting the White House in early January, family friend Nancy Saunders Toy mentioned that she had "never heard" the song, now so popular that one Washington store proudly advertised that "these records are scarce—But we have them." When Margaret Wilson promised to play the 78 record for her, his cousin Helen Bones joked: "What! In the White House!" But Wilson did not find it especially amusing, especially when Toy mentioned the recent Daniels controversy. "His fist came down on the table," she wrote in her diary. "Daniels did not give that order that Tipperary should not be sung in the Navy," Wilson barked. "He is surrounded by a network of conspiracy and of lies. His enemies are determined to ruin him. I can't be sure who they are yet, but when I do get them—God help them."

Strict American neutrality, Wilson continued to believe, was the wisest course to avoid war and leave the door open for involvement in the peace process. It was a stance that increasingly satisfied none of the belligerents. The growing flow of shell, shrapnel, and other munitions from Bethlehem Steel, DuPont, and other American companies to the Allies had begun to enrage Germany, especially in a struggle fast becoming, as TR's friend Arthur Lee noted, "a war more of ammunition than of men."

"I do not think that people in America realize how excited the Germans have become on the question of the selling of munitions of war by Americans to the Allies," Ambassador Gerard informed Washington. "A veritable campaign of hate has been commenced against America and Americans." The German-born congressman Richard Bartholdt, representing Deutschland-friendly St. Louis, sponsored a resolution to block such arms sales, which predictably got nowhere, since Wilson and even Bryan believed that neutrals had every right to sell munitions to countries at war. Germany could buy them if it wished; it was not America's fault that the powerful British navy gave the Allies a huge advantage in trade with the United States. And the German government had not shown the slightest reluctance to sell arms as a neutral nation to the Russians in their war against Japan a decade earlier.

The Germans had already begun to pursue other tactics, some legal, others pure espionage, to disrupt any American efforts that might benefit the Allies. Early that year, the German government secretly provided funds for the creation of the Bridgeport Projectile Company, designed to purchase vast quantities of powder and shrapnel-making machinery in the hopes of preventing American firms from fulfilling Allied orders. In February, a former German officer named Werner Horn, later declared insane, tried to dynamite the Vanceboro Bridge, which connected Maine and Canada, insisting he was performing a legitimate "act of war" against an enemy of Germany. Other plots included forged passports; attempts to buy American newspapers, including *The Washington Post*; and industrial sabotage in munitions plants, mostly with the knowledge and sometimes active involvement, at least financially, of Bernstorff and the German embassy in Washington.

But officials in Berlin believed their most important ace in the hole was the sizable German American population, who they were certain were itching to show their loyalty to the Fatherland. Arthur Zimmermann of the German Foreign Office warned Gerard in January that at present "there were five hundred thousand trained Germans in America who would join the Irish and start a revolution," should "trouble" occur. That Zimmermann and others actually believed such fantasies betrayed a complete misunderstanding of conditions in America (Spring Rice, the British ambassador, was equally clueless, suggesting that war with Germany might result in "something like a civil war" in the United States).

But Bernstorff knew better. Aside from a group of hard-core Germanophiles such as George Viereck, the average German American loved his new home as much as the old country. "Our greatest mistake," Bernstorff later admitted, "was to expect too much from them."

If Wilson had his hands full dealing with German accusations of partiality toward their enemies, the Allies were just as convinced that the United States leaned in the opposite direction. F. A. Mahan, brother of the recently deceased American naval luminary Admiral Alfred Mahan, whose writings on the significance of sea power profoundly influenced TR, depicted Paris as a seething cauldron of anti-Americanism. "You can have no idea of how strong the feeling against the United States is here," he wrote Roosevelt in February. "The people cannot understand how our country can so abandon all its old traditions of independence, right and justice, and fail to protest against and denounce everything which has gone on here."

Meanwhile, the British detected favoritism in virtually every move by the Wilson administration. Why, they asked, was America's first official protest of the war on December 26 lodged against British interference with American trade, instead of the German invasion of Belgium months earlier? And why was an American citizen (of partial German descent, no less) allowed to purchase the *Dacia*, a German ship interned in the United States, and use it to transport cotton to Rotterdam to be reshipped to Bremen? Threatening to intercept the *Dacia*, the British eventually thought better of it. The French did the deed instead in late February, a suggestion TR had made to Spring Rice. The British also saw disturbing unneutrality in Wilson's support of the Ship Purchase Bill, designed to alleviate the war-driven shortage of vessels needed to carry out America's commerce by acquiring German ships stuck in American ports. "There is danger in the present situation," *The Spectator* warned from London. "If the Washington Government think our difficulties will make us more compliant than in peace time, they are very much mistaken."

The thankless task of placating both sides had already begun to wear on Wilson. "Together, England and Germany are likely to drive us crazy, because it looks oftentimes as if they were crazy themselves, the unnecessary provocations they invent," he privately complained. "Both sides are seeing red on the other side of the seas, and neutral rights are left for the time being out of their reckoning altogether. They listen to necessity, not to reason, and there is therefore no way of calculating or preparing for anything." Still, the very real possibility that, as TR's friend Henry Cabot Lodge believed, "both sides heartily dislike and despise him" had not shaken Wilson's conviction that he was pursuing the wisest course for America. In a January speech in Indianapolis for Jackson Day, then an important event on every Democrat's calendar commemorating Old Hickory's defeat of the British in the Battle of New Orleans, Wilson offered a simple explanation for his current stance: "Do you not think it likely that the world will some time turn to America and say: 'You were right, and we were wrong. You kept your heads when we lost ours; you tried to keep the scale from tipping, but we threw the whole weight of arms in one side of the scale. Now, in your self-possession, in your coolness, in your strength, may we not turn to you for counsel and assistance?'"

Ironically, the President appeared less than cool or self-possessed during the speech, which contained a rather un-Wilson-like rant against the Republicans, who planned to do their best to block the Ship Purchase Bill. "The trouble with the Republican party is that it has not had a new idea for thirty years," he scoffed. "The Republican party is still a covert and a refuge for those who are afraid, for those who want to consult their grand-fathers about everything." It was the Democrats, not the Republicans, who were truly progressives and had "carried out the policies which the progres-sive people of this country have desired."

The speech predictably incensed GOP stalwarts like Lodge, who con-sidered it "angry" and "cheap," but even some of Wilson's own supporters thought he had gone too far. The President was not apologetic. "The Re-publicans are every day employing the most unscrupulous methods of par-tisanship and false evidence to destroy this administration and bring back the days of private influence and selfish advantage," he wrote a friend. "We must hit them and hit them straight in the face, and not mind if the blood comes."

The erratic (at least for Wilson) behavior reflected the labile emotional state of a man still recovering from an enormous personal loss. Physically, he felt fine, with the exception of some vague kidney issues, but sadness and thoughts of Ellen continued to consume him in the new year. Still, the talk of death that had so unnerved Colonel House back in the fall seemed to have disappeared; in fact, Wilson now seemed resigned to a second term if "only to keep Bryan out" of the White House. And his deep religious faith offered solace. "Never for a moment have I had one doubt about my religious beliefs," he remarked one Sunday that January. "There are people who *believe* only so far as they *understand*—that seems to me presumptuous and sets their understanding as the standard of the universe."

He still craved distractions from his grief and the increasingly vexing European situation. Mary Hulbert's woes continued to occupy him, so much so that he was not shy about passing along her article on afternoon teas to *Ladies' Home Journal* editor Edward Bok, who was more than happy to do the President a favor and paid fifty dollars for the publishing rights. The White House birth of his daughter Jessie's first child and his first grandchild also helped to raise his spirits, although he promptly quashed any talk of naming the boy Woodrow. The baby, he remarked, will be "sufficiently handicapped by being born in the White House." But Francis Bowes Sayre Jr., who lived another ninety-three years, would have an im-pressive career of his own as a prominent Episcopal minister and a fearless foe of McCarthyism, segregation, and the Vietnam War.

The press, of course, wanted pictures of the White House baby with Wilson, who had no choice but to comply. Such obligations were a mundane, but necessary, part of the President's day-to-day duties. AT&T, for example, requested Wilson to participate in the first-ever transcontinental telephone call, from Washington to San Francisco on January 25, during which he exchanged pleasantries with Alexander Graham Bell and Thomas Watson. "One hundred million people will have for their daily use a system of communication that knows no East, no West, no North, no South," boasted Bell phone system ads. "Truly, This is The Triumph of Science."

The new triumph of science was not cheap: $20.70 for a three-minute call that would take up to ten minutes to process (the equivalent of about $500 today). The luxury of a transcontinental conversation (one reporter envisioned a future where "every man may talk to anybody anywhere in the United States") was unfathomable for most Americans, especially in the midst of a weak economy yet to show the impact of increased war orders. Soup kitchens and breadlines were seen in New York, where Roosevelt had gone on recent fact-finding missions to better understand the plight of the unemployed and perhaps find ways to put them to work. At a lodging house on East Twenty-fifth Street, he mingled among the unfortunate men and women in the dining room, even partaking in their humble meal of pea soup. "Isn't it tough when an ex-president has to eat this stuff?" someone shouted. Later, TR gave a talk on his Brazilian adventures at the Metropolitan Opera House to raise money for the unemployed just one day after the historic phone call while pushing for the creation of a "federal employment bureau."

Colonel House, who saw the unemployment problem up close from his East Fifty-third Street residence, felt that Wilson was not sufficiently engaged with the problem and "does not realize the importance of these sociological measures." The President's "unimaginative, mediocre" (at least in House's eyes) labor secretary, William Wilson, did not help matters.

As a social worker, Addams understood the seriousness of the situation. In a world without unemployment insurance or federal welfare of any kind, unfortunates had little choice but to flock to institutions such as Hull-House, which was forced to dip into its coffers repeatedly that winter. Jobless men met there each Sunday and even took to the streets that

January bearing signs proudly proclaiming WE WANT WORK; NOT CHARITY, prompting some head bashing and arrests by the Chicago police. Not only did Addams succeed in getting the protesters out, but a judge also ruled that such parades were not illegal if kept under control. The appearance of hotheaded radicals, Russian and Irish, at subsequent unemployment meetings at Hull-House did not especially concern her. "Let them talk it out," she suggested. "They come from lands of oppression and they bring with them new and often crude ideals of freedom. It is only harmful when it is suppressed. I have found that they lose their radicalism in a few years and make highly respectable citizens."

As much as Addams may have wished to do more, her main focus was the upcoming women's peace meeting in Washington. That the gathering would be well attended was no longer in doubt, but some of her acquaintances fretted that the more militant wing of the suffrage movement, Alice Paul's Congressional Union for Woman Suffrage, which had split from the National American Woman Suffrage Association, would try to take over the gathering and steer the new organization down a more extreme path. But Addams again showed that ideological differences did not faze her. She was "not afraid" of the Congressional Union, she told an associate; in fact, a good many "friends . . . were in it." They would be given a place at the table, same as representatives from more conservative organizations, such as the National Woman's Christian Temperance Association and the Daughters of the American Revolution.

On Sunday, January 10, more than three thousand women from all walks of life jammed the ballroom of the New Willard Hotel, just two blocks from the White House, with hundreds more turned away by the fire marshal. ("In the crush," noted one journalist, "many gowns were torn.") The excitement in the crowd was tangible as they watched the birth of a new organization, to be known as the Woman's Peace Party, which boldly insisted in its Declaration of Principles that "women be given a share in deciding between war and peace in all the courts of high debate; within the home, the school, the church, the industrial order, and the State." Some of the more emotional types wept as they listened to speakers detail the war's devastation, such as Pethick-Lawrence, who also praised Wilson, a few miles away enjoying one of his usual motorcar jaunts with his cousin

Helen Bones. Others thrilled to Schwimmer's typical fire-and-brimstone address. "You have set the greatest record for women ever set in the history of the world," she roared. "You have always been a teacher to the women of Europe, and now you are teachers of the men. Until now, *might* has been the motive force of governments. Now we are coming to an age of reason when *right* shall substitute this."

But it was Addams's speech, labeled by one attendee as "the most convincing and forceful woman's Peace Speech I have ever heard," that commanded most of the attention. The war's negative impact on women, Addams began, had been enormous. The governments of the belligerent powers had unfortunately moved in a crude militaristic direction, whipping men into a patriotic frenzy "because they have been told that they must thus save their homes from destruction." What this meant for women, she argued, was "a world put back upon a basis of brute force—a world in which they can play no part." The war had also severely damaged the movement toward greater "sensitiveness to human life," which she deemed especially important for women. "I do not assert that women are better than men—even in the heat of suffrage debates I have never maintained that—but we would all admit that there are things concerning which women are more sensitive than men," she explained. And this heightened "sensitiveness" of women carried with it obligations, just as in days past when they had banded together to stop human sacrifices. Now, their duty was to speak out against the current and more frightening mass "sacrifice of life . . . unnecessary and wasteful. . . . If women's consciences are stirred in regard to warfare, this is the moment to formulate a statement of their convictions."

Along with Carrie Chapman Catt and several others, Addams had been hard at work on such a statement the day before, one that would eventually encompass eleven distinct resolutions, which she later described as "somewhat startling" to much of the world. The conference-of-neutrals idea, proposed by Schwimmer, was front and center, but the platform also called for arms reduction, "organized opposition to militarism" in America, peace instruction in the schools, "democratic control of foreign policies," votes for women, international cooperation among nations and the creation of some sort of law-based "organization of the world," an "international police," and the creation of a federally sponsored "commission of men and women . . .

to promote international peace." On Monday, an anti-preparedness resolution was added at a meeting attended by Ellen Slayden, whose journal entry was filled with her usual pungent observations: "Jane Addams presided in her gently great way—she is always so much the biggest woman present," Slayden wrote. "If we could get the women of the country to take as much interest in saving their sons from the shambles of war as they do in preventing everyone from taking an occasional drink, our influence might be tremendous."

That Addams should be chosen to head the WPP was not surprising. To Anna Garlin Spencer, a minister and pacifist also named to the board, her selection gave the new organization a legitimacy it would desperately need in the days ahead. American women interested in peace, she told Addams, "want to join something. . . . There is no woman in the country . . . that women of all classes will follow more gladly than you."

But Addams knew that the honor would come with a price. Continued high-profile involvement in causes, some outside her acceptable sphere as a do-gooding social worker, invited increased public scrutiny and outright criticism. A few weeks later at the Hotel McAlpin in New York, she overheard a "bright little matron from Georgia" loudly proclaim how Addams "had lost prestige and the applause of the world by her desire to undertake too much." Hull-House, the Georgian claimed, was falling apart because of too many "irons she has in the fire." Worst of all, Addams seemed a bit too willing to assist "foreigners who have ideas to exploit. . . . The Peace party is her fad just now." And her continued prominent presence in matters state and national did not sit well with some men, including one letter writer ("A Mere Man") to the *Chicago Tribune*. "Other nations have their hereditary autocrats," he wrote, "but America alone has a self-made dictatress."

The "dictatress" would have her hands full in the weeks ahead trying to get the new organization off the ground. As usual, drama surrounding the volatile Schwimmer posed a problem. Schwimmer had been selected as international secretary, but her occasional abrasiveness continued to irritate old-school pacifists and some WPP members, who were eager to drop her. And Addams found herself caught in the middle while serving as mother-confessor to Schwimmer, who informed her about plots "behind my back," along with the "jealousy" and "suspicion" of people who "personally dislike me." She even offered Addams the chance to distance herself from her on-going personal dramas: "If it would relieve you of difficulties with some of your co-workers, don't hesitate to throw me over."

Addams would do no such thing, but Schwimmer tried her patience. News about how a "nervous and hysterical" Schwimmer ranted about Wilson, Bryan, and Americans in general reached her, as did her continued, almost obsessive belief in a "Stop the War Now" approach, viewed as "absolutely foolish" by other members. Already, some were scared off by a platform seen as far too radical, even the votes-for-women plank. The antisuffrage crowd, a significant presence in New England and the South, wanted it out, but Addams and other WPP leaders viewed it as "fundamental to the undertaking."

For now, the immediate goal for the organization was getting its message out and building up membership in local branches. Seemingly, everyone wanted peace, but the press did not appear especially interested in promoting the WPP. The Washington papers had provided decent coverage, but most of New York's morning newspapers ignored the conference completely, preferring to devote their columns the next day to preparedness and the "man-killing in Europe." For Addams, the "usual lectures and peace literature" would not suffice, nor would a proposed "Jane Addams Peace Fund." Instead, she suggested that "plays and festivals" might be a more effective way to reach Americans. Marion Craig Wentworth's recently published one-act *War Brides*, the powerful story of a pregnant German woman who loses her husband in combat and then chooses to kill herself rather than offer up another child to the Fatherland, seemed ideal, as did Gilbert Murray's adaptation of Euripides' *The Trojan Women*. She approached officials at the conservative Carnegie Endowment for International Peace about financing a tour of Murray's play, only to discover they were "not in entire agreement" with the WPP platform and were "unwilling to be associated with it." Eventually, "in view of the respect and esteem" they had for Addams, Carnegie officials grudgingly agreed to a $5,000 contribution.

Publicity, while important, took a backseat to the more pressing need to get the organization's platform before the people—the men—who truly mattered. A WPP delegation visited Washington embassies in late January, hoping the ambassadors would then turn over the information to their home governments. British, Russian, and German representatives were polite enough, although the Germans were quick to insist that they bore no responsibility for the war. The French, however, informed them that they were not authorized to see "any peace delegations." Belle La Follette, the activist wife of the left-leaning Wisconsin senator Robert La Follette, managed to discuss the platform with Bryan, who was dubious about a conference of neutral nations, many of whom were linked to the belligerents in some way or another. Her own husband, "Fighting Bob," was also pessimistic, though he saw the value of the WPP as "propaganda."

Roosevelt would also be approached by the women. A few weeks after the conference, Julia Barrett Rublee, who campaigned for the Progressives in 1912 and whose husband, George, knew TR well, sent him the platform. After all, he was a Nobel Peace Prize winner and had advocated the same kind of international police force mentioned in the WPP platform. But Rublee should have been wary, especially if she had read Roosevelt's recent articles (anthologized in the recently published volume *America and the Great War*) and noticed their general contempt for pacifists and peace without "righteousness."

In any event, it was not the best time to reach out to TR for a favor or endorsement. Physically, his body was wracked with gout and rheumatism, worsened by an unpleasant return of his jungle fever at the end of January. Mentally, he remained in a funk, or as one friend later recalled, "as near despair as Theodore Roosevelt could come." With his influence limited, he lamented the time now spent "merely answering idiotic letters where the character of the writer forces me to be moderately civil, or holding dreary interviews on utterly unimportant or preposterous subjects with people I can't very well refuse to see." He could live vicariously through friends like Arthur Lee, who gave him the lowdown on the war situation in Europe while supervising British army medical services for Lord Kitchener. The Germans, Lee told TR, are "stout fighters—beyond all question—and still quite convinced, apparently, that they are going to win in the end." And this was a war that bore no resemblance to the old Rough Rider days when they had first met. "I have not once been on a horse," Lee explained. "This war is too serious a proposition for anyone but professionals (and up-to-date ones at that) to succeed in." Even Roosevelt seemed to concede that if he wished to get into the thick of things, it would have to be as "head of a brigade or a division. If I tried to go as a private or a junior officer I should be useless and I would make myself ridiculous."

For now, his raison d'être was twofold: promote preparedness in his writings and preach against the danger of what he called "hyphenated Americans," those he perceived as unduly loyal to their mother countries, an issue he had warned about as early as 1893. He perceived the "hyphen" as especially concerning in the current global war involving dozens of countries and nationalities. Every citizen, he believed, must be an "American-American" first, regardless of their ancestral home. "I don't care a rap where a man was born," TR explained. "If he is a good American without a hyphen, if he is straight United States; and just so long as he is a good American, I will stand by him exactly as much as if his ancestors had come over in the *Mayflower*."

More than a few German Americans, already extremely unhappy with him, interpreted his hyphen fixation as directed exclusively at them. Still, he did his best to show his impartiality. Despite warnings from friends, he attended a luncheon gathering in January of prominent German Americans at the home of Hugo Münsterberg, a distinguished German-born Harvard psychology professor and currently one of Germany's most persistent defenders in America. An English friend of Roosevelt, John St. Loe Strachey, the editor of *The Spectator*, wondered whether TR might be trying too hard to be evenhanded, especially after reading his latest book and what he perceived as its "coolness toward England."

Luncheons were not enough for *the Fatherland*'s George Viereck, who had been trying for months to get his old friend TR to embrace or at least understand the German cause. Viereck was both mystified and deeply hurt that Roosevelt, who had always been sympathetic to Germany (more so than England or France, at least in Viereck's eyes), was seemingly abandoning her in her time of need. A fiery exchange of letters followed, culminating in TR's labeling Viereck of not being "a good citizen" of Germany or America and advising him to return to his homeland and enlist. The two never spoke again.

To Viereck, the man for whom he had campaigned so actively in 1912 and who inspired his "Progressive Battle Hymn" had changed. He was not the only Bull Moose supporter perplexed by Roosevelt's attitude that winter. The firebrand who embraced virtually every liberal cause in recent years no longer appeared quite so estranged from conservative Old Guard Republicans, including his friend Henry Cabot Lodge. Their mutual antipathy toward the Wilson administration brought them closer together in the early months of 1915. "I never expected to hate any one in politics with the hatred which I feel towards Wilson," Lodge confessed to TR. Roosevelt felt the same: having exhausted his usual insults, he now insisted that Wilson was not "a real man."

To Roosevelt, Republican reactionaries such as Boies Penrose, William Barnes, or even Elihu Root (a TR cabinet member and one of the hated "burglars" whom he believed helped to thwart his 1912 Republican nomination) were preferable in the White House. That Roosevelt did all he could to assist Lodge in his successful effort to defeat Wilson's Ship Purchase Bill (America, TR believed, would ultimately "purchase a quarrel with every ship") and then hosted Lodge at Sagamore Hill for the first time in four years could not help but raise some eyebrows.

Roosevelt's hostile reaction to the Woman's Peace Party, then, was not surprising. In a lengthy letter to Rublee written on February 9, he attacked the platform as "silly and base," although he did concede that those behind the organization might be "high-minded" if extremely misguided. His reasoning was vintage TR. First, no peace organization or congress had ever accomplished much of anything, and "not one particle of good will" would result from any efforts of the WPP. Second, the WPP's platform pushed for "peace in the abstract" without any distinction between a "good" and a "bad" peace, not unlike the Copperheads of the Civil War who believed peace more important than the end of slavery and preservation of the Union. Third, if the women of the WPP wanted to do something, they should speak up for the crimes against Belgium and "demand that in the interests of peace the United States do what it can to put a stop to those wrongs. . . . Let them do something that shows that they mean what they say and that they are really striving for righteousness." In the meantime, "let every wise and upright man and woman refuse to have anything more to do with a movement which is certainly both foolish and noxious."

Roosevelt did not mention Addams in the letter, although privately he sneered at the "Jane Addams inspired idiots" of the WPP. On some level, he probably understood that it would not do to publicly attack a fellow Progressive party member, even one whose involvement had diminished. He was also aware of her still considerable influence, so much so that some believed TR was "afraid of her." They had maintained a cordial relationship of late, Addams supplying him with information on prison reform and investigating an elderly Chicago man who claimed to have served with TR. However, she knew that the ex-president was no longer a useful ally for any of her causes.

Wilson, the candidate she had rejected in 1912, now seemed a more likely possibility. She had met him at the White House for the first time after the WPP meeting, not to discuss peace but to voice opposition to a pending bill that would mandate a literacy requirement for immigrants. After Wilson vetoed the measure, she dashed off an appreciative note.

Whether their agreement on immigration could transcend their very real differences on other issues remained questionable. Addams's prized woman's suffrage cause was of no importance to Wilson. Publicly, he continued to insist that it should be "brought about state by state." Privately, he was far more candid. "Suffrage for women," he mused in an early January conversation, "will make absolutely no change in politics—it is the home that will be disastrously affected. Somebody has to make the home and who is going to do it if the women don't?"

Addams's and Wilson's widely divergent racial views presented another area of friction, starkly illustrated by their response to *The Birth of a Nation*, a new motion picture based on the Southern writer Thomas Dixon's racist Civil War and Reconstruction novel, *The Clansman*. Dixon, an old Johns Hopkins acquaintance, contacted Wilson in late January about screening a new "photo play," one that would "show him the birth of a new art—the launching of the mightiest engine for moulding public opinion in the history of the world." As a recent widower still in mourning, Wilson knew that theater attendance was out of the question, but he agreed to view the film projected "on the white panels" of the East Room on February 18, along with his family and cabinet members and their spouses, provided the screening was not publicized. The gathering then witnessed a breakthrough in movie history, thanks to director D. W. Griffith's pioneering efforts in cinematography and storytelling. The highly inflammatory racial content, including horribly stereotypical depictions of African Americans and a heroic view of the Ku Klux Klan, likely made little impression on those present, most of whom shared Wilson's views on segregation.

What Wilson actually thought of *The Birth of a Nation* remains uncertain. His oft quoted assessment ("It is like writing history with lightning. And my only regret is that it is all so terribly true"), derived from a single source more than twenty years after the screening, has been called into question. When news of the White House showing inevitably leaked, he made no attempt to endorse the film, a box office smash. Later, he told his secretary, Joseph Tumulty, that the film was a "very unfortunate production." But it is hardly a stretch to suggest that Wilson probably would not have found the content especially objectionable. The Civil War and Reconstruction section of his *History of the American People* depicted African Americans as either "devoted" slaves or "helpless" freedmen and -women "easily taught to hate the men who had once held them in slavery," and the film even quoted Wilson's writings on screen.

The Birth of a Nation deeply troubled Addams, who attended a showing in New York with Lillian Wald. She left the theater believing the film should be stopped. "The producer seems to have followed the principle of gathering the most vicious and grotesque individuals he could find among colored people, and showing them as representatives of the truth about the entire race," Addams wrote afterward. "The same method could be followed to smirch the reputation of any race. For instance, it would be easy enough to go about the slums of a city and bring together some of the criminals and degenerates and take pictures of them purporting to show the character of the white race. It would no more be the truth about the white race than this is about the black."

She was also horrified by the manipulative nature of the film: "Of course the spectators applaud the Klan. It is not shown to them except to stir their sympathy. Of course they applaud slights and contempt for the negroes; they are shown only as despicable brutes." And she recognized, perhaps earlier than most, the potential of film to distort history. "You can use history to demonstrate anything when you take certain of its facts and

emphasize them to the exclusion of the rest," she observed. The film generated protests across the country, including one in Boston spearheaded by
William Monroe Trotter, the "unspeakable fellow" who had dared to confront Wilson.

But Addams was a pragmatist, realizing that a valuable alliance was more
important than ideological purity. As she had cast her lot with Roosevelt
two years earlier despite his big navy notions, she could overlook Wilson's
less than progressive views on suffrage and racial issues. His actions during
the first six months of the war suggested that he was a friend to the pacifist
cause—if not to the degree of Bryan, who was now being seen in public
sporting a "dove of peace with outstretched wings" on his lapel. In the coming months, her goal, and that of other pacifists, was to strengthen Wilson's
ties to the peace movement and ultimately push him in a more aggressive
direction. The current Wilsonian neutrality policy to "ignore the war and
go on our way as if nothing were happening" was not enough. "Our neutrality should be a vigorous and dynamic kind that is not content to sit still with
folded hands waiting for Europe to cease fighting," Addams insisted. "Such
peace is not worthy of a great people. Nor is it enough to send shiploads of
food and clothing to destitute Belgians, splendid as that is."

Of course, she had no idea that one day after she visited the White House
to talk over immigration policy, Colonel House was arriving in Washington
to finalize the details of his latest secret European adventure, which perhaps might lay the groundwork for peace. Whether either side was eager
for any kind of outside intervention or mediation now or ever was questionable. "The more life and treasure spent in winning this war," Rudyard Kipling warned Roosevelt, "the less will the victors be disposed to
listen to any neutral's suggestions when the time comes to deal with the
loser."

Wilson apparently believed some good could come from another
House trip and made no attempt to squelch his scheme. House was
his closest friend, he trusted him, and perhaps the personal touch was the
best way to break the European logjam. Others did not agree. The Allied
ambassadors in Washington, especially Jusserand and George Bakhmeteff

House and Wilson, 1915.
(Library of Congress, LC-B2- 3527-3)

of Russia, thought any conversations with Germany were pointless, until House reminded them that it would show "how utterly unreliable and treacherous the Germans were." Bryan was especially displeased that House had usurped him as the "peace emissary," a job he very much wished to perform himself. "The President thought it would be unwise for anyone to do this officially," House coolly explained. Bryan "would attract a great deal of attention, and people would wonder why he was there for such a purpose when the matter could have been done quite as well from Washington."

Bryan was not pacified. A trip by House, the President's adviser, would "create just as much of a sensation," especially during a world war. Afterward, House reported the gist of the conversation to an annoyed Wilson, who concluded that the secretary of state was not the right person for "such a delicate mission," but "was so anxious to do it himself that the idea obsessed him."

That House might be just as "obsessed" did not occur to Wilson. In his mind, they were entirely simpatico. "You are the only one in the world to whom I can open my mind freely," the President told House during his visit, "and it does me good to say even foolish things and get them out of my system." With House, he could let his hair down and display a silly side that few except close family saw. One night at the White House, daughter Nell asked her father to pose in front of Seymour Thomas's portrait of Wilson. House and others roared as the President "made all sorts of contortions, sticking his tongue in his cheek, twisting his mouth into different positions, rolling his eyes, dropping his jaw, and doing everything a clown would do at a circus."

A few matters needed to be worked out, including a laughably easy code for their communications and a letter for House to present if necessary explaining his role and intentions. Otherwise, Wilson felt no need to go further, at least if House's diary account is to be believed. "We are both of the same mind and it is not necessary to go into details with you," he told him. His "most trusted friend" would do the right thing. Both men were emotional when they parted at the train station. "Your unselfish and intelligent friendship has meant much to me," Wilson told House. "Your words of affection," House wrote him the next day, "touched me so deeply that I could not tell you then, and perhaps can never tell you, just how I feel."

On Saturday, January 30, House and his wife headed for Europe on the Cunard liner *Lusitania* with 739 other passengers. Soldiers, journalists, and excursionists undertaking their usual late-winter trips to Europe were among the group, which also included Treasury Secretary McAdoo's daughter Nona, who planned to serve as a war nurse at a recently converted French château. Nona McAdoo and her friend provided a neat cover story for the curious press; the Houses would "chaperone" the young ladies until they reached their destination. It was "preposterous," House told a reporter, that anyone should think he was traveling for any other purpose. The President did his part in the deception. "His mission is a very simple one," Wilson said of House at a press conference. "In the first place, he often goes abroad just at this time. He is going abroad a little earlier than usual, because there are a great many things we want to keep in touch with—the relief situation and everything of that sort. There is no formal mission of any kind. The papers have been imagining that."

The Atlantic crossing took seven days. On the final afternoon, House and the other passengers noted something peculiar while crossing the Irish Sea. The British Admiralty, fearing German submarines, ordered the *Lusitania* to hoist an American flag while steaming at top speed to Liverpool, its final destination. While the British defended their action as a legitimate and previously employed (even by the United States during the Spanish-American War) *ruse de guerre*, especially with numerous Americans onboard, the use of the Stars and Stripes as a sort of supershield was troubling. Pressed by reporters after his arrival, House refused to weigh in on the merits of the English case. His concern remained the secrecy of his mission, though the American and European press sensed something was in the air.

During the week that the *Lusitania* sailed, the issue of submarine warfare suddenly took center stage. In response to the British blockade, the Germans countered with a startling announcement that a "war zone" would be established around waters surrounding the British Isles. Beginning February 18, all belligerent vessels in the zone, nonmilitary merchant ships included, would be fair game for German submarines without warning. And American and other neutral ships could not be guaranteed safety should they venture into the war zone, since they could easily be mistaken for Allied vessels.

Such a step violated international law, which required submarines and other warships to stop and search a merchant vessel before guiding it into port as a prize of war or destroying the craft if necessary. The warship was also responsible for the safety of the crew and passengers. Attacking unarmed merchant ships without warning was shocking and unthinkable, at least before the war. "It is something that has never been done in the history of civilized warfare except by pirates," Senator John Sharp Williams, a Mississippi Democrat, observed. Some believed the Germans would never stoop this low. "To sink even an enemy merchant ship, without stopping to inquire what would become of the non-combatant crew and passengers, would be ferocity," the *New York Evening Post* observed. "To sink a neutral vessel in that way would be ferocity tinged with *madness*."

But German naval officials such as Grand Admiral Alfred von Tirpitz, who had prodded the kaiser to go forward, believed Germany had no choice. "England wants to starve us," he had explained to an interviewer a few months earlier. "We can play the game. We can bottle her up and torpedo every English or allies' ship which nears any harbor in Great Britain, thereby cutting off large food supplies." The "starvation" claim was somewhat exaggerated; what the Germans actually dreaded most was the British blockade's continued effect on the import of much needed raw materials. Meanwhile, the kaiser and his chancellor, Theobald von Bethmann Hollweg, believed the interview did more harm than good and that Tirpitz should have kept his mouth shut.

But Tirpitz and his colleagues saw the submarine as their miracle weapon. Long viewed as hopelessly impractical because of its lack of speed, limited range, and navigation difficulties, the new-look *Unterseeboot*, or U-boat, had demonstrated its deadly efficiency back in September, when a single German submarine sent three British cruisers to the ocean floor in little less than an hour. American naval officials could not help but be impressed. "The submarine has come to stay," remarked Franklin Roosevelt, recently described by a reporter as a "man who will do much and dare much." "That it is useful for coast defense, for commerce destroying, for scouting purposes, and as a part of the protection . . . and attacking power of a battleship fleet is established."

But could the small fleet of 30 or so German submarines succeed to any large degree in stopping the 140 ships that reached Great Britain daily? James Norman Hall thought it "preposterous." "Doubtless some merchant vessels will be torpedoed," he wrote his father, "but the English navy is far too strong both in numbers and in the fighting quality of her ships." The more important issue, which the German naval officials seemed to minimize, at least initially, was the possibility that an errant torpedo might sink an American vessel or vessel carrying American passengers, inflame the folks back home, and bring the United States directly into the conflict. Some had already begun to speculate about a possible attack on the *Lusitania*, though Captain F. M. Passow of the American liner *St. Paul* believed Germany would never be so foolish. Otherwise, "it would involve her with every civilized nation in the world."

Wilson was now faced with his first real crisis of the war, one far more serious than the troublesome British interference with American trade. He realized that the situation easily could spiral out of control, exactly what he had feared since the war began, and just as it had seventeen years earlier when the sinking of the *Maine* in the Havana harbor helped to stampede the country into war with Spain. His options were relatively simple: order American merchant ships to stay out of the danger zone, a policy certain to have economic and political ramifications, or insist on our neutrality rights, likely to go over much better with the public, although that alone would not necessarily determine his course.

"He is conscious of public sentiment," Interior Secretary Franklin Lane observed of the President. "And yet he never takes public sentiment as offering a solution for a difficulty; if he can think the thing through and arrive at the point where public sentiment supports him, so much the better."

At a February 5 cabinet meeting, Secretary of War Lindley Garrison argued for a strong "public statement," one that "we must be prepared to back up by force if defied." With Bryan absent on a speaking tour in Indiana, his place temporarily filled by Robert Lansing, the State Department counselor, no one was prepared to offer a strong pacifist counterargument. Instead, Wilson seemed convinced. The current situation, he noted, was not unlike "boys drawing [a] line in sand & daring other to cross." Lansing subsequently went to work on a diplomatic note, while Ambassador Bernstorff, even without formal instruction from Berlin, took it upon himself to do damage control in the United States. The war zone announcement, he insisted, did not reflect a radical departure from practices in place since the beginning of hostilities, except that neutral vessels might be caught in the crossfire because of the British use of neutral flags.

The note that eventually went out on February 10, tweaked slightly by Wilson, did not go quite as far as Garrison might have wished. Through the haze of polite diplomatic language two ominous words stood out: "strict accountability" that Germany would be held to should an "American vessel or the lives of American citizens" be lost.

What that meant remained frustratingly unclear. Was the administration prepared to go to war or would any future action take on some other form? Was the note also insisting that American citizens must be protected even if traveling on belligerent ships? There was no immediate answer, and

Wilson likely was not entirely certain himself. Still, the note received a positive reception not only in America but also in the United Kingdom, which had received its own note about its recent use of the Stars and Stripes. That the British note included no warning of being held to a "strict accountability" confirmed to already dubious German officials that America was far from neutral. They had no intention of abandoning their submarine policy, but the chancellor and others were concerned enough about the possible impact on America to proceed more cautiously. The German reply sent on February 18 expressed a willingness to "deliberate with the United States concerning any measures which might secure the safety of legitimate shipping of neutrals in the war zone." And secret orders were also given to avoid torpedoing neutral vessels—American and Italian—if at all possible.

But the crisis was far from resolved. "We are liable, at any time, to have a disaster over there which will inflame public opinion," Bryan warned Wilson, "and we are not in a position to meet this outburst of public opinion unless we have done all that we can do to prevent it."

Roosevelt also sensed the danger. "We are now ambling in sidelong fashion dangerously near entanglement in the European War," he wrote a Republican senator. The fault, he believed, was the feeble and wishy-washy policy of the administration and its "professorial views of international matters" since the war began.

Wilson grasped at one last straw. Conversations with German representatives in Berlin and Washington suggested that they might go for a compromise, or what the diplomats called a *modus vivendi*, which would mostly involve the British navy permitting food to reach Germany in exchange for submarine warfare on merchant vessels limited to the previously accepted stop-and-search only. Such a scheme, if accepted, would be a diplomatic coup and cool off tensions considerably, if both sides accepted it.

But notes sent to both sides on February 20 produced nothing. The Germans, it turned out, were not willing to shelve their superweapon merely for food; they would expect raw materials also to be included in the agreement. The British also wanted more, perhaps promises to stop air bombing and improved prisoner care. Even then, Foreign Secretary Edward

Grey informed House that "it would not meet popular approval and the chances are that nothing will be done."

Instead, the British moved in the opposite direction. In early March, a new Order in Council countered the German "war zone" with a decisive effort to completely stop any trade directly with Germany or even through nearby neutral ports. Such a policy was in effect a de facto blockade, except that neutral ships would not be captured and confiscated but steered into British ports. Their cargoes would be purchased by the British government or sold, with the proceeds eventually turned over to their owners. It also meant that the British navy would now attempt to stop American trade with neutral nations, even in noncontraband materials, yet another example of international law falling by the wayside. "If this Order in Council stands and is enforced," Senator Thomas Walsh of Montana warned, "there are no neutral nations. They are all vassals of Great Britain."

Garrison, whose differences with Wilson were becoming more pronounced by the day, felt the time had come to talk tough and hold Great Britain to the same "strict accountability" imposed on Germany, a stance that might very well lead to serious conflict, even war, with the British.

To some, the possibility of America allying with Germany did not seem so far-fetched. "I am very much afraid of the possibility of our participation in the struggle," the journalist John Callan O'Laughlin wrote that March, "on which side I don't know." But again the President did not heed Garrison's advice, choosing a middle path of a note presenting the American perspective, but (in the words of *The Times* of London) "in the most friendly spirit." Not surprisingly, the British government didn't bother answering for almost four months.

Wilson believed he had no other choice. It did not make sense to "debate with the British Government," as the legal-minded Lansing seemed inclined to do. "We are face to face with *something they are going to do*, and they are going to do it no matter what representations we make," Wilson told Bryan. "We cannot convince them or change them, we can only show them very clearly what we mean to be our own attitude and course of action and that we mean to hold them to a strict responsibility for every invasion of our rights as neutrals." Whether Wilson recognized that a more assertive policy from the get-go might have made the British a bit more pliable in such disputes and the Germans a little less suspicious of American neutrality is uncertain. In any event, British leaders were convinced more than ever that unless they were guilty of committing an especially egregious violation of international law, they need not fear any serious consequences from America beyond peevish diplomatic notes. It did not help Wilson that his ambassador in London, Walter Hines Page, seemed to grow more smitten with his English hosts and their cause by the minute.

During this time, TR was in secret contact with British and French officials. He could no longer meet openly with Spring Rice, who kept Whitehall informed of Roosevelt's attitudes and even passed on his letters to Foreign Secretary Grey. The Allies were in the right because of Belgium, Roosevelt warned Spring Rice, but they would do well to exercise restraint and avoid doing "something wrong, something evil," lest he and others be forced to "clearly take the stand on the other side." And Great Britain should not flout its enormous "command of the seas," he wrote Grey, especially when she was benefiting far more from American trade than Germany. "I ask you merely to take careful thought, so that you shall not excite our government, even wrongfully, to act in such a way that it would diminish or altogether abolish the great advantage you now have." But TR was no more successful than Wilson in altering the British position. "We do what we can to avoid provoking neutrals, and especially the United States," Grey responded, "but, with German submarines round our coast . . . people here will not stand letting goods go past our doors to Germany."

House had requested a meeting with Grey soon after his arrival in London. In the past, he had not been especially impressed with the veteran statesman, who had long urged stronger ties with America and whose diplomatic work during the First Balkan War had won him plaudits. Grey, House thought, was "absolutely trustworthy and a man of high character, but without ability of the first order." It was not long, however, that House had fallen under his spell and those of other Englishmen eager to flatter "the President's friend." Within a few days, House happily recorded in his diary how Sir William Tyrrell, Grey's secretary, told him "that the war could be settled upon the right lines by the President . . . Grey and myself" and how much Grey was already quite fond of him. The man said to be "Grey by name and grey by nature" was proving to be quite charming. Soon not only were the two men discussing "nature, solitude, Wordsworth . . . by the fire" but the supposedly neutral House was also sharing correspondence from the German Foreign Office with Grey.

Even Wilson, normally content to allow House considerable latitude, began to question some of his decisions. Why, the President wondered, was House consulting with Grey and Prime Minister Herbert Asquith as to the best time to visit Germany? "You cannot go too far in allowing the English government to determine when it is best for you to go," Wilson warned his friend. "They will naturally desire to await some time when they have the strategic advantage because of events in the field or elsewhere." And the already suspicious Germans, he added, would then be justified in perceiving House "as their spokesman rather than as mine."

Such logic from so far away failed to sway House. If he went to Germany now, he believed the British would no longer be open to Wilson as a mediator in the future. Besides, his new friend Grey "looks upon the situation as fairly and dispassionately as we" and it would be best to "keep in as close and sympathetic touch with him." That Grey's agreeable persona, frank discussions of privileged Whitehall developments, and interest in American peace schemes might be strategic did not seem to occur to the decidedly amateur diplomat House (ironically, he believed that Ambassador Page "put too much trust in the people with whom he is thrown"). House was won over even more when Grey "confessed" to his correspondence with TR and allowed House to read it.

In House's mind and diary, he was accomplishing important things in England. Each day was packed with meetings and luncheons with luminaries of all kinds, ranging from James Bryce, the author of the much praised *The American Commonwealth* and former British ambassador in Washington, to Herbert Hoover, the head of the Belgian relief effort. There was even a trip to Buckingham Palace to see King George, who recalled TR as "a man of great force and charm" and was curious about House's earlier meeting with the king's cousin Kaiser Wilhelm.

The kaiser, House told the king, "seemed to like the English."

"I know he does, I know he does," the excitable little monarch replied. But moments later the king launched into a diatribe about how the Germans needed to be crushed and the inadvisability of any peace talk right now.

Taken aback, House thought it best not to let George V "know what was in my mind, nor did I let him know what was in the great Woodrow's mind." House had already decided that Grey was his partner in crime, although the king's blunt talk offered a more accurate description of the British attitude at present.

After securing Grey's approval and divulging the details of his next move, House was finally ready to depart for France and Germany in early March. In the meantime, he briefed Wilson on the important groundwork laid in England while reiterating his own lack of ambition. "I think constantly of the great part I feel sure you are to play," he wrote the President on March 8, "and my desires go no further than to have you preside over the convention composed of all nations."

As usual, Wilson saw no reason to question the purity of his friend's motives, nor did he question the exciting news House offered five days later that the French had "tentatively accepted you as mediator." Actually, nothing of the kind had come up during his conversation with Théophile Delcassé, the foreign minister who, like most of the French, was interested in neither peace overtures at the moment nor future American mediation. Meanwhile, House also discovered that many Americans in Paris and other European capitals were undercutting Wilson at every turn. "Roosevelt's friends," he told the President, "are particularly active."

House's trip to Germany and his conversations there with heavyweights such as Arthur Zimmermann, Foreign Minister Gottlieb von Jagow, and Chancellor Theobald von Bethmann Hollweg were just as unfruitful. Like the French and English, the Germans were more than willing to engage in polite academic discussions about peace with House, who tried to emphasize "points of common interest between us" and dangled a potential future "freedom of the seas," but they informed him that nothing could be done at present. He also found himself constantly badgered about American munition sales to the Allies. "It seems that every German soldier that is now being killed or wounded is being killed or wounded by an American bullet or shell," he wrote Wilson. And speaking English in public, he discovered, was a risk better not taken, especially with German bitterness and hatred of Britain mounting by the minute.

Nevertheless, House convinced himself that some good was being accomplished—namely, his dubious contention that Germany, like France, was now willing "to tentatively look upon the President as a proper mediator."

By the time he left Germany on March 28, House had a clearer sense of the current situation. With neither side enjoying the upper hand, any move for peace presented an unacceptable risk to the governments in Berlin, London, and Paris. "The world is upon a strain as never before in its history, and something is sure to crack somewhere before a great while," he informed Wilson. "It looks as if our best move just now is to wait until the fissure appears."

House had no intention of returning home just yet. There were more dignitaries to see, more opportunities to present the President's views. But he did not realize that his exalted position in Wilson's life was about to come to an end.

Unaware of what House was up to, Addams and other pacifists were hard at work combating preparedness talk. As much as Roosevelt continued to believe that Americans were asleep and "seem incapable of learning except by disaster," his message had shown more signs of sinking in, especially on the East Coast. In late February, a New York–based organization emerged known as the American Legion (unrelated to the veterans group created four years later); it was designed to address the lack of reserves by creating a national "card index system on a gigantic scale" of men with a military or other relevant experience who could be called on to serve in a crisis. That TR provided the movement with his name, his blessing, and a hefty check (supposedly refused) led some to believe the Legion was also doubling as an unofficial Roosevelt-for-President action committee. All the Roosevelt men joined, including the eldest son, Ted, who was listed on the incorporation documents. "I should be ashamed of my sons if they shirked war," TR declared, "just as I should be ashamed of my daughters if they shirked motherhood."

An Iowa pacifist was not impressed by TR's bravado. The Woman's Peace Party, she suggested to Addams, should "call for a Peace Army" of women brandishing "mopsticks and rolling pins" and "drive Mr. Roosevelt's unofficial American Legion home."

Much of the nation was also buzzing about the renewed interest in military training or drill in the public schools and colleges. To its supporters, such a policy would be a win-win situation for America. "The country would be infinitely better prepared to meet a sudden emergency," *The Washington Post* editorialized. And if no war came, "the boys would not have been losers, for they would have received a physical training and moral drill that would be useful to them in any walk of life." But to opponents, who were in the majority at present, training of this sort in the schools meant only one thing: a first step to mandatory military service, from which many immigrants had fled.

Not surprisingly, the pro-military training crowd encountered more than its share of roadblocks. A Spanish-American War vet lamented to TR his failure at New York University, thanks to a "peace society organizer who always seems to have more success with the Faculty than I have and of course, the manly boys have to yield to the (I must say) degenerates."

Addams was cheered by such successes. The news of the "shocking" and "unnecessary" American Legion had appalled her and further drove a wedge between her and TR. "To start a project like the American Legion with the purpose of preparing every one for war is very wrong," she insisted. "There is nothing that will drag us into war quicker than this increasing spirit of militarism." That the comment was an indirect swipe at her old Bull Moose colleague was not unnoticed by the partisan press. "Theodore, the militarist, and Jane, the pacifist, are at odds," chortled the *Philadelphia Record*.

Addams, like other pacifists, worried that Americans were already becoming desensitized to war, perceiving it as almost "a great sporting event." In speech after speech in Boston, New York, and Philadelphia that March, she did her best to give her listeners a cold dose of reality. "There was one man, a Polish Jew," she told a Columbia University audience, "who was spearing another man with a bayonet, think of that in these days! And as the other man succumbed he threw up his arms and repeated the prayer for the dying in Hebrew. It was too much for the man who had attacked him. His reason gave way." She told a packed Carnegie Hall (despite competing against the recently opened *The Birth of a Nation* a few blocks away) of a Hull-House resident who returned from the war with hundreds of photos, including one depicting a woman carrying her dead daughter "killed by the soldiers. . . . There never was so much brutality as in the present war."

But the answer to such horrors was not, Addams stressed, preparedness and militarism that threatened to change the very fabric of our nation. Instead, Americans should embrace the WPP program, one that would ideally prevent future wars. "Come and join this peace movement," she urged. "We will try to act wisely, calmly and carefully, and the more of us there are the more we can do."

Between speaking engagements, the demands on Addams remained considerable. Besides the activities of the WPP, which had already grown to fifteen state branches, no shortage of causes required her support, ranging from raising the mandatory school age in Illinois from fourteen to sixteen to blocking an attempt in Delaware to do away with the ten-hour-maximum workday for women. And Edward Bok was eager to interview her (with an "expert stenographer" present) for *Ladies' Home Journal* on non-peace-related matters, including her views on the current generation of American women. "They are simply more vocal," she explained in the feature that eventually appeared in the August issue. "They have dropped their old policy of repression and are talking—saying what they think and what they want. . . . I am sometimes a bit taken aback at the modern young woman; at the things she talks about and at her free and easy ways." Still, Addams believed that the growing "breakdown of prudery that has come has done them good," even though puritanical attitudes toward sex education persisted. "We say 'Teach it in the home,' and then mothers don't do it; and the result is that it is not taught at all," she lamented. "It must be taught more naturally everywhere—not as a dangerous subject that must be mysteriously and strangely treated."

Behind Addams's confident public persona was growing anxiety about her sister Alice. The cancer that her physicians had managed to control with surgery and radium treatments had now spread to her spine, forcing Alice to leave her home in Kansas and her duties as one of only a handful of women bankers in America to stay with Addams in Chicago. On March 19, she died, surrounded by Addams and other family members—among them her daughter Marcet, who watched as Aunt Jane sadly "drew down the lids over my mother's half-open eyes." With only one sibling alive, a brother afflicted with schizophrenia, she could not help recalling happier times "out of the long past and my childhood."

Mary Smith was always there to console her but, like Wilson, Addams had always found her work just as essential in coping with loss. The vitality of the women's peace movement energized her and provided her with ample opportunities to channel her grief into something productive. Every day, it seemed, new developments suggested something was happening, that women's voices were being heard as never before, and that peace was possible—if not now, permanently in the future. She was especially encouraged by rave reviews of a new plan developed by another foreigner, a young Canadian instructor of English at the University of Wisconsin named Julia Grace Wales.

Deeply disturbed by the massive casualties of the early months of the war to the point where they physically "sickened her," Wales had spent the Christmas break between semesters feverishly formulating a scheme to halt the carnage. As the WPP and others had suggested, she proposed that the neutral nations band together in a conference to stop the war. That alone, she recognized, would not be enough. Instead, the conference would constantly issue peace proposals to both sides on a regular basis in a process known as "continuous mediation."

The similarity of the plan to some of Rosika Schwimmer's ideas was not lost on the temperamental Hungarian, although she admitted that the Wales proposal was a "more academically framed sketch." And the Wales plan, soon to be dubbed the Wisconsin plan, did not call, as Schwimmer's did, for an immediate armistice.

Actually, Wales had no knowledge of Schwimmer's work, nor was she especially concerned about notoriety. Instead, she truly believed that her plan offered a real chance of success. More than a few pacifists agreed, so much so that the Wisconsin plan won the wholehearted support of Addams and others attending the national conference of the Emergency Peace Federation in Chicago called in late February. Wales, one pacifist wrote Addams, "is on fire with the conviction that the Wisconsin plan has in it the germ of salvation, and would develop into a sort of Joan of Arc if you could encourage her."

Addams did more than encourage Wales. She tried, along with others, to set up an early March appointment with the President to formally present and discuss the Wisconsin plan. Wilson, by this time burdened by an endless stream of visitors with various peace schemes (Addams herself received bizarre letters from correspondents claiming to bear messages from God or advocating mass telepathy for peace), begged off. Besides, he had no faith in any conference-of-neutrals plan, the most recent introduced by Bob La Follette (it quickly went nowhere). Nevertheless, the President chose his words carefully. "I should welcome a memorandum from you with all my heart," he wrote his new acquaintance. Wilson's apparent interest satisfied Addams. At least the plan was in his hands. Surely he would do something with it.

But something far more significant than a single meeting with Wilson was also in the air. Because the war had forced the cancellation of the scheduled biennial meeting of the International Woman Suffrage Alliance in Berlin, a Dutch feminist named Aletta Jacobs proposed that a large-scale woman's congress for peace should meet at The Hague in April. Jacobs, a remarkable though occasionally prickly figure who had made her mark in the Netherlands as a suffrage leader, pioneering female physician, and birth-control-clinic organizer, wanted a sizable American presence, ideally including key members of the WPP, which she had learned about from Schwimmer. And she wanted Carrie Chapman Catt to preside.

Catt was not interested. It was not simply that suffrage came first for her (she supposedly told a journalist that "I shall not leave New York until I get the vote"); she believed the notion of bringing women together from warring countries was a recipe for disaster, like "trying to organize a peace society in an insane asylum." Besides, the mines and the German U-boats concerned her. She "was willing to die for peace, or for suffrage," she told Schwimmer, but she "wasn't willing to drown myself for nothing at all."

The job fell to Addams, who also harbored serious misgivings. Despite the enthusiasm of firebrands like Emmeline Pethick-Lawrence, who viewed the congress as "the greatest, most unparalleled opportunity that has ever yet fallen to the lot of women in the world," Addams knew the venture would likely be criticized heavily and its chances of success were slim. She also was very much aware of the dangers involved in a transatlantic crossing. Still, she was game to embark on what she called a "moral adventure." "Women who are willing to fail," she wrote her friend Lillian Wald, "may be able to break through that curious hypnotic spell which makes it impossible for any of the nations to consider Peace."

The task ahead was formidable. In less than a month, while coping with the loss of her sister, Addams would need to assemble a sort of "dream team" of elite women to accompany her to Europe. She did not simply want pacifists but experts on labor, immigration, economics, and social work, all of whom would be expected to pay their own expenses, which would total at least $300 per person.

Old friends like Wald refused to go, even after Mary Smith privately informed her how much Addams wanted her to come. Emily Balch, an economics and sociology professor at Wellesley and passionate peace advocate, also declined, citing her teaching responsibilities. But Addams was persistent. "Don't you think," she wrote Balch, "that there is a certain obligation on the women who have had the advantages of study and training, to take this possible chance to help out?" Eventually, Balch accepted, a decision the future Nobel Peace Prize winner later described as the "turning point in my life."

As Addams sent letter after letter out in late March, lingering doubts persisted. "There are times when I feel very much aghast about the entire affair," she admitted. And she was not expecting a miracle, only to get the ball rolling for potential future peace talks. Still, as she wrote to Wald, "no one can predict—it is literally 'on the lap of the gods.'"

As the winter began to wind down and Washington temperatures began to rise, Wilson continued to fight his depression with a combination of his official duties, golf, motoring, and the company of close family. His daughter Margaret, the current White House hostess, was pleased to see her father enjoying himself in a family singalong one night. "My only trouble is with my spirits, which are distinctly bad, when I allow them to be," he wrote a friend.

One March day, his cousin Helen Bones brought a new acquaintance to the White House for tea after a walk at Rock Creek Park, a widow named Edith Bolling Galt. Bones had been introduced to Galt through Wilson's physician friend Cary Grayson, who was courting Galt's young acquaintance Alice Gertrude Gordon, who was nicknamed Altrude. Her shoes muddy, the stout, normally smartly dressed forty-two-year-old widow was somewhat embarrassed by her appearance until she bumped into Wilson and Grayson returning from a golfing outing, their boots equally filthy.

Wilson was immediately intrigued. Weeks earlier, he had seen the same "tall . . . dark-haired" lady "wearing a red rose" while motoring on Connecticut Avenue and had been curious about her name. It was not surprising that the man said to have "lived on feminine inspiration" was interested. But this was an era when widows and widowers were expected to wear black for at least a year and refrain from "worldly pleasures" such as "dancing or mingling in gay society." Slightly less than eight months had passed since Ellen Wilson's death. It would not do for the President to pursue a relationship or even the close (and highly uncommon for the time) friendships he enjoyed with Mary Hulbert and Nancy Saunders Toy.

He could, however, encourage Cousin Helen to continue to make Galt's acquaintance and invite her to dinner. Galt was not only delighted to accept but found herself enjoying the company of the President. "He is *perfectly* charming and one of the easiest and most delightful hosts I have ever known," she wrote a relative shortly after arriving home from the White House on March 23. "He was full of interesting stories and a fund of information." At the request of Helen, the President even read poetry, which did not fail to impress Galt.

Their mutual attraction was not surprising. Not only had both lost spouses, but Galt, like Wilson, was a child of Virginia (Wytheville, about 150 miles from Wilson's Staunton birthplace), the seventh of eleven children, whose family plantation near Lynchburg fell victim to the Civil War. Her father, William H. Bolling, whose "weak lung" had kept him out of that war, was a lawyer and later a judge, although the family's wealth never matched outward appearances.

Unlike Wilson's, Edith's life was never one of the mind. Even by the standards of the late nineteenth century, her formal education was minimal, with instruction from her grandmother, a governess, and then stints at Martha Washington College and Richmond Female Seminary. In 1895, at the age of twenty-two, she married Norman Galt, a cousin of her older sister Gertrude's husband, Alexander Hunter Galt. The Galt family owned a successful and long established jewelry firm in Washington on Pennsylvania Avenue, which eventually passed into the hands of Edith's new husband. His death in 1908, from what was called the "Russian influenza," left her with the business and an estate said to be worth over $250,000. In the seven years since then, she had led a comfortable merry widow's life, packed with European trips and occasional suitors.

It was not the life that Wilson's beloved Ellen, she of the artistic temperament and concern for Washington's poor, would have pursued. But Wilson found Edith's vivaciousness, like that of Mary Hulbert in her less troubled moments, especially appealing. And he still remembered that Ellen herself, after all, had told him to "marry again."

Five days after Edith's visit, a British steamer, the *Falaba*, was heading to west Africa from Liverpool. A German submarine accosted the vessel off the coast of southwest Wales, forced the *Falaba* to stop, and then fired a torpedo while the crew and passengers were still taking to the lifeboats. Not surprisingly, 104 of the 242 aboard went to their deaths. "It was murder, simply murder," remarked two officers present. One of the unfortunate 104 was a master mechanic from Massachusetts named Leon Thrasher, who was headed to the Gold Coast to work in the mines. For the first time, the blood of an American civilian had been shed in the Great War.

Chapter 4

A DISGRACE TO THE WOMEN OF AMERICA

MARCH 29–MAY 7, 1915

I do wish Jane Addams would come home! . . . She could have done more good here than by going off to that peace conference at The Hague. This is the time for Americans to stay at home.

—Anna Howard Shaw, May 1915

In early April, the journalist John Callan O'Laughlin received a disturbing letter from an acquaintance in the German diplomatic corps he had recently written discussing America's shifting attitudes toward the Great War. The unnamed official, posted to Italy—where his boss, Prince von Bülow, was doing his best to lure his currently neutral hosts to the German cause—bristled with resentment at what he considered unfair insinuations about Germany's motives and behavior. Most Germans, he informed O'Laughlin, now hated America thanks to its growing arms sales to the Allies and what they perceived as the Wilson administration's blatant partiality toward Great Britain. And war with America might actually be a blessing, as the devastating munitions shipments to Britain, France, and Russia would come to a halt. In any event, he doubted the United States would ever fight, in view of the "Japanese danger, the Mexican Imbroglio, the general unpreparedness for war and the huge German-Irish element."

O'Laughlin found the diplomat's attitude toward the safety of American travelers especially worrisome. The fault, his German acquaintance insisted, lay with the failure to curb England, which "rules the waves" but also "waives the rules." Germany, then, had no choice but to use submarine warfare to the fullest and, if Americans were caught in the crossfire, "they have only themselves to blame if they come to grief." A passenger liner such as the *Lusitania* would be fair game for German submarines, especially with its recent phony use of the Stars and Stripes. And even if "two or three hundred Americans might be drowned . . . nothing in the least would happen."

O'Laughlin strongly disagreed. The United States, he warned in his reply, was a sleeping giant. If war came, "a wave of patriotism would sweep across the land that would astonish Germany. . . . A man who dared to say anything against the Flag in such a crisis would . . . be suspended from a lamppost. . . . As surely as we become involved in this war, so surely will we become a military nation."

The letter so troubled O'Laughlin that he forwarded copies to both Roosevelt and Joseph Tumulty, Wilson's private secretary. The "insolent" tone and casual disregard of American power appalled TR. "Lord, how I would like to be President," he sighed once again. "That . . . letter is the kind of letter that, if I didn't keep a grip on myself, would make me favor instant war with Germany."

As usual, the administration did not share TR's views. As Bryan explained to Wilson, "the view they take is a natural one." Americans had been "warned . . . not to travel on British ships," the U.S. flag had been used as a subterfuge, and the Germans could not be blamed for considering the "drowning of a few people" insignificant when "there is no objection" to the British navy's attempt to starve Germany into submission. And the arms trade was becoming more problematic every day and "likely to get us into trouble."

Wilson did not accept the German rationale as wholeheartedly as his secretary of state, whose analysis was very much shaped by his obsessive eagerness for peace. Still, the President understood that American neutrality had entered a new phase, as had the war itself. On April 22, the Germans introduced a fearsome new weapon, poison gas, witnessed by the American William Robinson firsthand. Told by a British officer to wait in a dugout during the second Battle of Ypres, Robinson suddenly experienced an unpleasant sensation. "My throat and nose seemed to be burning, and my eyes commenced to water," he later wrote. "I couldn't draw a breath without sharp pain piercing my throat and lungs." The words "Run like hell, it's the gas!" saved his life, although two other officers present were not so fortunate.

If the Western Front remained a stalemate, there was still considerable optimism that the war would be over soon. A combined Anglo-French force was about to launch an ambitious land invasion of the Gallipoli peninsula, hoping to neutralize Germany's Turkish ally permanently. Betting New Yorkers were now offered 50/50 odds that the shooting would stop by October 1. James Norman Hall, now engaged in mock battles fought with blanks in preparation for deployment, thought it a very real possibility that the war might be over by the summer. "I expect to join the family for Christmas dinner if not before," he wrote his still worried mother.

For now, the war was still very much an uncomfortable reality for Wilson. An American civilian was dead because of a German U-boat attack. It was a situation that the President could not ignore, especially in view of his "strict accountability" statement. "I do not like this case," he admitted. "It is full of disturbing possibilities." And sorting out precisely what had occurred would not be easy when each side predictably blamed the other. The British claimed the German submarine gave the *Falaba*'s passengers and crew only five minutes to take to their boats before firing the fatal torpedo and then taunted the survivors struggling in the frigid water. The sub's commander, Baron von Forstner, said it was actually twenty-three minutes and that the rescue efforts were botched.

What Wilson did know was that the *Falaba* incident, described by one pundit as "barbarism gone mad," shocked and disturbed the American public. "In the light of international law the act was piracy," thundered Oswald Villard's ultraliberal *New York Evening Post*. "In the light of common humanity it was wickedness such as the history of war will find it difficult to match." That the death of *one* American in the midst of a bloody no-holds-barred global struggle elicited such journalistic fury could not help but puzzle Bernhard Dernburg, TR's recent "intellectual wrestling match" foe and Germany's mouthpiece in the United States. Thrasher's death,

Dernburg admitted, was "very regrettable. At the same time, any number of Americans have very unprovokedly enlisted with the Allies. These have had, of course, to take their chances of being killed in the trenches, just as they have tried to kill Germans. No protest has come from this country in regard to them. If a citizen or subject of a neutral country engages in war, or unnecessary sojourns in the zone of war, he takes the consequences."

Dernburg's comment persuaded few Americans, well aware of its pro-German slant. But Bryan believed there was at least some logic to the argument. "I am very much worried," he wrote Wilson on April 6, "the troublesome question being whether an American citizen can, by putting his business above his regard for his country, assume for his own advantage unnecessary risks and thus involve his country in international complications."

His legalistic colleague Robert Lansing did not agree. The matter was simple. Germany's violation of international law resulted in an American death. Not only did a "firm demand" seem warranted but he also reminded Wilson that "American public opinion will never stand for a colorless or timid presentation." Such a course, the State Department counselor admitted, would drastically worsen America's already shaky relations with Germany.

Without question Germany *had* violated international law as it currently existed. The *Falaba*, an unarmed, apparently unresisting merchant ship, had been sunk without sufficiently providing for the safety of passengers and crew. To Lansing, U-boats should be held to the same rules that torpedo boats had followed for the past four decades. Their attacks should be limited to enemy warships, as neither submarines nor torpedo boats were "capable of furnishing means of escape to passengers on board the ill-fated vessel."

The Germans, of course, thought it highly unfair to shackle the submarine to antiquated precedents that had not anticipated the destructive power of the new weapon. And the British were not playing by the rules either. They were arming their merchant ships (although the *Falaba* was not), which were also secretly instructed to attack submarines if necessary.

Bryan, more than anyone in Wilson's inner circle, perceived that Thrasher's death was not likely to be an isolated incident. He was convinced that the President must do his utmost to bring both sides to the peace table.

Wilson's response was not encouraging. "To insist now would be futile and would probably be offensive," he told a disappointed Bryan. "We would lose such influence as we have for peace." That his decision was also shaped by "what House writes me" could not help but further irritate the secretary of state.

Wilson toyed with the idea of sending a note to Germany but eventually decided against it. Better to deal with the Thrasher matter and others like it after the war, if at all possible, especially since the national anger in the United States dissipated as quickly as it had appeared. His goal, as before, was to keep a lid on America's passions, lest they carry the nation needlessly into war. American neutrality, he explained that spring to a gathering of the Associated Press in New York, was not driven by "self-interest" or a "petty desire to keep out of trouble," but a genuine wish to "help both sides when the struggle is over." And by avoiding the fight, refraining from taking sides, and maintaining "absolute self-control and self-mastery," the United States would earn the respect of the entire world and be fit to play a leading part in the future peace process. "Whom do you admire most amongst your friends?" he asked. "The man who will fight at the drop of the hat, whether he knows what the hat is dropped for or not? Don't you admire and don't you fear, if you have to contest with him, the self-mastered man who watches you with calm eye and comes in only when you have carried the thing so far that you must be disposed of? That is the man you respect. That is the man who, you know, has at bottom a much more fundamental and terrible courage than the irritable, fighting man."

More than a few journalists in the audience likely interpreted Wilson's reference to a hypothetical "irritable, fighting man" as a not-so-subtle swipe at TR, whose attacks on the administration, or what he now termed "a stench in the nostrils of decent American citizens," had continued. Roosevelt could not understand how Wilson could respond so passively to Germany's "return at least to the principles of the Thirty Years War and the buccaneer days of the Spanish Main." The Allies were no angels either, he realized, but the "brutal and overbearing" behavior of Germany could not be ignored, and Americans had every right to be partial. "I see by the morning paper that the President even bids us to beware of sympathy," he grumbled after reading Wilson's speech to the Associated Press. "Where would he lead us?"

In TR's mind, nowhere. The President seemed to be unaware of the very real global threats facing America now and in the future, from not only Germany, but even Allied powers such as Japan ("entirely ruthless . . . and indifferent to the rights of other weak peoples") and potentially Russia in the next fifty years if she could somehow match "German efficiency" and "ruthlessness." And it was delusional to anticipate that battered and bruised European nations would gratefully turn to the "self-mastered" America to make peace. Unless the administration drastically changed its current policies, the United States would be limited to the "position of international drum major and of nothing more, and even this position it will be allowed to fill only so long as it suits the convenience of the men who have done the actual fighting." Roosevelt did not believe, at least for the moment, that America should enter the war, especially with the current shoddy state of her military and navy apparatus, but Wilson should have "protested strenuously" against the Belgium invasion and other violations of international law and morality.

TR realized that his much repeated arguments still appealed to only a small segment of the population. Why get so worked up about Belgium, some asked, when China and Korea had been violated by Japan in the past without any American protest or intervention? And a sizable segment of the public discounted anything from Roosevelt as the jealous ravings of an aging power-hungry hack desperate to remain relevant. Even those who admired his astute political tendencies, such as Robert Pellissier, a Harvard-educated professor who returned to France to enlist in the army of his homeland, questioned TR's behavior. "What is the use of calling Wilson names?" he wrote a friend in late April. "Theodore's language strikes me as altogether too violent and self-contradictory. He says in the same breath that Wilson ought to have shown fight and that the navy is not ready."

But with each day, Roosevelt won a few more supporters to his perspective on the war. The cumulative effect of seemingly minor episodes such as the *Falaba* and the destruction of the wheat-carrying *William P. Frye* by a German cruiser back in late January, the first American ship to be sunk (though with all passengers and crew placed safely onboard the cruiser), could not help but unnerve even Wilson's strongest advocates. And in the weeks ahead, they would also learn of the clumsy German efforts just under way that spring to disrupt the hated overseas munitions shipments through strikes and incendiary bombs placed on outgoing merchant ships.

The sudden appearance of "invasion scare" literature that spring helped convince many that America was no longer safely tucked between two oceans. By late April, readers could choose to be frightened by Cleveland Moffett's "The Conquest of America" in *McClure's*, Francis Greene's *The Present Military Situation in the United States*, or J. W. Muller's syndicated "Invasion of America" newspaper series, all of which presented vivid scenarios of foreign armies and navies overwhelming our pitiful defenses, blowing up the Woolworth Building, holding J. P. Morgan Jr., Andrew Carnegie, and John D. Rockefeller for ransom, and other diabolical deeds.

TR especially approved of Hudson Maxim's *Defenseless America*, released in the last week of April. Maxim, like several of the other scaremongering scribes, was hardly an impartial observer. His brother Hiram had invented the Maxim machine gun thirty years earlier, and Hudson was instrumental in the development of smokeless gunpowder (not surprisingly, the DuPont company had secretly financed the publication of his book). Roosevelt was not particularly troubled by Maxim's obvious conflict of interest, nor was his new Oyster Bay neighbor J. Stuart Blackton, the English-born head of Vitagraph Studio, which he claimed was "the largest moving picture concern in this country."

As a supporter of preparedness, Blackton understood that a nationally distributed propaganda film about America's feeble defenses would be more effective than magazine articles, books, and speeches. "The motion picture is a very broad, powerful and far-reaching medium," he wrote TR. "I believe it has done more to educate and enlighten the world than any other thing since the invention of the printing press. We can reach immediately, millions of people." Roosevelt was interested, and in the weeks that followed, Blackton went to work developing an ambitious film, to be known as *Battle Cry of Peace*, inspired by Maxim's book. TR read the working script, and he could not help but be pleased by Blackton's plan to strategically employ his image in the finished product.

How long could Wilson resist the growing preparedness wave? It was easy to dismiss the charges of enemies like Roosevelt, criticism from reactionaries like Lodge, and pressure from Washington's influential "army and naval cabal." But other preparedness supporters were less easy to categorize: the Bull Moose liberals like Raymond Robins (a friend of Addams) and men in his own party such as Franklin Roosevelt. FDR, a fan of *Defenseless America*, had continued to share information with Gussie Gardner, informing him that spring that the navy had dropped to fourth largest in the world (a notch lower than TR's estimate). Ignoring the issue indefinitely was politically risky, and some observers from both parties believed Wilson "was making a grave mistake not to get behind this movement to some extent."

For now the President would not move in that direction. The friction with Germany and the Allies was troublesome but controllable at present. And if the Allies succeeded at Gallipoli, perhaps the war might end sooner than later, negating any need for an American military and navy buildup. In the meantime, there was also the chance that House's meetings and chats with European officials might somehow generate a pathway to peace.

House himself was not optimistic. A second round of talks with French leaders after his trip to Germany had not been fruitful. He was dumbfounded that the French appeared to believe that Wilson was pandering to the German American vote. "The ignorance of Europe concerning itself, to say nothing of America, is appalling," he wrote in his diary. By the end of April, he was back in London for more consultations with Sir Edward Grey, who he still believed saw the situation as he and Wilson did. "His mind and mine run nearly parallel and we seldom disagree," House wrote. "I know in advance, just as I know with the President, what his views will be on almost any subject."

Back in Washington, some of Wilson's cabinet sensed what House had been up to and thought it high time that he return. Walter Hines Page, whose position as the American ambassador to the United Kingdom had been undercut by House's presence in London, agreed. "Peace talk, therefore, is yet mere moonshine," Page wrote in his diary. "House has been to Berlin, from London, thence to Paris, then back to London again—from Nowhere (as far as peace is concerned) to Nowhere again."

Addams faced a similar dilemma. If peace talk was, as Page believed, "mere moonshine," did it make sense for her and the forty-odd American women she had assembled to cross the Atlantic in the midst of war for a hastily organized international gathering of female representatives from belligerent and neutral nations that she herself admitted might be a "fools' errand"? The very concept of such a gathering was too alien for most to grasp. Not surprisingly, most of Chicago's movers and shakers told her to stay home (at a Windy City gathering that April, Ellen Slayden heard barbed comments of how the "arch-feminist Jane Addams . . . had lost much of her influence"), but that made her all the more determined to go. It was the character trait that Clarence Darrow, a Chicago man himself, most admired in her. Miss Addams, he once told her niece, "has courage."

She would need every bit of it in the days before leaving. The attacks had already begun on the "silly women trying to accomplish in the excitement of war what the wise masculine brains failed to accomplish." Addams did her best to explain that this was a "women's conference" and not a harebrained stop-the-war meeting, although Schwimmer's flippant comments to the contrary made it an uphill battle at best. "We are not so foolish as to expect to end the war," Addams insisted to reporters. "The most we can hope is that we may perhaps be the entering wedge of a movement toward future peace." The ultimate goal was to "formulate plans for the settlement of the present international troubles when the time comes to consider terms of peace." After all, she reminded them, old-style diplomacy had utterly "failed. . . . Now is the time for women to assert themselves and attempt to bring about a settlement that will be a lasting settlement if it be possible to do so."

Her attempts to legitimize their efforts were dealt a serious blow when the press got wind of TR's February "silly and base" letter harshly condemning the Woman's Peace Party. Reporters, sensing a juicy tale of the two former Bull Moose pillars at odds, were eager to read its contents, although Addams thought some of it was better left private. "Colonel Roosevelt and I," she explained, "never did think alike about peace and war." Ultimately,

TR leaked the full letter to his friend John Callan O'Laughlin, whose own paper, the *Chicago Herald*, published it in its entirety. In the days that followed, almost every major publication printed excerpts.

Pacifists naturally rallied to Addams's support. TR's letter, a lawyer named Catherine Waugh McCulloch remarked, was the "cry of a barbarian out of his element. It is a half century out of date, and the longer the colonel lives, the more out of date he will become." Gertrude Pinchot, wife of one of TR's former Bull Moose colleagues and a member of the WPP's New York branch, agreed. Colonel Roosevelt's ideas on war, she observed, seemed to be suggesting that we should "make no effort to understand its causes with the object of future prevention; let us simply get ready to fight, and let the women stand out of our way, because they can only bear children and not arms, and when they organize to protest against war they come under the head of 'physical cowards,' who 'fear death or pain or discomfort beyond anything else.'" The *Springfield Republican*, a favorite of Wilson's and despised by Roosevelt, could not help but chuckle at the WPP being caught in TR's buzz saw: "It is hoped that by this time Miss Addams . . . may have an inkling of how people feel toward the colonel who have passed through the dreadful experience of not being as wise as he is."

Whether positive or negative, TR's views on the pacifists and, by extension, the Wilson administration's current policies received considerable exposure in the early weeks of April. It was a warm-up for a far bigger Roosevelt story about to unfold: his libel suit at the hands of the New York Republican boss William Barnes, touched off by an explosive TR campaign speech in 1914.

That Roosevelt found himself in such a situation revealed just how far his stock had fallen since leaving the White House. And the trial, he knew, was not about libel but the desire of Barnes and other conservative Old Guard Republicans to destroy him once and for all. He was not confident of the result. "The general feeling in New York in both the old parties . . . is so strong against me that there will be a very real effort made to have Barnes win, simply for the purpose of getting at me," TR lamented. "It will be a rather tough thing upon mother and the family. Even if I win, it will of course mean an expenditure of $30,000, and if I lose, it will cost me two or three times that."

But money was soon the least of his concerns. After returning from a funeral in New Haven (where protocol forced him into an awkward public handshake with his former friend William Howard Taft), he discovered that his wife's ongoing health issues had dramatically worsened. Up to that moment, TR had assumed Edith was improving, but he soon realized that she needed to be taken immediately to Roosevelt Hospital (named for a distant relative) in Manhattan. Surgery (probably a hysterectomy) was necessary. In an era before antibiotics, no operation was routine, but Edith pulled through, much to TR's relief. Before boarding the train to the trial on April 18, he stopped to check on Edith at the hospital. He was heartened to see her "propped up in bed in a pretty pink kimono and a lace cap with pink ribbons, and she had been able to eat and enjoy chicken soup and milk toast."

From the hospital, it was on to Syracuse, a change in venue from Albany requested by TR's lawyers, who believed he could not get a fair shake in Barnes's stomping grounds. During the last leg of the journey, TR and Barnes ended up on the same train together, where each man did his best to ignore the other. Their relationship had once been relatively amicable. Barnes was a reactionary, but he was a powerful force in state politics, and therefore could not be discounted. TR knew that he would be a formidable opponent. Barnes, one observer noted, "has intellect . . . and plenty of courage and he is not a bit afraid of the Colonel." There was also talk that Barnes was interested in running for the Senate.

Each side believed their case was strong. TR's legal team, headed by John M. Bowers, a former law partner of Wilson's German ambassador James Gerard, would be out to prove that the Republican Barnes in fact not only had huddled and colluded with the Democrats to suit his purposes but was guilty of corrupt involvement with state printing contracts. On the opposing side, attorney William Ivins would seek to show that Roosevelt was a holier-than-thou hypocrite guilty of everything he had charged Barnes with and more. Ivins, a brilliant, spiffily dressed, widely read, and onetime Republican New York City mayoral candidate, believed he had a gold mine of evidence—TR's voluminous letters over the past twenty years—to win the case and eliminate Roosevelt for good.

But TR was a celebrity whose personal appeal, though diminished since his presidential days, was still considerable. Thousands waited outside to see him ("circus day in a small town," quipped one reporter), and he was cheered as he walked into the courtroom. Even the jury selection process revealed that this was anything but a normal trial. "It appeared that every man summoned from farm or office or factory was a little more than eager to be accepted as a juror," observed the *New York Sun*. The Roosevelt team did their best to keep German Americans off the jury but two—a Boschert and a Beneke—were selected. That Boschert identified as a Progressive helped lessen the sting.

The next day, Bowers put TR on the witness stand. It was the moment that everyone had been awaiting. To illustrate his client's character, Bowers began by having Roosevelt recount his life to date, in case anyone needed to be reminded of his illustrious past and heroics, especially his days with the Rough Riders.

But TR's proud comment that "over a third" of his regiment was killed or wounded in Cuba was too much for Ivins, who sensed Roosevelt might be trying to dazzle the jury with his military exploits. Judge William S. Andrews, whose time at Harvard and Columbia Law coincided with TR's, agreed. "I don't think that is very important," he told Bowers. "We all know what the result of the battle was."

Roosevelt was hardly deterred that day or the next seven he spent on the stand. He was fighting for both his political life and his own legacy. "Neither rules of evidence, objections of lawyers or the admonitions of the Court restrained him," one reporter noted in wonder after the second day. "Whole sections of his testimony were stricken from the record when he was through, but not before they had been delivered to the jury in forceful and eloquent fashion."

And Ivins's cross-examination did not deliver the knockout punches he hoped. His witness, it seemed, had an answer for everything, whether it be questions about his state residency when running for governor or campaign contributions from big corporations. As far as his relationship with political bosses, TR admitted he had played footsie with them in the past out of necessity, but they could not "make him do anything he did not want to do." "When I do a thing it is right, substantially right, and I know it is right," he thundered. Ivins became increasingly annoyed by the ex-president's theatrics. "Instead of telling the jury things, I would like to ask you questions and have you answer them." He also attempted to curtail TR's overly animated body language. The Colonel, wrote the *Washington Times*, "drove home his points by banging a fist into the palm of the other hand, pounding the arms of the witness chair and snapping his jaws in his most vigorous manner." It was vintage Roosevelt.

After more than thirty-eight hours on the witness stand, Roosevelt still seemed raring to go. "You can't tire me out, Mr. Ivins!" he roared. No one realized that his health was less than 100 percent. His doctor, Alexander Lambert, had reminded TR to get plenty of rest in Syracuse with the help of automobile rides and "little sleeping powders" he prescribed. The physician was also concerned about an abscess that he advised TR to "keep . . . open" to prevent fever. Fortunately, TR's Syracuse hosts, the Bull Mooser Horace Wilkinson and his wife, Ada, made sure he was well cared for.

He had survived the first part of the trial, but there was still plenty of testimony to be heard. The Barnes team believed they had damaged Roosevelt's credibility. "We've made him rewrite his autobiography," Ivins chortled. But TR's friends felt differently. "You have already disposed of Barnes," his fellow Rough Rider Frank Knox, the future secretary of the navy, wrote him. "It would do your heart good to hear some of our reactionary friends curse him heartily, for giving you a chance to get at him."

Regardless of the stakes, the libel case and "Mr. Bawnes," as Roosevelt pronounced it, did not consume him. Edith remained very much on his mind, although her recovery now seemed assured. And the four hundred letters he received each day in Syracuse kept him abreast of national developments, including the reprehensible women's gathering at The Hague "to bleat about peace." If anything, TR's irritation with Addams and her "foolish, foolish associates" had only increased. He was glad, he wrote Cecil Spring Rice from the trial, that he had been able to publicly bash them. "I felt the keenest indignation as an American that American women should make such an unworthy exhibition of themselves," he explained. "They are a disgrace to the women of America."

S uch comments did not trouble Addams. As she prepared to sail on the
Noordam on the Holland America line, the more pressing concerns were
submarines and mines (the Noordam had already struck one back in October) potentially lurking in the North Sea and English Channel. Precautions for the ship's journey were already in place. "Through the mine
field she will be preceded by . . . 'soft-nosed tugs' . . . with a net swung
between them to gather in any mine that may be in the path," a reporter
explained. "Should the tug itself strike one its artificial proboscis of a soft,
yielding character strikes the mine so light a blow that the mine will not
explode." Addams dismissed those who marveled at women undertaking such risks. "It is no more serious than the trips that men make in the
course of the day's work," she insisted, "and I do not see that there can be
any more heroism in a woman doing the same thing." Her "greatest
fear" was not a sinking but the possibility of being "interned in some neutral
port."

The newspapers and newsreel cameras were out in full force in New
York on Tuesday, April 13, to see the forty-odd women and a handful of
men off (Schwimmer and a few others had already departed). They were,
as Addams noted, "all sorts" but an impressive collection of "sorts" nonetheless: the Pethick-Lawrences, a prison reformer, labor folks (the Boston
telephone operators union sent their president, Annie Molloy), pacifists like
Julia Grace Wales, socialists, suffragists, along with a substantial cadre of
her Chicago disciples ("those dreadful Hull-House people," Schwimmer
called them). But when Addams herself arrived at the dock at eleven thirty,
most of the three hundred or so onlookers were paying more attention to
a newly designed peace flag carried by her companion, Lillian Wald, sewn
that morning at the Henry Street Settlement. Up until the last minute, the
use of the simple white banner with the word "Peace" in blue had been in
doubt. Fearful that the use of such a flag might give Wilson's critics more
ammunition, she wanted State Department authorization, only to be told
that it was Holland America's call. Ship officials gave the green light, requesting that it not fly when sailing through the Channel.

Addams (second from left), Pethick-Lawrence (far left), and colleagues on the Noordam *before their departure, April 13, 1915.*
(Library of Congress, LC-B2- 3443-11)

Addams was the woman of the hour. The ship's captain immediately tried to give his celebrity passenger the *Noordam*'s finest cabin, only to be rebuffed. "Indeed, I can't take it," she told him. "The captain is very kind, but why should I be set apart from the others?" She changed her mind when her friend Florence Kelley told her it was big enough to double as a comfortable sick bay. And everyone wanted a final statement from Addams. "It will break the hypnotic spell when no one may talk of peace; this is one definite thing that will be accomplished—it is a big thing in itself," she announced. "Good-bye." But her farewell proved to be premature. Addams and the others sat through a two-hour delay, some eventually deciding to have lunch, while Leonora Reilly of the Women's Trade Union League ingeniously conducted business from the ship, "megaphoning messages with her hands" to her associates.

Around 2:30 p.m., the *Noordam* finally began her voyage down the Hudson River. "I don't know whether they're fools or world saviors," one gentleman on the docks was heard to say, "but, by Jove! they're a gallant lot."

The *Noordam* would be the women's home for at least a week. The accommodations, they were happy to discover, were quite comfortable, the food plentiful, the crew picturesque. "How can Dutch people so perfectly look their part," Emily Balch wrote in her diary. "There is one tiny little cabin boy directly off a Christmas card, rosy cheeks and all." But they soon noted an undercurrent of hostility from most of the male passengers, who seemed more intrigued with a "frivolous, high-heeled and flirtatious" *fräulein* heading home to see her boyfriend in the German army.

Addams and the delegates had no time for such nonsense. This would be no pleasure cruise; in fact, they were determined to devote as much of the voyage as possible to productive activities. With the help of Addams, a virtual mini-university was soon up and running, complete with peace library and twice-daily lectures and discussions. The delegates, along with Louis Lochner, served as the "professors," offering talks in their fields of expertise, including eugenics, social work, war-related illnesses, suffrage, and immigration. Peace, of course, remained the primary focus, although the radical author and suffragist Mary Heaton Vorse found it difficult to suppress her cynicism as she listened to Wales detail her much touted Wisconsin plan. "It is so simple and so naïve that it is as though a wee child ran into one of the cabinets of Europe and with a word showed the way out of all difficulties," she wrote her husband. "Such things haven't happened in real life since Jeanne d'Arc." Nor did she think much of Pethick-Lawrence, whose condescending talk on "working girls" and "slum children" had rubbed some of the Americans the wrong way.

One evening the *Noordam*'s onboard university featured a debate between Pethick-Lawrence and Addams on the topic "Is war ever justifiable?" The prison reformer Madeleine Doty could not help note the contrast between the two sides. Addams, in opposition, talked of Tolstoy, nonresistance, and the "sacredness of life." "Gentle, modest, clad in a dark silk dress, the light of her spirit shining in her tragic eyes, she seemed hardly of the earth," Doty remarked. "The Englishwoman in her Oriental dress of red and green was all passion and fire. . . . Both women were inspired by the same ideal. But one looked at life as a saint; the other faced reality."

Their philosophical differences aside, Addams got along splendidly with Pethick-Lawrence and the other delegates. "The women on the whole are as nice + friendly as 40 women, thrown suddenly together, could possibly be," she wrote Mary Rozet Smith. "Miss Addams is really having a good time," her physician friend Alice Hamilton confided to Smith. "She has made every woman on board feel that she is an intimate friend and they all adore her." Vorse was one of the new admirers. "I like her more than almost any woman I've ever known," she wrote her husband of Addams. "She has a quality of simple greatness." And with each day, Addams's understated presence provided a much needed bond to transform "a very heterogeneous group of most individualized women used to being leaders and playing a conspicuous role" into a cohesive unit determined to fulfill the object of the mission.

Eight days passed. She missed Mary. And the lack of contact from the outside world—no newspapers or letters—became increasingly irritating. The captain refused to share any of his wireless dispatches, fearful that news, perhaps war related, might cause conflict or anxiety among the passengers. With the *Noordam* now steaming near the Isles of Scilly close to the British mainland, everyone was thinking submarines, including the captain and crew. Back in Washington, Bryan wired Ambassador Gerard in Berlin requesting that he alert the Foreign Office about the *Noordam*, hoping to avert any "mistakes" by U-boats. Still, lifeboats were prepared, and large wooden letters, three-feet high, spelling *Noordam*, were now attached to both sides of the ship and lit at night. Anticipating the worst, Madeleine Doty's roommate "wore her best underclothing and silk stockings to bed," deciding that "if we were to be blown up, she wanted to dress for the part."

The war seemed to grow closer each day, though Addams tried to set an example of calm. An "evening of entertainment," she suggested on Thursday, April 22, might be a good idea. When the ladies finished their activities around ten o'clock, they suddenly heard a "shrill whistle and sound of running feet." An armed English cutter had pulled alongside the *Noordam*, and several officers had scurried onto the ship and were heading for the captain. "No one knew what was happening," Doty later wrote. Soon, more English vessels appeared. "We had a gun trained on us," WPP official Alice Thacher Post marveled. "Think of Jane Addams with a gun trained on her!"

The British, they soon discovered, were there to take two German stow-aways into custody. The two men—a steward and a carpenter stuck in New York on interned German ships—had emerged recently from the coal hold after running out of food. Addams and the others watched intently as the unfortunate pair were led off the *Noordam* with ropes around their waists in case they had any ideas about plunging into the Atlantic. As they boarded the cutter, one defiantly yelled, *"Hoch der Kaiser! Deutschland über Alles!"* his spirited words eliciting cheers from several of the onlookers. The au-thorities then proceeded to scrutinize the passports of the male passengers before allowing the voyage to continue.

The next day, their Dutch hosts at The Hague were relieved to receive a wire that Addams and the *Noordam* had reached the English Channel, giving the women plenty of time to arrive before the start of the congress on Tuesday. The ship then anchored at Dover for inspection, where pas-sengers and cargo (mostly grain) were deemed satisfactory. With the reso-lutions and preliminary program for the congress thoroughly hashed out, there seemed little to do except relax and enjoy the scenery, including the sight of a dirigible heading toward France.

Yet twenty-four hours passed without movement. Something was wrong. Addams learned that the British Admiralty had stopped all passenger traf-fic to Holland. The supposed reason was a big naval battle likely to unfold in the North Sea, but many delegates suspected a more sinister motive. The British government, they soon learned from newspapers brought on board by a "bribed" fisherman, had been less than thrilled about the "pea-cettes" and their upcoming "tea party," authorizing only 24 of a requested 180 passports. Like their American cousins, the two dozen Englishwomen allowed to travel to The Hague found themselves effectively blocked from their destination, a pleasing development to the foes of "peace babblers." "We are perfectly satisfied, and we have information which supports that belief, that the whole thing has been engineered by agents of Germany," insisted Emmeline Pankhurst.

As the weekend wore on, frustrations began to mount, especially when rumors surfaced that their confinement might last weeks. While the more conservative types were content to wait out the delay, others simmered with resentment that the British had the nerve to prevent the journey of a neutral ship to a neutral port. "We are not allowed to go on shore—except that the Captain and Purser might if they chose—nor can anyone but the English officials come on board to us," Emily Balch complained. "We are practically interned altho' neutrals." Addams, her own patience wearing thin, did her best to preserve the harmony and camaraderie she had nurtured for the past ten days. "Miss Addams shines, so respectful of everyone's views, so eager to understand and sympathize, so patient of anarchy and even ego, yet always there, strong, wise and in the lead," Balch recorded in her diary. In the meantime, Addams drafted letters to anyone she knew who might be able to help, including James Bryce, the pacifist future prime minister Ramsay MacDonald, and Lord Eustace Percy. She also reached out to an old acquaintance, Ambassador Page, who had worked with her in his days in the magazine and publishing world, explaining that they were "willing to risk anything" to get moving again. Page, whose distaste for any peace talk mirrored Whitehall's position, claimed his hands were tied (privately, he sneeringly referred to Addams and company as "Daughters of the Dove of Peace").

It was now Monday. Bryan was now aware of the situation and had wired Page himself, but they were running out of ideas and time. That day, they watched a tugboat pull up alongside the *Noordam,* probably to bring more provisions. Instead an officer boarded with the surprising news that the ship would be permitted to proceed to her destination (the would-be British delegates, they soon learned, were not granted the same privilege). No one was quite sure what had changed their minds, but the women were ecstatic. "We dance about the deck," Doty wrote. "We played tag and ran three-legged races to let off steam." But the captain thought it best to leave the following morning, especially after peering at a map of a mine-filled North Sea.

Early Tuesday, the *Noordam* finally began the much delayed final leg of its voyage. Untroubled by mines or submarines, she arrived at Rotterdam that afternoon, the peace flag proudly displayed on the side, a full two weeks after leaving New York. Addams and the others would have to hustle but there was still time to get to the informal opening of the conference at eight that evening. After hectic cab and train rides, they finally reached The Hague, the peace capital of the world and home of the Carnegie-funded Peace Palace, where the Permanent Court of Arbitration operated. The beautiful sights and sounds of Holland—gorgeous blue skies, fragrant, blooming tulips, "the wooden shoes, flaring white head-dress and gold hair-pins of a peasant woman"—reinvigorated the exhausted delegates by the time they entered the Zoological Gardens that evening (the Peace Palace rooms were too small for such a large meeting). "I'm so glad you're alive and not blown up, or at the bottom of the seas," remarked one of their hosts. "We didn't know what had happened."

The real work began in earnest the next day. Despite the logistical night-mare of trying to assemble such a gathering in the midst of war, when letters were censored and confiscated regularly, 1,100 delegates, 47 of them Amer-ican, took their seats that morning. The Dutch naturally sent the largest delegation, "big, fine, wholesome, clear-skinned . . . specimens of woman-hood," one American marveled, but neutrals such as Norway, Sweden, Den-mark, and Italy were also represented. Most striking was the presence of women from Germany, Austria-Hungary, Canada, and the three from Great Britain who managed to get to The Hague before the North Sea traffic stoppage. Somehow, they resisted the ridicule, hostility, peer pressure, and official and unofficial governmental interference that prevented any repre-sentatives from France, Russia, and Serbia from attending.

Addams was quickly made chairwoman and took her place on stage, intentionally flanked by representatives of both sides and the neutral na-tions. The reporters present waited expectantly for a quick blowup of some kind, perhaps involving umbrella-wielding lady delegates, but nothing of the kind occurred. Everyone was on her best behavior; in fact, a sense of restraint prevailed.

Addams's greatest difficulty on the first day was trying to ensure that everyone heard and understood the speeches and resolutions in a world where public address systems were not yet in use. Every speech had to be translated multiple times—French, German, English—but even the best translators could not help missing crucial words and phrases in the noisy hall. Addams herself asked the audience to indicate "by a gesture" when she was speaking too fast.

The subdued atmosphere shifted on Thursday and Friday. Schwimmer, whose speech had already electrified the public meeting on Tuesday evening, was in her usual fiery form. A comment by Alice Thacher Post suggesting that "we are not asking that there shall be no war, but we ask that there shall be no war except one wished by the people of the world," appalled Schwimmer. "I am very much embarrassed," she explained. "Yesterday it seemed as if we would unanimously say: we don't want any kind of war, whether democratically approved or not." The audience cheered. She also engaged in a bit of pageantry at the end of the business sessions on Friday, leading the gathering in a five-minute silent prayer for the war dead and their mothers.

But the most dramatic event of the day occurred earlier, when a band of five plucky Belgian women walked into the hall. Against all odds, they had managed to get passports from hostile German authorities, driven a borrowed car to Essen on the Dutch border ("where they were searched to the skin"), walked another two hours with their luggage to Roosendaal, and finally caught a train to The Hague. Addams was the first to greet them, but the more powerful gesture was the warm welcome from the German feminist lawyer Anita Augsburg. "1,000 women stood on their chairs and clapped and tossed their handkerchiefs in the air," the *New York Sun* reported. Such symbolic and sometimes shocking gestures between citizens of warring nations were not uncommon; the Pethick-Lawrences dined with Augsburg and her partner, Lida Gustava Heymann, one night. To the American delegate Alice Carpenter, their behavior was reflective of a "new type of women. . . . They had put aside their nationality and were citizens of the world." And they had done so at considerable risk: some of the German delegates would be jailed upon their return.

The conflict that the male-dominated press had anticipated never seemed to materialize, although Addams occasionally had to smooth some ruffled feathers. The English suffragist Amy Lillingston's criticism of "silly . . . platitudes" and her insistence that "for every hundred women that were willing to come to this Congress, a thousand women are ready to go to France and fight" elicited angry hissing, which Addams did her best to stop. "In this Congress every member must be able to say what she thinks necessary," she announced. "There must be free speech here." Everyone applauded her

masterful performance as chairwoman, her "statesmanlike handling of diverse personalities" and "extraordinary parliamentary skill." Addams, Leonora O'Reilly admitted, "pulled the best out of each of us, and made us
see that what came from us, as a unified body, was far bigger and better
than what came from any one of us alone."

Working harmoniously, the congress succeeded in hammering out a series of resolutions to bring about peace now and in the future, some of
which overlapped with the WPP's program. The more significant included
Julia Wales's continuous mediation idea, self-determination of nations, arbitration of international squabbles, peace instruction for children, "democratic control of foreign policy," votes and equal rights for women, a third
Hague Conference after the war, a new "Society of Nations," government
control of arms manufacture as a step toward global disarmament, freedom
of the seas, the end of secret diplomacy, the creation of an International
Committee of Women for Permanent Peace, and the calling of a second
women's congress at the same place and time of the peace conference.

On Saturday, May 1, the congress was preparing to wind down to an
uneventful conclusion. Only a few knew that Schwimmer, proud that she
had already "shocked the professional pacifists" in America, was about to
do the same thing at The Hague. When Addams innocently asked about
any resolutions too late to be published in the program, Schwimmer was
on her feet with a scheme she had been cooking up for weeks. Mere words
were not enough, she asserted. The congress must now take the bold and
unprecedented step of sending emissaries with the resolutions to the leaders
of European nations, belligerent and neutral, with the goal of stimulating
a peace settlement.

The proposal horrified Kathleen Courtney of Great Britain. "I don't
appeal to your heart but to your head," she explained to the congress. "Try
to keep your heart out of the matter and keep your head in the question
and then you will see that this is not a really possible proposal."

But Schwimmer had a ready response. "Brains—they say—have ruled
the world till to-day. If brains have brought us to what we are in now, I
think it is time to allow also our hearts to speak. When our sons are killed
by millions, let us, mothers, only try to do good by going to kings and
emperors, without any other danger than a refusal."

Judging by the animated response to Schwimmer's words, Addams could see where this was going. Her own impulse, and that of most of the American delegation, was opposition to such over-the-top silliness; in fact, she had it in her power to rule the entire proposition out of order since it had not first been authorized by the resolutions committee. Still, she allowed the congress to vote on the Schwimmer resolution or the more modest alternative of presenting the resolutions to the European ambassadors at The Hague. As she later explained to Mary, "you can never understand unless you were here, how you would be willing to do anything." After two votes, the motion carried. And as chairwoman, she would be part of the resolutions-bearing delegation, a task she did not especially relish.

Her ambivalence about the Schwimmer plan was offset by her realization that the congress had more than accomplished its goals. "The great achievement," she told a reporter, "is to my mind the getting together of these women from all parts of Europe, when their men-folks are shooting each other from opposite trenches." Arguments had arisen, but "no more . . . than at any Church meeting," and far less than hostile press accounts suggested. She was also pleased with the platform adopted, "which we do not claim contains all wisdom, but which we do believe contains some elements which will make peace more permanent and more just than it has ever been before." But she knew that she was about to embark on a journey likely to be harshly criticized and misinterpreted at every turn, even by Mary, whom she suspected might "think it 'silly and base,'" like TR. Still, she was compelled to try anything, she wrote her partner, even if "there is just one chance in ten thousand" of success.

While the congress was concluding its work at The Hague that Saturday morning, millions of Americans were waking up to find a peculiar item in their newspaper. A small advertisement, issued by the German embassy, alerted transatlantic passengers to a few unpleasant realities: there was a war on, the "waters adjacent to the British Isles" were a war zone, British and Allied ships passing through would be subject to sinking, and "travellers sailing in the war zone in ships of Great Britain or her Allies do so at their own risk."

The notice, which was originally scheduled to appear a week earlier, was largely the work of Ambassador Bernstorff, who believed the Wilson's administration's silence about American travel virtually guaranteed a major international incident that might plunge his nation into war with yet another power. The *Lusitania* was sailing from New York that day, but neither Cunard officials nor passengers were deterred, even by mysterious last-minute telegrams from the likes of "John Smith" and "George Jones" warning of possible torpedo attacks.

Bernstorff was aware that Berlin officials had ramped up the U-boat war, neutrals seemingly be damned. In the first three days of May, thirteen vessels were attacked by submarines off the British Isles, one of them an American oil tanker, the *Gulflight*, heading to Rouen, France, from Port Arthur, Texas. Just hours before the *Lusitania* departed, a torpedo struck the tanker's starboard side, forcing the crew to take to their boats. Most survived, with the exception of a sailor and wireless operator who jumped overboard and drowned, likely after struggling to swim in the oily waves. The unfortunate captain, Alfred Gunter, made it safely to a lifeboat, only to drop dead of heart failure a few hours later, nearly fulfilling his own prophecy that he would not live two years after the birth of his daughter.

Wilson was in Williamstown, Massachusetts, that weekend for the christening of his first grandchild, Frank. Dr. Grayson preferred that the President take more time off, but the demands of the job, even away from Washington, were too much. "I'm sentenced to hard labor for several years," Wilson quipped. When he returned to the White House on Monday morning, he was fully briefed on the *Gulflight* situation and the newspaper warning, which Lansing perceived as "highly improper" and "insolent," though Bryan saw it as a "friendly desire to evade anything that might raise a question." TR, meanwhile, believed the proper answer to the warning would be to send Bernstorff home—on the *Lusitania*.

Wilson would not and could not move in such a dramatic fashion. Still, he realized that the offenses were mounting at a frightening pace—the *Falaba*, the *Gulflight*, and an episode the prior Wednesday where a German plane dropped a bomb on the Standard Oil steamer the *Cushing* without causing much damage. He also recognized that Germany had directly or indirectly caused the deaths of four Americans. If not the "energetic action" demanded by TR and his followers, something had to be done. "I believe that a sharp note indicating your determination to demand full reparation would be sufficient in this instance," House wired the President from London. "I am afraid a more serious breach may at any time occur, for they seem to have no regard for consequences."

But it was equally clear that House's British hosts also had "no regard for consequences." Their annoying interference with American trade, in some cases delaying ships and cargo for weeks on end, had continued, so much so that Wilson's cabinet members had begun to "boil over . . . at the foolish manner in which England acts." Much of the country, Interior Secretary Franklin Lane noted in a letter to House that week, was pro-Allies, "but it would not have been as strongly with them, not nearly so strongly, if it had not been for the persistent short-sightedness of our German friends." The Allies, then, were winning the PR war in America by default. Lane assured House that most of the country seemed to approve of Wilson's cautious approach. "They do not love him, because he appears to them as a man of the cloister," he wrote. "But they respect him as a wise, sane leader who will keep them out of trouble."

Such heavy responsibilities weighed heavily upon Wilson. But his thoughts that week often drifted to a more pleasant diversion. He had fallen in love with Edith Galt.

It had happened quickly in a matter of weeks, far too quickly for a man still in mourning, at least according to etiquette. Almost overnight, she had become a fixture in his life, with the assistance of his cousin Helen Bones, usually present to quell any possible charges of impropriety, and White House usher Irwin Hood Hoover, who discreetly handled their messages. Throughout April, they had seen more and more of each other on motoring trips and at dinners at the White House. She had even appeared with him in public, as part of the presidential party at opening day of the Washington Senators (Wilson was a baseball fan, while TR preferred football). A photo of Wilson, Bones, Grayson, and "Mrs. Norman Gault [sic]" appeared the next day in the *New York Herald* and other newspapers, although no one suspected that she was anything more than a friend of the family.

Two weeks later, the President began to write to Galt, whose Dupont Circle home was only a little over a mile from the White House. The first letter, on April 28, only hinted at his growing affection: he was sending her a copy of *Round My House*, Philip Gilbert Hamerton's account of his experiences in rural France, from the Library of Congress while he waited for a copy on order (Hoover was hard at work tracking down the thirty-eight-year-old book). "I hope it will give you a little pleasure. I covet nothing more than to give you pleasure,—you have given me so much!" Wilson also included a coy invitation to "come around" that night for "a little reading" or, weather permitting, "another ride," with the closing "Your sincere and grateful friend."

Obligations to her mother prevented Galt from seeing the President that night, but the next day, she was back at the White House for another dinner. Clearly, she and Wilson were now friends, united in the loss of their spouses and their "loved Southland," but she still saw him as "the President," whose "high office set you apart." But Wilson wanted more than friendship. He decided that he would propose when he returned from the Massachusetts christening on Monday.

The international situation forced him to set his thoughts of marriage aside until Tuesday evening, when Edith again returned to the White House. After dinner he took her aside and poured out his heart to her. "It had taken possession of me," he later told her, "and I could not hold it back."

In her memoirs, Edith claimed she was shocked. It was too soon after Ellen Axson Wilson's death, she explained, and the President did not "really know" her yet. She would have to decline, at least for now. His disappointment lifted somewhat the following morning when Cousin Helen brought him a note Galt had written soon after coming home from the White House. "What an unspeakable pleasure and privilege I deem it to be allowed to share these tense, terrible days of responsibility," she wrote. "How I thrill to my very finger tips when I remember the tremendous thing you said to me tonight, and how pitifully poor I am, to have nothing to offer you in return." And Wilson had not jeopardized their friendship by his "fearless honesty. . . . There is nothing to fear—we will help and hearten each other."

More breakthroughs followed on Wednesday and Thursday: another automobile ride, hands touching, and a flurry of letters, each one seemingly more gooey than the last (the public would have been flabbergasted that the President, the apostle of self-mastery, was capable of getting so hot and bothered over a lady). "It will be my study and my joy to make you glad that you met me," he wrote on Thursday, May 6. "The wonderful woman I recognized and loved, and sought selfishly to claim, I shall seek to enrich, not impoverish. . . . I would rather see light—the light of joy and complete happiness—in those eyes than have anything I can think of for myself." A difficulty that needed to be overcome, he realized, was that she still had "not stopped thinking of me as the public man," though Edith was especially thrilled and delighted when he began to take her into his confidence about the "awful conditions" he faced.

For now he was in limbo. He would accept a "deep and tender friendship" from Edith if that was all she could give, but he hoped she would reciprocate his feelings. "All that you have to determine," he wrote her, "if you are going to be fair to me is, can you love me for my own sake and do you want me for your life's joy? All the rest it will be easy to take care of."

Friday, May 7. Wilson spent the morning dodging a persistent group of Philadelphia suffragettes representing Alice Paul's Congressional Union, who were incensed that he had preferred to hit the golf links the day before rather than see them (golf, they were told, was essential to the President's continued good health). After an eleven o'clock cabinet meeting and lunch, yet another game of golf awaited him in the early afternoon.

In Syracuse, the Barnes trial was wrapping up its third week. Franklin Roosevelt, who "described himself as a fifth cousin of Theodore Roosevelt by blood and a nephew by law" (FDR had married TR's niece Eleanor ten years earlier), had recently testified confirming the cozy relationship between Barnes and the Democrat boss Charles Murphy. TR was pleased by FDR's testimony, but he increasingly began to doubt whether he could win the trial. A defeat would knock his prestige still lower, although he took a philosophical attitude. "From 1898 to 1910," TR wrote his son Kermit, "everything went my way. . . . I have no complaint because, during the last five years, things have gone the other way."

At The Hague, Addams met with Dutch prime minister Cort van der Linden that day, along with Schwimmer and three other delegates. The discussion with van der Linden, a German sympathizer, did not get very far. The time was not right for mediation, he told them, and many women in the belligerent countries supported the war effort, although Addams tried to explain that "what you read in the newspapers are the opinions of only a handful of female writers." Afterward, she prepared to depart Holland for London.

House was still in the British capital. That morning, he had an outing with Grey at Kew Gardens, where they discussed a matter that was now on everyone's mind in Britain: the possibility of a liner's being sunk ("I almost expect such a thing," Ambassador Page had written his son a few days earlier). The conversation was cut short by King George's request to see House at 11:30 a.m. at Buckingham Palace, a prospect the President's friend did not especially look forward to. "The truth of the matter is, unless he was the gentleman he is, I would not care to see him," House recorded in his diary. Like Grey, the king wanted to talk about what the sinking of a liner with American passengers might mean, especially the *Lusitania*, which had entered the war zone recently and was nearing completion of its voyage. House was relatively certain that "a flame of indignation would sweep across America, which would in itself, probably carry us into the war." He was doubtful, however, that the Germans would ever stoop to such a level.

Sometime after 1:00 p.m., Wilson had finished lunch and was now preparing for his afternoon golf game. He was interrupted by his assistant secretary, Rudolph Forster, with a message. A German U-boat had torpedoed the *Lusitania* off the Irish coast.

Chapter 5

TOO PROUD TO FIGHT

MAY 7–JUNE 30, 1915

*I do not deny that the situation concerning Germany
is critical, but, if we had a jingo in the White House
this country would now be at war with Germany.*

—William Howard Taft, June 1915

T he news," one reporter at the White House noted, "came like the dropping of a bomb from a clear sky."

Wilson cancelled his golf game and retreated to his office to await more details. Because no reports of fatalities had been issued, a sliver of hope existed that perhaps all 1,959 passengers and crew had somehow survived. Early coverage in the afternoon editions of the *New York Evening World* and *Washington Evening Star* even provided optimistic reports and headlines proclaiming "NONE PERISH" and "THINK PASSENGERS ARE SAFE." But those who remembered the *Titanic* disaster three years earlier could not help but question how so many passengers could be saved. In New York, crowds began to gather around newspaper offices and the Cunard line headquarters, desperate for any information about loved ones. On Wall Street, the stock market plunged.

Bernstorff, meanwhile, was on his way to New York from the German embassy in Washington that afternoon. When his train stopped in North Philadelphia, he bought a newspaper. The man behind the warning a week earlier saw the news he had been desperate to avoid. "Do you think—had

I known it—I should have allowed three of the best friends I had in America to take passage on the *Lusitania*?" the anguished Bernstorff asked a journalist. "I not only let them go. I gave them friendly letters of introduction to certain gentlemen in London." He would later learn that his three friends—the multimillionaire Alfred Vanderbilt, the playwright Charles Klein, and Herbert Stone, the son of the head of the Associated Press— were not among the survivors.

By eight that evening, Wilson knew the full scope of the tragedy. On its way home after two days of stalking prey on the Irish Sea, the U-20 had sighted the *Lusitania*. The U-boat's captain, Walter Schwieger, immediately realized that the passenger liner, if she could be caught, was a sitting duck. Seventy minutes later, only 700 meters separated the two vessels, and Schwieger was ready. The U-20 fired, the torpedo ripped into the *Lusitania*'s starboard side, and the ship was soon convulsed with what Schwieger later described as "an extraordinarily great detonation."

What followed was a scene of unimagined terror and chaos. The *Lusitania* began sinking faster than anyone could have anticipated. Desperate passengers scrambled to reach lifeboats, lifebelts, or collapsible craft, but time ran out for most of them. In just eighteen minutes, the *Lusitania* was gone, taking 1,198 with her, including 128 American citizens.

The death toll meant that America was entering uncharted territory, far beyond the handful of lives lost in previous incidents. Wilson was now facing the most difficult decision of his presidency. Did these deaths of American men, women, and children in a deliberate attack on a passenger liner, albeit a British one, warrant severing ties with Germany, potentially leading to involvement in the bloodiest war in world history? If not, what path could he pursue that would maintain the honor of the United States and his own administration?

That evening, a troubled Wilson left the White House temporarily without Secret Service protection for a quick walk up to Corcoran Street and back, hoping that the instincts and intellect that had served him so well could find a way out of what some would label the "greatest crisis that has visited the country since Lincoln's day." The ultimate decision would be his and his alone, per his usual preference. As usual he had no desire to consult anyone, let alone his cabinet, which King George wrongly assumed would be a key part of the decision-making process. Still, the President had Edith Galt, whose role as confidant seemed to grow by the day, as a potential sounding board. "In the awful possibilities the extra papers hint at," she wrote him Friday night, "I know you need all the help and tender comprehension I can give."

If his temperament and ego would not allow for a consensus-driven decision, Wilson could not isolate himself entirely from other voices and influences. From Maine to California, the prevailing mood was profound anger. "I have not seen the country so stirred since the Civil War," marveled the elderly Henry Lee Higginson, a Union army veteran and founder of the Boston Symphony Orchestra. For the President, who had long feared unchecked emotions carrying the nation into war, it was his worst nightmare. Somehow, he would have to dissipate the public's rage or at least channel it away from a desire for bloodthirsty revenge, which was aptly expressed by James Norman Hall. "Thank Heaven I am where I am," Hall wrote a family member. "Were I at home in Boston I could not endure standing by! I should have to get into the fight to do what little I could to help put an end to such outrageous business."

The English press and public, Hall noted, were quite anxious to see whether America would join the Allies, especially in view of Wilson's infamous "strict accountability" note of February and the recent failure of the "war-ending" Gallipoli campaign. "Nobody but a damn fool could think it would not be of benefit to us," Lord Kitchener told House. Kitchener did not have to convince Ambassador Page, who was eager that his fantasy of "Anglo-American partnership" would finally come true (he already believed that "English-speaking folk must rule the world"). A dispatch from Page sent from London on Saturday, May 8, warned Wilson that "the freely expressed unofficial feeling is that the United States must declare war or forfeit European respect." If that was not enough pressure, Page also was certain that "a failure to act now will kill the [Democratic] party for a generation," though House managed to prevent such an expression of tawdry opportunism from reaching the President.

It was not difficult for Wilson to ignore Page, whose partiality was now well known to everyone in Washington. But Colonel House was a different story. His wire to the White House on Sunday offered another voice for war, albeit with an escape hatch. The President should "demand" that Germany promise never to repeat such behavior. If the German government refused, then the United States should "take whatever measures were necessary to insure the safety of American citizens." War might result, but this would benefit America by ending the hostilities faster and expanding her role in the eventual peace process. "Think we can no longer remain neutral spectators," House wrote. "We are being weighed in the balance, and our position amongst the nations is being assessed by mankind."

Both Page and House were sounding positively Rooseveltian at the moment. TR himself had learned of the *Lusitania* from a telegram handed to him in the midst of an especially tedious day in the Syracuse courtroom, mostly featuring testimony about printing issues. A copy of one of Aristophanes' plays—*The Acharnians*, given to him by Barnes's lawyer Ivins— helped pass the time. After the court adjourned, the press wanted a statement, although the death toll was unknown at the moment. For a change, Roosevelt exercised restraint. He would not bash Wilson. "I do not know enough of the facts . . . to make any further comment or to say what would be proper for this government to do in the circumstances."

Late that evening, a reporter contacted him at the Wilkinsons', this time with the full details. "That's murder! Will I make a statement? Yes, yes. I'll make it now. Just take this." The sinking of the *Lusitania*, TR began, "represents not merely piracy, but piracy on a vaster scale of murder than any old time pirate ever practiced." The time for negotiations or notes had ended. "It seems inconceivable that we should refrain from taking action in this matter, for we owe it not only to humanity but to our own national self-respect." The media soon wanted more. On Saturday, both the Wheeler Syndicate and John Callan O'Laughlin wired Roosevelt hoping for "detailed views" on the crisis and urging him to "take the lead in denouncing *Lusitania* crime." TR was game, but it would be through the *Metropolitan*, his regular outlet. Never a quick writer, he labored over the editorial much of the weekend before submitting it to his editor for publication in the June issue, although its contents would also be released immediately to the daily press.

"Murder on the High Seas" unleashed TR's full fury on Germany and the Wilson administration. The submarine attacks, he wrote, were atrocities and clearly indefensible, except for those who "would likewise justify the wholesale poisoning of wells in the path of a hostile army . . . the shipping of infected rags into the cities of a hostile country . . . the torture of prisoners and the reduction of captured women to the slavery of concubinage." Ignoring such evil to maintain "peace above righteousness" invited "measureless scorn and contempt. . . . For many months our government has preserved between right and wrong a 'neutrality' which would have excited the emulous admiration of Pontius Pilate—the arch-typical neutral of all time." Once again, he insisted that America must now "act with immediate decision and vigor" or "we shall have failed in the duty demanded by humanity."

Roosevelt's blistering comments came with considerable risk, both politically and personally. An ex-president attacking the current administration at this moment would not go over well among those who already hated TR. (Taft had chosen to say little "except to express confidence that the President will follow a wise and patriotic course.") He also had the ongoing libel trial to consider. Such venomous charges might very well cost him the goodwill of the two German Americans on the jury. "It is more important that I be right than to win this suit," he told his host Horace Wilkinson. "I've got to be right in this matter."

The brinkmanship approach of TR, House, and Page disturbed Bryan, who remained the strongest voice for peace in Wilson's orbit. One important issue, he felt, needed to be considered. The *Lusitania* was not merely a passenger liner; she was also carrying munitions, including shrapnel cases, cartridges, and fuses, even if she was not armed, as the Germans first claimed (the *Lusitania* carried three "hydroaeroplanes" during House's journey in February, although "two big guns" from Bethlehem Steel were not ready in time). On Sunday, May 9, Bryan sent Wilson a copy of that morning's editorial in *The Washington Post* ("as you do not read the Post"), which proposed that any ship transporting contraband should forfeit its right to carry passengers. "Germany has a right to prevent contraband going to the allies," he reminded the President, "and a ship carrying contraband should not rely upon passengers to protect her from attack—it would be like putting women and children in front of an army."

The suffragist Elizabeth Colt expressed a similar view after hearing the news. "The people of this country should stay at home," she told a reporter.

"I met, just before he sailed, one man who went on the *Lusitania*. He told me he knew the ship was likely to be struck, that his wife implored him not to go, but his 'business required it.' Must this country go to war because people are reckless like that?"

For Addams, who was now in London, assigning blame was not important. To her, the *Lusitania* sinking confirmed once again that a way must somehow be found to broker peace, ideally through the efforts of the neutral countries. She was relieved that her new associate Wilson, "a splendid man" and "absolutely safe," was in the driver's seat. "I am a great admirer of Mr. Roosevelt, but I am unable to agree with him that the United States should take sides with the Allies," she explained. "Colonel Roosevelt would take the bit in his teeth and go in for war. I think we will be able to accomplish infinitely more by staying out." American involvement would create enormous tensions among immigrants, Addams believed; already, a German American had been badly beaten in New York after excitedly tossing his hat in the air in response to the *Lusitania* news. Yes, the United States must demonstrate "an unflinching attitude against barbarity," but war, as Wilson himself believed, would destroy America's hopes of mediating in the future. Ultimately, Addams insisted that "nothing can be settled by force," a statement soon mocked by many a pundit citing the American Revolution and the Civil War.

At the moment, Wilson's own views did not differ markedly from Addams's. His gut impulse remained the same: avoid war if possible without sacrificing America's honor. He also realized that a declaration of war would be an extremely tough sell to Congress. For every eastern Republican like Gussie Gardner openly touting a Roosevelt approach that weekend, there were dozens of Bryan disciples in Congress from the South and Midwest determined to block any overseas involvement. And the President could not ignore the piles of telegrams arriving at the White House, the "majority," according to one press report, against war, though some demanded intervention "in the name of God." "War isn't declared in the name of God," Wilson told one of his stenographers, "it is a human affair entirely." But the voices of the people, pro or con, were merely another data point to consider and nothing more. "It is his problem," William

Stone, the Democratic chairman of the Senate Foreign Relations Committee, explained to a reporter, "and it is useless for others to attempt to advise him."

No one knew what the President was thinking, beyond a statement issued by Tumulty on Saturday night that Wilson was "considering very earnestly, but calmly, the right course of action." What the public and press saw that weekend was a man conducting his routine business much like any other day: golf, motoring, a flag-raising at a country club, and Sunday services at Central Presbyterian Church, where he sported a white carnation for Mother's Day, a new holiday created just seven years earlier. His unsettled situation with Edith Galt was not far from his thoughts, and he managed to see her on Saturday and exchange several more notes. She still had yet to fully reciprocate his love, but he promised to remain patient, even in the depths of his profound longing for her. "My love for you passes present expression," he wrote. "I need you."

Those words were penned Sunday night as a respite from two tasks of immense importance: putting the finishing touches on a scheduled speech he would give the next day in Philadelphia (where the pesky suffragettes of a few days earlier had hoped he would meet with their group) and crafting a note to Germany. The American people, he knew, would be scrutinizing every word he spoke tomorrow for clues to the administration's planned response to the *Lusitania*. The seemingly never-ending updates, mostly bleak, had only increased their anxiety. They learned of the deaths of the theater impresario Charles Frohman, the playwright Justus Miles Forman (whose *The Hyphen* about German Americans had just flopped on Broadway), and eight members of the Crompton family of Philadelphia, including an infant.

They also heard inspiring tales of survivors, such as the elderly man of seventy-five and the boy of seventeen who somehow clung to a plank together until rescue, and the newlywed who was sucked down by one of the ship's funnels only to be miraculously propelled to the surface by a subsequent explosion. Both she and her husband survived.

Monday finally arrived. Millions returned to work and school, Roosevelt to the courtroom. A threatened bombing of the German embassy failed to materialize, although a fresh rumor of Wilson's assassination soon surfaced, sending stock market prices tumbling until discredited later that afternoon.

By that time, the President was safely aboard a train headed for Philadelphia. He had lunched with Edith, who offered further words of encouragement. She would not reject his "wonderful love," she told him, if it could
"quicken that which has laid dead so long with me."

After arriving at Broad Street Station a little after 7:00 p.m., a relieved
Wilson and his entourage made their way up Broad Street to Convention
Hall, a temporary facility constructed to accommodate a German Ameri-
can choral festival two years earlier.

The atmosphere was predictably patriotic. Thirty thousand onlookers,
among them four thousand new American citizens, packed the building,
each clutching a small American flag. Strains of "America the Beautiful"
and "America (My Country 'Tis of Thee)" filled the air. On stage, the
message "Welcome—To a Government of the People, by the People, and
for the People" magnificently glowed in electric lights; it was soon to be
overshadowed by a group of one thousand bunting-clutching schoolchildren
who suddenly stood to create a massive American flag.

Wilson did not speak until 9:20. Before he took the stage, his picture
was dramatically projected on a screen, following a "series of pictures"
depicting the lives of Washington and Lincoln. Rudolph Blankenburg, the
city's German-born mayor, his accent still unmistakable, introduced the
featured guest. "I present to you—God bless him—the President."

After the thunderous applause subsided, Wilson began to speak. His
words, as usual, were eloquent and heartfelt, but they could have been
written months ago, when he first accepted this engagement. The new
citizens should not forget their native nations, the President began, but they
must become "thorough Americans. . . . America does not consist of groups.
A man who thinks of himself as belonging to a particular national group
in America has not yet become an American." (Such a statement would
have pleased the "hyphen"-obsessed TR.) Still, the hopes of newly arrived
immigrants revitalized America every day. And multicultural America possessed a unique "consciousness," one that "touches elbows and touches
hearts with all the nations of mankind." As such, "the example of America
must be a special example," one of peace, "the healing and elevating influence of the world." What followed were two sentences that no one in
America would soon forget: "There is such a thing as a man being *too proud*

to fight. There is such a thing as a nation being so right that it does not need to convince others by force that it is right." Five minutes later, the speech was over, amid much cheering and flag-waving.

Wilson had said nothing but he had said everything. America would not go to war over the *Lusitania*; in fact, he was merely reiterating his favorite theme of self-mastery in a different form. But the phrase "too proud to fight" was a peculiar, ill-advised comment providing more ammunition for those who already thought the President a wimpy academic. He himself recognized he had made a mistake ("I did not know before I got up very clearly what I was going to say," he admitted), even though he denied that the words had anything to do with the *Lusitania*. "I do not know just what I said at Philadelphia (as I rode along the street in the dusk I found myself a little confused as to whether I was in Philadelphia or New York!)," he wrote Edith the next day.

For TR's supporters, Wilson had sunk to a new low ("mawkish" and "made me gag" were among the choicer barbs). Roosevelt did not disagree. The President's words, he explained to reporters in Syracuse, put the United States on the level of feeble China, especially since the "policy of milk and water" favored by the administration had utterly failed. Something concrete needed to be done, such as an immediate halt to all trade with Germany to show them we meant business without resorting to more extreme measures.

"I do not believe that the firm assertion of our rights means war, but we would do well to remember that *there are things worse than war*," Roosevelt insisted. Such tough talk, prominently featured on many a front page, won some support, even from TR's enemies. "I dislike Roosevelt intensely," one told TR's friend Joseph Bucklin Bishop. "I wish to God he was President now!"

Unfortunately for Roosevelt, it was not a commonly held opinion. Most of the country did not see things his way, although he believed time would prove him right. "Truly Providence has been kind to the United States," one Brooklynite observed. "For the civil war we had Lincoln; for the present crisis we haven't got Roosevelt."

What especially frustrated TR was the praise heaped upon Wilson at the further expense of his own waning popularity. Unfairly or not, he found himself perceived by many as a "truculent and bloodthirsty person, endeavoring futilely to thwart able, dignified, humane Mr. Wilson in his noble plan to bring peace everywhere by excellently written letters sent to persons who care nothing whatever for any letter that is not backed up by force." Roosevelt could only hope that the public would finally come to its senses about the President. "If he does not stand up for our rights, and if he goes off into long futile negotiations, I think our people will condemn him," TR warned.

The speech won Wilson few friends in England. "TOO PROUD TO FIGHT" was plastered on newspaper sandwich boards all over London, the words soon finding their way into a music hall skit featuring two quarreling comedians on the verge of fisticuffs. Before a punch could be thrown, one walked off the stage with the words "I'm too proud to fight." The audience roared.

"What in the name of common sense does such an absurd statement mean?" a disheartened James Norman Hall asked. "I like to think that the president who has been so decidedly practical thus far, will not become a futile idealist." For Walter Hines Page, who already believed the President exhibited certain unattractive Jeffersonian qualities, it was already too late. Even House began to wonder about Wilson's thought processes.

Addams had no such doubts. Still, she could not have chosen a worse time to arrive in London bearing peace proposals. The Liberal government was in crisis mode that week, thanks to revelations of a shell shortage and the Gallipoli fiasco; in fact, a new coalition government of Liberal, Conservative, and Labour would emerge by the end of the month. Meanwhile, the *Lusitania* sinking unleashed an orgy of violence in the East End against Germans and their shops. "I saw men skipping rope in the street with strings of German sausage," Mary Chamberlain, one of the American delegates at the women's congress in The Hague, remarked.

The hostile atmosphere in London did not deter Addams, who set up headquarters at the St. Ermins Hotel, met with the press, and fielded requests to meet English friends and acquaintances. In the meantime, she worked on arranging meetings with Whitehall officials—ideally Prime Minister Asquith and House's partner in crime Sir Edward Grey (why they did not attempt to see House is unclear, unless they were unaware of his presence in London).

Whether it was her worldwide celebrity or the assistance of Ambassador Page (despite his own disdain for peace talk), Addams had no difficulty getting in to see Grey on Thursday, May 13, accompanied by her fellow peace envoys Aletta Jacobs and the Italian fashion designer Rosa Genoni. Grey, while always eager to cultivate American support, might have been tiring of well-intentioned Yankees butting into English affairs by this point. He was also likely distracted by his rapidly deteriorating eyesight. Nevertheless, he listened attentively to their presentation and appeared intrigued about the neutrals stepping in to facilitate peace negotiations since neither side could do so without appearing weak. When told the neutrals were apparently waiting for the "right moment," Grey then asked a question that might well have been presented to Wilson: "When do they think the right moment is going to come?"

That night, Addams spoke at Kingsway Hall before an audience of about fifteen hundred. The predominantly female crowd was mostly friendly, with the exception of one of Emmeline Pankhurst's henchwomen, apparently sent to disrupt the meeting. "What of Belgium?" she shouted at the speakers. "Shame, shame." The heckler continued to grumble, albeit more quietly, when Addams began her address by discussing the highlights of the recent congress and the prevailing spirit of internationalism. "I have had a long training in internationalism," Addams explained. "I have lived for many years in an emigrant quarter of Chicago into which there pours constantly people from all the nations of Europe, and they begin, of course, by not understanding each other in the least. But there is something in human nature that overcomes these differences, and in the end there comes to be a . . . curious understanding . . . of the important things, and a forgetting and a passing by of the unimportant things."

The following day, Addams saw Asquith alone. If anything, the sixty-three-year-old prime minister was even more distracted than Grey. Just two days earlier, his twenty-eight-year-old lover, Venetia Stanley, had informed him that their affair was over (his obsessive letter writing to Stanley, even during cabinet meetings, made Wilson's love correspondence seem positively restrained in comparison). Asquith, who apparently viewed most women as playthings, had actually had little regard for the congress, but did not openly discourage Addams's efforts. She left the interview and her whirlwind week in London in a more positive frame of mind than before. As she wrote Mary a few days later, the meetings had been "most favorable" and "some of the wisest men we met were in favor of the pilgrimage. I am going ahead with a better heart."

G ermany was Addams's next planned destination after a quick stop in Amsterdam. Whether she made it there depended very much on Wilson, who continued to work on the American response to the *Lusitania*. The issues to consider were formidable. How far should he go in demanding satisfaction? Would an apology and an indemnity from the German government be sufficient? Should Germany be pressured to guarantee the safety of American passengers in the future? Should he also protest the Allies' violations of international law? And just how strongly should the note be worded? Push too softly and another liner might be sunk with more American deaths. Push too hard and he might have a diplomatic break and eventually war on his hands.

House believed Wilson had to act decisively. "I cannot see any way out unless Germany promises to cease her policy of making war upon noncombatants," he wrote the President. "The question must be determined either now or later and it seems to me that you would lose prestige by deferring it."

But Bryan still desperately hoped for a peaceful solution. Informed by the Brazilian ambassador that neutrality no longer existed and the "world was against Germany," he remained defiant. "I am and will continue to be neutral," he responded. During the first gathering of the cabinet following the sinking, the secretary of state became increasingly irritated during discussion of the note. "You people are not neutral," he complained. "You are taking sides!"

Wilson immediately put him in his place. "Mr. Bryan, you are not warranted in making such an assertion. We all doubtless have our opinions in this matter, but there are none of us who can justly be accused of being unfair."

Bryan, certain the note's message and tone were moving in too harsh a direction, was now a man possessed, determined to head off the nation from plunging into the abyss of war. He peppered the President with several letters after the cabinet meeting, insisting that by ignoring the sins of the Allies, the note would "relinquish the hope of playing the part of a friend to both sides" and would play to the "jingo element."

The argument did not move Wilson, but he was intrigued by Bryan's suggestion to dangle the prospect of deferred settlement through future arbitration without resorting to war. This might be best achieved indirectly, the President believed, through a "tip" issued through the press. Bryan then made the mistake of telling Lansing, who feigned acceptance but promptly reported the plan to less sympathetic ears. Eventually, Tumulty convinced Wilson that any such statement would be ill advised. The disappointed Bryan began to wonder whether the President was as pacifistically inclined as he once believed.

On Thursday, May 13, six days after the *Lusitania* sinking, the note that left Bryan so uneasy was cabled to Germany. The German government's actions in the *Falaba*, the *Gulflight*, the *Cushing*, and finally the *Lusitania* had crossed an unthinkable line, "absolutely contrary to the rules, the practices, and the spirit of modern warfare," the cable read. It would do well to remember that the "lives of non-combatants . . . cannot lawfully or rightfully be put in jeopardy by the capture or destruction of an unarmed merchantmen" and must follow the "usual precaution of visit and search" to determine its flag and contraband status of its cargo. Since U-boats were incapable of following such rules and normally had little choice but to sink the merchant ship and force the "crew and all on board . . . to the mercy of the sea in her small boats," the submarine "cannot be used against merchantmen . . . without an inevitable violation of many sacred principles of justice and humanity." And every American had "indisputable rights" of travel "wherever their legitimate business calls them upon the high seas" without fear of acts "done in clear violation of universally acknowledged international obligations." Finally, the note concluded with three weighty demands: Germany should "disavow the acts," "make reparation," and "take immediate steps to prevent the recurrence."

The contents of the note reached most Americans in the Friday morning newspapers. Nationwide, the reaction was overwhelmingly positive. Even the increasingly critical Allies appeared to be satisfied. "I have an idea that Wilson is going to do big things for international peace," the Harvard professor turned French soldier Robert Pellissier wrote an American friend. "He may be big enough a man to give international diplomacy a brand-new character which will be a reflection of his own integrity and courage."

Somehow, Wilson had deftly managed to stand up for American rights without further escalating the situation. Nor had he issued any kind of ultimatum, which pleased Ambassador Bernstorff, who "went to dinner . . . with a sigh of relief." Of course, everything now depended on how far Berlin would go to pacify America and keep her from joining the Allies. When stripped to its essentials, the note insisted that Germany restrict its submarine use or face the severing of diplomatic ties and potentially war. In the midst of a no-holds-barred struggle, could the Imperial Navy allow a neutral government to take her best weapon out of her hands without severe political repercussions? If Germany refused, what then for the nation "too proud to fight"? Anti-German feeling was mounting by the day, especially after the Bryce Commission report, released by the British government that week, provided additional support for atrocities committed during the Belgian invasion the previous year. "When Miss Addams has read the Bryce report," *Life* quipped, "one may surely expect to hear of her cooperation in getting up an international rope and lamp-post party to swing off the whole house of Hohenzollern [the German royal family]."

For now, the pressure was off, and Wilson could bask in the praise while the administration waited for a positive response. Others were not as optimistic. "It is of course, natural that Wilson should receive applause for the note," John Callan O'Laughlin advised TR, "but I am satisfied that he will not get any satisfactory results and the negotiations will drag on."

Wilson had just experienced the most intense seven days of his pres-idency, if not his whole life. But only a handful of individuals knew that he was also simultaneously wrestling with an affair of the heart, one that he hoped to sort out during a trip to New York to review the Atlantic fleet. He would be traveling on the *Mayflower*, the Presidential yacht, and Edith, along with several others, would be on board.

She had never been far from his mind all week. In the midst of the crisis, he still found time to craft gobs of overheated prose to Edith. "I dream that some day you will take down the rusty keys and come out to me," he wrote her on May 11, "as sweetly and naturally as a child, with utter faith in your shining eyes and no quiver of doubt or dismay—coming of course, because I am waiting and am already your own." His persistence had begun to pay off. She finally admitted that she loved him, sending Wilson into raptures of ecstasy in his Friday morning epistle. "I love you, I love you, I love you! Smuggle me a line saying you love me."

It was a happy few days for Wilson. The crowds in New York treated him as a conquering hero, with the exception of two annoying Congres-sional Union suffragists, who demanded to see him and then scorned him as the "best little evader we know." He was rarely alone with Edith, but they often exchanged meaningful glances. "I think the proudest minute of my life," Edith wrote, "was when you turned your wonderful eyes to me—in the midst of all the people and their praise of you." And she was beginning to enjoy the perks her new status afforded her, including a dinner on the secretary of the navy's yacht, attended by several cabinet wives and Eleanor Roosevelt. "I feel like I was living in a story," Edith wrote her sister-in-law. Still, she continued to maintain a somewhat mad-dening distance without the "complete acceptance" Wilson craved. "You have not yet completely surrendered to me as I have to you, but have let little queries have harbour in your heart," he observed. "If I only could take you in my arms and interpret by my kisses my love for you in all that I long to prove it to be!"

As much as the President might have wished to do so, he could not dwell long on his thrilling yet unsettled personal life. The *Lusitania* crisis, he knew, had only just begun.

While Wilson was enjoying a much needed respite in New York, German officials were digesting the note. Foreign Minister Gottlieb von Jagow was scornful. "Right of free travel on the seas, why not right of free travel on land in war territory," he asked Ambassador Gerard. Admiral Georg Alexander von Müller, whose colleagues Alfred von Tirpitz and Gustav Bachmann already advocated a hard line toward America, viewed the note as "almost insulting." Meanwhile, Kaiser Wilhelm and Chancellor Bethmann were slow to grasp the crucial nature of Germany's current predicament, although both favored some sort of pullback in the U-boat war. The note must be answered, of course, but there seemed no pressing need to be especially conciliatory, especially when reports from the usually reliable Bernstorff in Washington seemed to suggest Bryan's peaceful views would be especially influential. Bernstorff did acknowledge that another such sinking might mean war, but he also cited the highly emotional nature of Americans that might easily dissipate: "They are easily carried away by their feelings and then become uncertain."

Discussions about the response were under way when Addams and the resolutions-bearing delegation arrived in Germany for their second stop at a belligerent capital, once again at a less-than-opportune moment. The German press had published Wilson's note, which she thought a bit confrontational, "not like him at all." She could not help worrying that war was inevitable. "It seems as though the whole world has gone crazy. There must be some little spot left where reason will rule."

Whether it would be in Germany remained to be seen. The entire nation was on a war footing. A horrified Addams watched five hundred German youths, all under nineteen, bouquets tied to their bayonets, "march gayly toward the slaughter." Able-bodied men were few and far between, their places on farms, on streetcars, and in offices taken by women, older men, and even children. In Berlin, casualty lists, bread cards, mourning widows, and war relief appeals were inescapable. Still, the city's prewar efficiency remained untouched, as Madeleine Doty noticed when she made her own trip to Berlin days after the The Hague conference concluded. "Even in the midst of war Germany is superbly run," Doty marveled. "The lawns are weedless, the flower-beds wonderful. The streets are clean."

But the German people, it became clear to Doty and other Americans, knew very little about the war other than what the government allowed to be published. The Fatherland, they insisted, had been forced into a war of self-defense against foreign invaders. And atrocity stories were ridiculous lies ("If you knew our good German soldiers," said one, "you'd see how impossible all that is"). The Germans also could not understand the American reaction to the *Lusitania*. After all, "she was carrying ammunition . . . the passengers had been warned, and had no more reason to complain than if they had deliberately entered a city that was being besieged."

As she had in London, Addams had to work in Berlin with an American ambassador frankly hostile to her mission. While Page had kept his thoughts to himself, Gerard made no attempt to hide his disdain. He and his wife, whose bags were already packed, were convinced America was about to go to war any minute and that any talk of peace in Germany was dangerous if not impossible. Gerard's dismissive attitude was all too common among the diplomats encountered by the Addams delegation and a second group of women sent by the congress to visit the northern European capitals. Steeped in tradition, not only did these men reject "all that does not answer to preconceived notions," but they believed that the foreign offices and ambassadors possessed "mysterious, almost superhuman knowledge" impossible for a layman or simple woman to grasp.

His rejection of personal diplomacy notwithstanding, Gerard managed to arrange meetings with the chancellor Bethmann and the foreign minister von Jagow ("to which they looked forward with unconcealed perturbation," he later claimed). That two of the most important figures in the government (the kaiser was in Galicia) agreed to see a woman in the midst of a major international crisis suggested the power of Addams's name and the understanding that a refusal would not look good in America.

Just as in London, Addams and her group did their best to see and talk to as many people as they could. Like House, they encountered many a local eager to argue with them about America's arms exports to the Allies.

Their explanation—that Germany had done the same in past wars and a change now would be anything but "neutral"—made little impression. Only the journalist Maximilian Harden, a onetime critic of the monarchy whose infamous writings about a supposed homosexual relationship between one of the kaiser's friends and a military official had rocked Imperial Germany, seemed to comprehend America's position. Since the Germans had no munitions shortages thanks to what Harden called their "enormous factories," the British could match them only by acquiring "the supplies she could not manufacture" from the United States. But he showed no such understanding of Belgium's position. Belgium, he informed them, was "like a little brother whom big brother has had to pull away roughly from bad playmates. Now little brother is in big brother's arms and he is pouting and his eyes are full of tears, but soon big brother will wipe away his tears and make him smile again."

Von Jagow met with Addams and Jacobs on May 21. As the English journalist Frederic Wile noted a year earlier, Jagow was a less than imposing individual with a "habit of glancing about him furtively, as if not quite sure of his ground." Peace, he told them, was desirable. He agreed with Grey that the neutrals would have to be the prime mover in any effort, but he questioned whether America was herself especially neutral. Would Miss Addams, he asked, be willing to go to Belgium to see for herself that the people were not being mistreated by the Germans? She was too shrewd to fall into his trap. It was not unlike a strike, she explained, when she would be invited by an employer to investigate a workplace and would "see only what the employer wished me to, and I should be forced to say that I had seen nothing to criticize, which would of course be interpreted as a complete defense for the employer."

The following day, she journeyed alone to the Chancellery for a noon visit with Bethmann Hollweg. Just twenty-nine days older than Wilson, he had been in power since 1909, often struggling to pacify the kaiser, the militarists, and other influential factions within Germany, though his subdued nature and personality were not always up to the task. "Of him it can well be said, as Mr. Roosevelt remarked of Mr. Taft during the late unpleasantness in the United States," Wile had written, "he is a man who means well feebly." At the moment, he was coping with the recent death of his son in combat, the American situation, and the disturbing possibility of Italy, a former German ally, joining the opposing side in the next few days.

The chancellor was more candid than he had been in his talk with House eight weeks earlier. The English, he told Addams, had no grasp of the German government and their desire to "crush German militarism" was the same as a desire to crush Germany. "He went on to talk in that half mystical way they do—so difficult for us to understand," Addams later recorded. "It is as if their feeling for the army was that of a church for its procession. It is part of it." Like Jagow, he claimed to have no objections to neutral efforts toward peace and also pushed her to see Belgium for herself, which she again declined.

In the span of just eight days, Addams had discussed peace with the civilian leaders of both sides in the middle of a major global war, an unprecedented feat for women and the pacifist movement. But whether her words or the proposals from the women's congress would have an effect remained uncertain. As she prepared for her next stop, Vienna, the German government was still considering its response to Wilson's note, a decision that might change the course of the war.

While Addams was in Germany, the Barnes trial was entering its final phases in upstate New York. Barnes finally had his chance to testify, but the tense international situation often relegated the coverage to the inner newspaper pages. TR had grown increasingly unhappy with the "very legalistic mind" of Judge Andrews, who had ruled out a good deal of the damning evidence Roosevelt's team had gathered about Barnes's shady public printing contracts. "I am simply unable to understand how he could have made so wicked a ruling," TR wrote to his daughter Ethel. "I believe this practically ends the case, so far as any hope of my winning is concerned."

Both sides landed their final blows during the closing arguments. This suit, TR's lawyer John Bowers insisted, was "the act of the machine to destroy Mr. Roosevelt's usefulness to the nation—Mr. Roosevelt, once a president, once a Governor, the people's true representative." Barnes's lawyer Ivins, meanwhile, did his best to remove the stars from the jury's eyes. "This man," he said contemptuously, "who attacks every man that does not

Roosevelt in Syracuse, flanked by his secretary John McGrath (left) and attorney William Van Benschoten, during the Barnes libel trial.
(Onondaga Historical Association, Syracuse, New York)

agree with him, got himself into the position in which we now find him by not abiding by the spirit of the letter he wrote when he retired from the Presidency, saying he would never try to attain that office again."

After sitting through almost four weeks of testimony, the weary jury began its deliberations on Thursday, May 20, at 3:45 p.m. TR returned to his friend Horace Wilkinson's home and waited by the telephone. There was no call that night. But at ten the next morning, signs seemed to suggest that a verdict of some kind might be forthcoming. The jury requested a private talk with Judge Andrews, who informed them that he could answer questions only in open court. They then continued their deliberations before emerging again an hour later, this time with a verdict.

No one knew whether the jury's apparent last-minute indecision might benefit TR or Barnes. Barnes and Ivins had already left Syracuse, but TR was present, "pale as a ghost, with set jaw and clinched fists." His very political future hung in the balance. Had his anti-German comments and political views cost him the trial?

The foreman, a grocer named Warren Somers, then spoke. "We find for the defendant, with the suggestion that the court expenses be divided equally." A relieved TR beamed. "I'd like to give you a big hug," gushed a "fashionably gowned and very handsome woman." "Madame, I wish that you could," he responded. "I sincerely wish that you could."

But the trial was far from over. Court expenses, Judge Andrews informed them, could not be attached to the verdict. The jury was polled, the first ten all finding for the defendant. Juror number 11, a red-faced, blue-eyed motorman named Edward Burns who had fallen asleep twice during the trial, then gave his answer: "For the Plaintiff." Some thought that Burns meant to say "defendant," but it soon became clear that he had only gone along with the original verdict provided court costs were shared. A hung jury situation now loomed, still a victory for TR, but not the complete exoneration he needed.

The twelve were sent back to the jury room, where deliberations continued until eleven that night and then resumed in the early hours of Saturday morning. At 6:00 a.m., Burns finally cracked, the not guilty verdict formally announced in court a few hours later. After shaking the hands of the jurors, including Burns, and presenting them with autographed photos of himself, TR prepared to return home to Oyster Bay. "I am happy, yes, intensely happy," he told an admirer at the Syracuse train station.

Roosevelt had won a remarkable victory. "We were all thrilled at Hyde Park," FDR wrote "Uncle Ted" the next day. "To get a unanimous verdict was to accomplish almost the impossible." And TR's political position was now stronger than it had been in a year, if not longer. But the trial, at least for the past two weeks, had grown to be a bothersome distraction to him. "My interest," he told a friend, "was so much greater in the things that were going on abroad," and the chance that America might go to war.

War, as much as most Americans did not want it, remained a possibility. Twenty-one-year-old Archie Roosevelt, bored with Harvard and eager for glory, implored his father in the last days of the trial to "telegraph me immediately what to do if war is declared." TR promised to do so, but was doubtful that Wilson and Bryan would fight "unless they are kicked into it. . . . Nevertheless, there is a chance that Germany may behave in such fashion that they will have to go to war."

Bryan had never stopped fearing this possibility. Other options needed to be explored, perhaps preventing munitions from being carried on any ship leaving an American port with American passengers. And it was time for the President to address the continued trade violations of the Allies in a message as firm as his recent note to Germany. But again Bryan found Wilson unwilling to see things his way. Certainly, it made little sense to do anything of the kind while the German situation was in limbo. Still, the President saw some validity in Bryan's argument. "It becomes more and more evident," he cabled House in London, "that it will presently become necessary for the sake of diplomatic consistency and to satisfy our public to address a note to Great Britain about the unnecessary and unwarranted interruption of our legitimate trade with neutral ports." If the British voluntarily relented, then Germany would not only look bad, but lose any justification for continuing the U-boat campaign. As usual, Wilson's appointed representative in London was largely left out of the discussions. "I fear," House wrote in his diary, "Page does not like the constant communications the President is sending me and in which he has no part."

Page believed the British would never go for it anyway, but House broached with Grey the same idea proposed back in February: allow food to get to Germany in exchange for restrictions on submarine warfare. The British foreign secretary thought the proposal might have merit, provided that the Germans also halted their use of poisonous gases as part of the deal. But House soon discovered the scheme had no chance of being accepted by the rest of the British cabinet. Nor did the Germans show much interest. Why consent to an agreement robbing them of two of their deadliest weapons in exchange for food when the nation, contrary to popular belief, was far from starving? They wanted more concessions, concessions that the Allies of course would not grant. Wilson was not surprised. "We are dealing with passion on the other side of the water, not with reason," he wrote Mary Hulbert.

The question remained of how best to deal with that passion. A strong note had been sent to Germany, but would it be enough? While Wilson waited, another incident revealed the continued vulnerability of American lives on the high seas. A German U-boat torpedoed the *Nebraskan*, an American steamer heading to Delaware from Liverpool, fortunately with no fatalities. That Germany had attacked a neutral American ship just days after the *Lusitania* (by accident, it would later be revealed) was yet another slap in the face of the United States. "Clearly no self-respecting power," editorialized the *London Daily News*, "can suffer this sort of thing to go on indefinitely." But Wilson also recognized that "no self-respecting power" could tolerate the blatant and continued interference with American trade to neutral ports. "England is playing a rather high game, violating international law every day," remarked Franklin Lane, his interior secretary.

House believed, though not as strongly as Page, that Britain's sins would have to be overlooked to a certain degree. "We are bound up more or less in their success," the Colonel wrote Wilson on the same day the *Nebraskan* was torpedoed, "and I do not think we should do anything that can possibly be avoided to alienate the good feeling that they now have for us. If we lost their good will we will not be able to figure at all in peace negotiations, and we will be sacrificing too much in order to maintain all our commercial rights." In any event, House sensed it would not be necessary. "I have concluded," he wrote in his diary on May 30, "that war with Germany is inevitable."

By then, House had seen the long awaited German reply to Wilson. It was not the conciliatory message that the administration and most of the American people were hoping for. The promise to make good on the *Cushing* and *Gulflight* incidents if warranted appeared acceptable enough, although the continued insistence that the *Falaba* had been given twenty-three minutes before sinking, rather than ten, was troubling. The tone became even more defiant, if not truculent, in the explanation of the far more important *Lusitania* episode. First, the German government "has already expressed . . . its keen regret" that neutral citizens had been killed. Next, the two governments seemed to differ in "certain important facts"—namely, that the *Lusitania* was not merely an "ordinary unarmed merchantmen" but was actually an "auxiliary cruiser" with cannon "concealed below decks"— which wasn't true. And since British merchant ships, the note argued, were known to use neutral flags and ordered to ram submarines, they could not be classified as "undefended." Finally, the Canadian soldiers on board (none in reality) provided additional justification, as did the cargo of munitions. "The quick sinking . . . is primarily attributable to the explosion of the ammunition shipment caused by the torpedo," the note insisted, though with virtually no proof. "The . . . passengers would otherwise in all human probability, have been saved." In other words, none of this was Germany's fault, and she had no intention of modifying her submarine warfare or guaranteeing the safety of American passengers as Wilson demanded.

Few Americans were satisfied with the response. "The real test of the statesmanship and the backbone also, let it be said, of President Wilson is about to be made," *The Philadelphia Inquirer* warned. "To put it plainly, Germany is trifling with the United States." The situation seemed to be back to square one, just as it was three weeks earlier, when the *Lusitania* went down.

Bryan was now becoming desperate, almost on the verge of a breakdown. He was losing weight and had recently been diagnosed with diabetes. At cabinet meetings, in letters, and in conversations over the next several days, he tried to prod Wilson toward solutions that would not lead to war. There was no need to reply immediately, Bryan vainly insisted, and the response should "take up the different points" and "treat them as we would if it were a case in court." He again questioned why the government could not "prevent our citizens incurring unnecessary risks." Was it not like a riot when "the authorities . . . order all citizens to remain at home in order to avoid the dangers"? And for the umpteenth time, he raised the issue of a "renewed protest to Great Britain" about trade abuses.

When it became clear that Wilson was not about to follow any of his suggestions, Bryan did a great deal of soul-searching. As a deeply devout man of faith (he had recently filled in for the evangelist and ex–major leaguer Billy Sunday at a revival, much to the chagrin of TR), Bryan genuinely hoped for a peaceful solution, even if his views occasionally leaned toward the extreme. "He is too good a Christian to run a naughty world and he doesn't hate hard enough but he certainly is a noble and high-minded man, and loyal to the President to the last hair," Franklin Lane had observed a few weeks earlier. But he had come to a fork in the road: Either continue futilely in an administration that did not share his views on the European war or resign. His millions of supporters, many of them rural "plain people" from the South and West, urged him to never surrender his principles. That he had grown tired of playing second fiddle to Colonel House also gave him pause. House, he later complained to Wilson, "has been Secretary of State, not I, and I have never had your full confidence."

Bryan decided he would have to go. He went to Treasury Secretary William McAdoo, who had recently become the proud father of Wilson's second grandchild, named after Ellen, and let him know his plans. McAdoo tried to get him to reconsider, as did Navy Secretary Josephus Daniels, who told Bryan "he was making the biggest mistake of his life." His wife, Mary, was also against it, but Bryan could not be moved. "I think I can do more to keep the country out of war out of the Cabinet than in," he insisted. "The President is wrong and history will not sustain him."

Ironically, the response to the German note that Wilson worked on in the early days of June was not especially belligerent. It rejected most of their claims concerning the *Lusitania*, suggesting that the ship's munitions cargo and possible role in the explosion were irrelevant to the underlying issue involved: the "principle of humanity." Wilson's note then reiterated the insistence on the "safeguarding of American lives and American ships, and asks for assurances that this will be done," but without mention of discontinuing submarine warfare altogether. Wilson had gone as far as he could, at least in his mind. Sources on Capitol Hill informed him that a declaration of war remained a tough sell to Congress. His goal was to continue to thread a very difficult needle: "carry out the double wish of our people, to maintain a firm front in respect of what we demand of Germany and yet do nothing that might by any possibility involve us in the war."

Roosevelt, of course, saw this as weakness, nothing more than a "policy . . . of words . . . which he tries to make strong enough to satisfy our people that something is being done and at the same to enable him to dodge out of doing anything to Germany."

Wilson was ambivalent about Bryan's plan to resign. On the one hand, as he explained to Edith "there is now a chance to do a great deal of constructive work in the State Department for which Mr. Bryan had no gift or aptitude." On the other, the President wondered how Bryan's departure would look to the belligerent powers. He also could not help feeling deeply wounded that someone "who has been your comrade and confidant, has turned away from you and set his hand against you," although he had "not for a moment lost hold of myself." And there was always the concern that Bryan might "do a lot of mischief," especially behind the scenes in Congress.

Edith did her best to reassure him. Ridding himself of such an "awful creature" would lighten his considerable load. Much of the press and public appeared to agree with her when the announcement was made on the evening of June 8. Even Roosevelt was pleased. By rejecting Bryan, perhaps the President "really had decided to be a man."

But when the second American note was published on June 11, TR was mystified. The note, at least to him, was "utterly worthless," filled with typical Wilson boilerplate language, certainly nothing to warrant Bryan's exit. If anything, it pleased much of the peace crowd, especially Addams, who noted that "part of his second note is quite pacific." Ambassador Bernstorff was also relieved. "I think the crisis is over now." For Bryan, it was likely less about the contents of the second note and more about Wilson's polite but firm refusal to pursue any of his suggestions, which he believed could prevent war. "No stranger man ever lived," Wilson marveled to Edith. "He suffers from a singular sort of moral blindness and is as passionate in error as in the right courses he has taken."

Had Bryan known what was then happening in Berlin, he might have reconsidered. The Germans had absolutely no desire to go to war with America at the moment. Bernstorff, who made a special visit to Wilson "to ask how he could assist to bring his crass government to its senses," had already made that clear. The situation had grown considerably more complicated. Italy was now in the war against Austria-Hungary, and the Fatherland wanted no part of another neutral turning against it (there was already fear that Holland might be next). Even before Wilson's second note reached the German government, the chancellor had been waging his own personal fight on the U-boat issue, against the wishes of most of the Imperial Navy leadership. Eventually, the kaiser agreed with Bethmann. According to a later conversation with Ambassador Gerard, Wilhelm "did not approve the sinking of the *Lusitania*, or killing women and children." He ordered that large passenger liners like the *Lusitania* would no longer be attacked without warning. The decision was kept secret, even from Bernstorff. Nor would it be mentioned when the Germans got around to answering Wilson's second note, which would not be for another several weeks.

Wilson's course seemed to be working. War had been avoided, and America's fitness to mediate in the future remained unblemished, at least in his view. But TR believed the President had botched things again by not looking ahead. Roosevelt was certain not only that the defeat of Germany would benefit America immensely from a global power perspective (a victorious Germany would likely attempt to extend its reach into Panama, Cuba, and the Caribbean), but that the United States would likely have to join the Allies at some point anyway. Wilson had blown his chance to go to war with most of America strongly on his side. "When the time comes and he . . . is forced into war," TR insisted, "he may find behind him an unprepared, divided, irresolute nation."

House also saw the possible advantages of American involvement. The war would end more quickly and America would be "in a strong position to aid the other great democracies in turning the world in to the right paths."

To Wilson, the war's horrifying brutality and death toll more than justified his stance. The Allies had made little progress on the Western Front; the ultimate winner, according to French general Philippe Pétain, would be "the side which possesses the last man." It was not surprising that James Norman Hall's regiment was finally to be thrown into the breach. Before departing in late May, he sent a sealed letter to his friend Roy Cushman to be opened in case of his death. To his family, he spun things more positively. "Most of the men who go to war come through little or any the worse for it; and I have just as much chance of being fortunate as any of them." After a haircut and reading a form letter from Kitchener warning the soldiers to behave themselves and "avoid any intimacy" with women, Hall boarded a troop ship bound for the Continent. "The great adventure," he wrote, "has begun."

After arriving in France, Hall was led in the darkness to his section of the trenches on the Western Front, about 340 yards from the German lines. The British regulars did their best to acclimate Hall and the other volunteers to the realities of trench life, the filth, the vermin, the lack of sleep, and the ever present danger. No major activity was under way at the moment, but shelling and sniper fire were constant. Soon he learned of two men near him picked off by German snipers, who proved to be far more accurate than English newspapers claimed. Hall, who had once claimed he was "happy" to be finally deployed, appeared less certain after his first rotation in the trenches. He had begun to understand, he wrote Cushman, "the tremendous sadness, the awful futility of war."

The dreadful impact of the war had become more noticeable as Addams continued her meetings with the heads of state. She discovered that Vienna, one of the two capitals of the dual monarchy of Austria-Hungary, had been far more adversely affected than Berlin. Signs of starvation were inescapable, "horses . . . so thin that one could count their ribs" and "pale, emaciated faces . . . hoping for a crust to be slipped to them." An Austrian acquaintance had Addams over for dinner, which proved to be a misnomer. "There was almost no food," she told her niece later. "They rose from the table nearly as hungry as when they had sat down."

Accompanied by Aletta Jacobs, Addams presented the resolutions to Stephan Burián, the Austrian foreign minister, who saw at least some of their merits, especially the possibility of a conference of neutrals, although not with America in the driver's seat. "What does the United States know about Europe?" he asked. The reactionary prime minister Count Karl Stürgkh, the victim of an assassin's bullet seventeen months later, listened to the two women's talk without comment, forcing Addams to attempt to break the silence. "It perhaps seems to you very foolish that women should go about this way," she sheepishly began, "but after all, the world itself is so strange in this war situation that our mission may be no more strange nor foolish than the rest."

Stürgkh suddenly came to life. "Foolish! No! This call is a relief. I am tired of seeing men who ask for nothing but more munitions and more soldiers," he shouted animatedly. "At last the door opens and two people walk in and say, 'Mr. Minister, why not substitute negotiations for fighting?' They are the sensible ones."

Neither Burián nor Stürgkh commanded as much influence as the Hungarian prime minister István Tisza, whom Addams would see alone in Budapest. Tisza, who resembled a "tall, broad-shouldered" Ulysses Grant and would be yet another victim of an assassin's bullet by the end of the war, spoke to her frankly. Hungary, he told her, was "getting nothing out of the situation." And unlike Germany and Austria, she had no hatred of Russia, whose peasant soldiers preferred tilling the land to fighting. The dual monarchy, he promised her, "would not be unreasonable about terms." Whether Tisza was truthful remained uncertain, but Addams had no difficulty openly discussing the women's congress before sympathetic audiences. At times, it was possible in Budapest to forget the war even existed. There was no bread shortage there, and the atmosphere seemed more American than that in Vienna or Berlin, at least according to Alice Hamilton, one of the members of Addams's entourage ("I only trail along as a lady's maid," she joked). The "Hungarian aristocrats reminded me of our Southerners," wrote Hamilton, "both because of their warmly cordial manner and because of their pride and their fierce independence."

Addams's next stop—Switzerland—yielded little. The small neutral states, she knew, were "timid" and not eager to rock the boat, lest they be drawn into the crisis. From Berne, the party headed to the latest country to take up arms, Italy. In Rome, they found the city war crazed. "Our hotel could serve us only our breakfast coffee and rolls," Hamilton recorded, "for cooks and waiters had been mobilized." Romans also excitedly awaited the impending return of Guglielmo Marconi, recalled by the Italian government from a patent case in New York to coordinate the military's wireless stations. Before sailing, the celebrated inventor had informed a reporter the exciting news that "within a short time persons communicating with one another by wireless telephone would be able to see one another."

Once again, Addams arrived at a foreign capital at exactly the wrong time. Certain that their entry into the war would mean a quick victory and gobs of Austro-Hungarian territory secretly promised by the Allies, the Italian foreign minister Sidney Sonnino and prime minister Antonio Salandra had no interest in peace talk. She noticed that Sonnino in particular seemed actually *glad* to be in the war. Her conversation with Pope Benedict XV, a former diplomat determined to stop what he called the "suicide of civilized Europe," proved to be far more intriguing. Before meeting the pontiff in Rome on June 10, Addams and Jacobs were instructed on the proper dress code: "long-sleeved and high-necked dresses" with heads covered by "veils of black Spanish lace." They were also expected to kneel, kiss his ring, and genuflect when departing the room, all of which the Protestant ladies managed to perform incorrectly or not at all. Hamilton, present as translator, was immediately struck by the diminutive Benedict: "very ugly, with a beaklike nose, sallow skin, and heavy-lidded eyes, but it was an ugliness that attracted, not repelled." The pope spent precisely thirty minutes with them, showing a great deal of interest in continuous mediation and a willingness to participate in a neutral conference anchored by the United States.

By this point, Addams had been away from America for eight weeks. The strain of train travel, passport delays, press interviews, and meetings with officials, friends, and well-wishers in each country had begun to take its toll on her stamina. Still, she soldiered on to Paris, where she had no reason to expect a favorable reception, especially with Germans occupying French territory.

Just as in Berlin, the only men in sight on Parisian streets seemed to be either old or maimed. And Frenchwomen, many dressed in mourning, were not at all sympathetic. They had already refused to attend the congress at The Hague, although some were willing to meet with the Addams delegation at the home of the French feminist and suffragist Marguerite de Witt-Schlumberger. Nor were the Americans in Paris especially neutral. One, a nurse, had amassed a "ghoulish collection she had made of German and Austrian helmets, knapsacks, fragments of uniforms, bayonet ends . . . bought from returned soldiers."

Prime Minister René Viviani and Foreign Minister Théophile Delcassé agreed to meetings with Addams and Jacobs, likely only because of the precedent set by the other belligerents. Predictably, they had little interest in the women's presentation. "We naturally did not try to force peace talk," Addams later explained, "any more than in going into a home in turmoil a caller would attempt to give advice." Delcassé, who had despised and distrusted Germany for years, was frankly hostile to anything other than a fight to the finish. The goal, he told them, was to "destroy Germany so that she would not come up for 100 years." Not surprisingly, the women soon discovered that the French police were shadowing them.

From Paris, the women headed to the French coast to Le Havre, home of the Belgian government in exile, for a talk with their foreign minister.

A few days later, they were back in London, where Addams dashed off a letter to Mary. The expedition, she told her, had "surely been interesting and I hope may be useful."

By this time, Addams had enough and was ready to sail for home, where she hoped to share her findings with Wilson as soon as possible. She did not want to wait another two weeks so that she could rendezvous in Amsterdam with the other set of emissaries who had yet to complete their interviews in Norway and Sweden. The receipt of "very exigent cables" from America about a vague "eastern situation" gave her a convenient excuse. She knew that Schwimmer would not be happy. "It will really be easier for me to come over again later in the summer, than to stay now," Addams explained. "I think you have been so fine through the whole thing, and I do hope you are coming to the U.S.A. soon, to find that we have Prest. Wilson."

Addams's last days in London before sailing were spent in a final frantic round of talks and meetings with journalists, MPs, reformers, and other influential people. She saw the Archbishop of Canterbury and the pacifist Bertrand Russell, who came away certain that she had "exactly the same outlook as I have. . . . War makes us grow daily more like the Germans." High-ranking government officials also granted her more interviews, including Lloyd George, the new minister of munitions, who proved as intractable as the French leaders. Grey, away on a leave of absence to try to save his vision, could see no point in meeting her a second time. "I have spoken more freely to Colonel House than I could to any other American, and he is more intimate with President Wilson than anyone else," Grey informed his secretary. Still, he understood that someone in the Foreign Office should speak with Addams, as "it would be very undesirable that less readiness to see her should be shown in London than in other belligerent countries." Ultimately, she was granted an appointment with Lord Crewe, the interim foreign secretary, who wrote up a five-page summary for his colleagues, mostly about her recent travels but also discussing the inherent difficulties in a neutral conference. A few days later, Addams boarded the New York–bound *St. Louis* in Liverpool. Her European jaunt was finally over.

In the days ahead, she could not help but look back on what had been accomplished. In the midst of war, a small group of women had not only crisscrossed the Continent but had presented their proposals to the most powerful leaders in Europe. "Never again must women dare to believe that they are without responsibility because they are without power," Emily Balch insisted. "When our unaccustomed representatives knocked at the doors of the Chancelleries of Europe, there was not one but opened." They had also elicited statements that seemed to suggest at least some of the belligerents were open to the idea of neutral nations facilitating peace. And the idea, Balch noted, was not at all far-fetched. In several instances over the past four decades, neutral nations had taken an active part in settling wars in the Balkans and China.

Could Addams, armed with her new information, push Wilson in that direction? As she crossed the Atlantic, her friends worked on arranging another tête-à-tête with the President. Wilson, who had already read the resolutions passed at The Hague "with the greatest interest and admiration," agreed to see her. Such news encouraged Addams. The President, it seemed clear, was the only man able to organize the neutral congress of nations and America "the only Power far enough away from the war to be able to do it."

For the moment, the extraordinary strain on Wilson had subsided. The second German note had gone out without any timetable for a reply. And his relationship with Edith was now closer than it had ever been. Not only was he finally secure in her love for him, but she would be spending time with him at the family's summer home in Cornish, New Hampshire, at the end of June. The Bryan crisis had seemingly cemented their relationship for good. It had also strengthened her position as more than just a lover—she had become a political confidant as well.

Edith relished her new status. "Much as I love your delicious love letters," she coyly wrote her "Lord and Master," "I believe I enjoy even more the ones in which you tell me . . . of what you are working on—the things that fill your thoughts and demand your best effort, for then I feel I am sharing your work and being taken into partnership." Already, she had put her stamp on the second note to Germany, criticizing the first draft as "flat and lacking color," which a dutiful Wilson was quick to address. She was more than eager to hear every tidbit about plans for the 1916 reelection campaign, Mexico, complaints about unwanted advice from his cabinet son-in-law McAdoo, and how to handle a certain William Jennings Bryan, civilian ("I will be glad when he expires from an overdose of peace or grape juice and I never heard of him again," she exclaimed).

Wilson was more madly in love than ever before, not only mooning over her photographs she had sent him but sending her a huge box of orchids. "I am complete in you, and nothing can really hurt me while you love me," he wrote her on June 21. "I wonder if the people about me here will realize that I am not really here at all—that my thoughts are away?" He was ready to propose again when they would be together at Cornish in a few days. On the way, he would stop in New York to see House, who had sailed home for America a few weeks before Addams.

Since returning, House had been brought up-to-date on the political situation and cabinet gossip, especially the resignation of Bryan and his replacement. Secretary of state was House's position for the asking, but he was more than satisfied with his current post as superambassador-adviser. To House, the obvious choice was the State Department counselor and interim secretary Robert Lansing, even though Wilson found him unimpressive. That, House explained to the President, was his greatest asset. Wilson wanted to be his own secretary of state anyway, and Lansing would be a "man with not too many ideas of his own and that will be entirely guided by you without unnecessary argument." And as an expert on international law, he would be especially valuable handling legal issues that would "keep him busy and happy."

Of course, House had another reason for preferring Lansing to a State Department outsider. Lansing was already familiar with Wilson's unorthodox foreign policy moves and "will be barred from complaining at the President's method of using me in the way he does." But other cabinet members, like Josephus Daniels, wondered whether Lansing was the right selection. Lansing, he later recalled, "was the sort of man who thought he was Daniel Webster!"

The Lansing matter would be one of the issues discussed with House when the President arrived at the Roslyn, New York, train station on June

24. "He greeted me with warmth and affection, placing both hands over mine," House recorded in his diary. What followed a short time later was what he described as "one of our most intimate conversations." Wilson had something important to tell House, "the only person in the world with whom I can discuss everything." He was ready to propose to a "delightful woman," he had met in March. What would the American people think? And when could he marry her? "My dear dead wife would be the first to approve if she could know," he remarked, "for she . . . talked to me about it and I am sure I would be following her wishes."

House was not surprised. His various informants had already let him know about the President's romance. The Colonel had no objection to a remarriage, provided the President wait until the spring of 1916. "I feel that his health demands it and I also feel that Woodrow Wilson today is the greatest asset the world has," he wrote in his diary. "If he should die or become incapacitated, it is doubtful whether a right solution of the problems involved in this terrible conflict and its aftermath would be possible."

Wilson remained the man of the hour, a frustrating yet undeniable reality for Roosevelt, who was back from a trip with his wife, Edith, to Louisiana to visit John Parker, a friend and Progressive colleague. Having narrowly escaped political oblivion, TR now had to consider his next move. For the good of the country, Wilson had to be ousted but how best to achieve that goal remained unclear. Roosevelt's constant attacks did not seem to be accomplishing much. Politically, the Progressive party was now a shell of its former self, though its members could still wield some influence. Should the Progressives and their leader merge with the Republicans in the hopes of moving the GOP toward the center-left? Was this even possible when TR himself admitted that "most of the Progressives approve of Wilson's infamous policy?" Should Roosevelt pursue another presidential run?

At the moment, such a course seemed unlikely. His health woes now included broken ribs, courtesy of a fall from a new horse presented to him after the Barnes trial. "I might just as well admit that I am old and stiff," TR lamented to a friend. "Much like a very rheumatic cow in a pasture."

And his enemies list had now grown to include thousands of German American voters, along with the usual embittered Old Guard Republicans like Barnes, who remained intent on "smashing me once and for all."

Nevertheless, House was already hearing rumors that Roosevelt and the Republicans would kiss and make up in an attempt to defeat Wilson in 1916. "I believe the President could beat him," House wrote, "but that will be determined by events between now and election day."

Chapter 6

"I DIDN'T RAISE MY BOY TO BE A SOLDIER"

JULY 1–AUGUST 19, 1915

*I see that it will naturally take very great
provocation to force your people into war.*

—Sir Edward Grey to Colonel House, July 1915

O n the evening of Friday, July 2, a solitary figure in Washington mailed a packet of identical letters addressed to Wilson and representatives of the local press. Signed by one "R. Pearce," who claimed to be an "old-fashioned American with a conscience," the letter attacked the continued export of munitions to the Allies. "Is it right to supply an insane asylum with explosives?" Pearce asked. "Let each nation make her own man-killing machines." But other passages suggested that Pearce had more than letter writing on his mind. "Sorry I had to use explosives," he wrote. "It is the export kind and ought to make enough noise to be heard above the voices that clamor for war and blood money. This explosion is the exclamation point, to my appeal for peace."

By the time the letter was opened the following morning, it had become clear that Pearce was more than a "crank" blowing off steam. Twenty minutes before midnight, a bomb had exploded in the Capitol's Senate reception room, the blast "felt as far downtown as the Post Office Department," though no one was hurt. While local authorities continued to piece together what happened, another disturbing development was unfolding on Long

Island at the plush Glen Cove estate of J. P. Morgan Jr., whose firm acted as the commercial agent for the British in America and was currently working on securing a $100 million loan for its client (the original administration policy that loans to belligerents would be unneutral would soon fall by the wayside). A slender, "very well dressed," .32-wielding man with a German accent named Frank Holt had forced his way into the home of Morgan, who was having breakfast with British ambassador Cecil Spring Rice. Holt's plan, such as it was, was to take Morgan's children and wife hostage until he exerted "his great influence to stop the shipment of explosives." Morgan's wife, his butler, and Morgan himself managed to subdue Holt, although not before he fired two shots into Morgan, which proved to be nonfatal. "I wanted him to be in the same danger . . . that we are imposing on Europe," Holt later explained.

Holt, said to be "in a perfect hell worrying over the war," was a clearly disturbed individual, a probable narcotics user who believed he "acted at the direction of God." Law enforcement soon discovered that he was most recently employed as a German-language instructor at Cornell and was about to start a position at the newly opened Southern Methodist University in the fall. Under further interrogation, Holt seemed to provide other important clues. Yes, he was the same "R. Pearce" who set off the bomb in Washington. No, he was "not influenced by any of Mr. Bryan's speeches." No, he had planned no assassination attempt on the President, although he believed Wilson "isn't doing anything to stop the war. He ought to do something" (ironically, Holt had written the President back in December to praise his stance against preparedness).

Still, many questions remained. Why would an "old-fashioned American" speak with a German accent? Was he telling the truth about other bombs placed on ships? And his close resemblance to one Erich Muenter, a German-born Harvard instructor who had disappeared after poisoning his wife with arsenic back in 1906, did not go unnoticed by his captors. But before they could learn more, an incompetent guard at the jail failed to keep an eye on Holt/Muenter, who proceeded to climb to the top of the cell block and hurl himself to his death.

Muenter, who had immigrated to the United States in 1889, had no clear-cut connection to the German government, but Berlin officials likely approved of, or at least sympathized with, his deranged behavior (the always excitable Spring Rice believed Holt had been blackmailed into terrorism by Germans who knew that he was a murderer). At that very moment, German and Austro-Hungarian officials in America were in the midst of overseeing ongoing secret campaigns to disrupt munitions production at Bethlehem Steel and other locations through work stoppages, luring away foreign-born workers with alternate employment, and attempts to purchase large quantities of liquid chlorine and phenol.

But such efforts, however successful they might be, could have only a limited impact on the rapidly expanding defense industry, ironically now a substantial driver of an economy overseen by a peace-loving administration. "The purchases of war munitions have stimulated industry and have set factories going to full capacity throughout the great manufacturing districts," Treasury Secretary McAdoo reminded Wilson. "Our prosperity is dependent on our continued and enlarged foreign trade."

The improved economy after the dismal winter of 1915 further strengthened the President's current popularity, a fact that irritated TR to no end (he now found the "continual praise of Wilson's English, of Wilson's style" particularly "sickening"). Had sophisticated political polling existed then, Wilson would have enjoyed a high approval rating, thanks to his handling of the *Lusitania* crisis. The "people are following you with the implicit faith of a child towards its father," wrote Assistant Attorney General Samuel Huston Thompson in early July. "Their attitude toward you as a personality is very similar to their reverence for the memory of Lincoln." Personality-wise, the reclusive Wilson was no Lincoln, but the public did seem to be showing him a greater degree of affection of late. On each stop on his train journey to Harlakenden, his New Hampshire vacation home, everyone wanted to slap him on the back or offer him words of encouragement. "I'm glad you're going to have a vacation," a Vermont woman gushed. "So am I," the President replied.

He would be spending most of July at Harlakenden with family and, most important, Edith. Within days after his arrival, they formally became engaged. "I promise with all my heart absolutely to trust and accept my loved Lord," Edith wrote, "and unite my life with his without doubts or misgiving." Work and the cares of the war, Wilson hoped, would not interfere with quality time with his future bride. "I think I shall have to send a confidential personal message to the Kaiser telling him why I should like the German reply held back until about the tenth of July," Wilson remarked. "If he is really human and has any heart in him he will understand and give me time to be with my Love."

Privacy would not be easy, especially with stepped-up security in the wake of the Muenter episode; still, Wilson was used to unstable individuals showing up at the White House, including one claiming to be "George Washington's grandson."

The President could not entirely escape his duties on vacation nor did he desire to do so. Long-distance calls kept him in touch with developments in Washington, and he continued to plow through a mountain of paperwork and dispatches each day. Still, most of his time was spent reading, golfing, playing billiards, and taking long drives through the countryside. His interactions with surprised fellow motorists and locals, some of whom became tongue-tied, soon became grist for newspapermen, who dutifully recorded the presence of Mrs. Norman Galt in the Wilson party. Their readers had not the slightest notion they were reading about the future First Lady.

While Wilson relaxed in New Hampshire, Addams was nearing the end of her voyage home on the *St. Louis*. The journey had been relatively uneventful, although two British destroyers had escorted the ship to the southern coast of Ireland in case any submarines might be lurking. The situation in America, Addams realized, had changed a great deal in the nearly three months she had been away. Thanks to the *Lusitania*, the possibility of American involvement in the Great War no longer seemed quite so remote, and the pacifist message had a chance to gain a more sympathetic hearing than ever before.

It would not hurt that the now unemployed Bryan was now devoting most of his time to the cause, quickly arranging high-profile appearances at Madison Square Garden and Carnegie Hall. His popularity and influence in the Democratic party remained considerable, and there was talk that he might try to run for the presidential nomination in 1916, thanks to a peculiar one-term plank inserted in the 1912 platform. Already he was toying with the idea of undertaking his own European mission, although he denied a belief in "peace at any price." "The words," he insisted, "are employed by jingoes as an expression of contempt and are applied indiscriminately to all who have faith in the nation's ability to find a peaceful way out of every difficulty, as long as both nations want peace."

Even the East Coast intelligentsia who had little love for Bryan or his rural following could not ignore a growing interest in peace. Just days before Addams left Europe for America, conservatives such as William Howard Taft and A. Lawrence Lowell, the president of Harvard, attended a Philadelphia gathering establishing a new organization known as the League to Enforce Peace. Its goal, the LEP's first president, Taft, was quick to explain, was not to "suggest a means of bringing this war to an end," but to prevent future conflicts through a world organization of nations agreeing to submit differences to a tribunal or face the combined military and naval strength of other members. Addams considered joining, but she was not comfortable with the willingness to resort to war, nor were many other pacifists, including Bryan. "You are using too much force," the former congressman and socialist Victor Berger argued. "You want more militarism to fight militarism. There is too much 'Teddy' Rooseveltism in it." Ironically, TR himself refused to join, despite similarities to his own "international police force" scheme he believed might be feasible in the future. Taft's involvement, of course, guaranteed Roosevelt would have no part of it, but TR also believed it would force America to "have to arbitrate everything," including such currently sensitive issues as Asian migration to the West Coast.

The issue of avoiding war, now and in the future, not only dominated the public discourse but also resonated in popular culture. The song "I Didn't Raise My Boy to Be a Soldier" had been a massive hit for months, selling thousands of copies of sheet music, player piano rolls, and 78s. Its homespun sentiments, imploring nations to "arbitrate their future troubles" and "lay the sword and gun away," could have been written by Addams herself. The continued popularity of such an "abject pacifist song" enraged Roosevelt, who believed its fans "would also in their hearts applaud a song entitled 'I Didn't Raise My Girl to Be a Mother.'" And any woman who did not raise her sons to fight for his country, he believed, was not "fit to be a mother."

For some reason, a New York advertising man named Henry Green thought it would be a good idea to invite TR to serve on the committee welcoming Addams home. Roosevelt's stinging reply to Green (whom TR privately labeled a "bustling fatuously-benevolent Jew") showed just that the gap between the former Progressive colleagues had grown even wider. The women at The Hague conference, he wrote Green, "have not shown the smallest particle of courage; and all their work has been done to advance the cause of international cowardice; and anyone who greets them or applauds them is actively engaged in advancing that cause." Once again, Roosevelt lumped the women with the hated "peace-at-any-price" crowd, claiming they fixated on peace "without regard to the redress of wrong," not unlike the Copperheads of the Civil War. As for Addams, she had once "rendered great and noble service," but now "she has identified herself with a movement that on the whole represents more damage to the fibre of American character than the worst crookedness in either business or politics." In other words, TR would be busy that day.

His absence did not dampen the enthusiasm of the gathering, many wearing "Welcome to Jane Addams" ribbons, awaiting her arrival at a Hudson River pier on a rainy July 5 morning. The photographers and press were also out in full force eager for pictures and statements. Once on land, Addams did her best to correct misinterpretations of her mission. "A great mistake has been made in thinking that in urging negotiations for peace we are urging peace at any price," she explained. "There is a great difference between the two things. Some substitute for war and the horrors of war must be found. The sooner it is found the better. And the sooner the best minds of the world cooperate in finding this way, the better." Did Miss Addams think the war might end soon? "No," she admitted. "How could I? But I see that the time has come for intervention, and it is only by intervention that the war will be ended. Left to themselves the warring nations will fight on and on."

That large segments of the media, most notably *The New York Times*, continued to distort her efforts as "peace-at-any-price" was enormously frustrating. "For months we have seen her flitting from capital to capital, asking the nations to lay down their arms," the *Times* snidely editorialized the next day. "She does not know it, but she and they have been doing what they could to bring about not peace, but war. They have been asking the democratic nations of Europe to drop their arms and give Germany time to make the next attack." For Addams, such unfair criticism confirmed that "there is evidently need to explain the situation in America," although she had no interest in participating in a proposed "Peace Train," on which she would make ten-minute whistle-stop speeches throughout America. Instead, she hoped that a major speaking engagement at Carnegie Hall that Friday, along with her meeting with Wilson, whenever he decided to see her, would not only help to clear up "a curious confusion of mind" but also determine the next step in the campaign for peace.

The campaign, Addams knew, remained at least partially dependent on battlefield developments. With the Central Powers now making substantial gains on the Eastern Front, the Allies were especially hostile to the idea of any peace overtures. And they still harbored peculiar fantasies about driving the Germans "back over the frontier" on the Western Front, despite horrifying casualties on previous attempts. "I was told by an officer who had served on the Western Front," Addams told a reporter, "that even on days when an engagement was not on, the loss was fully 2,000 lives every 24 hours—lives taken by sharpshooters, by firing from advanced trenches and by dropping bombs from aircraft."

Such "sad and really terrible" things on the Western Front had now become common to James Norman Hall, who had begun occasionally slipping grisly descriptions into his letters home unless the censor saw them first. "An evening or two ago," he wrote his Boston friend Roy Cushman that July, "a corporal a few feet from me, stood up on the firing bench and looked over the parapet. 'This is where you are to fire' he said to one of the men. And then he crumpled up limply on the ground with a bullet through his brain. One half minute, a living, thinking human being, the next, a bit of lifeless clay." In his weeklong stints in the trenches before going behind the lines, Hall could not help dwelling on his own mortality and the existence or nonexistence of an afterlife, although he admitted "there is real danger in thinking too much."

He deeply missed his family and friends, but was now convinced that the war would go on at least another year. "The chief factor in determining the outcome will be the economic one," he wrote. "And there can be little doubt that Germany + Austria will be economically ruined first. I wonder how long it will take?"

The brutal yet common experiences of the soldier on both sides would be an important part of the speech Addams would deliver at Carnegie Hall on July 9. News in the afternoon papers that the forthcoming German response to Wilson's second note would likely be unsatisfactory put a slight damper on the evening, although the venue was packed with well-wishers and representatives from suffrage, reform, pacifist, and civic organizations. When Addams was introduced at 8:15 p.m., a young man from the Inter-collegiate Anti-Militarism League shouted out, "Three cheers for 'the world's first citizen!'" The capacity crowd erupted. "It's good to see that peace can be as rousing as war," she remarked.

The cheering continued during her address, as usual delivered with consummate skill and poise. On the stump, she lacked the oratorical flourishes of Wilson and the heated passion of Roosevelt. Still, Addams's speeches were equally powerful and effective. "From the first word to the last she held the complete attention of her audience," her niece Marcet Haldeman-Julius later recalled. "Thought flowed into thought and at the end one had the satisfied feeling of having heard a well-rounded view. Her hands, always bare of rings, were exceptionally expressive—although she used them seldom, and then in brief, timely gestures rather than in sweeping ones."

Addams began her address that evening by recounting the recent congress at The Hague and her experiences visiting nine different governments. Each belligerent not only justified its decision to fight on the same basis, but also claimed it could not show interest in peace without appearing weak. At the same time, each government was open to outside propositions for peace. She also identified the growing power of the military at the expense of civil authorities, a disturbing development that might persist after the war if not held in check now.

She then turned to the men doing the fighting. "We heard everywhere that this war was an old man's war: that the young men . . . were not the men who wanted the war, and were not the men who believed in the war." She gave examples from both sides of men who did not want to kill while acknowledging that "there are thousands . . . in the trenches feeling that they are performing the highest possible duties."

In the concluding moments of her talk, she discussed the fallacy that the answer to militarism was more militarism, such as the conscription Britain was now considering. "It is quite as foolish to think that if militarism is an idea and an ideal, it can be changed and crushed by counter-militarism or by a bayonet charge." And bayonet charges themselves, Addams explained, were abhorrent to the humanity that still lingered in the heart of many a soldier. Without relying on notes, she illustrated her point by mentioning how each army needed to "make their men practically drunk before they can get them to charge" (the published version, likely edited, replaced "practically drunk" with "necessity for the use of stimulants"). "They have a regular formula in Germany," she explained, "they give them rum in England and absinthe in France. They all have to give them the 'dope' before the bayonet charge is possible." A few minutes later, the speech was over; it was followed by a startling rant from Meyer London, New York's new Socialist congressman, suggesting Frank Holt "was no more dangerous than living organizations such as the National Security League."

Underlying her talk was the simple notion that "negotiation rather than through military advantage" should be the way to peace. Unfortunately, she soon discovered that her message was almost completely overshadowed by the "practically drunk" comment that seemed to question the age-old concept of manly men courageously fighting for home and country. "Many Americans romanticized the war," Addams's friend Alice Hamilton later noted, "and resented fiercely anything that disturbed the picture they had created."

The backlash was almost immediate, the first major blow a vicious letter to *The New York Times* from TR's war-loving friend Richard Harding Davis. This "complacent and self-satisfied woman" had slighted every dead soldier. "Miss Addams denies him the credit of his sacrifice. She strips him of honor and courage. She tells his children, 'Your father did not die for France, or for England, or for you; he died because he was drunk.'"

The Davis letter soon unleashed an avalanche of attacks in editorials, letters to the editor, and private correspondence (Roosevelt kept quiet, likely because Davis said everything he would have wanted to say). Some merely attributed Addams's silly views to the ignorance of women, who could not comprehend the "joy of combat" or "understand how men can possess sufficient physical courage to charge into a cloud of shot and shell unless 'soused to the gills.'" Others descended into deeply personal insults. She was nothing more than an "ancient spinster," a "crack-brain old creature who ought to be restrained in some institution," and a "foolish, garrulous woman" who was "badly overrated" with views not unlike those of Emma Goldman, "who also is for anarchy."

"Look into the trenches, mademoiselle, or even into the ambulances," the French poet Jane Catulle-Mendès sneered. "You will learn there how they die, without nice words and for an ideal, which is surely worth more than the prattling for a vague and easy fantasy which costs nothing and which stimulates much publicity." That some women were equally scathing did not surprise Addams, who had encountered plenty of European ladies just as militant and bloodthirsty as their sons, husbands, and brothers.

Soldiers of all ages weighed in, mostly denying her claims. "Don't believe what Miss Jane Addams is telling or rather what she has been told," wrote Robert Pellissier to an American friend a few months later. "French soldiers don't get drunk each time they go into a bayonet charge. I took part in one, and not only had we nothing in our cans except water, but we had had nothing to eat since breakfast."

But some came to Addams's defense, including a Civil War veteran who attested to the age-old practice of providing soldiers with "dutch courage." "Sergeants and corporals poured whisky from their canteens into little tin cups to every private soldier at roll call before daybreak on the morning of an intended charge," he explained. Even Pellissier admitted that a Zouave informed him that he "had received a half-pint of brandy the night before the attack" at Vauquois.

Addams, stung by the ferocity of the attacks, did her best to try to explain that she was not implying anything about the courage of soldiers and was simply suggesting that some required artificial means to reduce inhibitions against killing in close quarters. As for her informants, she cited "a prominent official in the Paris War office," a "German lieutenant," and a "big Oxford University professor," all confirmed by Alice Hamilton.

But the damage was already done. Her status as America's foremost woman, under assault since involving herself in (shudder) partisan politics with TR in 1912, had taken yet another hit. The incident also gave the antisuffrage crowd ammunition to show that "foolish" women could not be trusted to "pass upon questions of war and peace." One even suggested that "it is uncertain whether the person who has done the greatest harm in the world is the Kaiser or Jane Addams."

The controversy's effect on the peace campaign concerned her more. The attacks on Addams, perhaps the most high-profile pacifist in the country after Bryan, revealed that powerful forces were eager to undermine the movement whenever possible. "I had my first experience," she later wrote, "of the determination on the part of the press to make pacifist activity or propaganda so absurd that it would be absolutely without influence and its authors so discredited that nothing they might say or do would be regarded as worthy of attention." Still, many remained in her corner, including a woman from upstate New York who sent her an encouraging letter a few weeks later. "Do not throw over this work, because a few shallow fools ridicule it in the papers!" she wrote. "Keep up your brave fight and emperors and kings and ministers will bless you for it for all times."

On the same day that most Americans learned of Addams's Carnegie Hall address, they also read the contents of Germany's reply to Wilson's second note. Anyone hoping the Germans would apologize and finally address the "principle of humanity" emphasized by Wilson were to be disappointed. Instead, the note trotted out the same arguments that Britain's violations of international law left Germany with no choice but to "adopt a submarine warfare to meet the declared intentions of our enemies." As for the *Lusitania*, the U-boat commander could not have acted any differently in view of the munitions carried, the British orders to merchant ships to "arm themselves and to ram submarines," and the likelihood of the "sure destruction of his own vessel" had he given the passengers the chance to get off the ship before firing the torpedo.

Turning to the travel issue, Germany would do its best to prevent harm to American vessels "engaged in legitimate shipping" and American passenger steamers would also be safe from submarine attack, provided they carried no contraband, bore "special markings," and were "notified a rea-sonable time in advance." But Americans on British ships such as the *Lu-sitania* could not "protect an enemy ship through the mere fact of their presence on board." As a solution, Germany offered a scheme influenced by James Gerard's suggestion by which American passengers would be guaranteed safe passage to England by traveling solely on the existing American liners and additional passenger steamers, neutral or enemy, that would be placed "under the American flag." Meanwhile, the note remained silent about the earlier secret decision to end attacks on any passenger liners, although yet another—the *Orduna*—had been mistakenly torpedoed the day before, with no damage or injuries.

That Berlin seemed prepared to debate the issue endlessly without yield-ing much of anything appeared increasingly clear. Asked about the German response as he waited to board a train at Grand Central Terminal for the Panama-Pacific International Exposition in California, an exasperated Roo-sevelt directed reporters to reread his post-*Lusitania* statement back in May during the Barnes trial. "What I said then applies now, and in the end the United States will have to recognize that fact," he remarked. Wilson, still vacationing in New Hampshire, was also not happy. The passage of two months and the exchange of four notes had seemingly solved nothing. "I think we might say to them," he wrote House, "that this Government is not engaged in arranging passenger traffic, but in defending neutral and human rights!"

Wilson knew he would have to leave his blissful New England vacation and return to Washington, at least for a few days. Besides the German crisis, ongoing instability in Haiti and Mexico needed to be addressed. On Monday, July 19, he was back in the White House, "invigorated," he told Edith, "by my three weeks with my darling." Wilson and his "darling" had already discussed the specifics of his planned response to Germany, but he dutifully shared an "outline of the argument" at the cabinet meeting the next day. Bryan, the major source of cabinet friction of late, was now gone, but Secretary of War Lindley Garrison would prove to be just as irksome to Wilson.

Even by the standards of the President's rather loose and dismissive cabinet relationships, he and Garrison had never worked particularly well together. "Garrison was an intensely argumentative man," Wilson later recalled. "He wore me out with argument." Garrison had already threatened to resign, and the President was prepared to accept if he tried it again. And the secretary of war's views on preparedness swung far more toward TR's perspective. Garrison, meanwhile, thought Wilson acted too much like a "schoolmaster" who "didn't like those associated with him to argue with him."

The President naturally saw things differently. Garrison, he told Edith, was a "solemn, conceited ass" who loved the sound of his own voice and "concentrates his entire attention on his own opinions and does not listen to mine."

Garrison followed his usual script at the July 20 meeting, arriving with and then reading his own proposed note arguing that Germany should be pushed "to a Yes or No or refusal to answer." "He seems to feel that he owes us this guidance," Wilson said later to Edith. "He does not expect us to see or think clearly enough to accept what he offers, but he feels bound in conscience to at least afford us the chance to be rightly and intelligently led."

Garrison's stance, the President felt, would simply prolong an already long back-and-forth, which would not go over well with a public no longer quite so charged up about the *Lusitania*. For now, Wilson's sense was that the majority of the American people wanted neither war nor a break in diplomatic relations; they simply wanted him to "insist on our rights." As such, he could not accept Germany's proposal to "limit our trade & travel to certain vessels. . . . We are entitled to whole & not part of rights." His plan, then, was simply to reiterate the same essential principles—namely, that merchant ships should not be torpedoed without first determining their "character and cargo" and noncombatants should be protected "unless the vessel resists or seeks to escape." Should Germany ignore those principles in the future, the United States would "consider that an intentional unfriendly act," with serious consequences to follow. Wilson would work out the final specifics that week with Lansing, whom Garrison noted "said very little" during the meeting.

Addams was scheduled to see Wilson the next day. She and other pacifists were somewhat annoyed that she had to wait sixteen days to see him, unlike the European statesmen who had accommodated her within five days. In the meantime, she had scheduled a meeting with Colonel House on Monday morning at his summer residence in Manchester, Massachusetts. Privately, House thought little of her expedition or, more likely, felt threatened by any peace strategy other than his own. "She has accumulated a wonderful lot of misinformation in Europe," he scoffed to Wilson. "She saw von Jagow, Grey, and many others, and, for one reason or another they were not quite candid with her, so she has a totally wrong impression." It never once occurred to House that possibly his friend Grey and the others might not have been always "candid" with him. Not surprisingly, he believed Addams had "nothing of value" to offer him during their conversation, but he did come away impressed with her "great poise and good sense." He was also pleased that she would see the President that week, "not that she can tell him anything he does not know, but it will please her following which is large and influential."

As far as Addams knew, her conversation with House went well, especially in light of the ongoing press attacks against her. She did not discuss any specific plans for peace with him, although they both agreed that at least some of the belligerents "would not resent negotiations, but would welcome them." But precisely which path to pursue remained unclear. Should she continue to back the continuous mediation idea and the neutral conference embraced by the recent women's conference at The Hague? She had begun to wonder whether a "bold stroke" was needed, which she sketched out during a conference the next day in New York with Lillian Wald and the Henry Street group of social workers and other reformers, now meeting for the third time since the war began. Official diplomacy had utterly failed, Addams explained to them. Why not move toward a gathering of internationally minded individuals who would work behind the scenes to broker peace the same way strikes had been settled? She had not fully worked out the details, but she envisioned a small group, perhaps sanctioned by the President, of three Americans, along with representatives from both sides, free from the restrictions imposed by "timid" neutrals and mainstream diplomacy. Some of those present proposed Addams as a key part of the hypothetical delegation (along with Colonel House, which showed how little they knew of him), but she knew Wilson would never

Addams and Lillian Wald (left) talk to reporters at the White House after their meeting with Wilson, July 21, 1915.   (Library of Congress, LC-H261-6624)

appoint her. Already, she was well aware that "the President is not 'for women.'"

The next morning, Addams and Wald headed to Washington for their noon appointment with Wilson. That he granted them a full hour in the midst of the strain of trying to finish off the response to the second German note showed that he was well aware of the importance of currying favor with Addams and her friends. She briefed him on her European travels without attempting to sway him in any direction, although she did touch lightly on her international commission idea. Afterward, a crowd of reporters, photographers, and newsreel cameramen awaited them outside the White House, eager to hear what had been discussed.

"Gentlemen, it is bewildering to be confronted by so many," she announced. "I really cannot tell you what I said to the president. That is confidential." The barrage of questions continued as she headed to her taxi. When did she think the war would end? "It may stop as quickly as it started. I'm too wise to try to predict anything about the war." When would Wilson mediate? She had no idea, but the President had already seen the resolutions passed at the women's congress. Had she read Colonel Roosevelt's recent attack on the female pacifists in the latest *Metropolitan*? No, she had not.

Someone then read her TR's comment about women who "were abroad, actively engaged in exciting contempt and derision for themselves and their country by crying for peace without justice and without redress of wrongs, at the very time that the *Lusitania* was sunk." She did not take the bait. "I believe in free speech," she told them with a smile.

"You're not afraid of him, are you?" a reporter asked.

The question irritated Addams. No, she informed the group, she was *not* afraid of TR. After the movie cameras got some shots of her on Pennsylvania Avenue, she had lunch at the Shoreham Hotel and then boarded a train for Chicago and home.

Addams felt the talk with Wilson was "encouraging," although the German note that was to go out in a few hours was paramount on the President's mind that day. The note would take a far more forceful tone than its predecessors, so much so that he believed it might lead to "the final parting of the ways." The latest German response, it read, had been "very unsatisfactory," and the U.S. government was "keenly disappointed" by the continued failure of Germany to abide by the established international law governing warfare and delay in "disavowing the wanton act of its naval commander . . . or from offering reparation for the American lives lost." Accompanying the tough language was an extremely important admission: that no one had envisioned the potential of the submarine when existing international law was written, and America was now "ready to make very reasonable allowance for these novel and unexpected aspects of war at sea," provided the U-boat commanders continue to refrain from attacking without warning and provide for the safety of crew and passengers. The final sentence ominously warned that another *Lusitania*-type incident would be "regarded . . . as deliberately unfriendly," a statement that would send the kaiser into a near tizzy. "Utterly impertinent," he wrote in the margin. "It ends with a direct threat!"

Wilson sent an advance copy of the note to Edith, who was still at Harlakenden. She could read it, he told her, to the others in the home, "whose departure for bed used to be our introduction to paradise." He fretted about the "momentous decision I have made," and the possibility that he might be "sacrificing millions of his fellow men to his own individual, almost unaided judgment." But there was nothing to do except wait for events to unfold. After all, the note did not demand a response. Germany would either toe the line he had set or flout it.

T he President had kept the country out of the Great War. That was enough for most Americans. It was not enough for Addams and other peace activists. They still implicitly trusted Wilson to do the right thing as far as peace was concerned, but they wanted him to take decisive steps in the near future and stop the interminable waiting for the perfect moment to act that might never arrive. For Addams, Wilson's job was simple. "The United States," she observed, "with all neutral nations, should throw every bit of its power into the scale for peace." That the President did not seem inclined to move in that direction at the moment was disappointing. And while they were told to "stand behind the president," the pacifist Louis Lochner complained that "nobody knows where the President is standing, or what he is making us stand for, or what his policy is." Wilson himself admitted that he was unsure from day to day "what the real duty of the country is."

If Wilson's mind was still in flux, then perhaps he could be converted. At least the pacifists hoped so. A few weeks after Addams's meeting with the President, Oswald Villard tried to interest Lansing in Addams's committee-type approach to mediation. The new secretary of state was not at all encouraging. Like House, he did not especially value anything she had learned in Europe, although he did agree to send the proposal along to his boss. Wilson, determined to keep liberals like Villard and Addams in his pocket for future needs, knew he had to proceed carefully. "I know these good people are not going to let the matter rest until they bring it to a head in one way or another," he wrote Lansing. "I must, I suppose, be prepared to say either Yay or Nay." Lansing then outlined his misgivings. Whether the civil authorities were open to mediation, as Addams claimed, was irrelevant since the military officials were most influential and "favor a continuance of the war" at present. And any attempt by the neutrals to act would likely "fail and . . . we would lose our influence for the future." The President did not disagree.

Villard's unsuccessful meeting was followed by yet another attempt to storm the gates of the administration, this time by Emily Balch, whose typewritten European impressions had already been presented to Wilson by Addams ("I think that he really takes things in better through his eyes rather than his ears," Addams told her). Balch first made a pilgrimage on August 16 to Colonel House, who handled her with aplomb. The President was on their side, he assured her. He "had his hand on the pulse of the situation" and would act when the time was right. And House himself would be glad to see Miss Addams again. The sympathetic hearing encouraged Balch, who had no idea that House disregarded everything she had to say about Europe. He was also rather pleased that "she and her associates evidently have no idea what the President has in mind or what he is doing."

Two days later, Balch spent an hour with Wilson, who confirmed that he would act at the right moment. "This was a comfort," she told Addams, "as I had feared that he really meant to stand aside." The two academics discussed the neutral conference proposal and Addams's unofficial commission idea, although the President cited the difficulty of selecting the appropriate internationally minded individuals. Balch also presented Wilson with a copy of Addams's Carnegie Hall speech and even mentioned the recent bayonet charge controversy, which did not concern him unduly. Balch departed with a sense that the President was truly sympathetic to their efforts, just as Colonel House had implied to her. But she was reluctant to press him too hard; in fact, she worried that she had stayed too long and allowed Wilson to instruct her on what to say to the press afterward.

She had misread him. A few hours later, he expressed his true feelings to Edith: Balch and Addams were pushing a "conference of neutral nations" that would "heckle the belligerent nations about terms and conditions of peace, until they are fairly worried (I suppose) into saying what they are willing to do." He did not believe it could work. "And yet I am quite aware that they consider me either very dull, very deep, or very callous."

Addams had already drawn certain conclusions about Wilson that summer. Virtually nothing would prompt him to act until he was ready. Still, she was not content to wait patiently for his next move. The continued slaughter in Europe deeply disturbed her, so much so that she believed it was better to do *something* rather than *nothing.* Her niece Marcet, who visited her in August at her summer home in Maine, was struck by her dedication to the cause. "I had the impression that Jane Addams was neither pessimistic nor optimistic," Marcet later wrote. "She felt—and there are few who will not agree in retrospect—that any gestures, any proposals of a pacific nature were infinitely more sensible than such mass murder."

Wilson believed he knew better. Should genuine peace opportunities present themselves through Colonel House's machinations, he was willing to follow them up. Otherwise, his approach to the war remained passive, beyond merely doing everything possible to keep America out of the conflict. The three *Lusitania* notes that had gone out to Germany were a key part of that strategy, a way of injecting a dose of sanity to a Europe "determined to commit suicide." The notes, he admitted, "alter no facts; they change no plans or purposes; they accomplish nothing immediate; but they may convey some thoughts that will, if only unconsciously, affect opinion, and set up a counter current. At least such is my hope."

But how long could such an approach succeed? Roosevelt was certain the steady stream of diplomatic notes merely delayed America's inevitable day of reckoning, either during this war or in the future when another nation behaved belligerently. When his daughter Alice Longworth mentioned that another note had gone out, TR could only grimace. "Did you notice what its serial number was?" he asked. "I fear I have lost track, myself; but I inclined to think it is Number 11,765, Series B." Using yet another historical precedent, Roosevelt then explained to Charles Thompson of *The New York Times*, present for this exchange at Sagamore Hill, just how Wilson had gone wrong. What would the fate of the Union have been, he asked, if, following the attack on Fort Sumter, Lincoln "had embarked on a series of notes to Jefferson Davis, just as logically perfect . . . just as stupendously reasonable, as those of Wilson"?

The President would likely have retorted that it was 1915 and not 1861 and that most Americans approved of the course he was pursuing to stay out of a foreign war that appeared irrelevant to most of their interests. To TR, this line of thinking epitomized the differences between the two men.

It was Wilson's *duty* to guide the people in the correct direction. "Men are easily puzzled; and it is easy to mislead them," Roosevelt explained. The "right kind" of president—one presumably like himself—"could have aroused our people. A bugle call from the White House will arouse many a slothful or timid or shortsighted or money-getting American who nevertheless deep down somewhere in him has the root of right feeling."

He could content himself with the knowledge that, after the *Lusitania*, his own call for preparedness and increased defense measures no longer appeared quite so extreme. Universal military service, a cause TR had long embraced, was now attracting support from the likes of administration officials such as Franklin Lane and FDR. House even discussed the idea with TR's friend General Wood, who advocated "a modified Swiss System. He thinks if our young men from eighteen to twenty-two had two months a year for four years, we would soon have a citizen soldiery that would practically make it unnecessary for us to have a standing army." And a number of school districts and colleges, mostly on the East Coast, had begun to explore the possibility of introducing military drill and instruction. Some, like Providence, Rhode Island, had already voted to make military training mandatory for all high school boys beginning that September, much to the horror of pacifists.

That July, TR's sons Archie and Quentin were among six hundred young men taking part in a five-week-long War Department–run military training camp at Plattsburg (then commonly spelled without an "h") in upstate New York. Such camps, a pet project of Wood's, had been held the past two summers without attracting a great deal of attention. Now, the press and public were intrigued, even more so in a separate camp for thirteen hundred well-to-do business and professional men that began on August 10 with more than its share of big names in attendance. Archie, Ted Jr., TR's son-in-law Richard Derby, and his private secretary, John McGrath, were there along with such luminaries as New York mayor John Purroy Mitchel, *Vanity Fair* editor Frank Crowninshield, ex–Secretary of State Robert Bacon, tennis superstar William Clothier, and Addams's recent nemesis Richard Harding Davis. Each paid his own way.

Anyone expecting, in Wood's words, an "ice cream and cake affair" was soon mistaken. "This is a very real thing," Davis admitted, "and *strenuous*."

The "recruits" were busy from five in the morning until ten at night with drilling, hikes up to twelve miles a day, instruction in various subjects, mock battles, and guest lectures. "It was a 'get-wise-quick' course," Davis later informed his readers in *Collier's*. "It was like trying in three weeks to train eleven men who never had handled a football to defeat Yale." And Davis, like many others, soon gained a greater respect for the craft of a soldier. But some wondered what possible practical purpose could the training of a fifty-one-year-old Davis or a fifty-five-year-old Bacon have, beyond publicity for preparedness and, perhaps, publicity for Roosevelt as well?

Wilson understood this well. The camp was overseen by the War Department, but he was not about to accept an invitation to review the proceedings, even if it made political sense to do so. Dudley Field Malone, a former State Department official under Bryan currently serving as collector of the Port of New York (Malone would find himself on opposite sides from his old boss in the celebrated Scopes "monkey" trial a decade later), pushed the President to come to Plattsburg to emphasize the Democrats' support of the movement. Wilson refused. He wanted no part of what he labeled a "Wood-Roosevelt affair." The President was also sure that "a speech on preparedness would be expected of me which Wood and his like would try to use to show that (in another sense) they had taken me into camp."

TR, of course, was already planning to show his face at Plattsburg, but he remained uncertain whether the current surge of preparedness interest was helping him politically. There had been some encouraging developments of late. Barnes was now less likely to bother with an appeal, since William Ivins, his lead attorney, had dropped dead a few weeks after the trial of Bright's disease, still insisting to the last that "the trial judge was wrong." And Roosevelt's trip to the West Coast for the Panama-Pacific Exposition confirmed that the people still very much wanted to see him. Enthusiastic crowds had greeted him everywhere, especially at the world's fair itself, whose exhibits TR predictably praised as "bully!" His two major California speeches, in San Francisco and San Diego, also attracted massive audiences, estimated at fifty thousand and thirty thousand, respectively.

That Theodore Roosevelt, *celebrity*, could still pack them in was not in doubt. But as he had discovered on the campaign trail the previous fall,

many present remained more interested in seeing him than actually em-
bracing his message, especially on the West Coast, where Bryan's appearances were drawing well. He sensed that his preparedness talk in San
Francisco (or what he called his "Damn the Mollycoddles" speech) and its
tried-and-true bashing of "professional pacifists . . . seeking to Chinafy this
country" did not quite catch fire as he hoped (as usual, he read a prepared
address, crumpling up each sheet and tossing it aside after completion). "It
would not be true to say that there was wild enthusiasm over my speeches,"
he privately admitted. Still, he reassured himself that "the audiences listened to me in each case for nearly two hours with the utmost attention
and with substantial assent."

His Bull Moose comrades on the coast were eager to meet with him to
map out strategy for 1916, although it remained questionable whether there
would be much strategy to map out. The two million Progressive votes in
1914, TR believed, did not mean a whole lot at this point. Clearly, many
of the reformers such as Addams had soured on him, especially since Roosevelt, who still proclaimed himself a "near-socialist," was now focusing
exclusively on what he called "great questions of national security and international duty." It would be best, he decided, for the party to "sit tight
and hold what we have got till next year" and remain open to "any olive
branch that may be proffered" from the Republicans.

TR said nothing about his own plans for 1916. The California Progres-
sive Meyer Lissner thought Roosevelt had made a good showing on the
West Coast, far better than Bryan, and that his "stock was on the uplift."
Colonel House naturally saw things differently. "Roosevelt is utterly dis-
credited as an extremist on the one hand," he wrote Page in London, "and
Bryan is discredited as an extremist on the other."

TR would not have disagreed with this assessment. His base at the
moment was still insignificant. Less than 5 percent of the population,
he believed, currently supported his view of America's responsibility in the
war, certainly not enough to mount any kind of successful presidential run
or even approach his 1912 showing. And a dual Progressive-Republican
nomination of Roosevelt, which the "Dough Moose" George Perkins appeared to be angling for, seemed unlikely, especially with the GOP "completely under the control of reactionaries," in TR's view. In any event, the

people did not want him, he told Perkins, and "it is of prime consequence not only that I should not ever attempt again to run for office but that no human being can have legitimate reason to have the slightest thought of ever again running me for public office."

Such feelings of self-pity were only temporary. Should a path to the presidency somehow present itself in the next year, Roosevelt was more than willing to take it. In the meantime, he would attack the administration whenever and wherever he could, and maybe, just maybe, the people would finally begin to listen.

Preparedness remained the administration's Achilles' heel. To House, the fault rested entirely with Wilson. "The President has never realized the gravity of our unprepared position," the Colonel wrote in his diary that July. "I urged him early in the Autumn to start in with some such program, and in my opinion, it should have started the day war was declared in Europe. If we had gone actively to work with all our resources to build up a war machine commensurate with our standing among nations, we would be in a position today to enforce peace."

At bare minimum, a "credible threat of force" might make a tremendous difference in dealing with Germany and the Allies. And every moment that passed made the task that much more difficult. "Preparedness is not the affair of a day," TR had reminded his San Francisco audience. "If we begin at once, a year or two must elapse before we shall have accomplished even a beginning."

Wilson had already concluded that his opposition to military and naval escalation expressed in his December message to Congress would no longer fly. The public did not want war, but "the demand for reasonable preparedness is clear enough," he admitted. On the same day he saw Addams, he sent letters to Garrison and Daniels requesting their input on the expansion of the navy and army. A few days later, news of the President's about-face was released to the press.

Roosevelt, pleased that Wilson would have to "eat his words of a year ago," thought it was a calculated political move, an empty gesture unlikely to amount to anything. Addams and other pacifists felt differently. Was their peace-loving president a closet militarist? They grew concerned when Wilson not only did not respond to their questions of whether the public would have any say in the military and naval programs but declined to see a delegation eager to change his mind on preparedness.

But the President was too smart a politician to ignore them completely. "I do not think there need be any fear that the country will go too far," he reassured Oswald Villard. "It will wish to see a course pursued that lies between the extremes in every particular."

If Wilson was well aware that no clear consensus existed as to the extent of preparedness necessary, he was certain that most of the country remained pro-Allies. Against considerable odds, he had managed to keep war-fueled emotions mostly under control, even during the worst difficulties of the past six months. Compared with the "hysteria" and "war mad" behavior seemingly everywhere at the time of the Spanish-American War, the country's response had been positively restrained. With no new German responses anticipated at the moment, he hoped for a period of relative calm as the nation enjoyed the remainder of the summer.

The quiet breather did not last long. While at Harlakenden in early August, Wilson learned from McAdoo of a recent episode involving two Secret Service agents, who had been trailing *The Fatherland's* George Viereck and an unidentified companion on the Sixth Avenue elevated train in New York. Viereck got off first at the Twenty-third Street Station, followed by his friend, later determined to be an embassy official named Dr. Heinrich Albert, at Fiftieth Street. As Albert, the money man behind the various German schemes and propaganda in America, made his way to the subway platform, he realized too late that he had left a large briefcase behind. One of the Secret Service men grabbed the briefcase, neatly dodged the frantic Albert, and then reported the find to his superiors (Albert, meanwhile, futilely placed a lost-and-found ad with a reward offered). What the Secret Service discovered was a treasure trove of documents, revealing the German government's involvement in mischief of all kinds, ranging from subsidizing pro-German periodicals such as Viereck's to plots to sabotage munitions plants via strikes.

Wilson was not immediately sure how to respond. The dossier, while invaluable, presented several difficulties. It had clearly been stolen, it contained nothing obviously prosecutable, and it was likely to unleash the passions that the President had tried to keep suppressed for a year. Those misgivings aside, he green-lighted a plan to leak the documents to the administration-friendly *New York World* to be published later that month, provided they disclosed nothing about the Secret Service involvement. House, who also weighed in on the final decision, thought it a sensible move, even if it increased the possibility of war. "The people will see things as those of us that know the true conditions have long seen them," House wrote Wilson, "and it will make it nearly impossible to continue the propaganda."

Ironically, the *World*'s sensational exposé would help to distract attention away from an ongoing troubling economic issue that had helped the German cause in America far more than months of often heavy-handed propaganda. Southern cotton growers and their champions in Congress— most notably, Senator Hoke Smith of Georgia—had long complained bitterly of the continued British practice of preventing their crop (not classified as absolute contraband, despite its use in explosives) from reaching neutral ports and eventually Germany and Austria. And the crisis now threatened to worsen. Not only did the British have no intention of changing their policy, but they had also decided by July to declare cotton absolute contraband, a move likely to dramatically increase friction with America.

"You of course realize fatal effect that would have upon opinion here," Wilson wired House. "Probably changing attitude of this country toward the Allies and leading to action by Congress cutting off munitions." That Senator Smith might lead such an effort in Congress was already recognized in London. Only the continued transgressions of Germany in August and the British promise to buy up most of the cotton market prevented the serious PR disaster for the Allies anticipated by the President. Once again, the Allies continued to win the propaganda war in America by default.

The daily strain of contending with what an unpredictable Germany and

Britain might do next was made bearable for Wilson only through the presence of Edith in his life. If anything, her role had grown even larger that summer, even though she was away with friends during much of August. Still, the two lovebirds were determined to "cheat our enemy, Space!" by using the technology then available: a constant stream of long-distance calls, telegrams (occasionally signed "Tiger"), and letters that often arrived within a day (sometimes on the *same* day), something that was not surprising in an era of frequent mail delivery. "I am as restless as any caged tiger if I cannot at least be pouring out my heart to you when I am free to come to my desk at all, before and after business," Wilson wrote. "I do not want you to go a single day without a love message from me if I can help it." By his own admission, he was now spending several hours each day engaged in letter writing, a poor substitute, he mused, for "a single kiss." And if his letters are any indication, he had also taken to smooching Edith's photograph on a regular basis. "Ah, Sweetheart, the glass over a picture is a cold thing to kiss, but surely you must feel the kisses I give these lovely pictures of my Beautiful Darling."

The President, to put it mildly, was obsessed with Edith, and it had become noticeable to the few who were in on the secret. Cary Grayson, his golfing partner and doctor, briefed House about what was going on. "It seems the President is wholly absorbed in this love affair and is neglecting practically everything else," House wrote in his diary. "Grayson says the President is using my approval as an excuse." House also learned from Grayson of some "rather disturbing" matters, presumably involving Wilson and Galt, "but which I do not care to put in the diary."

House, whose various informants kept him abreast of *everything* in the White House, likely had no idea that Galt not only was Wilson's lover but was also beginning to seriously challenge House's exalted advisory role. She freely admitted her formal education was spotty, her letters inelegantly crafted and punctuated. The President was unconcerned. "The capacity of your mind is as great and satisfactory as that of any man I know," he assured her. "I could not love or admire a blue-stocking or endure a woman politician!"

Edith, then, had no trouble manipulating the love-struck Wilson into divulging the most classified of information even after knowing her for less than six months. "I don't believe I ever made you know how perfectly happy I was when you would let me share your work," she wrote him. "And I thrill now when it comes back to me how . . . you would turn to me with love on your lips, and whisper the tenderest secret in the world." He was now sending her a "big envelope" on a regular basis, chockful of government documents and private correspondence, often with his own pungent commentary attached, and even apologized when he had nothing especially juicy to send her. The future Mrs. Wilson loved every minute of it and made no attempt to hide this fact. "If the afternoon mail comes with no big envelope, I feel cheated," she admitted. For a moment, Wilson wondered whether Edith was turning into a dreaded "lady politician." "You don't want it all business, do you, deeply as you are interested?" he asked. "You would miss the love letters, would you not, and the other confidences which concern only us?"

She, of course, assured him this was not the case. In the meantime, she felt confident enough to begin offering her critical opinions on Wilson's longtime associates. She did not care for the "common" Tumulty, whose Irish Catholicism and hard-nosed political background were alien to her. To his credit, Wilson tried to defend his secretary. Yes, he told Edith, Tumulty "was not brought up as we were; you feel his lack of our breeding," but he was "absolutely devoted and loyal" and skilled in handling the masses, "the great majority of the people who come to the office" who were "not of our kind."

She had already decided that she also did not think very highly of House, whom she knew only through his letters the President had shared with her. "I can't help feeling he is not a very strong character," she wrote Wilson. "I know what a comfort and staff Col. House is to you Precious One and that your judgment about him is correct, but he does look like a weak vessel and I think he writes like one very often."

Wilson, taken aback by the criticism of his closest friend, might have told his lady love to mind her own business. Instead, he tried to convince her of his excellent qualities as a trusted adviser. "But you are right in thinking that intellectually he is not a great man," he conceded. "His mind is not of the first class. He is a counsellor, not a statesman." Wilson was sure she would come around eventually, "if only because he loves me and would give, I believe, his life for me." That Edith felt the need to again comment on his deficiencies in her next letter suggested that she was undertaking a subtle campaign to undermine House's privileged status in the President's life.

O n Thursday, August 19, Wilson arose and penned his usual love ode to Galt, who would be returning to Washington in less than two weeks. "I've just come from kissing your picture before locking it up for the day," he dreamily informed her. The remainder of the day, he anticipated, would be routine: meetings, paperwork, and the usual golf outing in the afternoon. And the next day he was scheduled to see his "oculist" in Philadelphia to monitor his vision.

Not until later that afternoon did he learn what had just occurred off the coast of Ireland, not far from where the *Lusitania* had gone down four months earlier. The *Arabic*, part of the White Star Line's fleet (which had once included the doomed *Titanic*), was making its usual passenger run between Liverpool and New York and had sighted manned lifeboats on the open sea belonging to the *Dunsley*, a cargo steamer barely afloat after a torpedo attack. Hoping to rescue the crew, the *Arabic* realized too late that the U-boat was still lurking in the waters, about to unleash another torpedo. "Here it comes!" shouted one passenger. A bugle warning began to sound. Within seconds, the *Arabic* "staggered as though hit by a great fist," but the crew quickly sprang into action with lifeboats and preservers. The captain was especially impressed by the "magnificent courage of the women. . . . They sought to do their share with the men in the boats." Most passengers made it off in time, including a panicked Vancouver schoolteacher named Margaret Ross, who was tossed ten feet into a lifeboat by a member of an acrobatic troupe known as the Flying Martins.

Forty-four men and women were not so lucky. If any were Americans, Wilson realized he had another *Lusitania* situation on his hands. "If we assume that the *Arabic* was torpedoed without any warning and American lives have been lost, then the country must decide the grave question of what must be done . . . a question of doing, not talking," *The Boston Globe* editorialized. "President Wilson has exhausted all peaceful and usual means to protect American lives upon the seas. He cannot now repeat what he has already asserted three times."

Chapter 7

A SECOND CRISIS

AUGUST 20–OCTOBER 5, 1915

*Our people do not want war, but even less do they
want you to recede from the position you have taken.*

—Colonel House to Wilson, August 1915

I n a world without air-conditioning, Washington in August was not a
desirable place to be. Those with the means, like Wilson, fled to New
England summer homes; the less fortunate might take a day trip to a
nearby beach or lake to cool off and check out the new fashions in female
swimwear. Young women, it was said, seemed to have lost all sense of
propriety this year. At the Jersey Shore, Coney Island, and other East Coast
destinations, authorities did their best to stamp out the shocking appearance of bare shoulders, "tights without a bathing dress over them," "ballet
dancers' skirts," and one-piece suits of any kind, even wielding "measuring
sticks" to make sure that all skirts reached the knees. Those who didn't
comply found themselves sternly sent to the bathhouse with instructions
to change into something more decent. "We will be glad to have women
come here to bathe, but they must not make vulgar exhibitions of themselves," a Coney Island official warned. "Coney Island will be kept clean
and married women need not fear to permit their husbands to come here."

Try as they might, the older generation could not turn back the clock.
Skin, preferably tanned, was in. And the bathing suit, the journalist Jane
Dixon explained, was no longer just for swimming, but something to be

seen in on the beach and even in nearby public places. "Convention? What an old fashioned word! Comfort's the thing," she remarked.

Comfort was not easy to come by at the White House. The prior summer, Wilson had even tried working outside under a large tent in the Rose Garden, but soon found it unsuitable. In the midst of the new *Arabic* crisis, he had no choice but to stay put and contend with the D.C. humidity, although he did keep his eye appointment in Philadelphia on Friday, August 20. Unwilling to contend with a hot, stuffy train trip, he decided to go by automobile, at least one way. The long ride (the presidential party got lost in Baltimore trying to find the Philadelphia road) allowed him to collect his thoughts while he waited for more details, just as he had done after the *Lusitania* sinking. After arriving in downtown Philadelphia around one thirty, he saw Dr. George E. de Schweinitz, who deemed his left eye stable but informed Wilson that he had been wearing the wrong glasses while reading. Lunch at the Bellevue-Stratford Hotel and a brisk walk to the Broad Street Station followed, with six Secret Service men and Grayson nearby at all times. At first, no one paid much attention to the bespectacled gentleman clad "in a gray sack suit and a soft mohair automobile hat" purposefully striding down city streets, but someone soon recognized him. Within minutes, crowds of well-wishers were in hot pursuit. "What's all this?" one befuddled onlooker asked. "It's the President" was the response. "The President of what?" "Of the United States, you damned fool."

When Wilson returned to Washington, the news was not good. Two Americans were among the forty-four on the *Arabic* who drowned: Josephine Bruguiere, a wealthy socialite, and Edmund F. Woods, a Wisconsin physician. Bruguiere, unable to swim, had plunged from the ship in the arms of her son Louis moments after he had tossed her two bulldogs, both of whom survived, onto a life raft. "We were caught in the vortex," he explained later. "The force of the swirling water separated mother and me and struggle as I could, I could not reach her." As for Woods, a naturalized American citizen born in England, the unfortunate doctor apparently made the fateful decision to stay in bed rather than leave his cabin for breakfast.

That the death toll was insignificant compared with the *Lusitania* offered no comfort to Wilson. Three months of diplomatic exchanges had apparently changed nothing: Americans were still dying on the high seas because the Germans refused to stop torpedoing merchant ships and liners without warning and providing for the safety of passengers. And this time, they had no excuse, flimsy or otherwise. The *Arabic*, though a notorious hauler of munitions to the Allies, carried none this time since she was heading to New York from Liverpool. "It is just an act of wanton disregard of international law and of brutal defiance of the opinion and power of the United States," a disgusted Wilson wrote Edith.

For the second time in three months, the President faced a decision fraught with frightening implications for the nation and the war itself. His gut instinct remained the same. The country not only did not want to go to war but American involvement would be the "worst thing that could possibly happen to the world" since it would destroy any hope of the United States "moderating the results . . . by her counsel as an outsider." Still, he recognized his previous notes left him precious little wiggle room. Warnings had been made and now apparently flouted—was not war inevitable? This time, there was no Bryan to offer a counteropinion; in fact, his replacement, Lansing, believed Wilson would need to move aggressively. "Outside of the newspapers," the secretary of state wrote the President, "everybody I have met, official and civilian alike, takes the position that the declarations in our notes are so strong that we must act, that otherwise it will be said that our words have been mere 'bluff,' and that it would place the United States in a humiliating position to temporize."

Wilson was not yet convinced. At bare minimum, he wanted "all the facts" before even convening a cabinet meeting. He also wanted the input of House, whose opinion he valued infinitely more than the Anglophilic Walter Hines Page's in London and the "idiot" James Gerard's in Berlin. House, who frankly dreaded another note dispatched to Germany, tried to strengthen the President's resolve. The original *Lusitania* note, House explained, had made Wilson "the first citizen of the world. If by any word or act you should hurt our pride of nationality you would lose your commanding position over night." Germany, then, had to yield and in a concrete way by disavowing the sinking and promising that it would never happen again. If not, Wilson had to take "some decisive action" if he wished America to have "influence when peace is made or afterwards." Later, House congratulated himself in his diary: "The President has clearly put it up to me and I have not flinched in my advice," he wrote. "I am surprised at the attitude he takes. He evidently will go to great lengths to avoid war. He should have determined his policy when he wrote his notes in February, May, June and July."

Severing all diplomatic ties with Germany appeared to be the next logical step, one that would likely be strongly supported by the public. Sending Ambassador Bernstorff home would make a statement to not only Germany but the world, while preserving national honor. But even this relatively harmless move posed some degree of risk. The Germans might respond by declaring war. "If she does, we are at last caught in the maelstrom and our independence of action is lost," Wilson wrote his "sweet counsellor" Edith. "I must call Congress together and we are in for the whole terrible business."

To Roosevelt, severing diplomatic ties would achieve absolutely nothing and represent yet another "sacrifice of American honor and interests" by the administration. The President's original "strict accountability" note, he admitted, had been "excellent, if only it had been lived up to." Instead, the Germans soon grasped that Wilson did not mean business, and the *Arabic* was another in a series of Germany's "arrogant answers which this weakness has inspired." Now, "the time for words . . . has long passed" and "the time for deeds has come." Perhaps wisely, TR did not specify what kind of "deeds" he envisioned, though his criticism of the "unwisdom of our people in not having insisted upon the beginning of active military preparedness thirteen months ago" offered an obvious clue.

There was a core of truth in the midst of Roosevelt's usual scattershot criticism of Wilson, one that House himself would have recognized. The President had finally decided to embrace "reasonable preparedness," but any program of military and naval expansion he proposed would have to wait until Congress convened again in December. And even if Congress should pass any legislation, the global impact of a substantially larger American army and navy would not be felt until 1917, if not later. That Germany might prove more tractable in the current crisis in the face of a viable American military presence likely occurred to Wilson, but it was a path he still found unattractive, even distasteful. That week, a widely published newspaper story suggested that the General Staff and Army War College had already developed "comprehensive plans for the organization, training and mobilization" of the one million American troops likely needed in the event of war. Wilson, nearly apoplectic, demanded that the assistant secretary of war find out if the General Staff had in fact made such plans and if so, "relieve at once every officer of the General Staff and order him out of Washington." Eventually, Wilson came to his senses, but the incident revealed his essential discomfort with a military solution to the current difficulties.

His agitated reaction was consistent with that of a man whose nerves were shot and under almost unbearable pressure. He missed Edith terribly. Five days into the crisis, he finally had a chance for a breather when Bernstorff, whom Wilson viewed, somewhat unfairly, as an "impertinent Prussian," informed Lansing that Berlin wanted a chance to tell its side of the story. What this meant Wilson could not say. "I suspect some mere manoevre for delay," he wrote Edith on Tuesday, August 24, "but I cannot see how the German government can deny or explain away the facts and it is not likely that they will apologise and reprimand the commander of the submarine." House was also concerned. "I believe the President will do the right thing, but I fear he may do it in the wrong way," he recorded in his diary that day. "He is very slow to move in such affairs which sometimes works for good and at other times for disaster."

The businessman's camp at Plattsburg was in full swing that week. The big news was that TR would be gracing the thirteen hundred or so recruits with his presence on Wednesday. After a nine-hour train ride, he arrived that morning, clad in khaki reminiscent of his Rough Rider days, and spent most of the day with General Wood inspecting the premises and chatting with friends and family.

Like other dignitaries invited to the camp, Roosevelt was also there to make a speech later in the evening. Wood looked it over beforehand and immediately had concerns about comments critical of the administration. "Theodore, as an ex-President, you have presidential prerogatives on a military reservation," the general told his old friend. "You may say what you

Roosevelt and Leonard Wood at Plattsburg,
August 25, 1915.
(Library of Congress, LC-DIG-ppmsca-36425)

want. But I suspect that some of the things you are planning to say are likely to stir up a lot of trouble." The normally headstrong TR acquiesced to Wood's wishes. Around six thirty, they headed to the parade ground for his address.

As usual, everyone wanted to see Roosevelt. Besides the recruits and their regular army superiors, hundreds of locals showed up. The sun was beginning to set, and a lantern was placed on a photographer's tripod for additional reading light. Originally, TR had planned to give the prepared 2,500-word speech, but he threw in more than a few asides to extend his talk to an hour. Early on, a captain's pet Airedale terrier ran in front of him and then plopped himself on his back, legs in the air. "That's a very nice dog," TR remarked. "His present attitude is strictly one of neutrality." The crowd loved it.

Roosevelt was careful, probably due to Wood's intervention, not to explicitly mention Wilson or the administration by name, although he reminded his listeners that America had "played an ignoble part" in the war, especially toward Belgium. He praised the recruits for "fulfilling the prime duty of freemen," and demanded that the pacifist crowd, "college sissies," and "money-getters" should also do their part in a national crisis, be it digging "trenches and kitchen sinks. . . . I wouldn't mind our pacifists," he quipped, "if, in trying to test their ideas of Chinafying a country, they move to China, and I apologize to China when I say that." He talked up universal military service, citing the example of Switzerland, "the most democratic and least militaristic of countries, and a much more orderly and less homicidal country than our own." He took potshots at the "professional German-American," a disgrace compared to the "citizens of German birth or descent who are in good faith Americans and nothing else." The hyphenated Americans, he warned, "will fight beside us or they'll be shot. They'll be given their opportunity to risk a shot from the front or accept the certainty of being shot in the back." Finally, TR explained how the Plattsburg camp offered a splendid example to the nation of preparedness and the "path along which we should tread."

Having kept himself somewhat in check during the speech, Roosevelt then threw all caution to the wind to the press waiting for him at the train station. He issued a prepared statement defending his attacks on Wilson, though once again he never mentioned his name. He felt no obligation, he said, to "stand by the President" unless the President "stands by the country." And if the President or any other official had done wrong, "the prime duty of the citizen is, by criticism and advice, even against what he may know to be the majority opinion of his fellow citizens, to insist that the nation take the right course of action." If Lincoln, for example, had expressed his belief that the supporters of the Union "were too proud to fight" and had exchanged a series of notes with Jefferson Davis, then he would not have been deserving of the nation's support in 1861. TR concluded with one final dig at Wilson: "To treat elocution as a substitute for action, to rely upon high sounding words unbacked by deeds is proof of a mind that dwells only in the realm of shadow and of sham."

His comments were front-page fodder across the country the next day. In the midst of the delicate *Arabic* situation, Roosevelt not only had attacked the administration again but had done so at a camp run by the U.S. government. Even Plattsburg recruits like Willard Straight, a former beau of TR's daughter Ethel now involved with the fledgling *New Republic*, began to wonder about his judgment. "It was a mighty poor place to cast even indirect slurs on the Administration," Straight wrote to a friend. "He seems to have the unfortunate habit of deterring a great many people from supporting a perfectly good cause, for there were many who would be willing to stand for a better scheme of national preparedness who will now be frightened off."

It was Wood who would pay the price for Roosevelt's comments. Garrison, while a longtime supporter of preparedness, had already warned the PR-happy general about some of his high-profile activities. (Wilson, meanwhile, was not happy that Wood had recently urged the Plattsburgers to "use your influence as good American citizens in contrast to the ignorant masses.") "He was the most indiscreet man we ever had in high command," Garrison later described Wood to an interviewer. In fact, the secretary of war had already begun thinking that a court-martial might be in his future if Wood didn't watch his mouth. This time, Garrison sent the general a stern wire warning him that the Plattsburg camp was not the time or place for any talk of "issues which excite controversy, antagonism and ill feeling" and it had best not be repeated. TR, naturally, jumped to his friend's defense, claiming he alone was responsible for the speech, attendance was not mandatory, the speech was "delivered outside the line of tents," and that he had only spoken of "the nation, of the people, of the United States." He then engaged in a public back-and-forth with Garrison, who soon realized it was impossible to win an argument with Roosevelt. "I evidently drew blood from the Administration," TR chortled. "It was worthwhile to have one man state the things that ought to be stated." The speech also drew blood from Wilson's ever faithful lover, who fantasized about making Roosevelt "eat his words" or smashing "his disgusting teeth."

The day after the speech, a young writer named Julian Street journeyed to the *Metropolitan* offices in New York to begin research on an article about TR, "The Most Interesting American," to appear in a forthcoming issue of *Collier's*. Initially, he was somewhat taken aback that Roosevelt in the flesh did not quite conform to his boisterous public image. This middle-aged mustachioed man, he noted, resembled a "conservative banker of Amsterdam" and his handshake was frankly wimpy. But Street soon discovered that he was still the same vibrant Roosevelt, never at a loss for words and able to discourse entertainingly on a wide range of subjects. "He has not aged," Street decided. "He has simply ripened, matured."

TR was comfortable talking to Street, who had no intention of providing anything but a puff piece with a generous sprinkling of tidbits about his personal life. Roosevelt, Street informed his readers, didn't smoke or swear, and only consumed "a little light wine." He did not care for "joke-for-a-joke's sake" but "expects a joke . . . to do something." And TR did not think he possessed genius. "I'm no orator, and in writing I'm afraid I'm not gifted at all, except perhaps that I have a good instinct and a liking for simplicity and directness," he explained. "If I have anything at all resembling genius, it is in the gift for leadership. For instance, if we have war, you'll see that young fighting officers of the army want to be in my command."

The former president also spoke candidly about Wilson. He had not set out to attack the President; in fact, he would have been happy to "praise Wilson if he'd given me the chance," although he had long believed that "the pedagogic mind is generally too theoretical and abstract for politics." But the administration had proved to be a failure from the get-go. "'Too proud to fight!' And all these letters to Germany!" Worse, Wilson the former historian had highlighted America's remarkable lack of preparation during the War of 1812, only to repeat the same mistakes a century later such that America was now a laughingstock militarily. As to charges that he was a bloodthirsty warmonger, Roosevelt was quick to note that there had been no wars of any kind on his watch, unlike the Wilson administration's military adventures in Mexico and more recently Haiti ("apparently the kind of country we can handle now," he griped).

TR invited Street to see Sagamore Hill, "a house which, from the outside, does not look nearly so spacious as it actually is." Inside, he showed Street the library, crammed with books, animal skins and stuffed heads, along with paintings of his father, his wife, Lincoln, Washington, and Daniel Boone. The living room, two stories, was just as impressive, filled with "trophies and souvenirs of all sorts," though far from pretentious. In fact, Street claimed the Roosevelts "do not keep a butler or a footman."

Street was left with the impression that TR was essentially "one of us . . . a moving picture of ourselves as we should like to be . . . brave, hardy and adventurous," unafraid to confront liars or evildoers of any kind. The problem, of course, was that he sometimes took it too far. "He isn't quite safe," Street admitted. "He won't listen. He just goes roaring on like a steam engine in pantaloons."

To Wilson, Roosevelt was an undeniably persistent annoyance, but one he would not confront. "The best way to vanquish him is to take no notice of him whatever," he confided to Edith. "I wish Garrison had taken that course, richly as Wood deserved the rebuke he gave him." In any event, the President was far more concerned that week about the possibility of war, which he knew most Americans did not want but he might be powerless to prevent. "I feel like a pilot who has been so long at the wheel that he longs to be relieved," he complained, "but who knows that he has come to the most difficult part of the passage, where he is not even sure of his chart and holds his breath lest any moment the vessel under him should strike a reef."

How Berlin would proceed remained uncertain. The request for additional time had raised hopes that Germany might yield, as did an encouraging report from Ambassador Gerard detailing his conversation with Foreign Minister Jagow. If the reports of the *Arabic*'s sinking were accurate, Jagow informed him, then the submarine commander had violated the new policy established after the *Lusitania* (a policy yet to be officially disclosed to America or even to Bernstorff). A statement by Chancellor Bethmann promising "complete satisfaction" if the commander "went beyond his instructions" further hinted that Germany was not especially eager to go to war.

Once again, the chancellor was determined to preserve American neutrality. That the "attitude of a single submarine commander" could turn America into a belligerent was unacceptable. The kaiser not only agreed but soon decided to expand the original order to include *all* passenger

liners, large and small. A few weeks later, the U-boats ended their opera-
tions in the English Channel and west of the British Isles. It was too much
for Imperial Navy hard-liners such as Admiral von Tirpitz, who tried to
resign. He understood that German U-boat campaign, so boldly launched
back in February, had now been effectively neutralized, while others believed its relatively modest accomplishments to date did not justify the
considerable risk of involving America in the war.

All that was left to do was to inform Washington. A much relieved
Bernstorff, finally briefed about the submarine policy, met with Lansing
on the morning of Wednesday, September 1. Three months earlier, Bernstorff told the secretary of state, the German government had made the
decision that "liners will not be sunk by our submarines without warning
and without safety of the lives of noncombatants, provided that the liners
do not try to escape or offer resistance." Lansing thought this startling
news, a coup for the administration, should be publicized. Bernstorff
agreed, even though his superiors had specifically told him the policy
should remain confidential. It was not the first or the last time that
Bernstorff would ignore his instructions in the interest of preserving
peace.

A few hours later, virtually the entire nation—pacifists, Democrats, and
Republicans—was singing the praises of Wilson. Not only was there to be no
war, but America had apparently forced Germany to cry uncle. Oscar Straus,
a former diplomat himself, believed Wilson had just pulled off "one of the
greatest if not the most important diplomatic achievements in our history."
Wilson's predecessor Taft was also impressed. "This must and should be the
cause of profound rejoicing by every patriotic American and the occasion for
congratulation to the President," he told a San Francisco crowd.

Even TR publicly conceded the outcome was more than favorable,
though he believed Germany would need to do more, namely make "the
most ample amends" for the American property and lives lost to date.
Privately, he believed Wilson deserved little credit. Only a perfect storm
had allowed the administration to emerge from the crisis without a scratch.
Germany had simply calculated that "her submarine campaign . . . did not
pay" and "abandoned it," but "our tomfool people" did not seem to grasp

this. All they seemed to care about, he complained, was that Wilson had kept them out of war.

Wilson was a happy man that day. Not only had his diplomacy been decisively vindicated, but he would be seeing Edith later that evening after a several week absence.

Unfortunately, a slight problem had crept into their secret romance of late: it was no longer quite so secret. Wilson tried to reassure his fiancée that she need not pay attention to "Washington gossip. . . . If we keep within bounds, as we shall, and give them no proofs that they can make use of, we can and should ignore them." Besides, no one had any right to cast aspersions on his relationship. The love of a good woman, he maintained, actually helped him to perform his duties more efficiently. "I am absolutely dependent on intimate love for the right and free and most effective use of my powers."

Edith was especially horrified by an article that appeared in the *Washington Herald* and other newspapers the previous Sunday with the sly headline "WHO IS THE FIRST LADY OF THE LAND?" Since the President's daughter Margaret was now busy with her singing career, the job had supposedly fallen to his cousin Helen Bones, ably assisted by "her friend, Mrs. Norman Galt," who had become a rather significant figure of late, "completely at home . . . at the Summer White House" in New Hampshire. "From the very first Mrs. Galt was a success as a guest," the article explained. "During the later winter and spring she rolled around luxuriously in limousines bearing the White House crest. The President has taken a keen delight in having his niece's [sic] friend as a frequent, in fact, almost a daily guest, at dinner at the White House in the last few months." Reading between the lines, the meaning was clear: the widowed president had a new lady friend. "Everything is being watched and noted," Edith warned him.

Wilson was not concerned, but Edith wished to be more discreet. He was somewhat taken aback that she had decided on a new policy: no letters when they were not together. And their reunion proved to be less joyous than either had anticipated. Edith was not quite herself that night. The "wretched newspaper people" were beginning to bother her. She also fretted that Wilson might "not like me as well as you thought you did," and she was not comfortable that her lover began discussing "intimate things" in the presence of a third party, Cousin Helen. Wilson soon did his best to set things right. Their "precious intimate matters," he promised, would remain between the two of them. "I was foolish. It had been so long since I held your dear hands in mine that I could not govern myself." Meanwhile, he gently nudged her toward reconsidering her correspondence ban. "The mails, sent through the P.O., tell no tales to gossips; and we've got to risk the gossips anyway," he explained. By their next "date" on Saturday, everything had been resolved. Edith was now confident enough to display a photograph of the President on her piano, although she admitted she could "appear to strangers just as a patriotic person—and to myself as an adoring worshiper of my precious One." Now, all that remained was the timing of the announcement of their relationship and engagement.

A few days later, Wilson received a letter from Mary Hulbert, now living in Los Angeles. She had never entirely disappeared from his life, even after Edith appeared on the scene. Back in May, she had spent a day in Washington seeing the new presidential grandchild, motoring with the President and Helen, and watching him speak at Arlington Cemetery. Hulbert then resumed burdening Wilson with her personal problems, lamenting how her incompetent but now sober son Allen needed $7,500 for his latest scheme (a California avocado business of some kind), how no publisher was interested in her recipe book, and how she was trying to sell family property in the Bronx in a last-ditch effort to raise cash. As usual, she played the damsel-in-distress card to perfection. "It's illuminating to see the cold shoulders a woman encounters when she enters the province of the business world," she lamented. "Charm is not marketable, if one has it." Naturally, the gallant Wilson took the bait and agreed to buy the mortgages for $7,500.

Somehow, Cary Grayson learned that Wilson was sending money to that Hulbert woman, the same Hulbert whose name had been linked to the President for years. Perhaps she was blackmailing him. Alarmed, Grayson informed Treasury Secretary McAdoo, who then concocted a rather devious scheme to force the President to come clean. He had received an "anonymous letter from Los Angeles," he told Wilson, that Mary Hulbert was circulating his private correspondence. A stunned Wilson, certain that

Mary "must have fallen under some evil influence," maintained his usual composure and divulged nothing to his pushy son-in-law.

But he knew that he would have to tell Edith. He also decided to prepare a document to be released to the public if and when the scandal broke. While there had been nothing untoward in the relationship with Mary Hulbert, the President wrote that he was "deeply ashamed and repentant," especially since he knew he "did not have the moral right to offer her ardent affection" in the correspondence. His wife, Ellen, he intimated, was aware of his dalliance and had "forgiven" him, and he was especially relieved that "nothing associated with this correspondence could even in the least degree affect the honor of the noble lady."

To his credit, Wilson had no intention of taking the easy way out by claiming that the letters were phony, cooked up by his enemies. "A public man has always to remind himself that he owes to those who have trusted him to make frank admission of so much as is true when such disclosures come, and attempt neither denial nor self-justification. When he alone is responsible, he must not shield himself."

The revelation or "awful earthquake," as Edith called it, blindsided her. Wilson begged her to "stand by me" and not to "desert me," but she would only allow him to "hold the dear hands that seemed to be groping for support." She admitted that she had put her "Lord and Master" on an unrealistic pedestal, believing that he was "so fine I could breath[e] better in your atmosphere, that the very air was charged with purity and that this heart of gold had been given into my keeping." But her doubts soon passed. She now understood that while he was not a "superman," she still loved the "vital, tender, normal man" who was her "precious Woodrow." Their task now, she told him, was to "rebuild our City of Dreams on such a firm foundation that no other can shake it." Meanwhile, the President promised that he would discuss the matter with House, who would soon be in Washington.

House, naturally, knew what was going on, even before he saw Wilson (in fact, Edith would unfairly blame him as part of McAdoo's scheme in her less-than-accurate autobiography). After arriving in Washington, he saw McAdoo, who filled him in on the gory details while House waited for the President to return from his golf game. That evening after dinner, a sheepish but determined Wilson told House the whole story: how he had been friends with Mary Hulbert for years, how he "had been indiscreet in writing her letters rather more warmly than was prudent," and how she was now apparently spreading their contents all over southern California. He would not allow himself to be blackmailed, he asserted, and would take whatever public punishment he had coming.

House, knowing that McAdoo had lied but unable to tell Wilson, managed to talk the President off the ledge. After reading a few of the letters, House was also convinced they contained nothing especially sinister. A discussion about the timing of the engagement announcement and the wedding followed: mid-October and "by the end of the year," respectively, were deemed ideal. House felt the need to assure the future readers of his diary that Wilson loved his first wife dearly and their marriage was a happy one. But he believed that the President *needed* to marry again. "I have never seen a man more dependent upon a woman's companionship," he wrote. "None of his family are with him, and his loneliness is pathetic."

The next morning, a much relieved Wilson wrote to Edith about his conversation. House was a great friend, he told her, a "wonderful counsellor," who had sized up a difficult problem and helped to work through a solution. Surely, she would feel the same once she met him in a few hours at lunch. The Colonel, blissfully unaware of Edith's dismal assessment of his "strength," thought things went rather well during their first meeting. The next day, they had a more prolonged discussion over tea. The topic of a second term arose, House believing it would not be necessary "if the President were able to play the part I hoped for" in the peace process. He was sure, he told Edith, that "if our plans carried true, the President would easily outrank any American that had yet lived." The two then took a brief ride in her "electric runabout" before joining Wilson for dinner and an excursion to the National Theatre to see the stout vaudeville comedienne May Irwin (better known today for participating in the first-ever screen kiss, in 1896) in *33 Washington Square*, a new farce.

House returned to New York afterward, secure that all was well in his relationship with Wilson. To quell recent rumors of friction between the two friends, the President had even planted House prominently at the theater for all to see. And Edith seemed to have been won over. "He is just as nice and fine as you pictured him, and his admiration for you is sufficient to establish my faith in his judgment and intelligent perceptions," she wrote her fiancé. But House had no idea of how much of a sounding board the future Mrs. Wilson had become. His days as the President's sole confidant and adviser were at an end.

During their time together, House and Wilson had spent considerable time discussing the war, which showed no sign of retreating to the background that September, even after the apparent happy conclusion of the *Arabic* affair. Seemingly every day a new development emerged, threatening to send the country and the media into a fresh tizzy.

That the Allies could be as barbaric as the Central Powers had begun to occur to Wilson, who had recently learned of a disturbing incident involving the British. On August 19, the same day the *Arabic* was sunk, another submarine, the U-27, intercepted the *Nicosian*, a British vessel carrying American mules from New Orleans. After permitting all aboard to take to the lifeboats, the submarine began to sink the *Nicosian*, until another ship, the *Baralong*, flying an American flag, appeared, ostensibly to rescue the survivors. Angered by the *Arabic* news, her crew suddenly hoisted the British colors and then began blasting away at the U-27, which realized too late that they had encountered a Q-ship, or decoy vessel. Six German sailors managed to escape the quickly sinking submarine but all were promptly shot in the water. The remaining five crew members, who had boarded the still afloat *Nicosian*, died at the hands of British marines. To Lansing, who briefed Wilson on the incident, the "conduct of the British naval authorities is shocking." The President agreed.

Such incidents might have given a boost to the floundering German PR campaign in America, except for more revelations of the Central Powers' mostly bumbling efforts to make domestic trouble. The latest concerned Constantin Dumba, the Austro-Hungarian ambassador, who had sent several documents abroad through a sympathetic American courier that were confiscated by British authorities. One of the more inflammatory involved a letter to the Austrian foreign minister Stephan Burián, who had met with

Addams back in May, discussing how strikes and other schemes might "disorganize and hold up for months, if not entirely prevent, the manufacture of munitions" at Bethlehem Steel and other locations. It was too much for Wilson, who ordered his recall. "And yet," the President asked his secretary of state, "if Dumba, why not Bernstorff also? Is there any essential difference?"

Of course, there wasn't. The German embassy had been aware of and sometimes facilitated similar efforts. But Bernstorff remained an essential (if not *the essential*) cog in the ongoing touch-and-go dealings with Germany. And it was soon clear that he would be very much needed. Just days after the announcement of Wilson's stupendous "diplomatic triumph" on September 1, an unwelcome development threatened to undo all of Bernstorff's careful work in preventing war. Shockingly, another liner was sunk, this time the Montreal-bound *Hesperian*, victimized by the deadly efficient U-20 commander Walter Schwieger, whose torpedoes had taken down the *Lusitania* (he would later claim the *Hesperian* was armed and therefore fair game). Fortunately, no Americans were among the thirty-two killed. German officials deceptively claimed a mine was the culprit, and Bernstorff was quick to assure Lansing that "this case in no way changes our general policy with regard to submarine warfare."

Bernstorff had an even more difficult situation on his hands when the German Foreign Office sent its formal explanation of the *Arabic* sinking to Washington, blithely claiming that the submarine commander, thinking he was about to be rammed or attacked, had acted in self-defense.

The response was not what Wilson wanted to hear ("obviously disingenuous" he called it), especially since the *Arabic*, according to reports, had been struck in the stern or back of the ship. "I suppose the *Arabic* was backing into the submarine," Lansing quipped. Germany also announced that no compensation would be forthcoming for the loss of life. Grayson, in the thick of things at the White House, did not like what he was hearing. "Our situation with Germany now is worse than it has ever been," he wrote Altrude Gordon, his fiancée. "It may mean war with this country."

Wilson, wilting under the Washington heat and the stress of negotiations, could not help wondering whether Bernstorff had been stringing them along. The much celebrated *Arabic* pledge not to attack large and small liners apparently had a giant loophole—self-defense—which the German government seemed prepared to utilize when convenient. To the President, the situation was once again coming to a head. "The Secretary of State and I will be obliged," he wrote Edith on the morning of September 13, "to make some decision that may affect the history of the country more than any decision a President and Secretary of State ever made before."

A few hours later, Lansing laid down the law to Bernstorff, informing him that the recent note of explanation was completely unsatisfactory and he would need to make Berlin understand this. The German ambassador was more than willing, but he had begun to wonder if he had anything left in his diplomatic bag of tricks. "He seemed to be much depressed, and doubtful as to what he could accomplish with his Government," Lansing wrote to Wilson after the meeting.

Bernstorff was certain that no more notes should be exchanged and that he be the point man for settling the issue. He did his best to explain to Bethmann that Americans viewed the last communication as more "German bad faith—a sign that we may perhaps give way in principle, but will always in practice seek to evade our obligations." Another liner attack would almost certainly mean war. He soon managed to wrest a stronger promise from Berlin, that "no passenger vessel will be torpedoed in the future without notice, and that the ship will have the benefit of the doubt." But he knew that America would not settle for anything less than a "formal disavowal of the *Arabic*." Otherwise, Wilson explained, "the country would consider us 'too easy' for words."

For the second time in a month, Bernstorff took matters into his own hands. On October 5, he informed Lansing that Germany was yielding on all the important points—namely, that the submarine commander had attacked the *Arabic* against orders, that Germany "regrets and disavows" the action, and that a future indemnity would be worked out. His bosses back home, especially Imperial Navy officials, were incensed that he not only had gone far beyond his instructions, but had caved in without demanding a quid pro quo from the Allies. But Bernstorff believed it had to be done. He was sure that Germany would lose the war if the United States joined the Allies, which seemed very much possible if not probable if the current crisis was allowed to fester much longer. And with a major area of friction with Germany eliminated, he hoped Wilson would finally take on the bad behavior of the British.

At the moment, the Allies were in no mood to hear anything from Wilson or America. The war was not going well. And the Russians had suffered horrendous losses of late on the Eastern Front, so many that the Germans thought the tsar's government might be receptive to an offer of a separate peace. "There is no question that the Germans are well ahead," TR himself admitted. Hoping to turn the tide, the Allies launched a major offensive in late September on the Western Front. The French attacked at Champagne and the British at Loos.

Loos would be James Norman Hall's first major battle, a prospect both thrilling and terrifying. "'Ave you got yer wills made out, you lads?" asked the sergeant as Hall and his comrades marched. "You're a-go'n' to see a scrap presently, an' it ain't a-go'n' to be no flea-bite." Their immediate task, another officer told them, would be to "take over captured German trenches on the left of Loos." Losses had been heavy and they could expect furious German counterattacks. The trenches, Hall soon discovered, were filled with not only "souvenirs" of all kinds, including diaries, letters, canteens, rifles, and helmets, but also dead bodies, "literally blown to pieces, and it was necessary to gather the fragments in blankets." It was not long before Hall himself narrowly escaped death when a shell struck a dugout that he had just vacated, killing six of the seven occupants, most of them his close friends. "The worst of it," he later wrote, "was that we could not get away from the sight of the mangled bodies of our comrades." Not surprisingly, some cracked under the strain, including one who "picked up an arm and threw it" and then "sat down and started crying and moaning."

Back in Iowa, Hall's mother had become increasingly frantic. From the newspapers, she knew a battle was on and that her son, whom she had not heard from in weeks, was likely involved. "We can hardly stand this waiting to hear from you," she wrote in desperation. Hall, meanwhile, had sent off preprinted field postcards, carefully choosing the option "I am quite well," but none had made it across the Atlantic as of yet.

Somehow Hall managed to write a quick note to his mother and a longer, more revealing letter to his friend Roy Cushman. "I have lived a century in the past week," he wrote. He was "crawling with vermin," "filthy dirty," and had slept little while under a continuous bombardment. "I don't think men anywhere any time in the world's history have had to go through more terrible experiences or suffer greater hardships; and yet they stick to it with a cheerful determination that is absolutely magnificent." More than ever, he believed he was doing the right thing, although he now thought it would be a "miracle" if he survived. "Men don't count anyway," he explained. "It's the ideal which matters. I'm willing to die and can do so gladly if Germany can be defeated." And America, he believed, needed to understand that Germany *had to be beaten* "for the future happiness of all peace loving nations."

Hall's words would have warmed TR's heart, had he known of them. At least one American had not gone soft. "Life is not worth living unless it is also worth sacrificing," Roosevelt wrote an English friend that September. "America should be in this struggle." He still desperately hoped to get to the front someday, ideally with the volunteer division he had been organizing for months. Admittedly, he was still not in the best of shape and expected he would "break down" after thirty days from the prolonged strain of combat. Still, he was certain he would "more than pay for my keep up to that period."

In reality, he was not fit to do much more than observe, if a hunting trip to Canada that month was any indication. He managed to bag two moose with "good antlers," he told FDR, who had just returned from his own unsuccessful moose hunt in New Brunswick. Privately, TR was embarrassed by his performance. His shooting was terrible, his movements creaky, and his vision poor. "I shall never again make an exhibition of myself by going on a hunting trip," he announced. "I'm past it."

He was, he conceded, a "gouty old man," though he made no real attempt to lose weight or improve his physical fitness. In his mind, he believed he would be well enough to serve with honor when the time came. It was a hope that kept him going in a world he no longer recognized, where a horrid weakling like Wilson was admired ("What inspiration is this man Wilson to any boy?" he griped) and America had lost its heart.

To Addams, Woodrow Wilson was no weakling. His cool head had pulled the nation from the brink of the most devastating war in human history twice in four months, although her more jaded friend Carrie Chapman Catt believed "he should have shown more backbone at the beginning." But Addams knew that the President's winning streak would not last forever.

That her always unpredictable health forced her to the sidelines at such a crucial time was enormously frustrating. In August, an attack of bronchitis knocked her out of commission in Bar Harbor, where Mary Rozet Smith kept a close eye on her sometimes uncooperative patient. "She secretly thinks that she might stagger to New York," Mary informed Emily Balch, but that proved impossible. For the moment, Addams would have to keep abreast of peace developments through her correspondents and visitors.

Her recent preliminary idea of a behind-the-scenes delegation of private citizens working to broker peace was currently in limbo. Instead, the neutral conference/continuous mediation scheme was gaining momentum once again. In London, advocates continued their attempts to convert Edward Grey, who remained too savvy to reject them outright. In any event, he wrote Colonel House, any neutral conference would be entirely worthless without the participation of the United States.

To get such a commitment from America was the mission of Aletta Jacobs, the so-called Jane Addams of Europe, whose talks with the Dutch prime minister convinced her that her government would call a neutral conference once Wilson gave the green light. Balch, who privately thought Jacobs was especially intent "to have Holland . . . do this great thing," did her best to lay the groundwork for Jacobs to see Wilson after she arrived in the United States in late August. As a first step, the two women met with Lansing, who was completely unsympathetic if not hostile to the concept of continuous mediation through a neutral conference, especially with Germany ahead. "This was meddling in other people's affairs," the secretary of state told them. "The United States would never do anything like that." Besides, he argued that "nations in their international relations were purely selfish . . . they were never disinterested in any degree," America apparently included. When Balch countered with Roosevelt's involvement in ending the Russo-Japanese War ten years earlier, Lansing was scornful. His "absolutely amoral and cynical attitude" disgusted Balch, who could not believe such an individual, clearly pro-Allies, was now heading the State Department. Even House occasionally had his doubts about Lansing's Machiavellian sensibilities: "He believes that almost any form of atrocity is permissible provided a nation's safety is involved." House, meanwhile, also granted the two ladies an audience, with similar results, although he was smart enough to feign the "deepest sympathy with their general purpose."

Jacobs was getting nowhere. Worse, her mission was now threatened by the unwanted presence of a certain Rosika Schwimmer, who had taken it upon herself to traipse across the Atlantic with the British suffragist Crystal MacMillan, one of the peace envoys sent by the woman's congress, in tow, in the belief that Wilson should be seen by a full delegation "such as had visited the other neutrals." As usual, Schwimmer not only refused to be deterred by any objections, but somehow managed to get the International Committee of Women for Permanent Peace to cover her costs. Frantic cables telling her not to come arrived too late.

Jacobs had no love for Schwimmer and her headstrong ways. She did not want the strong-willed Hungarian in America potentially ruining her chance for an audience with Wilson, and she did not want her babbling to the press. Of course, Schwimmer promptly gave interviews after her arrival. "I hope," Jacobs wrote Addams from New York, "that you will and can come here to see these two firebrands" (Schwimmer/MacMillan). The two firebrands, meanwhile, were just as eager to talk to Addams. Once again, Mary intervened. Her patient now had pleurisy and traveling was out of the question, but they were welcome to come to Maine to see her, just as Jacobs had done already. In the meantime, the White House approved Addams's request that Wilson see Jacobs at noon on September 15. There was no talk of the two interlopers from Hungary and England tagging along.

Like Addams, Jacobs left the White House believing Wilson was on their side. "He was very kind and manlike as well as gentlemanlike," she wrote Addams a few hours later. "His answers were very *diplomatique*." With the international situation changing so rapidly, the President told her that he did not want to commit himself to any particular policy that might limit his options in the future. Nor could he "say a word" about peace at the moment. Of course, he did not inform her that he had already decided he was not only opposed to calling a neutral conference now but was not even sure that America would participate at the behest of another nation such as Holland. "It would necessarily depend on the occasion and on the whole European situation as it stood at the time of the call," he told Lansing.

By the end of September, reality had sent in. His *diplomatique* talk aside, Wilson was not going to do anything right now, especially while the Allies were mounting desperate offensives to turn the tide. Schwimmer was disgusted. "I loathe the neutrals more than the others," she bitterly complained. Other pacifists, such as Louis Lochner, were growing equally disillusioned. "People are getting so awfully callous regarding the war, and accept it as a matter of course," he lamented. Addams received further proof from a Maine woman, who wrote her that she was "surprised and almost dismayed at the hopeless, persistent prophecies of evil that I get from Christian people when I suggest thinking and talking Peace."

Still, Addams had no thoughts of channeling her energies into another cause. Along with the other pacifists, she continued to feel a strong moral obligation to do all she could to stop the carnage. And with the war barely into its second year, it still seemed possible that "sane and reasonable" people on both sides could somehow be reached. The worst outcome, Addams and the other pacifists believed, would be either side achieving a decisive victory. Such a result, Schwimmer argued, would lead to a "military peace—which means that after a generation war will begin again." Schwimmer had tried to make that very point to Wilson last year. "It is ignoring the psychology of the belligerent nations not to see that a decisive victory, an absolute defeat, would create such an arrogance on one side, and such a hatred on the other side, that all hopes for an everlasting peace would have to be abandoned," she warned him.

The question now was Wilson's role. Could anything be achieved without him? Veteran reformers like Addams recognized the importance of having the President on board. But should they wait politely on the sidelines for him to make a move, one that might never come? It was clear that their formal one-on-one conversations with Wilson, House, etc., while pleasant enough, were not accomplishing much. Crystal Eastman, the head of the New York branch of the Woman's Peace Party, suggested a different approach. "If we are to influence the head of the government, we must get the people to *want something*," she explained. "We ought to consider how the public can be got to feel and act."

Unlike future activists, most were too genteel to resort to angry protests or anything that might "embarrass" the President. Nor were they about to pursue extreme solutions such as the "sex strike" advocated by Marian Craig Wentworth, the feminist author of *War Brides*. Instead, they envisioned "mass demonstrations and rallies," circulating literature, anything to make the public sit up and take notice. Such an effort, of course, would require considerable sums of money, money that the conservative Carnegie peace people had but would never part with.

But another option had miraculously presented itself in the last few weeks. One of the richest men in America had just made a startling announcement that he would spend $10 million for peace and would "do everything in my power to prevent murderous, wasteful war in America and in the whole world." And this was no garden-variety tycoon, but a revolutionary genius. His name, known to every man, woman, and child in the country, was Henry Ford.

The creation of the Ford Motor Company in 1903, the development of the inexpensive yet reliable Model T five years later, the use of mass production techniques in his factories, and the introduction of the "$5 a day" concept (wages plus profit sharing, eligibility determined by "habits and conduct" of workers) had made Ford a household name. It had also made him extremely rich, with profits said to be close to $60 million by 1914 (about $1.5 billion today). The Model T was now an indelible part of the American landscape, so much so that Ford jokes and joke books had become all the rage. And the public seemed especially fascinated by the "sinewy, wiry," gray-haired Midwesterner who professed to care little for money, dressed unpretentiously, and preferred his wife's simple cooking to more sophisticated fare. The key to his success? "Find out something that everybody is after and then make that one thing and nothing else."

Ford was now a celebrity and the public was eager to hear what he had to say on a variety of subjects. Some already believed he should run for president. A few of his ideas were rather progressive for the time. He wanted cutting-edge technology at the new hospital he was building in Detroit and believed that drug addicts could be treated. He also believed Americans consumed too many calories, should "eat only when hungry," and should abstain from cigarettes, which he believed contained "poison." And he insisted that "employers must be taught the advantages of short hours and good pay." "I do not think that any man can do good work mentally and physically for more than eight hours per day," he announced.

At the same time, his intellectual interests were disturbingly narrow. The study of history, he believed, was worthless, as was art. "I wouldn't give five cents for all the art in the world," he told the writer Julian Street. Nor did Ford care for higher education or words longer than one syllable. His thinking, then, was often maddeningly concrete, simplistic ("there would be no hospitals . . . if people were temperate"), and superficial, except when it came to engineering principles.

The war in Europe, he concluded, was a disaster. In late August, he went public with a lengthy statement to the press. "I have prospered much," he wrote, "and I am ready to give much to end this constant, wasteful 'preparation.'" Preparedness, he believed, was "the root of all war," and he would have no part of the lucrative munitions trade. "I shall expect the sneers and condemnation of those whose business is war and of those who profit by war." A few weeks later, Ford announced that he was willing to spend $10 million on the cause. The key would be education of the American people. "They must learn how their taxes are used for military preparations in times of peace, only to be wasted along with their lives in times of war." And children must also be converted. "The first thing I would like to do is to tear out of the school histories the pages glorifying war," Ford explained. "Boys and girls now are taught that war is something to be proud of and that all soldiers are heroes. They are not shown the horrors of it, nor told the sordid facts about the selfish commercialism of the men who inspire it." As far as the current war, he believed it would end with "the uprising of the industrious people, those who have lost sons and brothers. Ninety-nine per cent of the world's population is made up of the industrious persons, and only one per cent of the people are parasites or money loaners."

Ford approved of the apparently pacific nature of the current administration in Washington, so much so that he met with the President on September 22. "This country ought to thank Providence that we have such a man," Ford proudly announced. The conversation was not especially fruitful, as Wilson soon discovered that "ideas took no root in his mind, which did not stir till you gave it a fact." Ford also saw Navy Secretary Josephus Daniels to discuss potential improvements in submarine technology and his current vague idea of a future fleet of wireless bombers, so terrifying that "nations would be afraid to engage in war." "I know that anything that we can imagine will happen," he told reporters. "Everything starts with our thoughts."

Ford's heart was in the right place, but he was obviously an eccentric and a sometimes unreliable individual (within days, he retreated from his $10 million peace promise). Still, every peace organization in the country was eager to spend his money. Already, Addams's associates made inquiries about getting her in to see him. Ford, they were told, was willing to talk to her, but he must not be "solicited for funds" under any circumstances.

Addams would have agreed to this stipulation, but she was still unable to travel. Her followers had begun to grow concerned. "May I take the liberty of entreating you to be very careful of your health, for we all need you," Julia Wales wrote her at the end of September. "I mean all this suffering world."

Chapter 8

PREPAREDNESS U.S.A.

OCTOBER 6–NOVEMBER 20, 1915

Our people are slowly, very slowly, waking.

—Theodore Roosevelt, November 1915

Even in the midst of depressing global developments, Americans had not forgotten how to laugh. In recent months, they had fallen in love with a young Englishman named Charlie Chaplin, whose brilliant comedic stylings and Little Tramp character in a string of popular silent movies had taken the country by storm. "Never was there such a popular player on the screens," one journalist observed. "There are Charlie Chaplin statuettes, Charlie Chaplin mustaches, Charlie Chaplin walking sticks and every other evidence of greatness. . . . He is the undisputed king of the film theatre today." *Shanghaied*, his eleventh two-reeler that year, opened in October, although his slapstick style continued to irritate some of the more conservative types. "The vulgarity of the Chaplin pictures cannot be denied," Heywood Broun remarked in a *New York Tribune* review. "They are a scathing indictment of public taste . . . and that is why we blush for shame in confessing that we laugh our head off whenever we see one."

If Chaplin allowed filmgoers to forget the world's troubles for thirty minutes, others saw the cinema as ideal for war-related propaganda. In September, the racist author Thomas Dixon, who had already managed to get *The Birth of a Nation* screened at the White House, once again reached out to his old acquaintance for possible encouragement and assistance for his latest project: an anti-pacifist/pro-preparedness polemic eventually titled *The Fall of a Nation*.

Not surprisingly, Wilson wanted nothing to do with the film. "There is no need to stir the nation up in favor of national defense," he curtly informed Dixon. "It is already soberly and earnestly aware of its possible perils and of its duty."

Roosevelt felt otherwise. That October, he enthusiastically praised the pioneering filmmaker J. Stuart Blackton, his Long Island neighbor, after attending a showing of his recently released *Battle Cry of Peace* at the Vitagraph on Broadway. "By George, those pictures drive home the truth that it should not be 'Americans for Americans,' but 'Americans for America!'" TR enthused. "They are the first primer, the public school and the college of education of Americans for preparedness."

Indeed, the film (unfortunately lost today) had taken New York by storm that fall, bolstered by endorsements from administration officials, including FDR and Lindley Garrison. That *Battle Cry* was rather heavy-handed propaganda, meant to be the *Uncle Tom's Cabin* of the era, did not seem to matter to audiences, who were subjected to a thirty-minute preparedness lecture that opened the film. What followed was a rather flimsy plot involving two families, the Vandergrifts and the Harrisons, meant to represent the peace and preparedness crowds. Too late the Vandergrift patriarch, tricked by a spy named Emanon ("No Name" spelled backward), realizes the error of his ways when an anonymous army launches a brutal invasion and attack on an unprepared New York. Critics marveled at the vivid scenes of "lower Manhattan in flames . . . in colors," "sinking of two American battle ships," machine-gunned citizens, bombs dropped on Times Square, and the mercy killing of one of the Vandergrift children by her mother to protect her from the "drunken soldiers." Lest the violence be too disturbing for 1915 audiences, the "victims of the invaders" later stepped out of character to show they weren't really dead after all.

Blackton insisted that the army was meant to represent no nation in particular, but the similarities to the German invasion of Belgium were inescapable. Germans in America such as Hugo Münsterberg, who had long believed Germany would have a better deal under a Roosevelt administration, were disillusioned by TR's support of the film and his later characterization of its opponents as "thoroughly bad Americans." The peace crowd, meanwhile, found *Battle Cry* just as disturbing. Pacifists, they noticed, were made to look stupid, clueless, and foolish at every turn, even holding peace meetings in the midst of the enemy's attack. It was hardly surprising that one wag thought the film deserved the title *The Trumpet Call of the Bull Moose*.

W ilson was not especially concerned with *Battle Cry*, which would not open in Washington until January. With the *Arabic* situation wrapped up satisfactorily and the always-simmering Mexican unrest quiet for the moment, his thoughts were on Edith. "Now," he wrote her, "we are free to be gay and happy!" He had now decided that he could not wait until mid-October to announce the engagement. "Is there anything to be gained by delay that is of sufficient importance to be weighed against the freedom that would be given me by an earlier announcement," he asked House, "freedom from all sorts of minor inconveniences and embarrassments connected with our seeing one another?" House did not stand in the President's way. "There is so much talk about him," the Colonel wrote in his diary. "The sooner the announcement is made and the marriage consummated the better for all concerned."

Others surrounding Wilson did not share House's view. More than a few Democrats, especially Joseph Tumulty, thought the President would be destroyed politically. The private secretary's loyalty to the memory of Ellen Wilson may have influenced his views, as did his probable sense that the future Mrs. Wilson did not especially care for his common background and Irish Catholic ways (Wilson had not helped matters by thoughtlessly informing Edith in advance that Tumulty would not approve of the match). Meanwhile, Navy Secretary Josephus Daniels and Postmaster General Albert Burleson were approached about talking sense into the President. Burleson thought it foolish to try to stop or delay the marriage. "It won't change five thousand votes," he insisted. And even five million votes would not have been enough to sway the smitten Wilson.

Accordingly, on the evening of Wednesday, October 6, Tumulty announced the engagement to the waiting press, with the warning that the news must be held until the morning papers. The marriage was not entirely a surprise to those in Washington who were paying attention to the society pages, which had dropped occasional hints about the President and Mrs. Galt. Almost immediately, Edith realized that her life of anonymity was over. Reporters weighed in on her "graceful, rather plump figure," her "fine white teeth," her nickname of "Sunshine" ("because of her cheerful disposition"), and her relation to Pocahontas. "I am of no importance," she tried to convince one persistent writer, "and the less the newspapers print about me at this time, the more I will appreciate their kindness, and so, I am sure, will the President."

Unfortunately for Edith, the unwanted attention worsened over the next forty-eight hours. The crowds and cameramen were everywhere during Friday's trip to New York with Wilson, her mother, and Wilson's Cousin Helen. Once again, the reviews were positive. "Isn't she stunning!" marveled one female onlooker. "Mrs. Galt is very handsome," conceded the *New York Tribune*. "And the world at large loves a good looking woman." Unbeknownst to the press, the President and Edith also picked out their engagement rings at Colonel House's apartment on Fifty-third Street from a selection sent up by the exclusive Fifth Avenue jeweler Dreicer & Company. The following day, the couple made another public appearance, this time at Shibe Park in Philadelphia at the second game of the World Series. Though both were baseball fans, observers noticed the two lovebirds paid more attention to each other than the action on the diamond. "They whispered and laughed and exchanged confidences," noted a Philadelphia newsman.

That Edith had passed her first public test did not mean that everyone approved of the marriage. The reaction of one German American was typical: "We all thought Wilson was devoting his days and nights to the terrible problems affecting the country and now we find he was courting a widow." The Progressive journalist William Allen White was also disillusioned that the President, who "had built himself up into the hero of a rather tragic, international scene . . . would let his personal affairs . . . obtrude so

Wilson and Edith Galt at Game 2 of the World Series at Shibe Park in Philadelphia, October 9, 1915. (Library of Congress: LC-B2- 3628-8)

ridiculously in a moment like this." To TR, Wilson's attitude appeared to be bordering on cavalier: "My wife is dead! Long live my wife!"

Ever the gentleman, the President informed Mary Hulbert of the engagement, although she did not receive the letter before the public announcement. Her response oozed with the usual helpless damsel-in-distress sentiments that Wilson found so bewitching. "The cold peace of utter renunciation is about me, and the shell that is M.A.H. still functions. It is rather lonely, not even an acquaintance to make the air vibrate with the veering warmth, perhaps of friendship. . . . Write me sometimes, the brotherly letters that will make my pathway a bit brighter." An exchange of letters continued into early 1916, mostly dealing with the Hulberts' avocado business in California and the need for the President to vouch for their good name. By that time, both she and Wilson recognized that their correspondence would have to end.

Hulbert may have largely disappeared from his life, but she remained an annoying Achilles' heel for Wilson, proof to his critics of the President's untoward dalliances with women. Within weeks of the engagement announcement, rumors began to surface that Wilson would soon face a "breach of promise suit." House, meanwhile, learned that rumors of the

"President's indiscretions" had even reached London. "There is a deliberate purpose to make the President appear before the country as a thoroughly immoral man," the Colonel wrote in his diary. "The most exaggerated stories are being told of him, none of them having the slightest foundation." Wilson bore it bravely, but the viciousness of his enemies shocked him.

As a man madly in love, he did not brood for long over such injustices. If anything, he was more obsessed with Edith than ever, to the point where some began to wonder whether she was proving to be a serious distraction. A recently installed private phone line between the White House and her home did not help matters. There was also the unavoidable question of the future Mrs. Wilson's influence on the President. Would she nudge Wilson toward peace? Addams did not think so. Other liberals fretted that her Southern upbringing would reinforce the President's less than enlightened attitudes toward African Americans. Of late, her family had even been incensed by the marriage of Edith's niece to a Panamanian.

Wilson tried to reassure her. "It would be bad enough at best to have anyone we love marry into any Central American family," he wrote Edith, "because there is the presumption that the blood is not unmixed, but proof of that seems to be lacking in this case."

House, ever strategic, had no intention of allowing Edith to stand between him and the President. He did his best to curry her favor, sending her a book of Wordsworth's poems. Still, the Colonel began to understand that Edith's role was larger than he anticipated, especially when he learned that Wilson had "shown her some of my European correspondence especially the cable gram I sent him regarding the *Lusitania*." A few weeks later, he had a "confidential talk" with Edith, who was in New York with Helen Bones. The gist of the conversation was that she should tune out those around her "urging her to influence the President" and "let the President alone to think out his problems in the future." This was House's way, and he recommended that she follow the same path. She also should watch what she said to "even the closest friends," but should "think aloud to the President and to keep nothing back." Edith agreed, although she may have questioned the purity of House's motives in offering such unsolicited advice about her relationship with her future husband.

House knew he needed to continue to have Wilson's ear. Edith was not likely to interfere, but her views, whatever they were, might place seeds of doubt in the President's mind. And it was now more essential than ever that Wilson and House should continue to approach the war situation as one mind, especially since House was now convinced that the time had come for a bold stroke.

He had broached such a notion during Wilson's post-engagement-announcement trip to New York. Like others, House realized that Germany had the advantage right now. If the Germans won, they might turn their attention to an unprepared United States, which would lack any viable backup. It was thus imperative that America not allow the Allies to lose. The Colonel's solution, then, was for America to "do something decisive . . . something that would either end the war in a way to abolish militarism or that would bring us in with the Allies to help them do it." The scheme appeared to be deceptively simple. First, the United States should discreetly determine whether the Allies would object to an outside "demand that hostilities cease" with a future free of militarism and navalism. If the Allies went along with this, the same offer would be tendered to Germany and the other Central Powers. Should they accept, House reasoned, "we would then have accomplished a master stroke of diplomacy." If not, their refusal would set off a chain reaction ultimately culminating in America joining the Allies. Wilson, according to House, was "startled" by his plan but did not reject it. And considering his surprising comment to House two weeks earlier that "he had never been sure that we ought not to take part in the conflict," especially if Germany was close to victory, he would not take much convincing.

House's grand scheme, of course, was not the impartial action favored by Addams or Bryan, especially since America apparently would make no move of any kind without the permission of the Allies. To House, this was justifiable. He was certain, as he put it, that "their cause" was "our cause," the war was a battle "between democracy and autocracy," and a failure to get in good with the Allies now might lead to postwar troubles of all kinds.

Lansing was easily won over, which pleased House immensely, although he occasionally wondered whether the secretary of state might eventually begin to resent House's enormous, yet unofficial, role in foreign policy. But Lansing was unlikely to make much of a fuss: according to Washington insiders like John Callan O'Laughlin, he had "absolutely no independence, and he is today as much Counsellor of the State Department as he was before his appointment to be Secretary of State."

Ultimately, Wilson chose not to stand in the way of House's superambassador fantasies. The President still trusted his unofficial adviser to represent his views abroad, far more than he trusted Lansing or his diplomats in London and Berlin. "I now have the matter in my own hands," House happily wrote in his diary, "and it will probably be left to my judgment as to when and how to act." He drafted a letter, one that might change the course of the war, to Sir Edward Grey on October 17, and then waited for Wilson's final approval.

The letter, the President believed, was "altogether right." Still, he had some misgivings. House's bold statement that "it would be necessary for us to join the Allies and force the issue" if the Germans refused to accept peace terms would not do. Instead, Wilson inserted a strategic "probably." "I do not want to make it inevitable quite that we should take part to force terms on Germany," he explained to House, "because the exact circumstances of such a crisis are impossible to determine."

House had to accept the change; of course, he had no choice. Besides, the British would be fools not to jump at the offer, one that House privately admitted would "practically . . . insure victory to the Allies."

Whether the Allies would be open to any peace talk remained a question. The fall offensive at Loos and Champagne had been especially bloody without accomplishing much of anything, making them all the more determined to try again in the spring.

James Norman Hall had survived Loos, although the "somewhat disorganized" state of mail from the battlefield meant that his family remained in the dark about his status well into October. "For the past month we have had a very interesting time of it," he wrote his mother. "Attacks and counter attacks day and night." Of the eight hundred men in his battalion who had crossed the Channel into France in May, only three hundred had not been killed or wounded. Thankfully, he was now out of the trenches and behind the lines attending a school of machine gunnery. "For of all the uncomfortable places on earth, trenches are certainly the worst," he admitted. "Being glorified earth-worms isn't so bad in summer; but at this time of year there isn't much to be said for the life."

Hall's time in the trenches would soon be at an end. His father was not well and he knew that he was needed at home. A request for a month's furlough was promptly denied. A discharge was an option, if it could be secured, but he was ambivalent about leaving. A few days before Thanksgiving in a water-filled trench at Hill 70, he was informed that he was going home (friends in Boston pulled the right strings to get him out—he was, after all, an American citizen). Back in America in early December, he told a *Boston Globe* reporter of the horrors he had seen and heard, the "Tommy's body nailed up against the side of an old barn" and the disturbed British sergeant who captured and then proceeded to slaughter twelve Germans.

Anyone reading the *Globe* article recognized that Hall had a unique and fascinating story to tell, one the war-hungry public would eat up. Not surprisingly, the prestigious *Atlantic Monthly* wanted him to write a series of articles about his experiences. The literary career that he had craved before the war seemed to be finally materializing. Yet he found himself strangely dissatisfied. Already, he began to think about returning to England to reenlist.

On his return, Hall could not help but be cheered by the intense anti-German feeling in Boston, similar to that in other places along the Eastern Seaboard. The German attempt to win the hearts and minds of Americans had continued to flounder, worsened by the recent execution of a British nurse, Edith Cavell, in Belgium in October, despite the efforts of American diplomat Brand Whitlock and others to save her. The by-the-book German authorities felt the sentence was appropriate since Cavell, along with others, had worked to smuggle Allied soldiers out of occupied Belgium into Holland. More rational German leaders realized that they had just handed the Allies yet another stick of propaganda dynamite. "Incredible stupidity!" lamented Admiral Müller in his diary.

The brutal death of Cavell, dubbed "Britain's Joan of Arc," horrified many Americans (the press rumor that she had been shot "while she lay in a faint on the ground" proved to be false, however). Germany, the *Boston Traveler* noted, had just added "one more to their list of shocking offences committed against humanity." Roosevelt agreed. "Such a deed," he maintained, "would have been utterly impossible in the days of the worst excitement during our Civil War."

Addams, while appalled, was uncomfortable with the fixation on Cavell's gender. "Every person, man or woman, killed in this war means as many inhuman acts committed. There should be no more talk over the execution of Miss Cavell than over similar shootings of men."

Addams realized that the Cavell case and other German blunders made it that much more difficult for peace efforts to gain traction in America. Stories of attempts to sabotage munition ships and facilities, along with suspected involvement in various Mexican intrigues, continued to mount, implicating the military and naval attachés of the German embassy, Franz von Papen and Karl Boy-Ed. Both were sent home, Von Papen later becoming a key figure in Hitler's rise to power eighteen years later. Once again, the administration chose to overlook Bernstorff's potential involvement with such shenanigans. Relations with Germany had to be preserved, House believed, and Bernstorff was "the best of the lot."

Bernstorff's position was safe for now, but he was under constant surveillance. This came as no surprise to him, although he apparently had no idea that the Secret Service had begun to tap his phones. It was not long before they discovered he was having an affair with a married American woman named Olive Moore White, who lived in an apartment across from Bernstorff's New York quarters at the Ritz (the Count's own wife, the American-born Jeanne Luckemeyer, had conveniently remained in Germany since the war began). To arrange their rendezvous and phone calls, the pair signaled availability by raising and lowering window shades. That other German officials were also carrying on with various American women soon became apparent. "A divorce lawyer," William James Flynn, the head of the Secret Service, later noted, "could have scanned our reports and found material enough to keep him busy for months." Whether Wilson knew is uncertain, but the surveillance would continue until January 1917.

The distrust and suspicion of the Fatherland further frustrated the Germans, whose hatred for America seemed to be growing by the day. In Berlin, Kaiser Wilhelm's prewar project—the statue-packed Siegesallee (Victory Avenue)—now also featured war booty. "Nearly every piece," noted an American observer, "be it aeroplane, submarine, or machine gun, is placarded: 'This was made in the United States.'" The kaiser, himself filled with bitterness toward America, refused to see James Gerard for months. Late that October, he finally granted the frustrated Amercian ambassador a meeting at the palace at Potsdam.

Clad majestically in military garb, the kaiser lectured Gerard about the U.S. partiality toward the Allies and its munitions sales. Like TR, his supposed "twin," the kaiser stood uncomfortably close to Gerard when speaking. Gerard then reminded him that Germany had sold weapons to combatants under similar circumstances, which somewhat pacified Wilhelm, who then drifted into a peculiar religious discussion. Was not the German success a clear sign that "God was on their side"? As far as peace was concerned, Wilson should not expect to be involved. "I and my cousins, George [King George V of England] and Nicholas [Tsar Nicholas II], will make peace when the time comes," he informed Gerard. And after the war, Americans should be aware that he "would stand no nonsense." Gerard was left with the distinct impression that Wilhelm viewed the "German, English and Russian peoples" as chessboard pawns and the war as little more than "a royal sport."

The kaiser's views notwithstanding, Bernstorff remained convinced that Wilson and the United States were very much essential factors in the war and the future of Germany. American pressure, he knew, could potentially accomplish what Germany could not: a relaxation of the crippling British blockade. The ambassador had continually dangled before his superiors in Berlin the promise that Wilson would finally turn his attention to the Allies once matters with Germany had been resolved, although the *Lusitania* negotiations continued to drag.

Politically, it made sense for the administration to protest against the continued Allied abuse of neutral rights. After all, American neutrality demanded that both sides be taken to task for their abuses. "There is not the slightest question," John Callan O'Laughlin wrote TR, "that England is maintaining a blockade that is illegal, that is discriminatory, and that works hardship upon our labor and industries." Even House agreed: "The British have gone as far as . . . possible in violating neutral rights, although they have done it in the most courteous way."

House, Lansing, and Wilson all believed that a stern note to the United Kingdom needed to go out, which was eventually dispensed in late October and made public a few weeks later. The British were then left with the question of how to respond. Their Washington diplomat Cecil Spring Rice thought concessions might be necessary. "The vital points for us are that this country should serve as a base of supplies and should not intervene by force, that is by convoy, to break the blockade," he wrote Foreign Secretary Edward Grey. "To obtain those ends we should be prepared to sacrifice a great deal." And Americans, the ambassador explained, could not be expected to blithely yield to British abuses solely based on the righteousness of their cause. "A large proportion of the American public have been brought up to make money and to make nothing else" (the perception of Americans as shallow materialists gleefully getting rich on European misfortunes was now widespread on both sides).

As the war progressed, Spring Rice himself was proving to be an unfortunate barrier to tranquil British-American relations. It was not simply his longtime friendship with TR (or what House called "his inclination to fraternize with the opposition"). Whether by temperament or untreated Graves' disease, Spring Rice had become disturbingly erratic in his behavior. When House initially attempted to broach the subject of a note to Britain, the ambassador launched into a diatribe about how Americans were quick to jump on the British when "our oil and copper shipments were interfered with" but had ignored far worse German transgressions of the "laws of God and man," and how Britain would never accept the American view of the blockade. Otherwise, it would be "all to the advantage of Germany whom you seem to favor." Nor did he wish to speak to any person in recent communication with Bernstorff or any other Germans. This was too much for the normally sphinxlike House, who told him bluntly that he "knew of no official anywhere who was serving his country as badly as himself." Mortified, Spring Rice replied that perhaps he should resign, to which House said that he should "use his own discretion as to that." Afterward, the Colonel discussed the matter with Wilson, who backed him up entirely and discussed potential suitable replacements. Spring Rice was not going anywhere, but he did his best to contain himself after this explosive confrontation with House (such confrontations with Americans were not uncommon; even a sympathetic editor admitted that he "never felt so much like throttling anyone" after a similarly charged conversation with Spring Rice). "He is a queer Sir Cecil," House maintained. Wilson agreed. "Some less childish man should take his place."

In London, Walter Hines Page was also the wrong man for the job, unable and unwilling to present the American case with forcefulness. The new note, the ambassador complained, not only lacked his input but was overly long, cold, and impersonal without a "word of thanks for courtesies or favours done us, not a hint of sympathy in the difficulties of the time." Wilson, who had already decided that Page was too enmeshed with the Allied cause to be of any value, should have canned him at this point, but he chose the more passive-aggressive approach of simply disregarding anything he had to say.

Regardless of their incompetence, neither Page nor Spring Rice could make or break the impact of the note. Its success would hinge almost entirely upon whether the British believed that the United States was prepared to back up its protest and hold them to the same "strict accountability" as Germany. But past experience had shown they had no real reason to fear American reprisals. And House's recent letter to Grey showed that the United States was not about to let the Allies lose the war. Accordingly, months would pass before the British bothered even to issue a response.

To Roosevelt, any British whining that American protests might "strike the weapon of sea power out of our hands" was ridiculous at best. Compared to the Germans, the British were clearly getting the better of America's neutrality deal, especially since the Allies would soon receive a $500 million loan administered by J.P. Morgan & Company (Henry Ford, meanwhile, promised to yank his considerable funds out of any bank that participated). But the British did not entirely see things that way. Americans, they believed, did not understand their struggle. And TR soon discovered that they were hypersensitive to even the mildest of criticism.

He had written yet another "wake up America" article for the *Metropolitan Magazine* that fall, this time including what he believed to be an innocuous paragraph asking his readers to learn from the British failure to adequately prepare, a view strongly advanced in one of his favorite books of late, F. S. Oliver's *Ordeal by Battle*. "After a year of war," Roosevelt wrote, "wealthy England . . . has failed to do her duty as Germany and Austria, as Russia, France, Serbia, Montenegro, and Italy have done theirs. Relatively to her population she has put an army of utterly inadequate size into the field, compared with what the other powers have done." The *Metropolitan* was not widely circulated in Europe, but the comment soon found its way into the pages of *The Times* of London and other periodicals.

That TR, a presumed staunch friend of the Allies, had made such a statement did not sit well with the British. Grey in particular was especially displeased. Roosevelt's words, he believed, would resurrect the nasty charge that the United Kingdom had contributed less to the war than her French and Russian allies. "It is really unfair to compare our efforts in numbers of men with those made by the Continental nations," Grey wrote Spring Rice. "They had prepared large Armies before the war." Nor did they have to contend with the needs of the powerful British navy, said to require the work of two million men on the home front, or the tens of thousands needed to keep the coal mines operating. That Britain had still managed to put one million men on the Continent was an impressive feat, one that he felt TR ought to recognize.

Grey's words were intentionally leaked to Roosevelt, who was frankly puzzled by the extreme reaction. Perhaps naïvely, he had not expected that "it would be read in England" (also in France, as it turned out). In any event, he insisted his essential point was to scold America, not the Allies, which he soon explained in a letter to the *New York Tribune*. And, as he reminded Grey, the British press had left out key sentences that might have softened the blow, such as "If England has not done well, she has done infinitely better than we would have done." Still, he did his best to atone by offering to write a public letter that would emphasize "the great work" performed by each of the Allies, an idea they liked but ultimately rejected. A few months later, TR went a step further by "correcting" the offending paragraph in a collection of his recent writings, *Fear God and Take Your Own Part*. Instead of suggesting that Britain was still militarily deficient "after a year of war," he now stressed that it had taken them a year to get up to snuff.

Privately, Roosevelt was contemptuous of the backlash. "The silly English," he noted, "had their poor feelings hurt" and seemed "rather jumpy." It was especially irritating since he had championed the Allied cause, at times at considerable political risk, since the war began. The episode reinforced his belief that the British ultimately did not understand Americans. "The average Englishman down at the bottom of his heart feels that the American is an alien," he observed. "I think the Englishman is right."

As much as TR despised Wilson, he could appreciate the President's increasingly difficult problem of contending with touchy Allies and an angry Germany (the other Central Powers were of minimal concern). It was now clear that no matter how "neutral" Wilson tried to be, neither side would ever be entirely satisfied. For now, each was willing to do what it took to maintain cordial relations with America. But a day of reckoning might lie in the future when one or even both sides would not be quite so pliable.

That day might never come, provided the war ended in the next six to twelve months, either by military victory or some kind of negotiated peace. The latter remained Addams's goal, even though she saw the considerable difficulty of trying to get Wilson—the "great original do nothing," in the words of one disillusioned pacifist—to budge from his cautious wait-and-see perspective.

By the fall of 1915, few would have blamed her if she had gracefully stepped back from high-profile peace work. Her public stature had taken a serious beating, thanks to the "drunk soldiers" comment, which she found difficult to shake no matter how many explanations she offered. And disapproval from many an old friend and ally remained significant. "So many around her," Louis Lochner observed that October, "are telling her that this thing must be fought to a finish, and that fighting to a finish will rid the world once [and] for all of war. You can imagine what a tremendous strain that must be upon her."

Addams also had to wonder how her views might affect Hull-House, whose finances were extremely shaky because of additional aid to the unemployed during the previous winter. Fortunately, wealthy friends like Anita McCormick Blaine, the daughter of Cyrus McCormick, the inventor of the reaper, were not scared off by recent attacks. After receiving a thousand-dollar donation from Blaine, a grateful Addams thanked her and enclosed a copy of a recent sympathetic *New York Evening Post* story "which states my position in the grossly exaggerated bayonet story."

In a post-*Lusitania* America, pacifism was becoming a risky cause to embrace, which woman's suffrage leaders such as Carrie Chapman Catt understood well. As much as she supported peace efforts, she could not help fearing that the movement might taint the suffrage cause, up for consideration in New York, New Jersey, Massachusetts, and Pennsylvania that fall. Catt intentionally kept Rosika Schwimmer from speaking in New York and was probably relieved that Addams's still fragile health kept her from doing much in the way of campaigning. Yet Addams remained a favorite whipping girl for the antisuffrage crowd. When Oswald Garrison Villard suggested in a Philadelphia suffrage debate that Addams would be ideal for a cabinet position, his female opponent was quick to remind the gathering of her ridiculous "peace at any price" beliefs and silly statements about the courage of soldiers.

Suffrage supporters were hopeful for a breakthrough that fall. They were encouraged that Wilson himself had announced that he would cast a vote for suffrage in New Jersey. Stockton Axson, the brother of Wilson's late wife, thought it a shrewd political move. "You have taken the wind out of Roosevelt's sail," Axson wrote the President. "But it is funny, the way the suffrage 'leaders' assume that you must now be for the Constitutional amendment." (The proposed Susan B. Anthony amendment, as it was called, had failed to gain much traction to date.) And Wilson had certainly not changed his mind on that issue, which Alice Paul viewed as far more important than a state-by-state strategy.

Nevertheless, the support of Wilson and several cabinet members stood

in stark contrast to reactionaries such as William Howard Taft, who pomp-
ously claimed that votes for women would "increase the proportion of the
hysterical element of the electorate to such a degree that it will be injurious
to the public welfare." Such views were not uncommon even among women,
including a forty-five-year-old New Yorker named Anne Lynch, who took
it upon herself to question ladies walking down Broadway whether they
believed in suffrage. Those who answered in the affirmative were promptly
socked. "Every woman needs a good beating once a week," she announced,
"and these crazy suffragists need one every day. If their husbands are not
men enough to do it I will." The police eventually took Lynch into custody,
but not before she warned the sisterhood of the dangers certain to accompany suffrage: "You don't know how lucky you are to have a man bringing
in the money. If you vote you'll have to go to work with the men."

The more mainstream suffragists did their best to show that votes for
women would not upset the normal social order. In fact, they even claimed
that many of the movement's leaders were adept at the womanly arts of
housekeeping and cooking. "Many of our suffrage campaigns," Catt announced, "have been financed by cookbooks." They also argued that plenty
of women very much wanted the chance to vote. "If my husband opposed
suffrage, I wouldn't feed him for a month," one New York woman told a
reporter. "I am tired of having laws made by men handed out to me," a
seventy-four-year-old complained. "I have more brains in my heels than
some of the men have in their heads."

Unfortunately, not enough men agreed. "They ought to take care of
children and bring them up instead of getting bees in their bonnets" was
an all-too-common view. Much to the chagrin of Addams, woman's suffrage failed to pass in a single state that fall. To Catt, the result was not
entirely unexpected. "In this reactionary period when nobody seems to be
able to see straight," she wrote Addams, "we probably did very well."

Much of the press, Addams believed, was contributing to the current
reactionary climate. She had grown disillusioned with what she
called its "unscrupulous power," especially when it came to the peace movement. The average American, she feared, still did not have a strong grasp

of what she and other pacifists were trying to achieve. They often found themselves aggressively questioned as to what they would have done if they had been in France under assault by the German army. "We could only reply that we were not criticizing France, that we had every admiration for her gallant courage, but that what we were urging at that moment was the cessation of hostilities and the substitution of another method."

Addams did her best to promote that message. In mid-October, a public "manifesto" under the auspices of the International Committee of Women for Permanent Peace was released to the press, signed by Addams, Emily Balch, and the three European members of the committee who had recently journeyed to America: Aletta Jacobs, Schwimmer, and Crystal Mac-Millan. As "conveyors of evidence," the five women argued that their multiple visits with foreign leaders during the spring and summer left no doubt that the "belligerent Governments would not be opposed to a conference of neutral nations," ideally including Spain, Switzerland, Holland, the Scandinavian countries, and the United States. To strengthen their argument, they disclosed several anonymous supportive quotes from their interviews, including one from a leader identified as one "whose name ranks high, not only in his own country, but all over the world" (British Foreign Secretary Sir Edward Grey).

The manifesto then attempted to puncture the widely held belief that peace terms could not be offered as long as one side was losing, since "the proposed conference would start mediation at a higher level than that of military advantage." Most important, it would break with the tired old diplomatic traditions that Addams had come to disdain by including representatives of an international bent far more concerned with "common service of a supreme crisis" than promoting parochial local interests. The neutrals, the manifesto warned, could no longer "absolve themselves from their full share of responsibility for the continuance of war" and needed to act now.

The committee claimed that three of the five neutral European nations were willing to go forward, although America remained a question mark. Whether the ringing words of the manifesto could succeed in its goal of waking up the "White House and . . . American public opinion" remained to be seen. "We think the United States, as the largest neutral country, ought to be one of the group," Addams insisted. "We have not asked President Wilson to call the commission together, but we do want him to participate in the creation of it once it is called." She hopefully forwarded the manifesto to Wilson and House, who acknowledged its receipt but offered no additional encouragement. Both saw far more promise in House's recent secret outreach to Grey.

Addams believed the President would eventually see the light. But with every day Wilson was finding it harder to present himself as sharing the same mindset as the pacifists, especially when they learned of the administration's formal proposals for army and navy increases. Navy Secretary Josephus Daniels recommended an expenditure of $500 million to expand the fleet of battleships, cruisers, submarines, and destroyers over the next five years. War Secretary Lindley Garrison's plan was even more startling: an increase in the regular army from about 108,000 to 142,000, along with the creation of a 400,000 reserve to be known as the Continental Army, one that would reduce the significance of the National Guard. Congress would ultimately make the final call, but Wilson clearly wanted some preparedness legislation passed.

Much to the horror of the peace advocates, the administration seemed willing to not only cave to the militarists and what would today be called the "defense industry," but also saddle the common people with a future burden of higher taxes. And a military and naval buildup, Addams and her associates feared, would be impossible to roll back once begun. "Militarism is like that popular confection known as 'crackerjack,' the motto of which is, 'The more you eat, the more you want,'" Louis Lochner noted. "It differs only in this—that even the most ravenous of youngsters will finally stop wanting crackerjack, while I have yet to find the militarist who is satisfied with the state of preparedness at any given point."

Addams was baffled by Wilson's leap into the preparedness camp. Such momentous decisions, she believed, should not be made when the country was too panicked to think clearly. In late October, she and other Woman's Peace Party officers dashed off a letter to Wilson, explaining that "we believe in real defense against real dangers but not in a preposterous 'preparedness' against hypothetical dangers." A military and naval buildup at present, they argued, would set off a chain reaction in other countries, who would "fear instead of trust us," and might very well "disqualify" him from a significant role in brokering peace.

Wilson believed their fears were unwarranted. Still, he remained sensitive to the political importance of Addams and other liberals in the pacifist movement, especially with an election a year away. He did his best to try to persuade them that he had not suddenly morphed into a saber-rattling Woodrow Roosevelt. His greatest desire, he assured Addams, was to "follow a wise and conservative course." And House skillfully played his part to further convince them that Wilson had not abandoned peace for preparedness. After meeting with House on October 25, the pacifist David Starr Jordan wrote his wife that the talk "strengthened my faith in the President." Nor should the peace forces fear the current military proposals, Jordan explained, "spread over six years and the disarmament of Europe would mean its abandonment." As for House, Jordan was impressed, finding him "soft-voiced, quiet, direct and amazingly well-informed."

Wilson was not the same president who had decisively squelched preparedness talk last December. Addams knew it, as did Roosevelt, who could not help but view it as a personal vindication. TR believed, and perhaps correctly, that he had "been the main factor in forcing Wilson to eat his own words." It was politically driven, he believed, but it was better than nothing. Perhaps Wilson finally was beginning to grasp that his long held contention that "unless America prepares to defend itself she can perform no duty to others."

Roosevelt still held no illusions that the country was ready to embrace his own take on America's role in the war and the world at large. One of his major talking points of late—universal service based on the Swiss and Australian systems—had converted few followers. More than ever, he was convinced that "the bulk of our people care for nothing but money-getting, and motors, and the movies, and dread nothing so much as risk to their soft bodies or interference with their easy lives." The manliness that he so prized seemed to be dead in the modern world of 1915. The signs seemed to be everywhere: the "Safety First" and "Thank God for Wilson" buttons some had begun to wear, the Harvard men talking up peace, even the "dissemination of pacificist literature" in the Boy Scouts.

TR's irritability with his fellow Americans matched his own personal frustrations about his physical decline. When his friend Charles Washburn visited him that fall, he was surprised to discover that Roosevelt believed that he could not take on a new historical book project because of the travel involved. "He recognized that there are some limitations to his capacity for work—something new for him," Washburn later recalled. TR had deteriorated, he sadly believed, into a "fat, rheumatic, blind old man," one whom the public listened to periodically but just as often tuned out. "Unless I write very briefly and along broad lines people do not read what I have to say," he admitted.

His children picked up on his depression, although their own tribulations—be they Alice's shocking new "pantalettes," Kermit's unhappiness in his banking job, or Quentin's involvement with the Harvard football team—provided a welcome distraction. And his wife, Edith, now mostly recovered from her surgery, remained the rock in his life. Like newlyweds, they took romantic boat rides together and spent evenings by the fire. "We sit and read," TR told Kermit's wife, Belle, "and she looks so pretty and charming that now and then I have to get up and make love to her—which is rather absurd on the part of a gouty old man." Edith, meanwhile, remained invested in her husband's work, so much so that the book title *Fear God and Take Your Own Part* was her idea.

As much as Roosevelt despaired about his influence, preparedness was now part of the public consciousness and his hated adversary had taken baby steps to embrace the cause and put words into action. Wilson had already met with the important movers and shakers of the Senate and House Military and Naval Committees, but his biggest and perhaps riskiest move to date lay ahead: his official "coming out" party for preparedness—a major address, or what Tumulty called a "National Defense Speech," to be made at the Biltmore Hotel in New York on November 4 to celebrate the fiftieth anniversary of the Manhattan Club, an influential Democratic social organization.

That Edith was already in New York "selecting gowns for her trousseau" made the occasion that much more sweet. She had hinted that she wanted to be present for the speech, but the President was not especially enthusiastic about the idea. If anything, the interest in even the most mundane of their doings had failed to dissipate. "Washington housewives are complaining that the President's calls at the Galt home delay their dinners," one reporter noted. "Delivery boys with wagonloads of urgently needed provisions are attracted by the throngs of nurse-maids, school children and strollers waiting for a glimpse of the couple as they start on their afternoon ride, and the deliveries are invariably late." Besides, Wilson told his fiancée, the speech was likely to be fairly dull, since he had decided to read it, "for prudence sake," rather than speak from memory and extemporaneously. Still, the President planned to see her beforehand. "To-morrow," he wrote her the day before, "I shall hold you in my arms and tell you how deeply and tenderly I love you and with what a passionate longing I have missed you these long drawn days in this empty town, but I cannot wait till then."

Within moments after his afternoon arrival in New York, he was taken to the Hotel St. Regis for a happy reunion with Edith for a few hours, before heading to House's apartment. Later that evening, while she took in a play, *The New York Idea*, Wilson headed to the Biltmore to schmooze with Democrats, some of them Tammany types like Al Smith, the new sheriff of New York County and future presidential candidate. A sumptuous "Buffet Présidentiel" followed, including oysters, oxtail soup, lamb, guinea fowl, turtle, salad, and a variety of wines and liquors. Not until almost midnight did Wilson get up to speak. That the President's thirty-minute speech barely deviated from the copy supplied in advance was immediately noted by the press present. They were also surprised to see that Wilson was apparently reading his address from shorthand, a rather valuable skill he had picked up years before.

America, he told the gathering, was now facing "new things about which formerly we gave ourselves little concern." While "there is no fear amongst us," some form of preparation was necessary, "not for war, but only for defense." This did not mean the massive military buildup that Addams and her friends feared but "an army adequate to the constant and legitimate uses of times of international peace." It would also be advisable to develop "a great body of citizens who have received at least the most rudimentary and necessary forms of military training . . . ready to form themselves into a fighting force at the call of the nation." He then reviewed the proposals to go before Congress: the increase in the regular army, the naval expansion, and the Continental Army reserve that he promised would not replace the National Guard (some Southerners were already fearful that the Continental Army units in their section might be largely staffed by "negroes"). "Does it not conform to the ancient traditions of America?" he asked. "It represents the best professional and expert judgment of the country."

The response of the thousand-person audience, likely ready for a nap after a heavy meal and several speeches, was subdued. It was not until the final moments of his address that Wilson finally caught fire. He transitioned to a discussion of an issue of "grave concern in recent months," the voices of certain Americans "which spoke alien sympathies, which came from men who loved other countries better than they loved America." The crowd suddenly erupted with cries of "Bravo!" Some began waving the miniature flags adorning each table. The statement was not as blunt as TR's ongoing battle against disloyal "hyphenated Americans," but it clearly struck a nerve. "These voices have not been many," the President admitted, "but they have been very loud and very clamorous." A few minutes later, the speech was over and Wilson was on his way back to House's apartment.

The next day, they lunched at the home of the President's wealthy friend Cleve Dodge in Riverdale, where House was annoyed by Wilson's loose lips at the table. "He said the day he got out of office, the first thing he would like to do would be to go out and shoot a reporter or two," House recorded in his diary. From there, they proceeded to Pennsylvania Station, where they nearly ran over an eight-year-old urchin named Mario Passi, saved by a quick-thinking Secret Service man. "I ain't hurted," the child told reporters.

Wilson's speech seemed to win over the majority of the public, soon to be made even more jittery by the report of nine Americans killed in yet another submarine attack. Heading for New York from Naples, the Italian liner *Ancona* was sunk on November 8 by a submarine under the Austro-Hungarian flag, later discovered to be secretly commanded by a German officer. The Austro-Hungarian government ultimately yielded to every American demand and agreed to pay an indemnity, but the incident seemed to confirm to many that the President's reasonable preparedness was a sensible approach. Even some pacifists, at least those of the more conservative bent such as Samuel T. Dutton of the New York Peace Society, approved. "What Mr. Wilson proposes," he noted, "would not be the scheme we would expect from Theodore Roosevelt."

TR would not disagree. He and other big army/big navy proponents saw the administration's proposals as woefully insufficient, "as absurd as Jefferson's gunboat plan [a much criticized attempt to use smaller and less expensive vessels to protect America's harbors in the early 1800s]." "Either we need to prepare or we do not," Roosevelt insisted. "If we do then we should prepare adequately." The regular army, he argued, should be 250,000, the navy should be second in the world, and the Continental Army idea ("an inefficient rival to the National Guard") should be tossed in the trash. He also took great pleasure that one of Wilson's postspeech comments defending his program alluded to the same biblical reference that TR himself had used in a recent article. Both men—purely by coincidence, unless Wilson was secretly reading Roosevelt's every word—had quoted verses from the Book of Ezekiel referring to the watchman's need to "warn the people" when the "sword came," and the people's responsibility to heed the call.

The story gave the public a good laugh, but the biblical scholar Bryan did not find it quite so amusing. He was not surprised that TR would look to the Old Testament for inspiration since "he would class Christ with the mollycoddles," a charge Roosevelt termed a "blasphemous falsehood." But Bryan could not understand why Wilson, "a Presbyterian elder," would "pass over the new gospel, in which love is the chief corner stone." Besides, Bryan argued, both men were interpreting the passage wrong. The verses were referring to an "attack actually made" and not "preparation against imaginary dangers. . . . What the world needs today is a Pentecost, not an Armageddon."

That Bryan seemed to be at increasing odds with Wilson could only please Republicans dreaming of a Democratic split in 1916 ensuring a GOP landslide victory. Some said Bryan could still sway 3.5 million fanatical voters, such as the "bewhiskered farmer" who so admired the Great Commoner that he planted a kiss on him after a recent appearance in Kansas. Bryan disliked the President's Manhattan Club speech as much as

Roosevelt, but for far different reasons. Wilson was breaking with precedent, he believed. America had "won its position in the world without resorting to the habit of toting a pistol or carrying a club. Why reverse our policy at this time?" And the United States should be "setting an example" rather than behaving in such a way to "encourage the nations of Europe in their fatal folly." Still, Bryan insisted there was no discord with the President. Privately, Wilson was not happy with his former secretary of state's comments.

Addams and other pacifists shared Bryan's views. Wilson, they believed, was making a colossal mistake. He had sacrificed his principles by failing to stand up to the militarists. It was also questionable whether he would benefit politically. "If, as the militarists assert, the country is in dire peril of attack, the President's proposals are ridiculously inadequate to meet the menace of the situation," the Reverend John Haynes Holmes, a Unitarian minister and Addams's peace colleague, boomed from his Church of the Messiah pulpit in New York. "If, as the pacifists contend, the country is safer from attack today than at any other time for a half century past, his proposals are ridiculously unnecessary."

The pacifists could not bring themselves to break with Wilson just yet. Still, they realized matters were reaching a tipping point. The President had refused to consider a conference of neutrals. Now he was supporting a military and naval buildup. If they would not directly attack Wilson, they recognized the need to immediately redouble their efforts to educate him and the public. Holmes and other Henry Street forces soon gathered to create a new antimilitarism organization, which went through several name changes before settling on the American Union against Militarism. And there were already plans under way for peace demonstrations and an onslaught of telegrams to the White House on November 8, followed four days later by David Starr Jordan's meeting with Wilson.

Louis Lochner, who would accompany Jordan to the White House, was hopeful Jordan would get results. After all, Wilson and Jordan knew each other from academia (both had been college presidents), although Jordan was far more well traveled than Wilson, with a deeper background in European affairs. Wilson granted them forty minutes, while they explained continuous mediation, reiterated Addams's European findings (of which

Wilson was well aware), and preached the gospel of a neutral conference. Wilson, Lochner wrote afterward, "kept wiping his glasses with his handkerchief," as he listened, but soon began to punch holes in their presentation. The other neutral countries could potentially "outvote" the United States in any conference. And the Allies "might object to mediation as a partisan measure." Jordan provided additional arguments until Wilson finally informed them that he had a cabinet meeting scheduled. He shook their hands, at which time Lochner took the occasion to ask a pointed question. "Then I may take the message with me that you will act?" The President was too clever to respond either positively or negatively. "No, that is for me to say when the right moment, in my judgment, arrives," he replied.

Afterward, Lochner wrote up a summary of the meeting. Wilson seemed more "mellow," more receptive than he had been in his talk with Addams during the summer. Jordan, who had known the President for twenty-five years, agreed. "Usually he was difficult to talk to, and rather haughty." On the other hand, Wilson gave absolutely no indication that he would adopt their plan, hardly surprising since he had recently authorized House's secret outreach to Grey. In fact, Lochner's main takeaway was that Wilson "has no plan outside of a fight to the finish, and secondly . . . he is afraid of what England, which he evidently regards as fighting the battle of democracy, may say to the proposal."

Neither pacifist was willing to publicly criticize the President; in fact, Jordan still saw him as "the most precious asset of the cause of peace." Lochner was not quite so effusive. Wilson was not a lost cause, he believed, but he would do nothing unless he faced public pressure far beyond what he had encountered in the past. Such a PR campaign would take vast sums of money. Their best bet, Lochner reasoned, was Henry Ford.

Ford had not been shy about continually expressing his unhappiness with the war and preparedness talk, much to the chagrin of TR. The celebrity automaker, Roosevelt had recently written to an official of the competing Packard company, "would make a good Chinese citizen of the old type" and "ought to wear a pigtail." More important for the peace crowd was Ford's dramatic promise that summer to invest his millions to end the war, although his handlers continued to try to stop their impulsive boss from doing any such thing.

Peace activity had begun to intensify around Ford's stomping grounds in Detroit, thanks to a plucky young woman named Rebecca Shelly (she later changed the spelling to Shelley), whose street corner speeches had attracted attention. Shelly was a University of Michigan graduate and former high school teacher whose minister father shaped her deep feelings about religion and peace. And like many other young women of the time, she had been strongly influenced by Addams. She had never forgotten when university officials refused to allow Addams to speak about suffrage on campus. "On that day," she later recalled, "I became a militant suffragist." She had quit her teaching job to join the American delegation to The Hague for the women's congress back in the spring, although she was just as interested in seeing her German fiancé, whom she had met during an earlier trip to Germany.

After failing in an attempt to see Ford, she began to organize meetings to invigorate the rather sluggish peace scene in Detroit. Addams, still feeling unwell, was not inclined to do much for her. Instead, Schwimmer, whose iconoclastic style Shelly had begun to find more appealing, spoke at a rally in early November, as did Lochner. All were eventually hoping to see Ford. Like TR, the industrialist had gone to visit the Panama-Pacific Exposition, where onlookers were thrilled to see Ford and his friend Thomas Edison take in the sights together.

In the meantime, Shelly and Schwimmer reached out to Reverend Samuel Marquis, an Episcopal minister and Ford friend who appeared at one of their peace meetings and would soon be put in charge of Ford Motor Company's "Sociological Department," which was designed to "improve" the lives of employees through close observation of their personal behavior and habits. They got nowhere, but someone, either Shelly or Schwimmer, got in touch with Ralph Yonker of the *Detroit Journal*, who knew Ford fairly well. Yonker talked to Ford when he returned and told him about a Hungarian pacifist who had seen the heads of Europe recently and now wanted to see him. The ever mercurial Ford promptly agreed, and Schwimmer was given an appointment at the Ford factory for 11:00 a.m. on Wednesday, November 17.

When she arrived, Schwimmer was disappointed to discover that she would not have Ford to herself. Marquis was there, as were Ford's attorney and others leery of her influence. At lunch, she was more encouraged that Ford was talking the pacifist talk as skillfully as she, at least until he abruptly decided to offer his interpretation of the cause of the war. "The German-Jewish bankers caused the war," he announced. "I can't give out the facts now, because I haven't got them all yet, but I'll have them soon." Her heart sank. Did he know she was Jewish?

Marquis then tried to get her to weigh in on the war's cause, but she refused. Ford then returned to a fairly coherent discussion of the war, occasionally interrupted by identical references to evil "German-Jewish bankers" or one in particular who had caused the war.

That a man who distrusted higher education would espouse such idiocies was not surprising, although casual anti-Semitism in various forms was hardly uncommon in 1915 (just a few weeks earlier, TR had alluded to the "considerable number of Jews" in the pacifist movement). Ford's unhinged views would grow more extreme in the years ahead, but Schwimmer would later claim that he never again repeated them in her presence. Perhaps this was true; more likely, Schwimmer felt Ford's anti-Semitism was a small price to pay to maintain a relationship with one of the richest men in America if not the world.

Schwimmer managed to do her sales pitch, casually throwing out Addams's name (which counted far more than her own) and the important work done by the women since the spring. The liberal reformer Frederic Howe, appointed by Wilson as the commissioner of immigration of the Port of New York, was also present and would later claim that Ford was ambivalent. If he was, he had changed his mind (again) by the time Schwimmer was preparing to leave. Come back tomorrow, he told her. And let me see the statements of the European statesmen in your black bag that you talked so much about. E. G. Pipp, another Detroit newspaperman and Ford friend who may have been at the meeting, thought Schwimmer still needed all the help she could get to succeed. Pipp wired Addams asking her to vouch for Schwimmer's "work at the Hague Conference as you observed it."

The next day, Schwimmer traveled to Ford's home in Dearborn, along with Louis Lochner, who had rushed back to Michigan at her request for an appointment with Ford that proved to be the figment of a deranged individual's imagination. When they arrived, Ford sent Schwimmer to talk with his wife, Clara, and then took Lochner and a reporter on a tour of his new tractor facility. He babbled about a variety of topics, including the evils of tobacco and alcohol, hiring ex-cons, his wonderful tractors, but nothing about peace. By this point, Lochner began to wonder if the whole trip had been a waste. Finally, Ford pulled him aside and grilled him about Schwimmer's talking points of the day before: a neutral conference and continuous mediation. This was the moment Lochner had been waiting for. Ford's money, Lochner told the Michigan mogul, could get the conference off the ground, at least until the U.S. Congress was ready to allocate the necessary funds. In the meantime, why not come to New York to talk with some of the leading lights in the peace movement?

Ford was sold. The idea of doing something bold, something concrete, was irresistible. "There is really one word to [describe] what we should do," he later explained. "I think the better word is not 'peace,' which is a negation. The better word is 'construction.' That is what every good movement is, everything worthwhile—it is construction." Meanwhile, his wife had succumbed to the persuasive Madame Schwimmer. Clara Ford was far from a public woman; in fact, she supposedly "gasped" when Schwimmer first suggested she get involved in the peace movement. But she was soon persuaded by Schwimmer's arguments that she had "assurances that every neutral nation is willing to partake in a conference for bringing peace" and was only waiting for the word from America. She was less receptive to Schwimmer's suggestion that she and Addams make a pilgrimage to talk peace with Wilson's fiancée, Edith.

Lunch with the Fords and their son, Edsel, followed, highlighted by Papa Ford's insistence that the poor were to blame for their predicament. Afterward they listened to Edsel drum along to a tune on the phonograph and then toured Ford's soon to be completed mansion, Fair Lane. As the hours passed, Schwimmer and Lochner sensed they had hit the jackpot. Ford not only trusted them both but was going to open up his wallet. It was eventually decided that Clara Ford would go public for peace and donate $10,000 to launch a mothers' telegram campaign, one that would ironically involve the childless Addams. Thousands of wires, all under Addams's name, would be sent to every conceivable women's organization: "suffrage organizations and anti-suffrage . . . lodges, granges, literary societies, Catholic, Jewish, Protestant societies, to Campfire Girls and college alumnae, to the National Daughters of the American Revolution and to debating clubs in the backwoods of Maine." The message would be simple. Send a wire to Wilson, "for the sake of all the anxious mothers," appealing to him to support a neutral conference "dedicated to finding a just settlement of the war."

For the cash-poor pacifists, the $10,000 gift, to be carried to New York by Rebecca Shelly and then handed over to Addams and the Woman's Peace Party, was a godsend, although Addams "positively refused" to be photographed with the check. But more significant was Ford's willingness to plug himself and his fortune into the existing peace movement. He was not only heading east, accompanied by Lochner, but he was planning to see House and Wilson. If Ford did not lose focus (a very real possibility, given what today would be called his attention-deficit-disorder tendencies), something substantial might very well be accomplished. Optimism was in the air. "It may be some time before peace wins the world," Shelly admitted, "but it's the greatest thing there is to work for."

Chapter 9

OUT OF THE TRENCHES
BY CHRISTMAS

NOVEMBER 21-DECEMBER 31, 1915

*I'm willing to spend everything I've got to stop the
bloodshed in Europe.*

—Henry Ford, November 1915

While Ford and Louis Lochner headed to New York, most Americans were thinking more of the upcoming Thanksgiving holiday that Thursday. The White House already had its turkey picked out, a thirty-five-pounder raised at the Kentucky farm of the clerk of the House of Representatives. Meanwhile, on Sunday, November 21, a syndicated feature by B. F. Roller, a physician who also doubled as a professional wrestler, offered tips to avoid "day after" stomach maladies. A few pre-Thanksgiving days of exercise and dieting, he insisted, "and you can eat all you wish, all your stomach can possibly hold, and enjoy the holiday . . . without suffering any inconvenience." And already prepared Thanksgiving dinners were a definite no-no. "Buy your food raw, whatever it is, take it home and prepare it yourself," he advised.

Since Addams had accepted a speaking engagement in Detroit on Friday, she would be spending Thanksgiving as a guest of Clara Ford. For now, she was in New York, eager to speak with Clara's husband to get a better understanding of his plans. All signs now suggested that Ford might be willing to underwrite the neutral conference idea that she and others believed in so strongly.

But she understood that official sanction and involvement from Wilson would strengthen the effort considerably. That Sunday afternoon, she had made another attempt to push the neutral conference idea to Colonel House, along with Schwimmer and Lillian Wald. No, he told them, the President would not move in that direction now, but Wilson would not stand in the way of a private unofficial effort. According to House, he then deftly succeeded in provoking "a controversy between themselves which delights me since it takes the pressure off myself."

He offered some hope by asking Addams for additional information on how the neutral conference could also function as a "clearinghouse" of various peace proposals, which she promptly sent, along with a copy of the recently published *Women at The Hague.* Ever the gentleman, House promised to share her comments with Wilson and read the book "with interest." It was unlikely he did either.

The next day, House heard the same neutral conference plan from Ford and Lochner, who had just arrived in Manhattan. The Colonel sized up Ford rather quickly, "a mechanical genius without education . . . who may become a prey to all sorts of faddists who desire his money." House was far more interested in hearing Ford's "plans for the uplift of his workmen" than his peace schemes, which he considered "crude and unimportant." Lochner, who dominated much of the conversation, prodded House to do something since he seemed to "agree . . . that something of that sort ought to be done." House, according to Lochner's possibly apocryphal account, then responded, "You see, I am not the Government." To which Ford remarked, "But you are pretty close to it."

Ford would see Wilson himself on Tuesday, November 23. He had already conferenced with Addams and other Woman's Peace Party leaders, now hard at work at the New York branch headquarters at 553 Fifth Avenue on the mothers' telegram campaign. The task at hand was enormous, requiring more than one hundred stenographers, typists, and filing clerks, along with the surprising cooperation of eighty Western Union and Postal Telegraph messenger boys, whose dawdling tendencies were legendary.

Addams, keeping a close eye on everything, could not help but be pleased that close to seven thousand wires, each costing about a dollar, went out to women's organizations in the first day or so. And the response had almost been instantaneous, as telegrams soon began flooding the White House, including one from Helen Keller. "I beseech you to help stop this war," she wrote. "We know that you believe in justice, mercy, and the brotherhood of man."

At the moment, Wilson was busy trying to finish his upcoming address to Congress. He did not especially want to see Ford, but Tumulty's counsel convinced him that it made political sense to do so. At their White House meeting, Ford soon made himself comfortable, draping his leg over the arm of his chair and then telling a "Ford joke" of his own creation about a man digging an unusually large grave. When asked why, he replied, "It's for me and my Ford. . . . It's pulled me out of many a hole before and I'm hopin' it'll pull me out of the last one." The President seemed to enjoy that one, so much so that he countered with a limerick.

Ford then got to the point. He was backing the women's plan of a neutral conference with continuous mediation. Would Wilson sanction it, especially since Ford was willing to foot the bill? The President, likely tired of being asked the same question, gave a diplomatic answer that he did not want to lock himself into any scheme when "a better plan" might come along in the future. Afterward, Ford disclosed little of the conversation to the reporters outside, except to say that Christmas would be an ideal occasion to launch the neutral conference. But Lochner noted that Ford appeared a bit disillusioned about Wilson. "He's a small man," he complained.

By this time, Ford had already made one of his typically impulsive decisions. Not only would he finance the neutral conference, but he would also pay for passages on what was to be called a "Peace Ship" to carry the delegates across the Atlantic. The idea, such as it was, germinated months earlier from the fertile mind of Rosika Schwimmer, who now had Ford's ear and was not prepared to let go. After all, publicity sold cars, why not peace? All that was left to do was to announce the plan to the press in New York on Wednesday, just in time for Ford to be the main topic of conversation at every Thanksgiving table in the country.

A t ten o'clock the next morning, a large group of reporters eager for a scoop waited at the Biltmore to hear what Ford had to say. They would not be disappointed. He explained that he was going to take matters into his own hands. The *Oscar II* of the Scandinavian-American Line would transport pacifists, including himself, to Europe, where a neutral conference would be established, all on his dime. Ford, hardly the most polished public speaker, then blurted out a typically impulsive statement he would soon live to regret. "We're going to have those boys out of the trenches by Christmas . . . and they're going to go home." (Some contemporary accounts recorded his statement as "we must get those boys out of the trenches by Christmas" or "we are going to try" to do so.)

The dumbfounded journalists exchanged glances. Did Ford just say what they thought he said? They began firing questions at him—namely, how exactly did he plan to accomplish this? "I can't tell you just how now. But we will use the wireless; we'll get the heads of the neutral nations together, and we'll get the press, the greatest agency for good, behind us. And we'll have those boys out of the trenches by Christmas! They'll walk out of their holes across to the men who are fighting them now from other trenches, and they'll shake hands in smiling agreement never to go back to those trenches again."

Lochner and the *Evening Post*'s Oswald Villard, who accompanied Ford to the press gathering, could see this was not going well. They did their best to explain how the ultimate purpose of the trip was to "erect the machinery by which peace can be brought about expeditiously when the time is right." Ford, meanwhile, talked of how they hoped to "appeal to the men in the trenches" and how the ship's Marconi radio transmitter, "the longest gun in the world," would spread their message as they crossed the ocean. "Get people talking about peace and you have taken a step forward," he insisted. And this entire effort would be a continuation of the women's congress at The Hague. "I'm on the job with the women for peace," he insisted. "The women may count on me."

Such words would have normally cheered Addams immensely. But she sensed that Ford, well intentioned as he was, had made a stupendous mistake. The Peace Ship and the "out of the trenches by Christmas" announcement had succeeded in creating a tremendous amount of publicity— front page in most newspapers—but he had also given an already dubious press ample ammunition to present a distorted message. Almost immediately, Addams called Lochner long distance trying to get him to emphasize the neutral conference and not the Peace Ship, which she believed to be completely unnecessary. It was too late. The world and Ford himself were now far more fixated on the magical ship that was going to stop the war than any possible conference that might result in the future. "The people in New York in charge of the enterprise believed that the anti-war movement throughout its history had been too quietistic and much too grey and negative," she later wrote. They were certain that "a demonstration was needed, even a spectacular one to show that ardor and comradeship were exhibited by the non-militarists as well."

Addams could easily have distanced herself from the whole scheme. Mary did not want her to go, nor did Alice Hamilton and other close friends. Her withdrawal would not have surprised Schwimmer and some of her followers, like Lola Maverick Lloyd, who believed Addams to be "tiresomely cautious. . . . If she would only drop the people who see no use in anything & go ahead with the hopeful!" But they had misjudged her. Addams continued to believe that any effort for peace, however unorthodox, was better than none. She decided to make the trip. "I had already 'learned from life,' to use Dante's great phrase, that moral results are often obtained through the most unexpected agencies," she later wrote. And by going, she also believed she could act as a stabilizing force for a mission that almost immediately appeared to be spiraling out of control.

The *Oscar II* would sail on December 4, which meant that Ford and his followers headquartered at the Biltmore had eleven days to assemble an appropriate and qualified delegation. Ford wanted some of his brilliant pals to accompany him, such as the botanist Luther Burbank, the naturalist John Burroughs, and especially Edison ("I'll make him go," Ford confidently announced), all of whom declined. Invitations (which strategically mentioned Addams's acceptance) were also sent to a hundred "representative Americans," among them politicians of all stripes and celebrities such as Clarence Darrow, the educational reformer John Dewey, and Helen Keller.

The curious press, of course, would be represented in full, along with photographers and newsreel men. In a strange irony, the man who disdained higher education had decided that college students should also be invited, an idea that Addams felt had little merit.

Her own preference to attract the best and brightest pacifists and reformers, as she had done for the Hague congress, proved difficult to achieve. Some simply could not leave the country on such short notice. Others, like David Starr Jordan, believed the "Peace Demonstration" component of the trip was overshadowing the more important work of mediation. The journalist Ida Tarbell also refused to go, even after Addams did her best to convince her in a thirty-minute phone conversation. "If you see it you must go, Miss Addams," Tarbell told her. "I don't see it and I can't. It is possible that standing on the street corner and crying, 'Peace, Peace,' may do good. I do not say that it will not, but I cannot see it for myself."

Addams was not discouraged enough to back out, but she recognized the trip would come with a price. After a warm welcome from a Chicago audience a few days later, she could not help remark that "after I sail on Mr. Ford's ship, I probably never shall be applauded again." Her Woman's Peace Party colleague Anna Garlin Spencer felt that Addams should reconsider. Spencer, who had thought about attending herself, was disturbed by the scene at the Biltmore, which had seemed to grow more chaotic by the day. As more and more rejections and regrets poured in, the berths on the ship were now being filled by individuals more interested in a free trip to Europe than peace, such as the pro-preparedness governor of North Dakota, who announced that he was going "to see what it looks like over there. . . . I want to see what the war has done to it." But Spencer was most alarmed by the prominent role of Schwimmer, who was clearly calling the shots, with Ford's apparent blessing.

Schwimmer was enjoying her new status. On the day after Thanksgiving, she and Ford were in Washington together for a rally at the Belasco Theater prior to another meeting with Wilson, which would be the dramatic culmination of the mothers' telegram campaign. The English suffragist and pacifist Ethel Snowden, who would accompany her to the White House, soon noticed Schwimmer's plush hotel quarters at the New Willard, all paid for by Ford. "Her rooms were filled with costly flowers," Snowden later recalled. "Her meals were served privately by waiters specially chosen for the work." For the normally cash-poor Schwimmer, it was a dream come true. "I do not sleep any more," she wrote Addams. "I feel new born."

Schwimmer was in her usual form at the Belasco, her speech filled with "passionate exaggerations" that "millions of men are praying for peace." Snowden presented it a different way. She told a story that had made the rounds in England of how German soldiers had put up a sign in the trenches saying THE ENGLISH ARE FOOLS, which elicited no reaction. Nor did the addition of a second line: THE FRENCH ARE FOOLS. It was not until the sign came up for a third and fourth time, this time reading, WE'RE ALL FOOLS. LET'S ALL GO HOME, that the British soldiers could not help but stop and wonder why they were fighting.

The final speaker of the afternoon was Ford, who with some prodding managed to mutter a few sentences, the same he had repeated ad nauseam for the past few days. "All I can say is: Remember our slogan, 'Out of the trenches by Christmas, never to go back.'" The crowd loved it anyway.

After the rally, Schwimmer and Snowden headed to the nearby White House, where they had a 5:30 p.m. appointment in the Blue Room. By this point, thousands of "mother"-grams had arrived at the White House, although Wilson likely paid little attention to them or to the roughly four hundred pacifists from the Belasco meeting waiting outside. It was to his credit that he was willing to sit through another sales talk about a neutral conference, the third in two weeks (the Peace Ship was not mentioned, since they knew he could not possibly sanction it). And the President did what he usually did in such situations: listen carefully, present possible roadblocks, and offer no real encouragement. But Snowden found herself liking Wilson, whom even Schwimmer conceded was "exceedingly nice" during the talk. She felt his heart was clearly in the right place, even if he would not act. Schwimmer, who had already met him last year, was less impressed, at least according to Snowden, who was far from her biggest fan. The fiery Hungarian, Snowden later recalled, became "voluble, bitter, insulting" and made snide remarks about America's "munition profiteering." Wilson, a bit defensive, suggested that the United States was hardly the only country to be guilty of this.

The President was not unhappy to see them depart. Peace was very much on his mind, but it was the peace that might result from House's secret correspondence with Grey, which no longer seemed quite so promising. On Thanksgiving, the Colonel had received a letter from the British foreign secretary that raised more questions than answers. Grey had already wired him a few weeks earlier asking whether the "elimination of militarism and navalism" House proposed meant America would get behind some kind of league of nations in the future? House, after consulting Wilson, assured him that it would, meaning a distinct break with America's historic avoidance of foreign entanglements. But the British, if Grey's Thanksgiving letter was any indication, were still not jumping at House's rather generous offer. They would need something more specific, Grey told him. Privately, Grey knew that most of his cabinet colleagues (no longer including Winston Churchill, who had recently resigned) were not especially interested in anything beyond a fight to the finish. House had begun to lose his patience. "The British are in many ways dull," he wrote in his diary that day, "or they would better realize what this country has done and is willing to do toward bringing about a proper settlement of the war."

Over the weekend, House saw Wilson, who was in New York for the Army-Navy football game at the Polo Grounds. The Colonel briefed the President on the Grey letter, which Wilson hadn't bothered to read. The President suggested that House would need to make another European trip to "let the Allies know how our minds are running," especially since he was convinced the ambassadors in London and Washington were worthless. Besides, Wilson was not keen on "putting our thoughts and intentions into writing." Better for House to do so in person. The final details and instructions still needed to be worked out, since the Colonel preferred to go in late December. For the third time in nineteen months, Wilson's so-called alter ego would be representing him in the halls of power in Europe.

During the President's weekend in New York, Addams was in Chicago wrapping up matters prior to the *Oscar II*'s sailing the following Saturday. She was not feeling especially well and her tendency toward seasickness made every ocean voyage an ordeal, but she was determined to make the trip. The constant brickbats hurled by most of the press disturbed her, so much so that she tried to explain once again that the neutral conference was not about trying to dictate peace terms to the belligerents. She discovered that even Hull-House residents and trustees would also need convincing, which she planned to address at a Tuesday evening meeting.

She would not get the chance. On Monday night, one of her kidneys hemorrhaged, a return of the tuberculosis she had contracted years earlier. She was taken to Presbyterian Hospital, where her physician, James Herrick, kept a careful eye on her, ordering X-rays and blood cultures. Surgery was not required, but she remained feverish and in no condition to sail. The hospital would be her home for the next few weeks, long enough for Wilson to send her a get-well letter, which somehow was sent to the wrong Addams (Ruth) at the wrong Presbyterian Hospital (Philadelphia).

Her friends, though worried about her condition, were privately pleased she would not be accompanying the Ford party, "an enterprise without a leader and without a rudder," as Carrie Chapman Catt labeled it. But Addams was ambivalent. Her absence, she knew, further undermined the already shaky legitimacy of the mission (there were some, like the poet Vachel Lindsey, who were supportive solely because of the involvement of Addams, "our best woman and queen"). And for the rest of her life, some believed, unfairly, that she had deliberately used her illness to avoid a trip shaping up to be fraught with problems.

Ford himself had begun to wonder whether the trip was such a good idea, but he had gone too far to back out now. In the meantime, regrets continued to pour in, including some from the Wilson administration. Colonel House, of course, begged off, as did a representative of Margaret Wilson. Frederic Howe was apparently interested, only to be informed by a fellow Democrat who had already talked to House that it would be best if he stayed home. Taft wanted no part of it either. Bryan was willing to join them but could not leave now. One of TR's Bull Moose colleagues, Ben Lindsey, the pioneering juvenile court judge, decided to go, even though

*Henry Ford (left) talks to skeptical reporters at the Biltmore Hotel on
December 2, 1915, two days before sailing on the Peace Ship.*
(Library of Congress: LC-B2- 3689-1)

he supported "reasonable preparedness" and doubted anything could be
accomplished. Lindsey informed Roosevelt of his decision a week before
sailing. "I am afraid that the Ford mission can do nothing but harm," TR
replied. "Your share in it, however, I am sure will be good."

Roosevelt had respected Ford's technological know-how and a few of his
ideas about labor relations. The problem, he believed, was that Ford didn't
actually know much of *anything* outside of those areas. "He is ignorant,"
TR told a friend, "yet because he has been so successful in motors, many,
many persons, hardly as ignorant as himself, think him wise in all things
and allow him to influence their views."

In the final days before departure, the Biltmore was a whirlwind of
activity, as passages and passports were finalized for the 160 or so peace
pilgrims, Ford officials, journalists, and students sailing on the *Oscar II*.
Most of the big names Ford had hoped to attract were not coming, nor
were most of the pacifist heavyweights, especially those most interested in
mediation. "Almost no one on our carefully selected original list actually
sailed on the *Oscar II*," Addams later recalled. Still, anyone making the trip
was guaranteed an enjoyable cruise. "Nobody can spend a cent," Ford insisted, "not even for tips." But the press, especially on the pro-Allies East

Coast, remained hostile, and Ford's continued befuddled statements did little to win them over.

"How do you expect to promote peace," one reporter asked him, "by taking a boatload of passengers to a neutral country in Europe?" "We want to show that there are enough Americans ready to drop their business—to make sacrifices," he responded. Why couldn't he do this in the United States? "To stop preparedness in this country," he explained. He then repeated one of his favorite phrases of late: "Preparedness is war." "Why go to Europe to stop preparedness in America?" another journalist asked. "To get any country, belligerent or neutral, to disarm." Just as Addams feared, the point of the whole trip—the establishment of a neutral conference— was largely forgotten.

Saturday, December 4, dawned, and as early as 10:00 a.m., the media and onlookers had begun to gather at the Scandinavian-American pier at Seventeenth Street at Hoboken to see the ship off. They had already learned an intriguing piece of news that morning; the President's wedding date had been set for December 18 at Edith's home, with the guest list mostly limited to immediate family.

Two bands, one on the ship, another on the dock, played peace songs, including TR's hated "I Didn't Raise My Boy to Be a Soldier." The appearance of Ford excited the crowd, as did the appearances of Bryan and Edison. Any last words? one reporter asked. "Yes," Ford responded. "Tell people to cry peace and fight preparedness." At one point, someone called for "Three Cheers for Jane Addams," while one wag asked if "Theodore Roosevelt was on board." At about 3:15, while Ford tossed the last of his American Beauty roses to the gathered spectators, including his wife and son, the *Oscar II* finally departed.

Ford still hoped Addams would find a way to join them. Two days later, she received a wire signed by Ford and dozens of passengers: "We love you, we respect you, we miss you, we expect you." Rosika Schwimmer, meanwhile, was having the time of her life without Addams to restrain her. The peace rebel, who had long resented that she lacked the cachet of Addams and other leading pacifists, was firmly in command, with no one to check her occasionally imperious tendencies and spendthrift ways. "I feel as though I were in Fairy-land," she remarked to Lochner. "All I have to do is wave my wand for what I think is necessary for our Peace Mission, and lo! it appears." Before sailing, Ford had even promised her $200,000, to be used by the International Committee of Women for Permanent Peace (which Addams wanted "kept distinct" from the Peace Ship scheme) with an initial payment of $20,000 to be sent in the near future. Almost immediately, Aletta Jacobs was skeptical. "Must we accept the 20,000," she wrote Addams from Holland, "if Rosika keeps for herself 100,000."

The harsh press criticism notwithstanding, most Americans remained curious what the Peace Ship would ultimately accomplish. That Ford had managed to pull together the mission in such a ridiculously short time suggested that perhaps he was not quite as clueless as the media appeared to make him. "Henry dares to be a clown, and probably has good martyr stuff in him, and that may make him a means of good, in spite of everything," remarked *Life*. "Let him do anything he will that is not against the law. If our country has had a fault in this war, it has been in being overcautious."

Wilson would not have agreed. Caution and restraint had kept the country out of war, and he intended his leap into preparedness to proceed along the same lines. The Manhattan Club speech in November had broken the ice; his message to Congress (not called the State of the Union address until 1934) on Tuesday, December 7, would further amplify his views, all in a calm, nonhysterical manner. In an hour-long speech, he again explained the proposals to beef up America's defense and the creation of the Continental Army reserve, all while insisting that he had "no thought of any immediate or particular danger arising out of our relations with other nations." He reassured his listeners that "we will not maintain a standing army except for uses which are as necessary in times of peace as in times of war." And he repeated his attack on "citizens of the United States . . . born under other flags . . . who have poured the poison of disloyalty into the very arteries of our national life. . . . Such creatures of passion, disloyalty, and anarchy must be crushed out." The words electrified the audience, much as they had done at the Manhattan Club a few weeks earlier. Meanwhile, the presence of Edith in the gallery turned more than a few heads. "She is rather pretty isn't she!" a newspaper cartoonist overheard one onlooker coo. "I don't see what he sees in her," scoffed another.

The message was generally well received, although everyone noticed the President's 180 degree turnaround from last year's sentiments concerning national security. To Roosevelt, this once again demonstrated that Wilson was the quintessential political opportunist. "What a smug thing that Message was!" TR wrote a friend. "Really it was difficult for me not to feel sick, as an American, when I read it." Roosevelt dashed off a fifteen-hundred-word response a few hours later, picking apart what he considered the address's numerous inconsistencies, although he did concede that the President was "entirely correct" in his "disloyal Americans" discussion.

"What does Mr. Wilson mean," TR asked, "when in one line he says that we have 'stood apart, studiously neutral,' because 'it was our manifest duty to do so,' and a couple of paragraphs later says that 'we demand security in prosecuting . . . self-chosen lines of national development for others'? He can take either of the two positions; but he cannot take both." The President's national defense discussion was just as confused. "He says; 'We will not maintain a standing army except for uses which are as necessary in time of peace as in time of war, and we shall always see to it that our military peace establishment is no larger than is actually and continually needed for the uses of days in which no enemies move against us.' What this means I have no idea, and I am certain that no one else has any idea."

Interior Secretary Franklin Lane, probably the most TR-sympathetic of all of Wilson's cabinet, thought Roosevelt had "lost his mind." Others were more intrigued by TR's latest colorful description of the President's language: like "that of a Byzantine logothete." No one seemed to know who or what a "logothete" was, and reference book definitions ("one who accounts, calculates or ratiocinates") did not seem to fit Wilson especially well. Finally, a reporter went to see Roosevelt.

"The Byzantine logothetes," TR explained, "were lawyers and orators, who believed in the efficacy of words and could not be persuaded to draw the sword." Did that mean he considered Wilson to be the spiritual descendant of these men? "Look in Bury's *History of the Later Roman Empire* or Hodgkin's *Italy and Her Invaders*. . . . You can find all about them in those books." Additional research still did not reveal any ancient Woodrow Wilsons of the Byzantine variety.

Regardless of their stridency, Roosevelt's attacks on the President had begun to bear fruit. TR's views on preparedness and hyphenated Americans no longer seemed as extreme as they had even a few months earlier. "The people are realizing that you are not so blood thirsty a person as some of them thought after your *Lusitania* statement," his Progressive colleague Dwight Heard wrote Roosevelt. The Republicans had also begun to take notice of their erstwhile leader, at least if TR's invitation to a December dinner at the Fifth Avenue home of Elbert Gary, the chairman of the board of U.S. Steel, was any indication. The party was small, but the attendees were among the most elite of the financial who's who, with names such as Vanderbilt, Belmont, and Guggenheim all present. Most had been violently opposed to Roosevelt in the past, especially after the Republican split of 1912. "Now they say that in preaching preparedness he was and is right," remarked one of the anonymous dinner guests.

Almost immediately, the gathering was seen as the opening blast in getting TR the Republican nomination for 1916. The man who had criticized the "malefactors of great wealth," one Democrat sneered, now seemed to be a "benefactor of great wealth."

Roosevelt claimed the dinner "had no political significance," but others were not so sure. A week earlier, a *New York Tribune* editorial, "Do They Want Roosevelt," had already raised the question whether the Republican establishment would forgive and forget. TR's national popularity had dipped after leaving the White House, but there had been a "real change in public opinion" of late. The reason was simple: "thousands and thousands of Americans believe that if Theodore Roosevelt had been President . . . there would have been no *Lusitania* tragedy." The *Tribune* suggested that TR was "the only man who can defeat Mr. Wilson, because he is the only man who has offered an honest substitute for Mr. Wilson's policy in the vital question of American honor abroad and security at home."

The editorial was widely circulated in the following weeks and generated considerable discussion throughout America. TR's supporters, like a New Yorker named D. W. Diggs, believed that "his election would do more to bring peace to the warring nations than a thousand Ford schemes." Other

Roosevelt men scoffed at accusations that TR was "dangerous." "I have a dangerous dog," said one New Jerseyite, "but he doesn't bite me, and you bet that no one who has no business here comes on to my place and takes my things." But his opponents were just as vehement that TR, a "faker supreme . . . braggart and the traitor to the Grand Old Party," should disappear into the political ether for good. "You little realize the contempt old Republicans feel for this man who tried to destroy the party because it did not nominate him in 1912," a Yonkers man noted. "Self-seeking, always and only."

Roosevelt himself understood that it would be extremely difficult, if not impossible, to win over the "extreme reactionary crowd" who still called the shots in the GOP. Too many were prepared to do everything in their power to prevent him from getting even a sniff of the nomination—behind the scenes, of course, lest the public witness another nasty factional struggle, as in 1912. His old friend Henry Cabot Lodge bluntly informed him that as much as he would "like to see you President again," the Republican nomination was unlikely. On the other hand, "unless the Progressives . . . reunite with the Republicans of course we cannot win."

What remained of the Progressive party remained a serious dilemma for TR. He knew that thousands of idealistic men and women had bolted the Republican party three years ago to follow him into the new organization. The well-meaning diehards who remained still trusted TR and believed he was a Progressive to the end, even if some of his recent activities, especially the Elbert Gary dinner with the fat cats, gave them pause. And TR insisted that he intended to stay the course with his Progressive friends, "unless there is a really vital national crisis." Still, he would not go as far as one New Jersey Progressive demanded: "some assurance" that he would run again as a Progressive and "one more unequivocal statement . . . that you have no part with the Republicans."

Another third-party run, he knew, guaranteed a Wilson landslide, an almost unbearable prospect for TR. His best chance would be at the head of some sort of Bull Moose–Republican fusion ticket, the dream of most of the remaining Progressives. The Old Guard Republicans, as much as they hated Roosevelt at the moment, might be compelled to go for it if they faced the disturbing possibility of a TR monkey wrench creating another hopeless three-way race. At the bare minimum, the GOP would presumably need to pick someone acceptable to the Progressives, even if not TR, who coyly claimed he was on the lookout for such an individual. "We hold the balance of power," the California progressive Meyer Lissner insisted, "we know it and they know it." Lissner was certain that TR would at least be able to choose the Republican vice presidential nominee, perhaps Hiram Johnson, Roosevelt's own running mate in 1912 and currently the governor of California. And Johnson might be effectively paired with the current Supreme Court justice and former New York governor Charles Evans Hughes, whose name seemed to be gaining traction in recent months. If Hughes decided to run, Colonel House wrote Wilson, this would be "interesting and important." The President agreed. "It is important if true."

Whether Hughes, TR, or anyone else could beat Wilson was uncertain. For now, most Americans were satisfied that the President had kept the peace without dishonoring America and appeared to be occupying the "sane" center between what some perceived as the extremes of pacifism (Bryan) and militarism (Roosevelt). "It is a common saying over here," the English journalist Sydney Brooks wrote, "that if there were an election tomorrow Mr. Wilson would poll nine or ten votes to every one that would be cast for Mr. Roosevelt." Although Brooks, who interviewed TR in November, was hardly the most reliable prognosticator, no one could doubt that Roosevelt would face the toughest political battle of his life in a one-on-one against Wilson. A day after Brooks listened to TR's rants against Wilson, the Englishman met with House, who was happy to provide the facts as he saw them. "I told Brooks," the Colonel wrote, "that for the first time in his career, Roosevelt was up against the real thing when it came to political sagacity, courage and a well equipped thinking machine."

Wilson was not especially concerned with Roosevelt at the moment. His major focus was House's upcoming journey, which he believed would "materially strengthen our position" with the Allies. But House discovered when he saw the President at the White House on December 15 that his friend appeared to have had several changes of heart. American involvement was not necessary or even desirable, Wilson told House, as it would "take too long for us to get in a state of preparedness" to make much

of a difference (a point that TR had repeatedly made). House again explained that America would need the Allies in any future fight with Germany. Wilson did not disagree, but he would not go as far as House—i.e.,
"let the Allies know we are definitely on their side"—and not allow a
German victory. (House had already inadvisably made a similar point to
the agricultural reformer Sir Horace Plunkett, who had close ties with the
Foreign Office, further weakening America's future bargaining position
with Britain.) "The last time we talked he was quite ready to take this
stand, but he has visibly weakened," House lamented.

Wilson had not weakened as far as the need for House to go to Europe
now. Peace could certainly be discussed, ideally accomplished in the future
through "disarmament and . . . a league of nations," but he should steer
clear of any talk of "territorial questions, indemnities, and the like." The
President also wanted House to lean on the Brits concerning their blockade's ongoing violations of international law. In the meantime, a few loose
ends needed to be addressed. House would be made a "special agent" of
the State Department to prevent certain senators from making a stink that
a private citizen appeared to be representing the country in foreign affairs
(there was also talk of a possible Senate inquiry into whether House had
been paid for his last European trip). The press would be given a story that
House was merely a courier, who would brief our ambassadors, who would
in turn give him the lowdown on the international situation. But not everyone was convinced, especially David Lawrence of the *New York Evening
Post*, who believed House was being sent to "canvas the prospects for peace,"
and perhaps to undercut the potential value of the Ford expedition. "What
an embarrassing political situation here if the Ford conference at The Hague
did start the ball rolling," Lawrence wrote. House and Wilson were furious.
The next day, the Colonel denied any "mission of peace." In fact, he had
"no idea of doing that, nor have I been asked to do that. . . . There is nothing
mysterious about my trip. . . . There is nothing to hide."

Wilson's other major concern was his upcoming nuptials on December
18. The nation seemed to want to know every last detail, especially
the specifics of Edith's trousseau, including her newly purchased gloves ("a

dozen of the two-clasp variety"), two handbags ("one of alligator skin . . . and another of dark blue grained leather, also fitted in silver"), and selection of glittering gowns. Not surprisingly, Edith had begun to receive letters from various "cranks" eager to relieve her of her pre–First Lady wardrobe. "You will have no need for your old gowns with a trousseau to replace them," wrote one nervy correspondent, "so while you are wearing your new things you may enjoy the satisfaction which comes of giving others pleasure by sending some of them to me." Others sent unsolicited gifts of all kinds, "many pieces of needle work, cut glass, china and silver." Those of any value were returned.

Wilson's wedding day began with a trip to the bride's home before heading to the bank to withdraw cash for the honeymoon in Hot Springs, Virginia. It was raining in Washington that morning, but a whistling Wilson did not seem to notice. "What was he whistling?" someone asked. "Couldn't exactly catch it," was the reply. "Sounded happy, though." By 11:00 a.m., the President was back at the White House, in time to attend his granddaughter Ellen Wilson McAdoo's christening. Last-minute presidential business also needed to be addressed, but he snuck out for a drive with Edith in the afternoon. After a family meal at seven, Wilson headed to Edith's home for the ceremony.

The crowd of onlookers outside the Galt homestead was not overwhelming, but police were there to make sure nothing got out of hand. If they expected to see Wilson's "best friend" Colonel House, they were to be disappointed. Officially, House was supposedly not attending so as not to offend others kept off the small list of invited guests (among them Edith's "awful" family, Wilson's daughter Nell McAdoo lamented), though some wondered whether the Colonel's exclusion suggested something of greater significance. The press was quick to note that Matilda Braxton, Edith's longtime "colored 'mammy'" was present, as were two other African American maids named Susie and Otey, who apparently were allowed to watch "from the doorway." The ceremony, Episcopalian for Edith, was over in about twenty minutes, followed by toasts, dinner, and the cutting of the cake. The "rich, dark fruit cake" did not follow the then common wedding tradition of including small articles for single women present to find (thimbles = will remain single; rings = will marry; penny = will become wealthy).

By ten, the Wilsons had departed for Alexandria to catch a train for Hot Springs, a clever ploy to outflank the hordes expecting them at Union Station. Just nine months after they had met, Wilson and Edith were now husband and wife.

The presidential wedding, lavishly covered by newspapers, which offered "splendid photographic reproductions" of the couple "well worth framing," temporarily distracted Americans from the Ford Peace Ship, which had reached Oslo (then called Christiania), Norway, at roughly the same time. The journey, if the hostile and distorted reports filed by the majority of boozing reporters on board were to be believed, was not going well. Beyond the massive quantities of food being gobbled down, little of note had been accomplished so far, except squabbling over Wilson's recent presidential address about preparedness, which readers in America were led to believe was a violent fight aboard ship. Meanwhile, Schwimmer gave reporters plenty to write about, thanks to her ubiquitous black bag supposedly filled with secret documents (the gist of which had already been disclosed in the manifesto of October) and her occasionally abrasive ways. And as dedicated, passionate, and creative as she was, she had neither the temperament nor the personality to work effectively as a manager and administrator, as Addams had done so many times. "I think of her daily and indeed almost hourly," Julia Wales admitted. "We miss her so."

They still hoped Addams would join them. The chances were better since she had been discharged from the hospital and was back at Hull-House under a nurse's care. A few days after their arrival in Norway, Ford (or more likely Louis Lochner under Ford's name) wired her that she should not believe the barrage of negative press reports about the expedition. "Hope your faith in our mission is as unshaken as ours. Norwegian people are splendid." Addams made sure the telegram was distributed to the dubious press and then sent one of her own to Schwimmer, insisting that she had "never wavered in my allegiance" although she would be likely unable to travel overseas until late February at the earliest.

It was Ford who had begun to waver. Even in the most ideal of circumstances, the fear that the expedition might be somehow compromised by his unpredictability was always present. By the end of the voyage, he was coping with a nasty bug, supposedly triggered by a wave that had soaked him on deck. And Reverend Samuel Marquis, who had opposed the scheme from the beginning and had accompanied him to Europe at the behest of Clara Ford, was in his ear constantly, so much so that it did not take much for Ford, already weakened from his own fasting treatment and frigid Norwegian temperatures, to yield. In the early hours of December 23, a taxi whisked him away from the Grand Hotel, along with Marquis. Passages to New York that evening on the *Bergensfjord* awaited them.

Before leaving Norway, Ford insisted that he was not abandoning the peace movement or its goals. And Schwimmer was still in charge, with the Ford millions presumably behind her. But everyone knew that his departure had punched another damaging hole in an expedition desperately in need of legitimacy. On Christmas Eve, the front page of virtually every newspaper in the United States reported on the return of the man who had promised to end the war by Christmas.

Naysayers could not suppress their glee. Ford, one report claimed, was "broken by the apparent failure of his mission." He was "pathetically foolish," the *Washington Times* insisted, and "will look better a thousand times to all the American people in his coming back . . . than ever he looked to anybody in his going away."

The news of Ford's return punctuated an especially profitable holiday season for America's retailers, enjoying the fruits of the booming warfueled economy. More than a few stores managed to integrate the war into their sales pitches. "The Big Vital Issue is Preparedness," the Washington-based R.P. Andrews Paper Company announced. "Our big store is headquarters for Christmas Preparedness. Let us help you out of the gift dilemma so you can be free to have an old-fashioned Christmas of complete happiness." And there was no shortage of toys available, although the Germans could no longer dominate the market as before. Some of the old favorites, like the named-after-TR teddy bear, remained popular ("a greater favorite with children than any bear at the Zoo," gushed one ad), but parents were warned that old-fashioned Noah's arks and girls' sleds pulled by a rope would no longer do. For boys, the recently introduced erector sets were popular, as were war toys such as "Battleship Target Games, Armored Automobiles and Trains, Red Cross Ambulances, 'Bleriot,' 'Curtiss' and 'Taube' Aeroplanes." For the girls, Indian squaw play suits and "Kitty Twinkle Toes . . . the Kitten who walks and purrs" were easy gift choices.

Christmas at Sagamore Hill was a happy one for TR. Most of the family was there, and he was pleased to see that two of his male grandchildren, Ted and Richard, both under two, "liked some of their more simple and vivid toys, and played hard." At the urging of his wife, Edith, Roosevelt had written poems "or a picture letter" as a special addition to the Christmas stockings. "My cave-man efforts were received with rapture," he wrote Kermit and Belle.

Several states away, the Wilsons were spending their first Christmas together at the Homestead Hotel in Hot Springs. On Christmas Eve, they attended a special holiday musical performance by the African American employees of the hotel. "The negroes put on a vaudeville show, which included a cake-walk and a long list of songs," one reporter noted. "Mr. and Mrs. Wilson liked especially 'Back in Dixie Land,' as they are both Southerners" (in contrast, TR had spoken twelve days earlier at Tuskegee Institute in honor of the recently deceased Booker T. Washington). After rain interrupted the honeymooners' golf game on Christmas Day, they retreated to their hotel room to enjoy their five-foot-high Christmas tree with "electric lights of green, blue, red, and gold" and a turkey dinner.

In Manhattan, Colonel House received a letter on Christmas from Wilson, one he considered "as important . . . as he has ever written me." The President seemed to believe House's upcoming trip might be successful. "It is possible that we are on the eve of some real opportunity," Wilson wrote. "I pray it may turn out to be so!" House was certain that he and the President were entirely of the same mind. He did not recognize, or chose not to, that Wilson had a very different view on what American "intervention" actually might mean. "He clearly places the whole responsibility back on my shoulders where I would gladly have it, for if I am to act, I wish to act with a free hand," the Colonel wrote in his diary.

On the battlefields of Europe, there was to be no Christmas truce this year. If anything, the war had grown more cruel and barbaric with each passing day. America had been rocked by news of the slaughter of hundreds of thousands of Armenians at the hands of the Ottoman Turks, Germany's ally. Roosevelt, like others, was horrified, but he saw no point in protest meetings unlikely to result in concrete action to right the wrong. "We refuse to do our duty by Armenia; because we have deified peace at any price," he observed.

Neither side had lost the will to fight. The Central Powers had gotten the better of their foes so far, but the Allies were already preparing for a massive summer offensive on the Western Front in 1916. Writing to friends that Christmas, the American ambassador Walter Hines Page recounted a recent conversation with a member of the British cabinet, who now believed the war would go on at least into 1918. "That," Page believed, "isn't possible."

Chapter 10

A WORLD ON FIRE

JANUARY 1–FEBRUARY 25, 1916

We need to prepare now. Not a cent should be cut
from the army and navy appropriations sent to
Congress.

—Franklin Roosevelt, January 1916

In the early days of 1916, a taboo subject found its way into most of the nation's major newspapers. Margaret Sanger, the thirty-six-year-old woman who had coined the term "birth control," was finally to have her day in federal court in New York. She had recently returned from Europe, where she had fled in 1914 to avoid prosecution for "obscene" material she had published in her monthly periodical, *The Woman Rebel*. Her supporters, "many . . . known as 'free thinkers' on sex problems," packed the courtroom on the opening day of the trial on January 18. Sanger herself was defiant. "I am guilty of no crime," she announced, "and will fight to the bitter end." She could content herself with the knowledge that the movement was slowly taking hold. "My reports from the west say that thousands of birth control pamphlets are being distributed there among working people," she told a reporter. "They are being photographed, type-written, mimeographed, even copied painfully out by hand, so that the information . . . may be spread from family to family." To Sanger, nothing was more important for women than the birth control movement, not even suffrage. "Women simply can never hope to advance without it."

A group of her British supporters, including her future lover the novelist H. G. Wells, reached out to President Wilson hoping for clemency. It was not an issue that he or any national politician would touch, regardless of their own personal feelings on the subject (years earlier, Wilson had written his first wife, Ellen, reminding her to "bring the little bundle of rubbers in the bottom drawer of the washstand"). Roosevelt, meanwhile, had long believed women, especially white Anglo-Saxon women, should bear as many children as possible, much to the chagrin of Sanger. Nevertheless, the feds dropped the charges a few weeks later. Sanger was free, only to find herself behind bars later that year for opening the nation's first birth control clinic in Brooklyn.

Such controversial matters did not trouble Wilson and Edith, now enjoying their honeymoon in Hot Springs, "happy as children off on a holiday," as Edith wrote her mother. Their days were filled with automobile rides, golf, walks, and even a two-hour trek up the nearby Warm Springs Mountain. As usual, reporters and photographers were documenting their every move, including a tender scene when the gallant President caught his bride when she "jumped down from a slight but abrupt terrace."

Miles away in New York, Henry Ford had just arrived home on the *Bergensfjord*. Now recovered from what was then called the "grip," he was not especially eager to talk to the press but eventually offered his latest pearls of wisdom to reporters at the Waldorf-Astoria Hotel. First, he did not regard the trip as a failure. "We have started the people to talking," he explained. "When you do that you start them thinking, and when people start thinking they think right and something good comes of it." Next, Ford had changed his views on the war. The people, he now believed, were entirely to blame for being uninformed and electing the wrong kind of leaders who were bent on war (that nondemocratic nations such as Germany and Russia were major participants in the war did not seem to enter into his equation). "So far as neglectful citizens go, I suppose I'm as bad an offender as any," he admitted. "I've only voted six times . . . only because Mrs. Ford made me do it." Before leaving for Detroit, the automaker also informed reporters that it was Jane Addams who had planted the peace seed in him, before he had ever talked to Rosika Schwimmer, a charge Addams felt necessary to deny.

The return of Ford was overshadowed by yet another disturbing international development. On New Year's Day, the country learned of the
sinking of the *Persia*, a British liner heading to India. Survivors, such as
Charles Grant, an American vacuum oil salesman, told a tragic tale that
had become eerily familiar. "I had just finished my soup, and the steward
was asking what I would take for my second course, when a terrific explosion occurred," Grant recounted. "It was a horrible scene. The water was
black as ink. Some passengers were screaming, others were calling out good
bye. Those in one boat sang hymns." More than three hundred people went
to their deaths in the Mediterranean, including two Americans: Homer
Salisbury, a missionary, and Robert Ney McNeely, a government official on
his way to his post in Aden, Arabia, who had elected not to take a neutral
Dutch ship to his destination. A few days after his death, McNeely's mother
received a letter from her son; written in December, it reassured her that
his upcoming voyage was "entirely safe" because the *Persia* was "convoyed
by cruisers and destroyers all the way."

The Wilsons were forced to cut short their honeymoon and return to
the White House, where Edith would assume her duties as First Lady (with
her African American servant, "faithful old Susie," in tow) and her husband
would cope with the latest crisis. All the facts were not yet in, but it appeared likely that the *Arabic* pledge of the previous fall not to attack passenger liners had been violated (that the *Persia* was armed confused matters
somewhat and German involvement was not clear-cut at the time). A few
hours after the President's arrival in Washington, he was in conference with
Joseph Tumulty, who urged a forceful response while warning of a growing
perception of a "lack of leadership."

This was too much for Wilson. He would not deviate from his current
course, he told Tumulty, even if it meant electoral defeat in November and
"if every last Congressman and Senator stands up on his hind legs and
proclaims me a coward." And "the sober-minded people," the President
insisted, "will applaud any efforts I may make without the loss of our honor
to keep this country out of war."

If not war, then what? Congress, back in session after the holiday break,
was demanding answers, many of them men of Wilson's own party, who

still believed in the doctrines of the Great Commoner Bryan. One of them was Thomas Gore, a forty-five-year-old blind senator from Oklahoma (and the future grandfather of the author Gore Vidal). The day after the President returned to the capital, Gore introduced Bryan-approved legislation designed to solve the submarine crisis once and for all. First, any American or neutral ships hauling munitions should be prevented from also carrying American passengers. Second, any country at war should not be permitted to transport American passengers to or from any port in the United States. More important, passports should be denied to any American attempting to travel on the ships of a belligerent nation. In a not-so-subtle reference to the unfortunate McNeely, Gore argued that "no single citizen should be allowed to run the risk of drenching this nation in blood merely in order that he may travel upon a belligerent rather than a neutral vessel."

To critics who accused him of making America "a nation of cowards," the senator had a stinging response his prickly grandson would have appreciated. "It is a little strange that you men with pale faces and chattering teeth are constantly upbraiding those of us who are unafraid with being cowards. It is those of you who are engaged in the wild rush for swords and guns and pistols who are really displaying the white feather. Moral courage despises such physical, mental and moral cowardice. . . . What you really need is a little fresh air, sunshine and exercise. Those are the best antidotes for hysterics."

At the moment, Gore's resolution was unlikely to go anywhere. But Wilson realized that the situation was reaching a crisis point. Even after his months of carefully crafted notes, negotiations, and promises, nothing seemed to be able to keep Americans from being caught in the crossfire. Even the most pacific-minded citizens were losing patience with these episodes and the possibility they would lead to war.

Germany was also losing patience. And the argument the Germans had raised again and again—that they should not be forced to abide by existing international law that had not foreseen modern submarine technology—was beginning to appear more reasonable. "It seems to me to be an absurd proposition that a submarine must come to the surface, give warning, offer to put passengers and crew in safety, and constitute itself a target for merchant ships, that not only make a practice of firing at submarines at sight but have undoubtedly received orders to do so," Ambassador Gerard wrote House from Berlin.

The Germans had already confirmed that such orders existed. Back in the fall, they had confiscated British documents confirming that some commercial vessels were in fact armed with instructions to "fire in self-defense, notwithstanding the submarine may not have committed a definite act such as firing a gun or torpedo." How, then, could U-boats possibly know which merchant vessels could be approached safely and which could not?

Lansing broached this issue with Wilson in the days following the *Persia* sinking. The international situation concerned him. A final disposition of the *Lusitania* affair had yet to be achieved, the main sticking point being an insistence that Germany disavow the act. Lansing also suspected that hard-liners in Germany would soon push for a resumption of unrestricted warfare. That, he knew, would almost certainly embroil America in the war.

The secretary of state had a deceptively simple idea to be presented to both sides. The Allies would agree not to arm any of their nonmilitary vessels. In return, German U-boats would not attack them without warning and would provide for the safety of passengers and crew.

In one fell swoop, Lansing's offer seemingly solved several problems. Allied merchant ships would no longer face the specter of deadly underwater attacks without advance notice, German submarines would no longer be sitting ducks for armed merchant ships, and American passengers would be spared a watery grave. Wilson was supportive, and a note went out a few weeks later.

Whether the belligerents would agree was another matter. Why should the Allies give up a right established in international law (and guaranteed to keep the Germans and Americans at loggerheads) in the midst of a no-holds-barred struggle? And what about the obvious loopholes in the agreement? A German submarine might justify a surprise attack by claiming the vessel in question was armed. Not surprisingly, the always excitable Cecil Spring Rice was horrified. "They can hardly expect that any nation should submit to such a doctrine," the ambassador wrote Foreign Secretary Edward Grey. "If the U.S. persists in the line they have taken we must be prepared to face a serious situation."

Cooler heads in the British Foreign Office were not as concerned. In a lengthy memo that January, Lord Eustace Percy, a diplomat who had served in the British embassy in Washington in the past, boiled current Anglo-American relations down to their essentials. The Americans, it was true, were not "inspired with sentimental Anglo-Saxon feeling . . . do not love us and will not actively help us." Still, "they want us to win" and "serious conflict . . . is a possibility so remote as to be negligible." And he deduced that Wilson was unlikely to push the United Kingdom too hard for political reasons. "If he does anything against the Allies, he exposes himself to an immediate attack from Roosevelt . . . who only needs a handle to turn the country upside down." Ultimately, Percy concluded that the Allies had nothing to fear from the United States. "We can, I believe, so far as America is concerned, adopt any naval policy that we please."

Wilson had yet to grasp that the British were unlikely to yield on anything of substance. (TR himself advised his English friend Arthur Lee that "it would be well for your people to make any unimportant concessions they can and to do it with a great flourish of trumpets, but not to yield on anything that is vital.") The President had approved of House's newest mission in the hope that he might stimulate peace talks and also get the British to bend in their interference with American shipping. The Colonel had departed on the *Rotterdam* on December 28 with two other celebrity passengers onboard: Brand Whitlock, the U.S. ambassador to Belgium, and the recently deported Karl Boy-Ed of the German embassy (minus his American fiancée); and he would have been joined by a third, Addams, had her health woes not interfered. When House arrived in Europe, he was not happy to discover that some intrepid soul had cleverly created a doctored photograph to make it appear the three luminaries had "posed together on the *Rotterdam*. . . . This incident illustrates the worst phase of American journalism."

House immediately went to work, conferencing with Grey and former prime minister Arthur Balfour, who was now First Lord of the Admiralty. The President, he told them, was committed to the United States' participation in "an agreement with the civilized world upon the broad questions touching the interests and future of every nation," including "general elimination . . . of militarism and navalism." But House's rather feeble attempts to bring up the impact of the British blockade on American shipping achieved little. The British public, he was told, would not stand for any relaxation of the blockade, and Grey himself, the lynchpin of House's efforts, would likely be forced to resign.

House made no real attempt to argue the point or press any advantage he might have had, given America's enormously important role in providing the Allies with munitions. Instead, he gave the British absolutely no reason to make even a minuscule concession. Within a week of his arrival, he blithely told cabinet officials that "the United States would like Great Britain to do those things which would enable the United States to help Great Britain win the war." And this attitude, House told them, was shared by the American people, virtually all of Wilson's cabinet, and the President himself. He also yielded to Munitions Minister Lloyd George's preference that Wilson's vague planned "intervention" should occur after the "big battles" of the summer, presumably after the Allies had bettered their military and bargaining position.

Intentionally or unintentionally, House had again reassured British leaders that America was on their side, no matter what they might say or do. He chose not to inform the President of his comments. Strategically, he believed this was the proper course, one certain to lead to peace and a new Wilsonian world order.

Before leaving for France on January 20, House was in constant contact with Wilson, each wire read by British intelligence, who found it child's play to break the simple code they had created. As usual, House laid the flattery on thick, informing the President he could very well "find yourself the potential factor in concluding peace" and that Lloyd George had told him that "no man had ever lived with such an opportunity, and that if the world went on for untold centuries, history would record this as the greatest individual act of which it had record." (House had no inkling that Lloyd George was known for suavely pretending to support causes he actually opposed. The Welshman, meanwhile, would later describe House as "not nearly as cunning as he thought he was.") Still, House would not go as far as to recommend future military involvement, as much as the British would have loved to hear of such a commitment. "I believe I have convinced those to whom I have been able to talk freely," he told Wilson, "that it is best for all concerned for us to keep out, conserving our strength so at the proper moment, we may lead them out of their troubles."

House's secret diplomacy favoring the Allies would have appalled Rosika Schwimmer and her Peace Ship colleagues, had they known what he was up to. Their own long cherished plan—to create a Neutral Conference for Continuous Mediation—was still very much alive, even after the somewhat embarrassing departure of Ford, if not his money, from the mission. With most of the original freeloaders, college students, press representatives, and various hangers-on now on their way home, the true believers were now ready to get the conference, to be based in Stockholm, off the ground. The first step was for the neutral nations, including America, to select permanent members.

Schwimmer realized that an unofficial conference of this kind needed world-renowned peace superstars present to have even the slightest trace of legitimacy. As much as she wished it were so, she did not quite fit the bill, and her connection to a belligerent power as a native of Hungary was also problematic. Everyone wanted Bryan as part of the American delegation, if they could get him, but they especially hoped to get Addams. "We need you," Schwimmer wrote her. "The world needs you."

Addams was willing to go even if she was not at 100 percent. "She has always been able to do miraculous things where her own body was concerned," one friend noted. Addams had made some modest improvement in late December, getting dressed for the first time in weeks and taking automobile rides, which were then believed to promote good health. Yet she was still a sick woman. She now knew that she had tuberculosis of the kidney, likely to require treatment and possibly surgery, although the diagnosis was a relief for those who feared she had cancer. But she felt she could not remain a Hull-House shut-in, not with all the work that needed to be done, especially the upcoming annual Woman's Peace Party meeting in the nation's capital.

Somehow, she managed to drag herself to the Washington gathering in early January. The WPP, she recognized, had made impressive strides in the past year, with more than twenty thousand members and with local chapters throughout the country, including an especially aggressive New York branch. The New Yorkers had recently sponsored Helen Keller's Carnegie Hall speech on "Militarism and the Workers," which included a pointed reference to "war-mad persons, like Colonel Roosevelt." But the organization as a whole had tried not to frighten off potential supporters with excessive radicalism. One member fearfully informed Addams about two young party members who were linking the WPP to the Anti-Enlistment League, which urged young men to pledge not to serve in any future war: "Cannot something be done to squelch these two zealous young women?" Even Addams received a considerable amount of grief about the perceived connection of the Peace Ship with the WPP, although not enough to prevent her reelection as chairman.

Publicizing the party's activities and goals, especially to skeptical government officials, remained difficult. California Representative William Kent, the husband of a WPP member, forwarded *Women at the Hague* to cabinet members and congressmen, few of whom appeared especially interested, even if they did profess to admire Miss Addams's "kindly impulses," if not her pacifist ways. "Where the power of wrong takes actual form in oppression, it must be resisted,—peaceably, indeed, if we can, but forcibly if we must," Secretary of Commerce William Redfield pontificated to Kent. "Were Miss Addams in personal danger, you and I would fight in her defense and she would not think us wrong."

The same condescending tone was apparent when Addams and a delegation of WPP members appeared before the Senate and House Foreign Relations Committees on the last day of the convention. She was forced to correct Henry Cooper, a Wisconsin congressman who insinuated that the silly women had not been taken seriously in their visits to the European powers the previous year. The Senate's behavior was no more enlightened. "With all these charming ladies and so many of them southern ladies," John Sharp Williams of Mississippi, a Wilson man and the supposed "official peace disciple" of the Senate, cooed, "I came not only to listen, I came also to look, and I have enjoyed doing both, I can assure you." He then proceeded to tell a folksy story of an "old Confederate soldier" who had once informed him that it was the fear of the women back home that kept him fighting.

Some of the WPP members were disgusted by the response of Williams and his ilk. But Addams was used to such treatment from men in high places. Most, she knew, believed that politics, foreign relations, and other worldly affairs were no place for women.

The Progressive party, or what was left of it, still valued Addams's involvement, or at least her name. She was invited to a national committee meeting in Chicago, but the WPP get-together made it impossible for her to attend, or at least provided her with a convenient excuse. It was clear to her that the party had continued to drift from its original ideology. Her Progressive friend Harold Ickes, the future secretary of the interior, conceded as much. "Our people just now are stale on questions of industrial justice and social betterment; they simply aren't interested," he observed. And Addams's peace activities had made her persona non grata to TR, virtually the sole reason the party still existed.

Roosevelt himself did not attend the national committee meeting, although his secretary, John McGrath, was present and a TR greeting was read to his followers. Two important developments emerged. The Progressives, the vast majority of whom had been Republicans, made abundantly clear their interest in a reunion with the GOP behind the same candidate ("the Bull Moose and the Elephant kissing each other," quipped one of Wilson's cabinet members). They also decided to hold the Progressive convention in Chicago on June 7, the same day and location as the GOP gathering. "We are all hopeful that both parties may agree on some one," George Perkins announced, "and it NEED NOT NECESSARILY BE MR. ROOSEVELT."

No one was fooled by Perkins's statement. The Dough Moose had just sent out a mailing to determine the degree of support for TR throughout America. Anecdotal evidence seemed to suggest that Roosevelt's political strength was gaining by the day. In Baltimore, Spokane, and New York, movie audiences "went wild" when he appeared on screen in *Battle Cry of Peace*. A Seattle editor informed John Callan O'Laughlin that "men who a little while ago were irreconcilable and ready to froth at the mouth at the mention of his name" were prepared to support TR wholeheartedly in June. "We want a President who is a man to respect and uphold and not one who ought to be in petticoats," a Syracuse factory worker wrote Roosevelt, begging him to run.

TR could not help but enjoy his return from political irrelevance. "Sometimes I have felt that my voice was crying in the wilderness; that there were no hearers," he admitted. Still he was not fooled into believing the majority of the country was behind him, not yet anyway. However noble his determination to "wake up our people to unpleasant facts by telling them unpleasant truths," his efforts had cost him popularity and potential votes, as had his constant jabs at Wilson. TR, some believed, had grown far too "brash," and his "continually dealing in high explosives" in his speeches was a turnoff. At times he seemed to recognize that the ferocity of his attacks was counterproductive, but it was not in his nature to exercise caution or restraint, especially at a time of a "great world crisis" when America would need to determine what kind of nation she would be, now and in the future.

For now, Roosevelt would keep a low profile, at least for him, although his monthly articles in the *Metropolitan*, an occasional public address, and even a preparedness talk in Paramount's new *Pictographs* newsreel magazine kept him in the public eye. Everyone wanted to know his political plans. When he arrived in Philadelphia that January for a speech, crowds greeted him at the Broad Street Station with shouts of "T.R.—next President!" "Come back, Teddy!" and "Oh, you, 1916." Reporters thought he looked well, "a good deal younger than his fifty-seven years and in the pink of condition, with no sign of gray in his sandy hair, less stout than he has been and with no trace of his throat trouble." The following day he was an observer at the Domestic Relations Court, where he listened with great interest to the sad tales of prostitutes arrested by the vice squad. "What sort of women are these?" he asked. "Are they hardened and coarse, or are they merely persons who indulge their wills without restrictions?" Every case was different, he was told, but these unfortunates were not beyond redemption.

The election was still months away, plenty of time for Wilson and the events in Europe to blunt Roosevelt's growing appeal. For now, TR was satisfied. The country, he observed, might not "turn to me, but I am absolutely certain that it will have to turn to the principles I am advocating, and that is the vitally important matter."

The country had already turned. Preparedness, the cause Roosevelt had trumpeted for over a year, was now the word of the hour. Every public figure of note, be they New York Giants manager John McGraw ("Giants are strong for adequate preparedness") or Thomas Edison ("every young buck should be trained as a soldier"), felt the need to weigh in on the issue. Even Al Jolson managed to slip in a reference in his new vehicle, *Robinson Crusoe, Jr.* Jolson's blackface character, Good Friday, a reviewer noted, found himself "surrounded by a throng of dusky cannibals, flourishing spears and knives." "Men of Pittsburgh!" he shouted. "I am glad to know you believe in preparedness."

Such jokes did not go over well with pacifists, who feared America was fast coming to a crossroads. A wrong turn now, they believed, would lead the country permanently down the path of militarism. The signs seemed to be everywhere. School districts, including Chicago's, were considering requiring military drill. Others were pushing for the introduction of rifle practice, a horrifying prospect to Addams. And women seemed as enthusiastic as the men. That January, an annoyed Ellen Slayden wrote in her diary of solicitations from "the Women's Section of the Movement for Preparedness." Even an American Woman's League for Self-Defense had recently been created, its goal to "enlist every able-bodied woman in the United States and to have her ready to do her bit."

That preparedness might lead to a draft especially concerned the pacifists. Such an undemocratic policy was bound to tilt the country rightward. A high-powered business tycoon informed Addams's friend Lillian Wald that conscription would be a fine thing since it would teach workers "how to obey" and "the necessity of doing what they were told." "That," Wald lamented, "is the greatest danger of conscription."

Wilson's recent preparedness proposals, of course, had said nothing about conscription. In fact, it was soon obvious that the administration would find it difficult to get any program through Congress. Large blocs of Democratic congressmen from the rural South and Midwest, many of them Bryan disciples, were opposed to any kind of increase, such as the eighty-year-old Isaac Sherwood of Ohio, the only Union officer currently serving in the House and a veteran of more than forty Civil War battles. "It is proposed to tax a patient and tolerant people that an overpowering *army of idlers* may be rendered to consume the savings of the industrial classes; increasing the already high cost of living and producing nothing but discontent and trouble," the ancient Sherwood sneered. "It is a crime against the republic, without sanity and without excuse." Naturally, Bryan was pleased.

More moderate congressmen were prepared to vote for some kind of increased defense measures. Two distinct proposals dominated the discussion. Garrison continued to advocate for what TR called a "small and insufficient increase in the regular army" to 140,000 and the creation of a 400,000 Continental Army reserve. The alternative was a plan backed by the Virginia Democrat James Hay, the chair of the House Military Affairs Committee, calling for a modest boost in the regular army and the National Guard under federal control. The war secretary, in his usual imperious manner, virtually demanded that Wilson take his side, especially since he viewed the House of Representatives as a bunch of know-nothings. The President, recognizing the mood in Congress and the considerable influence of the state National Guards, would do no such thing. He would keep an open mind, an answer that irritated the already prickly Garrison, who had begun to see the struggle in intensely personal terms. Hay, he later insisted, had a "hatred of the North" and by extension, Garrison, a New Jersey native.

Five weeks of congressional hearings, from January 6 to February 11, would determine the fate of the dueling plans and Wilson's preparedness program in general. Addams, representing the WPP, was permitted an audience on the morning of January 13 before Hay's committee. In the first week of hearings, the committee had already been bombarded with pro-military arguments, facts, and figures from Garrison, Assistant Secretary of War Henry Breckinridge, and two generals, Hugh Scott and Tasker Bliss.

In her opening statement, she admitted it might seem "absurd" for a woman to speak before a committee of this kind. Still, decisions made in Washington had an enormous impact on the women of America, especially now when the country was so afflicted with "war contagion . . . a good deal like the case of a man living in the middle of Kansas who, hearing that there were a great many burglaries in New York City, thereupon immediately armed himself against the advent of burglars, although there were none in Kansas."

Addams then presented her case. The world after the war would present unprecedented opportunities for arms reduction among the major powers. If America "were at least to postpone this proposed policy of military expansion, we could go in for such an international program with clean hands" and be in a position to spearhead any efforts in that direction. "It would be a great mistake," she insisted, "if the United States did not take advantage of the opportunity which presents itself to turn the world, not toward a continuation of the policy of armed peace, but toward the beginning of an era of disarmament and the cessation of warfare."

And why did Congress and the administration feel the need to act so hastily? "The lessons of the European war," she explained, "are not yet learned." Why, for example, invest millions of dollars in dreadnoughts (early battleships) that might prove obsolete in a few years? Why not first create an impartial fact-finding commission (a favorite scheme of every progressive reformer) to analyze the army and navy budgets, already consuming 30 percent of federal revenue, and see "whether it is really an increase in the Army and Navy which is needed?" Such a commission, created by Congress, could also look into the "motives" of the individuals and groups most vociferously pressing for preparedness. Six months, Addams believed, should be sufficient for the commission to do its work and head off the current hysteria, a good deal of which seemed to be fueled by the supposedly cool, calm, and collected male of the species. "I do not like to say that men are more emotional than women, but whenever I go to a national political convention and hear men cheering for a candidate for 1 hour and 15 minutes, it seems to me that perhaps men are somewhat emotional. I think the same thing is true in regard to this war."

Questions then followed. That the very first inquiry, from Ohio Democrat William Gordon, was an obvious attempt to contrast Addams's current pacifism with her support of Roosevelt in 1912 could not help but annoy her. She had joined the Progressive party, she explained, because of its "program of what seems to me to be a very remarkable political expression of social justice."

Gordon was not satisfied. "But as you understand it," he began, "a great many other citizens supported Mr. Roosevelt—"

"He was not talking as he is now," Addams interrupted. Her gallery of female supporters burst into applause. "He was talking minimum wages, the protection of children and women in industry, and things of that sort."

Gordon continued his TR questioning. Was Roosevelt's preparedness crusade sincere or just a means to discredit Wilson?

It was sincere, she told the congressman. "There are people of a certain type of mind, such as Col. Roosevelt, who are ready for a challenge and who think that the only way to defend the national honor is to fight for it. I do not think that type represents a large body of people." Once again, the ladies present cheered.

The committee finally moved away from questions about Roosevelt to hear Addams's views on the press ("distinctly misleading"), the volatile Mexican situation ("I admire the President for keeping peace"), and military instruction in the schools ("outrageous . . . very much to be deplored"). But several of the cagy congressmen seemed intent on making her look foolish. Hadn't wars existed, one asked, long before there was ever a "munition trust"?

"I did not claim that that was the only reason for war, nor even the chief reason," she retorted.

Frank Greene, a Vermont Republican and Spanish-American War vet, reminded her that "the doctrine of physical force has played a tremendous part in the evolution of civilization."

Yes, she replied, "war has persisted but society may get rid of it as it has gotten rid of other things, the black plague, for instance." Greene, thinking he had trapped her into an inflammatory statement, pressed his advantage.

Was Miss Addams actually suggesting war and diseases were "on the same plane"?

No, she was not saying that, she explained. "You spoke of war having been inevitable and I made the illustration that certain diseases, at one time considered inevitable, are now obsolete."

A few hours later, she repeated her arguments before the Senate committee. Some wanted to know more about the women's meeting at The Hague of last year. "All we tried to do," Addams explained, "was to get out a set of resolutions, looking to permanent peace. . . . We had a very fine set of resolutions all looking toward the establishment of peace. They have been highly spoken of in European countries, and President Wilson said that it was the best series of resolutions he had seen up to that time." She spoke of a future where a world organization of some kind might effectively use economic sanctions to maintain peace and how such an organization might have been sufficient to prevent the current conflict. And she was definitely not recommending "peace at any price" or eliminating the army.

Once again, she sparred with a committee member, this time Thomas Catron, an elderly Confederate veteran now representing New Mexico as a Republican. Catron did not accept Addams's contention that the United States was not France with an ancient and heavily armed foe in her backyard. America, he told her, "should get ready."

Politely but firmly, she put him in his place. "It seems to me," she interjected, "that to get ready for a hypothetical enemy, which does not exist, and spend our people's money for something in the air, is absolutely wrong."

Between her House and Senate testimony, Addams managed to squeeze in a quick interview with the President. At the moment, there was not much to discuss, although Wilson indicated that he remained familiar with the resolutions passed at the women's congress at The Hague. Presumably, the Ford expedition came up in the conversation, Addams likely reassuring him that the press reports were exaggerated.

With minimal stamina, she had accomplished a great deal in Washington, but she knew she needed to go home to continue her recuperation under Mary's careful watch. Addams was heartened that Bryan and others thought she had done well in her testimony. Much of the press and public did not agree, again choosing to attack the woman they had once venerated. Miss Addams, they insisted, fancied herself the "world's Messiah" and had no right butting her nose into military affairs. "Somebody ought to lead Miss Jane Addams back to social service," the *Minneapolis Journal* scoffed. "She may know how long it will take Hull-House to get a job for a woman out of work, but does she know how long it takes to turn raw recruits into seasoned troops?" A Utah paper was even more vicious: "About the best thing that could happen to Miss Jane Addams . . . would be a strong, forceful husband who would lift the burden of fate from her shoulders and get her intensely interested in fancywork and other things dear to the heart of women who have homes and plenty of time on their hands."

Back in Chicago, Addams soon discovered that even "fancywork" would be beyond her capacities for the foreseeable future. She was told she had "several tubercular foci in her system," such that an operation on the affected kidney was unlikely to solve her health issues. Instead, she was ordered to leave for California for two months, where the climate and "serum treatment" (probably tuberculin, today used to detect but not to treat TB) would hopefully cure her condition. Mary, of course, would accompany her.

There was now no chance that she could go to Europe to join the Neutral Conference. Both Schwimmer and Lochner pleaded with her to find a way to come, Schwimmer even suggesting that Europe might be an ideal place to recuperate. "Your coming and that of Mr. Bryan is to my mind absolutely essential to the success of this movement," Lochner wrote her. "Your coming will give the prestige to the Conference almost as nothing else could do." Privately, he wondered whether this might be a "friend's trick" (Mary?) and urged his colleague Alfred Kliefoth, now sailing home on the *Rotterdam*, to "try to prevent it. Essential she come here."

It was too late. Addams's doctors would not permit an ocean voyage. Nor was Bryan coming: he felt his greatest value now was in the fight against preparedness. With Addams, Bryan, and Ford nowhere to be seen, Schwimmer and her colleagues knew the Neutral Conference would be facing a desperate struggle for relevancy.

W hat Ford was thinking at the moment was a mystery to everyone. Not only had the promised $200,000 failed to materialize, but pacifists had found Ford almost impossible to reach since he arrived home.

There was talk that one of his handlers did not want him to see Addams and that Ford had been "poisoned by adverse criticism" of her. Strangely, he had also taken it upon himself to invite Roosevelt to Detroit, perhaps to explain his much misunderstood recent activities.

TR, taken aback, reminded Ford that he was "emphatically out of sympathy with you (just as I am radically out of sympathy with my friend, Miss Addams), as regards this pacifist agitation." Perhaps Ford might wish to rescind his invitation. If he did come, Roosevelt warned, his host could expect to be lectured that he should "use your great influence" toward achieving the proper kind of peace, a peace of "righteousness."

Ford (or, more likely, one of his secretaries) wrote back a very pleasant letter explaining that he would be happy to talk peace with TR, even if they disagreed. "Honest criticism of my efforts in any direction have always been beneficial to me in working out problems." Although Roosevelt then agreed to "go over at length with you this pacifist business," he eventually decided against it for now.

Addams and other pacifists recognized that Ford remained an unpredictable, albeit invaluable, commodity. They could take heart that preparedness, the issue that had stirred Ford's mind in the first place, continued to encounter roadblocks in Congress. "There is no enthusiasm on the 'hill' for preparedness," Tumulty warned Wilson a few days after Addams's testimony. And the people themselves seemed to be befuddled about how to proceed. Now was the time for the President to present his case as a reasonable alternative to the extremes of the pacifists and the militarists. "They are reluctant to follow Mr. Roosevelt except in sheer desperation, and they are waiting for you," Tumulty explained.

Wilson did not disagree. It would also be a good chance to show that it was he, and not a certain William Jennings Bryan, who now controlled the party. Bryan himself thought the President would benefit from mixing with his constituents. "He will find that the mass of the people are not frightened by imaginary wars," the Great Commoner observed.

The plan was that Wilson would spend a week away from Washington, concentrating his speeches mostly on the preparedness-ambivalent Midwest. On Thursday, January 27, he gave a few warm-up addresses in

New York before leaving on the tour. One was at the Waldorf-Astoria, where a determined group of Congressional Union suffragettes, eventually numbering over two hundred, parked themselves for hours, hoping to get an audience with the President before his speech. An annoyed Wilson eventually appeared for a few minutes, offering no encouragement on the Susan B. Anthony amendment.

"The labor men didn't have to wait for 'state by state' growth when they got the Clayton-Sherman anti-trust bill through," one suffrage advocate complained afterward. "We are going to hold President Wilson to *strict accountability* on this issue."

The tour began in Pittsburgh (still spelled *sans* "h" by some). Wilson, while an accomplished speaker, was a bit out of practice and his two addresses were more professorial than spellbinding. About 6,500 present at the two venues listened to Wilson tell them of his love for peace, his opposition to a large standing army, and his desire for a substantial reserve of trained men. Why did America need this? Because peace, as much as both he and the country wished it, was no longer entirely within their control. "The world is on fire, and there is tinder everywhere," he warned. "The sparks are liable to drop anywhere, and somewhere there may be material which we cannot prevent from bursting into flame." He also managed to slip in a jab at TR, mentioning "other counselors, the source of whose counsel is passion, and with them I cannot agree."

As usual, everyone wanted to see Edith. She refused to cooperate with the photographers, who tried vainly to get her to stop obscuring her face with various periodicals, although one intrepid cameraman finally got a good shot. On stage at Memorial Hall, she sat alongside her husband, reporters noting how the newlyweds "chatted and smiled at each other as only true lovers can." And the reviews of her outfit and appearance were enthusiastic. One onlooker noted that the new First Lady, "although she is a large woman," was "winsome," blessed with a "clear complexion" that "shows her health."

In speeches over the next five days, Wilson returned to the same themes. The world was in flames, "our own house is not fireproof," and he was not a superman able to keep American peace and honor indefinitely. Preparedness of some kind, then, was necessary. This preparedness, he emphasized,

Wilson speaks to a crowd in Waukegan, Illinois, during his preparedness tour, January 31, 1916. (Library of Congress: LC-USZ62-131813)

would be entirely reasonable, a middle ground between those who "tell you that we have no means of defense, and others [who] tell you that we have sufficient means of defense." Without naming names, he similarly presented himself as between those "preaching war" in America and those "preaching the doctrine of peace at any price." The reference to "preaching war" was another swipe at TR, as was a similar comment about "the loudest voices have been the irresponsible voices. It is easy to talk and to say what ought to be done when you know that you do not have to do it." Still, the President continued to avoid using any names, though at times it was obvious to everyone present. A reference to "some men are so hopelessly and contentedly provincial that they cannot see the rest of the world" elicited a cry of "Do you mean Bryan?"

His arguments grew more forceful and specific as the days went on. The United States had an "army so small that I have not had men enough to patrol the Mexican border," he warned. And its current navy had the nearly impossible job of patrolling an "enormous stretch of coast from the canal to Alaska—from the canal to the northern coast of Maine. . . . No other navy in the world . . . has to cover so great an area . . . as the American navy, and it ought, in my judgment, to be incomparably the *greatest navy in the world*." The St. Louis crowd loved it, but Wilson would later sheepishly admit he had gotten swept up in the moment on the stump, "intoxicated by the exuberance of my own verbosity."

The trip was taxing and sleeping conditions were less than ideal, with most nights spent on a noisy train. There was also the very real danger that any president faced appearing in public. William McKinley's assassination was less than fifteen years ago and TR himself had been shot during the last presidential campaign. At Cleveland, Wilson's second stop, rumors surfaced that he had dodged an assassination attempt; the rumors were later traced to the presence of a harmless Armenian immigrant, carrying a razor blade in his overcoat, who claimed to have no knowledge that the President was in town. Two more threats awaited him in Chicago, one from a New Yorker who eventually jumped to his death from the fourteenth floor of the Blackstone Hotel and another from a disturbed individual promising to "kill the President with a pair of scissors."

Security was especially beefed up in Milwaukee, said to be the "Munich of America," a place where department stores expected their hirelings to be fluent in German. But Wilson did not seem to be especially concerned. The reporters noted that the President ate heartily and consumed his typical breakfast of "oatmeal, bacon, two boiled eggs, coffee and rolls." And the people, even where preparedness was an afterthought at best, seemed to be hanging on to his every word. They roared when he said "America is not afraid of anybody" and shouted "yes!" when he asked if they would "back me up and come to my assistance . . . knowing what you are about." (An unfortunate but all-too-typical anecdote during his Milwaukee speech about an "old darky preacher" likely did not go over well among any African Americans present.)

The man said to lack the common touch appeared to be more popular than anyone realized. Frigid weather in Des Moines did not deter one Wilson follower, who proclaimed "I don't care if my ears do freeze, I'm going to see Woody!" During a whistle-stop in East St. Louis, another admirer ran after the departing train, shouting, "Put it there, Wilson," who happily obliged him. The crowds especially enjoyed bantering with Wilson about Edith. "Get out of the way so we can see her," they called to Wilson on the train platform in Rock Island, Illinois. At the Moline, Illinois, train station, a boy with a "kodak" made a similar request. "I admire your taste,"

Wilson replied before moving aside. "And we admire your taste," one wag quipped.

By the time Wilson returned home on February 4, reporters estimated he had covered four thousand miles in the past week, made twenty-five separate stops, spoke to roughly 130,000 people, and had been seen by perhaps half a million. That the trip was a tremendous success seemed to be taken for granted. "He is incomparably stronger than when he started," a *New York Tribune* correspondent conceded. "He has gained in every way— support for his policy, personal popularity, political standing and leadership, and, most important of all, in his ability to reach and move the people." But how much the President gained remained uncertain. Most of the audiences who came to hear him were not the rural folk most fearful of militarism. And his "furious shouting that he is now for preparedness," as TR dismissively labeled the tour, concerned the pacifists, who heard disturbing echoes of Teddy himself in some of the speeches.

Wilson was pleased with the tour, "a most interesting and inspiring experience, much fuller of electrical thrills than I had expected." Still, he did not have long to enjoy his triumph. He returned to a Washington simmering with tension. Germany had continued to refuse to admit that the *Lusitania* sinking was illegal. If some concession was not made soon, a diplomatic break was likely, and then possibly war. The kaiser himself was alarmed. "He had spent half the night a prey to the thought that he was responsible for now having involved the unhappy German nation which had already made such huge sacrifices, in a new war," Admiral Müller wrote in his diary that week. "To console him I said that America wanted war— this is my firm conviction—and had given her pledge to England that she would intervene when the time was ripe." Judging by the content of House's recent conversations in London, Müller was not that far off.

House himself believed that it would not be ideal for America to enter the war now based on the lack of a "suitable apology" over a "nine months' old issue," especially when the Germans were likely to do something equally outrageous in the future. The Germans eventually came through with a reply close enough to Wilson and Lansing's demands: "profound regret," a willingness to accept "liability" (rather than admitting any illegality), and an offer to pay reparations. The *Lusitania* affair was finally put to bed.

But the submarine crisis was very much alive. Lansing's January proposal suggesting that Allied merchant ships be unarmed in exchange for immunity from German surprise attacks had gone nowhere. Instead, the Germans were preparing to shift the submarine campaign in a far more aggressive direction. "Time," as Chief of Staff General Erich von Falkenhayn conceded, "was against us." But unrestricted submarine warfare, coupled with an upcoming go-for-broke assault on Verdun, could potentially bring the war to a close this year.

The kaiser was ambivalent about moving forward. Albert Ballin, director of the Hamburg-America Line, warned him that at best the submarines would not be enough to do more than "greatly inconvenience England." Equally unenthusiastic were Chancellor Bethmann and Karl Georg von Treutler of the German Foreign Office, who believed it would result in a certain "alliance with America for which England has always striven, an alliance which will spell our utter ruin."

The combined naval and military pressure was too strong. As of February 29, all enemy merchant ships that were armed would be subject to attacks without warning, with the likelihood that neutral passengers (namely, Americans) would be caught in the crossfire. (Much to his embarrassment, Lansing recognized that his own recent scheme provided additional justification for classifying armed merchant ships as warships.) And German naval authorities were still not entirely satisfied, hoping that full-blown unrestricted warfare without limitations of any kind would be the next step.

The "tinder" that Wilson had warned about seemed ready to ignite, this time for good.

O n Capitol Hill, the preparedness situation remained muddled. The secretary of war was not going to get his Continental Army. That much was certain. Garrison had begun to talk of some sort of "compulsory enlistment for training," a favorite TR idea, but one that Wilson could not stomach. Southern representatives were especially hostile, fearing the prospect of thousands of African Americans receiving military training. Nor did Wilson fully agree with Garrison's opposition to recent congressional

moves regarding the timetable for returning self-government to the Philippines. The two men were not especially fond of each other and had never
agreed on much, if Garrison's frequent threats to resign were any indication. When Garrison submitted his latest resignation on February 10, Wilson accepted. "I think Wilson was damn glad to see me go," Garrison
recalled years later. The former professor wanted a "school-boy type," he
believed, and Garrison was not that.

Rumors flew that Colonel House, Interior Secretary Lane, or perhaps
even Franklin Roosevelt would take Garrison's place. But Wilson chose to
go in a different direction, eventually selecting Newton Diehl Baker, a man
he had known since his Johns Hopkins days who had already declined the
secretary of the interior job. On paper, the diminutive, bespectacled Baker
(said to resemble "a miniature edition of Woodrow Wilson") seemed like a
solid choice: lawyer, good Democrat, and former progressive mayor of
Cleveland. But his past involvement with peace organizations (he was said
to be "in sympathy" with the peace ship) and lukewarm attitudes toward
preparedness made him a somewhat puzzling choice as secretary of war.

The anti-Wilson elements of the press did their best to present Baker
as some sort of sissy who did not play with tin soldiers as a child and loved
flowers. Baker himself immediately disclosed his sordid pacifist past to the
President, who was not at all concerned. The new secretary of war would
prove to be a perfect fit for the cabinet, a good foot soldier who worked
well with Wilson, far from the obstinate and somewhat egomaniacal Garrison. And Baker soon discovered that the President "had a deep-seated
religious belief that someway and somehow the U.S. could keep out of the
war, and that an opportunity would come for the government to act as the
great pacifier."

The day after Garrison's departure, TR and his wife left Oyster Bay to
begin his several-week trip to the West Indies, supposedly to strengthen
Edith's health after her operation the previous spring. The air was chilly
at the East River pier, but press and newsreel cameras came out in force
to get Roosevelt's thoughts on Garrison's resignation (they were advised to
read his just published book "now on sale by all booksellers") and the

Lusitania ("if a man's wife's face is slapped and he talks about it for eight months it is of no earthly consequence what action he then takes"). Would Roosevelt do any hunting? No, the West Indies were not exactly hunting territory. Meanwhile, a well-wisher present was shocked that TR not only knew his name but remembered that he had last seen him almost eighteen years before, during the Spanish-American War, as the commander of a vessel bringing him home from Cuba.

A thirteen-year-old Brooklyn girl named Marjorie Sterrett was also there to meet Roosevelt. A week earlier, she had written a pro-preparedness letter to the editor of the *New York Tribune*, enclosing a dime to start a fund to "help build a battle ship for Uncle Sam" to be called *America*. Within a few days, the *Tribune* had already collected $133.30, including ten dimes from TR himself, one for each of his four grandchildren and six for future offspring. "Grandchildren and battleships go together, you know," Roosevelt announced. "We have to have the battleships to protect the grandchildren." Sterrett was starstruck. "He looks just like the cartoons, doesn't he?" she asked. "His teeth are so square and white. I think he's dandy."

One reporter made an interesting observation. TR seemed to leave the country "when things political got hot and everybody in politics was guessing what you were going to do." Roosevelt made no response. He was not about to show his hand. A few minutes later, the *Guiana* sailed away. Photographers and newsreel cameramen looked in vain for TR, who had disappeared from view.

Wilson was likely not unhappy to see TR disappear for a while. "There are only two things he is afraid of," Roosevelt had scoffed before leaving. "I am one and the Kaiser is the other." (Ambassador Bernstorff reported the comment to Berlin as a sign of TR's growing "madness.") The submarine situation was growing more delicate by the day, even though the *Lusitania* matter was apparently closed. The President and Lansing had backed away from trying to broker some sort of compromise involving the conduct of submarine warfare, which neither side wanted. The matter now at hand was Germany's new and dangerous policy, which was taking effect in two weeks. If German submarines would soon be treating all armed merchant ships as quasi-warships and attacking them without warning, American travelers would be putting themselves and their country at risk.

The day-to-day pressure on Wilson was enormous. Ida Tarbell sensed it when she spoke to him at a dinner party at the home of Navy Secretary Josephus Daniels in Washington a few days after the President returned from his speaking tour. "No one can tell how anxious it is," he told her. "I never go to bed without realizing that I may be called up by news that will mean that we are at war." His primary task, he explained, was "not to see red" and keep events from spiraling out of control. Meanwhile, Tarbell noted that Wilson appeared in good spirits, sharing stories and limericks, although she felt his wife "didn't reach him in distinction."

The President already knew that evening that trouble was brewing in Congress. Two days later, Jeff McLemore, a Texas Democrat and Bryan disciple said to have "little schooling, because of his aversion to teachers," introduced a resolution that American citizens should be warned against traveling on armed merchant ships. That, along with Senator Gore's earlier attempt in January to deny passports to Americans traveling on armed belligerent ships, spelled serious difficulties for the administration.

Wilson made his current position crystal clear in an hour-long evening meeting at the White House on February 21 with three leading Democrats: William Stone, chair of the Senate Foreign Relations Committee and who was already suspicious of the administration's favoritism toward the Allies; Senator John Kern, the unofficial majority leader; and Representative Henry Flood, chair of the House Foreign Affairs Committee. They listened as the President explained that he would not and could not support any congressional attempt to stop Americans from traveling on armed belligerent ships. Nor would he tolerate a German attack on armed merchant vessels, which would likely mean a break in diplomatic relations. His stance appeared dangerously rigid to his listeners, who feared it might lead to war. The always in-the-know John Callan O'Laughlin heard that "there was a good deal of profanity exchanged." Stone, according to one colorful report, "banged his fist on the president's desk and said: 'Mr. President, would you draw a shutter over my eyes and my intellect? You have no right to ask me to follow such a course. It may mean war for my country. I must follow my conscience in this matter.'"

But Wilson was prepared to follow his own conscience. For better or for worse, he had positioned himself as the champion of neutral rights; to surrender now would undo every agonizing effort expended in that direction since 1914. It would mean that Bryan and not Wilson dictated the fortunes of the Democratic party and that Congress, not the President, dictated foreign policy. And it would also effectively destroy his standing among the belligerents and any hope that he might mediate in the future.

The legitimacy of his presidency hung in the balance over an issue that many Americans still struggled to fully comprehend, especially those residing in the hinterlands who had no need or desire for international travel. Those who did saw things very differently. Since there were only a handful of American ships, anyone contemplating a trip to or from Europe for legitimate purposes usually traveled on European vessels of either a belligerent or neutral country (Addams and Ford, for example, had made their journeys on Dutch and Danish liners). In 1915, steamships under a belligerent flag carried more than a quarter million passengers between Europe and the major ports of the United States, almost five times as many as American ships. And in certain parts of the world such as Africa, travelers had virtually no choice but to book passage on European ships.

At the moment, few of the Democratic leaders in the House were prepared to stand with Wilson. The McLemore resolution, then, had a good chance of passing. It was now up to the President to muster his inner strength and determination to win what could prove to be an unprecedented battle on Capitol Hill.

Wilson had disclosed nothing of what House was currently up to in Europe. The Colonel had reached Germany on January 26 after brief stops in France and Switzerland. The Germans had him "under constant surveillance," as he had been in England and France. As usual, everyone went out of their way to see the President's "friend," recognizing his importance if not quite understanding his position. Bethmann, then in the midst of the struggle over the new submarine campaign, spent more than an hour with the supposedly neutral House, who did his best to convince him that the British were a "stubborn race" determined to win or fight to the last man. The Colonel noticed that the German chancellor quaffed a generous amount of beer, which "did not apparently affect him, for his brain was as befuddled at the beginning as it was at the end. Into such hands are the destinies of the people placed." While in Germany, House picked up a fifty-mark coin inscribed "Gott strafe England and America" (God punish England and America), which he later gave to King George V.

As usual, the Colonel kept Wilson apprised of his comings and goings. Nothing could be done now, he told the President, since he expected (correctly, as it turned out) that "hell will break loose in Europe this spring and summer as never before." Afterward, Wilson's chance would come. In the meantime, House continued his peculiar strategy of letting the Allies know that they could count on the future assistance of the United States. "I again told them that the lower the fortunes of the Allies ebbed, the closer the United States would stand by them," he wrote in his diary. He informed French officials of the "necessity of helping the United States to help them" and intimated that America would be involved "before the end of the year," provided a sufficiently explosive "incident" occurred. Shocked, the French diplomat Jules Cambon specifically asked House to repeat his statement a second time, wrote it out in English, and then had House confirm it. "Exactly," he told Cambon.

Not surprisingly, the Colonel once again did not disclose the precise details of this conversation to Wilson, which went far beyond what he would have authorized (instead he left the President with the impression that the intervention promised would not be of the military kind; House would later claim that the French misunderstood him). At times, House appeared to forget Wilson altogether, while he basked in the fawning attention of foreign dignitaries. The French themselves could not help but notice how the Colonel's head had been turned. After talking to him a few weeks later, Jules Jusserand, the French ambassador to Washington, observed that the President's friend was still swooning and "congratulated himself enormously on the courteous welcome he had received" in Paris.

On House's return to London on February 9, newsmen, both British and

American, were eager to pick his brains about a variety of subjects, including TR's recent statements about Wilson. But the Colonel offered them nothing of value. He also conferenced with Walter Hines Page, whose Anglophilia continued to worsen (one British editor told House that the American ambassador was "more British than any Englishman he knew"), so much so that he was now openly bashing Wilson and the administration. "Everything the President was doing was wrong, the contempt of the British and Europe generally for us was growing stronger every day, and the United States was in bad odor everywhere," Page told a highly annoyed House. The usually mild-mannered House "literally flayed him," but it seemed to have little effect. Each man viewed the other as a nuisance. "House is doing a lot of harm here," Page wrote in his diary.

The Colonel did not see it that way. His talks with Sir Edward Grey led him to believe that "the beginning of the end of the war" might be in sight. They had agreed on a basic plan: Wilson would "demand" that the belligerents consent to a peace conference in the very near future, the Allies would go along, but if the Germans refused, "we would throw all our weight in order to bring her to terms." (Page, finally clued in, was disgusted by what he called "a carefully sprung trick!") The problem was that House's pet scheme did not excite Grey's colleagues at all. Any minister in favor would likely feel the wrath of the British public who might "even go so far as to smash his windows," according to Grey himself.

Between his discussions with Grey, Asquith, Lloyd George, generals, editors, and other leading lights, House had ample time to amuse himself. He took in the play *Caroline*, a comedy by W. Somerset Maugham, whose literary stature had soared since the publication of *Of Human Bondage* the previous summer. The distinguished Hungarian-born artist Philip de László painted his portrait, adding House to an already impressive list of the high and mighty who had sat for him, including the kaiser and TR.

After thirteen days in London, the Colonel saw Grey for the final time. Grey had written a document, later to be known as the House-Grey Memorandum, laying out precisely what had been proposed. Wilson would call a peace conference when the Allies decided the "moment was opportune." If the Germans declined to participate, America would "*probably* enter the war against Germany." If by some chance Germany *did* participate, the

Allies could expect an agreement "not unfavourable" to them. If no agreement were reached and Germany was "unreasonable," the Allies could expect America to join them in the fight. Finally, the offer was not good indefinitely. If the Allies waited too long and American intervention would no longer turn the tide, then "the United States would probably disinterest themselves in Europe." Still, Grey did not commit himself fully. He would have to "inform the Prime Minister and my Colleagues" and "could say nothing until it had received their consideration." The other Allies would also have to be consulted, as would Wilson, of course.

The Colonel was more than satisfied, as apparently was the British foreign secretary. They talked of how in some not-too-distant time House might visit Grey, no longer troubled by the cares of war, at his home in Northumberland. "You and I speak the same language," Grey told him. Privately, Grey was not nearly so optimistic. The House scheme, he believed, could not be ignored, since it might be another weapon in the British arsenal if their fortunes faltered. On the other hand, if the Allies were nearing victory, it had no value whatsoever. Time would tell.

An excited House believed he had single-handedly pulled off a sensational diplomatic coup. Before sailing for home on the *Rotterdam*, he wired Wilson that he had "much of great importance to communicate that I dare not cable" (the Colonel remained unaware that British intelligence was reading most of his messages). But Page, who was now certain that the latest submarine crisis would put America in the war very shortly, believed House had accomplished absolutely nothing. "He cannot come again—or I go."

Chapter 11

A TEST OF STRENGTH

FEBRUARY 24–MARCH 24, 1916

*The President, in his unreasonable and obstinate
stand in the present submarine controversy, is
making the biggest mistake of his life.*

—Representative Claude Kitchin, February 1916

olonel House's efforts notwithstanding, the outlook for peace did not appear encouraging at the moment. The sheer scale of the recently begun German attack on Verdun suggested that months of fighting still lay ahead. And the bitter struggle in Washington over travel on armed vessels frightened pacifists who feared that the issue might drag America into the war. Edward Krehbiel, a professor and peace advocate, briefed Addams's friend Lillian Wald about the current situation on Capitol Hill. "No one seems to think that war is really possible," he informed her, "but on the other hand, they do not see any way out of it unless Wilson or Germany backs down, and one of the congressmen frankly said that he believed that Congress would not support Wilson if he brought this matter to a breaking point."

Addams, now in California, remained hopeful that the Neutral Conference (the "Counsel of Imperfection," as she called it) might prove invaluable now that it was up and running. But the reports from Europe were not encouraging. The press had gotten wind of a December wire she had sent instructing the International Committee of Women for

Permanent Peace to keep separate from the Ford party, forcing Addams to reiterate her own personal support of the Peace Ship mission. Even worse, the failure of Schwimmer to come up with Ford's promised $200,000 to the International Committee was growing more embarrassing by the day, both sides burdening the always sympathetic Addams with their version of events.

A growing number of complaints about Schwimmer's role in the conference had reached Addams, but she tried to give the tempestuous Hungarian the benefit of the doubt. Schwimmer, Addams was well aware, was an impassioned and truly gifted woman, whose devotion, nay *obsession*, with peace was unmatched in Europe or America. From the moment she set foot in America in September 1914, she had accomplished great things: the interviews with Wilson, the speeches that inspired the women's peace movement, the visits to the belligerent powers, and the alliance with Ford. And her supporters were sure she had pushed Addams in a more aggressive direction.

But Addams had also witnessed Schwimmer's unfortunate faults: her haughtiness when challenged, her secretiveness, her self-pity, her considerable ego, her inability to handle money—all of which were dramatically amplified with Ford's millions behind her. Julia Grace Wales saw firsthand that Schwimmer was not the right person for the job. "The trouble with her is just that she is ambitious, that she craves credit, that above all she craves power, and that the craving has practically become mania," Wales wrote her family. "She is rather a tragedy, for I think she started sincere, and supposes herself to be sincere still." Her support eroding, Schwimmer resigned from her position with the Neutral Conference at the end of February, though she promised Addams that she would eventually hear the "true story."

Schwimmer's departure allowed the Neutral Conference to go about its business in the months ahead: developing, disseminating, and publicizing peace terms and proposals. Wales, Lochner, and others did their best under difficult circumstances (and increasing belt-tightening ordered by Ford) to try something that had never been tried before. But missing were the pacifist heavyweights who might have given the conference greater gravitas. "A ship-load of amateurs, enthusiasts and hangers-on may serve for a

demonstration," David Starr Jordan wrote Addams. "But mediation requires elements quite different."

That Addams could not be there was tremendously frustrating (at one
point, she had hoped that she and Emily Balch could alternate as one of
the representatives), although she tried to offer advice through letters.
"There is no time of my life when I would rather not have had such a severe
illness," she told Schwimmer, "but apparently I was given no choice in the
matter." Alarmingly, Addams's condition seemed to be worsening, forcing
her back into bed under the care of Mary Rozet Smith (David Starr Jordan's
wife, Jessie, who visited them in San Francisco, thought Mary was her
"secretary"). Addams's mood grew increasingly depressed, so much so that
her niece Marcet made a special trip to see her. Almost immediately her
spirits improved, but Marcet would later acknowledge that her aunt "felt
her distance from momentous events."

Addams was still close enough to the domestic situation, which continued to center around Wilson. Like other pacifists, she could not help
but feel some disenchantment with the President's recent preparedness
speeches, which seemed to be bordering on TR's views. On the other hand,
Wilson had not cut the peace crowd off and was willing to hear their arguments and proposals. And his progressive credentials remained more
than intact, especially after his recent controversial selection of Louis
Brandeis, considered by some to be "an extreme radical surcharged with
what are generally denominated socialistic proclivities," as the first Jewish
justice to sit on the Supreme Court. (Some believed the nomination was a
secret quid pro quo for buying Mary Hulbert's stash of correspondence with
Wilson.) That Addams knew Brandeis, and his wife, Alice, was a Women's
Peace Party member offered even more encouragement.

The question remained whether it was finally time to directly criticize
the President. The risks were considerable. Some feared that such a stance
would lead to a TR victory over Wilson in the November election. Better,
then, to attack the President's policies, but not the man himself.

David Starr Jordan, among others, believed such a policy was wise.
Wilson, he continued to insist, was "'the most precious asset of the cause
of peace, for he has held us from war and will continue to do so.' I do not
want to do anything to make his position harder."

At the moment, Wilson was facing perhaps the greatest political challenge of his career. Three days after their explosive meeting on Monday, February 21, Senator Stone sent a letter to the President warning that "members of both Houses feel deeply concerned and disturbed by what they read and hear" and reiterating his own belief that it would be catastrophic for America to become involved in the war simply because of individuals "recklessly risking their lives on armed belligerent ships."

Once Stone's letter arrived at the White House, around noon, Tumulty advised the President that an immediate public answer was essential. Wilson went to his study with orders not to be disturbed. For the next several hours he worked on a response, refusing to stop to meet with three influential Democrats—Flood, Speaker of the House Champ Clark, and House Majority Leader Claude Kitchin, a fierce preparedness opponent and Bryan loyalist from North Carolina—who were forced to settle for a 9:00 a.m. conference the next day. Later that evening, while Edith held a tea on the floor below, the President put the finishing touches on the letter. He would continue to "do everything in my power to keep the United States out of war," he wrote Stone. On the other hand, he could not "consent to any abridgment of the rights of American citizens in any respect" since "the honor and self-respect of the nation are involved." It would also be wise to consider that if America yielded to "expediency" in this situation, the door would be open to "further concessions. Once accept a single abatement of right, and many other humiliations would certainly follow, and the whole fine fabric of international law might crumble under our hands piece by piece." The letter, released after ten that night and published the next morning, let Stone, the rest of Congress, and the world know that Wilson would not be moved from what one pacifist called the administration's "stand-up-for-our-rights program." The President's assertion that any kind of concession would be disastrous was somewhat of an exaggeration, although it made Germany and the Allies take notice.

While millions of Americans that Friday read the dueling Wilson and Stone letters in their morning newspapers, Flood, Kitchin, and Clark trooped to the White House for their morning meeting, later dubbed the Sunrise

Conference. They informed the President that the infamous McLemore resolution would have an excellent chance of making it through the House by a 2-to-1, perhaps 3-to-1, majority. The issue of what more American deaths on an armed ship might mean was also raised. Wilson made it plain that a break in relations with Germany and likely war would follow, which might bring the conflict to a quicker conclusion. He was not at all pleased when it was mentioned that some believed the President was itching for a fight with Germany. Kitchin himself believed Wilson wanted war.

Meanwhile, Bryan was watching the situation from afar while sending an occasional telegram to his friends in Congress. "A Mayor keeps the people of his city out of the danger zone during a riot," Bryan wired on Thursday, February 24. "Can our government afford to do less when the world is in riot?"

Over the weekend, tensions cooled somewhat. McLemore gave a statement saying he was willing to delay consideration of his resolution for now, while insisting it had been "deliberately misinterpreted" and blaming "certain rabid pro-English papers of the big Northern cities that have underground wires to Wall street and want war at any price." In the Senate, Thomas Gore had also decided not to press his resolution further, since he believed he had already won the battle by "its introduction and attending public discussion." The Germans helped matters along by backing off somewhat on their new policy. Passenger liners, it was announced on Monday, would not be attacked without warning, even if they were armed.

The momentum was shifting in Wilson's direction. He decided now was the time to kill the revolt once and for all. He would demand a vote on the McLemore resolution, a move very much fitting in his stated belief that a "politician to be successful must be 'audacious.'" One reporter noted that Democrats and even Republicans were impressed, viewing Wilson's decision as "one of the boldest moves ever made by an American President." If the resolution passed, Wilson would be virtually impotent in any future submarine negotiations with the Germans and possibly a one-term president. If it failed, Wilson's dominance over Congress and his own party would be virtually unassailable.

The stakes were undeniably high. Still, administration officials were confident. The news of the weekend had changed some votes, as had not-so-subtle warnings to Democrats about the potential loss of patronage jobs if they crossed Wilson. Some predictably grumbled that Wilson was "playing politics" and trying to "out Roosevelt Mr. Theodore Roosevelt." A canvass by the *New York Herald* on March 1 suggested that the Senate would reject the resolution soundly. In the more troublesome House, Wilson had 142 definite votes at the moment, 76 short of a majority. Some suggested that a "compromise resolution" might solve the issue—i.e., a statement backing the President but also warning Americans off armed ships. But Wilson would not settle for a partial victory. "Does not the president realize," one Democratic congressman asked, "that if he gets this thing in the House now the vote will be so close that a victory would be barren?"

Rumors surfaced that Wilson might resign or perhaps not run for reelection if the resolution passed. In the meantime, Gore stirred the pot in the Senate by stating that he heard "that certain Senators and certain members of the House" had spoken to Wilson, who intimated that a war "might not be of itself and of necessity an evil to this republic, but that the United States by entering upon war now might be able to bring it to a conclusion by midsummer and thus render a great service to Civilisation." Stone immediately denied that Wilson had said any such thing, but he would not give specifics of the conversation. "What the President said to me . . . is something I do not care to repeat."

The next day, the Senate prepared to vote to table Gore's resolution. At the last moment, the Oklahoman changed the content of his resolution entirely to state that the death of an American citizen on an "armed merchant vessel" sunk by a German submarine would be a justifiable cause of war. With the First Lady and her mother watching the proceedings, the Senate tabled the motion by a 68–14 vote, although more than a few senators were no longer sure what they had voted for.

Wilson was satisfied, even if the result was muddled. Four days later, it was the House's turn. The Capitol was packed with more than a hundred reporters and a sizable crowd of spectators, including numerous women. Hours of debate and speeches followed.

"The question is," insisted Kentucky Democrat J. Campbell Cantrill,

A new Wilson for 1916.
(*New York Tribune*, January 29, 1916)

"Shall the House stand by the President or desert him in the hour of need? I propose to stand by the President until the end." John Farr, a Republican from Pennsylvania, agreed. "To vote against tabling the McLemore resolution is to vote for a yellow streak in the American flag." When the final tally was counted, 276 congressmen voted to table the resolution, almost double the 142 voting against. Wilson had won handily.

Bryan wondered whether the President had "won" anything. "The question was presented in such a way that there is little significance in the vote," the Great Commoner told a reporter. "It does not represent the sentiment in Congress." Still, on paper at least, Congress and his own party had upheld Wilson's leadership. His potential role in ending the European crisis was safe for now.

In the midst of the excitement on Capitol Hill, Colonel House and his wife arrived home in New York. As usual, he offered smooth nonanswers to queries about the details of his trip and a clever quip when a fawning reporter expressed a desire that House would someday be president. But a question about his writing career caught him off guard. Evidence now pointed to House as the author of the 1912 anonymous novel *Philip Dru, Administrator*, published by B. W. Huebsch, a member of the Ford Peace Ship and Schwimmer disciple. Was it true?

"Ha!" was the Colonel's response. "All sorts of stories have been started about me, but I never affirm or deny anything."

The next morning he left for Washington to see Wilson. After breakfast at the White House and chats with various cabinet members, he joined the Wilsons for an automobile ride, where he fully briefed them on his trip (even Edith was "crazy to hear all he has to tell us"). Lansing received a similar courtesy at the State Department for an hour before House returned to the White House for a lengthy private conference and discussion of the House-Grey Memorandum with the President.

As far as the Colonel could tell, Wilson was pleased. "I cannot adequately express to you my admiration and gratitude for what you have done," he told House. "It would be impossible to imagine a more difficult task than the one placed in your hands, but you have accomplished it in a way beyond any expectations."

House responded that he "could see [Wilson] sitting at the head of the counsel table at the Hague."

But the two friends were not completely of one mind. Wilson requested an important change: the insertion of that tricky word "probably" before "leave the Conference as a belligerent on the side of the Allies, if Germany was unreasonable." Clearly, the President was not willing to go quite as far as House had led the Allies to believe. Still, the Colonel remained confident. Wilson, after all, could have killed the memo then and there but did not. The man who had repeatedly assured the country of his peaceful intentions was not standing in the way of a proposal that could very well put the country in the war by the end of the year.

House's conferences with Wilson and other great men delighted him more every day. Being part of decision making likely to affect the entire world was an intoxicating drug. "The life I am leading transcends in interest and excitement any romance," he wrote in his diary a few days later. "I believe I am the only one who gets a view of the entire picture. Some get one corner and some another, but I seem to have it all."

Miles away, the Roosevelts were enjoying the weather and sites of the West Indies. Everywhere TR was greeted enthusiastically, although the "irritating publicity and functions" proved tiresome to him at times. At his first stop, St. Thomas, then under Danish control, the locals shifted the date of their carnival ball so TR could be present. In Antigua, the people "strewed flowers in his pathway"; in Guadeloupe, homes and ships were festively decorated in his honor with WELCOME, ROOSEVELT! signs everywhere, requiring him to give an impromptu speech in French.

His final stop before returning home was Trinidad, an area where access to American news was limited. As a zoology enthusiast, he made a special trip to see what the natives called the guacharo, a noisy bird that lived in caves by day and foraged for food at night. So eager was TR to watch these oilbirds in their natural habitat that he slept on a rather short, borrowed table from a nearby plantation, which he still preferred to the hammocks used by the others in his party. He thought he might have discovered a new species, only to learn when he returned home that the existence of the guacharo had been known for at least one hundred years.

His adventures with the oilbird were secondary to his main purpose in Trinidad: the release of a formal statement on March 9 responding to an attempt by some Massachusetts Republicans to place him in the state's upcoming presidential primary. Henry L. Stoddard, a TR supporter and the editor of the *New York Evening Mail*, was responsible for wiring the message back to America. The statement, he understood, was not just about Massachusetts but Roosevelt's overall plans for 1916. It would be best, Stoddard believed, for TR to position himself as a possible candidate to prevent any contender from co-opting his message, even if he made it clear that he had no interest in the nomination.

Just about everyone reading the statement understood that Roosevelt was still very much interested in being president again. He insisted that he did not want to be in any primaries, had no desire to be nominated, and was "not in the least interested in the political fortunes either of myself or any other man." His goal now, as it had been for more than a year, was to alert Americans to "unpleasant facts." But he left one important door open. "It would be a mistake to nominate me," he wrote, *"unless* the country has in its mood something of the heroic" (or as he privately put it, "a reasonable amount of iron in its blood . . . because I certainly shall not pussy-foot"). And heroism, TR believed, was sorely needed in a time when America was facing a test on the scale of the American Revolution and Civil War, "where the action taken determines the basis of the life of the generations that follow." It was crucial, then, for the Progressive and Republican conventions to choose someone especially prepared to address the "mighty tasks of the next four years" and someone who would support a "programme of clean-cut, straight-out, national Americanism, in deeds not less than in words, and in internal and international matters alike." That "someone" was apparently Roosevelt himself.

The statement generated considerable comment, although it made po-litical sense. Primary victories, as TR had seen, were not enough to guar-antee the nomination, and a poor showing would almost certainly kill his candidacy. Better to stand still for now, see where the winds were blowing, and hopefully influence enough uninstructed delegates to his side at the convention.

Bryan could not take the statement seriously. "Ever since [Roosevelt] found that he could not build up a successful party himself he has been working his way back to the Republican party," Bryan wrote in his monthly periodical *The Commoner.* "He will be back in line this year, getting any crumbs he can, but back, no matter how humiliating the terms."

In reality, even hard-core TR-haters in the GOP machine were willing to take him back, perhaps as "adviser in chief," but certainly not as a pres-idential candidate. Their problem was that the best alternative to TR, Su-preme Court Justice Charles Evans Hughes, threatened to be as troublesome as Roosevelt, if his stint as New York governor was any indication. "Hughes has never 'done business' with politicians," John Callan O'Laughlin ex-plained in a letter to Gerard, Page, and other American ambassadors, "and the stand patters realize that he is a hard man for them to handle." And Hughes had continued to deny he was a candidate, although most expected he would accept the nomination if offered.

Roosevelt had much to contemplate as he sailed for home. Tennis, billiards, and whist occupied his time, along with writing and socializing with the other passengers. The weather was favorable until late in the voyage, when the ship was pounded by a ferocious storm. TR woke up to find his cabin flooded, thanks to a huge wave that had enveloped the ship. With the help of a steward, he cleared out the water and went back to sleep.

Back in New York, reporters wanted to know his plans and his thoughts on the current political situation. Except for a smirk about Newton Baker's resistance to tin soldiers as a child, Roosevelt had little to say. Nor would he say much about the current Mexican crisis, touched off by a disturbing Pancho Villa raid on Columbus, New Mexico, three miles from the Mexican border, resulting in the death of eighteen Americans. The answers, TR told reporters, could be found in the Mexican chapter in *Fear God and Take Your Own Part*. "Everything I have said and have for the last three years applies exactly." Within a week, he was far more critical of America's failure to overcome what he called a mere "bandit raid." A "hideous disaster," he warned, would likely await us "if we were ever menaced by a serious foe."

Mexico had long been a thorn in Wilson's side, "a situation I do not understand," he once admitted. The administration had recently thrown its lot with the Carranza government, which continued to face guerrilla warfare at the hands of Villa, Carranza's former colleague. The current Villa "invasion" was especially dangerous, since it might lead to a full-scale war, one likely to preempt full American involvement in Europe should the need ever arise. (That Germany was actively involved in making mischief on the U.S.–Mexican border was suspected by everyone as a way to tie up American forces in the event of U.S. entry into the European war.) Wilson sent a force under General John Pershing after Villa, although House heard a rumor that the President almost changed his mind after hearing a report, ultimately untrue, that the Carranza forces would attack American troops crossing the border. Such a decision, the Colonel believed, would have been disastrous. "It would not only destroy him in the United States, but it would destroy his influence in Europe as well."

House had become increasingly bold about second-guessing his friend, at least in his diary. But Wilson's other moves appeared to be working out quite well of late. The preparedness legislation he wanted would soon become a reality, now that the House had approved the Hay army bill by a 403–2 margin. He was also happy with his new secretary of war, Newton Baker, who proved to be one of his better cabinet selections. And the once bleak situation with Germany was now looking promising. Bethmann had emphasized to his colleagues that the recent developments in America suggested that Wilson was serious about breaking diplomatic relations if another incident occurred. The United States would then join the Allies, dooming Germany. The chancellor rejected the counterargument, enthusiastically trumpeted by navy leaders such as Tirpitz, that unrestricted submarine warfare was the best way to end the war quickly, regardless of its effect on the neutrals. The kaiser sided with Bethmann, and the renewed submarine campaign on armed merchant vessels, begun on February 29, would not be expanded to unrestricted status until at least April. Tirpitz then resigned, a move that Bethmann thought would play well in America.

Wilson had just experienced what he described to a friend as some of the most grueling weeks since the start of the war. He had managed recently to take a brief weekend breather on the *Mayflower* with Edith, enjoying their stop at Newport News, where they watched pilots perform a series of dazzling flying maneuvers. Other such opportunities for rest and relaxation might be possible that spring if the international situation remained quiet.

But it was not to be. On the afternoon of Friday, March 24, an unarmed French steamer named the *Sussex* was carrying at least 325 passengers, 25 of them American, across the English Channel to Dieppe. At about 2:55 p.m., an American bacteriologist named Edna Harde felt what she later described as "a very sharp, quick explosion, over at once, accompanied and followed by a tremendous crash as of wood and glass." Panicked passengers tried to find life preservers, many of which were useless, although one woman later reported that two different men yanked them out of her hands. Meanwhile, a French naval officer on board did his best to calm the passengers, insisting, correctly as it turned out, that the *Sussex* would remain afloat. Others desperately plunged into the sea or took to the lifeboats, one of which capsized. The damaged *Sussex* was eventually towed into port, but early reports suggested that at least 50 were dead.

Harde was unsure what had caused the explosion, although some passengers insisted they had seen a torpedo. Wilson knew that if a German submarine had attacked the *Sussex* without warning and if Americans were among the dead, he faced a new crisis. And his previous tough words about "strict accountability" would leave him precious little room to maneuver.

Chapter 12

TEETERING ON THE ABYSS

MARCH 25–MAY 20, 1916

*These are certainly times that try men's souls and I
hope that the fire will purify the whole nation.*

—Woodrow Wilson, April 1916

I n a world where sea travel was almost impossible to avoid, future *Sussex* incidents seemed likely to recur. But some already believed a new world was coming, one dominated by aviation. Exciting accounts of "aerial combats" during the bloody struggle at Verdun featuring aces such as Jean Navarre of France and American volunteers in the newly created Lafayette Escadrille confirmed the growing importance of what many then referred to as the "aeroplane," or what one of TR's correspondents called "the great weapon of slaughter in the future."

In America, the exploits of a twenty-five-year-old aviatrix named Katherine Stinson fascinated the public. Her New York appearance that spring at the Sheepshead Bay Speedway attracted crowds eager to see the "young Queen of Speed" perform a variety of daredevil maneuvers, including topping 90 miles an hour in a plane-versus-car duel and deftly "bombing" an "imitation fort" with blanks. "I want more girls and women to fly," Stinson told a reporter. "There's no reason why any woman with average health and strength, a cool head and the sporting instinct shouldn't fly her own plane." And as much as the public seemed to enjoy her stunts, she looked forward to a day when aviation was "commonplace, an everyday affair," as routine as the reconnaissance missions of modern-day warfare. The military had supposedly rejected her own attempts to assist in the Punitive Expedition in Mexico to get Pancho Villa, but she had already decided that "if America went to war tomorrow I'd be an army scout."

In the wake of the *Sussex*, it was no longer improbable that America might be going to war immediately. If the *Sussex* had in fact been torpedoed, as many already believed, then the proverbial "last straw" had come. At least the secretary of state thought so. Germany's "illegal and inhuman conduct" had been permitted for too long. Note writing should stop, Lansing wrote Wilson, and "whatever we determine to do must be in the line of action and it must indicate in no uncertain terms that the present method of submarine warfare can no longer be tolerated." A diplomatic break seemed appropriate, unless Germany fulfilled a series of conditions, including compensation for the American travelers wounded and/or killed (none died on the *Sussex*, as it turned out, though four were injured), abandonment of its current undersea tactics, and the acknowledgment of "the *illegality* of submarine warfare in general." That Germany would swallow such an ultimatum appeared unlikely. A break in relations, then, followed by a subsequent declaration of war, seemed to be the most probable course.

Whether Wilson would approve such a drastic stance remained uncertain. Colonel House was pessimistic. "I am afraid he will delay and write further notes when action is what we need," he wrote in his diary before leaving for Washington to consult with the President. On arrival, he soon discovered that Lansing, just like his predecessor, was beginning to show signs of irritation at House's outsized role in affairs normally delegated exclusively to the State Department. Still, the secretary of state shared his recent communication to Wilson with House, who approved of its contents. But the Colonel's conversations with the President suggested that Wilson did not feel the same way. For one thing, there was no definitive proof yet that the *Sussex* had been torpedoed and there were "many particulars to be considered." For another, he had no idea whether this signaled a new campaign of unrestricted warfare or an unfortunate error by a German commander. House sighed. "He does not seem to realize that one of the main points of criticism against him is that he talks boldly but acts weakly. It would be better to talk weakly and act boldly."

Wilson feared that a diplomatic break would only prolong, rather than shorten, the war, and "there would be no one to lead the way out." House, somewhat embarrassed that the President was adopting one of House's prior talking points, explained that such was not the case. In fact, House proposed a new pie-in-the-sky scenario where Wilson would "make a dispassionate statement of the cause of the war and what the Allies were fighting for," followed by a new House mission to Holland, where he would "open negotiations directly with Berlin, telling them upon what terms we were ready to end the war" (not before the Allies had given their say-so, of course). Wilson would then step in and "preside" over the peace conference sure to follow. According to House's diary, Wilson was "visibly pleased," although he must have known that there was no way in hell Germany would have been interested.

House left Washington after two days. Nothing had been decided, but the evidence that a submarine had attacked the *Sussex* began to mount. Additional eyewitness accounts from Americans on board, along with unique metal fragments preserved from the explosion, left little doubt that the culprit was a German-built torpedo. Still, Wilson gave no clue to anyone, with the possible exception of Edith, as to how he would proceed. The cabinet and other administration officials, House claimed, were "as ignorant of his intentions as the man in the street." And rumors of war had begun to spread. George Viereck, the *Fatherland*'s editor, even disclosed in a wiretapped phone conversation that he had learned from his Washington correspondent that "war will be declared by the end of April to win the Morgan support and take the wind out of Roosevelt's sails."

Wilson had no desire to go to war. The question remained whether he could resist the tide pushing him in that direction, as he had done since the *Lusitania* sinking eleven months earlier. Back in New York, House tried to steel the President for what might be coming. Entering the war, the Colonel wrote Wilson on April 3, "would not be without its advantages in as much as it would strengthen your position at home and with the Allies." There would be no need to invite any neutrals to the proposed peace conference and the President's position there "would be enormously enhanced." And perhaps Sir Edward Grey should be contacted now to see if the Allies would prefer Wilson's diplomatic intervention, as envisioned in the

House-Grey Memorandum, to occur *now*, before the situation with Germany came to a head (again, House was thoughtfully allowing the Allies to dictate American foreign policy).

Two days later, House returned to the capital. There was no longer any doubt that the *Sussex* had been torpedoed by a German submarine without warning. Wilson had already told Lansing to write up something to be sent to Ambassador Gerard in Berlin for presentation to the German government. The document pulled no punches: relations with Germany would be severed, with no ifs, ands, or buts. Wilson had yet to see it, but House knew that it was unlikely to go out in its current form.

The next morning, Thursday, April 6, House had a heart-to-heart with Wilson. A break was "inevitable," and the President needed to "definitely make up his mind what he intended to do." If House's assessment of the situation rang true, then Wilson needed to "prepare for it from today in order to give us the advantage of two or three weeks' time to get ready before the Germans knew of our purpose." In the meantime, the President would draft a cable to Grey asking whether the British were ready for his diplomatic intervention, since American involvement would likely extend the war. (In reality, British leaders such as Lord Kitchener believed American participation would drastically *shorten* the war; Grey conceded it would be "of incalculable advantage.") Their conversation continued in the afternoon, this time with Lansing present, although the Colonel much "preferred talking to the President alone" about such matters. Lansing gave Wilson the fateful document calling for a break with Germany. Wilson did not have time to digest it fully, but he read enough to understand what it meant.

Later that afternoon, House went to see Secretary of War Baker to discuss whether troops would be available to protect the great metropolises in the event of war (New York was supposedly crawling with German reservists stuck there since 1914) and whether the possible withdrawal of troops from Mexico would be necessary, as the Villa expedition had tied up a large chunk of America's already modest armed forces.

That the United States was on the brink of war was not a surprise to Roosevelt. Months of what he considered to be wishy-washy behavior had apparently resulted in a crisis from which Wilson was unlikely to extricate himself. That same Thursday, TR wrote to George Perkins explaining his feelings in his usual colorful way. The President, he again insisted, was like the man whose reaction to his wife being slapped was to "think it over" and send notes "telling the other man he must not do it" ad infinitum. "Moreover I feel that there would not have been any trouble if in the first place he had had it clearly understood that if anyone slapped his wife's face there would be a fight."

On one level, Roosevelt was correct. A more muscular foreign policy from the onset of the war might have made Germany more pliable. "We would be far safer from danger of war if I were President than we are now," TR insisted. But such a policy required a stronger American military and naval apparatus, one that did not exist a year earlier and was *still* being hashed out in Congress at the moment. Was that Wilson's fault? Roosevelt believed it was. Even House felt that Wilson could have moved sooner on preparedness. The question remained whether the country would have backed him in the early months of the war. TR would have grimly admitted that the answer was no, at least outside of the East Coast.

Roosevelt's ultimate view was that the United States could not be a force for good around the world without the ability to project American power (or the *threat* of American power) globally. "There are certain nations which can be withheld from wrongdoing only by fear of the consequences," he explained to Perkins in the same letter. Germany had no fear of the consequences from America and thus was willing to administer "continual kickings. . . . In the end we shall either have to accept war at a great disadvantage or suffer hideous permanent humiliation and loss, such as the taking away of the Panama Canal, Hawaii or Alaska."

But the problem TR faced was twofold. Many Americans, he knew, had virtually no knowledge of foreign affairs and could not grasp some of the finer points he tried to put across in his speeches and writing. Others simply believed Roosevelt was being exceptionally unfair to a man doing his best job under very trying circumstances. Again and again, TR's followers suggested that he should tone down his attacks. "When you hit him they feel as though [heavyweight champion] Jess Willard had punched some little clerk," his friend Julian Street explained. Roosevelt agreed, but he found it difficult to restrain himself. Lincoln, he claimed, had been even more vicious in comments about his predecessors Franklin Pierce and

James Buchanan. "I have been scrupulously careful never to do him an injustice."

Few would have agreed. TR's attacks on Wilson appeared deeply personal at times. The President truly confounded Roosevelt, and it frustrated him enormously. Worse, Wilson was no dummy politically. Even TR had to admit that the "hypocritical word-juggler" Wilson was "infinitely more astute" than his Republican adversaries, who "have neither courage nor convictions and therefore can do little against him." In Roosevelt's view, the President was an especially "dangerous man . . . for he is a man of brains, and he debauches men of brains."

That Wilson seemingly had the upper hand with Roosevelt was not surprising. Three years in the White House had only enhanced Wilson's already formidable mix of smarts and "unscrupulous cunning" to become the "cutest little Machiavelli we have ever produced," according to one of TR's friends. The journalist Ray Stannard Baker had spent time with Taft and Roosevelt, but found himself especially impressed with the White House's current occupant when he interviewed him that spring. "I have never talked with any public man who had such complete control of his whole intellectual equipment as he," Baker wrote afterward about the President. "He pounces upon things half said and consumes them before they are well out of one's mind. And his pounce is sure, accurate, complete. He instantly adds what you give him, whether fact or opinion, to his own view of the situation, so that to an extraordinary degree, you go along with him, and arrive at that meeting of the minds which is so rare a thing in discussion."

To his friends, Wilson was a master politician, expert at thwarting his opponents while keeping his own party firmly in line. He continued to avoid mentioning TR's name publicly, which never failed to infuriate Roosevelt. "A campaign between Wilson and Roosevelt," the *New Republic*'s Herbert Croly observed that April, "is likely to be one of the most venomous and heated campaigns that we have ever had."

While the *Sussex* situation was unfolding, Addams was on her way home, bypassing a planned stop in El Paso due to the flare-up in Mexico. The West Coast air and treatment had not improved her as much as she hoped. Back in Chicago, it was thought best that she stay at the home of her wealthy friend Louise de Koven Bowen at her upscale Astor Street mansion for continued recuperation, especially since doctors had identified "diabetic complications." Still, she planned to go to Hull-House when she could and keep a close watch on pacifist developments. And Mary would offer emotional support during a difficult time when she wanted to be in the thick of things. At the same time, Mary was not shy about giving her a dose of reality when needed. "The love and understanding between them," Addams's niece Marcet noted, "was so limitless that Miss Smith could and did furnish Aunt Jane with a tender, tonic criticism that she found nowhere else." Mary also kept her spirits up. "Her natural gayety did much for Aunt Jane, who on her part was inclined to be a little too somber."

The news of her still shaky health was national news, even reaching the President, who took time from the stressful *Sussex* deliberations to have roses sent to a grateful Addams. "There are some compensations in being ill," she wrote Marcet. Wilson may have been genuinely concerned about her well-being, but he also knew it was smart politics to keep Addams and her followers on his side, especially with an election in seven months.

If the pacifists were still in Wilson's camp, they were willing to challenge him more than in the past. His preparedness speeches in January and his statement in St. Louis that those opposed to defense increases "ought to be encouraged to hire large halls" so their "folly" could be heard and then ignored had prompted them to take him at his word. The American Union against Militarism, an outgrowth of the Henry Street group and which included Addams as an executive committee member, decided to counter Wilson's tour with one of their own: the "Truth About Preparedness" campaign. On the evening of April 6, hours after Colonel House's frank "war-is-coming" White House talk with Wilson, a packed Carnegie Hall listened to a series of speakers ranging from Amos Pinchot, an ex–Bull Mooser whom TR now considered part of the "lunatic fringe," to socialists such as the Pennsylvania labor leader James Maurer. The less threatening but no less passionate Lillian Wald spoke first, attacking the hysteria that seemed to be inescapable, especially on the East Coast. "People are 'seein' things at night,'" she explained. "In all sincerity one man declared that at two o'clock in the morning he *saw* a company of Germans drilling in Van

Cortlandt park. . . . Yesterday I was told by a Boston friend that ladies there are registering their automobiles as available to 'carry the maidens inland' if necessary." (The American Woman's League for Self-Defense had even concluded that pants would be the preferred attire "to guard your home against marauders" while the men were away.) Meanwhile, the crowd went wild at the mere mention of the name "Ford," whom one speaker insisted would be remembered long after the "bludgeon of Oyster Bay" had disappeared from the scene.

In the next ten days, the tour visited ten more cities and eventually reached forty thousand listeners, including Addams in Chicago and Ford in Detroit, neither of whom spoke. Wilson, as had been decided beforehand, was not explicitly targeted, but an occasional cutting remark snuck through. In Des Moines, the fiery progressive Rabbi Stephen Wise suggested that the crowd Wilson had drawn in the same building back in January had little to do with preparedness enthusiasm. "You wanted to see the president," he insisted. "We only elect twenty-five of them every 100 years."

Wise also told the audience that Americans "do not want to be treated as children" and Wilson should share his "inside information" about the global threats necessitating a military buildup.

To some, the questioning of the need, expense, and financial beneficiaries of preparedness was dangerous, if not treasonous. The National Security League sent out stenographers to capture every word spoken, hoping to record an explosive comment or two to undermine the cause. In Des Moines, Wald claimed that National Guardsmen "improvised a bowling match . . . to prevent the speakers being heard." And press coverage was lukewarm to hostile in most communities. In Buffalo, one newspaper gave "four times as much space to a dog fight"; in Cleveland, the News intentionally provided the wrong locale in pre-event publicity. "It is a mortification," Bryan sadly observed, "to live in a country where the newspapers lie so." The pro-Wilson New York Times was especially vicious, blasting the "socialists and the pacifists who preached the gospel of cowardice" and would "sow through the country the seeds of national degradation and disaster."

That the tour still managed to draw respectable audiences suggested that the pacifists' essential point was correct: Americans remained deeply

divided about preparedness. And the crowds, they suspected, might have
been even larger if the country did not appear to be lurching toward war
at any moment.

With each day, Wilson faced increasing pressure to make up his mind
how far to go in the current crisis. The emphatic Lansing note severing relations with Germany, he knew, had to be revised. Meanwhile, the
Germans had already decided on how they would respond, eventually sending a rather feeble explanation claiming that the only vessel torpedoed in
that area appeared to have been a "war vessel," a "mine layer of the . . .
Arabic class." The submarine commander had even provided a sketch as
"proof" that this craft looked nothing like the *Sussex* picture the Germans
had available (the *Sussex* had actually been modified since the beginning
of the war). The unfortunate *Sussex*, then, must have struck a mine, although Berlin was willing to hear other evidence and perhaps submit the
matter to a future "commission of inquiry." Virtually no one—the press,
the administration, or even Ambassador Bernstorff—was happy with the
German response. "The German alibi . . . is weak," the *Philadelphia Evening
Bulletin* editorialized, "and it ought not be permitted to serve its obvious
purpose of delaying action."

On the evening of Monday, April 10, Wilson went to work on Lansing's
draft. He was not feeling well from what the press called a "severe cold,"
although House identified the culprit as a "digestive spell." The Colonel
himself was back in the White House the following morning for more discussions about the note, joined by the First Lady. Neither was entirely satisfied with Wilson's rewrite. House believed the "last page. . . . inconclusive . . .
opening up the entire question for more argument," while Edith "declared
it weak and unsatisfactory at the end. He patiently argued the matter with
her, but refused to admit any sort of weakness in it." To the President, anything stronger would probably result in a declaration of war, which would
require the approval of a still reluctant Congress.

Their discussion ended at eleven for Wilson to go to a cabinet meeting,
although he had no intention of letting his colleagues know his specific
intentions. "He said he did not care for their opinion and was afraid to trust

them with it," House wrote. Later, the President complained "he had been bored for two hours with a lot of childish talk."

The Colonel returned to New York that evening believing that a diplomatic split was inevitable. He kept in touch with officials about possible troop needs in New York. He also heard from Bernstorff, who as usual was eager to find any kind of solution. By this point House had been briefed about the dalliances of Bernstorff and other German officials, revealed in intimate and occasionally explicit detail through wiretaps, which House opposed "even in wartime." (Bernstorff had begun to become more suspicious; "the telephone is very dangerous right now," he remarked to his lady friend that week.) Nevertheless, House could not help finding the German diplomat preferable to Spring Rice and Jusserand. "The difference between Bernstorff and the representatives of the Allies is that the one never complains and is always ready to see our side."

Wilson remained under considerable stress, "a killing load," he admitted. Keeping a lid on America's emotions, his formidable task for the past twenty months, was becoming almost impossible, especially since another case of would-be German espionage was uncovered in the midst of the crisis, this time involving attempts to place bombs on Allied merchant ships departing from America. Over the next week, the President did his best in his public addresses to convey a sense of calm, while even getting in another shot at TR. "This country has not the time, it is not now in the temper, to listen to the violent, to the passionate, to the ambitious," he told a Jefferson Day gathering. And America, he explained to a meeting of the Daughters of the American Revolution four days later, would never fight "merely for herself" but only in the "interests of humanity." One of the wiretaps caught a German propagandist mocking Wilson's comment: *"Er ist verrückt"*—"He is crazy."

With Lansing's input, the President had continued to perfect the note until he deemed it ready to be transmitted on April 18. It was not as strong as the secretary of state's original, but it was an ultimatum nonetheless. The next morning, Wilson briefed the Senate Foreign Relations and House Foreign Affairs chairs, Stone and Flood, along with the ranking Republicans on the Senate and House committees, TR's friend Henry Cabot Lodge and Henry Cooper, the same congressman who had irritated Addams during her testimony. Everyone on Capitol Hill wanted to know what the President had told them. "What does he ask us to do?" "Does it mean a break?" An Associated Press correspondent had already warned that a split would almost certainly mean war, since there had been "only one instance in modern diplomatic history in which a breaking of diplomatic relations between two first-class powers has not eventually been followed by war."

At one o'clock, Wilson appeared before a joint session of Congress. The galleries, normally occupied by reporters and a few curious onlookers, were packed. Edith and her mother were there, as was the cabinet that the President had such little regard for. Wilson, one onlooker noted, "looked tired and worn, yet determined" as he read from the speech, "written on small sheets of White House stationery, single-spaced on the President's own rickety typewriter." At roughly fifteen minutes, the address was brief and to the point. Promises had been made, but the "Imperial German Government has been unable to put any limits or restraints upon its warfare against either freight or passenger ships." If Germany wished to continue to "prosecute relentless and indiscriminate warfare against vessels of commerce by the use of submarines" in violation of international law, then relations would be broken.

The Democrats and a good many Republicans applauded. Privately, some were not so sure. Republicans such as Lodge, whose hatred of Wilson matched TR's, approved the speech, but others, such as House Minority Leader Jim Mann, believed the President was clearly bent on provoking war. "We have some complaints against Germany, though the President exaggerated them this morning," he told a reporter afterward. "We have some complaints against Great Britain, but the President doesn't care about this."

Bryan, meanwhile, had decided even before Wilson's speech that he needed to be in Washington. Before boarding a 12:02 train from St. Louis, he announced that "it would be a crime against civilization for this country to go into this war."

A few hours after Wilson's address to Congress, reporters gathered at the *Metropolitan* offices in New York to hear Roosevelt's take. To TR, the matter was very simple. It had taken Wilson an absurd length of time to reach this point and his waffling along the way had only made matters worse.

"If Germany now does as the President demands it will be proof positive that if he had chosen to take the proper position at the time of the 'strict accountability' note the lives of all those women and children and other non-combatants would have been saved and the causes of friction with Germany would have been removed."

Taft, the other living ex-president, approached the situation very differently. Republican or Democrat, the country was in crisis, and everyone should rally behind Wilson. "This is neither the time nor the place to indulge in political personalities," Taft announced. That he had chosen, once again, not to attack Wilson publicly did not surprise his former friend. "He has done some real damage by his consistent backing of Wilson," TR had remarked a few months earlier, "and after all he does not get the Supreme Court and sees it given to Brandeis!"

Taft, like every other Republican, was watching the political situation very closely. That more than a few of his colleagues were starting to consider the once fantastic possibility of TR as the GOP nominee was now obvious. A few days after the *Sussex* torpedoing, the nation's front pages were filled with the startling news that Roosevelt had apparently offered the olive branch to one of his bitterest enemies, Elihu Root, his former secretary of war and secretary of state. Like Taft, Root had once been a warm friend of Roosevelt, but his role as temporary chairman of the explosive 1912 Republican convention had destroyed the good feelings that existed between the pair.

The two men met at the Park Avenue home of Robert Bacon, an old friend of TR who had succeeded Root as secretary of state in the final days of the administration and was now a major force in the National Security League and other preparedness organizations. Two other Roosevelt pals were invited—Lodge and General Leonard Wood. Later, everyone present claimed that nothing had been discussed except preparedness, but Wood's diary told a different story. "Roosevelt cussed out Wilson as did Root and Lodge," the general wrote. "Opinion that the country never so low in standing before."

Afterward, TR headed down the street to the home of George Perkins, who was certain something important had just occurred. The Root/ Roosevelt reconciliation, Perkins believed, could only mean one thing: the Republicans were beginning to see the light and would ultimately turn to TR at the convention. At bare minimum, the meeting showed that Roosevelt, supposedly still a devoted Progressive party member, no longer viewed the Republicans as the enemy. Root, whose supporters would soon begin to work for his nomination without his active involvement, privately admitted that he hoped the meeting would grease the paths for TR's return to the GOP.

But die-hard Progressives were not happy. Breaking bread with a conservative like Root, they believed, was inexcusable under any circumstances. Would poor old Will Taft be next? Why was their leader behaving this way?

Roosevelt did his best to soothe the hurt feelings, again providing a historical precedent. Lincoln in the early years of the Civil War, he reminded them, "had to work with every man (no matter what that man might think on other matters)." The goal, then, was to bring together "good and patriotic citizens, no matter what their past political beliefs . . . in support of some man who shall stand as he ought to stand, on the questions of Americanism, of national preparedness and international duty."

That man, TR hoped, would be himself, even if his wife, Edith, did not want him to run. "Every time I have gone against Edie's judgment I have gone wrong," he admitted a few months earlier. But the signs were increasingly encouraging. The *New York Tribune* endorsed him in April. The libelous William Barnes said he would support Roosevelt if he got the nomination, although he soon issued a furious denial. Even the "psychic astrologer" Willie De Kerlor, who arrived in New York from France that spring with his wife, the then unknown design legend Elsa Schiaparelli, had announced that America's next president would be "a man whose name begins with an R," with an "l" and "t" in his name.

The Progressive nomination, of course, was already TR's for the taking. Now the Republicans needed to be converted. And Roosevelt, Perkins, and his supporters were doing all they could behind the scenes to make that happen, without explicitly announcing his candidacy, ranging from the formation of the Roosevelt Non-Partisan League to seeking common ground with the press magnate and failed Democratic politician William Randolph Hearst, who had long despised TR.

The most worrisome obstacle was the man who had beaten Hearst in the New York gubernatorial race ten years earlier, Charles Evans Hughes. To some, a Hughes candidacy checked all the right boxes. As a Supreme Court justice since 1910, he had no part in the catastrophic Republican split four years earlier, nor had he any need to take sides publicly on any of the most controversial war-related issues likely to impact voting behavior. And his past record suggested he was liberal enough to lure some of the less committed Bull Moosers back into the GOP. A flurry of efforts to get Hughes to commit himself as a candidate got nowhere, although he privately remained ambivalent. "I do not want the work that is before the next president," he remarked to TR's friend Henry Stoddard. "He may wear a crown, but it will be a crown of thorns."

Taft, among others, believed Hughes would be the ideal choice. In the midst of the *Sussex* crisis, the former president wrote to Hughes twice in two days pushing him to run. Taft certainly did not want Roosevelt, who in any case "cannot be elected" even if he somehow got the nomination. The German Americans would not vote for him, and plenty of Republicans might desert the ticket rather than support TR. But Taft knew that Roosevelt would do almost anything to stop Wilson's reelection. "He has put himself in a position which makes it absolutely necessary for him to support you if you are nominated," Taft explained. "Moreover, he will, after his disappointment, do so with fervor." The question at hand, then, was simple. Would Hughes "save the party from Roosevelt and the country from Wilson"?

Hughes was fifty-four years old. As the child of an evangelist and a former schoolteacher, he had grown up in relatively humble circumstances in upstate New York. At a young age, it was clear that Hughes was brilliant, so much so that he received most of his education at home, rather than in the local schoolhouse. He was only fourteen when he entered Madison University (now Colgate), where his parents hoped he would receive the necessary training to enter the Baptist ministry. But Hughes chose a different path. After transferring to Brown, where he earned a bachelor's degree at nineteen, he tried his hand at teaching before pursuing a career in law at Columbia, the same school where TR had abandoned his legal education a year earlier. Hughes soon realized that he had found his calling. He finished first in his class and then scored a sterling 99½ of a possible 100 on his New York bar exam in 1884.

For the next twenty years, Hughes practiced law in New York, aside from a two-year stint teaching at Cornell Law School. Now married with four children, he had built a reputation as an outstanding attorney, albeit one who largely toiled in obscurity. But his life was about to change. In 1905, New York Governor Francis Higgins appointed him to head an investigating committee into the gas and electric utilities. Hughes's publicized discoveries of rampant price gouging and other abuses not only resulted in much needed regulation and legislation but also made him a household name in New York, as did his involvement in a separate investigation into the life insurance industry.

With TR's prodding, the Republicans nominated Hughes for governor in 1906. After beating Hearst, he was reelected a second time in 1908. His honest, competent, and reform-oriented administration won high marks among liberals, including Addams's friend John Palmer Gavit of the *New York Evening Post*. "He is everything that Roosevelt has pretended to be," Gavit told a friend a few months into Hughes's first term.

Unlike Roosevelt, Hughes refused to play the political game while in office. He would not work with the bosses nor would he dole out the usual generous patronage plums to his loyal supporters. "Mr. Hughes is a very strong-willed, forceful character," the journalist Oscar King Davis wrote. "He is extremely dogmatic, and, when he has reached a conclusion for himself, is impatient of argument on the other side." As early as 1908, there was talk of nominating Hughes for president, but he refused to make any real effort. "He would rather be Hughes than President" was a contemporary quip. Nor was he especially enthusiastic about potentially following TR in the White House. "I was sure that, although out of office, he would still desire to have a dominating influence," Hughes later wrote, "and that he would have a large following which would make the way of his successor hard," an unfortunate reality that Taft would soon come to discover.

In 1910, Taft appointed him to the Supreme Court. Aside from an occasional high-profile case (he was one of two dissenters in the Court's decision to uphold the conviction of Leo Frank, who was later lynched), the "calm bewhiskered Buddha," as Ellen Slayden called him, remained largely out of the public eye. Slayden, as a congressman's wife, crossed paths with him more than once. "I often see him walking down New Hampshire Avenue, generally alone, as stiff as any tradesman's dummy and not unlike one with his whiskers parted to a hair and his trousers knife-creased."

Hughes was in an unenviable position. If he agreed to the nomination, he not only would have to step down from the Supreme Court but also might face a hopeless battle if Roosevelt decided to mount another third-party campaign. For TR, Hughes's decision was crucial. If Hughes decided to stay put, the Republicans, even the reactionary Old Guard hard-liners, might have to accept Roosevelt as their standard-bearer.

The current international situation would also have an impact on Hughes's decision. If a break with Germany and war followed, Wilson would be especially hard to beat as a sitting president in the midst of a national crisis. But Wilson, who knew and respected Hughes more than Roosevelt, was not thinking about the election at the moment. His note had reached German hands on the evening of Thursday, April 20, with no expectation that a reply would be forthcoming over the upcoming Easter holiday.

In the midst of enormous pressure, Wilson tried to project his usual air of calm to the public. That same afternoon, he threw out the first ball at the Washington Senators season opener, followed by a reception for the Daughters of the American Revolution in the Blue Room. The next day, Good Friday, was summerlike in Washington, with temperatures cracking 80 degrees. Still, the Wilsons boarded a train that afternoon to head to Philadelphia to see his new granddaughter, Eleanor Axson Sayre, born to Jessie and her husband, Frank Sayre, a few weeks earlier. Back in the capital on Saturday, they took in an evening performance at Keith's theater, where they watched the great Harry Houdini escape from a water tank.

If Wilson was calm and collected, Bernstorff was anything but. He believed he would be sent home in the next few days. "I tried hard to prevent them from sending that note, but it's gone," he told his lover. "My life has been unbearable for the last eighteen months." The German ambassador's conversation with Colonel House over the weekend encouraged him somewhat. The President had to be tough on the Germans, House explained. Otherwise, the Allies would never take him seriously as a peace intermediary. Meanwhile, the Allies had somehow thought now was the time to answer and politely dismiss America's November note about blockade abuses. "The British Government is not lacking in stupidity," House complained. "The sending of their answer to our notes at this time is an incredible performance." In the coming days, the British would have their hands full with the outbreak of the Easter Rebellion in Ireland.

In Germany, the mood was not optimistic. American women and children were already leaving the country in droves for Denmark and Holland. Bethmann, who understood what the note meant, tried to alert the kaiser, who "refused to interrupt his *skat* [card game]" and strangely believed that Wilson "by demanding other methods against armed merchantmen had left the door open and was holding out a helping hand to us." Other German leaders were also in denial, such as Admiral Henning von Holtzendorff, who offered the peculiar theory that an "English submarine using a German torpedo" must have been the culprit in the *Sussex* attack.

Bethmann, like Bernstorff back in America, strongly believed a break had to be avoided and concessions would have to be made. Once again, a bitter struggle was shaping up between Bethmann and the naval and military authorities. And the impact on the civilian population, who were not eager to face another enemy but did not wish to see Germany submit to America, also had to be considered. The German public, Bernstorff was informed, could never accept his suggestion to stop all submarine warfare while negotiations were unfolding. The most feasible solution, which Bernstorff conveyed to House (as usual, far more important in the negotiations than Lansing), was a promise that Germany would not abandon the submarine but would restrict its use to the same rules followed by cruisers. "Under this a submarine must be used only as a cruiser can be used, for 'visit and search,'" the *New York Herald* explained, "and it must take upon itself the full responsibility of real, not fictitious, safety of passengers and a crew before any vessel is sunk." Of course, the submarine's main strength—the element of surprise—would be eliminated.

As usual, the kaiser was undecided. In one ear was Chief of Staff General Erich von Falkenhayn, who prodded the weak-willed monarch to stay firm. A German victory at Verdun, about to begin its third bloody month, depended on the submarine campaign in its current form, as did Germany's ultimate fate in the war. The campaign, then, could not and should not be modified. By Sunday, April 30, Falkenhayn had apparently won the kaiser over, much to the horror of Bethmann and some of the more far-seeing navy officials such as Admirals Holtzendorff, Eduard von Capelle, and the diarist Georg Alexander von Müller. But the kaiser again vacillated after reading a memo from Holtzendorff suggesting in emphatic terms that the submarine was most decidedly *not* an acceptable trade-off for the enormous negative impact of American involvement on the side of the Allies. "His Majesty changed round immediately, obviously relieved by the thought of having shed the burden of war with America, an idea which is a nightmare to him," Müller recorded.

The next day, Ambassador Gerard was granted an audience with the kaiser at the General Headquarters in Charleville, France ("a great mistake," Müller wrote, especially in view of the kaiser's tendencies toward "impulsiveness"). But their talk was relatively calm. "Do you come like a Roman Pro-Consul bringing peace in one hand and war (in the other?)," Wilhelm asked Gerard with a smile. After the ambassador denied that was his intention, the kaiser pontificated about the "rough and discourteous tone" of the note, the British blockade, which "justified any means of submarine war," and how international law needed to be adjusted for the submarine. Besides, "if an American travels on a cart behind the battle lines and is hurt by a shell what right has his nation to complain?" The battlefield, Gerard countered, was "a far different case" than the sea. Afterward, Wilhelm and Gerard continued their conversation during lunch, this time discussing less weighty matters ranging from woman's suffrage to Henry Ford. The kaiser gave no indication that a break was forthcoming.

Bethmann, whom Gerard now respected and saw as a Lincolnesque figure, had won. For the good of Germany's future, America would be pacified. Falkenhayn tried to resign in protest but eventually stayed put. To Müller, the chief of staff's position was a grandstand play, a smoke screen to obscure the stalemate at Verdun. "He is not in a position to win a decisive victory," Müller wrote, "and is therefore shifting the blame on to the U-boat war question. It will be exceedingly difficult for him to prove any connection between them."

That Germany had made its decision was not yet known to Wilson. House returned to the White House yet again on May 3, for what he expected to be his last visit for several months, at least until the summer heat dissipated. The President, he discovered, was showing more backbone than previously in the submarine matter. He now believed that Germany had no choice and would have to yield, even if war might result.

"He spoke with much feeling concerning Germany's responsibility for this world-wide calamity, and thought those guilty should have personal punishment," the Colonel wrote. House, as usual, took credit for imbuing Wilson with a new sense of grit during his last trip to Washington, although he now wondered whether he had created a monster. Unlike Roosevelt, Wilson was not eager to be a war president. Nor was he enthusiastic about a second term. He told House that he wished he could step down, but of course that was out of the question.

The next day, German Foreign Minister Jagow handed Gerard the official response for transmission back to Washington. An unofficial copy would also be released by wireless to the American press. On the morning of May 5, newspaper extras began to appear with excerpts. United Press provided copies to House, who made sure the German ambassador also received them. The "harsh tone" of the early paragraphs disheartened Bernstorff. "Then it is war," he sadly concluded. But his mood changed by the time he had read the entire response. Germany was backing down. He shared the news with his mistress, who as usual was interested in the impact on the market, so much so that she encouraged her apparently clueless husband, Archibald White, to buy stock now. "B. is here in the other room," she told White at 12:27 p.m., "and he says the note is in and everything is settled and as the market is way down . . . now is the time to jump in" (it was later claimed that Bernstorff and other German embassy officials also made killings on the stock market, thanks to their inside information).

Wilson and his cabinet had dissected the note that morning. Like

Bernstorff, they immediately detected a somewhat "insolent" attitude. Germany, it began, resented and rejected America's unfair claim that the submarine campaign had been a "deliberate method of indiscriminate destruction of vessels of all sorts, nationalities and destinations," especially since no "concrete facts" had been provided. In fact, Germany had "imposed far-reaching restraints" on the submarines because of the neutrals—unlike the Allies, who had done nothing of the kind. Admittedly, "errors" happened, but these could not be helped, especially when engaged with "an enemy resorting to all kinds of ruses, whether permissible or illicit." And Germany had offered ways to minimize the risks to neutral travelers in the war zone, only to be rejected by the United States. Had the American government pursued this path, the "greater part of the accidents that American citizens have met with" could have been avoided. As for America's concern with the "sacred principles of humanity" and international law, why did this not also apply to German women and children, suffering at the hands of the British blockade? Why were the Allies always let off the hook with "protests" rather than ultimatums?

After the tart litany of complaints, the note addressed the major issue. Under a new order, submarines would operate under the rules of cruiser warfare, meaning merchant vessels would not be sunk without warning or providing for the safety of those on board, as long as the ship did not "attempt to escape or offer resistance." However, Germany expected that America "will now demand and insist that the British Government" toe the line and follow the "rules of international law." If the United States did not succeed, then Germany would have the right to revisit the submarine issue.

Lansing was not pleased. "It has all the elements of the 'gold brick' swindle," he wrote Wilson the next day. But House was encouraged. Admittedly, this note, the so-called *Sussex* pledge, was not perfect. Still, since Germany had sufficiently yielded on the major point, a diplomatic break and war were hardly justified. The attempt to link German concessions to America getting tougher on the Allies should be ignored, of course.

Wilson agreed. A brief acknowledgment went out to the Germans, emphasizing the expectation that the new policy would be followed to the letter. A few days later, the Germans issued an apology and promise to punish the submarine commander who had torpedoed the *Sussex*. The crisis was over, almost exactly a year to the day that the *Lusitania* had sunk.

A combination of Wilsonian firmness and the uncertainty of the German military situation had averted war. But everything now depended on Germany's future behavior. How long would it be before Germany decided that using an effective new weapon to its full capacity was more important than keeping America neutral? And would Wilson now have no choice but to take the country into war if another incident occurred? The long-suffering Bernstorff could not help but betray his pessimism. "We will settle this crisis," he lamented to John Callan O'Laughlin, "and have another one in two months."

For Addams, the *Sussex* confirmed the need for continued peace efforts. She was pleased that the now Schwimmer-less Neutral Conference in Stockholm had succeeded in issuing an Easter appeal to the belligerents, calling for self-determination of nations, freedom of the seas, disarmament, an international organization where disputes could be arbitrated, a World Congress, and the replacement of secret treaties with "parliamentary control of foreign policy." The appeal received coverage in Europe and the United States, though far less than if Addams or Bryan had been directly involved.

Even on the sidelines, Addams remained an influential figure. Wilson's roses showed he recognized this, and it was now TR's turn. His Progressive comrade and Addams friend Harold Ickes planted the seed of Roosevelt's seeing Addams when he came to Chicago for a late April speaking engagement. "I know also that she has a very warm personal regard for you even though she does differ with you in the matter of preparedness, etc.," Ickes wrote TR. "I am merely suggesting this interview as something that I will try to bring about if you desire it." Roosevelt consented, as did Addams, although she admitted that "I know I must be a thorn in the flesh to the Progressive Party."

She was also one of the hated "pacificists" TR had railed about nonstop for more than a year. On the way to Chicago, he had been in the presence of another—the elderly bearded minister Jenkin Lloyd Jones, one of the

Ford pilgrims and the uncle of the architect Frank Lloyd Wright. "I'm not afraid of him now," Jones said of Roosevelt. "I don't think he'll have me put off the train, even if I am against preparedness."

Chicago still loved Teddy. When he arrived on Saturday, April 29, the streets were jammed with well-wishers, including one determined woman desperate to have her ten-year-old son shake TR's hand. "Glad to meet you; glad to meet the boy; glad to meet everybody," he boomed. A few hours later, he made a pilgrimage to the Bowen home, where Addams was recuperating, his arrival noisily signaled by a two motorcycle escort. Curiosity got the best of the tony Astor Street set, who could not help but peer outside to see who the famous visitor was. Addams, clad in a "tea gown of gray silk," eventually showed her face to the reporters, though she did not look well.

The two spent a half hour together alone. So much had changed in the nearly four years since Addams had seconded his nomination for president. What they talked about on this occasion remains uncertain, but he brought her two books; undoubtedly, *Fear God and Take Your Own Part* was one of them. He almost certainly was interested in whether she would actively oppose his candidacy this year. At least one issue—suffrage—still bound them together, especially since TR had already announced his support of the federal amendment, rather than the piecemeal, state-by-state approach favored by Wilson.

For now, Addams's major priority remained the war. She knew that the Peace Ship, in its own clumsy way, had done some small good, and the Neutral Conference's work in Sweden was contributing to peace. But a more dynamic campaign was now needed, both to keep America out of the war and to stop the hostilities. And she and other pacifists also realized that a specific program would correct the still commonly held view that they were weak-kneed namby-pambies peddling utopian fantasies about the brotherhood of man. A reconsideration of America's foreign policy and defense, they recognized, could be only one part of a larger progressive-oriented agenda with such proposals as an "army of conservation," "democratizing our military service and turning it into a training school," and even "compulsory social service for every man and woman." Some, like Stephen Wise, believed a new "fundamentally progressive" party was the answer, albeit one nothing like the 1912 organization concocted "to elect a most fascinating gentleman to the Presidency."

Addams, like many reformers of her era, never lost her faith in the good sense of the American people. Surely, they would be persuaded and rally to the pacifist cause once they heard and understood the message. But reaching the public was becoming more difficult that spring, as a growing number of media outlets restricted and even eliminated any peace-related content altogether. By May, Ellen Slayden complained that many seemed unaware that "there was such a thing as a peace movement. All news of it is systematically excluded from the press." The belligerent countries, Addams believed, were even worse. "They will not permit any discussion of peace," she explained. "The people of one warring country who desire peace are induced to believe that those of the enemy country are all for war whereas a large portion of the population in the other country are equally anxious for peace."

If the press would not cooperate, other ways of spreading the message had to be found. Ford and his millions remained the best option, even if he had cut back on his funding of the Stockholm conference and had apparently forgotten most of his big-money promises to peace organizations. To his credit, he had refused to abandon pacifism, even in the face of press bashings and ongoing pressure from the worried suits at Ford. Addams sensed the automaker was still with them when she had finally managed to see him in Detroit in April, as did David Starr Jordan, who found that Ford was not the guileless bumpkin portrayed by the press and actually had a "very bright mind and sharp wit." And he still was willing to spend money for peace, sponsoring splashy full-page ads in national newspapers under his name. "For months the people of the United States have had fear pounded into their brains," one dramatically read. "All the wild cry for the spending of billions, the piling up of armament, and the saddling of the country with a military caste has been based on nothing but *fiction*."

To Roosevelt and others, the Peace Ship had already confirmed that Ford was a crackpot. That many did not agree was confirmed by Ford's April wins in the Michigan and Nebraska Republican primaries without lifting a finger. Another 20,000 voted for him in Pennsylvania as a write-in or "sticker" candidate. Baffled pundits suggested Ford's polling strength had something to do with the quality of his automobiles or the loyalty of the thousands of workers employed in his factories.

Hoping for a scoop, reporters were eager to talk to Ford when he came to New York later that month. He assured them he was not running for anything. "I just can't think of taking seriously this movement to put me into politics," he announced. "I can't even talk or think of such a thing. It is incredible." He was more interested in visiting with Louis Enricht, a Long Island inventor/con man who claimed he could "make motor fuel out of water for two cents a gallon" with the addition of a mysterious green liquid.

If Ford was not seeking office, what did his support mean? At minimum, pacifism was far more common than some recognized, especially in the heartland. To Roosevelt, it was another troubling indication that the country was not feeling especially "heroic." The prospect of a President Ford someday so horrified him that he told John Callan O'Laughlin that "even Wilson is infinitely preferable."

Who Ford might back in the fall remained unclear at the moment, but Wilson appeared far more likely to attract Ford's endorsement than Roosevelt, regardless of their friendly correspondence earlier that year. And the President had continued to do everything possible to show that he was on the side of Addams and the peace crowd. A few days after the *Sussex* crisis wrapped up, he welcomed a delegation from the American Union against Militarism, who came to brief him on their recent antipreparedness tour. Privately, he was not eager to "have these people come and make speeches to me," but Tumulty wisely advised him that Lillian Wald, their spokesperson and Addams's friend, could not be ignored.

Beforehand, Wald and her colleagues decided to focus only on preparedness, the issue that Ford had tapped into so strongly of late, rather than any discussion of peace or foreign policy conduct (such a strategy, they believed, would reduce the potential of being promptly "bathed in the typical Wilsonian speech, all generalities and righteousness"). Once again, Wilson gave a virtuoso performance. For every concern about militarism they raised, especially proposed legislation in New York requiring "compulsory military training for all boys" ages sixteen to nineteen, he had a compelling response. "I don't need to tell you that I am just as much opposed to militarism as any man living," the President told the pacifist group. But some degree of "reasonable preparation," even a 250,000-man army, was nothing to fear, especially in a country of 100 million people. At times, he sounded positively Rooseveltian in his justification of a military buildup. It was 1916, "a year of madness," and not 1895. And if the United States was seen as "helpless," then her influence with other nations would be "negligible. . . . If the world undertakes, as we all hope it will undertake, a joint effort to keep the peace, it will expect us to play our proportional part in manifesting the force which is going to rest back of that. Now, in the last analysis, the peace of society is obtained by force." Wald tried to pin him down on "universal compulsory training," TR's favorite talking point, but Wilson refused to dismiss it entirely. "I didn't say I believed in it. . . . I would say merely that it is not contrary to the spirit of American traditions."

Wilson appeared so reasonable, so sensible, so willing to listen that only later did the delegation realize that he had not given them an inch. Rabbi Wise, who had been present, began to see the President as an insincere phony, although most of the others kept the faith. Addams still thought Wilson could be persuaded to call an official neutral conference, perhaps motivated by its impact on his reelection. Still, she recognized that he preferred to ride, rather than resist, the preparedness wave now sweeping America, especially in the East.

The signs were everywhere. Five days after the meeting with Wilson, New York celebrated "Preparedness Day" with a massive thirteen-hour parade up Fifth Avenue from Washington Square to Fifty-ninth Street, said to be the largest in America since the end of the Civil War. Estimates suggested that more than 130,000 marchers participated, some chanting "We-we-we-want peace, with-with pre-par-edness," while another million watched from the sidelines, happily waving flags and dodging pickpockets. Organizations from virtually every walk of life were represented: teachers, jewelers, haberdashers, garment salesmen, engineers, grocers, even doctors. Two hundred different bands marched, including one from the American Telephone and Telegraph Company, which appropriately played "Hello Frisco," the hit of the previous year celebrating the first transcontinental phone call. The biggest name present was the sixty-nine-year-old inventor

TR promotes preparedness with a group of Boy Scouts at Sagamore Hill,
May 13, 1916.   (Ag1984.0324: Doris A. and Lawrence H. Budner Theodore Roosevelt Collection,
DeGolyer Library, Southern Methodist University)

Thomas Edison, who had publicly endorsed TR for president that week.
Beyond donning special "rubber-heeled shoes" for the march, Edison made
no attempt to spruce himself up for the big occasion. "His pants hadn't
been creased in some days," a *New York Sun* reporter noted. "He looked as
if he had just got up from a laboratory bench over in his wizard's laboratory
in New Jersey."

TR had been invited but chose to stay at Sagamore Hill, where a mini-
parade of Boy Scouts, schoolchildren, Bible students, and others marched
on his lawn, toured his home, and learned about some of his more interesting trophies, including the "chair I sat in when I was President keeping
order in the nation and having Uncle Sam respected abroad." The Roosevelts were represented in the main affair in the city by his wife, Edith,
and his daughter Ethel, along with an older gentleman at Thirty-seventh
Street who waved a large framed photo of TR while shouting "Three cheers
for Theodore Roosevelt and preparedness!" Most took his cheers in good
stead, except for a member of the engineers' division. "Sit down," he complained. "T.R. hasn't got a dog's chance."

The Woman's Peace Party, socialists, and other left-wing organizations tried to mount counterprotests. At 208 Fifth Avenue, the WPP's ongoing exhibit, "War against War," featuring a large papier-mâché dinosaur named Jingo (said to be extinct because he was "all armor plate—no brains"), attracted 11,000 curious visitors even with law enforcement ready to harass radicals on the premises such as Emma Goldman and Becky Edelsohn. They also hung a dramatic banner that everyone on the nearby reviewing stand could see: "To the Marchers: There are only 100,000 of you. You are not the only patriots. Two million farmers, half a million mine workers and organized labor throughout America are against what you and Wall Street are marching for. Are you sure you are right?"

The most striking demonstration that day was a brave group of fifty young women in white, bearing the sign REAL PATRIOTS KEEP COOL, who handed out antipreparedness literature and pamphlets. Lella Secor, a twenty-nine-year-old journalist who had journeyed to Europe with Ford, was one of them. "I have never had anything affect me more deeply," she wrote her mother. "I could not look at those long lines of fine looking men, marching so gaily along, and with so little realization of what it all means, without a fresh outburst of tears."

Addams and other pacifists also found the parade deeply troubling, especially its corporate and financial connections. They knew that a good many men and women had been either forced to march by their employers or offered a free day off (the Saturday workday was still common in 1916). Even worse, copycat parades were soon organized in Boston, Chicago, Hartford, Memphis, and other cities eager to prove they were as patriotic as the folks in the Big Apple.

Whether the big cities and the New York press represented the true feelings of the nation remained to be seen. Parts of the West Coast and the Midwest, if TR's correspondents that spring were accurate, not only continued to fear the cost of a military buildup but also displayed a "most intense distrust" of the munitions industry and "every cent they are making out of the war." And most of the country's young men remained stubbornly resistant to the civic duty of military service. Enlistments to assist in the Mexican mission had been pitiful to date, and the country was clearly not ready for the mandatory military commitment championed by Roosevelt. Brooks Adams, the grandson of President John Quincy Adams, told TR that Americans would someday accept the idea, although it would clearly take time, especially in a nation that was "too materialistic. We set a money value on everything."

To the relief of the pacifists, the much debated National Defense Act signed by Wilson a few weeks later mentioned absolutely nothing explicit about a draft. Nor was the expansion of the army to 206,000 in peacetime and the federalized National Guard to 425,000 as dramatic as they had feared. Perhaps the President could still be trusted. In any event, there was nothing that Addams or anyone else could do at the moment. Verdun was raging, and the Allies would likely launch their own assault this summer. Best for Addams to sit tight for the next few months while "keeping the peace powder dry" until ready to be sparked again at the opportune moment. In the meantime, she would try to get better. There was also to be a new member of her extended family to meet, a young Jewish socialist named Emanuel Julius, who had become engaged to her niece Marcet. She suggested to Marcet that perhaps they might wish to hyphenate their names, a then highly unconventional idea that horrified Mary Smith but appealed to the young couple, who both took the name Haldeman-Julius.

For Rosika Schwimmer, a waiting strategy was a return to the bad old days of 1914, when the mainstream peace movement sat on its hands while the world burst into flames. She had begun to wonder whether the pacifists would ever accomplish anything. And women were still stuck on the sidelines powerlessly "preaching," rather than getting things done. "I wish I were a man," she wrote her wealthy friend and disciple Lola Maverick Lloyd. "I wish I were a millionaire. I would like to show what could and ought to be done." But now Schwimmer was a mere observer while others did the work she believed she alone had started.

The unhappy end to her role in the Neutral Conference had crushed her emotionally, leaving her bedridden for weeks. The thought of "wickedness, meanness . . . selfishness, lies . . . triumphant" sickened her. "The injustice of the whole thing nearly chokes me," she bitterly complained. "I get physically weak, and have a sensation, as if the indignation would run in fluid state through my veins."

A few days after the New York preparedness parade, Houghton Mifflin published James Norman Hall's *Kitchener's Mob*, touted as an "uncensored" account of his experiences in the British army. The reviews were almost universally favorable. "One of the best books that have come out of the war," the *Chicago Tribune* raved. *Town and Country* agreed. "The most vivid, coherent, logical, intelligent, well-balanced account of what being in the British trenches was like that we have yet encountered. . . . [I]t deserves to become a classic." Within a month, the book was in its third printing, and it eventually sold fifty thousand copies, an impressive start for a first-time author. Hall's literary dreams were coming true, but his old life continued to call him, so much so that the former British tommy signed up for the "rookie" training in Plattsburg, where he was soon promoted to squad leader. With his father's health now stabilized, he was ready to return to Europe in the summer, anxious to get away from the "hum-drum life of peace." War, he admitted to a friend, "despite all the horror and the bloodshed—has its attractive side."

Chapter 13

LAST STAND OF THE
BULL MOOSE

MAY 21–JUNE 10, 1916

*I now have a considerable following, whereas a year
and three quarters ago, I had none; and indeed until
six months ago I had practically none.*

—Theodore Roosevelt, June 1916

The "attractiveness" of war notwithstanding, Wilson hoped that peace would somehow come in the next several months. He understood all too well that every minute the Great War went on, the chances of America's being involved dramatically increased. After almost two years, the Allies had made little headway. "The general situation is none too good," TR's English friend Arthur Lee confided to him in May. "I do not mean that the Germans are winning but their powers of resistance are still but little impaired and the vitality—both military and economic— of the Central Powers is still enormous." Eventually, he believed, one side would be worn down to the point of "sheer exhaustion," but that day was a long way off, especially since the British had introduced conscription and had recently extended the net to married men.

Not surprisingly, the Germans saw the value of ending the war sooner rather than later. Buried within the *Sussex* note was a reference to the German government's "readiness to make peace on a basis safeguarding Germany's vital interests." "Safeguarding," of course, would mean keeping most of what Germany had gained in the war to date. Arthur von Gwinner, the managing director of the Deutsche Bank, explained it this way: "Germany is like a poker player who has gathered in all the money on the table and naturally is willing to break off an all-night session and retire with his winnings, while the others persist in continuing, in the hopes of recouping some of their losses."

The Allies, then, were not about to welcome any peace efforts or any of the Wilsonian "intervention" envisioned by Colonel House in his discussions in London that winter. Grey had informed House of as much during the *Sussex* crisis. "Everybody feels there must be more German failure and some Allied success before anything but an inconclusive peace could be obtained," the British foreign secretary wrote. House tried to push him, warning that more waiting might prove disastrous, but neither Grey nor his colleagues were convinced. Even House had begun to wonder about the Allies. "I see evidences of the Allies regaining their self-assurance and not being as yielding to our desires as they were when they were in so much trouble," he wrote Wilson. "We have given them everything and they ever demand more." Privately House was more cynical. "What the Allies want is to dip their hands into our treasure chest."

The Colonel believed the longer the Allies waited, the more American public opinion would turn against them, especially since matters with Germany had cooled down at the moment. Intentionally or not, the British appeared to be doing all they could to antagonize Americans of late. The swift and vicious suppression of the Easter Rebellion ("a very sad business . . . far more serious than the censored news allowed the world to know," Roosevelt's correspondent Sir Horace Plunkett informed him) shocked American sensibilities. And the British not only were continuing their ongoing interference with American trade, but were now intercepting and examining mail from neutrals.

This was too much for TR, who claimed he would have sent the "mail over on war-ships." Still, he refused to accept the argument that British abuses should be addressed the same way as the Germans'. "The difference," he explained, "is the difference between the offense of the blackhander who kidnaps your child, and the offense of the man who trespasses upon your ground, and who steals your fruit."

Wilson agreed. As usual, there would be no ultimatums for Great Britain and what he himself called their "altogether indefensible" behavior. But his patience with the British was nearing a breaking point. It was obvious that they did not want his intervention for peace. Nor did they want him to make what Grey called "embarrassing demands" about American neutral rights. The President decided Great Britain could not have it both ways and let them know as much. But the message was not strong enough to get results from Grey, who offered a batch of new and old excuses. The other Allies would have to be consulted. And it would be a mistake for Wilson to intervene too early, since "it would be interpreted as meaning that he desired peace on a basis favourable to Germany." As for the "great scheme," aka a future league of nations, Grey believed it would need to be linked to a "peace favourable to the Allies."

By this point, even House appeared to dimly recognize that the Allies wanted Wilson's intervention only as a last resort if they could not decisively crush Germany. He also began to believe that the "French and English are prolonging the war unnecessarily." Perhaps the time had come for the President to do something, even if the Allies advised against it. Tumulty made the same point to Wilson. The peace process was bound to be lengthy. "Why should we wait until the moment of exhaustion before ever beginning a discussion?" he asked his boss. Tumulty suggested some sort of note to the belligerents inviting them to join the United States at The Hague to "discuss means for making peace, and for establishing a world court or international tribune to safeguard the peace of the world after the close of the war." The suggestion was not unlike some of those made by Addams and other pacifists, who would have jumped for joy had they known someone so close to Wilson was speaking their language.

The President was already convinced of the growing need to do something concrete for peace. The question was *when* and *how*. Neither he nor House believed he could move forward now. Still, he was ready to articulate how peace might be achieved and America's essential role in the process. And he had a perfect opportunity, an invitation to speak before the first annual meeting of the League to Enforce Peace at the New Willard Hotel in Washington on May 27. Taft, who sent the invite, privately was no fan of Wilson, whom he labeled in a letter to Hughes as the "greatest opportunist and hypocrite ever in the White House" (Wilson, meanwhile, thought Taft weak and wishy-washy). But Taft understood that the appearance of the President would further legitimize the organization, which had more than its share of heavy hitters in the political, economic, and business world involved. Addams herself received an invitation to attend, but she and other pacifists had flatly rejected the "Enforce" part of the league's message. "When we turn from moral suasion to force we step down and not up," explained Bryan. "I don't care to have this nation a policeman."

House and Lansing were lukewarm on the LEP, House believing it "impracticable" right now and the secretary of state fearing its potential to embroil America in global struggles of all kinds, but Wilson would not be there to rubber-stamp the LEP's program anyway. In the days before the speech, he worked on the main points to get across—namely, that a postwar world must ensure self-determination for all peoples, the "integrity and sovereignty" of small states, and the "right . . . to be free from every disturbance of the peace that proceeds from aggression." But the biggest bombshell would be the President's announcement that the United States would be more than willing to participate in a global organization to guarantee these rights in the future. Grey and House, of course, had privately discussed this possibility for months, but this would be the first time the American public would be clued in on such a seismic foreign policy change.

The press recognized that this would be no ordinary speech. Taft, newly reelected president of the organization, was on stage with Wilson, as was the usually low-profile vice president, Thomas Marshall. Edith was also present, as were two of the President's daughters. Wilson decided in advance there would be no extemporaneous content. He wanted his message to be understood and consumed exactly as he had conceived of it on paper.

After a series of speeches, including one by his sworn enemy Henry Cabot Lodge, it was the President's turn. His address was relatively brief. Wilson explained that the issue of peace was becoming increasingly significant. As the president, it was his duty to explain the "thought and purpose of the people . . . in this vital matter," especially since America, while not a participant in the current conflict, was very much involved in the "life of the world" and the preservation of peace. The old ways of "secret

counsels" and "arbitrary force" must give way to a "new and more wholesome diplomacy," in which the United States would do more than its part.
He then outlined the three "fundamental things" America stood behind—
self-determination, the "territorial integrity" of small states (undercut
somewhat by the United States' recent involvement in Haiti and Santo
Domingo), and the resistance to "selfish aggression"—and spoke of the willingness to join a postwar congress of nations. Finally, Wilson highlighted
America's potential role in making peace. Specific terms could be decided
among the belligerents, he announced, but the United States would support
a "universal association of the nations," one that would not only guarantee
freedom of the seas but secure the "territorial integrity and political independence" of all countries.

The speech was well received by much of the nation's press, aside from
some of the more hostile Republican newspapers. "Pacifists and militarists,
big army men and little army men, peace leaguers and security leaguers,
can accept it, laud and embrace it," remarked *The New York Times*. Not
surprisingly, some feared the "entangling alliances" the Founding Fathers
warned of, but Wilson had a ready answer. He would never "consent to an
entangling alliance," he explained, "but I would gladly assent to a disentan-
gling alliance," especially one that would "unite the peoples of the world
to preserve the peace . . . upon a basis of common right and justice."

The speech contained one major faux pas. Early on, Wilson made a
seemingly innocuous and truly "neutral" comment about the war: "with its
causes and its objects we are not concerned." This, along with a remark a
few weeks earlier referring to the "rest of the world" being "mad," enraged
the Allies. Was the President making no distinction between the Allied
and German causes? Page, as usual eager to convey the London party line,
immediately informed House that the British suspected Wilson didn't understand what the war was really about and was preaching to "the gallery
filled with peace cranks Bryans and Fords and Jane Addamses."

House felt the British were being a tad oversensitive, if not ungrateful.
Wilson had done them more than a few favors since the war began. Now,
the Colonel told Grey, the Allies "pick out some expression he makes giving
it a meaning and importance he never meant. If we are to take part in
maintaining the peace of the world we could hardly be indifferent to the

war and its causes and the President never intended to leave such an impression."

Privately, House believed Wilson's blunder was of his own making. At times, he noticed that the President seemed to care more about mundane "domestic matters," like filling a postmaster position in New York, rather than international affairs. "If he would keep himself informed," House confided in his diary, "he would not destroy his influence abroad as he does from time to time by things he says in his speeches."

House's frustrations with Wilson once again suggested that he believed, deep down, that he knew more than the President. The Colonel's already considerable ego had grown larger since his return from Europe. The man who supposedly had no desire to receive credit admitted that April that his diary keeping was at least partly driven by a desire to record the "work I have done," which he believed had not been sufficiently documented during his past career in Texas politics. "If this diary had not been kept, no one would ever know the part I took in the making of the Federal Reserve Act," he wrote. And fawning mentions in the *North American Review* and the more mainstream *Collier's*, one of the country's most popular magazines, further boosted his self-esteem. The *Collier's* piece, an editorial entitled "A Man" (ironically written by Mark Sullivan, a Republican and friend of TR), waxed poetic about House's "self-effacement," his "modesty," and his high-minded lack of interest in holding office. The President's adviser "is a pretty important figure in the world," Sullivan wrote. "There aren't many things in America more worthy of emulation by Youth than Colonel House and his career." House was pleased, but he couldn't help wondering how Wilson might respond to such glowing mentions. "I hope the President is too big a man to allow them to affect him."

Wilson was not at all jealous. He still trusted House implicitly, far more than he trusted his cabinet, which remained in the dark much of the time. The President had praised House obliquely in two speeches of late, referring to "men" (likely using the plural to throw off the public) who never thought "about themselves for their own interests. And I tie to those men as you would tie to an anchor." Foreign observers such as the French ambassador

Jules Jusserand were amazed by the Colonel's role. "The status of Mr. House remains truly extraordinary," he wrote his superiors in Paris. "Especially with regard to Europe, the President does nothing without consulting him. The State Department is constantly in communication with him by a telephone service specially controlled to avoid indiscretions."

The greater House's role, the more he found fault with Wilson, all of which he recorded in his diary. The President moved too slowly, he believed. The President was avoidant and "dodges trouble." The President has "intense prejudices against people. He likes a few and is very loyal to them, but his prejudices are many and often unjust. He finds great difficulty in conferring with men against whom, for some reason, he has a prejudice and in whom he can find nothing good." By June, the Colonel had also decided that Wilson was a poor administrator and "does not get the best results from his Cabinet or those around him." House, naturally, believed his own superior ideas could correct this problem, but he had no intention of sharing them with Wilson. Otherwise, he understood "there would be no place for me, for it is to supplement his deficiency in these directions which make my endeavors valuable to him."

House was also not above participating in various palace intrigues to replace major administration officials, surprisingly with the help of Edith Wilson. Edith, who had resigned herself to House's role, conspired with him in the midst of the *Sussex* situation about finding a way to get rid of Josephus Daniels and Joseph Tumulty as "helpful" moves for the President's benefit. Daniels's running of the Navy Department had been under fire for three years, and Edith had never liked Tumulty, whose Catholicism remained an issue. "Many Protestants do not believe that communications reach the President," the Colonel admitted (he had also recently learned of "some of Tumulty's activities against me"). Daniels's departure was to be House's responsibility, while Tumulty would be left to Edith, but neither would succeed in these cloak-and-dagger activities. The Colonel also made sure that Wilson learned that Page resented House's presence in Britain (there was "no place in one country for two Ambassadors," Page complained). "It lowers my opinion of the man immensely," Wilson told House. They both agreed that Page could be best rehabilitated by a return home "to get some American atmosphere into him."

If the Colonel was not the singular force in Wilson's life he had been before Edith came into the picture, his influence had diminished only slightly. The President even wanted him to handle the reelection campaign, but this was too much even for House. For one thing, it would interfere with his efforts in foreign affairs. For another, he realized that the public would begin to ask serious questions, if they hadn't already, about why Wilson delegated so much responsibility to a single individual and perhaps wonder who was really the president.

By late May, Roosevelt understood that Wilson would be extremely tough to beat in November. No matter how often TR tried to point out the President's deficiencies, the public seemed to be satisfied. The economy was good, and war had again been avoided without loss of American dignity. The novelist Owen Wister, who had written a snarky anti-Wilson poem that had caused controversy early in the year, warned Roosevelt that the "hallucination that Mr. Wilson has kept us out of the war will be the strongest ground for his re-election in many minds. These minds must, if possible, be disabused of the hallucination, and made to understand that it is Germany who has kept us out of the war because she did not want to go to war with us."

But how to accomplish this remained difficult. Vast segments of America believed TR meant war and Wilson meant peace, no matter how many times TR tried to stress that no American soldier had died on his watch as president or that Wilson had already sent troops into Mexico and launched what Roosevelt called "little wars" against "Santo Domingo and Haiti . . . killing and wounding some hundreds of badly armed black men." At times, he could not help but grow frustrated that the American people did not always grasp his message. "Mere outside preaching and prophecy tend after a while to degenerate into a scream," he wrote his sister. "After that point has been reached the preacher can do no good, and had better keep quiet."

It was not in TR's nature to keep quiet, even if he was not feeling well. Since returning from the West Indies, a bad cold with an even worse cough plagued him, so much so that he saw a specialist who sprayed his throat. The health of other family members also concerned him—namely, his wife,

Edith, who was "not very strong," and Kermit's wife, Belle, a new mother, now afflicted with typhus. Still, TR kept up his usual frenetic pace at home at Sagamore Hill and at the *Metropolitan* offices in downtown Manhattan. Much of his days were eaten up by the piles of mail he received and the hundreds of people who wanted to see him, mostly regarding matters of minor importance. And all were convinced that Roosevelt did not give them enough time, even though another twenty might be waiting outside the door hoping for a second with him. Victor Murdock, one of his Progressive lieutenants, marveled at TR's remarkable ability to multitask when he came to see him that spring. "He was signing letters and talking at the same time, greeting callers and bidding them goodbye. Over in one corner jangled the telephone. The afternoon newspaper men were outside, asking for him. He rushed out. He rushed back. He went on signing letters."

Offers to write for Allied periodicals or visit the front lines did not interest him. His current focus was to alert the sleeping American public to their responsibilities in three broad issues: preparedness, Americanism, and international duty. Beyond that, the ultimate goal was to get rid of Wilson.

The weeks leading up to the June conventions would determine whether TR would be the man for the job. There was no longer any doubt that he was running. He had officially approved the work of the Roosevelt Non-Partisan League, which sponsored (with Perkins's money) a four-page advertisement, "Why Roosevelt would be our best guarantee of Peace," in the *Saturday Evening Post*, one of the most popular magazines in the country. The "open letter" tried to demolish Roosevelt's warmonger reputation, explaining how his own skillful brand of personal diplomacy had averted conflicts with Germany, Japan, and Britain, among others, while touting his Nobel Peace Prize for his efforts in ending the Russo-Japanese War. And a new organization, the Roosevelt Republican Committee, headed by George von L. Meyer, Taft's former navy secretary, was now actively in the field trying to find a way to drum up the 493 delegates needed for the GOP nomination. Most were already pledged to other candidates through the primaries or party machinery, but the hope was that enough could be swayed to jump on the TR bandwagon at crunch time.

Roosevelt knew that his task ahead was daunting. Somehow, the men who controlled the party and the convention, a "sordid set of machine masters," as TR called them, would have to be convinced that Roosevelt, and Roosevelt alone, could lead them to victory in November. The Old Guard conservatives of the party would be a tough nut to crack. They remembered with seething rage every nasty attack TR had rained upon them in 1912 and how he had almost wrecked the party. "Some of the republicans frankly say that before accepting Mr. Roosevelt they would burn up their homes and leave the country forever," one reporter observed. But those odious objections might be set aside if faced with the prospect of another three-way race and a humiliating defeat. A number of Progressives, such as Charles Sumner Bird of Massachusetts, believed this was TR's best, if not only, hope. "If the Progressives would nominate T.R. at once, and adjourn, Hughes would be eliminated; he would refuse to be a candidate with Col. Roosevelt in the field and with Hughes out of the way the Republicans would have to nominate Roosevelt," Bird explained to Perkins. "You are playing for big stakes and must take a big chance." But Perkins and TR both preferred to see how things unfolded at the Republican convention first. More than a few Progressives had a sneaking suspicion that TR would not run unless he also received the Republican nomination, a charge he denied. It would all depend, he insisted, on whether the Republicans chose "to act so that the Progressives will be able to act with them."

If TR somehow managed to get the Progressives and Republicans united behind him, he still faced the very difficult challenge of beating Wilson. Wilson had only captured about 42 percent of the total vote last time, but the world of 1916 was far different from 1912. Pacifists and the Henry Ford crowd certainly would not vote for TR this time around, even those like Addams who had been attracted to the visionary Bull Moose social reform program. And more than a few hard-core Progressives had lost patience with Roosevelt's current fixation on the war and lack of interest in "social and industrial justice." Nor did they care for his recent chumming around with the likes of Lodge and Wall Street bigwigs. But friends like the former Republican congressman and Roosevelt biographer Charles Washburn advised TR not to concern himself with the "lunatic fringe" among his supporters. "Remember that you owe more to the country than you do to anyone who followed you in 1912."

Most Democrats believed that Roosevelt would be easier to beat than the still silent front-runner Charles Evans Hughes. Wilson, while he would not go that far, conceded that Hughes would be a formidable foe. "Roosevelt deals in personalities & not argument upon facts & conditions," the President told the journalist Ray Stannard Baker that May. "One does not need to meet him at all. Hughes is of a different type. If he is nominated, he will have to be met."

The unpleasant possibility that Hughes might ultimately get the Republican nomination was never far from Roosevelt's mind. What his next step would be in that scenario remained uncertain. Everyone knew he did not like Hughes. It was not the almost obsessive hatred he felt for Wilson, but more of a general disdain for Hughes as a man and politician. Their relationship had begun pleasantly enough ten years earlier. Roosevelt then viewed Hughes as a "sane and sincere reformer," and went to bat for his gubernatorial nomination in 1906. But he soon discovered that Hughes as governor was not interested in Roosevelt's advice or involvement in state or party affairs. Nor did he appreciate Hughes's goody-two-shoes unwillingness to make sure loyal Republican workers were taken care of. By 1908, Roosevelt had almost completely soured on Hughes personally, although he conceded the governor was "entirely an honest man and one of much ability." That year, TR again helped in Hughes's reelection and also stepped in when Hughes waged a futile attempt to get a direct primary bill passed shortly before leaving Albany for the Supreme Court.

During the primary bill fight, Hughes disclosed to TR his belief that the state Democrat and Republican bosses were colluding, a charge Roosevelt later repeated publicly, resulting in the Barnes libel suit. When TR tried to get Hughes's help, the now Supreme Court Justice wanted no part of it. "He declared that he did not recall the conversation and that he had no recollection that such a state of affairs had existed," Roosevelt bitterly complained. "That is the way Mr. Hughes stands up." From that moment forward, TR privately had little good to say about Hughes, whom he liberally doused in his favorite adjectives usually reserved for Wilson: "powerful, cold, selfish . . . obstinate, narrow." (Rumors even surfaced that Roosevelt had called Hughes a "Baptist hypocrite," a charge TR was quick to deny as "just as preposterous as if it had been said that Mr. Hughes had called me a 'Dutch reformed dinosaur.'") To Roosevelt, Wilson and Hughes were of the same ilk, even if he suspected that Hughes would be a much better president than Wilson. Worst of all, no one knew what Hughes's views were about any of the current issues or if he knew much of anything about foreign affairs. "In international matters and in the present situation I know I am worth two of Hughes," Roosevelt insisted.

Many Republicans would not have disagreed. But Hughes was undeniably a safer bet at the moment, even if the Old Guard conservatives did not want him. "There are some of them," TR observed to the journalist Charles Thompson, "who would prefer me to Hughes, because, they say, 'He understands politics; if we got in back of him he would play fair. If we accepted his ideas, he would let us have the Post Offices.'" But the common mind-set among most Republicans desperate to take back the White House, one journalist explained, was this: "We MIGHT win with Roosevelt . . . but if we want to take EVERY PRECAUTION to prevent defeat, Hughes is the man."

TR was not giving up. He had three speeches scheduled in the Midwest in late May designed to boost his profile further before the conventions. The first stop was Detroit, where everyone wondered whether Roosevelt would see Ford after their cordial correspondence earlier in the year. TR's friends advised him against it, especially since Ford had recently made a fresh batch of controversial and somewhat bizarre statements, gleefully trumpeted by the hostile elements of the press. A preparedness advocate named Henry Wise Wood had picked Ford's brains on a number of subjects including the potential for disaster because of America's weak defenses (Wood was "full of Eastern scare gas," Ford told him), history (useless and "need not be studied nor considered"), wars ("created artificially by bankers," two in particular), and patriotism ("last resort of a scoundrel"). Ford also announced that he thought little of the flag and promised that he would contribute nothing to the munitions trade if America went to war. To his credit, Roosevelt was still not averse to seeing the eccentric automaker, who was eager to show him the Highland Park plant, where a car could now be assembled in seventeen minutes. Beforehand, TR was warned by Gustavus Pope, a wealthy Detroit manufacturer, that Ford was a bit of a strange fellow, to say the least, with a "simple childlike nature" and the

"faith of an early Christian in human nature. . . . I just want you to remember that you are dealing with a person who is not like other people in
many ways." Their meeting never did materialize, although TR sent Ford
a copy of his main speech in advance.

Detroit, Roosevelt understood, was not friendly territory, with its thousands of Ford supporters and sizable German American enclave. The possibility of assassination was never far from his mind. "Some pacifist may
kill me in order to prove how devoutly he believes in peace at any price,"
he quipped. He could not avoid the sometimes overwhelming crowds, who
remained as anxious to see him as any Hollywood star. Julian Street, covering the trip for *Collier's*, could not help noticing the heavy price of celebrity TR paid. Roosevelt, he noted, was like "an animal forever on
inspection. . . . Fancy his not being able to ride on streetcars, or walk freely
about . . . without being mobbed by eager strangers, holding out their hands
politely or even poking them toward him wildly and shrieking: 'Hello,
Teddy!' directly in his face."

Thousands stood on the streets between the Detroit Athletic Club and
Detroit Opera House, desperate to get a glimpse of him, shouting, "We're
for you here!" and "You can trust us!" Those waiting to hear him speak at
the Opera House in the morning were surprised to hear TR say he had no
ill will toward Ford and "very genuine admiration" for his accomplishments.
But he soon switched gears, linking Ford and the pacifists to "the men who
denounced and opposed Washington" and "the men who denounced and
voted against Abraham Lincoln." The remainder of the speech was a mixture of the usual calls for preparedness ("we have to decide whether we
are to be in good faith a people and able and ready to take care of ourselves") and pleas for Americanism ("we must set our faces like flint against
any effort to divide our people along the lines of creed or of national ori-
gin"). A few attacks on the administration were thrown in for good measure, especially the "prolonged and excessive indulgence in note-writing"
and ultimatums that were not "ultimate."

The most dramatic moment occurred when Roosevelt began speaking
of universal service. A woman named Anna Neuer stood up. "I've got two
sons to go," she proudly announced (ironically, one worked for Ford). The
crowd at first did not react. Seconds later, it erupted. "Madam," TR began,

"if every mother in our country would make the same offer there would be no need for any mother to send her sons to war."

Ford was not impressed by TR's visit. Roosevelt, he told a reporter afterward, did not "understand the trend of events" and "does not keep with the times." The automobile magnate was also not bothered by TR's criticism, which he believed would only give his cause additional publicity. "The people are important," Ford insisted. "I am not. And at the proper time the people will attend to Theodore Roosevelt."

TR spent a week at home before resuming his speaking engagements, enjoying the growing flurry of campaign activities on his behalf. On May 27, the same day that Wilson spoke before the League to Enforce Peace gathering, hundreds of rowdy Roosevelt supporters gathered at Pennsylvania Station, where they boarded special trains to Oyster Bay. There, they marched three and a half miles to Sagamore Hill, merrily singing "We'll Vote for Theodore Roosevelt" ("to the tune of 'Glory, Glory, Hallelujah'"). And TR was there to greet them all: men, women (some who sang "We *Did* Raise Our Boy to Be a Soldier"), African Americans, even a gentleman of German descent, who assured Roosevelt that he was not a member of the dreaded hyphenate crowd. "Fine, fine!" TR boomed. "Come back, I want to shake hands with you again."

The next day he was back on the train for two more speeches, scheduled in Kansas City and St. Louis. His first stop was a four-hour layover in Chicago, the scene of the Republican and Progressive conventions the following week, where reporters heard him scoff at the pacifist notion that "preparedness means war." If that were true, then "we shouldn't permit our sons to learn how to write in school lest they become forgers." A few hours later, he arrived in Kansas City on Memorial Day (then commonly known as Decoration Day), where the waiting crowds at the train station and city streets were even more impressive and animated than what he had experienced in Detroit (a story that someone had thrown a knife at his car proved to be exaggerated if not false). The city's over-the-top welcome deeply touched him, as did a special demonstration in the lobby of the Muehlebach Hotel, where he was staying (ironically, in the same suite used by the President and the First Lady in January). A group of small girls, patriotically attired in red, white, and blue, serenaded TR with the previous year's hit, "America I Love You" and then a special "Teddy Battle Cry": "Rah, Rah Teddy! You're the Boy, Get Them Ready! Hooray!"

His speeches in Kansas City and the next day in St. Louis teed off on his usual targets. Wilson's talk of "visionary plans about world action in the future," Roosevelt explained, was utterly ridiculous until America took care of its own business—namely, preparedness and an end to "reckless promises which cannot, or ought not, or will not be kept." And the President's recent support of something called "universal voluntary training" came under an especially withering attack. It was no different, TR insisted, than imposing mandatory schooling for "all children except those who preferred to stay away." To Roosevelt, Wilson was indulging in more of his favorite wishy-washy phrase making, or what he called "weasel" words (the amused media thought TR had invented a colorful new expression until they discovered its use dated back at least sixteen years).

The German-American Alliance, the largest group of its kind in the United States, also felt the sting of the Roosevelt lash. Its refusal to partic-ipate in a preparedness parade in St. Louis did not sit well with him, nor did its threats to vote for the candidate most sympathetic to Germany, the very antithesis of Americanism. This organization, TR announced in an ad lib from his speech, "seems to forget that next fall we are going to elect an American President, and not a viceroy of the German Emperor." Ultimately, he viewed the Alliance as little better than the dreaded pacifist crowd (the "old women of both sexes"). "The professional pacifists do not serve good," he explained. "They serve evil."

After his speeches, an exhausted Roosevelt did his best to relax during the more-than-daylong train trip back to the East Coast, which was enliv-ened by a stop in Pittsburgh, where a touring group of Friars Club mem-bers, featuring luminaries such as George M. Cohan and Irving Berlin, entertained TR. Whether his Midwestern trip had hurt or helped his cause before the conventions remained uncertain. That thousands wanted to see and listen to him made at least a few Republicans look up and take notice. "The plain people are with you to a man," the celebrity evangelist Billy Sunday assured him in Kansas City. But Roosevelt's speeches further destroyed his standing among most German American voters, a substantial group national politicians feared to antagonize.

More concerning, his shrill attacks on pacifists accomplished little. For E. W. Rankin, an advertising man from Topeka and a Roosevelt supporter, the Kansas City speech had crossed the line. "Of course he is wrong when he describes the pacifists, so-called, as weak, selfish, ease loving, devotees of the auto and of the movie rather than of the country, copperheads, ignorant," Rankin wrote TR's friend William Allen White. "Is that the characters of Jane Addams" and others like her?

Roosevelt was not about to apologize. For almost two years, he had made his fight and allowed the chips to fall where they may. Either the country and the Republican party were heroic or they were not. He would find out in the next ten days.

The nation turned its attention to Chicago, host of the Republican and Progressive conventions for the second time in four years. Addams, in the thick of things in 1912, would only be a bystander this time as she continued her recuperation at Louise de Koven Bowen's home. There, she tried, as much as she could, to keep her finger on the pulse of the Woman's Peace Party, both nationally and locally. Chicago's 100,000-strong giant preparedness parade, scheduled for the Saturday before the conventions started, troubled her, as did the strong presence of women among the marchers. At its headquarters on Michigan Avenue, the WPP tried to display the same twenty-seven-foot-long antipreparedness banner used in the New York parade, only to have the police yank it down and arrest the two men (one the son of the WPP's secretary) responsible.

That weekend, delegates from every state in the country, every journalist worth his salt, thousands of interested spectators, and the leading lights of the suffrage movement began to converge upon the Windy City. TR's "short, stocky and efficient" secretary John McGrath was already there, as was George Perkins, who had set up headquarters in a Blackstone Hotel suite facing Lake Michigan with a direct long-distance phone line hookup (said to cost a whopping $900 a day) to the "Gun Room" at Sagamore Hill. Everyone wanted to know whether Colonel Roosevelt was planning on making a dramatic appearance at one or both conventions, but for now the answer was no. The press did not seem to believe him. Their typical line of inquiry went this way: "Colonel, what train are you going to Chicago on?" "I am not going to Chicago." "Then, Colonel, what train are you not going to Chicago on?"

The Old Guard Republicans believed they had the TR threat sufficiently squelched at this point. At most, they believed he might be able to rustle up perhaps 200 of the necessary 493 delegates. "If I were a betting man I would lay odds of ten to one that Roosevelt will not get the nomination," Reed Smoot, a conservative senator from Utah, smugly announced. But Perkins believed the odds were far better, provided a number of ifs came to fruition. If Roosevelt could at some point pick up the delegates earmarked for some of the "favorite son" candidates, if the largest states would "rise up and demand" his nomination, if the Old Guard decided that Roosevelt was preferable to Hughes, then TR was still very much in the game. And Perkins had come to Chicago ready to wheel and deal with the Republicans, who understood that TR held the power to defeat whatever candidate they nominated. They were prepared, then, to allow TR considerable say-so in picking someone, provided he backed out of the contest himself. The more radical elements of the Progressives continued to favor a quick Roosevelt nomination and absolutely no negotiation with the Republicans, but were prepared to go along for now.

The Roosevelt supporters had already taken over the town, shouting or singing his name at the top of their lungs with little encouragement. In the Congress Hotel lobby, a persistent "bunch of Roosevelt bullfinches" used an electric xylophone to accompany their evening renditions of a new TR song, "Teddy, You're a Bear" with lyrics by the journalist and short-story writer Ring Lardner. ("You'll make 'em treat us right; You're not too proud to fight . . . We're tired of reading notes; You'll get ten million votes.") A Missouri Progressive epitomized the current stance of the TR devotees. His delegation, he explained, was willing to accept any of five possible Republican nominees: 1) Theodore Roosevelt; 2) Col. Roosevelt; 3) "Teddy"; 4) T.R.; 5) "The Man from Oyster Bay."

In the forty-eight hours before the conventions opened, TR was in constant contact with Perkins. A stenographer also listened in, capturing every word at the request of Roosevelt, who had feared his conversations with Republican and Progressive leaders might be "misquoted." The news so far was both positive and negative. There was some indication that the crucial Pennsylvania delegation might move in his direction, especially since its leader, the reactionary senator Boies Penrose, had decided he preferred Roosevelt, even though TR had labeled him the "representative of all that is worst in our political life" four years before. But TR was prepared to forgive and forget. The nomination was more important than past principles. "Supposing that matters come about so that I am nominated; I want to say to you what I have said to Mr. Perkins," he told Penrose when Perkins put the Pennsylvanian on the line, "that you will be the leader in the Senate at that time" (this conversation would have sickened TR's more militant supporters, had they known). But Penrose and Lodge, who also got on the phone, informed Roosevelt that the Hughes wave was becoming more and more irresistible. That Hughes had privately praised TR's "wonderful fight" and believed he "was entitled to be nominated" was no consolation.

On Wednesday, June 7, the two conventions opened, the Republicans at the Coliseum and the Progressives about a mile away at the Auditorium. Many of the delegates making their way to their destinations in the rain talked not of Roosevelt, but of the death of the man on the famous British recruiting poster, Lord Kitchener, whose ship had struck a mine (his unfortunate demise gave fresh publicity to Hall's recently published *Kitchener's Mob*). "From his own standpoint how could a man die better," Roosevelt mused. Whether the tragic news would help TR by showing the instability of the international situation remained to be seen.

The Republican convention proved to be a bore on day one. Twelve thousand made their way into the Coliseum, their eyes immediately drawn to a large portrait of Abraham Lincoln, painted during the Civil War and making its sixth convention appearance. They then listened to Warren Harding, a conservative Republican senator from Ohio, give the keynote address, which promptly killed any talk of his being a contender for the nomination. Everyone agreed that Harding was a good-looking man (secretly in the midst of a long affair with Carrie Fulton Phillips) and spoke well, but his address was something out of the last century, full of stale

James Norman Hall. By June 1916, Kitchener's
Mob *was already in its third printing.*
(Grinnell College Libraries Special Collections)

patriotic platitudes and clichéd references to the likes of John Paul Jones. "When Mr. Harding got through his speech the crowd got up and yelled for joy and I didn't blame them," Lardner quipped.

Fortunately, there were other distractions. Hundreds of hardy suffragists marched in the driving wind and rain down Michigan Avenue to the Coliseum, where they hoped to strong-arm the Republicans into a plank supporting the Susan B. Anthony amendment. Spectators not scared off by the horrendous weather were rewarded by such colorful sights as a "living flag" of marchers outfitted in red, white, and blue, a baby elephant from the New York Hippodrome dubbed "Suffrage Plank" decked out in the traditional yellow suffrage colors, and a group of Iowa women in squaw costumes mocking the recent vote given to 180 Sioux: "Red men, white men, black men vote—Why are women the silent note?" By the end of the route, the suffragettes' long skirts and shoes were soggy and caked with mud, their umbrellas turned inside out, but their spirits were undaunted.

Addams was with them, although her condition forced her to participate from the safety of an automobile.

The suffrage parade was somewhat overshadowed by the dramatic beginning of the Progressive convention. A few minutes after 1:00 p.m., the keynote speaker, Raymond Robins, mentioned the magic "R" word for the first time, unleashing a frantic burst of pent-up Rooseveltian emotion and energy. "Red bandanna handkerchiefs, the distinguishing mark of the convention four years ago, were pulled from pockets and flapped in the air," a *New York Tribune* reporter recorded. "Flags waved. The band struck up. . . . As if by magic, banners theretofore not visible, but evidently stored somewhere handy in case of emergency, appeared." An excited Perkins climbed on a table and "began gyrating like a cheer leader at a football game." Not until almost two forty-five did the demonstration peter out, a new convention record surpassing Bryan's eight years earlier. Through the modern miracle of long-distance telephony, TR was able to hear the excitement live. Afterward, John McGrath spoke to him on the Perkins phone hookup from the Blackstone, already rumored to be tapped. "They are right up in the air and it is as much as we can do to keep them from nominating you," he warned.

Roosevelt and Perkins still wanted the Progressive delegates held back. The Republicans were far more important right now. Perkins had already made a gesture to Senator William Borah, an Idaho Republican who leaned progressive, offering to surrender the Bull Moosers lock, stock, and barrel to the GOP, provided they nominate TR with a sufficiently liberal platform, but nothing came of it. Growing impatient, William Jackson, a concerned Republican ex-senator from Maryland, decided to take matters into his own hands. At 9:10 that evening, he wired TR explaining that a "complete reunion" between the Progressives and Republicans was absolutely essential, but it would require a "perfect understanding between you and the Republican convention." If Roosevelt came to Chicago, Jackson promised to do his best to get him before the delegates.

He was willing to go, TR telegraphed Jackson, if the convention formally requested his presence (some Republicans had already proclaimed that the only way Roosevelt would ever be allowed on stage would be after he repudiated his Progressive affiliation). In the meantime, TR warned of the "professional German-Americans . . . seeking to terrorize your convention" into choosing someone soft on the Fatherland, presumably Hughes, rumored to be a favorite of the German-American Alliance. The best scenario, Roosevelt concluded, would be for both parties to rally behind a candidate, a man utterly unlike Wilson, and "join for the safety and honor of our country to enforce the policies of genuine Americanism and genuine preparedness."

The reading of this telegram on Thursday afternoon to the Progressive delegates succeeded in keeping the convention controlled for another day. Up to its reading, Perkins and his lieutenants appeared to be fighting a losing battle. Not only did the convention want to nominate TR immediately, but the delegates were also against any kind of proposed outreach to the Republican convention. Why did the Progressives have to "get down on our knees" to the GOP? "The one thing you ought to send to the Republican convention," Victor Murdock boomed, "is the nomination." William J. MacDonald, a former Progressive congressman, was even more defiant. "The Republicans," he warned, "never intend to nominate Roosevelt. . . . The only message that a man with red blood . . . can send to those people—I do not mean the rank and file, but those dominating them—is to go to hell as soon as possible."

But Perkins, who had invested so much in the party, got what he wanted in the end. The Progressive convention passed a resolution to invite the Republicans to a "harmony conference," which was quickly accepted.

Perkins, one of the Progressives appointed to the ten-man joint committee, soon discovered that the Republican willingness to meet meant almost nothing. Several hours of talk at the Chicago Club brought TR no closer to the Republican nomination, nor was there any agreement on a compromise candidate. Charles Bonaparte, who had served in Roosevelt's cabinet and was also present, already sensed that the Republicans, mostly of the Old Guard variety, were not negotiating in good faith. The convention leaders not only did not want Roosevelt, Bonaparte suspected, but preferred another loss to his nomination. But the biggest stumbling block was TR himself. The Republicans had a strong hunch that TR would not run again as a third-party candidate, provided they put up a passable warm body "right" on most of his pet issues.

Roosevelt, following every twist and turn by telephone, refused to commit himself. "I don't want those burglars to get any idea that I will not run on a third ticket," he told William Allen White, "and at the same time I want our people to understand that it is a very very serious thing and that I must have the right to reserve my judgment about doing so." He wanted to see how things played out, although he already understood he would likely be facing a difficult situation in the next few days. "Roosevelt's great embarrassment," Dudley Field Malone reported to Wilson from Chicago, "is he does not see how he can refuse [to] accept Progressive nomination without being called a traitor."

Friday, June 9. The conventions began their third day. The rain, which had let up briefly on Thursday, showed signs of finally stopping for good. Local businesses were now charging double the normal price for a humble ham sandwich. The morning newspapers were stuffed with the latest convention developments, although the *Tribune* ran an ad from the American Union against Militarism signed by Addams and others. The *Tribune* also included an interview with Helen Keller, who was in town to speak on behalf of suffrage and other causes. Who was Miss Keller's ideal man? Colonel Roosevelt? "T.R is not patient, not statesmanlike," she quickly responded. "I should never marry a man like T.R."

The considerable number of female Progressive delegates would not have agreed. They, along with their male counterparts, adored TR and were ready to nominate him that day, especially when they learned the harmony conference had failed. By the evening, the entire Auditorium seemed to be singing in unison: "Why Not, Why Not Nominate Now?" to the tune of the familiar hymn "Why Not Come to Jesus?" But this was neither Perkins's nor Roosevelt's wish. Both men continued to hope that events at the Coliseum would turn their way.

Perkins remained optimistic. The uneventful Republican convention suddenly came to life when Senator Albert Fall of New Mexico (later imprisoned as part of the Teapot Dome scandal) nominated TR. Most of the delegates, likely on order from the Republican bigwigs, barely reacted. But the galleries were a far different story. A local woman named Katherine Davis, who had jump-started a TR demonstration four years earlier, got things started, wildly waving flags and bunting until the cops made her calm down. Another Chicagoan, Kate Rutherford, was just as enthusiastic, tossing her hat into the crowd of delegates and then swinging two fistfuls of flags to the band music, ignoring the cries of "Sit down, Grandma!" But the proudest woman of all during the forty-minute demonstration was TR's daughter Alice Longworth, who got the crowd to sing "America (My Country 'Tis of Thee)."

At eight that evening, an excited Perkins was on the phone reporting the good news. "I really feel hopeful tonight for the first time," he told Roosevelt. At that moment, the Republicans were in the midst of their first ballot. Hughes, as expected, was doing well, leading with 253½ votes. A few days earlier, Perkins believed TR would get at least 81 or 82 and build his strength on subsequent ballots. Instead, only 65 delegates supported him.

It would now take a miracle to get the Republican nomination. Gifford Pinchot, who had worked closely with Roosevelt in conservation efforts and in the formation of the Bull Moose Party, got on the phone with his old friend and presented the situation in stark terms. The Republicans were confident TR would not run unless they nominated someone as distasteful to him, as say, Taft. "We have been playing poker with them substantially without chips," Pinchot explained. But if Roosevelt would intimate that he was planning to run anyway, "it would very much strengthen our case."

TR again rejected this idea, even when Pinchot warned that the Progressive party would collapse if he did not run. "There is a very wide difference between making a young colonel and a retired major general lead a forlorn hope," he responded. "I have simply got to reserve judgment."

By ten o'clock, the Republicans had completed their second ballot. After picking up 16 delegates, TR was at 81 votes. The hope that dozens of delegates no longer committed to various favorite sons or primary winners like Henry Ford might leap on the Roosevelt bandwagon had failed to materialize. At the Congress Hotel, one wag thought he would have some fun with the TR fanatics nervously waiting for news. He announced that his secretary had just told him that the Republicans had nominated Roosevelt. Ten minutes of wild celebration followed until the same man stood up and claimed he had a second bulletin to read. "It's all a mistake." The would-be comedian soon found himself trying to dodge the flying fists of an angry crowd.

Hughes, meanwhile, had jumped to 328½, a disturbing trend to the conservative Old Guard, who managed to temporarily halt his momentum by preventing a third ballot that evening. But they realized that unless something drastic happened in the next twelve or so hours, they would be facing the unpleasant reality of a Hughes nomination. Meanwhile, the news of his likely opponent reached Wilson, who heard preliminary convention reports issued from the stage while attending a vaudeville show at Keith's. Tumulty briefed the President more fully when he returned to the White House and then issued a statement denying that Hughes had already stepped down from the Supreme Court.

At that moment, a second Progressive/Republican harmony conference was under way at the Chicago Club. None of the Republicans, it was obvious, was going to budge. To Nicholas Murray Butler, one of the five Republicans on the committee, the main issue at the moment was not Roosevelt but stopping Hughes. After the meeting broke up in the wee hours of Saturday morning, June 10, Butler went to the Blackstone at Perkins's request to talk to TR long distance. Roosevelt was no fan of Butler, the president of Columbia, a Root supporter, and a mainstream pacifist before the war. Butler, he believed, was "about the cheapest fake there is," but Perkins convinced TR the conversation might have value, "all along the line of trading out before morning."

Butler got straight to the point. The nomination of Hughes would be a "desperate calamity. . . . I regard it as impossible to elect him. . . . I regard it as assuring four more years of this awful Wilson." But Hughes could be blocked if Roosevelt would put his stamp of approval on a compromise candidate, one whom the Progressives would also support. He tossed out three names: Root, TR's vice president Charles Fairbanks, and Philander Knox, who had sat in both Roosevelt's and Taft's cabinets. Root and Fairbanks were obviously too conservative for the Progressives, and TR believed Knox had mishandled Mexico while secretary of state.

It was Roosevelt's turn. How about General Wood, the apostle of preparedness? Butler thought the Midwest and Southwest would not stand for a military candidate. William Borah? No, the senator had "personal habits that are objectionable" (the notorious womanizer Borah had a long affair with TR's daughter Alice and even fathered her only child nine years later).

"Apparently only Wilson can get away with anything of that sort," TR snorted.

Roosevelt had also proposed his friend Henry Cabot Lodge. Butler was not especially enthusiastic but TR had come to believe he might be the best compromise. Lodge had voted for TR on the second ballot and was thoroughly "right" on foreign policy and preparedness, even if he was not a reformer of any kind (a few days earlier, he had opposed a woman's suffrage plank). "I know Lodge's record like a book," Roosevelt told Perkins afterward, although he conceded that "he does not have as advanced views as you and I." That TR did not seem to believe this would rule Lodge out showed that he was out of touch with many who had followed him in 1912. "Next to Penrose there is nobody in the country more distasteful, to the real Progressive, than Lodge," David Starr Jordan later observed. Still, that morning Roosevelt worked on a telegram recommending Lodge, whom he wanted both conventions to consider when they resumed in a few hours.

At the Auditorium, the Progressive delegates were ready to go at 10:40 a.m. They were in an ornery mood, especially when they learned the final conference with the Republicans had failed. Three days of delays and negotiations, they sensed, had been pointless. Their mood did not improve when TR's proposal to unite the parties behind Lodge was read. Anguished shouts of "No, no!" soon filled the vast hall. Perkins, whose orchestrations had controlled the convention all week, wanted them to wait to see how the Republican convention would respond to the Lodge idea. He soon discovered that no one at the Coliseum, except the Massachusetts delegation, appeared to be especially excited about a Lodge candidacy.

It was now past noon. The Progressive convention learned the Republicans were in the midst of a third ballot with Hughes far in the lead. Perkins could no longer stop the determined group of men and women who had been waiting to nominate since Wednesday. "There comes a time in the life of every man when he is up against the gun," California Governor Hiram Johnson told the gathering. "You are up against the gun now. . . . There is just one way out. Put it up to the man who never yet has shirked responsibility." Moments later, the delegates nominated TR "by acclamation" at virtually the same time the Republicans chose Hughes. The Bull Moose convention then adjourned until three, when they would complete the ticket and finish up other business.

Perkins went back to the Blackstone for a discussion with TR, who had much to decide. If he accepted the nomination, his adversary would almost certainly be reelected, probably by a bigger margin than in 1912. On the other hand, if he refused, the Progressive party would be unalterably destroyed. But Roosevelt's own political future also had to be considered. If he returned to the Republican fold this year, the GOP might come calling in 1920 if they lost again in November. The prodigal son would only turn sixty-two that year, not too old to rule out another presidential run.

When the delegates reconvened, they were informed that a message from TR would be read in the next two hours. "I hope to God it will read, 'I am your candidate now without qualification,'" Victor Murdock announced. In the meantime, they sat through the selection of a running mate (TR's friend John Parker of Louisiana, a former Democrat) and Murdock's bitter complaints that the Progressives had nearly lost their souls that week by meeting with the Republicans. He gestured to Bryan, present as a reporter, suggesting that the Great Commoner had "at least stood by his convictions." Whether TR would do the same remained uncertain, but the faithful were confident. One of Bryan's friends was not. "Roosevelt is going to refuse this nomination in a few minutes," the friend told Bryan. "He hasn't the courage to run. Why don't you lead this crowd, you would get 5,000,000 votes."

Shortly before five, Raymond Robins announced that he would be reading the wire from TR. The crowd waited expectantly. Roosevelt, Robins reported, was "grateful for the honor," but "cannot accept it at this time." He wanted to know the views of Hughes "toward the vital questions of the day." If they needed a response immediately, he was refusing, "but if you prefer it, I suggest that my conditional refusal to run be placed in the hands of the Progressive National Committee." The National Committee could then determine if Hughes was an acceptable candidate. If so, then TR's rejection would be a moot point. If not, then further consultations with Roosevelt about what path to pursue "to meet the needs of the country" would follow.

A few minutes later, the convention was over. The stunned delegates, described by a reporter as "cheerless, depressed, bewildered," filed out of the Auditorium, trying to process what had just occurred. It was not long before reality sunk in. Unless TR had a change of heart, the man they had blindly followed and idolized for four years had abandoned them in a cold, almost impersonal manner in what one observer called the "least creditable document he ever wrote."

"It was a sad scene," Bainbridge Colby, one of TR's trusted Bull Moose lieutenants, recalled fourteen years later. "The personal following Col. Roosevelt had gathered about him in the course of the Progressive movement was one of the finest imaginable, and it snapped in an instant." "Big bronzed men were openly weeping," John Reed reported.

Others, while disillusioned, were willing to wait to see what TR would have to say in the days ahead. At a bare minimum, Roosevelt would have to do or say something to keep them on his side. "If ever there was a time when they needed guidance it is now," the industrialist and inventor Thomas Robins wrote TR the next day. "The Progressive Movement is to them a religion. Their faith is shaken. You alone can preserve it."

Chapter 14

SUMMER OF ANXIETY

JUNE 11–SEPTEMBER 30, 1916

The situation is a very puzzling one. Which ever
course I take is very unsatisfactory.

—Theodore Roosevelt, June 1916

It was a heartbreaking street scene all too common in New York that summer. One July day, an ambulance appeared in a predominantly Polish neighborhood in Brooklyn with a grim task: the removal to the hospital of a baby afflicted with "infantile paralysis," or polio. The driver and the physician who accompanied him to 159 Twenty-seventh Street were not surprised by what they encountered: a frantic, hysterical mother unwilling to let go of her offspring until her husband finally intervened. But the sight of his child carried away and his wife's screams were too much for him. The father yanked the baby out of their hands and fled back into his home while neighbors and friends congregated menacingly. The ambulance driver sensibly went on to complete the rest of his rounds, not before picking up two policemen, who proved to be more than necessary at their remaining stops. "In the Italian district, where we found four cases, we were denounced as 'Black Hands,' come to steal babies and hold them for ransom or murder them," the driver told a reporter.

With seven babies now in tow, the ambulance motored back to Twenty-seventh Street for a second try. "One of the policemen held the father downstairs," the driver reported, "while the other slipped up behind the mother and snatched the baby. She pursued him, sobbing and shrieking, and neighbors began pouring into the street from every tenement, some of them carrying bricks and clubs. I started the car at full speed. We left the policeman still trying to quiet the baby's father and mother and drive back the crowd."

The first cases had appeared in New York City in early June, normally the beginning of the dreaded "polio season." The city had not experienced a serious outbreak in nine years, and only thirteen New York residents had died of the disease in 1915. But local health officials soon recognized they were dealing with an epidemic. By early July, more than a thousand were afflicted, 238 were dead, and panic had begun to set in.

The problem was that polio research was in its infancy, although important breakthroughs in recent years raised hopes that a vaccine of some kind might be feasible in the future. For now, most specialists were certain of only a few things—namely, that infantile paralysis was a communicable disease of some kind, predominantly struck the young, and tended to peter out in the cooler months. But its cause remained very much a mystery. Was it "dust and dry weather," as some had speculated? the "stable fly"? rats? mysterious "magnetic currents" of some sort? vaccines? Aware of the epidemic's beginnings in the immigrant neighborhoods, some believed poor sanitation had to be the answer, only to be baffled by cases among the tony Fifth Avenue set. The public was especially shocked to learn of the frighteningly rapid death of Walter Hines Page's twenty-five-year-old daughter-in-law Katherine in "surroundings . . . considered ideal" in Garden City, Long Island. On Tuesday and Wednesday, she experienced coldlike symptoms and a fever. Over the next two days, paralysis of her neck and respiratory muscles set in. By Saturday, she was gone.

In less extreme cases, the medical establishment experimented with a variety of treatments. Adrenaline injections and electric currents were tried, as were serum injections of blood from exposed and unexposed individuals, which seemed to offer some promise. But some preferred to take their chances with various patent medicines and folk cures. One charlatan made a brisk living hawking one-dollar bottles (the equivalent of twenty-five dollars today) of a "guaranteed cure" containing "alcohol, turpentine, red pepper, sassafras and water," before authorities caught up with him.

Others were victimized by a would-be health inspector who gained entrance by claiming he needed to "spray rooms with a disinfectant." Before leaving, the scam artist noticed that he had somehow forgotten his wallet. Could the man or woman of the house lend him fifty cents? The grateful citizen was usually willing, especially since the nice man offered to leave behind a deposit of his "heavy gold ring," a ring that turned out to be worth all of a nickel.

Regardless of what treatment was prescribed, most survived. What was especially feared was the very real possibility of permanent paralysis. If the last epidemic, in Buffalo in 1913, was any indicator, at least 40 percent of those who contracted the disease would suffer some form of paralysis for life. Anxious parents did their part by keeping their children away from Sunday schools, churches, July 4 celebrations, and public gatherings in general (the city had already ordered movie theaters to bar children). And thousands were shipped out of the city to the country or towns in Connecticut, Pennsylvania, and New Jersey, many of which began to quarantine any young New York visitors potentially exposed to the disease. By the end of August, twelve thousand cases in thirty-eight states had been reported, the worst polio epidemic America had ever experienced.

Like other communities, Oyster Bay took the standard measures to keep the epidemic under control. At the train station and on the roads into town, local authorities turned away children from New York City, at least when they could catch them. Roosevelt, meanwhile, took the lead in spearheading aggressive sanitation efforts. "The hygienic conditions of this town are something scandalous," he announced. "The American people never learn by experience until they are hit by disaster. The same principle of the sanitary unpreparedness of this town applies to the unpreparedness of the nation." But the community was not spared. Not far from Sagamore Hill, four children from the same family were stricken and their estate soon placed under quarantine. As a growing number of cases began to appear in early August, the mere *suspicion* of polio in the home could result in a six-week quarantine. TR became concerned enough that he questioned whether his daughter Ethel should keep away from Oyster Bay for now since "it has killed one girl of her age here" already. A few days earlier, one of his correspondents, W. D. Elger, sent him a surefire polio cure, "AMYL-KIJO," and a list of its not-so-special ingredients. "You will, doubtless, receive little encouragement from the medical profession," Elger admitted, "but, if you get to work with your usual energy and have eight or ten barrels . . . made, and also secure thirty or forty atomizers . . . you will clean up Oyster Bay in very short order."

The situation in Washington was less dire, although eighteen cases were recorded in the district by late August, three times as many as the prior year, enough that Franklin Roosevelt requested his wife, Eleanor, to delay their children's return from their New Brunswick summer home, Campobello. For Wilson, his greatest concern was his year-old grandchild Ellen McAdoo. In August, her mother, Nell, fled the capital for the safety of the Jersey Shore, only to be stricken there by another dangerous 1916 illness: typhoid fever. To the relief of Wilson, Nell recovered and baby Ellen escaped polio, but the worried family continued to take precautions for weeks. "We haven't even seen Ellen for fear of carrying Paralysis germs to her," Margaret Wilson told her sister Jessie in early September.

News of the "New York plague" eventually reached London, which had a handful of cases to contend with that summer. Still, the British Isles had never faced a serious polio outbreak on the scale seen in the United States. At the moment, every English family was far more concerned about the Allied offensive on the Somme launched on July 1, a battle they hoped would end the war. The casualties were staggering: twenty thousand British soldiers were killed on the first day, the deadliest in British military history. The American poet Alan Seeger went to his death in the first week of battle, as did a young Philadelphian named Dillwyn Starr two months later. Three days before he was killed, Starr tried to reassure his family back home. "No news is good news, and you will find out from the War Office immediately [if] anything happens to me, which I don't anticipate," he wrote. "They hope here that we shall break through the German lines, but I have my doubts. There is a chance, however, and if we do it, it will make all the difference in the world."

How much "difference" remained uncertain. The hostilities, now on ten different fronts, appeared to be growing uglier and more brutal by the day. "This war has already cost the lives of some 3,000,000 men and filled the old world with widows, orphans and cripples," William Jennings Bryan lamented. More frightening, a belief had begun to emerge that the "war to end all wars" was just the prelude to a far greater apocalyptic struggle in the future. Harvard President E. Lawrence Lowell warned that the "next war, thirty or forty years hence," would be "more destructive than the present one and probably will involve the whole world." The English novelist H. Rider Haggard told an American journalist in July that Germany and England were destined to fight again. "Have you seen anything in the German temper to indicate that they will take this defeat—and defeat is certainly before them—as final?"

The war—especially the combat and emotional connections to comrades in arms—continued to tug at James Norman Hall, who sailed for Europe in July. He was determined to get back to the front in some capacity, even if most of his original battalion had been killed or wounded. Hall was especially devastated to learn of the death of one of his closest companions. "The loss of one of my own brothers could not have affected me more," he wrote.

Ellery Sedgwick, the editor of *The Atlantic Monthly*, was interested in having Hall write some more first-person accounts on the war, especially since *Kitchener's Mob* had sold so well. For Hall, his goal was to "accompany various battalions when they went up to the firing line" and "be a spokesman for the men" in the trenches, but the Allied military authorities were predictably slow in granting him permission. Realizing that it might be months before they made up their minds, Hall began digging into a more promising topic while in Paris: the American pilots fighting for France in the Lafayette Escadrille. Writing began to take a backseat as he became increasingly fascinated with the men, the "peculiar cast of mind that flying gives them" and the dangerous lives they led. Once again, the thirst for thrills that had prompted him to enlist two years earlier proved impossible to resist. By the early fall, he had joined the Escadrille. "I'm as happy as a lark," he wrote his Boston friend Roy Cushman, "for this next experience will be more exciting, more adventurous than any I have had thus far." It would also be difficult and dangerous: months of training with the possibility that he would not make the cut.

Roosevelt would have gladly traded places with Hall. Almost immediately after the conventions ended, he was contending with fourteen reporters sitting in his library at Sagamore Hill, waiting to hear what he would do next. He had nothing to say, TR told them, beyond what he had already wired the Progressive convention. No pictures or filming that day would be permitted; in fact, he announced he did not want journalists hanging around in the future since he was now "out of politics."

His sister Corinne soon made a pilgrimage to comfort him. "Theodore— the people wanted you," she insisted. "It seems terrible to me that they could not have you."

"Do not say that," he replied. "If they had wanted me hard enough, they could have had me."

Corinne could tell that her brother, despite his denials, was deeply depressed by what had occurred. As much as TR had told everyone that he had no chance of winning, he and Perkins had hoped up to the last minute that a double nomination was possible. And with the Progressives and Republicans behind him, he believed that he could have taken Wilson in November. He was everything that Wilson was not, and he was sure that enough Americans saw things his way. Now he would be forced to watch Hughes or Wilson tackle the issues so crucial to the nation's future. "I would have done my best work in connection with the European war, the Mexican situation, and the Japanese and Chinese situation; and also in connection with universal military service," Roosevelt wrote a friend. "I would, moreover, have fought for the industrial regeneration of this country along the lines of the 1912 platform."

He could not help wondering what his next step would be, especially when his health problems flared again in the week following the convention. While on his way with his wife, Edith, to welcome Kermit and his family home at a Hudson River pier, he began coughing violently, the same cough that had plagued him for months. At one point, he experienced a sharp pain, so bad that he had trouble walking up the gangplank, and onlookers noticed "his face would flush and then get pale." His worried daughter Ethel called a physician, who promptly had X-rays taken, while rumors soon spread that TR had dropped dead from a heart ailment. The eventual diagnosis was a torn tendon from the coughing episode.

At his request, the press minimized the incident as much as possible. "I don't want any 'Roosevelt Critically Ill' headlines that will scare my friends to death" he told them. His condition, he explained, reminded him of a cartoon he had once seen showing a reluctant man about to mount a horse that appeared anything but docile. "Is he quiet?" the man asked the groom. "He is perfectly quiet," he replied, "if you don't cough, or sneeze or touch your hat." "That is the way with me," TR explained sadly, "it pains if I cough, or sneeze, or touch my hat."

That same day in Washington, another massive preparedness parade was under way, one that would also celebrate Flag Day, recently officially designated as such by Wilson, who would lead the marchers. The President, flag in hand, was smartly dressed in what a reporter described as "white duck trousers, a double breasted blue sack coat" with a "boutonniere of red, white and blue carnations." One onlooker noticed that Wilson "walked with a jaunty swing, that kept a large pompous gentleman on his left pumping the whole distance."

As the President approached the Treasury Building on Pennsylvania Avenue, he could not escape the sight of a large banner at Lafayette Square, courtesy of the always pesky Congressional Union suffragists, with the message "Be Prepared—If You Care about Ninety-one Electoral votes, Consider Us." Eventually, he joined the First Lady and others at the reviewing stand to watch the thousands of enthusiastic flag-bearing marchers pass by. Many were government workers given the day off, including a good-sized Navy Department contingent led by FDR in the absence of his boss Josephus Daniels. There were also patriotic floats galore to enjoy: Pocahontas, the thirteen original colonies represented by "thirteen pretty girls in white robes," and even a "Historical American Women" showcase. The most vivid and appropriate for the day's festivities was the "Wake Up" float, depicting a slumbering Uncle Sam with an angel above him imploring him to awaken to the horrors of war, graphically displayed by the "ruins of a home in Belgium."

After the parade, Wilson made a speech that once again sounded positively Rooseveltian. The word "hyphen" was not used, but he alluded to a

Wilson marching in the Washington preparedness parade, June 14, 1916.
(Library of Congress: LC-H261-7504)

certain small subset of individuals in America more loyal to their European roots than their adopted home. Such "disloyalty . . . must be absolutely crushed," the President warned. "There are those at this moment who are trying to levy a species of political blackmail, saying, 'Do what we wish in the interest of foreign sentiment or we will wreak our vengeance at the polls.'" House, among others, viewed the statement as a first slap at Hughes and his rumored German-American Alliance supporters.

"No matter what Hughes may say or do," Colonel House wrote Wilson the next day, "it will be firmly fixed in the minds of the voters that a vote for Hughes will be a vote for the Kaiser. Say what he will, do what he will, he cannot get from under that."

The strategy of the Wilson reelection campaign was already becoming clear that week at the Democratic convention, held at the Coliseum in St. Louis. The keynote address, by Martin Glynn, the diminutive former New York governor, set the stage. Glynn, whose lifelong crippling back pain led to suicide eight years later, dramatically illustrated that Wilson's preference for negotiation before war was the American way. As the crowd listened in the sweltering heat of the arena, Glynn cited multiple past administrations—those of Grant, Harrison, Lincoln, Pierce, Van Buren, Jefferson, Adams, even Washington—that had faced dangerous provocations from foreign powers. Each example concluded with a simple phrase:

"But we didn't go to war," the delegates and galleries then raucously shouting, "What did he do?" (although one wag shouted "What would Teddy do?"). The president at the time, Glynn explained, "settled our troubles by negotiation, just as the President . . . is trying to do today."

Roosevelt predictably found the proceedings horrifying ("one of the most degrading spectacles we have ever seen," he complained to his sister). "The convention," TR later wrote, "went frantic with delight whenever one of its 'keynote speakers' uttered sentiments praising the peace of cowardice, the peace obtained by refusing to help the weak to whom we were pledged, and by refusing to protect our own women and children who were murdered on the high seas or in Mexico."

The rest of the Democratic convention was anticlimactic. Wilson was nominated the next day with Thomas Marshall again on the ticket. Bryan's presence in St. Louis had left some Wilson loyalists uncomfortable, but the Great Commoner had already accepted that Wilson would be the nominee, regardless of the one-term plank in the 1912 platform. Wilson now controlled the party, and there was little Bryan could do about it. What Wilson wanted Wilson got. He demanded and got a vigorous Americanism plank in the platform, along the lines of his recent Flag Day address.

A new peace organization, the American Neutral Conference Committee, had sent Lella Secor to St. Louis hoping to get the Democrats to consider an official neutral conference plank. Addams, who was on the advisory board of the ANCC, gave Secor a letter of introduction to Bryan, who met with her, as did Secretary of War Newton Baker and Senator William Stone. But the party bigwigs were not at all interested. To Secor, the convention proved a bit underwhelming. "It was so frightfully cut and dried," she complained. "There was evidence everywhere that a group of political dressmakers had cut and basted the pattern."

Afterward, she headed to Chicago to meet with Addams for the first time. Addams knew all about Secor and her friend Rebecca Shelly and their ongoing attempts to shake up the pacifist world like their hero Rosika Schwimmer. The two firebrands had recently been brainstorming a "tremendous international young people's movement" for peace but finally decided the much discussed official neutral conference idea remained the only feasible solution. That two young women under thirty were the driving force behind the ANCC surprised the feminist author Charlotte Perkins Gilman. "It seems funny to see you kittens running things," she told Secor.

Secor was eager to speak with Addams about the convention and ANCC developments. Unlike some of the "peace hacks" Secor and Shelly despised, Addams was more open to nontraditional approaches. And she especially liked their enthusiasm. Shelly, she believed, was "perhaps more devoted than wise, but devoted she certainly is and sometimes her wild plans come out extremely well." To Addams, "all effort is to the good." The official neutral conference idea, a now two-year-old idea, might be a long shot but it deserved her support.

Secor enjoyed her talk with Addams. "She is so sweet and simple," Secor wrote a friend, "in fact one might easily expect her to be an every day sort of mother to an every day sort of family." Still, Secor remained frustrated with the general direction of the movement. "Rebecca and I," she wrote her mother a few weeks later, "stand for radical action, and we have to fight the old pacifists every step of the way."

A ddams was still not well enough to fully dedicate herself to the movement, a movement TR increasingly believed "should close now." Like other pacifists, she continued to have misgivings about Wilson, especially his recent prancing at the head of a preparedness parade. For now her main goal was to get well enough to move off the sidelines and into the thick of things once again. "They told me in the beginning that eight months was the shortest possible period and that it might take three years for a complete recovery," she told a friend. "In my great desire to take the shorter route I have tried to do everything they told me and I gleefully count off six months." But she was disappointed she had been unable to attend her niece Marcet's recent wedding. The two newlyweds did stop to see her in Chicago, where Marcet was surprised to see wine served, none of which Addams consumed. Her aunt, Marcet later recalled, was "consistent both in her tolerance and in her own complete abstinence."

Shortly after her meeting with Secor, Addams left for Bar Harbor, Maine, where she would stay at Louise de Koven Bowen's summer home.

Fortunately, the polio plague had not struck this playground of the wealthy. The sea air seemed to agree with Addams, so much so that within a few weeks, she was well enough to move back into the nearby cottage she and Mary owned. There she worked on a new book, *The Long Road of Woman's Memory*. Like TR, she was not a fast writer. "She had a compulsion to find exactly the right word and she needed to write, rewrite and write again," Marcet recalled. In a world without computers, one of her preferred strategies consisted of "cutting paragraphs or sentences out of one page of her manuscript and pinning them as inserts in their shifted sequence on another page."

Only one of the manuscript's six chapters involved the war. In "Women's Memories—Challenging War," she wrote of conversations she had in Europe with mothers on both sides who had sent their sons into combat and an early death. "The suffering mothers of the disinherited," she wrote, "feel the stirring of the old impulse to protect and cherish their unfortunate children, and women's haunting memories instinctively challenge war as the implacable enemy of their age-long undertaking."

But the general public appeared to be more interested in reading the chapters on the "Devil Baby," an "old wives' tale" that proved to have staying power in the early twentieth century, especially among elderly immigrant women, who showed up at Hull-House demanding to see the mysterious creature. Not surprisingly, Sedgwick at *The Atlantic Monthly* was happy to publish material from the noncontroversial Devil Baby chapters. "This is the Miss Addams in whom we all believe—militarists, pacifists, progressives, and the rest of us," he wrote her. "It is the Miss Addams about whom no two Americans have a right to think differently."

Such occasions of universal public acceptance were now rare. She was no longer an American saint, at least to the sizable and vocal portion of the population who did not care for her peace and antipreparedness activities. She had also continued to antagonize some of the wealthy benefactors of Hull-House, some of whom were already unhappy with her past political involvement and support of union causes. But if some of the masses had turned against her, she understood that her efforts had legitimized causes ignored by the mainstream media. "Your peace mission to Europe made it possible for us to publish a whole lot of radical propaganda (which very

much needed publishing) for which we would otherwise have had no excuse," *The Boston Globe*'s Lucien Price told her. "You have no idea of the
respect and affection which you are held by the radical young men of this
country." Louis Lochner, still plugging away in Stockholm with Ford's unofficial neutral conference, felt the same. "You have been the greatest influence for good that ever came into my life," he wrote her that summer,
"and I want to assure you that, though you are not with me, I keep asking
myself, what would Miss Addams advise me to do were she here."

Addams faced an important decision of her own that summer: which
party to support in the fall. She was, at least in theory, still a member
of what remained of the Progressive party, although her involvement had
been minimal for two years. She knew she could not vote for TR, if he
ultimately decided to run again, but she still believed in the party's noble
ideals. Her friend Louise de Koven Bowen had already decided what to do:
she would support the Republican ticket, as she believed "all good Progressives" should do.

In the days after the convention, the Progressives were in limbo, waiting
to see what course TR would follow. Some still hoped that there was a
chance, admittedly an extremely slim one, that he would accept the nomination if he found Hughes lacking in some way. After all, why would
Roosevelt want to get behind a man he had long scorned as a second Wilson,
nominated by a convention he considered to be "composed of as sordid and
cheap politicians as we have ever seen"? And how could he possibly abandon an organization whose visionary program made both parties stand up
and take notice? Its very existence, some argued, had forced the Republicans to nominate someone with a reform record like Hughes, something
inconceivable a few years earlier. "The people of America need this party,"
Ida Tarbell insisted during the convention. "I am not for Roosevelt. But I
am for this party."

On the other hand, there was no shortage of letters and wires pouring
into Sagamore Hill imploring him not to run. A third-party campaign
would only benefit "Wilson and his party of unlettered swine," TR's friend
Owen Wister warned. The elderly Boston philanthropist and Civil War

veteran Henry Lee Higginson even invoked Roosevelt's beloved father, whom he "knew well," and "his great public spirit without asking anything in return." Higginson and others alluded to TR's political future. If he did the right thing by the Republicans this year and Hughes lost, his chances in 1920 looked very good. Roosevelt was not so sure. In four years, he noted, "no human being can tell what the issues will be. I am already an old man, and the chances are very small that I will ever again grow into touch with the people of this country to the degree that will make me useful as a leader."

His friend John Callan O'Laughlin laid out the situation for him. He "could not possibly win" if he ran again and he would attract less support than in 1912. "You would be accused of inconsistency, of self-seeking ambition, and you would find that your influence would be seriously impaired," the journalist warned. But supporting Hughes was a win-win situation. If Hughes was elected, then TR would be in a "position of authority" in the new government. If Hughes lost, which O'Laughlin thought quite possible, TR would be the go-to candidate in 1920. Of course, this meant Roosevelt would have to reject his faithful followers and "kill your own child," the Progressive party.

The multitude of phone calls, wires, letters, and conversations did not particularly sway TR one way or another. He had decided early on that he would not make another hopeless third-party run and that Hughes had to be supported enthusiastically to ensure the defeat of the "worst President we have ever had." If that meant abandoning his supporters, so be it. Another viable option—staying out of the election entirely and encouraging the Progressive party to continue to function—did not appeal to Roosevelt, especially when the organization was a shell of what it had once been. "The trouble with the Progressive Party now," he believed, "is that it is suffering the fate of all noble movements when the cup has been drained and only the dregs are left."

His formal announcement came in the form of a June 22 letter to the Progressive National Committee. The party had done wonderful work by advancing the causes of the progressive movement itself, he wrote, and he predicted that their causes would someday "be embodied in the structure of our national existence." But since the country had shown it would not accept a third party and the Republicans had nominated someone who was not a reactionary, the best course was to "strongly support Mr. Hughes," as he planned to do, and not run a candidate. After much discussion, the party leaders then voted to accept both of TR's recommendations (a few disgruntled Progressives later put up John Parker to run for vice president). The Bull Moose movement was over.

But shock, anger, and resentment from some of the more left-leaning Progressives would linger for weeks if not years. They believed TR had frankly betrayed and used them and that he should have been honest about his unwillingness to accept anything but a combined Progressive-Republican nomination. Roosevelt refused to concede the point. Hadn't his Trinidad statement and others made it clear that he would not run as a Progressive if a candidate acceptable to both organizations could be found? As for the "unspeakably foolish" charge of abandonment, TR reminded his detractors how many Progressives had scurried back to the Republicans after the dismal showing in the 1914 midterm election. "It was not I who deserted the Progressive Party, it was the Progressive Party who deserted me," he insisted.

His explanation did not sit well with J. A. H. Hopkins, the head of the New Jersey Progressive organization, who had desperately tried in person and by letter to change TR's mind in the days following the convention. Roosevelt and Perkins, Hopkins believed, had not been honest. Back in April, Hopkins had even written Perkins suggesting that "if there is the remotest doubt as to Roosevelt accepting our nomination . . . let him say so now." The silence then was deafening. And Hopkins was appalled by TR's claim of "desertion" by party members. "I cannot believe that you really mean to say that because every man did not stick to the Party this justifies in the slightest degree the betrayal of the men who went to the Chicago Convention," he told him. Worst of all, he could not understand why Roosevelt, who had told him in person that Hughes was "a little, and perhaps some, better" than Wilson, was now enthusiastically behind the Republican nominee.

TR as usual was incapable of admitting he might have done something wrong or that his overwhelming hatred of Wilson had more than a slight impact on his decision. He believed that most Progressives agreed with him.

As for Hopkins, he threw his lot in with Wilson a few weeks later. Whether other Bull Moosers would follow remained to be seen.

The Republicans were hopeful that most of the Progressives would fall in line behind their erstwhile leader. Hughes immediately reached out to Roosevelt once he learned the outcome of the Progressive National Committee meeting, inviting him to have dinner with him at his eighth-floor suite at the Hotel Astor in Times Square. TR, of course, accepted, although he could not help feeling ambivalent about dining with the man he had privately labeled a "skunk" a few weeks earlier.

Their first meeting in six years went surprisingly well. "Colonel Roosevelt, welcome!" Hughes greeted him warmly. For the next two and a half hours, the two men chatted while enjoying a variety of delicacies, including squab chicken, brook trout sauté, potatoes doria, and cold asparagus. For a change, TR did more listening than speaking. His main contribution to the conversation was advice to the candidate that he would need to "make an aggressive fight of it. . . . He must hit and hit hard."

Roosevelt, now fully satisfied that Hughes was the right man for the job, agreed to make a few speeches for the candidate once the campaign got under way. It was essential, TR believed, that anything he did for Hughes should not "make me look as if I was trying to keep the center of the stage." But whether Hughes could win even with Roosevelt's support was debatable. The President, the Hearst columnist Arthur Brisbane observed, had an almost irrefutable argument: "I HAVE KEPT YOU AT PEACE AND HAVE FILLED YOUR POCKETS—WHAT MORE DO YOU WANT?"

Hughes did have some weapons if he chose to use them. Wilson's German policy was especially vulnerable; the difficulty would be convincing the people that a Republican would have done things better or differently under the circumstances. Better yet, Hughes needed to somehow find a way to show the people that the President's moves had actually been more likely to *provoke* war, rather than *prevent* it, and had kept the country teetering on the abyss for almost two years.

The Hughes campaign had already decided on one obvious target, Mexico, or what TR called "our Balkan Peninsula." The Punitive Expedition had not only failed to turn up Villa, but the Carranza government was growing more and more annoyed at the intimidating presence of American troops making their way deeper and deeper into Mexico. Tensions finally exploded on June 21 at Carrizal, where the two sides engaged in a small battle with disturbing if not humiliating implications for the administration. At least twenty American soldiers were killed or wounded and another twenty-three were taken prisoner by the Carranza forces. Wilson, who had already called out the National Guard to the border, was now facing exactly what he had long dreaded: a war in Mexico certain to siphon away men and resources needed for any potential involvement in Europe. House, as usual, was trying to steel him for what lay ahead. "It looks now as if it [war] were inevitable," the Colonel told the President. "If it comes to that, I hope you will prosecute it with all the vigor and power we possess."

A full-scale war, Wilson believed, would be a nightmare, a quagmire from which America might not extricate herself for years. His immediate predecessor agreed. "I do not want war," Taft announced. "If it does come, an army of at least 250,000 will be required, and we will have to seize and occupy every town and port in the entire country, then send forces out scouring the mountains for bandits." Still, Wilson began preparing a message to Congress to authorize military intervention in Mexico.

Roosevelt, who had long violently disapproved of Wilson's Mexican policy, perceived at least one possible benefit from the administration's current predicament: the chance to indulge in his long cherished fantasy of raising a division of volunteers, the Rough Riders redux. A military adventure would also provide a much needed distraction and escape from his recent political setbacks. He had been secretly working on the plan for months, even inquiring about horses from the New York Police Department, though he recognized the War Department might nix the idea. "If the administration is wise and wishes to shut my mouth," TR wrote John Parker, "it will then let me raise a division; for I can't talk when in uniform." After his plan went public, hundreds of applications to join the unit, dubbed "Teddy's Tigers," poured into Sagamore Hill, overwhelming the local telegraph office.

The possibility of war disturbed Addams, who was hopeful Wilson would find a way out, perhaps along the lines of the American Union against Militarism proposal of an unofficial gathering of Mexican and

American representatives. She contacted Bryan about doing something, but he doubted he would get very far with administration officials or Mexican President Carranza. Addams and other Woman's Peace Party leaders also wired Wilson pushing for a "direct conference" or mediation to avoid war. His response was not especially optimistic. "My heart is for peace," he wrote her, "and I wish that we were dealing with those who would not make it impossible for us."

The President knew that most of the country, aside from perhaps Roosevelt and his ilk, was not eager to go to war, especially after Carranza released the American prisoners. "Mr. President, keep us out of Mexico," a railroad engineer told him before he departed from a train. The next day, Wilson made it abundantly clear that war would be a last resort, in an address reminiscent of the infamous "too proud to fight" speech of the previous year. "The easiest thing is to strike," he told a New York Press Club audience at the Waldorf-Astoria. "The brutal thing is the impulsive thing. No man has to think before he takes aggressive action. But before a man really conserves the honor by realizing the ideals of the nation, he has to think exactly what he will do and how he will do it." House approved. "The people do not want war," the Colonel wrote Wilson the next day, "least of all with a country like that."

Carranza soon grabbed for Wilson's not-so-subtle olive branch. He agreed that Mexico would participate with the United States in a newly created high commission to work through their difficulties. Addams and the AUAM, whose representatives had already met unofficially with a Mexican delegation, were delighted. If war in North America could be averted this way, then why not in Europe?

Naturally, Roosevelt was bitterly disappointed. The President, once again, remained an implacable barrier to his ambitions. "This man will never declare war on Mexico," TR complained to a newspaperman. "The only way that war will come will be by Mexico declaring war on us. . . . Later on as election draws near he may do something, but—bah!" To Roosevelt, death in combat would be a fitting end to his career and life. "I would like to finish in such a manner," he wrote in a condolence letter a few days later to British ambassador Cecil Spring Rice, whose fifty-two-year-old brother had been killed in action in France.

TR continued to believe that in Mexico, as in Europe, a more forceful policy from the get-go would have prevented the situation from ever reaching the crisis stage. But Wilson felt that was not a feasible option. The country and most of Congress, he was certain, would not have stood for a war with Mexico, nor did they see the need, at least until recently, for a strong enough military to keep the threats at the border to a minimum. That the Republicans and Hughes would be blasting away at his Mexican policy for the next several months did not concern the President; in fact, he never had any doubt that he was doing the right thing. Some Democrats, like Homer Cummings, the vice chairman of the DNC, could not help but detect some of the early signs of the messianism that would become more apparent in the future. "I think he has been inspired by the idea that to him has come an opportunity to aid in the uplifting of a fallen people," Cummings wrote after discussing Mexico with Wilson, "and he means to be true to this vision, even if it should cost him the election."

Fortunately for Wilson, the passing of the Mexican crisis came at a time when relations with Germany were at their best since the war began. If the Germans continued to abide by the *Sussex* pledge, there seemed no reason that the two nations could not coexist peacefully for the foreseeable future.

German Americans began to notice a slight but noticeable shift in attitudes that summer. The entire country was transfixed by the exciting exploits of the *Deutschland*, a German submarine that showed up in Baltimore harbor one Monday morning that July carrying dyestuffs and mail (thus qualifying as a merchant ship instead of a warship). The "super-submarine" not only had bypassed the British blockade, but had also traveled a record-setting 3800 miles in a sixteen-day nonstop voyage from the German naval base at Heligoland. Many had believed such a voyage was impossible, including a *Times* of London writer who speculated that the submarine must have been "sent to America in sections, and reassembled on this side of the water."

For the next two weeks, captain and crew were the toast of America, especially the large German population of Baltimore. Everyone wanted to

know the details of their amazing journey, including American naval officials. Rear Admiral Albert Grant tried to explain to the press the difficulties of life in a submarine. "While operating in any kind of weather,
submerged, the men live below in an oil vapor saturated atmosphere. The
food has to be cooked below. The toilet arrangements are below. There are
certain gases generated by the storage batteries charging and discharg-
ing. . . . The ventilation on board is extremely poor. . . . The quarters are
exceedingly confined." Captain Paul Koenig explained that the *Deutschland*
had actually remained above water as much as possible, "submerging every
time he sighted smoke or a vessel."

What did they do for boredom, reporters wanted to know? A well-stocked
library featuring Shakespeare ("Germans are fonder of Shakespeare than
Englishmen," Koenig observed), Dickens, Bret Harte, among others, along
with a variety of tunes on the gramophone: "German marches and waltzes
and all sorts of things. Sometimes they tried out an Italian record and one
of the most popular records was a good old American ragtime air." Bernstorff, who visited the submarine, could not believe what the men had been
through. "It must have been 110 degrees or more in there," he marveled.

Crew members, not eager to return to what they called the "coffin,"
journeyed to nearby Washington, where they appeared on stage at Keith's,
in between picking up a speeding ticket. They also spent time seeing the
sights of the city, including the Capitol and the White House. At the Navy
Department, the crew was especially eager to see "the man who is like our
Grand Admiral von Tirpitz," but had to settle for FDR, who chatted with
them in German. But to some, the voyage had less happy implications. "The
Preparedness maniacs," Ellen Slayden complained in her diary, "are making
the most of the proven menace of U-boats to our unprotected shores." Koenig himself had even suggested that "great Zeppelin machines" were now
under construction that would "sail through the air to the United States."

In the final days of the *Deutschland*'s stay in America, two events heightened Americans' sense of vulnerability. Ten people were killed and forty
more wounded at a preparedness parade in San Francisco on July 22 after
a suitcase containing a bomb, "nails, cartridges, slugs, and other missiles"
suddenly exploded. Local authorities immediately blamed the city's radical
element, specifically a union organizer and socialist named Tom Mooney,

though photographic evidence conclusively proved he was nowhere near the site of the explosion. After a sham trial marked by bribery, coached witnesses, perjury, and doctored evidence, Mooney was sentenced to death, later commuted by the governor, at Wilson's suggestion, to life imprisonment. Not until 1939 did Mooney finally walk out of San Quentin a free man.

Eight days after the San Francisco suitcase bombing, residents of Jersey City were awoken shortly after two in the morning by the sound of a violent explosion at the Black Tom piers, where much of the overseas munitions shipments to the Allies originated. What followed was a devastating chain reaction of fire and exploding shells so relentless that the blast was felt as far north as Connecticut and as far south as Delaware. Seven died, hundreds more were injured, and thousands of windows were broken. In Jersey City, fearful locals congregated in the parks in the minutes that followed while "panic-stricken women wheeled baby carriages about, some of them praying and others screaming." Across the harbor in New York, frightened residents frantically blew police whistles, fearing the city was under attack, while resourceful crooks looked for looting opportunities in the Maiden Lane jewelry district. At nearby Bedloe's Island, the main door of the Statue of Liberty was "wrenched off its hinges as by a giant hand," although Miss Liberty was relatively intact, suffering only some minor shrapnel damage. The culprits, it was determined years later, were German agents (FDR supposedly used this incident to justify the decision to intern Japanese Americans during World War II).

Such a revelation would have been catastrophic to Germany, which wanted nothing less at present than a potential break or controversy with America, especially in the midst of the bloody Allied offensive at the Somme. And the German government had more than enough to deal with in its own backyard that summer: food riots, a protest strike, and growing unrest about the war. The situation in Berlin was also less than stable, especially the position of the chancellor, under increasing fire for caving in to the Americans. Admiral Müller, who believed Bethmann's decision had prevented a fateful alliance between Britain and the United States, admitted that discontent was in the air. "There are men who say: 'Our youth is shedding its blood in the trenches because the Chancellor has not the guts to start an aggressive U-boat campaign,'" Müller wrote to his brother-in-law.

The behavior of the increasingly erratic kaiser did not help matters. Wilhelm's sudden interest in the "deciphering of the Hittite language" puzzled one German military leader, who wondered why the kaiser didn't have "more important things to worry about." "What more important things?" he roared. "The breaking of the Hittite script is as important as the whole war. Had the world busied itself more with the Hittites a war would never have broken out, for France and England would have recognized that the danger always comes from the East and would never have become allied to Russia!"

In Great Britain, the domestic situation was not quite so chaotic. The Allies, despite tremendous losses, were making gains ("winning at last," Lloyd George, the new war secretary, wrote House, somewhat prematurely) and had the Germans fighting a more defensive war. Still, they remained uneasy about their relationship with America. The suppression of the Easter Rebellion and the subsequent execution of Roger Casement, who had visited TR at Sagamore Hill in 1914, would turn many Irish Americans against them (Roosevelt himself had "always favored Home Rule for Ireland"). And the mail issue, despite a State Department protest in May, remained a constant annoyance. Americans not only wondered why some innocuous letters never made it to their destination on the Continent but began to suspect that the more than two hundred British censors might be pilfering "trade secrets." But far more disturbing was the July 18 publication of a blacklist of American firms who had traded with the Central Powers. Wilson was furious. "I am, I must admit, about at the end of my patience with Great Britain and the Allies," he wrote House. "I am seriously considering asking Congress to authorize me to prohibit loans and restrict exportations to the Allies." Such a drastic move would have finally gotten their attention, but he was not prepared for the political and economic fallout likely to occur, nor did House encourage him. Instead, another protest was sent out, ignored by the Allies until October, when they defended the practice as legal.

Spring Rice, author of many a hysterical "sky is falling" letter about Anglo-American relations, warned London that "all indications are that an unpleasant time is coming." The ambassador floated all kinds of dire possibilities, including a premature peace move by Wilson or America "heading a league of neutrals," the very thing Addams and other pacifists had hoped for since 1914. The United States, Spring Rice reiterated, had no special feelings for the British, despite their historic ties. This country, he wrote Sir Edward Grey, "is anti-German, anti-British and somewhat pro-ally. All these sentiments are those of the spectator who has no desire to leave the stall for the stage."

That the two nations did not always understand each other was unde-niable. "They are just as much foreigners to us as the Germans, Russians, or French," Roosevelt admitted. The British, meanwhile, viewed most Americans as blind to their struggle. Wilson's controversial League to En-force Peace speech had made that clear. The British people had gone to war in defense of Belgium and were now fighting what they believed to be a battle for democracy; shouldn't the Americans support them as much as possible and at the very least overlook a few inconveniences that could be adjudicated after the war? But even House, who tended to see things through the eyes of the Allies, did not agree that Britain's motives had been entirely pure. "The stress of the situation compelled her to side with France and Russia and against the Central Powers," he wrote in his diary; "primarily it was because Germany insisted upon having a dominant army and a dom-inant navy, something Great Britain could not tolerate in safety to herself." As for the "violation" of Belgium, "all the great powers have been, at one time or another, guilty of similar offenses." He also believed that the Allies had unreasonable expectations of American friendship and would not be content "unless the United States is willing to sacrifice hundreds of thou-sands of lives and billions of treasure."

Their differences, though significant at times, were never irreconcilable. The Allies needed American money and munitions, which allowed the United States to prosper as never before. "Judged by figures alone," Spring Rice observed, "America has never been so rich." The British had also long realized that Wilson's words, as much as they could be irritating, meant far less than his actions. They had never faced a "strict accountability" ultima-tum and it appeared unlikely that one might never be forthcoming. But the President knew he had to continue to lean on the Allies to some degree, at least if he wanted to show an increasingly dubious Germany that the United States was truly neutral. The question was how far he should go. Push too hard and he might harm the Allied cause, a cause some believed was essential to American national security in the future.

If peace or an armistice could be obtained and soon, Wilson's dilemma would vanish. House still believed there was a chance if the Allied offensive on the Western Front did not accomplish what they hoped by October. "If they are not ready, I believe you should seriously consider making the proposal without their consent," the Colonel wrote the President. "There is a strong sentiment in both England and France favorable to peace and I believe a majority of the people in those two countries would demand that their governments accept your offer of mediation if they knew actual conditions."

The costs of the war were growing exponentially by the day. The French had already spent close to 2 billion francs; the British were spending over a million dollars *an hour*. After two years, more than 15 million men had been killed, wounded, or missing, at least if press estimates were accurate. But the monumental sacrifices on both sides made peace more elusive than ever. Grey was no longer even pretending to be interested in anything he had discussed with House in February. The President's lack of concern with the "objects and causes of the war" and his talk of freedom of the seas, the foreign secretary explained to House, did not go over well. Besides, until the Somme was decided, everything was up in the air. Privately, the British also doubted the Americans would ever commit to a postwar league of nations, which they recognized would be impotent without U.S. involvement.

At the moment, the Allies were interested in Wilsonian peacemaking if a battlefield victory was not possible. "The only conditions on which such a proposal might be listened to," Grey's secretary Eric Drummond explained, "would be . . . if the French came to us and said 'we are exhausted and can no longer continue the war and feel bound to make peace.'" Otherwise, the Americans might be useful to bring the parties together or to act as what TR scorned as "a make-believe umpire, a fetch-and-carry go-between."

For Addams and other pacifists, what could and should be done right now was a difficult question. Fighting domestic militarism remained important, although the main preparedness battles had already been fought and largely lost, except for the blocking of more extreme legislation. The Hay army bill that prompted Secretary of War Garrison's resignation had been signed in June and Congress was now about to pass a massive naval expansion, salvaged somewhat by a provision calling for a path to future international disarmament and arbitration (to help pay for the defense increases, legislation calling for higher income taxes and America's first inheritance tax would pass in September). Addams had not given up on the Neutral Conference in Stockholm, now functioning on Ford's modest $15,000 monthly contribution. That pacifist causes always had to scrounge for cash in the face of what she called "American apathy" was enormously frustrating, especially when the flush Carnegie Endowment continued its wartime hibernation. Already, she was strategizing to raise money for a planned postwar conference of women, which she now realized might be several years in the future.

The hope remained that Ford, whose company claimed to have made a $59 million profit in the last year, would give them another blank check or something close to it. The automaker, at least if a lengthy interview conducted by the socialist writer John Reed in June for a future profile in *Metropolitan Magazine* was any indication, still seemed passionate about peace. "I don't believe in war; I don't think it settles anything," he told Reed. "I'll stand up and be shot for that." War, he believed, was "foolish . . . it's not only the people that are killed and wounded—I don't lose any sleep about that—but it's the extravagance and waste of it, and the oppression of people that follows it." As usual, his relatively sensible comments were accompanied by various bizarre musings, among them his insistence that alcohol had contributed to the war ("alcohol makes people suspicious. I think it made the French and Germans suspicious of each other"). To Ford's credit, he refused to disavow the Peace Ship, except to reconsider his shipmates. Next time, he announced that he would "take the whole village of Dearborn—men, women and children. I meant to advertise Peace, and I did it."

Ford's next move remained unclear. That he was growing closer to Wilson was now obvious. When the President came to Detroit for a speaking engagement on July 10, Ford met him at the train station, rode with him in his automobile, and acted as his guide at the Ford plant, where a banner, designed by the great man himself, was hung for all to see, inscribed with the words "We take our hats off to the man who kept us out of war." The cheers of the twenty thousand men and women on the day shift, along with a noisy symphony of factory whistles, made it impossible for Wilson to be heard when he tried to make a brief speech extolling Ford and his company. Ford was pleased. The President, he told reporters, "is on to the interests. He knows who is the cause of war and he isn't afraid to say it."

But Ford was no longer inclined to make large contributions of any kind to pacifist causes, especially those with women involved. The Schwimmer fiasco and the absence of Addams on the Peace Ship (he still believed she had been faking) had permanently soured him, as had the increasing misgivings of his wife and colleagues. When Emily Balch returned to the United States that summer hoping to get additional funding for the Stockholm conference, Ford made it clear that he would not be financing her return to Europe.

Addams was appalled. "Poor Mr. Ford is simply out of his depth," she wrote Balch. "If you are not expected to go back, I will be disgusted with the situation."

Rosika Schwimmer, meanwhile, still dreamed of a reconciliation with Ford and his millions. In late July, she decided to sail for America, where she hoped to tell her side of the story and attract support for her new organization, which was known as the International Committee for Immediate Mediation, or what she called an "independent offspring of Mr. Ford's Neutral Conference." Almost immediately, she showed up in Detroit trying to see Ford, only to receive a cold refusal carried by one of his associates. She also got nowhere with his wife. "The way Mr. Ford's name and money was used was shameful, and you were the leader," Clara Ford tartly wrote Schwimmer. "You and your followers cared not if he died, just so long as he went along to lend his name and provide money to be squandered." Yes, she had done "some good work, but used such poor judgment . . . and did not want to take any one's advice. . . . Mr. Ford knows what you have done, and what you should not have done, and I am positive he will not see you or give you money." The always dramatic Schwimmer was devastated. The "incredible brutality" of the letter, she told Addams, gave her "a severe fit," especially since she now believed Clara Ford had played an important role in "ruining everything."

Addams was sympathetic. She was more than happy to see Schwimmer in Maine in August and politely listen to her rage about the misguided direction of the conference since her departure and the wicked treachery of various peace colleagues such as Julia Wales (now "on the road to insanity," Schwimmer insisted). But Addams's attempts to remain impartial naturally did not sit well with the fiery Hungarian. "I am . . . disgusted with Miss Addams," she wrote her friend Lola Maverick Lloyd afterward. "She was very 'sweet' but I believe she believes more what the others tell her."

Schwimmer was also annoyed that Addams would not involve herself in any of her current schemes. When Schwimmer learned Ford was in New York at the Biltmore Hotel (where he was slapped with a lawsuit from the Vitagraph Company for comments about their *Battle Cry of Peace*) during her last week in America, she desperately wired Addams to urge Ford to see her. Addams refused. For one thing, she had not witnessed the Peace Ship events firsthand. For another, "Mr. Ford firmly believes I exaggerated my illness . . . and of course can have very little respect for the opinion of such a quitter."

A few days later, Schwimmer sailed back to Europe, having accomplished little. That she had been criminally wronged by everyone was obvious to her. "The indignation, the sorrow and all the other painful emotions," she wrote Addams, "are still dominating me more than they should after so much hardening." She would not return to America for another five years.

Addams, though unwilling to lift a finger for Schwimmer, did her best to set up an appointment for Balch to see the President so she could brief him on the doings of the Neutral Conference. Wilson readily agreed. "I will search my calendar for the earliest possible hour at which I may see Miss Balch," he eagerly responded. Privately, he also knew it was good politics to be so receptive. A few days after the President met with Balch, the journalist Norman Hapgood, now tasked with recruiting Progressives to the Democrats, reminded him of Addams's importance. Addams,

Hapgood explained, was among a group of influential individuals "who can be kept in line by constant contact and explanation." The hope was that she would eventually "take a public stand on our side, as she counts very heavily."

Obligatory meetings with the likes of Balch and others remained a substantial part of Wilson's daily grind, one that frequently left him exhausted by the end of the day. And he never had much patience or interest in the million mundane tasks needing his attention. "I must admit that I am often bored," he once remarked. His typical day that summer might begin at 6:00 a.m. with breakfast, followed by retreat to his second-floor study with his stenographer, Charles Swem, to clear away some of the mounds of paperwork requiring his signature or attention. Every day, his secretaries sifted through hundreds of letters and telegrams with requests of all kinds: morphine for a neuralgia sufferer, help in getting a book published, a Wilson photograph for "good luck," and the usual demands for commissions and pardons. Then came meetings with various congressmen, cabinet members, and administration officials, along with a never-ending stream of outsiders, first screened by Tumulty and his associates, who wanted a moment of his time to pitch a cause or proposal. In the evening, the day's major developments had to be absorbed, especially those concerning the international situation.

But even during the busiest of times, Wilson was not afraid to enjoy himself. Golf provided a welcome respite most afternoons (thirty-one times in July and August alone), as did the comforting automobile rides with his wife and weekend trips on the *Mayflower*. "I dote on fun," he told Edith. "I have never fully grown up. Things that amused me and pleased me when I was a boy please and amuse me still. I play as hard and fast as I work and with more interest!" Those who still perceived the President as the prim-and-proper professorial type would have been much amused, as was House, to see him walking in the White House that May with a heavy dictionary "balanced on his head very much as the Negroes in the South balance pails of water."

His family was never far from his thoughts. The First Lady was his rock, increasingly willing to offer her two cents on matters large and small. Treasury Secretary McAdoo, according to House, was certain that "the new

Mrs. Wilson was antagonistic to him and to several other friends of the President's"; Wilson himself once teased his bride about her capacity to "hate." He doted on his grandchildren, though he believed parents had grown entirely too permissive ("the trouble with children to-day is that they aren't *made* to do anything," he told his cousin Helen Bones). And that summer he worried about the health of his only sister, Annie Howe, who was in New England trying to recuperate from peritonitis. Still, he did his best to relax in the final weeks before his reelection campaign began in earnest in the fall.

For many Americans, especially those on the East Coast, it was a summer of anxiety. It was not only the polio epidemic but an unprecedented wave of shark attacks at the Jersey Shore. In an eleven-day span in July, four swimmers were killed, the youngest an eleven-year-old boy. One shark even appeared at Oyster Bay, as TR's neighbors, the Blacktons, sighted a ten-footer not far from the private beach on their estate.

The tragedy was not enough to deter the hordes who continued to flock to the seaside resorts. As usual, there was no shortage of unusual sights. At Long Beach, New York, young girls zipped along on their motorized "autopeds"; in Atlantic City, New Jersey, a pet monkey was now the latest "thing" for fashionable ladies to be seen with while strolling along the Boardwalk. And the new slit-skirted bathing suits attracted just as much attention.

That some communities had begun to reconsider the need for women's bare legs to be covered while swimming suggested America was taking much needed steps away from still lingering Victorian sensibilities. But the celebrated novelist Theodore Dreiser would not have agreed. That August, the New York Society for the Suppression of Vice had decided that the sexual content in Dreiser's latest novel, The "Genius," was absolutely unacceptable. "There is something just absolutely sickly about the whole mental attitude of this country," a disgusted Dreiser complained. "Are we going to succumb to Puritan thought, or is it possible for the United States to accept a world standard of thinking? . . . They see that on page, say 78, there is a reference to a stocking or a leg, and that is 'lewd' to them."

Dreiser could take some comfort in the knowledge that the war had already disrupted age-old perceptions of sexual morality, at least if the prevalence of "war babies" and high rates of venereal disease on both sides were any indication. And the United States, try as she might, would find it difficult to resist to such currents in the future, whether she joined the war or not.

Since Wilson would not be campaigning that summer, the Republicans had the field to themselves for the moment. Everything seemed to be proceeding as planned. Hughes had selected a campaign manager who would also serve as RNC chairman (his friend William Willcox, a member of the Public Service Commission and a former New York postmaster appointed by TR), most of the Progressives were hopefully coming home to the GOP, and the public was eager to hear what the candidate had to say during his upcoming formal acceptance speech. The Hughes coming-out party, scheduled for July 31 at Carnegie Hall, would also be Roosevelt's first appearance at an official Republican function in four years. When he arrived with his wife, strains of "Auld Lang Syne" were heard. "Who's all right?" someone shouted. *"Roosevelt!"* the crowd roared. TR could not help but smile.

A few minutes later it was Hughes's turn to speak. Eight thousand words and ninety long minutes later, many wondered whether Hughes had said much of anything. His attacks on the administration pleased Roosevelt, but the press and audience could not help wishing for fewer vagaries and more specifics. And former Progressives, listening intently for signs of sympathy to their cause, were alarmed that Hughes seemed to be bending over backward to placate mainstream GOP opinion. Wilson, meanwhile, read enough of the speech the next day to sense that Hughes had whiffed. The man on the street, at least those randomly canvassed throughout America by the *New York Herald*, agreed. "Don't think much about the speech," a Manhattan policeman remarked. "Teddy is the boy for me." A Boston book dealer was also unimpressed. "What I read of it was uninteresting and very dry." To a New Haven man, the speech was unlikely to make a difference one way or another: "you can't beat Woodrow."

Hughes, away from politics for six years, was clearly rusty. "A term on the bench takes the punch out of many men," TR had once observed.

Hughes had always been known as an outstanding speaker; veteran politicos still talked about his devastating takedown of Bryan during the 1908 Taft campaign. The plan was to get him on the road during August in the Midwest and West, where he would build momentum. "What the average voter wants is not an etching, but a poster, a statement so broad and clear and in such simple language that he can thoroughly understand it," TR reminded Hughes.

Hughes and his handlers believed the administration's inefficiency and wastefulness should be a major target, along with the disastrous mess in Mexico. But attacks on Wilson's European policy, they believed, should be deferred, lest his campaign statements limit Hughes's options as future president. It was soon clear that the strategy was not an especially wise one. TR's numerous correspondents began flooding his mailbox with reports that Hughes was bombing. His speeches, they complained, remained "shockingly superficial"; the crowd response was similar to what a "Chautauqua lecturer encounters." Worst of all, the candidate's instincts were all wrong, prone to accept the wrong kind of advice or ignore sensible suggestions altogether. In California, he did not see the state's leading Progressive, Governor Hiram Johnson (some later blamed Johnson), nor would he endorse his legislative accomplishments. "In political circles the failure of the two to meet is regarded as ominous," the Hearst columnist William Hoster wrote. Some already speculated it might cost Hughes fifty thousand votes.

Hughes needed the Progressive vote in California and elsewhere to win, but he seemed to believe that a middle-of-the-road, offend-nobody approach was the best path to victory. Since the bulk of the Progressive vote was theoretically in the bag, there seemed no need to talk Bull Moose principles, at least according to most of the Republican leadership. But Roosevelt's old supporters saw things differently. Hughes's statements and speeches to date had given them little reason to vote for him, except for a general belief that a Hughes victory would move the Republican party to the left.

The liberal *New York Evening Post* journalist John Palmer Gavit was baffled by Hughes's performance, especially since he believed the GOP nominee "worth six of Wilson, in straightforwardness, sincerity, executive ability and knowledge of the world." In private, Gavit noticed that Hughes had talked tough about Wilson's German policy. "If there had been a strong man as Secretary of State, and a strong man . . . at Berlin," Hughes told him, "there never would have been any *Lusitania*. Germany would never have dared to touch a hair of an American head!" Just as assertively, he had scoffed at the mixed messages sent by the administration: "forcefully worded notes" undermined by "whispers that they didn't mean what they said." But on the campaign trail he said nothing of the kind.

That Hughes might not possess the necessary drive to win the election had become distressingly obvious to the Republicans. Hughes himself had already betrayed a sense of ambivalence. He was "better adapted" to the Supreme Court, he confessed to Henry Stoddard of the *New York Evening Mail* before his nomination, than to the White House. "I am not the kind of man for that sort of work. Your friend Roosevelt could do in an hour there what would take me a day. And he would enjoy it, while I enjoy the court." It was hardly surprising that a common cry began to be heard among GOP circles: "I would thank God if we just had Roosevelt in this fight."

TR continued to insist he was "out of politics." Five or six speeches was the extent of his current commitment. The suggestion that he go to Europe to avoid the campaign did not appeal to him. "I don't wish to be put in the position of an outsider, and an ambulatory globe trotter, a mere looker in, visiting trenches where men are spending their lives like water for a great ideal," he explained. And there were other matters to occupy his attention that summer: his grandchildren; the poet Edgar Lee Masters, whom he invited to Sagamore Hill; and an offer to write a series of columns for *Ladies' Home Journal*. But beating Wilson, even if it had to be done vicariously through Hughes, was never far from his thoughts. The lack of enthusiasm for Hughes concerned him. "Of course he is 'better than Wilson,' but what sort of thing is that to say of a man?" a Chicago newspaperman wrote TR.

As much as he hated to admit it, Roosevelt also knew that plenty of Americans believed that Wilson was doing a first-rate job. Except for a far less substantial war chest than the GOP, the Democrats seemed to be in the driver's seat at the moment to elect their first two-term president since

Andrew Jackson in 1832 (Grover Cleveland also served two terms, but nonconsecutively, between 1885 and 1897). "They [the Republicans] haven't anything to put up and will have to shut up," Wilson told a group of party members. "They haven't any rival policies, any policies worthy to rival ours." The President had already decided to let his considerable first-term legislative successes do most of the talking. If the country was truly more progressive than not, as Bryan and others believed, then Hughes could not match the Federal Trade Commission, the Federal Reserve, loans to farmers, federal aid for road construction, and antitrust legislation, among other accomplishments. Even a TR disciple like John Callan O'Laughlin conceded that "the President's internal legislative program unquestionably is excellent, and the Republicans are not attacking it, and indeed cannot do so."

Vance McCormick, the former mayor of Harrisburg and an unsuccessful candidate for Pennsylvania governor who had been endorsed by TR in 1914, was the new chairman of the Democratic National Committee. Unlike Willcox, whom few Republicans were happy with, McCormick had the support of virtually everyone who mattered, especially Colonel House and Edith Wilson. The President himself had no strong ideas about how the campaign should be conducted ("I am not fertile as a suggester of campaign methods," he admitted), but he was certain that he did not want to make an extensive speaking tour. Nor would he respond to any of Roosevelt's criticisms directly. As for Hughes, whom he knew casually, Wilson understood he need not do anything right now, since Hughes seemed to be doing a fine job sabotaging his own campaign.

But Hughes managed to outflank Wilson in at least one area: the still sensitive suffrage issue. Initially, Hughes had refused to support the Susan B. Anthony amendment. After getting nowhere with him, Alice Paul of the Congressional Union journeyed to Sagamore Hill with Alice Carpenter hoping TR might work his influence. Roosevelt, while sympathetic, made them aware of Hughes's limitations and his tendency to move slowly. "The great trouble is, in politics, that people don't seem ever to quite master this thought, that you not only have to be right, but you have to be right in time," he told them. "He just hasn't mastered the idea if he should be president. . . . that he must be right in time and let the world know." With

TR's prodding, Hughes came out for the amendment the day after his Carnegie Hall acceptance speech. "That killed him with me," cracked a Chicago salesman.

Hughes's endorsement stood in stark contrast to Wilson's continued preference for a state-by-state approach, which everyone knew would take far longer. Paul's Congressional Union suffragists, unlike Carrie Chapman Catt's less militant National American Woman Suffrage Association, had already decided to crank up the pressure on the President. They showed up on July 4 at Wilson's appearance at the dedication of the new American Federation of Labor building on Massachusetts Avenue in Washington. In the middle of Wilson's comment about "common understanding," a young Quaker woman from Nevada named Mabel Vernon stood up. "If you sincerely want common understanding," she shouted, "you will get out of committee the national suffrage amendment." Wilson said nothing, although angry cries of "Shut up!" and "Throw her out!" could be heard. A few minutes later, she resumed her heckling. "Answer, Mr. President! Why do you block the national suffrage amendment?" At this point, Vernon's breach of proper female decorum was too much for the local police, who hauled her away.

For Paul and the Congressional Union, Hughes was now the obvious choice for the four million women voters in the twelve suffrage states, where the National Woman's Party, an offshoot of the CU, would be campaigning against the President. But Wilson was hopeful the more patient elements of the suffrage moment would not abandon him. He insisted that following Hughes's lead now would make him look like an unprincipled "angler for votes." And he did his best to present himself as friendly to the cause, accepting an invitation to speak before the NAWSA convention in Atlantic City in September. Afterward, he and his wife attended a charity musicale where the audience called for a speech. Instead, the man who loved limericks gave them an old favorite: "For beauty I am not a star; There are others more handsome by far. My face I don't mind it, Because I'm behind It; It's the people in front that I jar."

Such whimsical moments helped Wilson vault ahead in the all-important likability factor, especially since Hughes was perceived as frosty and distant. Still, the Democrats recognized that the European war was the issue that mattered most of all. The simple phrase "He Kept Us Out of War" had begun to pick up steam as a made-to-order rallying cry, hardly surprising to campaign officials such as the journalist George Creel. "People do not read; they are governed by slogans," he would later remark. Wilson, who knew everything could change in an instant, was not comfortable with the slogan's implications, but McCormick was not concerned. If in the unlikely event war came before the election, the people would rally behind the President anyway.

Of course, Wilson's involvement in bringing peace or an armistice in the next few months would seal the deal for him. That other neutrals were interested in joining with him at any time was apparent. Spain, supported by the pope, had put out feelers months earlier, which Wilson did not acknowledge until August. House, meanwhile, was told by the Dutch ambassador that if Wilson "could get them to parley, it would be impossible for them to resume fighting no matter how impossible it was for them to arrive at terms." The Colonel did not disagree, but nothing could be done as long as the Allies believed there was a light at the end of the tunnel. "Any offer of mediation at this time, or even a hint of it," Arthur Draper, the London correspondent of the *New York Tribune*, explained, "would have the same effect upon the British as a red flag on a bull."

The Germans had begun to feel differently by the end of the summer. They were far from losing the war, but they knew that time was not on their side and they could not sustain their enormous losses indefinitely. Bethmann well understood this. "We must make peace soon while we are still in the position of victors," he told Admiral Müller during an August 25 conversation. The kaiser, in a lucid moment, agreed: "No chance of making peace must be rejected." And America could be valuable to initiate the proceedings, but there would be no Wilsonian mediation.

Two days later, the Central Powers received disturbing news. Romania, like Italy lured by a secret promise of postwar territory, declared war on Austria-Hungary. The prospect of a new enemy opening up another front devastated Wilhelm, who was sure the war was lost. Wiretaps revealed that these anxieties were shared by German sympathizers on the other side of the Atlantic. In New York, Edmeé Reisinger, daughter of the celebrated brewmaster Adolphus Busch, expressed her fears to her lover Heinrich

Albert (the German official who'd lost his suitcase on the elevated train the year before). "I am worried for the first time," she told him. Albert agreed. "It is a very very serious thing, there is no doubt about it. It would be foolish to deny that."

Cooler heads in Berlin managed to convince Kaiser Wilhelm that Germany was still in a good position, but the Romanian crisis sent shock waves through the country's military and political leadership. Out went Falkenhayn as chief of staff (Müller reported that the kaiser "shed tears"), replaced by Paul von Hindenburg with Erich Ludendorff as his quartermaster general, moves that would ultimately strengthen the military's influence in civil and political matters. Bethmann himself realized that his ability to hold off the ongoing demand for a return to unrestricted submarine warfare would not last forever. If Wilson wanted to bring the belligerents together, now was the time to do it. The chancellor began prodding Bernstorff to plant the seed in Wilson's mind, even floating the possibility of Germany's giving up Belgium. Bethmann also realized there might be other benefits to a Wilson peace move. Should the Allies reject it out of hand, Germany not only would gain the upper hand from a propaganda standpoint but would have a convenient rationale for resuming the submarine campaign.

Addams and other pacifists, unaware of Bethmann's thoughts, continued to believe it would be better for Wilson to do something rather than nothing. "The opinion is growing that the chances of peace are not likely to be any better two years from now than they are at present," Emily Balch explained. Three days after Romania entered the war, Balch had made a second pilgrimage to the White House as one of the representatives of a Committee of 100 put together by the American Neutral Conference Committee. Addams was not well enough to go, but her name helped bring in a few of the nonpacifist "business and professional" men (the inventors Luther Burbank and John Kellogg joined) the ANCC deemed essential to the committee makeup. Not surprisingly, a number of establishment figures—such as American Federation of Labor head Samuel Gompers, two of TR's former cabinet members, and Harvard president and League to Enforce Peace member A. Lawrence Lowell—were openly hostile to the idea.

Once again, the indefatigable Lella Secor and Rebecca Shelly had been the driving force behind the idea. Secor had originally hoped to have most of the 100 boldly show up in Washington, only to find the ANCC's "conservative wing" unenthusiastic. Instead, a thirty-person delegation made the trip on August 31. At the White House, Secor noticed the President, clad in a "white flannel suit," was "rather interesting to look at. . . . His eyes—small but brilliant—look very steadily through eye-glasses which are NOT tortoise shell (thank God for that)." Wilson patiently listened to their speakers, among them David Starr Jordan and Hamilton Holt (one of the conservative, go-slow "peace hacks" disdained by Secor and Shelly), pitch the neutral conference idea for the umpteenth time. By this point, Wilson ("less frightened than anyone else," Secor noticed) was skilled at batting away their arguments while appearing interested and sympathetic. An official conference of neutrals would be problematic, he explained, because other neutral nations would be looking for some sort of material gain from the agreements, unlike the United States. "Their point of view is utterly different from ours, and their object is utterly different from ours." Then there was the problem of including South American countries and their ability to outvote the Europeans. (Months earlier, he had been far more candid to the journalist Ray Stannard Baker, explaining that "he thought it would hamper rather than help us to be associated with a group of little nations.") But he did not want to discourage the delegation. "I believe that a psychological moment will come," he said soothingly. "I am praying it will come very soon, when some suggestion made out loud by somebody [presumably Wilson himself] that they have to listen to will be irresistible, that they will have to begin to parley." Moments later, Wilson had politely rid himself of the pesky pacifists, without giving them a chance to respond.

It was another virtuoso performance. Secor herself had momentarily been swayed. "During the moments when he was speaking, I thought him a truly wonderful man," she admitted. She soon realized that Wilson had played them. No matter what argument was presented to him, the President was not going to act in concert with other neutrals. It would be solo or not at all. A few days later, Secor briefed Addams, who was eager to hear the details, although she knew in advance not to expect a breakthrough. The ANCC was not giving up, Secor explained, even if some of the more timorous types remained fearful they might "offend" the President. The newest plan was a petition to push American mediation in any form likely to be successful, neutral conference or whatever. Secor conceded that Addams might not be especially excited about what was admittedly an old idea. "But it does seem that if within the next two months great numbers of Americans (personally, I hope for millions) voice through this petition the positive wish that our government make active efforts to mediate, such expression of public opinion cannot fail to react upon the belligerent peoples."

Secor was aware that Wilson could be a lame duck in two months. She was not convinced that Hughes would be much better and expected he would be "far more belligerent in his attitude." Other pacifists were not quite sure what they would get with a Hughes administration. Would TR be lurking in the background, pulling the strings? Or would Hughes ignore him as he had done while governor? A group from the Americans United against Militarism had gone to see Hughes in July to sound him out on militarism, internationalism, and the war's negative impact on social reform. The *Evening Post*'s Oswald Villard, who had long soured on Wilson, was impressed with Hughes's "fearlessness, courage, independence" and thought he might have potential. Amos Pinchot disagreed. After talking with Hughes, he decided he would vote for Wilson. "There is hope in Wilson and he often speaks as if he had a real idea of democracy." Hughes, he believed, was "a wooden man, honest but impossible to educate."

A victorious Hughes, of course, would not take office until March and by then the war might be over. If not, the Allies knew that Hughes might undo all of Wilson's policies. The British were already wondering whether the former Supreme Court justice might approach the British blockade in a particularly legalistic fashion. As far as mediation, Hughes would likely have an even more difficult time than Wilson. "Hughes's international reputation is at present exactly nothing," Arthur Lee informed TR.

By the end of August, Hughes's reputation in America was not much better. Establishment Republicans, as much as they still couldn't stand Roosevelt or the returning ex-Progressives in general, were happy to see TR finally get into the campaign. His first speech was scheduled for August 31 in Lewiston, Maine, a state whose September presidential elections (until 1960) were believed to predict November outcomes ("As Maine goes, so goes the nation"). Roosevelt decided in advance to focus only on Wilson's Mexican policy, blasting the futile attempt to get Pancho Villa and the "several hundred men . . . killed and wounded," supposedly more than those killed by Spain during the Spanish-American War (some thought his comment comparing Wilson's lack of concern for American deaths in Mexico to that of a farmer watching "rats killed by his dogs when the hay is taken from a barn" went too far). "It is a mere play upon words to say that these were not 'wars,'" TR told the gathering. "They were wars, and nothing else: ignoble, pointless, unsuccessful little wars; but wars. They cost millions of dollars and hundreds of lives. . . . And yet Mr. Wilson's defenders say that he 'has kept us out of war.'"

Most Republicans were pleased with the hard-hitting tone of TR's first appearance, so much so that there was talk that he would take a much more active part in the campaign than originally intended. A few days later, a campaign film was shot at Sagamore Hill of TR greeting William Willcox, the RNC chair and Hughes campaign manager, along with scenes of Progressives and Republicans shaking hands. The director, Hal Reid, noticed that most of the politicos needed acting lessons. "Walk right up, shake hands and try to look like live ones," he shouted. "I've got to have action here."

Wilson as usual had no response to Roosevelt's attacks. His hands were full with a possible national railroad strike, one with the potential not only to tie up the entire country, but also affect the troops on the Mexican border and disrupt war shipments to Europe. The main issue was the eight-hour day; the railroads were determined to fight it and refused the President's recommendation to yield. Wilson, disgusted by the attitudes of the railroad plutocrats, decided he had no choice but to forge ahead on his own. He pushed for immediate legislation, and the undisputed master of Congress succeeded once again with the passage of the Adamson Act on September 2. Politically, the legislation was likely to be a big hit, especially among "everyone who works with his hands," as John Callan O'Laughlin observed.

Earlier that day, Wilson had officially launched his campaign with his nomination acceptance speech at Shadow Lawn, a West Long Branch estate at the Jersey Shore that would double as the "summer White House" and campaign headquarters this year. Family members, cabinet members, and thousands of other Democrats high and low filled the spacious grounds of the beautiful mansion, decked out in red, white, and blue, to hear Wilson speak, although his voice could not hope to reach beyond the first few rows. Unlike Hughes, he kept the address a reasonable length, highlighting the administration's accomplishments while continuing the outreach to disgruntled Progressives. "We have in four years come very near to carrying out the platform of the Progressive Party as well as our own; for we also are progressives," he reminded the audience. "The Republican Party is just the party that cannot meet the new conditions of a new age. . . . It tried to break away from the old leaders and could not." As for foreign policy, he insisted that America's "traditional provincialism" had come to an end. "We are to play a leading part in the world drama whether we wish it or not." In an exciting finish, the crowd watched American flags shot into the air parachute to the earth while the band played a suitably patriotic song.

The differences between the two candidates were becoming increasingly obvious. Wilson, it was beginning to appear, was the true liberal reformer, except when it came to suffrage and segregation (although he did express his deep discomfort with racial violence in response to a letter sent by an African American clubwoman that summer). Hughes not only disliked the Adamson Act, the new eight-hour law for railroad workers (as did TR, who thought an investigatory commission should have been created instead), but also rejected a new Child Labor Law for legal reasons (the bill was declared unconstitutional in 1918). And influential endorsements had begun to fall into Wilson's lap. In early September, Edison announced his preference for Wilson as a second choice to his favored candidate, TR. A few days later, Ida Tarbell also threw her support behind the President. Wilson, she argued, was the real Progressive all along, not Roosevelt, who "does not and never has really understood what the Progressives are fussing about."

Tarbell's statement appeared in the morning papers on September 11, the day of the Maine election. By this point, both sides had poured in money and high-profile speakers there, hoping to turn the tide for their candidate. The Republicans usually had the lock on the state, but Wilson had shockingly won there in 1912, the first Democrat in sixty years to do so. This time, Hughes captured 51 percent of the vote to win Maine and its six electoral votes. That Wilson would have won with a mere switch of 2738 votes led many to believe TR's Lewiston speech had been the deciding factor. "I think we have good reason to be cheerful," Hughes wrote Roosevelt afterward.

TR was cautiously optimistic, though he still had his doubts about Hughes ("too much of a judge," he complained). He understood that his relationship with the candidate was shaping up as a crucial issue. But his speeches, he believed, must not appear as necessary to save a floundering campaign. And harmony between the two must be preserved. "It has been no light task for me in my speeches to avoid seeming to clash with Hughes and, at the same time, not to go back on any of the things for which I stand," Roosevelt admitted.

Wilson learned the results while in New London, Connecticut, to see his sister, who had only days to live. He did not share Tumulty's grave concern about losing Maine. Hughes, he still believed, had shown very little thus far and the people would see through him in the end. While in New London, a Republican informed him that he would be voting for Wilson in 1916. "That's music," the President replied. The sassy response, the press reported, was likely a lift from a "recent Southern song," probably one of the ragtime tunes Wilson enjoyed on his phonograph.

Back at Shadow Lawn, the campaign to reelect Wilson began in earnest. Executive offices were established four miles away in the Asbury Park Trust Company Building, complete with a considerable support staff of clerks and an assortment of telephone and telegraph operators. Wilson maintained his usual schedule of work alternating with golf, although he occasionally indulged in billiards with Edith, who was known to beat her husband a time or two. Reporters, desperate for something to write about, filed dispatches about the "nuts" who had shown up wanting to see the President and about a black cat that turned up in Tumulty's office. Dubbed Omega, the feline was seen as a good omen and soon attracted fan mail requesting photographs.

By the end of September, there had been little newsworthy to report from Democratic headquarters. Wilson had begun making front-porch speeches to various groups, but he had not changed his mind about stumping the country. There was no reason for an incumbent president to do so, he believed, since "the record is there, and he can't change it." The President himself admitted that the campaign had not yet captivated the public's fancy. "For a little while I myself expected that this campaign would be an interesting intellectual contest," he explained. "But I am sorry to say I have found nothing to interest me."

The campaign suddenly became much more interesting when a telegram arrived at Shadow Lawn from a lawyer and militant Irish sympathizer named Jeremiah O'Leary. O'Leary, the head of the pro-German, anti-British American Truth Society, had voted for Roosevelt in 1912, but came to despise what he considered TR's sympathy with the "menace" of "Anglo-Saxonism." Now it was Wilson's turn. The President's pro-British attitudes were costing him votes, O'Leary warned. "Your foreign policies, your failure to secure compliance with all American rights, your leniency with the British Empire, your approval of war loans, the ammunition traffic, are issues in this campaign. . . . Anglo-maniacs and British interest may control newspapers, but they don't control votes."

The "hyphen" issue had died down of late, thanks to the improved relations with Germany. But Wilson, seeing a perfect opportunity to position himself as the champion of Americanism, could not resist teeing off on a fat pitch thrown down the middle. "Your telegram received," he responded. "I would feel deeply mortified to have you or anybody like you vote for me. Since you have access to many disloyal Americans and I have not I will ask you to convey this message to them." The Democrats gleefully publicized Wilson's fiery reply, one that TR probably wished Hughes had uttered. To House, the telegram was a brilliant coup for Wilson, "the best thing so far in the campaign and will do more good than you can realize."

Day by day, Wilson was growing stronger as a candidate. He had also begun to show that he could sling mud with the best of them. The day after he received the O'Leary telegram, he presented to a Shadow Lawn gathering of young Democrats a rather fearful vision of what a Republican administration might bring. "All our foreign policy is wrong, they say," the President explained. "And if they are going to change it, in what direction are they going to change it? There is only one choice as against peace, and that is war. . . . So that the certain prospect of the success of the Republican party is that we shall be drawn, in one form or other, into the embroilments of the European war." (Unfortunately for Hughes, the Republicans had no idea that Wilson might just have easily plunged the nation into the dreaded "embroilments," at least if the now abandoned House-Grey Memorandum had come off as planned.)

With less than six weeks left in the campaign, reelection appeared within the President's grasp. Still, he could not escape the same sense of resignation and dread that he had experienced since the war began. The feelings surfaced at his sister's funeral in Columbia, South Carolina, where he resumed acquaintances with family members (an elderly aunt greeted him with "Tommy," explaining to Edith Wilson that "since he took to writing books he calls himself Woodrow"). Later, he and Cary Grayson visited the home he had lived in for several years as a teenager, Grayson asking one of the four boys residing there "if he expected to be President." Wilson offered the young man no encouragement. "I would not wish anything like that on you."

Chapter 15

AN ELECTION AND A PEACE MOVE

SEPTEMBER 30–DECEMBER 25, 1916

*Everything I believe in chains me here. Nothing is
finished. Is it wise that the country should change
now, leaving so much at loose ends?*

—Woodrow Wilson, October 1916

During his South Carolina trip, Wilson could not help but hear talk of an issue increasingly disturbing to the white residents of the South. For the past several months, thousands upon thousands of African Americans had departed for the big cities of the North, where social conditions were far less dire and war-fueled factory opportunities plentiful thanks to labor shortages. What became known as the Great Migration was now under way, its main cheerleader the *Chicago Defender*, a widely circulated African American weekly. A Southern transplant now residing in Pennsylvania named C. D. Douglas was thrilled with the *Defender*'s efforts. "You are doing the best work for the Race since the death of John Brown—that is, by instructing our people to leave those hellish states and come north and do the things that are right and enjoy a little freedom," Douglas wrote the *Defender* that fall. "If all the Negroes in the south would leave and come north and be honest and do right they would find themselves better off in many ways."

Southern officials were not happy. Without the black man, who was going to work the fields for a princely sum of fifty cents a day? They tried their best to paint the North as a fearful place where African Americans would surely freeze and starve without the assistance of their kindly white friends down South. The Wilson administration was also concerned. Were these Negroes being brought north into "doubtful states" solely to cast their votes for Hughes? Few northern blacks were prepared to vote for Wilson, who still seemed disinclined to make any gesture to win their support. "You have grievously disappointed us," W. E. B. Du Bois wrote the President in October. But Wilson remained incapable of understanding his anger. In his own mind, he believed he was doing all he could for the Negro. He was permanently stuck in his childhood Old South mind-set, where segregation was desirable and references to an "old darkey" (a term that the First Lady was also known to use) in a political speech were perfectly acceptable.

The President's racial policies never became an issue during the campaign. With the exception of liberal reformers like Addams and her ilk, most whites remained either oblivious of or hostile to the plight of African Americans. Even TR, who was more open-minded on the subject than Wilson, was not enthusiastic about any new effort to enforce black voting rights in the South. Most southern blacks, he believed, currently were "wholly unfit for the suffrage," and if allowed to vote, "would reduce parts of the south to the level of Haiti."

For Roosevelt, the "race problem" was an insignificant domestic matter, not worthy of mention right now, especially when the President had so many other glaring deficiencies to highlight. In his second major political address of the campaign, TR offered a devastating two-hour critique (in "high falsetto") of Wilson before a crowd of ten thousand under a circus tent in Battle Creek, Michigan, on September 30. The Byzantine logothete, he charged, was not only a weakling who tamely submitted to foreign powers and "big labor leaders" alike, but an insincere political chameleon constantly shifting his views for votes. This joke of a president, he reminded the crowd, "argued for preparedness and against preparedness. He stated that our army was ample, and that we did not have enough troops to patrol the Mexican border in time of peace. He said the world was on fire and that sparks were liable to drop anywhere and cause us to burst into flame, and he also said there was no immediate danger." As usual, Roosevelt was not shy about boasting how he had handled similar crises as president and even digressed from his prepared speech to weigh in on the *Lusitania*. "I would have seized every German ship interned in an American port and then I would have said to Germany: 'Now you tell me what you will pay and I'll tell you how much the United States will take.'"

That some newspapers gave the Battle Creek speech more ink than Wilson's Shadow Lawn address that day concerned some Democrats, although they could take heart that TR's *Lusitania* comment bolstered his (and by extension, Hughes's) reputation as a warmonger. Others could not help but notice that Roosevelt's mentions of the Republican candidate were relatively minimal. To *Life*, TR's Battle Creek message seemed to be "Mr. Wilson is not a bit like me . . . I am right, and he is dead wrong. Gentlemen, vote for Hughes!"

But the Hughes campaign was so pleased with Roosevelt's efforts that they convinced him to commit to a more extensive speaking tour in October. They had already persuaded him to show up at a big Republican shindig honoring Hughes on October 3 at the Union League Club in midtown Manhattan, a decision that did not sit well with former Progressives, especially since Taft would also be present. They could not understand why TR would appear with Taft, "a fat-headed and impossible reactionary," as one Progressive labeled him, or other Old Guard Republicans who had stolen the nomination from him in 1912. "You strengthen them in public estimation when you meet them; they only weaken you," his friend Henry Stoddard warned.

The press was out in force to document the potentially awkward interaction between Taft and Roosevelt, who had been seen together only twice since 1912, both times at funerals. Afterward, no one was sure exactly how their meeting went, although the gist seemed to be that someone, New York Governor Charles Whitman in one version, presented TR to Taft. After shaking hands and exchanging the obligatory "How do you dos," the former friends then separated and did not speak the rest of the night. Following Hughes's speech, interrupted by Roosevelt's enthusiastic "Good!" and "Right!" the audience began shouting, "Teddy, Teddy, Teddy." Moments later, TR launched into a blistering attack on Wilson's supporters, "people with shoulders that slope like a champagne bottle . . . people with timid hearts and quavering voices, who say that he has kept us out of war."

Four years earlier, no one could have envisioned Roosevelt making nice with Taft, let alone appearing at the same venue as reactionaries such as Boies Penrose, former Massachusetts senator Murray Crane, and Nicholas Murray Butler. "It is very galling to have to take any action which helps these scoundrels," TR admitted. But Roosevelt had made his decision months before. If necessary, he would compromise his principles to make sure Wilson was defeated.

Addams, away in Maine for much of the summer, had yet to make a final decision on the campaign. But she knew that most of her colleagues and friends who had recently met with Hughes had not been especially impressed. In any event, her health would not allow her to do much more this year than vote for her preferred candidate, a right granted to Illinois women since the last presidential election. In early October, she left Bar Harbor for Chicago to join the thousands of others who would need to renew their registration in time for the upcoming election. Local observers claimed that some "steerers" were combing bars and saloons in search of easily manipulated voters. This year, the steerers offered ten cents a head to register, a far cry from the one and two dollars tendered in other campaigns.

She was glad to be home, "home" being the residence of Mary, who would continue to keep close tabs on her. More than ever, Addams needed the support and comfort of her dearest friends and allies. Her views on the war had continued to drive an unpleasant wedge between herself and former supporters and acquaintances. "I think that there never was a time," she sadly told one associate, "when one so needed the companionship of like minded people." And the vicious hostility faced by some pacifists distressed her. "If we have war," one angry preparedness advocate wrote Amos Pinchot, "I think you pacifists deserve to have your wives and daughters raped and yourselves killed first."

Addams tried to resume a semblance of a normal life, putting in a few hours a week at Hull-House, although she was forbidden to live there that winter. A new Montessori school at the settlement house, serving twenty-three pupils "representing eight nationalities," pleased her, especially since she had met Maria Montessori during the Italian educator's American tour three years earlier. Her friend, the poet Vachel Lindsay, wanted Addams to join him at a showing of the latest "photoplay" everyone was talking about, *Intolerance*, D. W. Griffith's follow-up to *The Birth of a Nation*. But she was unlikely to be interested. *The Birth of a Nation* had probably soured her on Griffith, whom Lindsay admitted was a "southerner of the virulent type." And her own feelings about film, especially its impact on the young, remained ambivalent at best.

But the presidential campaign intrigued her. Ford had already come out for Wilson. He had hinted as much in early September when the press began to hound him. "I am a Republican," he admitted, "but we must admit that Wilson has somehow managed to wiggle the country out of war." A few weeks later, Ford formally endorsed the President. "I know Hughes," he announced. "'Teddy' and Wall Street are behind him." As for the man he once deemed small, Ford now believed Wilson had "grown a mile" in the past year.

The Democrats, Wilson included, were overjoyed to have Ford in the fold, even if the *Chicago Tribune* had recently denounced him as an "anarchist," who was both "ignorant" and "deluded," statements that would result in a $1 million libel suit (TR was happy to assist in the *Tribune*'s defense). They were especially hopeful that Ford might throw some of his millions into the campaign, especially since the Republicans supposedly had "$5 for every $1 that the Democrats have collected." (Ford eventually financed one ad under his own name, far less than what the Democrats hoped.) When Ford showed up at Shadow Lawn in early October to see the President, House took it upon himself to educate him about all of the good things Wilson had accomplished but without much success. Ford, he discovered once again, had no real knowledge of politics or international affairs and seemed fidgety and uncomfortable. Still, the Colonel admitted that Ford was a likable sort, an "idealist" with "many fine qualities . . . I believe if I saw more of him I might derive some pleasure from his company."

House and other Democratic leaders were reasonably confident. The preparedness legislation and the Adamson Act (railroad men had taken to calling him "Eight-Hour Wilson") had helped the President a great deal, but it was the peace issue that seemed to connect most with the voters. The phrase "He Kept Us Out of War" was now inescapable, in speeches, advertisements, campaign songs, even on movie screens. "They are making votes every day with the phrase," one Republican sadly admitted. Still, the President would need to make at least a few speeches outside of Shadow Lawn, even if he believed that the voters would instinctively make the correct choice. "To hear him talk you would think the man in the street understood the theory and philosophy of government as he does, and were actuated by the same motives," House complained in his diary.

The day after seeing Ford, Wilson left for Omaha for his first campaign speeches away from Shadow Lawn. On the various whistle-stops along the way, he increasingly sensed the importance of mingling among the people. At Lima, Ohio, one local called out that Wilson didn't need to give a speech; "we wanted to see our President." "I don't think much of my speechmaking," he retorted, "but I think it is better than I am to look at." "I heard a republican say today he was going to vote for you," someone yelled out at Wooster, Ohio. "He must be a good man," Wilson cracked. The banter continued at Valparaiso, Indiana, where a man asked the crowd, "Aren't we glad he hasn't got whiskers?" (the Hughes/Fairbanks team was the first bearded ticket in years, a definite negative among the younger set, who believed whiskers were hopelessly old-fashioned). "You are a clean shaven crowd yourself," Wilson remarked.

It was not just the average man and woman who were drawn to Wilson. A growing number of Addams's friends and disciples had decided to vote for him, including Louis Lochner, Harriet Thomas of the Woman's Peace Party, and Alice Hamilton, who just that week publicly endorsed the President in the pages of *The New Republic*. The rumors that Addams would be next were finally confirmed by announcements that both she and Lillian Wald would back Wilson—although Wald, like other women, could not vote in New York.

Addams's decision was not a surprise. Not only did Wilson seem to be truly invested in peace, but he had made a point to indulge her requests. A new administration, one possibly beholden to TR, would likely grant her no such access.

Almost immediately Wilson wrote to thank her. "I cannot deny myself the pleasure of telling you how proud I am and how much strengthened I feel that I should have your approval and support," he gushed. Two days later, their alliance was further solidified by Wilson's afternoon appearance in Chicago at the Auditorium before a gathering of "non-partisan women," Addams among them and prominently seated in a box not far from Edith. But her coming-out party for Wilson proved to be embarrassing for both. Outside, a group of National Woman's Party suffragists was silently protesting the President's appearance. Wilson had seen their banners ("Wilson Is Against Women" and "President Wilson! How Long Do You Advise Us to Wait?") when his automobile pulled up to the venue, but he had no idea what was about to occur after he went inside. His supporters, male and female, increasingly enraged by the suffragists, began yelling "Shame!" "Disgrace!" "Where's your baby?" and "Back to the kitchen!" Finally, they took matters into their own hands. "There was a swift surge outward," one reporter wrote, "and the thin line of women sashed in the colors of the party rumpled up like a rank of paper dolls." Canes and umbrellas crashed down on the banners and their unfortunate bearers alike, while Chicago police looked the other way. "Pitch 'em in the lake," someone shouted. "Scratch her eyes out."

The suffragists beat a hasty retreat to their headquarters, but not before all of their signs were destroyed. To Alice Paul, the "violent attack . . . shows the seriousness with which they take our campaign."

Paul was hopeful that Addams would have something to say about the episode. She soon discovered that Addams was not about to get involved. "It is strange that Miss Addams declines to be interviewed," Paul remarked. "She was in here yesterday . . . and said that she was surprised that no paper had asked her opinion on the attack." But Addams, like TR, had made her decision. Wilson may have been wrong on suffrage, but he was right on peace. For now, that was enough.

It was not enough for everyone. "I still believe in suffrage first," Elizabeth Thacher Kent, one of Alice Paul's followers, insisted. "We will never have an end of war until women have a responsible voice in public affairs. . . . I believe Miss Addams is mistaken in her attitude." Others wondered how she could stomach Wilson in view of the administration's treatment of African Americans. A Chicago African American, Mrs. K. J. Bills, was especially disappointed that Addams was assisting "a party whose policy is to disfranchise and oppress one-tenth of its citizens for no other reason than race hatred." The so-called reformer Wilson may have done something for the railroad men and child labor legislation, she argued, but he had ignored 10 million American citizens, most of whom remained socially and economically oppressed in the South.

The socialist Morris Hillquit thought Addams was too naïve, too willing to believe Wilson's good intentions, just as she had bought TR's progressive bill of goods four years earlier. But Addams, fundamentally a pragmatist, knew exactly what she was doing. Such a stance was bound to annoy some of the more doctrinal types in both the peace and suffrage movements. "You can never be quite sure what she is," the suffrage leader Anna Howard Shaw complained earlier that year. "We have had our great trouble the past few years because of her being on both sides of so many things in the suffrage that you could not depend upon her taking a stand and keeping it."

Wilson's enthusiastic reception in Chicago, which TR had won in 1912, did not bode well for the Hughes campaign. Roosevelt would be speaking in the Windy City in a week, the last of his five major addresses scheduled over ten days. The fears he had after the Chicago conventions in June that the people no longer loved him were soon put to rest by the thousands who turned up to see him in Louisville for his first speech, on October 18. "Louisville went wild over him," Edwin Lewis, covering the TR tour for the *New York Tribune*, wrote. But Lewis also detected a "touch of sadness . . . in his face," perhaps a realization that his time had passed and might never return again.

Like so many others, Lewis found himself charmed by Roosevelt. How many ex-presidents would have waited to eat before the boys from the press got lunch first? How many former presidents were so *funny?* "He tells us stories and gives us opinions which if put on the telegraph would convulse the country," Lewis wrote his mother. And TR's still formidable intellect was constantly on display, whether he was conversing fluently in German to a group of citizens in Washington, Missouri, or reciting his friend William Allen White's famous "What's the Matter with Kansas" editorial from memory.

But Wilson was never far from Roosevelt's mind. Every carefully crafted speech, every off-the-cuff remark at small-town whistle-stops was devoted to one goal: educating the people about the hypocrite in the White House. "Instead of carrying a Big Stick Mr. Wilson speaks harshly, but carries a powder puff," TR told one audience. A favorite device was to gesture to a small child in the crowd. "Just 103 babies of about her age were drowned on the *Lusitania*," he explained, "and all President Wilson did was to say that we are too proud to fight. That's all he did, my friends."

Roosevelt's Wilson fixation made him an easy target for hecklers, some of them Democratic plants, others spontaneous. Cries of "Hurray for Wilson" greeted him wherever he appeared.

"That's right; cheer for Woodrow," he snarled. "Then, with the spirit of cowardice in your heart, cheer also for the murder of the babies on the *Lusitania*! Cheer for the murdered men and women in Mexico. . . . That's the cheer for a man who is 'too proud to fight.'" Tiring of listening to TR's complaints about the President's preparedness policy, someone in a Denver crowd jeered, "What did you do?" TR did not hesitate. "I'll tell you. . . . I made the United States navy the finest in the world." The crowd erupted.

Everywhere the audiences loved him. One Midwestern woman could not restrain herself. "You're the best President we ever had!" she roared in the midst of one speech. But whether the enthusiasm for Roosevelt would translate into Hughes support remained uncertain. "We know you're all right," another lady yelled from the gallery. "What about Hughes?" "Mr. Hughes can be trusted to keep his word," TR replied. "He means what he says." Some were not convinced. More than once he heard the cry of "we're for you, Teddy, but not for Hughes," although Roosevelt did his best to steer them in the candidate's direction. "If you're for me you've got to be for Hughes this year."

Privately, TR had begun to grow increasingly ambivalent. Hughes, to use one of Roosevelt's favorite pejoratives, had pussyfooted his way through the campaign so far. Nor had he made much effort to ingratiate himself with the reporters covering him or heed any of their suggestions. A TR clone he decidedly was not. Hughes, Roosevelt sighed, "is the kind of a man who would in this campaign vote for Woodrow Wilson!"

If TR was not satisfied with Hughes the campaigner, more than a few

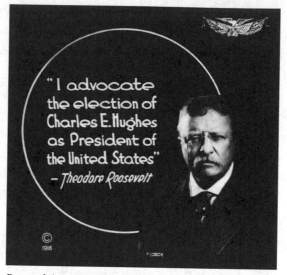

Roosevelt in campaign material for the Hughes campaign.
(Library of Congress: LC-DIG-ppmsca-36786)

Republicans had begun to worry about the content of Roosevelt's speeches. After his Denver address, top GOP honchos leaned on him to soft-pedal any preparedness or "hyphen" talk at the tour's final stop in Chicago, for fear it might antagonize women and foreign-born voters. For TR, this was the last straw. He threatened to pull out of the engagement altogether.

While on the train waiting for their response, he angrily vented to Donald Richberg, an old Progressive comrade. "There was nothing incoherent in his wrath!" Richberg later wrote. "With knife-edged words he explained what he thought of the campaign—its blunders, its hypocrisies, its consistent double-dealing." The Republican campaign managers soon caved in.

TR proceeded to Chicago, where he gave two uncensored speeches, one before a group of women, including Addams's close friend Louise de Koven Bowen. The response was better than everyone expected. "Results in Chicago proved that was the correct course," Roosevelt mused. "The honest course always is."

But Taft thought TR was more concerned about doing what was best for Roosevelt instead of what was best for Hughes. Every TR comment, Taft understood, was grist for the Wilson campaign, which had already started circulating complete copies of the explosive Battle Creek speech throughout the West and in German American communities. And as much as Roosevelt tried to deny that he was an "issue" in this election, the Democratic leaders wanted the voters to see Hughes and TR as a package deal, for better or worse. "Wilson and Peace with Honor? Or Hughes with Roosevelt and War?" one Democratic ad blared. "Roosevelt says that following the sinking of the *Lusitania* he would have foregone diplomacy and seized every ship in our ports flying the German Flag. That would have meant war!" Another fearfully warned of a Hughes administration with Roosevelt as secretary of state. "How many men do you suppose there would be to march? How many would have two legs to march with?"

Wilson himself had kept to his promise never to acknowledge Roosevelt directly in public. "Why doesn't he name me?" TR growled. "Is he too timid?" But the President made his feelings crystal clear with barbed references to the Republicans' sole "articulate voice, a very articulate voice" that "professes opinions and purposes at which the rest in private shiver and demur." This "vocal element," Wilson explained, "prefer a peace that is produced by the methods of those who defy, of those who brag, of those who threaten." His audiences did not miss a beat. "Give it to Teddy!" they roared. "Soak 'im good."

In speech after speech, the President presented himself in stark contrast to Roosevelt's views on the war and America's international responsibilities. He did not feel the need to defend his own record. "All that I have tried to do was to keep my ears open and do what I thought you wanted me to do," Wilson explained. Nor would he blame either side for the current conflict or hazard even a casual guess as to its causes. "Have you ever heard what started the present war?" he asked a Cincinnati audience. "If you have, I wish you would publish it, because nobody else has. So far as I can gather, nothing in particular started it, but everything in general." But the United States could no longer stand aloof, "confined and provincial," as she had once been. Now, "she belongs to the world, and must act as part of the world." Going to war might be in America's future someday, he admitted, but only "when we can find something as big as American ideals to fight for." For now, the nation would not lose its head "when all the rest of the world seemed to have lost its poise." America would stay the course it had taken for two years, "saving ourselves for something greater that is to come," a postwar league of nations in which the United States would play a significant role.

Roosevelt had long believed that America should stay out of any new international organizations until it had shown she could keep existing obligations. Back in England, Grey was also dubious. Could a country whose citizens were now hysterically rallying behind a president who "kept us out of war" be expected to do very much in any future league of nations? Still, the British foreign secretary understood that America must participate. "Unless the United States is a member . . . and a member that could be depended upon to intervene," he wrote that fall, "the peace of the world would be no more secure in [the] future than it was in 1914."

As October progressed, Hughes continued to avoid any detailed discussion of America's role and responsibility in the Great War. But during a speech in Louisville, a Democratic heckler named Gus Bizot put the candidate on the spot. "Justice Hughes, just a moment, please. Permit a respectful interruption. What would you have done . . . when the *Lusitania* was sunk?" Cries of "Put him out" and "Go on, you boob" were heard, but Hughes ignored them while trying to shush an angry audience.

"Sir, I would have had the State Department, at the very beginning of the Administration, so equipped as to command the respect of the world," Hughes began. The audience began to cheer, Hughes again requesting quiet. "Next, I would have so conducted affairs in Mexico as to show that our words meant peace and good will, to the protection at all events of the lives and property of American citizens." His listeners liked that even more. "And next . . . when I said 'strict accountability' every nation would have known that that was meant; and, further, when notice was published with respect to the action threatened, I would have made it known in terms unequivocal and unmistakable that we should not tolerate a continuance of friendly relations through the ordinary diplomatic channels if that action were taken; and the *Lusitania*, sir, would never have been sunk."

The crowd went berserk. For the first time in two months of campaigning, the "old Hughes," the one who had impressed so many as governor, seemed to be making an appearance. Four days later in Omaha, he connected again with a jab at Colonel House. "It might be said that the present Administration has been in a large measure an administration of *unofficial spokesmen of mysterious influence*," Hughes remarked, "and I may say in entire good humor that I desire government through two *houses* and not three." The next day in Sioux City, the candidate silenced a group of hecklers trying to embarrass him about his labor views by citing the union support he had enjoyed in New York.

The "bearded iceberg" was showing signs of life. Whether it was too late to undo the common belief that Hughes was nothing but a "fault-finder" unwilling to confront major issues such as the Great War was unclear. Up to this point, the voters had seen only fleeting flashes of the man who had courageously investigated the insurance companies and had been willing to put principle over party without concern for his political future. "If the Republican party can't stand the doing of the right thing," Hughes had once told John Palmer Gavit, "so much the worse for the Republican party." But now, Gavit observed, Hughes appeared to be perceived, fairly or unfairly, as a political hack, nothing more than an establishment "candidate of the outs who desire to get in."

That the Republicans were desperate to return to power was obvious. They reminded voters that the President, the so-called friend of the workingman, had once claimed that "labor unions drag the highest man to the level of the lowest" and had even previously claimed to be a "fierce partisan of the open shop." They also dug into Wilson's past writings for material, especially *A History of the American People*, which referred to immigrants as "the coarse crew that came crowding in every year," including "men of the lowest class from the south of Italy and men of meaner sort out of Hungary and Poland, men out of the ranks where there was neither skill nor energy nor any initiative of quick intelligence." And they accused the President of planning to weaken the second *Lusitania* note by adding a Bryan-proposed "postscript" offering the prospect of arbitration, eliminated only when other cabinet members threatened to resign. Wilson soon issued a furious denial, although he did not disclose that he had briefly considered at the time of the first *Lusitania* note Bryan's suggestion of a supplementary statement that would dangle the prospect of a "cooling-off" treaty to Germany.

The Republicans believed they had one final ace up their sleeve: Wilson's relationship with Mary Hulbert. As early as June, rumors of the President's dalliances ("fiendish lies," he called them) were being circulated, so much so that Democratic leaders realized they would be raised again more seriously during the campaign (some believed the suffragists were involved). The candidates' personal lives had always been fair game; back in 1884, the Republicans had taunted Grover Cleveland, who had fathered a child out of wedlock, with chants of "Ma, ma, where's my Pa?" This time, there was wild talk that Hulbert had filed a breach-of-promise suit, supposedly defused by a Democratic lawyer named Samuel Untermyer, who had been rewarded by the appointment of a fellow Jew, Louis Brandeis, to the Supreme Court. GOP operatives even tracked down Hulbert and tried to buy her letters, but the cash-strapped divorcée remained loyal to her old friend and his new bride, even though she would grow to despise Edith. To TR, "petty gossip" of this sort was "a waste of time," especially since the people would instinctively jump to the President's defense. Besides, Roosevelt doubted it would be effective. "You can't cast a man as Romeo who looks and acts so much like the apothecary's clerk," he remarked.

The increasing viciousness of the campaign disgusted the Democrats. "Misquotations and misrepresentations—yea, lies—have been used by the President's opponents," Franklin Roosevelt told a Providence audience. "I say lies because that is a good 'Roosevelt' word to use." Wilson was especially disappointed with Hughes, a man he had once respected. "I have such an utter contempt for Mr. Hughes now," the President told a newspaperman on the last day of October. "He has sunk so low." For the good of the country, Hughes had to be defeated. "The election of Mr. Hughes with the motley crowd that is behind him would be a national calamity," Wilson insisted.

In the final week of the campaign, both sides publicly professed their confidence. But veteran pundits knew there would be no landslide, even if Wilson would start with 126 electoral votes from the former Confederate states (plus another 10 from Oklahoma), all of which religiously voted Democrat and disfranchised their black residents. An extremely close race seemed likely unless something dramatic—say, an armistice in Europe—occurred. Colonel House had already come up with a plan, endorsed by Wilson, to allow for a quick transition of power in the event of a Hughes victory. Wilson would request the resignations of Vice President Marshall and Secretary of State Lansing, appoint Hughes as Lansing's replacement, and then resign himself to allow Hughes to succeed him as president immediately instead of waiting until March.

Roosevelt was not feeling optimistic. Hughes had made some gains of late, but TR still believed he had "not made Wilson fight. As matters are, the people do not know where Hughes does stand—they look upon him as another Wilson when they do not look upon him as a man without a policy." Still, Roosevelt agreed to do a final round of speeches over a three-day period in Ohio, Connecticut, and locally in Manhattan. These addresses, he knew, would be his last chance to get his message across to the American people, not just to his listeners but to the millions who would read the accounts the next day.

His speech at Cooper Union, where Lincoln had delivered a famous address fifty-six years earlier and Wilson had appeared earlier in the week, drew the most attention. Once again, TR tried to draw parallels between the crisis of the 1860s and the present. "The times have needed a Washington or a Lincoln," he explained ("A Roosevelt," someone shouted). "Unfortunately we have been granted only another Buchanan." As usual, Roosevelt refused to concede that he had been unfair to Wilson. Everything he had said about the President was "absolutely accurate and truthful. . . . I spoke of him at all only because I have felt that in this great world crisis he has played a more evil part than Buchanan and Pierce ever played in the years that led up and saw the opening of the civil war."

His stance now sufficiently rationalized, TR then proceeded to unleash one of his most furious attacks, the culmination of four years of his growing hatred of Wilson. The President, he explained, had "adroitly and cleverly" bamboozled the American people with a "shadow dance of words . . . a spangled shroud of rhetoric. He has kept the eyes of the people dazzled so that they know not what is real and what is false, so that they turn bewildered, unable to discern the difference between the glitter that veneers evil and the stark realities of courage and honesty, of truth and strength." Worst of all, Wilson was the quintessential waffler, who one minute proclaimed a "neutrality that would make Pontius Pilate quiver with envy," and the next insisted that "never again must we be neutral!"

The speech built to a final dramatic conclusion, alluding to Wilson's current residence at Shadow Lawn. Roosevelt, one reporter noted, "spoke slowly . . . pausing solemnly between phrases until he had reached the end." "There should be shadows enough at Shadow Lawn—The shadows of men, women and children who have risen from the ooze of the ocean bottom and from graves in foreign lands. The shadows of the helpless whom Mr. Wilson did not dare protect lest he might have to face danger; the shadows of babies gasping pitifully as they sank under the waves. . . . Those are the shadows proper for Shadow Lawn; the shadows of deeds that were never done; the shadows of lofty words that were followed by no action; *the shadows of the tortured dead.*" After an obligatory call to vote for Hughes, the speech was over a few minutes later, the frenzied audience frantically trying to get to TR as he exited the venue.

Roosevelt was delighted with the reaction to what he modestly called "rather a good speech." His work on the Hughes campaign was over, beyond an address in Bridgeport the following day and an election eve talk at the Oyster Bay opera house. Except for toning down his content, no one could say that he had not done everything asked of him.

Addams was not in a position to do as much as TR in the final week. Still, the Wilson campaign found creative ways to use her name and influence. A press release with a photo of Addams, "America's foremost citizen," reminded voters that she was supporting the President, "a matter of intense interest to every righteous American." Another ad listed her, along with Henry Ford, Thomas Edison, John Dewey, Luther Burbank, and others, as some of the "biggest thinkers in America" backing Wilson. And Addams herself managed to contribute an article appearing in dozens of newspapers in the last days of the campaign. She had joined the Progressive party in 1912 because she and others believed that neither the Democrats nor Republicans possessed the will to push through federal legislation necessary to address "abuses inevitably developed by an uncontrolled industrialism." But she was now an enthusiastic Wilson convert, thanks to his impressive slate of domestic and international successes. (Wilson had recently proclaimed: "this country is progressive . . . I am a progressive.") That her endorsement meant a great deal was trumpeted in a Democratic ad in a small-town Illinois newspaper telling of how Addams's stance had convinced an "intelligent woman" to vote for Wilson: "the women know that Jane Addams could not be fooled."

Wilson had begun to show the strain of the campaign in its last days. After he arrived in New York on November 2 for his last major speech, he immediately launched into an angry diatribe about the city and its "moneyed class" to House. He was especially furious about the giant full-page Hughes ads running in all the local newspapers, even those friendly to the Democrats. New York, he told him, was "rotten to the core" and should be "wiped off the map." His mood did not improve after a disastrous appearance at Madison Square Garden, so crammed with supporters that leading Democrats and family members could not get inside or had to resort to the fire escape like the Wilsons. After the giant crowd of sixteen thousand cheered the President for nearly thirty minutes, thousands soon discovered they could not hear a word of his address and began to leave in the middle of his speech. "Apparently New York had come to see Mr. Wilson, not to hear him," one local reporter wrote. "Mr. Wilson was visibly annoyed."

He could console himself in the heartfelt adulation and affectionate greetings ("We're with you, Woody!") he received every time he showed his face that day. But House sensed Wilson's irritability had something to do with the pending election. "The President reminds me of a boy whose mother tells him he has ridden long enough on his hobby-horse, and that he must let little Charlie have a turn," the Colonel mused. "If left to the boy it would never be Charlie's turn. His attitude is not unlike that of T.R. who has never forgiven the electorate for not continuing him indefinitely in the White House."

Tuesday, November 7. The entire nation anxiously awaited the results of a potentially history-changing election, one that might dramatically shift not only America's current European policy but the Republican party's direction for years to come. Two days earlier, the Republican-leaning *New York Herald* published the results of its national straw poll of 250,000 voters throughout the nation; it showed Wilson leading in the electoral college. House had assured the President that the Democrats' "infinitely more accurate" polls also forecast his victory. "The fight is won," the Colonel told him. As a last-minute push, 100,000 Wilson college men were each deputized to call five of their friends to remind them to vote for the President.

At Shadow Lawn, Wilson would be kept up-to-date on the voting by phone through Tumulty, who would receive detailed reports at the Asbury Park offices. For much of the rest of the country, newspaper extras and bulletins at the newspaper offices themselves would provide the latest information. In Chicago, results would be available in some movie theaters, ballparks, and hotel lobbies or flashed on special screens, some of which were using the "teleautograph stereopticon . . . a huge shadow pen reproducing on the screen each figure or letter as it is written by the operator." For the final result, locals were told to listen for the sound of explosions and then "look toward the Hearst Building" for white fireworks (Wilson) or red (Hughes). In New York, a "steady horizontal beam circling the horizon" from the Herald Tower would mean a Wilson victory; a "zig-zag" beam his defeat (within eight years, the growing popularity of radio would render such colorful services needless).

Early Tuesday morning, Wilson left for Princeton to vote. Hughes had already marked his ballot at 7:00 a.m. at a laundry on Eighth Avenue in New York City, the thirteenth person to cast his vote there that day, which he thought might be a good omen. Two hours later, Wilson and Edith arrived at their polling station, an old firehouse on Chambers Street where students greeted him with the old "Princeton yell" and unsuccessfully tried to coax a speech out of him. After voting, he headed back to Shadow Lawn for lunch and then golf with the First Lady. The rest of the day would be spent with family.

The polls opened at six in the morning in Chicago, where Addams would cast her first-ever presidential vote. Illinois women, still unable to vote for judges or the two amendments up for consideration, were given two ballots to complete instead of the three men received. They were also warned in advance of "careless scratching" that might disqualify their ballot, with some suggesting that a single "x" for the straight ticket was the safest course. Reporters were on the scene to get a quote from Addams after she exited the polling place. "It was indeed a thrilling and impressive experience to be voting for President," she told them. "I believe that every voting woman in Chicago is feeling moved and thrilled by the experience, which is one of deep significance." That women could still not vote in New York remained enormously frustrating to Lella Secor, especially when she watched "Negroes and half drunk foreigners going into the polls" that day.

Around 11:45, Roosevelt showed up at the Oyster Bay firehouse to cast his vote, accompanied by his son Archie. Curious onlookers watched TR's chauffeur recklessly drive over the sidewalk and smash a few planks in the process. "Stop! Don't break down the polling place!" Roosevelt roared. "It would be terrible if I had to pass this day in jail." Hughes, he believed, was going to win. But he was also sure it was going to be "so close that it will be several days or a week before the result will be positively known." And Hughes would have been a lock, TR complained to his son Quentin that day, if he had only consistently run the kind of campaign Roosevelt wanted.

In the early evening, the first returns began to be recorded. Hughes was sweeping the East, including New York's 45 electoral votes. A devastated Tumulty tried to remain calm, insisting that Wilson could still win even without New York, New England, Indiana, Illinois, and New Jersey. But the news did not improve. By 7:30, two New York papers, the *Herald* and the *Tribune*, had already called the election for Hughes. And when the *World* and the *Times*, both hard-core Wilson supporters, followed suit an hour later, Tumulty knew his boss's odds did not look good. He briefed the President on the current situation, although Tumulty was certain it was far too early to concede to Hughes, who also remained cautious. "We will wait," Hughes told his supporters. "They might take it back."

The Republicans were jubilant. Owen Wister dashed off a few lines to Roosevelt, mocking Wilson: "What mode of polished cant will you now choose / To tell us all how gracefully you lose." Around 9:45 p.m., reporters showed up at Oyster Bay, where TR issued a statement. Judging by the returns he had received from Republican headquarters, Hughes had won. "I wish to express my profound gratitude as an American proud of his country that the American people have repudiated the man who coined the phrase about this country, that is 'too proud to fight,' and whose

administration had done so much to relax the fibre of the American conscience and to dull the sense of honorable obligations in the American
people."

Some shocked Democrats already believed they were defeated. Franklin
Roosevelt, in New York getting the returns at the Biltmore, began to con-
sider what his next step would be, perhaps a return to the law. Others
worked on sympathy letters and wires to Wilson. House and Attorney
General Thomas Gregory went to the Bar Association to look into how
Wilson's resignation might be handled and when the Senate could confirm
Hughes as secretary of state.

House was not entirely convinced that Wilson had lost. Many western
states had not been heard from yet. By midnight, encouraging results had
begun to trickle in. Wilson was doing well in Nebraska, Utah, and California.
"We're not dead yet," an elated Tumulty announced. He had seen this before
in other close elections, where newspapers had prematurely called a winner.
A few minutes later, Wilson went to bed at Dr. Grayson's insistence, instructing aides to awaken him only if something "definite" occurred.

By Wednesday morning, it was clear that the pendulum had begun to
swing toward Wilson. The 28 electoral votes of Nebraska, Kansas, Washington, and Nevada were likely his, and California was also leaning Wilson's
way. *The New York Times* not only retracted its earlier Hughes prediction
but as of 5:30 a.m. had Wilson ahead in the electoral college, 264–251. The
President, who had calmly accepted whatever news was provided to him
since the voting began, continued to remain on an even keel.

"How's it going, Joe?" he asked Tumulty.

"Gov, it's okay," Tumulty answered.

"That's fine, Joe."

He was content to wait for more results before heading out for an automobile ride with Edith. "Bully for you Wilson, four years more," someone
shouted from the road. Later he went golfing with Grayson, who was
shocked that a relaxed Wilson not only beat him but "played the best game
I ever saw him play."

The entire nation, many of whom had gone to bed the night before
convinced Hughes had won, was transfixed. No one had seen anything like
this since the Blaine–Cleveland contest of 1884, when the outcome had

been in doubt for several days. Calls flooded every newspaper in the country for up-to-date information, the *Washington Times* alone logging more than six calls a minute. "He kept us out of *sleep*," cracked one telegraph operator, punning on the DNC's popular campaign slogan. Everyone wanted to hear the latest on the close races in Minnesota, New Mexico, North Dakota, and especially California, whose vote count was far from completed. By the afternoon, it was increasingly clear that Wilson had shifted from underdog to favorite ("Wilson Has a Winnin' Way" they gleefully sang at the Democratic headquarters). Later editions of the *Times* and the *World* now declared Wilson the winner, and House was confident enough to do the same. "I make this statement on the basis of that sixth sense which any man who has dabbled in politics for forty years is bound to develop," he humbly observed.

But it was not until late Thursday evening that it became certain that Wilson was going to win California by a very slim margin (the final plurality was fewer than 4000 votes out of nearly 1 million cast) and the election. Wilson and Edith were on the *Mayflower* on their way to Rhinecliff, New York, to catch a train to Williamstown, Massachusetts, for the baptism of his granddaughter Eleanor Axson Sayre when a telegram arrived from Tumulty, who had been waiting for Associated Press confirmation of the California result (the Republicans and Hughes would not officially concede until November 22). The final tabulation gave Wilson 277 electoral votes to 254 for Hughes and a plurality in the popular vote of 594,000. Had just 1887 voters changed their Wilson votes to Hughes in California, a state that everyone believed Hughes had blown by his disastrous August appearance, Wilson would have lost the election (a pronounced shift of California's socialist voters to Wilson also helped). In the weeks ahead, some politicians on each side proposed eliminating the electoral college, which Taft warned might raise the controversial "question of the Southern ballot."

Wilson, though dreading the possibility of a second term with "problems . . . even more difficult" than the first, could not help but feel vindicated. The President, the Roosevelt-supporting *New York Tribune* grudgingly admitted, was undoubtedly the "strongest man politically in the nation . . . a man to be reckoned with because of his hold upon popular imagination and public approval." For TR, forced to endure a parade of

Democrats noisily marching around Oyster Bay after Wilson's reelection was assured, the defeat was not entirely unexpected, though it did nothing to lessen his hatred for the President. The English journalist Sydney Brooks told House about visiting Roosevelt a few weeks later and listening to him excitedly rant and rave about a number of topics, including Wilson's so-called cowardice. "The fact that Wilson shrinks from flinging a hundred million people into war is the only excuse Roosevelt has for such an accusation," House complained. "He probably would feel differently himself if he were President."

House, like a number of other political pundits, already believed Roosevelt would be nominated by the Republicans in four years and Wilson would have to run against him for an unprecedented third term. But TR would say nothing about his future. "No amount of calls or talk can induce me to speak of the 1920 nomination," he announced. "I do not discuss pipe dreams."

Addams was delighted by the results of the election, suffrage defeats in South Dakota and West Virginia notwithstanding. She was particularly pleased that Montana had just elected the country's first congresswoman, a thirty-six-year-old Republican named Jeannette Rankin, whose background interest in social work, suffrage, and peace mirrored her own. The media soon reassured the public that Miss Rankin was not one of the dreaded short-haired "lady politicians" Wilson so disdained and was said to be a master at the womanly arts of bread baking and sewing.

For Addams, the question now was whether Wilson was going to justify her support, especially since she believed he had received "an unequivocal mandate from the people 'to keep us out of war'" (there were even rumors that the President had recently informed his cabinet that he was "bound to nothing and nobody, except the pacifist West"). As much as she admired Wilson, she had nagging misgivings about his willingness to "carry out the will of the people" and wondered whether he actually preferred to sagely guide his befuddled constituents in the direction where "in his judgment their best interest lay." Still, she would not sanction any attempt by the Woman's Peace Party to pressure the President about peace at the moment, even though some members were frustrated that the organization was not doing nearly enough. She hoped he would finally do the right thing, whether it be mediation, a conference of neutrals, or some other way to halt the bloodbath.

The nearly five-month struggle at the Somme was winding down with a minimal Allied gain of about six miles. Like the Verdun offensive earlier in the year, the casualties were astronomical, both sides suffering losses of at least a half-million men. James Norman Hall, immersed in flight school at Buc in southwest France and trying to master the Bleriot monoplane, had no reason to fear that the war would end before his planned return to combat in the late spring. For now, his greater concern was some of his American colleagues who didn't take their training seriously, despite the death of two American pilots in France that fall. "They are heavy drinkers," he wrote a friend, "and every time they go to Paris on permission they get uproariously drunk, get into trouble with the authorities at the school and get the rest of us into hot water."

During one of Hall's own trips to Paris that winter, he stopped at Brentano's bookstore, where he discovered a volume chronicling the mutiny on the British ship *Bounty* in 1789. Intrigued, he purchased the book to read when he had a spare moment back at flight school.

B ack in America, the realities of the Great War continued to grow closer. One Saturday afternoon in October, yet another German submarine had showed up on the East Coast, this time in Newport. Unlike the *Deutschland*, the *U-53* was a war vessel armed with torpedoes. No one was quite sure why it had come, although local curiosity seekers were allowed to go on board during the three hours it remained in port, some handing out American coins as souvenirs to the crew. Meanwhile, the captain, Hans Rose, visited with naval officials and dropped off mail for the German embassy.

The next morning, the *U-53*'s mission became more obvious. After positioning herself beyond the three-mile territorial limit of American waters, the sub began sinking Allied merchant vessels off the island of Nantucket. Wireless distress signals frantically warned other Allied ships to change course or make for the safety of American waters. But the *Stephano*, a Red

Cross passenger liner, heading to New York from Canada, was not fast enough. Crew and passengers, some of them Americans, were forced to abandon ship, which was torpedoed and sank a few hours later. No one was harmed, except the ship's cat, thanks to American destroyers on hand to scoop up the *Stephano*'s survivors and those of the five unfortunate merchant ships (three British, one Dutch, and one Norwegian) sunk.

To one passenger, there was "something ludicrous in the matter of fact way the German commander went about his business," while U.S. destroyers did nothing to stop him. The furious Allies naturally felt the same. But America was neutral and the Germans had played by the new "rules," providing warning in each case and carefully following the *Sussex* pledge (although the *Stephano* attack seemed to fall in a gray area). And beyond complaints of lost trunks and money, no one had any reason to object to the *U-53*'s behavior. "Except for destroying our vessels the Germans certainly were good to us," one crew member of the *West Point* told reporters. "They hitched our boats to the submarine and towed us."

Still, Roosevelt was not satisfied. "Putting . . . non-combatants in open rowboats in the October seas is no way to guarantee their safety," he insisted.

The greater concern was the sobering reality that if one German submarine could do so much damage, what was to stop an angry kaiser from sending a flotilla across the Atlantic to prey upon American shipping someday? "The *U-53* has shown us how accessible our shores are to Europe, the pacifists to the contrary notwithstanding," Rear Admiral Bradley Fiske warned. TR, among others, believed the whole incident grimly illustrated once again that the war was getting closer and closer "until it stares at us from just beyond our three-mile limit, and we face it without policy, plan, purpose, or preparation."

Roosevelt as usual was prone to hyperbole. Wilson's preparedness program had put the country on a better footing than a year ago. But since it would take months if not years to see substantial improvement, peace, if it could be had, remained the best immediate solution to the agonizing problem the President had kept at bay for two years: the constant threat of being sucked into the death struggle in Europe.

The signs from the Allies were not encouraging. In late September,

British War Minister Lloyd George, whom Wilson later compared to TR as a man who "loves to play to the public," gave a controversial interview to an American reporter. The "British empire has invested thousands of its best lives to purchase further immunity for civilization; this investment is too great to be thrown away" prematurely, George explained, especially by the actions of well-meaning neutrals. And since Germany wanted a "finish fight . . . we intend to see that Germany has her way. The fight must be to the finish—to a knockout." Grey, among others in the British cabinet, was not at all pleased that George had now done all he could to scare off Wilson permanently. The president, Grey had long believed, was an option that should be retained as long as possible.

The Germans continued to be more receptive. Throughout the presidential campaign, they had explored various ways to get Wilson to initiate a peace move of some kind, after which he would ideally make himself scarce while the belligerents hashed things out. Or, if the Allies refused to meet, then Germany would have the upper hand from a global public relations standpoint and abundant rationale to resume unrestricted submarine warfare. Before Ambassador Gerard left Berlin for a visit back home in September, Chancellor Bethmann and Foreign Minister Jagow let him know that Germany would favor some sort of American peace initiative to head off the relentless demands of the annexationists and militarists who wanted the *Sussex* pledge scrapped. Even the kaiser took it upon himself to write a memo in English for Gerard to give to Wilson, prodding the President to act while warning that Germany might have to return to unrestricted submarine warfare otherwise. The memo, which an alarmed Bethmann sensibly managed to keep out of Gerard's hands before sailing, eventually made its way to Bernstorff in Washington, who turned it over to House in late October. "Clearly a threat," House wrote to Wilson, "their idea being to force you before [the] election to act, knowing if you are defeated nothing can be done by anyone for many months to come."

Wilson never had any intention of doing a thing before the election. Even then, he would have to weigh his options carefully. Lloyd George's statement was discouraging, but hardly enough to stop him. A bigger problem was the current fractious state of Anglo-American relations, thanks to the ongoing blacklist and the mail situation, neither likely to be solved anytime soon or ever. It did not help that Walter Hines Page's Anglophilia seemed to worsen every hour the war continued. The British, the ambassador now believed, were "the only invincible people in the world . . . the best race yet mixed & developed on this globe" (not included in his thoughtful analysis were the Irish, "a sort of yellow dog," or the Welsh with their unfortunate "tendency to lying"). He dreamed of a future British-American alliance, so much so that State Department officials suspected that Page's typical presentation of an American protest went something like this: "Here is another damn fool request from our Government which you need not pay any attention to."

Page's own visit home in August had not gone well. He had been brought back to the United States for a much needed "bath in American opinion," but he viewed his visit very differently, as a chance to persuade Washington to see things the Allies' way. After two lunches with Wilson and others, he recognized that no one in the administration was interested in hearing his highly colored view of the war. And the more resistance he encountered, the more disillusioned he became. Lansing he saw as an unfeeling "manikin," a "law-book-precedent man" who "writes big-sounding Notes to England and publishes them!" (Little did he realize that the secretary of state was privately as much on the Allies' side as he was.) And Wilson, a man he had once venerated, seemed disturbingly isolated, except for Colonel House. "He is surrounded by the feminine Boneses and Smiths [his cousins]," Page scoffed. "The men about him (and he sees them only 'on business') are nearly all very very small fry, or worse, the narrowest twopenny lot I've ever run across. He has no real companions. Nobody talks to him freely and frankly."

Page was determined not to leave until Wilson consented to a one-on-one conversation. Even House thought the President should see the ambassador for "his point of view, contrary to his own though it may be." In late September, Wilson finally granted Page an audience at Shadow Lawn. Almost immediately, the President made it plain to Page that he did not see the war as purely a matter of good and evil. Back in 1914, Wilson said he had been pro-Allies, "heartily in sympathy . . . as any man could be," but his feelings had shifted, thanks to Britain's "doing anything she wished, regardless of rights of others." As for the war itself, Wilson told the ambassador it was "a result of many causes. . . . He spoke of England's having the earth, of Germany's wanting it. Of course the German system is directly opposed to everything American. But this didn't seem to me to carry any very great moral reprehensibility."

A disheartened Page sailed back to England a few weeks later, realizing Wilson would never see things his way. The ambassador offered his resignation after the election, which the President ignored for months, until Lansing finally communicated Wilson's desire for him to remain. A frustrated Roosevelt probably would have ditched Page months earlier. But the President could not face either the likely political blowback or the discomfort of splitting with a onetime close friend. Instead, a virtually useless ambassador (from Wilson's standpoint) remained in London. The two men never saw each other again.

If Wilson's Anglophilic tendencies had long worn off by this point (he even told House that "if the Allies wanted war with us we would not shrink from it"), the British were just as disenchanted with the man who appeared to present himself as the "sane Saviour" in a world gone mad. Many did not greet his reelection enthusiastically. "It is safe to say that had Roosevelt secured the nomination, British opinion would have been dangerously un-neutral in regard to the Presidential election," Sir Horace Plunkett wrote House. Grey, despite his many talks with the Colonel since the war began, also wished that Wilson had been more like Roosevelt in his stand toward the war. "We think Wilson might have taken advantage of such things as the 'Lusitania' incident to make his country play a great part," Sir Edward observed. "But, if it be true that the country really wanted at all costs to keep out of war, we admit that he has great difficulties."

America, Grey noted, was "not popular here right now." That the Yanks were getting rich off the war was a major annoyance. That the Allies were now totally dependent on America's financial help and supplies was an even greater source of irritation. Wilson had alluded to the issue during the campaign. "We have become, not the debtors, but the creditors of the world," he told one audience. "We can determine to a large extent who is to be financed and who is not to be financed." The British understood this unfortunate truth. "We have to pay $10,000,000 every business day in the United States . . . a prodigious amount to find every six days," Reginald McKenna, the Chancellor of the Exchequer, announced in October. A few days later, he privately admitted that "if things go on as at present . . . by next June or earlier the President . . . will be in a position, if he wishes, to dictate his own terms to us."

Wilson remained unwilling to aggressively wield that fearful club, no matter how effective it might be in forcing the Allies to accept any peace move (although he later supported the Federal Reserve's November decision to discourage banks from making unsecured loans—without collateral—to the Allies). Neither he nor most of the American people had the stomach for any kind of "trade war" with the Allies, not with the country's current booming prosperity at stake. And the question remained whether it was in the national interest to do anything potentially harmful to the Allied cause. Lansing and House were certain it was not. The Allies, House admitted, "are irritating almost beyond endurance," but "if we are to have war, let it be with Germany. . . . The situation demands, for our own protection that we hold with the Allies as long as we can possibly do so with dignity."

As long as Germany maintained its U-boat promises, the chances of war remained remote. The kaiser was opposed to restarting the unrestricted submarine campaign, especially since the U-boats had shown they could still be very effective following the cruiser rules. Admiral Müller agreed. "I prefer a restricted U-boat warfare sinking 400,000 tons of shipping per month to unrestricted warfare with sinkings of 600,000 tons and the risk of war with America," he observed. But the pressure to use the submarine to its full capabilities had grown more intense that fall. Serious food shortages, thanks to the ongoing British blockade and a weak harvest, were now a reality for German civilians, many of whom would subsist on turnips during the upcoming winter. That reality, along with ongoing claims from naval officials such as Admiral Holtzendorff that the war could be won now if only the burdensome submarine restrictions were lifted, would become increasingly difficult for both Bethmann and the kaiser to resist.

The American embassy in Berlin warned Wilson of what might be coming. Ambassador Gerard even touched off a small panic during his visit home in October by indiscreetly informing a journalist that Germany was about to resume unrestricted submarine warfare. Once again, Wilson was not eager to see one of his presumably most important ambassadors, but he eventually consented to a meeting at Shadow Lawn before the election. Edith was also present, surprising Gerard with her "deep knowledge of foreign affairs." A few days later, Gerard had a more candid conversation with TR's friend Leonard Wood. "Gerard states that the Germans hate us and will come after us at the first opportunity," General Wood wrote in his diary. "He says U-boat work will commence in a ruthless fashion as soon as the days are a bit longer." Like Page, Gerard was not at all happy with the administration. "They pay no attention to me," he complained.

By the time Gerard finished his lunch with Wood, newsboys were on the streets booming a disturbing development that the administration could not ignore. The *Marina*, an armed British steamer carrying horses from the United States, had not only been sunk off the coast of Ireland, apparently without warning, but six American crew members drowned. A full report was not yet available, but Wilson had already made up his mind that even if Germany had broken its promises, it still would not justify war. "I do not believe the American people would wish to go to war no matter how many Americans were lost at sea," he told House. Besides, he thought the *Sussex* pledge covered only passenger liners, a misconception a horrified House did his best to correct.

Had Addams and the millions of others who would vote for Wilson a few days later heard the conversation, they would have been ecstatic. The man who "*kept* them out of war" was planning to "*keep*" them there, regardless of pressure. Wilson was not nearly as confident, especially after an armed passenger liner, the *Arabia*, was sunk a few days later (on election day), also without warning and with an American on board (a wiretap captured a German embassy official admitting "That is against all the rules, you know"). Unless Germany came up with a suitable explanation, a diplomatic split would follow, if the President were to be consistent with his demands a month earlier. And if a split occurred, war would likely result, whether he wanted it or not.

For Wilson, there was no longer any doubt in his mind. At long last, the time had come to move for peace.

For the moment, a disheartened TR continued to remain publicly silent about Wilson and the election. "I can only reply to your request," he told reporters, "by quoting the remark of the old New Bedford whaling captain to his mate. . . . 'All I want out of you is silence, and damn little of that.'" There were other matters to keep Roosevelt busy: plans for a February trip to the Polynesian islands with his wife, Edith, and the strange but lucrative gig for *Ladies' Home Journal* requiring him to produce twelve inexplicably anonymous (perhaps not to violate his exclusivity agreement with the *Metropolitan*) 3000-word articles on topics such as "Man and the Church" and "Man's Relations in Industry." The November issue contained TR's uncredited musings about the relations between men and women. Women, he explained, were "entitled to a full equality in rights with man," provided they fulfilled their "full duty to the commonwealth and to the race." American husbands, meanwhile, should not be overly fixated on money at the expense of family life, nor should they be "guilty of . . . sex wickedness. I do not believe that over-much talk about sex evil is healthful. There should be as little as possible; but it should be absolutely *truthful*."

The war was never far from Roosevelt's thoughts. The French and British both wanted him to come over to review troops after the election. But TR had not changed his mind about going to Europe. "I would like to visit the Front at the head of an American Division of 12 Regiments like my Rough Riders," he wrote his friend Arthur Lee, "but not otherwise."

On the Monday after the election, House received a wire from the President, asking him to come to Washington to "spend a little while with us." Soon after the Colonel's arrival at the White House, Wilson revealed the real reason he wanted to see him. He had decided to move for peace, he told House. "Unless we do this now, we must inevitably drift into war with Germany upon the submarine issue." And the Allies might support such a move, if there was as much "peace sentiment" in those countries as many believed.

House, who had never favored an independent action of this kind unless the Allies had given their consent beforehand, immediately tried to pour cold water on the President's scheme. First, the Allies would regard it as "an unfriendly act," since their military position was stronger than it was a year ago. Second, the Allies would believe Wilson was doing this solely to escape a nasty confrontation with Germany over the latest U-boat situation. Finally, House suggested that it would not look good and might be interpreted as if the President "wanted to reward Germany for breaking her promises to us."

It was not the answer Wilson wanted to hear. Could his friend give it additional consideration? The two men talked again later in the evening, although neither changed his mind. Wilson now suggested that House might go to England and France, in time for the peace proposal to be released shortly after his arrival. House winced. "Hades," he wrote in his diary, was preferable than being in "those countries when such a proposal was put to them." The Colonel tried to push the President to do nothing for now, but Wilson believed the "submarine situation would not permit . . . delay." By eleven o'clock, the conversation ended, the President now "deeply disturbed."

House was equally disturbed. The next morning, he continued to chip away at Wilson's resolve. Wasn't the recent news of the harsh deportation of thousands of Belgians to work in Germany another reason not to act now? And what would happen if the Germans embraced his outreach and the Allies rejected it?

The President would not budge. He would write something up and then he and House would revisit the issue again. Their current disagreement did not affect Wilson's fondness for the Colonel. He was disappointed that his "best friend" could not stay longer and invited him to return at any time for as long as he wished.

Back in New York, House fretted about Wilson's plan, which Lansing and State Department counselor Frank Polk also opposed. The three of them would have to keep a close eye on their wayward president, especially since "his tendency to offend the Allies in order to keep clear of war with Germany is likely to lead us into trouble with the Allies." More than ever, House was convinced it was he, and not Wilson, who was the foreign policy expert. "The President," he explained, "must be guided, for he has no background of the European situation."

What bothered House more than the President's supposed lack of knowledge was his unwillingness to see the war the same way House did. Unlike the Colonel, who had already decided that the United States would have to side with the Allies eventually, Wilson was trying to be as neutral as humanly possible. The big picture, he believed, had to be considered. "I have tried to look at this war ten years ahead, to be a historian at the same time I was an actor," he told Ida Tarbell during the campaign. "A hundred years from now it will not be the bloody details that the world will think of in this war: it will be the causes behind it, the readjustments which it will force."

Wilson understood that whatever moves he made in the coming weeks would likely have an enormous impact on America, Europe, and the world. That month, he had read and saved a memo by Norman Angell (one of England's "reprehensible pacifists," according to TR), which had argued that the "entrance of America into the international policies of Europe would in any case be a step *as radical as any taken* since she became an independent state, and should be taken, if at all, with a searching of mind on the part of the American people as to their ultimate objects." Angell had also warned what might follow should America join the Allies who then proceeded to defeat Germany. The inevitable "resentments" would follow, the Central Powers would attempt to recoup their losses, and America "would in future conflicts be likely to see the lives and trade of her citizens exposed to even greater risks than they have suffered in the present war."

Wilson was eager to get started but there were other matters needing his attention, including a devastating cold. There was also an uncomfortable personnel issue confronting him. Edith and House again wanted the troublesome Tumulty out as the President's secretary, and this time Wilson went as far as to offer him a position at the Customs Service, which he promptly rejected. Only through the intercession of the journalist David Lawrence, who reminded Wilson of Tumulty's unshakable loyalty, was his job saved. It would be Tumulty who received Hughes's long delayed concession telegram on November 22, which Wilson saw when he returned with Edith from a performance of the Ballets Russes at the Belasco. Three days later, Hughes sent a handwritten thank-you letter to TR, whom many blamed for his defeat. "I have no regrets," Hughes told him.

By Thanksgiving (on the last day of the month that year), Wilson had recovered sufficiently to begin working on the peace note. First, he outlined his general thoughts on the current situation in a "prolegomenon," or introduction to be used in some future writing. The fundamental question, he wrote, was how to obtain a "lasting peace" when the outcome of the current war almost guaranteed another bloody conflict in the future. In his draft of the more formal peace note, he focused on several key issues: the utter devastation of the war, the disturbing impact on neutrals, the lack of specific terms demanded by both sides, the willingness of America to "join a league of nations," and the likelihood that a war ending in a victory that "overwhelms and humiliates" would not bring future peace. It was thus "within my right as the representative of a great neutral nation" to find a way to "define the terms upon which a settlement of the issues of the war may be expected," ideally through a conference involving the belligerents and neutrals. He was not, he explained, pushing his mediation or "proposing peace." But the time had come for the belligerents to disclose their peace terms, so America could "intelligently determine its future course of action."

House, recognizing that Wilson could not be swayed, now set out to soften and delay the message. It was the Colonel who had pushed the President to insert a passage that he was "not trying to mediate or demand peace." But House was still not happy with the draft. Wilson, he complained, continued to make the "same error of saying something which would have made the Allies frantic with rage," this time his insistence that the "causes and objects of the war are obscure." The Colonel also wanted the President to "prepare a better background" for the note to be received by the Allies. Show them we don't favor the Germans by condemning the Belgian deportation, he argued (privately, Wilson thought it "one of the most unjustifiable incidents of the present war"). That the Germans would immediately distrust Wilson even more than usual did not seem to concern House, who wanted him to wait as long as possible. "If you do it now," the Colonel wrote the President on Thanksgiving, "there does not seem to me one chance in ten of success and you will probably lose your potential position for doing it later."

Wilson no longer accepted this tired line of reasoning, which had been fed to him for nearly two years. Still, he elected to wait a bit longer, while hoping the Germans understood there could be no more "incidents" or controversies in the meantime.

The Germans were growing impatient. The American election was over and Wilson still had not done anything. House had told Bernstorff that Wilson was going to act soon, which the German ambassador reported to his superiors in Berlin while reinforcing the need to keep things status quo for now. (Bernstorff completely misread House, believing the Colonel was prodding a reluctant Wilson to action.) But before the message reached them, Jagow sent a confidential cable to Bernstorff. Depending on the military situation, Germany in the near future would express its willingness to enter into peace talks. Bernstorff was sworn to secrecy. The Germans remained hopeful that such a move might not be necessary if Wilson acted soon.

Bernstorff was elated, so much so that he told House, without any confirmation, that Germany would be willing to get out of Belgium and France as part of any peace settlement. It was not the first time that the ambassador exceeded his instructions from Berlin, and it would not be the last. He continued to be virtually the only German of importance to grasp that Germany's fate was likely to be determined by America and Wilson in particular. He had even worked quietly behind the scenes for Wilson's re-election, instructing George Viereck to curb any politicking for Hughes in the pages of *The Fatherland*.

It had not been an easy month for Bernstorff. Armgaard Karl Graves, who had made a name for himself writing about his not-so-successful spy work for the Germans, tried to blackmail Countess Bernstorff, recently back in the United States for the first time since the war began, by threatening to publish personal letters from a woman friend back home "full of endearing phrases, such as one woman uses to another." Graves was arrested, but his continued babblings to the press contained occasional nuggets of truth—namely, the German embassy's willingness to share info to help certain Wall Street investors and its awareness of and involvement with various espionage schemes in America.

More damaging was the publication in the London-based *Sketch* of a bathing-suit-clad Bernstorff with his arms around two American women, one of them his paramour Olive Moore White. The American press caught wind of it, perhaps on a tip from the Russian ambassador in Washington, and began poking around, even showing up at the Whites to ask questions. Bernstorff, as usual, kept his wits about him. He told a reporter from the pro-Allies *New York Tribune* that the picture was "faked. . . . I don't want the picture published. I don't care about myself, but for the lady's sake." The *Tribune* decided against publishing, as did other American newspapers, although the photo did appear in Canada.

If Bernstorff was uneasy about his personal life, he was now more confident that a way out of the hostilities was on the horizon, at least if a wiretapped conversation with Minnie Townsend, a well-known hostess on Washington's Embassy Row, was any indication. The two discussed the possibility of a move by Wilson, a doubtful Townsend observing that "he has been slapped in the face so many times already." Bernstorff reassured her: "He would not be slapped in the face this time I know. This is the opportunity, this is the moment. The time is just ripe for it."

Increasingly, Americans sensed that two years of fighting had solved very little. Peace talk, often discredited by the mainstream media, was now appearing in strange places. *The New York Times* had begun running a series of articles titled "All Want Peace: Why Not Have It Now?" written by a mysterious "Cosmos," later revealed to be the conservative Nicholas Murray Butler. "It makes the British so mad to think that their own paper [the strongly pro-Allies *Times*] is taking the lead in the campaign," Bernstorff chortled. And stories of new peace petitions, peace organizations, and even a plan for children residing on the East Side of New York representing "each nationality" to leave resolutions with Wilson filled newspaper columns during the last week of November.

Like other pacifists, Bryan was delighted by the turn of events. When he saw House briefly in New York, Bryan confidently informed the Colonel that "he expected to be at the Peace Conference" in an official or unofficial capacity. Once there, he was sure he could bring about peace if Wilson gave him the "proper authority and credentials." After all, both sides were "Christians and not pagans, and I could talk to them in a christianlike way and I am sure they would heed." House was astounded, although it was not the first time Bryan had made such a proclamation. "The deluded man sincerely believes this."

For Wilson, Bryan and the potential that he might "muddy the waters" was another reason to act sooner rather than later. House tried to reassure the President: Bryan would get nowhere with the Allies if he tried going over now. The best way to handle Bryan was to treat him respectfully, so as not to create any public sympathy for the Great Commoner, who already appeared to be thinking of a fourth run for president in 1920.

With peace on everyone's lips, the Woman's Peace Party could not have picked a better time to meet for its third national meeting in Washington on December 8. Addams, deemed well enough to make the trip to the capital, had been following the latest developments carefully, but other issues continued to concern her. She and other pacifists had been alarmed by an obscure clause in the big army bill passed that summer, the so-called Hayden Joker, which authorized the federal government to draft men for the National Guard reserve units if voluntary enlistments were not sufficient at a time of war, potentially making "conscription a part of our institutions." They had exchanged several private letters with Wilson, hoping he would push for its removal. While sympathetic, the President had yet to take any concrete steps in that direction, nor would he mention it in his upcoming address to Congress.

As usual, the pacifists trusted Wilson to do the right thing and decided not to do anything to "embarrass" their president for the time being. But the socialists had no such reluctance. During the presidential campaign, their candidate, Allan Benson, repeatedly mentioned that the "word 'draft' was smuggled into the bill." Wilson had said nothing publicly about it, he observed, and the press had been just as complicit in burying the issue.

At its national meeting, the WPP discussed the distasteful Hayden clause but without any condemnation of Wilson for signing the bill in the first place. The main concern among the disappointingly small gathering of about fifty women was the continued insidious growth of militarism in American life. Amos Pinchot, whose wife was a WPP member, had noticed the changes in recent months. "They are jailing boys and men for talking against the National Guard," he warned. "They are making the flag a kind of silly fetish, not realizing that the flag will be and ought to be respected only in proportion to the humanity, justice and democracy which it represents." Already, many states were trying to find a way to shove military training into the curriculum, which the WPP hoped to combat by promoting an alternate general program of physical education in the schools. The women also were determined to stop the possible passage of the Chamberlain Bill, which would require military training for all young men between the ages of twelve and twenty-three.

Addams, reelected chair, spoke briefly, emphasizing the importance of internationalism while reinforcing the idea that the pacifists were just as patriotic as the preparedness types. She remained in Washington after the close of the meetings on Sunday, December 10. On Tuesday, she testified before the House Judiciary Subcommittee in support of the federal Susan B. Anthony amendment. The WPP, she explained, supported suffrage "because we believe that women ought to have the chance to vote on the great subject of peace or war, or, rather should vote for the men who decide on a policy of peace or war." And the women, she reminded the Democratic majority subcommittee, had voted for Wilson in force based on his peace credentials. Almost immediately, the National Woman's Party suffragist Anne Henrietta Martin demanded to address the committee, noting that Illinois women had voted against Wilson in significant numbers. But Addams shut her down. Not only did Addams want the committee to view women as a potential Democratic voting bloc, but she was now a loyal supporter of the President, who had already invited her to the White House for a state dinner that evening.

Just about everyone in Wilson's circle was present at the affair: family members, House, Tumulty, Vice President Marshall, and most of the cabinet and their wives. It was likely the first time Addams had met Edith Wilson, said to be "slenderer than she was a year ago" and "extremely handsome in a gown of black net, with silver embroideries and trimmings." Dozens of pink roses and the strains of the Marine Orchestra completed the elegant atmosphere.

But everyone present was distracted by a surprising report received a few hours earlier. Chancellor Bethmann had spoken before the Reichstag at noon. Germany, though in an enviable military position, very much emphasized in the speech, was ready to enter into peace talks. No terms of any kind were mentioned, nor was the involvement or mediation of Wilson. The kaiser, meanwhile, issued a statement to be read to his troops: "Soldiers: In agreement with the sovereigns of my allies and with the consciousness of victory I have made an offer of peace to the enemy. Whether it will be accepted is still uncertain. Until that moment arrives you will fight on."

German Americans, at least those interviewed by reporters, were hopeful. "My parents are in Germany, and I have not heard from them in two years," a New York waiter explained. "I must tell my wife about that," remarked a shoemaker. "She has two brothers in the army and half the time she is crying about them." Addams was less optimistic. It was certainly positive that such an offer was being made, but she knew that the Allies, smarting from the recent German capture of Bucharest, the fifth capital to fall into the hands of the Central Powers since the war began, were unlikely to bite. Still, she had long believed that "any time" was a good time to start talking. And the ice at long last had finally been broken.

Bernstorff had known that a peace move was coming that day (his intrepid lover was desperate to learn anything since "the market is terribly depressed today"), but he was not privy to the decision-making in Berlin. Bethmann had decided Wilson was not the answer. Germany might not only wait forever for him to do anything, but Wilson might also try to present himself as mediator or offer concrete terms to accept or reject. If Germany was to make any offer, now was the time. Hindenburg was demanding with increasing persistence that unrestricted submarine warfare must otherwise resume in a few weeks, which could potentially win the war or blow up in the Empire's face. And the recent Romanian victory showed everyone that Germany was not trying to bargain from a position of weakness.

Whether the Allies would respond positively was uncertain, especially when the note felt the unfortunate need to boast proudly of the Central

Powers's "unconquerable strength" and "lines . . . unshaken." But Bethmann and Kaiser Wilhelm himself thought there was at least a slight chance the French in particular might be willing to talk. And they understood the immense value of initiating a dialogue, even if it was rejected. "If the Allies refuse to confer they will thereby assume responsibility for continuing the war and at the same time make it appear that they are fighting an aggressive and not a defensive war," a *New York Tribune* reporter observed. "If they accept the offer it will be regarded as a confession that they have given up the idea of bringing Germany to atonement."

Bernstorff hoped Germany's salvation was at hand. "It is all up to London," he told Minnie Townsend in another wiretapped conversation. "I don't think they can refuse, so I think there will be something out of it anyway. Because even all the pro-Ally press in this country says they cannot refuse." He was also optimistic that "Mr. Limerick," the code name for Wilson used by the German embassy (House was "Mr. Palace," Lansing "Mr. Saber"), would add his own endorsement to the note.

But Wilson was not happy. For a month, he had struggled to complete his own peace note while contending with an unending series of distractions and roadblocks. The annual message to Congress had to be prepared and delivered on December 5. There, a group of Congressional Union suffragists interrupted him by suddenly unfurling a banner over a gallery balcony with the message "Mr. President, what will you do for woman suffrage?" He watched silently as a page, hoisted up by officials, pulled down the offending message. Some onlookers saw disturbing echoes of the militant suffragettes in England, especially when the same stunt was repeated four days later at the Gridiron Club dinner, but Harriot Stanton Blatch of the Congressional Union was not concerned about such controversial associations. "We're going to let down banners and keep on letting down banners till we get what we want."

On the same day as the Gridiron Club incident, Wilson received news that would further delay him: a change of government in Britain. After nineteen months, the Asquith ministry had fallen apart, to be succeeded by a coalition government headed by the new prime minister, Lloyd George, whose recent "fight to the finish" speech made his feelings about peace disturbingly clear. House, hoping to sidetrack the President from his current scheme, floated the possibility of a letter to Lloyd George remind-ing him of their discussion earlier in the year about Wilson's intervention. The Colonel remained baffled "why the Allies did not accept our proposal made in February." But the President shot him down. "We cannot go back to those old plans," he told House. "We must shape new ones."

House's continued lack of enthusiasm did nothing to boost Wilson's confidence about his decision to go forward. It did not help that Lansing was equally hostile about an American peace move, even though he was somewhat more subtle about his objections. The secretary of state had already made up his mind that America should fight alongside the Allies, "for we are a democracy." And the recent *Marina* and *Arabia* sinkings and the usual "explanations" offered by Germany convinced him that diplo-matic ties should be severed now. That this was hardly the time for such a matter to be considered while Wilson was putting his final touches on a potentially game-changing document did not seem to occur to Lansing. It was at times like this that Wilson likely missed the unflinching pacifist support of Bryan, as inane as he could be at times.

He continued to perfect the note while soliciting more feedback from Lansing, who conceded that it was "probably the only step which can be taken offering a possible way to prevent an open rupture with one side or another." But how would Wilson handle a possible rejection "from the belligerents whom we could least afford to see defeated" (meaning the Allies)? Like House, the secretary of state was emphatic that the President should not attempt to strong-arm either side into a response, even if he had the ability to do so. House himself got another look at the document when he came to Washington on December 12 for the White House dinner at-tended by Addams. The German offer had come through earlier that day, and House found Wilson understandably "depressed" over the develop-ment. He tried to reassure the President that the United States would be needed more than ever in the future peace conference.

Wilson now had several options. He could abandon his note altogether and see how the Allies responded to the German offer, which would be formally presented by America and other neutrals. After all, the press had been repeatedly told of late that the administration had absolutely no plans to make any peace appeal at the moment. Or he could throw America's weight behind the proposal, what Addams and virtually every other pacifist prayed he would do, even if his track record was not encouraging. "Is Wilson to lose all by once more letting delay, expediency, fear of ruffling somebody's feathers, cost another opportunity to add undying lustre to the American flag?" Oswald Villard asked in the *New York Evening Post*. "One feels like crying out: 'In heaven's name, is there never to be one single action to be taken without this never-ending weighing of consequences, and without wondering if this is really the right moment to do a noble deed?'"

Wilson had no intention of backing out now. Still, he knew the situation was even less ideal than before. Not only would he need to wait to release his note so as not to seem to be piggybacking onto the German move (even then, it would be almost impossible for many to separate his effort as a "me too" initiative), but he would also need to act before the Allies had a chance to dismiss the German effort and show themselves categorically against peace. And the signs, especially warlike comments by Allied Prime Ministers Aristide Briand and Lloyd George, were not encouraging. To Frank Simonds, covering the war for the *New York Tribune*, no peace move could work now, since both sides still believed they could win and that the cost of continued fighting, no matter how horrendous, was worth the goal of ultimate victory.

On Monday, December 18, Wilson went over Lansing's final suggestions and deemed the message ready to be sent. It was also his anniversary, the Wilsons spending part of the day playing golf on a course speckled with ice and snow. Later, they saw a film at the Belasco, the Australian swimmer Annette Kellerman's controversial vehicle *A Daughter of the Gods*—the leading lady's nude scene could well have shocked the moralistic president. In between, during the first press conference he had held in months, Wilson discouraged any questions about the foreign situation, his listeners unaware that a peace note was about to be sent later that evening.

House saw the note on Wednesday, a day before the American public learned of it in Thursday's morning papers. Wilson was apologetic in the covering letter. "Things have moved so fast that I did not have time to get you down here to go over it with you," he explained. The final draft, House noticed, was filled with changes, reflecting the note's long germination and outside input. It now included an admission that the President was "somewhat embarrassed" that his note might be perceived as linked to the German peace move but requested that it be "considered entirely on its own merits." Otherwise, the note broadly followed Wilson's original concept: a request that both sides state their terms to provide an opening wedge to peace, a move more than warranted by the "exceedingly hard to endure" plight of neutrals such as the United States. The more explicit call for a conference in the original draft was no longer present, nor was any reference to America's need to "determine its future course of action." "It may be that peace is nearer than we know; that the terms which the belligerents . . . would deem it necessary to insist upon are not so irreconcilable as some have feared," the President wrote.

House congratulated Wilson on the message, but he was not happy that the President had repeated the same "error" from the original draft, an insistence that the "objects" of the war, at least as presented by the leaders of "both sides," were "virtually the same." Try as the Colonel might, he could not shake Wilson from "that thought, and he cannot write or talk on the subject of the war without voicing it." That unfortunate statement, House believed, would not only inflame the Allies but probably knock Wilson out of any significant role in the future peace conference.

At times like these, House's frustrations with Wilson, along with his own ego, became apparent. "I find the President has nearly destroyed all the work *I have done* in Europe," he testily wrote in his diary (although a few days earlier he claimed that his own "desire for peace is so much keener than my wish to bring it about *personally*"). Once again, House felt the need to document all of Wilson's many shortcomings, especially his personal grudges and his poor administrative skills. And the country was still terribly unprepared and vulnerable to foreign attack, although House believed "the greatest security for peace at this time would be complete preparedness for war," sentiments that would have cheered TR had he read them.

House was uneasy about the future. "I am convinced that the President's place in history is dependent to a large degree upon luck," he wrote. "If we should get into a serious war and it should turn out disastrously, he would be one of the most discredited Presidents we have had."

For Addams, the note justified her faith in Wilson that some of her own friends had questioned. She wired the President immediately expressing her support, while suggesting that both sides would eventually understand the need to disclose specific terms "after the first hypersensitive reaction subsides." The most important thing, she believed, was to get them together, even if they were miles apart at the moment. From that inauspicious beginning, peace might finally result, followed by the creation of an international organization allowing for the world to be "organized politically by its statesmen as it had been already organized into an international fiscal system by its bankers."

Bernstorff, who thought a conference was now definitely coming, relished the displeasure of the Allied ambassadors in Washington at the latest developments. An angry Jules Jusserand thundered that "it is not for a stranger to say when a nation shall stop dying" and France "would never forgive the United States." And Cecil Spring Rice, Bernstorff suspected, was just as incensed, his already sour feelings about Americans likely to worsen further. Minnie Townsend, who knew everything going on in the diplomatic community, confided to Bernstorff that Spring Rice had recently declared, "I loathe and detest the Americans so much that I would rather be a Turk than an American." "The funniest thing is that they all say they never expected it, and I can't see where they have been living if they didn't," Bernstorff told her.

The Allied ambassadors did not remain angry for long. Lansing, behind Wilson's back, met first with Jusserand and then Spring Rice to talk them off the ledge and downplay the significance of what had just occurred. The President, he reassured them, favored the Allies. The secretary of state then went a step further in a chat with reporters a few hours after the first morning newspaper reports appeared on Thursday. He blithely announced that the President's message wasn't really a peace note at all and was more about America's being on the "verge of war" and needing to know the peace terms of both sides so "we may regulate our conduct in the future."

Lansing's comment set off a panic on Wall Street, which would experience its "wildest day" in fifteen years. Meanwhile, an alarmed Tumulty, never a fan of Lansing, immediately alerted Wilson what had just occurred. Furious, the President ordered Lansing to the White House. The secretary of state would immediately need to find a way to undo his statement about the possibility of war. "The whole atmosphere of our present representations may be altered by that reference," Wilson warned Lansing, who meekly complied. By four o'clock, he had given a second statement following his boss's instructions.

But the damage was done. If America was on the brink of war, presumably with Germany, then the force of the President's supposedly "neutral" peace note vanished. Most presidents would have sent Lansing packing, but Wilson refused to wield the ax. An emotional confrontation of that sort was unpleasant to him. He also knew that another shuffle in the State Department would signal a divided administration, precisely what he did not want to convey to the belligerents. As for Lansing, he knew exactly what he was doing: he had to undercut Wilson, even at the risk of his own humiliation, so the Allies would not perceive the message as backing the German peace move and favoring Germany in general.

For now, Wilson would wait for the Allied response to both notes. The domestic editorial response had been positive, although the British and French press were hostile (a "most terrible thing," the legendary French actress Sarah Bernhardt proclaimed to reporters in Philadelphia). With Christmas in a few days, the matter would be on hold for several more days at least. The talk of war had little effect on the American holiday season. A "Western woman" traveling to New York marveled at the vast crowds of female shoppers, all demanding their packages and change as soon as possible while griping about how slow the help was moving. And authorities everywhere preached the gospel of the "safe and sane" Christmas, with no candles on the tree and decorations kept away from gas jets.

Addams, still forbidden from living at Hull-House during the winter, spent a quiet holiday at West Walton Place with Mary. Roosevelt, while disgusted by the note and its "immoral and misleading" statements, celebrated on the twenty-second by handing out gifts, fruit, and candy at Cove Neck School in Oyster Bay, which most of his children had attended. The enthralled pupils also listened to TR's tale of an elephant he and Kermit had hunted one Christmas in Africa and his stern advice not to "let anyone bully you." Reporters present naturally were more interested in Roosevelt's take on the Wilson/Lansing affair. "The antics of the last few days," he told them, "have restored to me what self-respect I lost supporting Mr. Hughes."

Even in the midst of an eventful month, Wilson's Christmas season was surprisingly traditional. Locals were surprised to see him shopping in Washington jewelry, leather, and book stores. As per tradition, there were also turkeys to be handed out to the married men on the White House staff. On Christmas Eve, he found time to join in a mass carol singalong on the steps of the Treasury Building. At the White House the next day, presents were exchanged after breakfast, Wilson's grandniece Josephine Cothren and his granddaughter Ellen McAdoo attracting most of the attention. Twenty-two family members and friends then gathered for dinner, followed by a rousing game of charades. It was a perfect day for Wilson, a "very happy Christmas."

Chapter 16

PEACE IN SIGHT

DECEMBER 26, 1916–MARCH 4, 1917

*This war is so unprecedented that we are justified in
abandoning precedent in our effort to keep out of it.*

—William Jennings Bryan, February 1917

A few days after Christmas, Wilson received word that a group of
suffragettes wanted to present him with resolutions written in
honor of the recently deceased Inez Milholland Boissevain, a leading light in the votes for women movement and one of the pilgrims on the
Peace Ship. That the increasingly annoying Congressional Union was behind the request raised Wilson's suspicions, although he agreed to the meeting on January 9, so long as they kept it small and did not try to use it for
propaganda purposes.

Wilson was not happy when he saw three hundred eager women waiting
to see him in the East Room, especially when two of their leaders began
pushing him once again on the suffrage amendment. "I had not been apprised that you were coming here to make any representations or would
issue an appeal to me," he said with more than a trace of irritation. "I,
therefore, am not prepared to say anything further than I have said on
previous occasions of this sort." And regardless of his own "private personal
convictions," he was helpless "until the orders of my party are changed, to
do anything other than I am doing as a party leader." With that, Wilson
stormed off in a huff.

Most of the women present thought Wilson's response was ridiculous, if not disingenuous. "It is only when women go to the President that he hides behind his party and says he is bound by it," snapped Sara Bard Field. "He holds his party in the hollow of his hand," Harriot Stanton Blatch insisted. "He is not willing to lay a finger on his party on behalf of women—one half of the people of the United States." Almost immediately, they decided Wilson's do-nothing policy had to be answered, this time with a campaign of "silent sentinels" picketing the White House gates, considered by one reporter to be the "most militant move ever" by American suffragists.

At nine the next morning and over the days that followed, a determined contingent and their banners became the latest Washington tourist attraction. Onlookers were impressed that the rotating group of women did not flinch from the frigid weather and refused offers to warm up in the East Room, preferring to use hot bricks (were they going to "throw them at the President?" one wag asked). Naturally, the antisuffrage crowd was appalled. The sentinels were embarrassing the President, they insisted, and perhaps even endangering his life by their banners, which might provide cover for a deranged assassin. What Wilson thought of them remained a mystery to the public, although reporters tried their hardest to figure out whether his smiles to the sentinels were friendly or scornful. To his cousin Helen Bones, the whole campaign was "suffrage idiocy. . . . They could stand there till time passed and eternity began and they would make no impression on WW."

Undoubtedly, suffrage was a low priority for Wilson in the early days of the new year. The international situation and the more hopeful outlook for peace were foremost in his and everyone else's mind. On New Year's Eve, simultaneous peace demonstrations under the auspices of the American Neutral Conference Committee were held in Washington Square in New York, where thousands chanted, "Ring out old wars, ring in world peace!" as midnight approached, and Orchestra Hall in Chicago, where Addams made her first public appearance in months. She tried, once again, to convey that they were far from foolish "peace-at-any-price" types. "What we desire," she explained, "is peace at once, and a peace founded on justice and law. We desire to get away from the blind, old stupid method of going to war, for we believe that the universal public opinion is against war. . . . We don't seek to lay down any terms, but merely to ask that the nations now at war somehow stop their fighting long enough to see if they can determine among themselves just what it is they desire."

This, of course, was exactly what Wilson had tried to do before Christmas: get both sides to state their terms with the hope it might lead to peace. The results so far had not been encouraging. Unlike Bernstorff, the German Foreign Office and the kaiser himself viewed Wilson's peace move as more of a hindrance than a solution to their problems. They decided almost immediately that they were not prepared to offer their terms publicly nor did they want an American president perceived to be pro-Allies involved in the eventual peace conference beyond bringing the parties together. ("I won't go to any conference!" an irritated kaiser scribbled on the cover letter enclosing Wilson's statement. "Certainly not under his chairmanship!") The quick response Berlin sent off to Washington after Christmas made those points abundantly clear, although it did express interest in participating with America in the "great work of preventing future wars" when the "present struggle of the nations" was finished. The Germans, it was obvious, were not tempted by "diplomacy in the open," what Addams hoped would become the new norm.

The Allies, still considering their answer, were relieved by the German response. Had Berlin showed any willingness to meet Wilson halfway, the pressure on the Allies to do the same would have been considerable. By this time, their initial anxieties and anger about the President's peace move had been largely allayed, thanks to the secret assurances of Lansing and then House, both of whom shamelessly undermined Wilson. Still, America would have to be handled carefully, unlike the Allies' tart rejection of Germany's offer (the "'poisoned chalice' peace note," TR called it) made a few days later. After much discussion, the decision was made to give Wilson what he wanted. The terms included in the note sent to Wilson on January 10 placed the Allies on the moral high ground, calling for the Central Powers to not only give up all of their wartime gains but also pay indemnities and reparations. "Such terms would be accepted only by a crushed and beaten enemy," one Boston journalist remarked, "and Germany is not."

Bernstorff, already disappointed by his government's reply to Wilson, betrayed his bitterness in a phone conversation with a reporter a few hours after the Allied response had come through. "They asked for everything in the world. I think the note is a huge joke. We might just as well write the Secretary of State and tell him we want New York." Whether anything could be accomplished now depended on the President and "whether he was going to use the authority of the United States for starting something, or whether he was going to be satisfied with two notes. . . . Practically both sides of the belligerents want someone to force them into peace. I think Europe will be very grateful if someone forces them into peace, because there is no other way of getting it."

To Roosevelt, the only accomplishment of Wilson's peace note was to enrich speculators on the stock market believed to have been tipped off in advance. (A subsequent congressional investigation into the supposed "leak" failed to turn up much, although the name of Wilson's brother-in-law, R. W. Bolling, surfaced, as did that of Archibald White, the husband of Bernstorff's paramour, who admitted his association with the ambassador but claimed no "business relations.") All along, TR had believed the note was a farce, "profoundly immoral," especially in what he believed to be the President's implication that "both sides seem to be fighting for the same thing." And how could Wilson talk about America's future willingness to "secure the future peace of the world" when he had flopped miserably for close to four years in Mexico, where thousands of National Guardsmen were massed at the border? Even now, Pancho Villa was still at large, and plans were already in motion to halt the Punitive Expedition in a few weeks.

TR's usual anti-Wilson rant notwithstanding, the note never had more than the slimmest chance of bearing fruit. Unlike Roosevelt in 1905, who had stepped in to bring the Japanese and Russians together, Wilson had little assurance of success. Its timing, so soon after the German move, was hardly ideal, but the more serious issue was the President's overly optimistic view that both sides could find common ground and accept something less than complete victory at this stage of the war, when enormous sums of blood and treasure had been expended (unofficial figures suggested that about 4.2 million soldiers had perished). Wilson not only miscalculated the true degree of peace sentiment in the warring nations but also failed to recognize that "hard-line interests" now controlled most of the belligerent powers and believed the war to be winnable.

In his defense, Wilson was still, to some degree, a foreign policy amateur. He had only the sketchiest knowledge of what was truly going on behind the scenes in Europe, imprecisely gleaned from House's travels, diplomatic reports (many of which he discounted, such as Page's), the press, and impressions from Americans such as Addams who had traveled to the warring countries. The administration could not yet conceive of a more bare-knuckles approach to intelligence gathering, such as the German spying program or the secret British interception and decoding of American cables (even the domestic wiretapping of Bernstorff and other Germans was halted that January after Tumulty found out that one of his friends had been targeted).

Even without a substantial military apparatus in place, the very thing TR had pushed for since 1914, Wilson still had one considerable card to play: the Allies' utter and growing dependency on American financial assistance. "The President could force the Allies to their knees any time," the former Chancellor of the Exchequer Reginald McKenna observed. With that card, perhaps supported by the other neutrals as Addams had wanted, Wilson might have pushed harder for a peace conference, as he had in his original draft. But he had long ruled out such a strategy, either from his own personal Allied sympathies or the possible economic fallout in America.

No one knew what the President would do next. The White House correspondents suggested another peace note to the belligerents would be forthcoming, a prediction that annoyed Wilson, who despised "conjectural journalism." Harold Ickes, while less hostile to the President than his friend TR and conceding that Wilson "may be a real progressive," remained uneasy about the country's future under Wilson. "I have a feeling," he wrote an ex–Bull Mooser that January, "that I do not know what his policies are going to be from day to day and that he does not know himself."

At the moment, Addams was satisfied that Wilson was doing everything possible for peace. He had finally taken concrete action in that direction. That alone justified her recent support in the election, even if he continued to waffle on suffrage and was privately opposed to the planned postwar gathering of Addams and other women at the same location and time of the eventual peace conference. To some State Department officials such as Frank Polk, Wilson's pacifist tendencies had gone too far of late. Polk, Colonel House recorded in his diary in early January, "thinks he [Wilson] is for peace almost at any price." A few months earlier, House had felt the need to reassure future readers of his diary that Wilson's "desire for peace is partially due to his Scotch Presbyterian conscience and not from personal fear, for I believe he has both moral and physical courage."

The rejections by both sides did not faze the President, especially when another opening seemed to materialize after the initial German response. Bernstorff and House hashed out an alternate scheme where Germany might confidentially disclose her peace terms to Wilson, who would in turn use that information to spark more formal negotiations. An enthusiastic Bernstorff floated the idea to Berlin, assuring them that they need not worry about leaks ("both Wilson and House are rather skilled in keeping secrets" unlike most gossipy Americans) and that the President was not interested in settling territorial issues. Bethmann, at least, was intrigued, but others, including the new foreign minister, Arthur Zimmermann, were not. Zimmermann reiterated to Bernstorff on January 7 that he should keep talking peace but America's involvement would have to be limited to a separate conference where such matters as disarmament, freedom of the seas, and a league of nations could be discussed. By this time, Bernstorff sadly recognized that his superiors in Berlin would never share his view that "American mediation" was the "only possible way out of the war."

Wilson, unaware of Berlin's attitude, had already decided on a more dramatic approach. During House's visit to Washington in early January, they discussed the President's next move, a speech to the Senate in the coming weeks where he would articulate what he believed the peace terms should be and how the emphasis should be the "future security of the world against wars." And the address, of course, was not meant merely for American consumption, but the whole world, especially the belligerent populations. "You are now playing with what the poker players term 'the blue chips' and there is no use sitting by and letting great events swamp you," House told Wilson. "It is better to take matters into your own hands and play the cards yourself."

For House, the two-day trip was a mixture of excitement over Wilson's upcoming speech and anxiety about some of the things going on in the White House. Lansing complained to the Colonel about Wilson failing to keep himself or the State Department in the loop and that "his mind is a vacuum during your absences." And the President's steadfast reticence to go to war even began to alarm House, who heard from Lansing that Wilson "did not believe the people . . . were willing to go to war because a few Americans had been killed." The Colonel had tried to broach the issue of how the nation was still "totally unprepared," only to be coldly shot down. "There will be no war," Wilson told him with more than a trace of exasperation. "This country does not intend to become involved in this war." Besides, America was now the "only one of the great White nations that is free from war today, and it would be a crime against civilization for us to go in," especially if some future apocalyptic battle against the "yellow races," namely Japan, might occur.

House had other reasons to be concerned. Edith Wilson, he recognized, remained ambivalent about his role in her husband's life. To the Colonel's discomfort, a discussion about replacing Ambassador Page in London suddenly shifted to the First Lady questioning him whether he would take the job. That Wilson was in favor suggested the two had already talked it over. House, smooth as ever, managed to convince Wilson that an ambassadorship would limit his all-important "activities" to London, and the matter was soon dropped. (House's "activities" had grown so large that a new joke was making the rounds: "Do you know the 'new way of spelling Lansing'? . . . H-O-U-S-E.)

House could never be sure how much influence Edith wielded. He knew she could not stand the overambitious McAdoo, and her dislike of Tumulty had never abated. She still believed and presumably hoped Tumulty might resign at the end of the current administration. If so, House observed, "the little circle close to the President seems to have dwindled down to the two of us, Mrs. Wilson and myself." The lack of confidants such as Mary Hulbert had begun to take its toll on Wilson. "I feel very lonely sometimes," he told House, "and sometimes very low in my mind, in spite of myself."

Throughout early January, peace talk appeared to be gaining momentum. Bryan, despite his misgivings about Wilson, approved of the President's recent course, and Taft, still promoting the League to Enforce Peace, predicted that pacifism would become mainstream in the future. "The important thing to consider," the former president explained, "is whether after the war we are going to let things go on just as they did before the war or not." A number of peace groups, including the American Union against Militarism and the Woman's Peace Party (sans Addams, whose tuberculosis flared again), busied themselves in Washington testifying against legislation for universal military training. Ford had also gone on record against "any kind of military service . . . fostered by the same class who in earlier years participated in and sanctioned witch burning, duels and feuds."

Such a statement, along with Ford's contention that "an army or navy is a tool for the protection of misguided, inefficient, destructive Wall Street," seemed to suggest that he had not lost his passion for peace or the Neutral Conference, now reconfigured as an International Commission at The Hague. Louis Lochner, the man overseeing things there, hoped so. In the fall, Ford had assured him of his continued support of the conference, so much so that Lochner thought he would ask to double the budget, to $20,000 a month, when he returned to the United States on January 14. And things looked promising, especially when Ford showed up in New York to greet Lochner and called Tumulty the next day to get him in to see Wilson. Lochner brought along a Hungarian named Ferdinand Leipnik to the meeting, explaining that Leipnik's contacts with the British Foreign Office indicated that they might be more amenable to peace talks if Germany signed a Bryan "cooling-off" treaty with America.

Lochner's enthusiasm soon disappeared when he learned Ford was actually thinking of *halving* his support. The news worsened when he went out to Detroit a few days later. The first bad sign was the presence of Ford's antipeace secretary and loyal company man Ernest Liebold—the man Lochner called the "evil genius"—at their Friday, January 19, meeting. The second was Ford's "hurried talking" and "troubled look" during the short discussion. Something seemed off. But the final bombshell came later in the conversation. "Well, I don't think this war ought to stop now," he told Lochner. "Those people over there haven't suffered enough yet. So long as they don't themselves refuse to go on with the war, we in America should do nothing to help them."

Lochner was stunned. The next day he headed to Chicago to brief Addams. Ford seemed to be wavering, Lochner told her, but he hoped his mercurial mind would change again. Addams thought Lochner needed to return to The Hague as soon as possible, lest Ford's interest completely disappear. She herself was still hopeful that Ford might make a generous donation to the planned postwar women's conference. That same day, the pacifist Lillian Holt visited with Clara Ford to discuss the conference and the possibility of meeting with Addams to learn more. But Holt, like Lochner, did not receive an encouraging response. "I am afraid," Holt wrote Addams, "Mr. Ford has turned his head against women in any movement."

Ironically, Ford's weakening came at a time when Wilson and House were at their most optimistic. The President's upcoming speech had already been completed, coded, and sent out to the embassies, who would hold the message until Wilson spoke before the Senate. The Colonel approved it except for a statement that the "war was brought on by distrust of one another," which Wilson agreed to remove. (The press was told that dinner, and not peace talk, had been House's motivation for coming to Washington.) Earlier in the week, House had a positive talk with Bernstorff, who suggested that Berlin was still very interested in peace, so much so that Germany was "willing to submit to arbitration as a means of peace" and sign a Bryan "cooling-off" treaty. The ambassador often spoke for himself rather than his government, but the Colonel was intrigued. "If Bernstorff has stated his Government's proposals correctly, peace is in sight," House told Wilson.

Since Wilson wanted to know more, House pressed Bernstorff for more specific details during the week, without much success. They planned to meet again on Monday, January 22, but Bernstorff abruptly cancelled on Saturday. In view of their recent conversations, the somewhat cryptic letter the Colonel received must have been puzzling to him. "I am afraid, the situation in Berlin is getting out of our hands," Bernstorff wrote. "In Berlin they seem to believe, that the answer of our enemies to the President has finished the whole peace movement for a long time to come, and I am, therefore, afraid that my Government may be forced to act accordingly in a very short time."

House had declined Wilson's invitation to attend his speech before the Senate that Monday. Thanks to unusual efforts to minimize any advance leaks, few on Capitol Hill knew what Wilson was planning until midmorning, followed by Vice President Marshall's more formal communication to the Senate at 11:00 a.m. that Wilson wanted to address them about foreign affairs. By noon, the Senate galleries had begun to fill. The "constant 'chatter' of women," one reporter observed, "interfered with the regular business of the Senate." And everyone present—the senators, the scattered congressmen, and cabinet members—wondered whether it meant war or peace. (TR's daughter Alice was also in the audience: "I enjoyed intensifying the dislike and resentment I felt by hearing him speak rather than waiting to read it in the papers.")

For twenty-five minutes, the gathering—Edith and Cousin Helen among them—hung on Wilson's every word, delivered with what a Washington reporter described as a familiar "staccato, yet well-measured precision." The President recounted the results of the outreach he had made in December and how he believed a future international peacemaking league of nations was now "that much nearer." America, of course, would play a great role in this organization, but "so far as our participation in guarantees of future peace is concerned, it makes a great deal of difference in what way and upon what terms" the current conflict ended. It must, he insisted, be a "peace that is worth guaranteeing and preserving . . . not merely a peace that will serve the several interests and immediate aims of the nations engaged." This peace, he went on to explain, "must be a *peace without victory*. . . . Victory would mean peace forced upon the loser, a victor's terms imposed upon the vanquished." Such peace, "accepted . . . under duress," would be pointless, short-lived, and doomed to failure.

As Wilson and, by extension, the United States saw it, the future peace would depend on certain essential principles and conditions: a separate and free Polish state, freedom of the seas, self-determination for all peoples, "government by the consent of the governed," and arms reduction. All, the President said in closing, were "American principles, American policies. . . . And they are also the principles and policies of forward looking men and women everywhere, of every modern nation, of every enlightened community. They are the principles of mankind and must prevail."

The applause that followed was mostly Democratic. "Mr. President, that was a great state paper," Senator Stone congratulated him. "I hope," Wilson responded, "that it will be taken as it is intended and that its meaning will not be mistaken."

But everyone grasped that his assertion that America should not only participate in a future league of nations but also become involved in determining and maintaining the peace of a European war represented a dramatic, almost shocking shift in American foreign policy. "The President thinks he is President of the whole world," sneered one Republican senator. "The most startling proposal in the history of our national life," marveled another.

Within hours, Roosevelt was giving out a statement denouncing the speech, especially the deplorable "peace without victory" sentiments. Page, who had seen the speech several days earlier, had already urged Wilson to substitute something more acceptable to the British, such as "peace without conquest," a suggestion the President chose to ignore. The *London Morning Post* expressed a common Allied sentiment: "When the war between Spain and the United States was still unsettled, would Americans have been satisfied if the European Powers had intervened and said—'You must make peace without victory, because any other peace would leave the sting of resentment and a bitter memory'?"

If the thousands of telegrams pouring into the White House were any indication, Wilson's speech was a home run, "the most powerful expression of the idea of universal peace which the world has heard," Ida Tarbell told Addams. Addams herself was elated. Wilson had again justified her support. "Isn't it fine," she wrote Lochner, "and isn't the cause moving along?"

But some, including an African American from New York named

C. Valentine, thought Wilson's supposed concern for humanity was hypocritical. "Would not a note on 'Justice Without Lynching' be far more appropriate from an American President, and President Wilson in particular, than
one on 'peace without victory,' and just as logical?" Valentine wrote in a
letter to a New York newspaper. "Or is justice and fair play only for
Europe?"

The general Republican disapproval of his message in the Senate discouraged Wilson. Still, he believed that all the elements were in place
to bring about peace talks now, if the Germans would cooperate. Bernstorff
should be informed, the President wrote House, "that this is the time to
accomplish something, if they really and truly want peace. . . . Do they in
fact want me to help? I am entitled to know because I genuinely want to
help and have now put myself in a position to help without favour to either
side."

Bernstorff very much wanted Wilson to help, but a few days earlier he
had received a distressing message from Berlin likely to make it impossible.
As of February 1, unrestricted submarine war would be resumed, neutral
shipping included. The ambassador was instructed to inform the American
government of this unpleasant fact on January 31, a mere nine days after
Wilson's speech, which had seemed so promising.

The fateful move had been made earlier that month. After the half-
hearted German peace note failed to accomplish much of anything, the
military and naval clique was in a stronger position to impose their will.
Hindenburg, Holtzendorff, and Ludendorff had decided they had waited
long enough for the return of unrestricted submarine warfare, neutrals
included. If Bethmann did not agree, then he would have to go. The decision was formalized at Pless castle in Silesia on January 9. The kaiser and
the chancellor offered no serious resistance to what was already a fait
accompli. The new submarine campaign, they were told, would end the
war within six months. If America became involved, she was unlikely to
make a military difference for a year, long after the war had come to a
close.

The plan rested on the optimistic belief that German U-boats unleashed to their full potential could disrupt food imports enough that a starving British population would be ready to surrender by the late summer of 1917. No one in the higher circles could conceive of another path to victory or the possibility of a compromise peace. Nor were they aware of the frighteningly shaky state of British finances, now projected to run out by the end of March, which might have been exploited and caused more damage to the Allies than the submarines themselves.

In desperation, Bernstorff sent a flurry of messages to Berlin asking for delay. "We can get a better peace by means of conferences than if the United States should join our enemies," he wrote. "The power and resources of the United States are very great." Since Wilson had no interest in territorial issues, why not accept his mediation and disclose Germany's peace conditions? If the future Wilson-proposed conference broke down, then Germany would be in a better position to resume unrestricted submarine warfare without the fear of American involvement. In the meantime, Bernstorff began to discourage his many American friends from booking any transatlantic passages in the near future.

Bethmann, somewhat intrigued, did send to Bernstorff peace conditions to be shared privately with Wilson, conditions that would have been tolerable to only a thoroughly defeated Allied side and that had little value except to possibly pacify America a little longer. But the chancellor told Bernstorff that it was too late to stop the new submarine campaign. Perhaps its likely success would prompt the Americans to "think twice" before declaring war.

Bernstorff knew better. He understood the United States, some said, much more than his British counterpart, Cecil Spring Rice. Only a miracle would stop America from joining the Allies.

In the chaotic days in Berlin following the decision at Pless, a Foreign Office official named Hans Arthur von Kemnitz resurrected a scheme he had been pushing for months: a possible informal alliance with Mexico, provided she lure the far more important Japan onto their side. The Mexicans, in declaring war on the United States, would even have the opportunity to obtain lost territory in Texas, New Mexico, and Arizona. War with America, he believed, was coming and the specter of a Mexican invasion at the border and the Japanese threatening the West Coast would neatly halt any American military intervention in Europe.

Under normal conditions, cooler heads would have killed such a preposterous proposal immediately. Instead, no one, not even Foreign Minister Zimmermann, whose name the communication to Mexico would bear, did anything except to change the contents slightly to emphasize Mexico's role and stress that the offer was good only if war should be declared with America (Bethmann, it is believed, never saw the note until much later). Thanks to the use of State Department cables, generously and some said foolishly opened to Germany to expedite communication between Washington and Berlin, the message reached the embassy in Washington on January 19, the same day Bernstorff was informed of the return of unrestricted submarine warfare. There, it was decrypted, enciphered under a new code, and wired to the German embassy in Mexico City, this time using Western Union.

Bernstorff was shocked and disappointed by the telegram. His superiors once again failed to grasp American conditions. Still, he did not believe it was his place to prevent the message from reaching Mexico. The submarine campaign, and not Mexico, would determine Germany's future relations with America.

Bernstorff, after exhausting all options, had no choice but to inform Washington of Germany's new submarine policy on the last day of January. Shortly after four that Wednesday afternoon, he handed the document to Lansing. The ambassador's mood was somber and apologetic. "I know it is very serious, very, and I deeply regret that it is necessary," he told Lansing, who quickly read that neutral and Allied ships would now enter the "barred zones" at their own risk, subject to attack without warning, although one specially marked American passenger ship per week would be permitted safe haven to Falmouth, England.

Lansing was not entirely surprised. He had long anticipated such a move was coming, but thought the Germans would wait until warmer spring weather returned.

After Bernstorff departed, Lansing tried to call Wilson, who was not available. Not until later in the evening did the papers reach the President, who immediately summoned his secretary of state to the White House.

Lansing, who for months had advocated a diplomatic split and had written a private "Certainty of War with Germany" memo three days earlier, believed he had sufficient arguments to force Wilson's hand. Had not America promised to sever ties if the *Sussex* pledge was violated? The nation, and the President himself, would look ridiculous if the United States did not follow through now. But Lansing was discouraged to find Wilson hesitant, still musing about the importance of America maintaining what he called "white civilization." He would not be pushed into anything, Wilson told Lansing, "unless he was convinced that viewed from every angle it was the wisest thing to do."

House, briefed by Frank Polk, reached Washington in the early morning hours of Thursday, February 1. The Colonel, like the President, had been optimistic that the spring would bring peace talks. Now House agreed with Lansing that the time had come to split with Germany. Wilson, he soon noticed, was "sad and depressed," but he did concede that Germany was a "madman that should be curbed." Why then, asked the Colonel, should the Allies be solely responsible for the "curbing"? Their conversation, later joined by Lansing, increasingly seemed to come closer and closer to a consensus that a break with Germany could not be avoided. Beyond that, Wilson was determined to keep America out of war. Otherwise, he believed it would be "impossible to save Europe" in the future.

Later that afternoon, after House had left for New York, Wilson met with a shocked Louis Lochner, who had been convinced that the civilian leaders had control of the situation in Germany. The appointment, scheduled before the submarine announcement, was originally planned as a last-ditch attempt to get a Wilson endorsement of the Neutral Conference/International Commission, without which Ford was planning to pull the plug on future funding. Lochner had even tried to get Addams to contact the President on his behalf, but she declined. Still, she was eager to hear the results of their talk. Wilson, Lochner wired her, "looked haggard and distressed" but listened patiently. He had no objection to their activities but his greater concern was the German submarine decision, which he thought *"may change the whole world."* Was there a "peaceful way" out? Lochner asked.

"If it can be done," Wilson responded, "I certainly wish it with all my heart."

News of the new submarine policy, a "supercrisis," as one reporter called it, shook the nation. In New York, crowds not seen since the early days of the war clamored around newspaper offices desperate for the latest bulletins from Washington. Surveying the scene, an old Civil War veteran believed war was coming. "I look about this crowd of American citizens and hear their silence—for there are some silences one may hear—I think it means war. I think the temper of the American people is about stretched to the breaking point." To George Perkins, the fault was Wilson's. "I now think he will be fortunate if he escapes impeachment."

Roosevelt, as usual, took the opportunity to remind everyone that this never would have happened if Wilson had pursued a stronger course after the sinking of the *Lusitania*. The next day, Friday, February 2, TR lunched at the Langdon Hotel in Manhattan with the German-born Oscar Straus, a Jew and moderate pacifist who had served in his cabinet. Among the topics covered was Straus's suggestion that he might serve as a go-between for Wilson and Roosevelt to discuss the crisis. After all, he had helped bring Hughes and TR together last summer. Roosevelt was dubious, especially since his own current recommendations would likely not agree with the President's. "He [TR] said he would promptly assemble our fleet," Straus recorded. "He would place marines on the interned German ships and thus show Germany we were indeed earnest and that unless she withdrew her announced purpose of sinking merchantmen without observing the rules of civilized war he would promptly take ships to protect our rights." Wilson, TR believed, would likely try to work out some wishy-washy deal with the Germans sparing American ships from the general order against neutrals. For now, the Roosevelts would not cancel their upcoming planned trip to Jamaica, but TR had already requested the War Department to contact him if war broke out.

That afternoon, Wilson met with his cabinet for more than two hours, with close to a hundred reporters outside awaiting the outcome. To those present, he appeared to be still struggling with a decision. When Lansing suggested that "for the interest of the world," America "should join the Allies," the President merely replied: "I am not so sure of that." To the shock of most present, he also claimed that "he didn't wish to see either side win . . . both had been equally indifferent to the rights of neutrals." Ironically, the suggestion that Addams and other pacifists had pushed for months—some sort of coordination of the neutrals—seemed to finally appeal to him at this late hour, but others argued that it might "put some of the small powers in a delicate position."

Some of the more bellicose cabinet members were disappointed, but Lansing believed Wilson's comments were merely an attempt to elicit opinions. After the meeting, the President went to the Capitol to talk to William Stone and other members of the Senate Foreign Relations Committee, but found most away or unavailable. Stone and fifteen other Democratic senators who happened to be around met with Wilson in his office in the Capitol to discuss possible options: namely, breaking with Germany, waiting for an incident, or a "final warning." Stone, long wary of any involvement, thought nothing should be done unless Germany actually followed through, but most of the others did not agree. Afterward, reporters wanted to know what had been decided. "That depends on how I feel in the morning," Wilson quipped.

Bryan was in New York that night for a Madison Square Garden rally arranged by the American Neutral Conference Committee weeks earlier to support Wilson's "Peace without Victory" speech, one that Bryan admired except for the league of nations idea. Some wars, he explained to the thousands present, were justifiable. If America was attacked, "we ought to fight until the last man is dead. But I don't believe that a single mother's son should be carried across three thousand miles of ocean and made to die on European soil in settlement of European quarrels." America should tell any of the "madmen of Europe" that "we will not get down with you and wallow in the blood and mire to conform to your false standards of honor." And he assured the gathering that the President wanted to keep America out and was capable of doing so.

Afterward, Bryan headed to Washington. The next morning, Saturday February 3, he spoke to Tumulty with a message to give to Wilson. Addams, meanwhile, wired the President with the old plea to unite with the neutrals as a possible "beginning of a league of nations standing for neutral rights" and to minimize the danger of war.

But it was already too late. Wilson had come to the conclusion that he had no choice but to sever ties with Germany. At ten o'clock that morning, Tumulty informed reporters that the President would be speaking to a joint session at the Capitol at 2:00 p.m. A stampede to the phones followed.

The speech itself lasted about fifteen minutes. When Wilson announced the diplomatic split, most of the audience erupted into prolonged applause, even his harshest critics such as Henry Cabot Lodge. "For the first time," Republican Senator Warren Harding explained later, "the President has said something that I can applaud." Still, Wilson expressed doubt that the Germans would stoop to this level and "destroy American ships and take the lives of American citizens. . . . Only actual *overt acts* on their part can make me believe it even now." The next step, he warned, would be congressional authorization for steps to safeguard American sailors and travelers.

The pacifist Ellen Slayden was pleasantly surprised by Wilson's performance. "He was almost modest," she wrote, "not dogmatic and schoolmasterish but like a normal man seeking advice and help of other men in a moment of awful responsibility."

The decision met with widespread support. "We have to show our virility as a nation," Senator Willard Saulsbury, a Democrat from Delaware, exclaimed. In France, James Norman Hall was just as pleased that America had finally "taken the right stand." Others were less certain. "I believe in standing by the president," an Indianapolis salesman told a reporter, "but I can't understand the necessity at the present time of breaking with Germany." Such ambivalence was overwhelmed by a surge of unrestrained patriotism. Just miles from Hull-House, a Chicago audience at the Auditorium Theater wildly waved flags to the strains of "The Star-Spangled Banner" played by John Philip Sousa's band. At the Garrick in the Loop, a similar scene unfolded, led by Al Jolson, who urged the crowd to "show the President we stand behind him."

Security was naturally beefed up at the White House. No longer would strangers be allowed to traipse around the grounds or indoors, especially since many feared the possibility of foul play by "German sympathizers." But many German Americans, while disappointed, accepted the news philosophically. It was too bad that Great Britain wasn't getting the same treatment, one admitted. "But between Germany and America, we are Americans, first, last, and all the time."

Roosevelt was delighted. The volunteer division he had been working toward for two years was that much closer to becoming a reality. It would all depend on Wilson, of course, but TR had already convinced himself that he could remain silent and loyal if given the military position he craved. He even had Gifford Pinchot pay a visit to Colonel House on Monday, February 5, in the hopes of arranging a meeting. House decided it was not a good idea to see Roosevelt right now, although he was willing to do so if war was declared. TR's offer, the Colonel observed, was one of dozens pouring in at the moment. "It saddens me to see how blithely people go into war," he recorded in his diary. "They are much the same in all countries and in all times."

For Bernstorff, the moment he had dreaded for more than two years had finally arrived. His passport and those of his wife and the hundred or so others in the German embassy were handed to him just as Wilson was getting ready to address Congress. "I don't care what happens to me now," the ambassador told reporters. "I am out of politics forever; my life work has failed." But even the most pro-Allied elements of the press admitted Bernstorff had done his best under extremely trying circumstances, especially when some of his superiors not only discounted his advice but tried to sabotage the efforts of a man they considered a "rank Social Democrat" (Zimmermann was completely blindsided by the decision to sever ties, although German leaders were relieved that other neutrals did not follow the American example). Bernstorff's greatest flaw was his knowledge and occasional oversight of the various espionage and propaganda schemes attempted in America, most of which accomplished less than anticipated and made his job even more difficult.

On his last day in Washington, Bernstorff took in a movie (Chaplin's

Count Johann von Bernstorff, the German ambassador to the United States, whose herculean efforts to prevent a diplomatic split with America finally failed in February 1917.
(Library of Congress: LC-H261-7093)

latest, *Easy Street*), before boarding a train for the Hoboken pier and the *Frederick VIII*. There, the photographers wanted a few last pictures of him. "Sure thing," he replied, impressing onlookers with his command of "American slang." And every precaution was taken to ensure his safety, the same treatment his American counterpart Gerard would expect when leaving Germany. A few peace workers tried to board the ship and hand out literature but were turned away, as was a "demented" young "crank" bearing a letter. But Bernstorff was too depressed to care about any potential dangers. "Oh, well, if we go down, I've had an interesting time of it," he announced. "It is quite possible that my official career is finished."

To the bitter end, he continued to misjudge House's neutrality. "Tell him he is the best friend I have in America," he told Dudley Field Malone before his departure. "But for him it would have been impossible for me to have remained as long as I have." The Colonel, meanwhile, saw "something pathetic about this message." His own dealings with Bernstorff were not about friendship, House claimed, but "merely in line with my duty, as I saw it, to the President and to my country."

Addams and the other peace forces were deeply troubled by the latest developments. A panicked Lochner had wired her and David Starr Jordan, warning that Washington and New York were both "war mad" and the country might be plunged into the conflict within days without "personal appeals" to Wilson. Woman's Peace Party members, "many . . . disturbed and bewildered," also reached out to Addams, desperate for "some reassuring expression." She knew something needed to be done, but she did not think it advisable to push Wilson too hard in the telegram quickly sent out under her name and those of the WPP executive board. It merely expressed confidence that the President's "wisdom can devise a new way out of the present difficult situation," hopefully through an official neutral conference that might "make a very genuine beginning of a league of nations."

That her fragile health (this time bronchitis) again would not allow her to do more for the cause was enormously frustrating. While she convalesced with Mary in Chicago, New York was the focal point for the pacifist movement. Almost overnight, the Emergency Peace Federation (different from the identically named Chicago-based organization established back in 1914) emerged to coordinate the work of the varying pacifist organizations under one large umbrella; it was headquartered in Greenwich Village at 70 Fifth Avenue, already the home to various peace and liberal organizations, including the National Association for the Advancement of Colored People. And Rosika Schwimmer's two faithful protégées—Rebecca Shelly and Lella Secor—were very much involved and eager to move the new entity in a more aggressive direction in the current crisis, even if some believed the "two young ladies . . . are intolerant of all who do not stand on the extreme left." The EPF had a good deal of promise, Addams believed. "It can move quickly and effectively."

Almost immediately, the EPF planned an ambitious agenda. Branches would need to be established in every congressional district, cards and letters sent to every representative, and a substantial war chest raised through newspaper solicitations. The President, one ad explained, "declares that we 'earnestly desire to remain at peace.' . . . Believers in the President's peace policy are uniting to support him and to make manifest to Congress the peace sentiment of the American people." Within three months, the EPF would succeed in raising more than $76,000 (about $1.5 million today), especially remarkable at a time when any overt show of pacifism was viewed suspiciously. A few days after the split with Germany, a Secret Service man showed up at a peace gathering at the Congress Hotel in Chicago. A week later, Oswald Villard noticed law enforcement snooping around during his talk in Brooklyn opposing "universal military training." "This is not Russia; this is America," he complained. "This country has come to a pretty pass if the fear of war sends police in plain clothes to a peaceful meeting like this."

The EPF and other peace organizations increasingly came to believe that the best way to demonstrate the country's firm opposition to war would be through a referendum, a common ballot measure of the previous twenty years thanks to the efforts of progressive reformers such as Addams, who had mentioned the idea in the last telegram to Wilson and thought it might be "our best hope." "It at least makes for delay," she explained, "and is in the line of extending democratic control." Bryan agreed. "If it is worthwhile to consult the voter on village bond issues and franchises it is certainly worthwhile to consult him as to whether he shall be called upon to spill his blood upon a battlefield," he insisted.

But "what would Germany be doing," a reporter asked, while the United States went about the time-consuming process (some said it "could be secured through the Census Bureau and postmasters in twenty-five days") of conducting and tabulating a nationwide ballot? The Great Commoner did not flinch. If Germany or any other country attacked America, he explained, then the referendum should obviously be called off. In the meantime, the American Union against Militarism sent out 100,000 postcards asking respondents in five different states to answer two "essential questions" and then forward their replies to their congressman. First, did they support American entry into the war? Second, did they support the idea of a referendum? And friends on Capitol Hill already had begun to introduce resolutions for a referendum, although without a great deal of success. When Addams tried to interest one of her senators, the Republican Lawrence Sherman, he informed her that it was "impracticable." She also contended with some WPP members who felt the whole thing was terribly embarrassing to Wilson.

Addams sensed that some pacifists were getting cold feet. In an emotional AUAM meeting, Rabbi Stephen Wise shocked the gathering by confessing that he now saw war "as the only way to throttle the greater evil," although he promised to give it more thought. That same week, Carrie Chapman Catt, who had always believed suffrage more important than the peace movement, announced that the National American Woman Suffrage Association was prepared to do its part for the war effort. "A miserable crawl to get the vote," scoffed one WPP member. When Ellen Slayden saw Catt in Washington a few months later, she was not impressed. "She is handsome and well dressed but, judging by her expression, is not in the same class spiritually with Jane Addams. . . . There is more calculation in her eyes, less sweetness."

But the most disheartening defection that week was Ford. He had shown up in Washington the day after Wilson's address to Congress and informed the President that he would turn over the Ford factory to the government in the event of war. Puzzled reporters wanted to know whether Ford had abandoned his supposed "peace-at-any-price" philosophy. "I never said I would not fight," he insisted. "I never said I would not do all for the country that I was able to. I am a pacifist, but I want to say to you that a pacifist is the hardest fighter you ever saw when he finally is crowded into taking up arms." If war came, the unpredictable inventor continued, "look out for President Wilson. You will see a real pacifist in action, and he will show you fighting that these roaring lions never dreamed of." In the days ahead, funding of the peace work in Europe stopped and Lochner was abruptly let go, never to see Ford again. It did not come as a complete surprise to Lochner, but he had somehow "hoped that the old Henry Ford would come back." But he was gone for good, thanks to his handlers, his wife, and probably his own bipolar tendencies.

The news eventually reached Schwimmer, now back home in Hungary and unable to leave the country. She would have to stay put, since her unrelenting pacifism, the prime minister believed, would signal to the world that Austria-Hungary was "war weary," exactly what the German ally did not want to convey. For now, there was little she could do. "Living in a belligerent country," she wrote a friend, "is just like being shut up in a cell."

To some Americans, the EPF and the referendum advocates were delaying the inevitable. War was coming and it was best to prepare for it. Even parts of the normally isolationist sections of the Midwest appeared to be resigned, such as Des Moines, where Ida Tarbell claimed there were "long lines waiting to enlist." A few miles from Hull-House, authorities recorded six hundred enlistments in a single day, figures not seen since the Spanish-American War. One young man on State Street refused to be taken in by all the patriotic rah-rah. "Why should I join the army?" he told one recruiter. "I'll stay home and read the death lists." And corporate American powerhouses, which once regarded Wilson as a foe, were now eager to show that they too were gladly willing to turn over their plants in case of war, among them General Electric, DuPont, Bethlehem Steel, Johnson & Johnson, and U.S. Steel. But Wilson was not naïve. Big business smelled massive profits ahead. It troubled him to think that if war came, "the steel, oil and financial magnates . . . will run the nation."

An undercurrent of fear in many American communities was now inescapable. The famous explorer Robert Peary warned that New York and other East Coast cities might face aerial bombing raids "within thirty days." Not surprisingly, some New Yorkers not only had taken to scanning the skies for zeppelins but were also convinced that they saw soldiers on the top of the Park Row Building. Already, extreme anti-German prejudices began to surface. Stories of German lessons being abruptly terminated and the boycotting of "songs by German composers" were now common. "Does patriotism demand that we draw the dagger at a dachshund's approach?" Villard's *Evening Post* sarcastically asked.

Everything now depended on what the Germans did next. After the brief grace period was over, would German submarines attack American ships entering the danger zone? (A wheat ship, the *Housatonic*, had already been sunk the same day Wilson appeared before Congress, but plenty of warning had been given by the *U-53*'s Hans Rose, the same commander who had stopped in Newport the previous fall.) An incident of some kind would immediately throw the country into war, exactly what had occurred nineteen years earlier when the *Maine* blew up in the Havana harbor. For now, American shipowners were on their own. The Wilson administration was not yet willing to arm them nor prevent them from leaving home. The passenger liner *St. Louis*, scheduled to leave New York for Liverpool with 280 passengers in early February, looked to be the first test, if and when its owners decided to run the risk.

A tiny sliver of hope remained that the Germans might be bluffing and might make some last-minute concession, as they had done before. But H. L. Mencken, one of a group of American journalists now trying to get out of Berlin, was doubtful. The attitude there, he sensed, was that they had no choice, at least according to a German officer, who boiled down the situation to its essentials to one of Mencken's colleagues. The war, he explained, was not unlike a "prize fight" between Germany and Britain with America as the referee, a referee whose decisions tended to favor the Allies. "Now our opponent grasps us about the neck and tries to choke us. . . . We appeal to the referee, but get no relief. Instead the referee gives aid to our opponent. Well, there is but one thing for us to do, and we do it. That is, we strike *below the belt*."

W ilson knew that Germany's current "good behavior" would not last long. If there were other means to avoid war, he was more than willing to consider them. Before leaving for home, Bernstorff had heaved one last desperate Hail Mary pass for peace, a plea to reopen negotiations offered through Paul Ritter, the Swiss representative in Washington who would oversee German affairs in America. Wilson was willing, but only if Germany agreed to either cancel the return to unrestricted submarine warfare or come forward with genuine and actionable peace terms. Both were highly unlikely if not impossible, unless a revolution or coup occurred in Germany. Lansing, skeptical of the whole thing, told the President he sensed that Bernstorff was behind it along with "certain Americans . . . antagonistic to your policy" and the "firm position which you have taken." One of those "Americans" was Bryan, at least according to House's suspicions, though there was no proof of his involvement.

Wilson still hoped something could be done with the neutrals, although his attempt to get them to follow America's break with Germany failed. The Dutch ambassador explained to House that Wilson's previous attitude was to blame. The neutrals (and Addams) had been pushing the President "for two years to cooperate with them" but he "had refused until a crisis arose."

Wilson's reluctance to work with the neutrals until recently doomed one of the better suggestions to come before him in the days following the break with Germany. A Columbia history professor named Carlton Hayes, an antimilitarist who would later serve as FDR's ambassador to Spain during World War II, offered a viable course that might preserve American integrity, avoid war, and satisfy much of the country. In an article in *The Survey*, Hayes cited historical precedents where neutral countries had joined together to resist the abuses of belligerent powers on the high seas without declaring war. The United States had participated in a similarly undeclared naval "Quasi-War" against France between 1798 and 1800. Perhaps sensing that conflict of some kind was inevitable, the WPP and other peace forces immediately threw their support behind this plan, hoping the President might be persuaded. They briefed House and Tumulty, both of whom forwarded copies of the Hayes article to Wilson.

"We are very well aware that to a great historian these facts are known, but your friends have thought deeply upon this matter and hope that they have something that may be of suggestive value to you," Lillian Wald wrote to the President. And the "league of neutrals" might be a first step to American involvement in the league of nations sketched out in the "Peace without Victory" speech. Wilson undoubtedly read the article, but he was not tempted—especially since he knew the other neutrals would not agree to such a plan.

For now, he wanted to do nothing to make America appear as an aggressor. "If we are to have war," the President remarked, "we must go in with our hands clean and without any basis for criticism against us" (according to FDR and a contemporary journalist, Wilson genuinely fretted about the judgment of "some historian" of the future). Not only did he refuse to authorize any seizure of the nearly one hundred German ships in American ports (a strategy favored by TR), but he would not be persuaded by arguments to convoy American merchant ships, which some believed was "physically impossible" anyway and might create a "double target" for German U-boats. Nor was he enthusiastic about the idea of arming merchant ships, loudly championed by Lansing and Franklin Lane in the cabinet. Lane was especially frustrated that Wilson remained ambivalent toward "any great preparedness" and continued to believe that "Europe would be man and money poor by the end of the war. I think he is dead wrong in this."

But the President understood that Washington and New York were not the United States and that Americans remained deeply divided over what course to follow. Arming ships would be risky and might precipitate a war that large segments of the country did not want. More than two years into the war, many Americans were still not convinced by TR's argument that the success or failure of the Allies would dramatically affect the future of the United States. And dozens of congressmen quietly shuddered at the thought of being forced to commit themselves on such a controversial issue. Already, one representative had supposedly received seven hundred letters, 90 percent against war. Bernstorff himself believed that about 60 percent of the country was "entirely indifferent" to either of the two sides fighting.

The pacifist cause had shown surprising strength, especially when most of the mainstream media was decidedly against it. A sizable delegation from the EPF traveled to Washington for a demonstration and interviews with individual congressmen and senators on Lincoln's birthday, February 12. Before they began their mission, they posed for the newsreel cameras with their banner: "War or Peace; Take a Referendum." The reaction on Capitol Hill proved to be far less hostile than they anticipated: Stone even bluntly informed them he was on their side. They tried to see Wilson, but had to settle for Tumulty, who patiently listened to their resolutions and arguments. To one of the speakers, Fanny Garrison Villard, the absence of Addams's wise counsel that day was especially painful. "How many people there are in the world who would give anything they possess to restore you to perfect health!" she wrote Addams a few days later.

The following Sunday, Addams did make it to a mass peace meeting in

Chicago at the Coliseum, although she let others do the talking, among them John C. Kennedy, the city's fiery socialist alderman. "If we are to have a war, it should be a war against ignorance in this country," he roared. "This country is more threatened from within than from without."

The pacifists assumed that Wilson had no objection to any of their stepped-up activities since they had heard nothing from those close to the President to lead them to believe otherwise. Privately, Wilson had begun to show signs of annoyance. When informed that Rose Dabney Forbes, head of the Massachusetts WPP, one of the more conservative branches, was looking for guidance whether to back the EPF campaign, he let it be known that she should be told such activism was counterproductive in the current crisis: "I think that the best way to support my efforts just now is to show that the whole country, at any rate the thoughtful element of it, is back of me." In other words, it was ultimately his call and others would merely muddy the waters.

The usual domestic issues and presidential stressors only added to his burden. An unstable Massachusetts man showed up at the White House on February 10 wanting to discuss battleships with him. A few days later, W. E. B. Du Bois prodded Wilson to say something about lynching in his upcoming inaugural address (he didn't). And the pesky silent sentinels continued their campaign, now with a new banner: "American women can be depended upon to support American ideals. Let them vote."

To critics insisting this was neither the time nor the place to picket, Alice Paul had a ready response. "When the civil war began Susan B. Anthony was told the same things we are being told today," she explained. "If she'd only drop her suffrage work and become an abolitionist, women would be given the vote as a reward as soon as the war was over." Anthony had been bamboozled, and women were not going to repeat the same mistake.

But the most disturbing episode that February was a food crisis in New York. Prices had skyrocketed of late, attributed to various factors, including crop shortages, fewer rail cars available because of submarine-shy merchant ships reluctant to sail, and perhaps even dastardly German espionage. In one local grocery, onions had jumped from six to sixteen cents in a month, the price of potatoes had doubled, and the cost of other staples had also soared. Herbert Hoover, the Belgian relief commissioner, would soon testify that starving Belgians were paying less for bread than New Yorkers.

In Manhattan on the morning of February 20, several hundred East Side women reached the breaking point. An angry mob shouting "We want bread!" marched to City Hall demanding to see Mayor John Purroy Mitchel, who, luckily for him, was nowhere to be found. Hastily closed gates kept the women from making a ruckus inside, but they refused to leave, shocking one official who called it the "worst scene that City Hall has witnessed in years and the most difficult crowd to break up." Another determined group proceeded to Rivington Street, where they menaced hapless fruit and vegetable peddlers, overturning their pushcarts, pouring kerosene on vegetables, and "raiding the cellars of green grocers." When similar riots spread throughout the city and other nearby communities, some feared that another French Revolution might be in the making. The famed labor organizer Mother Jones even showed up in New York, promising to "lead all the women who'll follow me down to the Mayor."

In the days that followed, the press offered helpful suggestions to combat the high costs of living. One reporter proposed following the example of the Italians, who seemingly were not as dependent on meat and potatoes. "The Italian family gets along very well with their diet of bread . . . and spaghetti," prepared "with a tomato or meat sauce." Others suggested rice, then seen as a poor and unfamiliar substitute for the tried-and-true potato portion of the nightly meal. But authorities insisted there were no food shortages of any kind in America, and the crisis eventually petered out, even if prices remained undeniably higher than they had been two years earlier.

The bread riots provided a brief distraction from the ticking time bomb of American ships and citizens on the high seas. On February 12, a German submarine sunk another vessel, the schooner *Lyman M. Law*, but advance warning was given and no lives lost. Neither this incident nor the *Housatonic* nine days earlier qualified as the explosive "overt act." Perhaps the German "frightfulness," as the press called it, would not come at all.

The waiting to see what the Germans would do next left Lane and some other cabinet members "feeling humiliated." For Roosevelt, it was merely more of the same from Wilson. TR would support the President now if he "meant business . . . but I doubt if he does mean business." As Roosevelt bitterly griped to one of his old Progressive colleagues, "I don't think that he has the slightest feeling against men who merely injure the country. I don't think he has much feeling against any man who humiliates him, if the man also inspires him with physical fear." It particularly disturbed TR that the likes of Hughes, Root, and Taft were now calling for everyone to stand by the President, although Taft at least had begun to partly redeem himself in TR's eyes by supporting universal service (Taft had even signed up for the Connecticut military census and touted his ability to ride a horse, although he admitted his 265 pounds might be "hard on the horse").

That a declaration of war and his own ability to go overseas was in the hands of Wilson, a man he believed wanted to "sneak out of going to war," was almost unbearable to Roosevelt. Still, if the President somehow backed his way in, TR was determined to find a way to serve. Of course, the trip to Jamaica was off, and he had already sent two letters to War Secretary Newton Baker, whose noncommittal responses offered little encouragement (hardly surprising, since Roosevelt had mocked Baker's supposed fondness for knitting in several campaign speeches the previous fall). If blocked by the administration, TR had even begun to consider an alternative: raising a division of American troops in Canada, which would serve under the Allied forces (perhaps, he quipped, with a "bull moose in the corner of the British flag"). He floated the idea to his ambassador friends Spring Rice and Jusserand, asking them to run it by their governments, neither of which was likely to authorize any such thing, especially if the scheme did not sit well with Wilson.

Day by day, Roosevelt grew more obsessed with the idea of getting into combat. "I am praying that we go to war," he wrote the British novelist Mrs. Humphry Ward. He refused to accept that his age might be a deterrent. After all, a few weeks earlier, Frederick Selous, the sixty-five-year-old British explorer and a friend, had been killed in action in Africa. "I think I could do this country most good by dying in a reasonably honorable fashion, at the head of my division," TR explained. He preferred that he should die rather than his sons. Not only would it be a perfect finish to his career, but it would also erase the pain and disappointments of the past few years and give meaning to a life that had lost its zing.

Not surprisingly, the German press refused to take TR's military ambitions seriously. "Please, Teddy, don't hurt us," mocked the *Berlin Gazette*. "Strip off your leather war paint and stay in your wigwam. Don't be grumpy, Teddy Bear. . . . Stop where you are and, please, please, leave me my scalp."

The great burning question with us in America now is, 'Are we going to become involved in the war?'" Roy Cushman wrote James Norman Hall from Boston in late February. "The number of those who urge a declaration of war against Germany at once is growing every day. . . . For myself I can not take that position." In Washington, officials were now giving a stock answer to the same inevitable question: "I don't know . . . but I can't see how we are going to avoid it." It would all depend on the "overt act," an act that Wilson was determined not to precipitate. Someone had asked the President exactly what form the "act" would have to take. On the scale of the *Lusitania*, for instance? "I can't define it," he explained, "but I think I should know it, and so would the country, if it occurred."

But should the act occur and America declare war, would it be justifiable? To David Muzzey, a pacifist and colleague of Carlton Hayes in the Columbia history department, the case for war hinged on three arguments. First was the notion that the Allies were fighting "the cause of humanity" and "are fighting our battle as well as their own." Perhaps there was some validity in this argument, Muzzey admitted, but he saw the war as something that had evolved from "Europe's rivalries, and it will be settled (whatever part we take) by Europe's arms and Europe's councils." As far as the second argument, that the United States should fight as the champion of neutral rights, the other neutrals had not "asked or wished us to do this." The third and perhaps strongest justification for war would be to "protect American rights and lives" currently endangered by Germany's failure to abide by international law, much of which promptly became obsolete in 1914. But did this warrant sending American troops across the seas to Europe? Muzzy didn't think so. The Germans were absolutely wrong and their behavior had been "inhuman and barbarous," but American interests would be better served by avoiding the danger zones for now.

For Wilson, war had always been an extremely unattractive option, undertaken only as a last resort when all viable paths had been exhausted. "No present opponent or future historian can charge that Woodrow Wilson was bent on embroiling this nation in foreign wars," the *New York Evening Post* editorialized. "He has resisted enormous pressure, and rivalled Abraham Lincoln in patience." But the President was now facing an entirely new situation from the crises of 1915 and 1916. Germany was no longer willing to placate the United States to keep her out of the war. His decision would be whether to respond passively or aggressively, or somehow find a middle path. And if war came, he would also have to decide how far to go. The American public, Spring Rice advised his superiors back in London, would not stand for sending a "large force abroad." In fact, the ambassador warned that "it will be extremely unwise to count with any certainty on the United States entering the war."

For now, Wilson decided on a middle course: a request for congressional authorization to arm American merchant ships. It had been a path he had chosen reluctantly, supported by the more militant cabinet members, several of whom he suspected were trying to stampede the country into war. The decision was kept under wraps, but press leaks clued much of the country that something would be happening by the close of the congressional session on March 4. Wilson's supporters were all for giving him as much authority as he needed, at least as much as he had been given during the Mexican crisis in 1914, when American troops occupied Veracruz. But others were horrified by the thought of Wilson having complete say-so over the international situation until Congress reconvened months later. Some Republicans already were prepared to launch filibusters to force an extra congressional session.

On Monday, February 26, news broke early that the President would be going before a joint session of Congress at 1:00 p.m. "Are we going to put on our armor?" Vice President Marshall asked. The answer came in Wilson's relatively simple speech. As yet, America had been spared the worst effects of the return to unrestricted submarine warfare, beyond ships being un-willing to leave U.S. ports. And the infamous "overt act" had still yet to occur, although the nation's luck might run out at any moment. Since di-plomacy had failed, "armed neutrality . . . for which there is abundant American precedent" would be necessary and he was requesting congres-sional authority to go forward. To those, like Senator Stone, who saw war in the message and thought it a "serious blunder," Wilson insisted that he was "not now contemplating war or any steps that need lead to it." (Colonel House, meanwhile, seemed to believe otherwise. Three days earlier, he told a British official that "we want to be your reservoir for everything that America can supply—Food, Munitions, Money and Men.")

Privately, Wilson knew how close the country was coming to war. Shortly before addressing Congress, he had learned of another sinking, this time an armed English passenger liner, the *Laconia*, on its way to Liverpool from New York. That no warning was given and three American lives were lost distressed the President a great deal. Austin Young Hoy, whose mother and sister perished, soon fired off an angry telegram to Wilson: "I call upon my Government to preserve its citizens' self-respect and save others of my countrymen from such deep grief as I now feel. . . . If it stultifies my man-hood and my nation's by remaining passive under outrage, I shall seek a man's chance under another flag." True to his word, Hoy soon joined the British army.

To Hoy, armed neutrality was a far cry from what was needed in the current crisis. But Addams was not happy with Wilson's new direction. She had come to New York a few days earlier for a WPP executive com-mittee meeting and other conferences with peace forces before heading to Florida, on doctor's orders, to recuperate from her "wretched bronchitis." On the way south to rendezvous with Mary, she would stop in Washington as part of one of two pacifist delegations scheduled to see the President on Wednesday, February 28, meetings that now seemed especially crucial in the current climate.

Addams, like her colleagues, believed Wilson could be reached. He had never stopped responding to their telegrams, listening to their suggestions, and promising them that he did not want war. Wilson, they were still cer-tain, was one of them. "Thank God Woodrow Wilson is President," one pacifist gushed. "We know no one in the whole country more truly aiming for peace than our national leader," one of Addams's WPP colleagues had written her a few weeks earlier. And Addams herself still admired the President tremendously, although she was willing to disagree with some of his policies. After all, she noted, even "the highest patriotism does not exclude conscientious discussion of public measures."

Two days after Wilson's appearance before Congress, Addams and other pacifists converged upon Washington. Bryan was one of the first to arrive that morning, meeting with Lochner, Secor, and Shelly of the EPF. "I hope the friends of peace will be as free to speak for peace as the proponents of war to advocate war," the Great Commoner told reporters. But he was not opposed to arming American ships. His objections remained the same: American ships should not carry munitions and American travelers should stay off belligerent ships.

Addams and Emily Balch arrived in Washington by noon, soon joining the other two members of their group: William I. Hull, a Swarthmore College history professor who had been a student of Wilson's at Johns Hopkins, and Joseph D. Cannon, a socialist and labor organizer. At two o'clock, they were ushered into the President's office. After several visits to the White House, Addams knew the drill by now. Wilson would give them the time he had promised, about an hour in this case, and no more or less.

As a scholar, Hull reminded Wilson again of how America had found ways in the past to avoid full-blown wars, such as with France during the John Adams administration and with Britain during the Civil War. Cannon informed the President that the vast bulk of the country was against the war and that most would back whatever Wilson tried to do to keep the peace. Balch, meanwhile, stressed her belief that the "German people" did not want war with America and if the President offered a peaceful solution, "they would force their government to consider it."

When it came Addams's turn to speak, she relayed her own experience of what she had seen at Hull-House and the growing fears within the immigrant community. "Your President will not go to war," one had told her hopefully, "because he is a man of peace." And as a fellow progressive, she presented Wilson with a depressing picture of what war would mean for reform. Just the previous week, the Senate had passed an onerous spy bill likely to seriously curtail civil liberties if the House went along with it.

Addams noticed there was something different about Wilson this time. He batted down every suggestion—referendum, neutral conference, appeal to The Hague tribunal—with increasing irritation, almost anger. And he insisted that war, though he did not want it, would allow the United States, and Wilson himself, to have a much greater say in the peace and the direction of the postwar world (Prime Minister Lloyd George had stressed as much in a recent fawning comment to Page about Wilson that he knew would be passed on to Washington). Otherwise, the President would be lucky to get into the conference "through a crack in the door," something he clearly found unacceptable (ironically, TR had been repeating the same point since 1914).

At that moment, Addams began to have serious doubts about Wilson. The President, she sensed, seemed to believe that his involvement in the peace process was absolutely necessary, not unlike the Thomas Carlyle "contention that the people must be *led* into the ways of righteousness by the experience, acumen and virtues of the great man." "I found my mind challenging his whole theory of leadership," she later wrote. "Was it a result of my bitter disappointment that I hotly and no doubt unfairly asked myself whether any man had the right to rate his moral leadership so high that he could consider the sacrifice of the lives of thousands of his young countrymen a necessity?"

It was obvious to the entire pacifist delegation that Wilson believed Germany was a lost cause. At one point during the conversation, he made a cryptic and disturbing remark: "If you knew what I know at this present moment, and what you will see reported in tomorrow morning's newspapers, you would not ask me to attempt further peaceful dealings with the Germans." What that meant Addams could only imagine. The meeting, she realized, had been a failure.

The President was sitting on perhaps the biggest news story since the *Lusitania*. Three days earlier, he had been briefed about the existence of the Zimmermann Telegram, which had been sent in late January. Blinker

Hall, the head of British naval intelligence, and his remarkable code-breaking team in Room 40 of the Admiralty Old Building, had intercepted and decrypted the communication. Page was eventually informed, and the news was then passed on to Washington. A shocked Wilson immediately sent a copy to Colonel House, who was not especially surprised. The Germans were expecting war and it made sense to House that they would want to "stir up all the trouble they could in order to occupy our attention."

How to handle the disclosure of the telegram had been on the President's mind even as he spoke to Addams and her group. Later that afternoon, the decision was made that the Associated Press, rather than the administration, would release its contents, so no one could suggest Wilson was trying to sway Congress to support the pending armed ship legislation. At 10:20 that evening, the AP sent a message to its subscribing editors that an "important war story, probably two thousand words, will be sent about eleven o'clock, Eastern time." Fifteen minutes later, the story was sent over the wires.

The news—a virtual "act of war," some said—sent shock waves through America, especially the telegram's infamous line: "it is understood that Mexico is to re-conquer the lost territory in New Mexico, Texas and Arizona" (a subtle but significant mistranslation of the original German from "*consent on our part* for Mexico to reconquer." Zimmermann himself claimed he "merely wanted to prompt the Mexicans through this encouragement to invade the said provinces"). Even the more isolationist regions fairly bristled with indignation. A "most diabolical plot," one Cedar Rapids paper called it. The telegram "reveals a spirit of national deviltry to a degree that is astounding," thundered the *Atlanta Constitution*.

Roosevelt, meanwhile, offered a warning. "What Germany attempts to do now, even should it fail at the moment, it will surely try to do some time in the future." Privately, he was furious with Wilson, so much that he even cursed before a group of reporters at the *Metropolitan* offices. "This man is enough to make the saints, and the angels, yes, the apostles swear, and I would not blame them," TR told them. "My God, why won't he do something? It is beyond me."

Others believed the story was overblown, arguing the country was no more threatened than it had been since the war began. If so, then why was there no talk of returning the National Guardsmen recently withdrawn from the Mexican border? "The idea of such collusion as suggested in the note is ridiculous," the socialist and former congressman Victor Berger insisted. "So far as Mexico is concerned, I believe two companies of Texas Rangers could march from one end of the country to the other. We have about as much to fear from Japan as from the Martians." For German Americans, the report was almost unfathomable. "I cannot believe any sane statesman would have written such a note," John Walz, a Harvard professor of German, observed. Oswald Villard noted that his "pro-German" acquaintances had "thrown up their hands. . . . The only explanation they can give me is that Berlin has gone crazy, absolutely crazy. . . . Certainly the Zimmermann episode would seem to indicate that what is now needed in Berlin is a kindergarten for men dealing with foreign affairs."

Once the initial anger wore off, uncomfortable questions of how and when the United States obtained the telegram began to surface, especially since everyone recognized its strategic importance in the pending armed ship legislation. The administration vouched for its authenticity, but refused to give more information, even when Senator Stone began asking whether the Allies were responsible, since he heard rumors from a reporter that the British were involved. Fortunately for Wilson and Lansing, Zimmermann strangely decided he would confirm that the telegram was legitimate almost immediately (had he pronounced it a fraud, the administration might have been forced to reveal its source). From that point on, no one appeared interested in digging deeper or seriously challenging the widely held belief that America had obtained the telegram through the dogged efforts of its own clever agents. House, of course, knew of Blinker Hall's involvement, but even he did not know that the British had been sitting on the document since January. And neither he nor Wilson had any idea that the British were also secretly decrypting American messages sent over the same State Department cables, likely among them House's communications to Washington last year.

Bernstorff, now back in Europe on his way home, had a better understanding of what had happened. "Somehow or other the English or American secret police obtained knowledge of the key whereby the message was decoded," he mused. But he soon found himself being blamed in Germany for the whole fiasco, some insinuating that his incompetence had allowed the document to find its way into American hands. Zimmermann was especially anxious to condemn Bernstorff, although some of his colleagues in the Foreign Office believed the "idiot" Kemnitz and the "yes man" Zimmermann deserved more than their share of the blame. "What rubbish regarding Mexico," Kurt Riezler, Chancellor Bethmann's assistant, wrote in his diary. "It would have been better, even if the scheme is not betrayed, to do without this minor [Mexican] assistance, and let the Americans, if they are bent on war, deal with their strong domestic opposition."

Bernstorff, who had once thought he had a chance at becoming vice chancellor, discovered he was now persona non grata back in Germany. Ludendorff objected to his peacemaking attempts in America, and the easily swayed kaiser had also soured on him. Still, Wilhelm ultimately approved Bernstorff's new appointment several months later as ambassador to the Ottoman Empire, even though he disliked the Count's "democratic views." Those same ideals would lead Bernstorff to oppose the rise of the Nazi regime in the future.

The revelations of the Zimmermann Telegram gave a new urgency to the armed shipping legislation. With much of America highly excited and spoiling for a fight, few congressmen, Republican or Democrat, were prepared to stand in the way of what Wilson wanted, especially since Congress had always gone along with the President in similar crises. Twenty-four hours after the release of the telegram, the House voted 403–13 to authorize the arming of merchant ships.

Attention then shifted to the Senate, which had a stronger bill under consideration. The President knew the Senate would not be quite so pliable. Not only were there pockets of opposition, but the Senate had no limit of any kind on debate, even at the end of a session. "Every Senator may speak in the same legislative day, each time as long as he likes, on one and the same measure, and he may speak again on any and every amendment he and his friends or his opponents choose to offer," C. W. Gilbert of the *New York Tribune* explained. "A strong lunged orator much in earnest has been known to talk for half of a day to defeat a measure."

That Robert La Follette of Wisconsin was the most likely senator ready to take up such a challenge was recognized by veteran observers on Capitol Hill. A devoted progressive Republican (too far left for TR, who disliked him intensely and labeled him "a damaged and dishonest hoopskirt") and suspicious of militarism (his wife, Belle, and daughter, Fola, were both WPP members), he was a champion filibusterer known for "grandstand plays on the Tariff law, the Currency law and other bills." La Follette also believed Wilson had never been neutral and was leading the country in a dangerous direction. This bill, he believed, not only would give the President "extraordinary and autocratic power" until the new Congress convened in December, but ultimately and unquestionably "meant war." He was determined to throw every possible monkey wrench at the bill to stop it.

At sixty-one, "Fighting Bob" La Follette was still a striking figure, whose "short, energetic body and leonine head, with its mass of shaggy hair," as one suffragist described him, commanded everyone's attention. Even before the Zimmermann Telegram's release, he had blocked an attempt to fast-track the Senate's version of the bill from being referred to the Foreign Relations Committee. The Senate had already agreed that, if any senator objected, no business would be undertaken before a vote on a pending revenue bill, and La Follette was more than happy to be the unpopular dissenter. He was also happy to add to the delay by beginning a filibuster in the early hours of March 1, stopping only when assured that debate on the Senate's bill would not begin until the next day.

Wilson was keeping close tabs on events. He believed a bill would go through—preferably the Senate version—although time was running out. When the Senate convened on the morning of Friday, March 2, the recently released Zimmermann Telegram was very much on the mind of every senator, few of whom were willing to oppose the bill publicly. Still, La Follette had a core group of about ten supporters ready to speak and eat up as much time as possible. After the naval appropriations bill was dispensed with, hours of interminable debate on the armed ship bill followed with no vote taken.

Finally, an attempt was made late that evening to set aside the Senate bill and consider the House version instead. La Follette and his supporters eventually agreed not to stand in the way, only if the Senate adjourned until ten the next morning. For nine precious hours, the Senate would be idle, and only twenty-six remained in the session to pass the bill Wilson wanted so much. A lengthy filibuster now had more than a good chance of success. La Follette himself had once spoken over *eighteen hours* nine years earlier.

On Saturday morning, La Follette and his group were ready to go. They were joined at the last minute by Stone, who tied up most of the afternoon with a marathon four-hours-plus speech, a crucial split with the administration likely to have serious repercussions. (Wilson was furious. "I'll not even shake hands with him again.") By that point, hundreds of curious onlookers strained to get inside the already jammed reserved galleries, admittance granted only to those with specially printed pink tickets handed out by senators. As midnight drew closer, it was clear that La Follette's gang had the advantage (ironically, their opponents' speeches had actually wasted far more time). And desperate attempts to clear the way for a last-minute vote had no hope of succeeding, as long as La Follette and his followers were prepared to object every time. At one point, seventy-five senators signed a statement attesting that they would vote for the measure if permitted. In the final hours, Fighting Bob himself was hoping to have the last word, but his frustrated colleagues, some of whom were ready to beat the living daylights out of him or worse, would permit no such thing. Finally, at noon on Sunday, March 4, four crashes of the Senate gong signaled that the session was over and the bill was dead. "Bob," a friend told La Follette moments later, "they'll crucify you. But God bless you."

As expected, pundits throughout the country immediately turned their ire on La Follette and what one editorial called his "little group of perverts" who had supported him. But the situation was far more complex than the average American grasped. La Follette himself recognized that there was considerable ambivalence about the bill and that a number of senators were secretly rooting for him, even though they were not about to risk their political future by potentially being on the "wrong side" of such an explosive issue. A few of the more disingenuous types even spoke in favor of the bill on the Senate floor, knowing their speeches were actually helping La Follette by consuming valuable time. And those who now bitterly attacked La Follette's skillful use of the filibuster seemed to be conveniently forgetting how other senators had been cheered for employing the same strategy—for instance, twenty-seven years earlier when a Republican attempt to introduce federal oversight to elections in the South had been similarly thwarted. Others suggested that the filibuster would have failed if Wilson had not waited until the last week of the session to push for legislation, so late that "any small group of Senators," as TR noted, could stop it.

Roosevelt found it difficult to get especially excited about legislation he doubted would accomplish much. Armed neutrality, he sneered, was nothing more than "feeble and timid war." He also could not understand why the public was so worked up about La Follette and company when they were merely parroting what Wilson had said "again and again." To TR, La Follette and Wilson were a pair of interchangeable "skunks," although he knew any criticism of the President right now would backfire. For now Roosevelt would try to continue the "good" behavior he had adopted since the break with Germany while somehow keeping his always volatile emotions in check. His nephew Theodore Robinson and his family were especially concerned. The Robinsons, Leonard Wood wrote in his diary, "are anxious I should do all possible to keep Theodore out of some foolish break, such as going on before war is declared, etc., etc. He is now surrounded by all kinds of fakers."

Addams, on her way to a winter home owned by Mary's brother in Oakland, Florida, was relieved. Armed neutrality in conjunction with other neutrals had seemed reasonable a few weeks earlier as a way to buy time, but the administration's plan seemed to many pacifists to be a direct stepping-stone to war, "too much armed and too little neutrality," as one WPP member observed. The peace forces seemed energized, at least according to the socialist writer Louise Bryant, the wife of John Reed. A day after the filibuster episode, she went to 70 Fifth Avenue to talk to WPP members. Had the Zimmermann Telegram changed their minds? "I'm not defending German morality!" one angrily told her, but this was no more than "an extra complication—not a cause for war." Bryant also visited the offices of the EPF, "perhaps the most radical peace organization," and marveled at how much they had accomplished in just a few weeks. "Before the war," Louis Lochner told her, "the peace movement was a parlor affair and 'goody-goody.' Now it has reached the people in the street."

Most had not lost their faith in Wilson, although at least one WPP member could not understand why. "Some of us believe that the President is inclined toward pacifism, and it is best for him to have all the power," she told Bryant. "They take the attitude that Congress is more belligerent than the President, and that is not at all true."

Chapter 17

THE FINAL BATTLE

MARCH 4–APRIL 10, 1917

It seems to me that exactly the same thing is going on here as in Germany in 1914. The newspapers tell the same lies. The fair weather pacifists make the same excuses for sliding into the abyss, and the faithful stand out without thinking just as they did in Germany.

—David Starr Jordan, April 1917

A few minutes after the tumultuous end of the congressional session, Wilson took the oath for his second term in his small office in the Capitol. House, who had come to Washington the night before, had been invited but elected not to show his face. "I never like to be conspicuously in evidence," he wrote in his diary. "There is enough jealousy abroad without accentuating it unnecessarily."

When the President returned to the White House, the Colonel noticed that his usual self-possession had disappeared. After hearing Wilson rant about what had just occurred in the Senate, House suggested that the President might share his anger with the public. A mention in his upcoming inaugural address did not appeal to Wilson, but he was willing to make a statement sometime that week. House thought that was too long a wait. Why not do it now and "strike while the iron was hot"? Wilson agreed.

Throughout the afternoon, the President worked on a statement to be released to the press that evening. The gist of it was simple. The current rules of the Senate needed to be changed since they had allowed "a little group of eleven Senators" to block legislation to "safeguard the country or to vindicate the elementary rights of its citizens" (a few days later, the Senate would vote during a special session to approve a new cloture rule creating a pathway to limit discussion and prevent filibusters). But Wilson's indirect attack on La Follette and company in the final paragraphs attracted the most attention: "A little group of *willful men*, representing no opinion but their own, have rendered the great Government of the United States helpless and contemptible."

With those words, the President succeeded in further intensifying the growing resentment and hatred of what Ambassador Spring Rice called the "twelve Iscariots," especially La Follette, a man Wilson had once praised on the stump and the only Republican to support his eight-hour railroad legislation. The President seemed unable or unwilling to see the actions of La Follette as anything other than defiance to the wishes of someone who knew better. That La Follette and his colleagues had shown remarkable political courage in opposing what some called "de facto war"—the same political courage that Wilson had demonstrated taking unpopular positions in the past two years—did not seem to occur to him. It was an out-of-character response by Wilson, who later admitted that he might have gone too far.

That evening, trains full of tourists poured into Washington for the public inauguration, which was scheduled the next day. Vendors did a brisk business selling armbands labeled "We stand by our President," a rebuke to not only La Follette but the suffragists whose White House demonstration that rainy afternoon was ignored by Wilson and mocked by his secretarial staff. The increasing pressure to conform disturbed Ellen Slayden. "Will our people," she wrote, "ever reawaken to the good old American belief that disagreeing with a President is not 'treason'?"

Administration officials were relieved that the rain finally let up on Monday, March 5, perhaps more of the Wilson good weather that seemed to come his way during any important occasion. But most of the thousands present could not make out more than a few words of the inaugural address as they shivered in the cold. "The high wind made it impossible for those more than a few feet away to hear," David Lawrence wrote, "and many of them began to leave." Those close enough heard the President repeat his commitment to armed neutrality and his warning that "we may even be drawn . . . to a more active assertion of our rights." And Americans, he explained, "were provincials no longer" but "citizens of the world" committed to the principles outlined in the "Peace without Victory" speech.

It was a happy day for Wilson (less happy for thirsty onlookers, who discovered the Washington saloons had been closed). Afterward, he, Edith, and House watched the fireworks together from the south portico of the White House, the Colonel musing how the Hughes family could easily have been occupying their very seats. Later, they took a ride together, a somewhat questionable decision since a potential assassination had been on everyone's mind all day. When their car got stuck in traffic, House was so concerned that he nervously fingered his pistol. But the crowds were good natured, boisterously shouting for their president. Some were already thinking a third term might be possible.

For House, the only unpleasantness that day was yet another nudge from the First Lady that he take over for Walter Hines Page whenever Wilson finally decided to get rid of his troublesome ambassador. House could only wonder how much Edith distrusted him and whether the President might be swayed to see things her way someday.

Wilson developed a bad cold immediately after the blustery inauguration, further proof to some that the March 4 date should be switched to later in the spring. Cary Grayson, who was about to be confirmed as a rear admiral amid considerable controversy, ordered Wilson to bed, where he would remain for more than a week with few visitors permitted. But the armed neutrality controversy was not about to disappear. The President and other administration officials already believed he had the legal right to arm merchant ships even without congressional authority. By Friday, March 9, he had decided to make it happen. From his bed, he dictated a statement that would be given out to the press later that day under Tumulty's name explaining the President's rationale. At the same time, the press learned that Wilson was convening an early congressional session to begin April 16 since "so much necessary legislation is pressing for consideration."

What this meant remained uncertain. According to one reporter, those in "administration circles" believed the country had never been "so near war with Germany as it is tonight," although some believed the kaiser and company might come to their senses. If the Germans refrained from attacking armed American ships, then a crisis would be avoided. If not, then what? It would all depend on Wilson. Was he willing to go beyond armed neutrality? Henry L. Myers, a Democratic senator from Montana, didn't think so. The President, he told a colleague, "would not declare war on Germany even if the Germans bombarded New York."

New York remained the most war-mad city in America. Two days after Wilson's announcement, churchgoers experienced what some called a "War Sunday" as preachers throughout Gotham boomed fiery patriotic sermons supporting the President and his course ("I think our ministers are going crazy," Wilson had remarked a few weeks earlier). Few went as far as the Brooklyn minister Newell Dwight Hillis's bluntly titled "Why We Should Go to War with Germany," whose mention of TR, "the swiftest racehorse in the world turned out to pasture," sent his Presbyterian congregation attending an evening service into near hysterics.

At that moment, Roosevelt was at a private dinner in Manhattan at the Metropolitan Club, where the topic was the future defense of the city and surroundings. The gathering of twenty or so was heavy on Republicans, but also included the tycoon J. P. Morgan Jr. and Franklin Roosevelt as an administration representative. FDR's star among preparedness types had continued to rise. The rumor was that only through FDR's prodding was the supposedly incompetent Josephus Daniels taking real moves to strengthen the navy. One of House's navy informants even told him that more than a few wanted FDR in and Daniels out, although the Colonel believed the constant criticisms of the secretary of the navy were seldom justified.

The dinner appeared to be mostly harmonious. Few present could disagree with Leonard Wood's contention that America was still "unready and could do very little" (Wood would soon be transferred out of New York to a new command in Charleston, which he was certain was payback from the administration). It was only when Wilson's name was mentioned that tempers flared—namely, TR's. Elihu Root's mistake of parroting what Roosevelt called the "general idiot cry" to stand by the President predictably set off TR, forcing Wood to intervene to keep the peace. But Roosevelt was not completely pacified. "The people who have at each turn of events shrieked that we must 'stand by the President' are only less guilty than he is," he grumbled.

Addams and other pacifists, while disappointed that their victory in the armed neutrality fight was short-lived, still would not make the final break with Wilson. Addams's friend Emily Balch wired Wilson immediately after his inaugural address to praise his allusions to "international idealism and constructive peace" and predicted the President would do great things for "world peace . . . if this country does not become involved." Between the flattery, she expressed her own fear of armed neutrality "as a probable prelude to war" and her opposition to "war as a tolerable policy even under far greater provocation than we have suffered." Perhaps such talk would give Wilson pause. "The President has changed his mind before," Lella Secor noted, "and we will fight the arming of these boats to the end."

The pacifists were convinced, probably rightly, that most Americans still did not want war. The Zimmermann Telegram hysteria had already worn off, judging by its rare press mentions by the second week of March. The problem was how to channel the war opposition into something concrete. The Emergency Peace Federation established a "Commission of Inquiry," where participants discussed ways to resolve the differences between Germany and America. "Militarists" such as Roosevelt were even invited, although TR naturally had no interest in appearing at one of the daily sessions. The EPF also hoped that La Follette's recent stand would spark more resistance on Capitol Hill, but the signs were growing bleaker by the day. "The discouraging thing about it all is that our friends in both houses are convinced that we are drifting right into war, no matter how much they may try to save the situation," Louis Lochner observed. "Privately they tell you, 'After all, what's the use.'"

The vilifications, the effigy burnings, the demand for recall could not help but weaken the resolve of even the most peace-loving politician. Pacifists, critics now sneered, were nothing more than "anarchists" and advocates of "pro-Germanism" and should no longer be tolerated. And institutions and individuals of all stripes continued to fall into line. Major league baseball players were now drilling, some with bats, during spring training. In Chicago, the public schools began to require the pledge of allegiance and instituted military training for all high school boys. At Columbia University, the board of trustees floated a plan to stop the "preaching of disloyal doctrine in the classroom," while students now felt free to rough up two young men who tried to speak out against a reserve battalion. In Boston, 106 social workers signed a telegram sent to Wilson and Massachusetts congressmen indicating their hearty support of armed neutrality instead of the "peace at any price propaganda of certain eminent social workers, for instance, Miss Jane Addams."

Addams had never been peace at any price. That many people still believed she was showed just how garbled the pacifist message had become. The difficulty of getting accurate peace news into the mainstream media had always frustrated her and the problem had only worsened of late. There were some, including her friend the educator John Dewey, who believed the pacifists might have a better chance at success by pursuing more realistic goals in the first place. "It is not sensible to work for things that are impossible of attainment, such as keeping the country's ships . . . off the ocean, or letting them be destroyed indefinitely and doing nothing about it," he explained.

To such practical arguments, the pacifists might point to miraculous events in Russia, where the war had become extraordinarily unpopular. While Wilson was deciding on armed neutrality, protests were brewing throughout Russia, culminating in the shocking overthrow of Tsar Nicholas and the establishment of a new liberal government. Virtually every American greeted the news with excitement. On New York City's Lower East Side, crowds of happy Jews celebrated the end of the monarchy with cries of "Nicholas has at last got his medicine" and "the Almighty has revenged our brethren whom he caused to be slaughtered in pogroms." Roosevelt was just as excited. "Russia is wonderful!" he wrote a friend. House, as usual, used the news as another opportunity to butter up Wilson: "I am not too sure that the present outcome in Russia is not due largely to your influence."

Everyone understood the revolution in Russia was likely to change the course of the war. Pacifists hoped it might bring it to a speedy conclusion.

"The Russian Socialists may save the world yet!" Rosika Schwimmer's close friend Lola Maverick Lloyd wrote Louis Lochner. "They are demanding peace—& the thing may prove contagious."

Unfortunately, the Russian Revolution did not prove to be a harbinger for peace, at least not immediately. The new provisional government ultimately continued the fight, a fateful decision that contributed to its overthrow by Lenin and the Bolsheviks later that year. And the American situation was growing more tenuous by the day. On Monday, March 12, the American tank steamer *Algonquin* was intercepted on its way to London by a German submarine and destroyed after the crew and captain abandoned ship. (Three weeks earlier, the same captain had pooh-poohed travel in the war zone as less dangerous than "trying to make my way about New York streets and dodging taxicabs.") Since no lives were lost and the *Algonquin* was technically fair game, as she had been transferred from the British to American registry after the war began, the episode was another "gray area" sinking in the vein of the earlier *Housatonic* and *Lyman M. Law* incidents, not the dramatic "overt act" everyone was awaiting.

The news reached the White House on Wednesday morning. Wilson's cold had improved enough that he was preparing to go back to his office by the end of the week. Outside the confines of the Executive Mansion, the city was convulsed by the outbreak of a streetcar strike. To get to work, most Washingtonians took cabs or walked, while a few brave souls rode trolleys operated by strikebreakers. They soon became the target of angry brick throwers, some of whom chalked the word "scab" on the cars.

More concerning for Wilson was the very real possibility of a nationwide railroad strike. The eight-hour Adamson Act of the previous fall was supposed to go into effect on January 1, but the railroads had delayed compliance until the Supreme Court ruled on its constitutionality. Tired of the foot-dragging and fearing that war might further delay the new policy, the four major railroad brotherhoods announced that a strike would begin on Saturday, March 17. A strike of this kind, Wilson knew, could not come at a worse time, especially if the National Guard or army had to be deployed to keep the trains running. A mediation committee that included both

Franklin Lane and William Wilson from the cabinet was quickly assembled in the hope of bringing the parties together.

The pressure on Wilson that weekend was unyielding. The first armed American ship, the *St. Louis*, departed. Many wondered whether America's initial battle with a submarine would follow. (The kaiser, meanwhile, flatly rejected any talk of reopening negotiations at this late date. "If Wilson wants war," he wrote on Sunday, "he can make it and then have it!") And the stream of the usual eccentrics showing up at the White House added to his stress, including a confused Russian woman named Anna Rahlicka. "God sent me to see the President," she announced. "He told me to instruct him as to the best methods of settling the conditions of the working girls in Russia and in the United States." The next day, two men who had walked part of the way from Toledo tried to call Wilson from Union Station to brief him about a "bullet proof armor" used by the Japanese and a special glass allowing one to see objects one thousand miles away.

On Sunday afternoon, March 18, Wilson was out with Edith enjoying one of their usual automobile rides. Like most of the country, he was encouraged by the announcement the day before that the strike action had been delayed for forty-eight hours, which proved to be long enough for the parties to come to an agreement, even before the Supreme Court upheld the Adamson Act on Monday. When the President returned to the White House, Tumulty was waiting with bad news. German submarines had sunk three more American vessels. The *Vigilancia* had been torpedoed without warning on Friday morning, its survivors adrift in lifeboats until rescued on Sunday afternoon. Fifteen did not make it, six of them American citizens. On Saturday afternoon, it was the *City of Memphis*'s turn, off the southern coast of Ireland, although the men made it onto lifeboats after a warning was given. Finally, a Texaco tanker known as the *Illinois* went down without warning near Alderney, one of the Channel Islands, on Sunday with no casualties, the fourteenth victim that week of the *UC-21*.

Was this finally the long awaited "overt act"? Many Americans who learned of the sinkings in Sunday late editions or the Monday morning paper thought so. Three U.S. merchant ships had been attacked, two without warning, and six American citizens were dead. The Germans obviously were not going to spare American shipping this time. At minimum, the sinkings strengthened the argument that armed neutrality was not only desirable but should have been done weeks earlier. And German submarines might think twice in the future, now faced with the possibility of being sunk by a "four-inch shell" at the hands of the "*St. Louis* or some other American liner," as one reporter wrote.

Upon hearing the news, TR predictably abandoned his promise to keep silent. "I felt that it would not do for me to fail to speak at this moment," he explained to Lodge. In a statement to the press crafted on Monday, Roosevelt insisted that since Germany had committed "overt acts of war" and was "already at war with us," there was nothing left to do except to "decide . . . whether we shall make war nobly or ignobly . . . and regain the right to look the whole world in the eyes without flinching." He also sent off a wire to Newton Baker, who again offered not the slightest encouragement to TR's desire to "raise a division for immediate service to the front."

Roosevelt would not be deterred. War was coming and he had to be part of it. On Tuesday, March 20, he attended a gathering of Republican leaders at the Union League Club, where he repeated his arguments that the country was already at war and needed to "go to war hard." Afterward, he talked with Hughes and Root about his desire to go overseas and die for his country and how he would need their help to persuade Wilson to let him go.

"Theodore," Root told him, "if you can make Wilson believe that you will not come back, he will let you go."

The Union League meeting provided comic fodder for Will Rogers, who was appearing at the National Theatre in Washington that week as part of the Ziegfeld Follies, along with Fanny Brice, W. C. Fields, and other luminaries. "Mr. Root and Mr. Hughes and Mr. Roosevelt," Rogers began, "had a meeting the other night in New York and declared war all by themselves. . . . Mr. Hughes told the meeting what he would have done in the eight hours that he was President. . . . According to Mr. Roosevelt we've missed three years of good war already." Wilson, in the audience with his daughter, Margaret, and Helen Bones, could not help but chuckle.

It was not a laughing matter for Roosevelt. In his more introspective moments, he sensed that there would be no battlefield glory and told Leonard Wood as much. Still, TR was a long way from giving up. The proposed division was just about ready, although applications continued to pour in, some even from children eager to serve as drummer boys or nurses' assistants. A good many applicants were African Americans, who were told the War Department would likely not permit integrated units. For now, there was little Roosevelt could do except wait. He had already made plans to accompany Russell J. Coles, a Virginia tobacco dealer and celebrated outdoorsman said to be a ringer for Taft, on an expedition to hunt devilfish, "the big game of the seas," in Florida. (When he heard about the expedition, Taft joked that he hoped the "Devil-fish would make up for the failure of the lions to do their duty" when TR had gone to Africa.)

"I am old," Roosevelt told Coles, "and not fit for much exertion; my eyes are bad, but I can sit in a boat during a fight with a Devil-Fish, and after a while might take part myself in it." That TR could make such statements and still believe he should be sent to France is startling, as photographs from spring 1917 show a plump Roosevelt looking older than his fifty-eight years.

Before departing, TR took the time to fire off yet another letter to Baker, reminding the secretary of war that he was a "retired commander in chief of the United States Army . . . eligible to any position of command over American troops to which I may be appointed" and providing other helpful information about his past military service. This time, Baker shared the correspondence with Wilson, who was appalled. "This is one of the most extraordinary documents I ever read," the President wrote Baker. "Thank you for letting me undergo the discipline of temper involved in reading it in silence!"

On March 19, the Monday following the three weekend sinkings, Wilson agonized over what to do next. As usual, Lansing pushed for immediate action. Why not call Congress in sooner and have its members contemplate a declaration of war? The secretary of state dangled the possibility that involvement "would aid the Russian liberals and might even cause revolution in Germany." But the President shuddered at what an unpredictable Congress might do, especially the "out-and-out pacifists" and the likes of William Stone. Wilson's apparent preference for doing nothing unnerved

Lansing and Frank Polk, so much so that Polk frantically called House twice in New York that day complaining of the President's "inertia" and requesting House's presence in Washington to "stir him into action." The Colonel stayed put, but he did send off a letter to Wilson that day. Like Roosevelt, he suggested that "we can no longer shut our eyes to the fact we are already in the war." And American involvement against Germany was "bound to break their morale and bring the war to an earlier close," a premise strongly rejected by some pacifists.

But the President still had serious doubts about going beyond armed neutrality. That afternoon, he expressed his misgivings in a conversation with Frank Cobb, the editor of the administration-friendly *New York World*, who later misremembered the date of the conversation as occurring two weeks later. War, Wilson told him, was an extremely unappealing path to pursue. American involvement would result in Germany being crushed, the very opposite of the "peace without victory" he had advocated in January. The President also fretted about the likely domestic impact. A nation under arms would "forget there ever was such a thing as tolerance. To fight you must be brutal and ruthless, and the spirit of ruthless brutality will enter into the very fibre of our national life."

As much as Addams and others might have hoped, Wilson was not a pacifist. He bristled angrily that week when a visitor told him that "people believed he would not fight under any circumstances." War, he believed, was sometimes justifiable and unavoidable, even if he personally found it distasteful. But he genuinely recoiled at the thought of sending thousands of young Americans to their deaths and had once fretted that "God would hold him accountable." And as much as the charge of Anglophile would be hurled at him in the future, he did not entirely trust the Allies or their ambitions (he would soon learn of their secret treaties promising territory to coalition members). Maintaining the current state of armed neutrality, then, seemed a reasonable option.

But deep down inside Wilson likely recognized that TR was right. Armed neutrality was in fact "timid war." If American ships were going to be free to blast away at German U-boats, then why not declare war officially and assume the advantages formal participation would bring? Only then would the United States have the seat at the peace table Wilson wanted so badly.

He knew there were other factors to consider. As much as the city dwellers on the East Coast were ready to go to war, vast sections of the Midwest, South, and West were indifferent. House himself admitted that the true "sentiment of America" bore almost no resemblance to the noisy clamor on the Eastern Seaboard. Wilson, David Lawrence explained, "must decide which is the truer Americanism. He must interpret the will of America. . . . He must mould a new foreign policy or stand squarely on the old and traditional doctrines that have done so long." The stakes were enormously high, likely to "shape the destiny of the United States for generations, and perhaps centuries to come."

Wilson very much understood the gravity of the decision, but it was one he was prepared to make himself. Still, he knew that much of the cabinet was leaning toward war. "We're at war," one anonymous member told a reporter, "why not fight?"

The Tuesday afternoon cabinet meeting loomed as one of the most important of Wilson's presidency to date. The question Wilson brought before them was whether to convene Congress sooner than April 16 in view of the current crisis and what action he should request of them. McAdoo, Baker, Lansing, Agriculture Secretary David Houston, and Commerce Secretary William Redfield all favored bringing in Congress sooner with the intention of obtaining a declaration of war; they differed on whether American involvement should extend beyond finances and naval support. Labor Secretary William Wilson, who according to Lansing tended to "temporize with the German Government," also fell into line, as did Attorney General Thomas Gregory and Postmaster General Albert Burleson.

Wilson then asked to hear from Josephus Daniels, the most dedicated pacifist of the bunch and a Bryan devotee. Surely, he would resist. But Daniels, "eyes . . . suffused with tears," according to Lansing, agreed that war was the correct choice. "I could not but wonder whether he spoke from conviction," Lansing wrote, "or because he lacked strength of mind to stand out against the united opinion of his colleagues." Franklin Lane, the tenth and final cabinet member to speak, merely added his assent to the chorus, although he annoyed the President to no end by suggesting the public pressure "would force us to act even if we were unwilling to do so."

"I do not care for popular demand," Wilson had already informed them. "I want to do right, whether popular or not."

By the end of the meeting, Wilson had decided Congress would be brought back in just thirteen days, on April 2, or two weeks earlier than originally planned. The fifty or so reporters gathered outside were not alerted to the decision, but the usual cabinet leakers, Lane and McAdoo, informed a few of their press pals of what was coming.

The next morning, Wilson signed the proclamation changing the date to April 2 in time for the news to reach the afternoon editions. In the afternoon, he went for a two-mile walk with Edith. To Thomas Brahany, one of Wilson's secretaries, the President seemed relatively calm, albeit a bit disengaged. Wilson, Brahany recorded that day, "apparently . . . is not in a working mood" and "spends nearly all his time with Mrs. Wilson, reading, playing pool or visiting."

The news shocked Addams, who was finding the Florida sunshine especially beneficial to her health. The peace forces, she realized, now had just days to stop America from being hurled into war. La Follette believed Wilson had intentionally pushed up the date to make it more difficult for the pacifist cause to gain traction in Congress (Bryan, among others, believed "every day of deliberation will increase opposition to war"). But at least one of the new members of the incoming congressional class appeared to be on their side: Jeannette Rankin was eager to talk with Addams about how she might help the cause in the House. At the moment, Rankin had eclipsed Addams as the most high-profile woman in America. TR had supported her congressional run in the fall, and the press had fawned over her every move and appropriate femininity ever since ("she has neglected to become mannish," wrote one reporter approvingly). Rankin was handling the press crush remarkably well, deflecting questions about her possible pacifist ways. "My hair isn't red, and neither are my policies," she announced.

Addams planned to be in Washington on April 10. At that time, a rendezvous with Rankin might be possible. For now, Addams would follow developments from afar, recognizing that pacifists would need to make a herculean effort to get their cause heard. Even Ford was hit up for money (which he ignored), and a group made a pilgrimage to see Colonel House on Sunday, March 25. As usual, House congratulated himself on his skillful handling of his visitors. "I think I satisfied them that the President knew more about the situation than they did, and was quite as anxious to keep out of war."

Mass meetings, demonstrations, wires, and literature would be the main pacifist strategy in the brief time remaining. Surely, Congress would follow the will of the people if it could be clearly expressed to them. That the pacifists' chances were slim did not dampen their ardor, at least those who had not jumped ship in the last few days. "It's great fun we are having," Louis Lochner remarked. "We are likely to lose out, but we shall die hard."

Lochner was involved in the first big event of the campaign on Saturday, what he called a "counter-demonstration" at Madison Square Garden in response to a superpatriotic meeting/TR lovefest held two days earlier, heavily attended by "Wall Street employees under orders," according to David Starr Jordan. Jordan, one of the Saturday speakers, made a benign reference to Roosevelt as a man who had once spoken for peace. A chorus of angry boos followed, punctuated by a single "H'ray for Teddy," which immediately prompted a brawl. The anger toward TR that night was inescapable. Speakers openly scorned "our bloodthirsty ex-President" and denounced him as the "greatest moral coward in America." The city planner Benjamin Marsh, who had waded into the prowar meeting on Thursday, only to be "ejected and beaten up," was especially bitter. "Let us all pray for the death of Root and Roosevelt before April 2," he shouted.

That twelve thousand people showed up with hundreds more unable to get inside provided a ray of hope, especially since signs announcing the event had been vandalized and most of the press had not been helpful. But espousing the pacifist viewpoint publicly was becoming increasingly risky. That same day, a San Francisco man soliciting signatures for a war referendum found himself being arrested after a woman complained, only to be released when police discovered he was guilty of nothing. General Horatio C. King, a Civil War veteran and onetime Bull Mooser, could see nothing wrong with the police pursuing such an aggressive strategy. "A few arrests now," he wrote in a letter appearing in the next day's *New York Herald*, "would not be ill timed."

The attacks directed at some pacifists were becoming more personal and vicious. "You contemptible white livered cowardly dogs," a Chicagoan angrily fumed in an anonymous letter to a local pacifist organization for daring to leave a flyer titled "The People Do Not Want War" in his mailbox. Some communities, fearing the potential of coordinated German uprisings if war was declared, began to make lists of their German American citizens. In Baltimore, home of a large German community, police were said to be interested in acquiring two machine guns, to be "used only during riots." Even at the White House, an "inoffensive German employed . . . to tend the fires" attracted suspicion. "The people are now in a hysterical condition; like a mob that cannot be reasoned with," the old pacifist congressman and Civil War vet Isaac Sherwood lamented.

In such a heated atmosphere, was the die cast for war? Some believed Wilson still had another option: ask Congress for a "vigorous policy of protection without a war declaration," a path believed to have considerable support in the West and one that Amos Pinchot implored the President to consider. But Wilson no longer appeared interested in appeasing the pacifist element, as Jordan discovered when he tried to make an appointment to see him. "The President," he wrote his wife, "has lost his nerve."

If Wilson had not lost his nerve, he was showing signs of being overwhelmed. When House came to Washington on Tuesday, March 27, six days before the new congressional session, he found Wilson bothered by a headache, more than likely stress related. A few days earlier, he learned that another American ship had been sunk, this time a Standard Oil steamer named the *Healdton*. But the President, House noticed, still seemed uncertain about several issues, namely whether to "ask Congress to declare war" or "say that a state of war exists, and ask them for the necessary means to carry it on." Wilson also appeared uncomfortable about potentially filling the role of a war president. The Colonel conceded the point, admitting that "a man of coarser fiber and one less a philosopher than the President," was better suited to "conduct a brutal, vigorous and successful war." But he offered him encouragement. All Wilson had to do was follow the template other countries had already established during the Great War. And House reminded the President that someone who had enjoyed such remarkable success controlling the disparate elements of his party should have no trouble succeeding even in an admittedly unfamiliar situation.

The two men discussed Wilson's upcoming message to Congress, which had begun to take shape. House was pleased that the President would make a distinction "between the German people" and their leaders. Once again, the supposedly self-effacing House eagerly recorded in his diary that "I believe I suggested this to him" two years earlier. There was also cabinet talk, Wilson railing about Lansing's mediocrity but unwilling to dump him. The recent rumors of the possible formation of a new coalition cabinet with TR as secretary of war were absurd, but House did suggest to the First Lady that it might be wise for Wilson to consider greater outreach to Republicans. It would not be easy, Edith told him, as "neither of them could endure people they did not trust or like."

Miles from Washington, Roosevelt was in a one-room houseboat with Russell Coles and his crew in the Gulf of Mexico, basking in the afterglow of his recent battles with the devilfish. On their first day out, on Monday, March 26, they had spied a school of the exotic creatures. Originally, the plan was for Coles to demonstrate the proper killing technique before giving TR a chance, but time was now of the essence since Roosevelt had cut the trip to a single week. With Coles's coaching and help, TR bagged his first devilfish after an eleven-minute struggle. "He jumped up and down and yelled with myself and the rest of the crew over his victory," Coles later reported. After towing it back to shore, they returned to the school, where they speared another of the "big game of the sea," this one a monster over thirteen feet wide, Coles generously giving most of the credit to Roosevelt. The remainder of the expedition was less successful (TR's loud snoring ensured no one got much sleep), but he had enjoyed the experience immensely. "It is a good sport," he later observed, "but not exactly the kind to recommend to a weakling, or one at all nervous of a little danger."

With less than a week remaining, the Emergency Peace Federation decided to focus much of its final efforts on a gigantic demonstration in Washington on April 2. "We are going to invade the Capital," a mass mailing explained, "to tell Congress and the President that the American people will not be forced into war—not to fight the battles of other empires, not to gratify financial powers, not to uphold 'American rights' when far more precious rights would have to be sacrificed in the process." In preparation, the EPF sent an advance group to Washington to establish headquarters at 1221 Pennsylvania Avenue, less than a mile from the White House, and planned to secure a parade permit from local authorities. The strong likelihood they would be egged did not deter them, but D.C. officials eventually put the kibosh on any march.

They desperately needed money for telegrams to flood Congress and the mountain of literature they needed to distribute. On Thursday, March 29, the Woman's Committee of the EPF ran ads in the major New York dailies hoping to raise $200,000 in the next day. "This pitifully small sum may save countless thousands from a horrible death. . . . Send in what you can NOW. Don't delay." Some Gothamites were infuriated that the press agreed to accept bleeding-heart pacifist advertising in the midst of a crisis, but others were touched by the appeal. The next day, Emily Balch watched in amazement as lines began to form at the EPF's Fifth Avenue headquarters. Poor immigrant women from the East Side arrived clutching dollar bills, as did a young bootblack. A few factory girls kicked in $6.85. One mother contributed five $20 gold coins. "I don't want my boy to go to the trenches and be killed," she told them. Sacks of mail brought even more donations, so many that empty trash cans were used as temporary storage. "Please let also this dollar do its share in preserving Peace, and save our Husbands," a Harlem woman wrote. "We voted for President Woodrow Wilson for Peace, and we Americans of the west would like Peace," a northern California woman asserted.

By Friday noon, the EPF had added $35,000 (approximately $700,000 in 2020 dollars) to its coffers, an impressive sum in such a short time. That so many were willing to give suggested the very real ambivalence that persisted, even after the Zimmermann Telegram and the recent sinkings. The *New York Tribune*, a longtime supporter of the Allies, surveyed twenty-four congressmen from the West and found that only nine supported war. And scattered referendums, including in three small towns in La Follette's Wisconsin, reflected further opposition. If America was to go to war next week, it would be with a sense of grim acceptance, rather than enthusiasm.

Still, the hurdles facing the pacifists remained almost insurmountable, especially on the more war-mad East Coast. That week, they found their meetings blocked at Princeton, intentionally disrupted at Harvard, and cancelled by local authorities in Philadelphia (one of the proposed speakers was let go from his teaching position at the University of Pennsylvania a few days later). The war, David Starr Jordan lamented that Friday, "even the prospect of it, the eager hope for it has raised an incredible flood of hate, intolerance and absolute lying." (That week he had informed an audience that "it costs $50,000 to kill one German. How many do you want to kill at that price?" "All of them," they shouted.)

More disturbing was the intense pressure to accept the inevitability of war and show one's patriotism as conspicuously as possible. And as Addams had long recognized, women were just as susceptible as men. A few days earlier, a twenty-year-old named Loretta Walsh made history as the first woman to enlist in the navy as a yeoman in the reserve. In Boston, female employees of the Shepard Department Store had already begun drilling at Fenway Park. In Salina, Kansas, a group of women clad in military dress accosted male passersby demanding to know "why they had not enlisted in" the National Guard. At Herald Square, a Manhattanite named Julia Wheelock, soon to be known as one of the best navy recruiters in the country, appealed to young men to join up immediately. "The pacifists are robbing us of our moral courage," she told the crowd. "But don't let them. Enlist today and show them just where you stand." Not surprisingly, J. Stuart Blackton's newest "photoplay" highlighted the patriotism of women, supposedly at the behest of TR, who appeared in the film. *Womanhood, the Glory of the Nation*, about to debut in New York that weekend, was another slice of preparedness propaganda in the same vein as Blackton's *Battle Cry of Peace*, this time featuring a female "martyred patriot" who "died that America might live."

The Washington demonstration on Monday, April 2, the pacifists hoped, would be a powerful answer to such patriotic hoopla, the dramatic culmination of months of effort. Originally, they planned on marching from New York until they realized its impracticality. Instead, the main vanguard, sporting white tulips and "Keep Out of War" armbands, left from Pennsylvania Station after midnight, with other delegations to follow (they crossed paths with House, who left for Washington only minutes before). That the gathering was not quite as large as they hoped was not entirely surprising. Only the diehards seemed willing to cough up the fourteen-dollar round-trip fare and face the scorn likely to be heaped upon them in the capital (the sociologist Franklin Giddings had already denounced the "alleged males" planning to attend).

Lochner reached out to Addams earlier on Sunday, trying to get her to reconsider coming to Washington. But she turned him down, just as she had rejected a request a few days earlier to add her name to yet another telegram to the President. Her last meeting with Wilson had convinced her that he was no longer interested in pacifist arguments, if he had ever been in the first place.

By Sunday, April 1, Wilson was putting the finishing touches on his address to Congress. It had taken him ten hours to complete typing it himself. "I write with difficulty," he told House a few weeks later, "and it takes everything out of me." No one in the cabinet had any idea precisely what he would do, hardly surprising since he often found them more nuisance than help. The outstanding question was how far he would go the next day. "Many here remain convinced that if there is a middle course remaining that middle course will be found," remarked a Washington correspondent.

TR, his fishing trip over, hoped there would be no middle course. "There are some who advocate giving France a billion dollars," he told a crowd in Lakeland, Florida, that evening. "If we are to enter this war, let us enter as Americans . . . and not stand back and pay someone else to do our fighting." At ten o'clock, his train departed. If everything went as scheduled, he would be in Washington by Tuesday. For what reason, no one knew.

In the early hours of Monday morning, the pacifists began to arrive at Union Station. The signs of war were everywhere: American flags, recruiters, even an electric sign on Pennsylvania Avenue with the message THE NAVY

NEEDS YOU—AMERICA FIRST! They were to report to headquarters, where badges and armbands would be provided to anyone not already equipped. Viewing the scene, Ellen Slayden acknowledged a greater tolerance for pacifists since the Spanish-American War. "A young man wearing such a thing then would have been mobbed." Once organized, the "peace pilgrims" (who had been followed into D.C. by the rival "pilgrims of patriotism," headquartered a few yards from the EPF) were to make every effort to see their congressional representatives that morning before they convened at noon.

Around eleven, a group from Massachusetts showed up at the office of Senator Henry Cabot Lodge. Lodge naturally told them he had no interest in any of their arguments and planned to support a declaration of war. "Any one who is a pacifist at a time like this is a coward," he said. "Any one that wants to go to war is a coward," responded Alexander Bannwart, a thirty-six-year-old Swiss-born Wilson supporter and former minor league ballplayer from Boston. "You are a damned liar," Lodge roared back. "I might return the compliment," Bannwart remarked.

All hell then broke loose. The account that most Americans read the next day suggested that Bannwart had hit Lodge, and the Massachusetts patrician had returned the blow. At that point, a Western Union messenger and Lodge's secretaries jumped Bannwart, beating him badly and accidentally hitting a female member of the delegation. The police soon arrived and arrested Bannwart, who was released the next day, when Addams's wealthy friend and WPP colleague Elizabeth Glendower Evans bailed him out.

Lodge eventually dropped the charges, but Bannwart insisted he had done nothing wrong. "He just hauled off and hit me as hard as he could," Bannwart explained. "Why, if I had hit Senator Lodge first I wouldn't have a leg to stand on." Most of the press chose to downplay if not ignore Bannwart's version of events. After all, where was the story if the sixty-six-year-old Lodge hit the pacifist first? Stacks of telegrams soon poured into Lodge's office, congratulating him for putting "a fist in pacifist." But two years later, the truth finally came out. After a threatened lawsuit, Lodge was forced to admit that Bannwart had acted in self-defense. It was too late to undo the damage to Bannwart's reputation.

At the time the Bannwart brawl ended, the new congresswoman Jeannette

Rankin was on her way to the House Office Building, before convening with the rest of the new Congress at noon. Earlier that morning, she had been the guest of honor at a remarkable breakfast at the Shoreham Hotel, where the two feuding wings of the suffrage movement temporarily set aside their differences to jointly celebrate her accomplishment. On one side of Rankin sat Carrie Chapman Catt of the National American Woman Suffrage Association, on the other sat Alice Paul of the National Woman's Party. Rankin was already feeling tremendous pressure on her first day. Her suffrage friends, she knew, wanted her to do nothing that would harm their cause. Support Wilson now, and the suffrage cause would be sure to benefit. If she didn't, it would show "female emotionality and sentimentalism and would set back the whole movement," they told her. Her brother, who had worked hard for her election, also pushed her to take the most expedient course. But the pacifists pleaded with her to stand strong with them this week. The hordes of newsreel cameras, reporters, autograph seekers, well-wishers, and "cranks" of all kinds following her every move since she arrived in Washington on Sunday only added to her stress.

Loud cheering and hearty handshakes from members of both parties soon greeted her when she took her seat in the House chamber for the first time. "Something I never expected to see," remarked an elderly messenger. "But I like her. There's nothing stuck up about her." The selection of the Speaker of the House and other routine bits of business followed, but the presence of the lady from Montana provided a temporary distraction from the more pressing concern of what the President was going to do that day.

Wilson's message had gone to the printer before breakfast. Afterward, he was out on the golf links in Virginia with Edith before returning to the White House in time for lunch. The cabinet still had no idea of its contents, although Wilson read the complete message to House, who had arrived at the White House at seven that morning. That the President had apparently only shared it with him (and perhaps the First Lady) pleased House immensely, almost as much as the speech itself. The Colonel was certain that much of the address was heavily influenced by his many discussions with Wilson. "It would be interesting to know how much of his address the President thinks I suggested," House observed. "He does not indicate, in any way, that he is conscious that I had any part in it."

Wilson did not want to wait until the next day to speak before a joint session of Congress. He also did not want to speak after three, fearing "it would make a bad impression" and "that he was unduly pressing matters." Everything depended on how quickly Congress finished its organization. When his three o'clock deadline proved impossible, he agreed to the 8:00 p.m. time offered by House Majority Leader Claude Kitchin. There was nothing to do now except wait. As the hours passed, the enormity of what lay ahead became apparent to the President, who uncharacteristically began to betray "signs of nervousness," according to House. Wilson knew that he was about to make the most important speech of his life, if not in American history.

The pacifists' day had not gone as smoothly as they hoped. Their attempt to demonstrate on the steps of the Capitol at noon was broken up by law enforcement. "They have discriminated against us," one complained. "While they allowed the militarists to keep their stations up here, they drive us to the street below." The so-called pilgrims of patriotism soon showed up to heckle the pacifists, cheering when the police pushed them back. Afterward, the pacifists headed for a business meeting at Convention Hall, also used by National Guardsmen, who had already hung up "ludicrous cartoons" mocking them as "Dangerous Citizens." When they heard Wilson would be speaking later that afternoon, they raced back to the Capitol only to discover that it was a false alarm. David Starr Jordan, whose speaking engagement in Baltimore the night before had turned violent thanks to an enraged group of local "business men, professors. . . . and students," had already made a futile attempt to meet with Wilson. Jordan himself understood it was likely useless. "I have known the President for more than twenty-five years," he later remarked. "but I can think of no common grounds upon which we could possibly meet this week."

Wilson had frittered away most of the remainder of the afternoon at the White House, except for quick visits to the offices of Daniels and Lansing. Around six thirty, he dined with House and family members with no talk of what lay ahead. A few minutes after eight, it was time to go. House,

Pacifists demonstrate on the steps of the Capitol, April 2, 1917.
(Library of Congress: LC-H261-2930-B)

two of Wilson's daughters, Helen Bones, and a few others left first, followed by Wilson, Edith, Tumulty, Grayson, and Colonel William Harts, the President's military aide. At the northeast gate, Wilson heard a crowd singing "The Star-Spangled Banner," "Dixie," "Yankee Doodle," and then "America" as the car departed. Heavy security was everywhere during the brief trip, which veered off into side streets to throw off any potential assassin among the crowds of enthusiastic onlookers lining the usual route to the Capitol. When he arrived around 8:40, he noticed the exterior of the Capitol brightly illuminated as an additional security measure, augmented by the presence of cavalrymen from nearby Fort Myer who made sure no one got in without special passes.

At the first sighting of the President inside, the packed galleries, most of the Supreme Court, the cabinet, Franklin and Eleanor Roosevelt, several ambassadors present, and most of Congress erupted in applause. La Follette, who did not sport the miniature American flag Senator George McLean of Connecticut had given out to his colleagues, elected not to join in, nor did at least two other "willful men." The press made a significant fuss about this later, but Wilson himself was not comfortable with the enthusiastic applause during such a momentous occasion. After House speaker

Champ Clark called the gathering to order, the President made his way to the clerk's desk to speak.

His voice, the audience noted, was quiet at first ("the voice of a tired man," one reporter remarked) and grew louder as he progressed. "To my mind," the suffragist Maud Wood Park later wrote, "there was no animation or appeal in the cool voice that went on slowly, clearly, collectedly." David Lawrence thought the President looked "visibly nervous . . . his fingers trembled. His face was pale." Wilson began by recounting the German decision to undertake unrestricted submarine warfare, "a warfare against mankind" and "a war against all nations." Five weeks earlier, he had believed that armed neutrality was the appropriate response, but now he saw this as "impracticable." Germany had already suggested that neutral crews who fired upon their submarines in the restricted zones would be treated "as pirates." Armed neutrality, then, could never work as intended and would "likely . . . produce what it was meant to prevent"—war (the very point La Follette had made, for which he had been vilified). "There is one choice we cannot make, we are incapable of making," the President continued, "we will not choose the path of submission." For the first time, the audience cheered. "With a profound sense of the solemn and even tragical character of the step I am taking and of the grave responsibilities which it involves," he was recommending that Congress take the fateful step to declare war. And those who had predicted financial involvement only were startled to hear Wilson state that half a million men would need to be added to the armed forces.

For what was America fighting? Not for material gain or profit but for the "same things" he had outlined in his earlier addresses this year: upholding the "principles of peace and justice . . . against selfish and autocratic power" and establishing some kind of organization of democratic nations to maintain peace in the future. Imperial Germany could never participate in such an organization, although it was not its people who were the enemy but its leaders, the same leaders who had done everything in their power to cook up conspiracies of all kinds in America since the war began, culminating with the recent Mexican note. Germany, then, posed a unique threat that must be quelled. "The world must be made safe for democracy," he insisted. "Its peace must be planted upon the tested foundations of political liberty."

Wilson had now spoken about thirty minutes. Adding to the drama was news spreading through the Capitol that an armed American ship, the *Aztec*, had been sunk, with twenty-eight deaths. Now on his final paragraph, the President again expressed his reluctance to reach this decision. "It is a fearful thing to lead this great peaceful people into war [La Follette supposedly "cleared his throat twice sharply"], into the most terrible and disastrous of all wars, civilization itself seeming to be in the balance," he admitted. "But the *right* is more precious than *peace*" (words that would have delighted Roosevelt), and America would go to war for the noblest of principles: "democracy . . . the right of those who submit to authority to have a voice in their own governments . . . rights and liberties of small nations" and the peacekeeping organization of "free peoples" that Wilson had already mentioned. "To such a task," he concluded, "we can dedicate our lives and our fortunes, everything that we are and everything that we have, with the pride of those who know that the day has come when America is privileged to spend her blood and her might for the principles that gave her birth and happiness and the peace which she has treasured. God helping her, she can do no other."

Thunderous applause followed. In a shocking moment, Wilson's archenemy Lodge, his face still bruised from battle, went to shake his hand. "Mr. President, you have expressed in the loftiest manner possible the sentiments of the American people," Lodge told him. But even in his moment of triumph, Wilson remained torn. On the way back from the Capitol, one of the Secret Service agents noticed he was still "visibly nervous and quite pale." According to Tumulty, whose subsequent recollections are more colorful than reliable, the President's uneasy mood did not change when he got back to the White House. As they sat together in the Cabinet Room, Wilson again expressed his sorrowful discomfort with the cheering that evening. "My message to-day was a message of death for our young men. How strange it seems to applaud that." But House recorded no such ambivalence in his diary. Back at the White House, they had merely rehashed what had just occurred "as families are prone to do after some eventful occasion. . . . I could see the President was relieved that the tension was over and the die cast. I knew this would happen."

The news soon reached the mass peace meeting at Convention Hall, heavily guarded to stop a mob of "several hundred young men from colleges and universities, eager to get in and 'have some fun.'" The disappointment in the crowd was palpable. "There is little hope that the Congress will have the manhood and the courage to oppose the proposition of the President," Rabbi Judah Magnes remarked. "The United States is going into a reactionary war at the very time when a social revolution is breaking out all over the world," shouted John Reed.

The conservative backlash that Addams and Wilson himself had feared began to materialize almost immediately, especially in New York. At 125th Street and Seventh Avenue, a socialist named Henry Jager, who made the mistake of beginning an antiwar talk at the same time news of Wilson's speech was posted on a bulletin board, found himself pummeled by an angry mob, some of them chanting, "We want war! We want war!" Jager, accused of calling the President a "murderer," eventually was given a six-month sentence in the workhouse. "You are the type of character who has taken advantage of the privilege of free speech," the sentencing magistrate scolded. At the Rialto, a couple who did not stand and cheer when the news was reported had to be removed from the theater amid a cry of "wring their necks." Such behavior was also seen in the heartland communities such as Havana, Illinois, where a German tailor was fired and the flags of his homeland he displayed in his lapel and above his workbench burned. He was more fortunate than a "stranger, believed to be German" in Thermopolis, Wyoming, who was nearly lynched for drunkenly shouting "*Hoch der Kaiser*" ("Hail the Kaiser") in a saloon.

For some pacifists, the speech confirmed what Addams already realized: the President was not who they thought he was. "Wilson has no true moral courage else he would have prevented the war," Fannie Villard observed a few days later. "His fine phrases really mean nothing when put to the test." The Canadian pacifist Elsie Charlton agreed. Wilson's latest speech, she argued, was nothing more than "not very original cant about fighting for the peace of the world, liberty, democracy, etc." That some pacifists had believed in the President in the first place and continued to do so mystified the Brooklyn socialist and physician James Warbasse. Contrary to popular belief, Warbasse wrote his American Union against Militarism colleague Amos Pinchot that week, Wilson did not necessarily want peace. In fact, everything he had done had virtually guaranteed a war with Germany would be the end result.

Most of the pacifists who had taken part in Monday's EPF activities left for home. Those who remained discovered their literature had been vandalized and their Washington headquarters decorated with the coward's color of yellow: first with crepe paper and then paint splashed on the windows. And the white armbands they had donned on Monday invited hoots and hisses, so much so that some thought it best to remove them altogether. But the faithful such as Lochner had no intention of giving up. "Congress has the power to declare war, and we shall try to stop them from voting for it," he remarked. "We are still pacifists."

There would be no vote on Tuesday, April 3. A war resolution was reported to the Senate, where La Follette used the rule requiring unanimous consent to consider a bill on the same day reported to delay things for a day. At the White House, there was little concern over the parliamentary maneuver. Instead, the staff sorted through the thousands of telegrams congratulating Wilson on his message.

At 2:35 in the afternoon, White House guards were shocked to see a familiar figure pull up. It was TR, accompanied by his daughter Alice. He had a thirty-minute train layover in Washington before heading home, he explained, and wanted to see Wilson. "Tell him I'm all alone—and just want a minute." The two men had not seen each other in person in three years, and the meeting was likely to be an awkward one, at least for the President. But since Wilson was in a cabinet meeting, all Roosevelt could do was leave his card. "Tell the President that I'm prepared to go any length to back up his utterances," he instructed the White House usher Ike Hoover. "And all of my family and friends are at the disposal of the President and the nation under present circumstances."

He had come to see Wilson, TR told the press later, to congratulate him. "The President's message is a great State paper which will rank in history among the great State papers of which Americans in future years will be proud," Roosevelt explained in a dictated statement (privately he viewed the speech as personal vindication, an "endorsement of what I have said and done during the past two and a half years"). That TR was actually saying something positive about the Byzantine logothete was almost incomprehensible to the reporters gathered around him at Union Station. But his comment seemed less surprising when they heard the remainder of his statement, especially his desire to "raise a division for immediate service at the front."

Wilson said nothing for publication, but he knew the matter would eventually need to be addressed. Already, he had no shortage of advice. House had informed him last week of a rumor that Roosevelt had 54,000 men ready to go and suggested TR's interest might wane if "three regiments of regulars" were sent to France first. Within a day after Roosevelt's stop by the White House, Mississippi Senator John Sharp Williams advised Wilson that TR had an "obsession that he is a military genius" and at best was "about competent enough" to serve as a lieutenant colonel, as he had during the Spanish-American War. Williams had nothing against Roosevelt personally, he explained, but TR's actual experience was minimal. And there were signs that the military establishment agreed. Reports soon surfaced that the General Staff did not want TR's volunteer division and that the presence of a former president would create difficulties for Allied officers, who would feel obligated to "consult him."

Roosevelt did not see things that way. He was willing to serve as nothing more than a brigade commander, subordinate to a major general who would head the division itself (several years earlier, he had expressed a desire to be a major general). If necessary, he was prepared to make a second trip to see the President to make his pitch, although his friend General Wood advised him to stay silent for now.

Wilson and Newton Baker, meanwhile, would face a difficult decision if war came to pass. Grant TR his wish and he would be effectively silenced for the duration. But it might also set a precedent for other militarily inexperienced politicians to demand similar opportunities. More concerning, Roosevelt's first combat experience had propelled him into the White House. Who was to say that a second round might not return him there in 1920?

Wednesday, April 4, arrived and the Senate galleries were packed to see the debate and eventual vote unfold. Special tickets were required for admission, dispensed by senators, who had been given five apiece. The city was increasingly on edge. Law enforcement was now watching and arresting those who spoke "irreverently or disrespectfully about the flag, the President, or the country," all with the cooperation of "patriotic Washingtonians." There had also been disturbing news of a possible "Negro uprising" in the South about to erupt, incited by Germans offering "absolute social equality" as a lure. W. E. B. Du Bois thought this was nonsense, the demented product of Southern fears of black soldiers. To George Harris, the Republican editor of the black weekly *New York News*, any supposed "disloyalty" of African Americans was not toward the country but to the Wilson administration. "The only way that President Wilson can get many Negro recruits for the army," Harris insisted, "is to appoint Theodore Roosevelt Secretary of War."

For thirteen hours, the Senate debated the resolution. In all, seventeen spoke in favor and five against. Those present in the galleries, instructed not to cheer, likely found most of the speeches forgettable at best. "Many years hence," David Lawrence of the *New York Evening Post* wrote, "when historians scan the pages of the record to examine the reasons for America's entry into the war, they will find that among the many speeches made in the Senate yesterday, very few give an adequate summary of American grievances or American purposes." The highlight was La Follette, who rose to speak before four o'clock. In his three-hour address, he did his best to punch holes in Wilson's Monday speech. If Germany was waging "a war against all nations," then why didn't other neutrals wish to join with the United States? And if, as Wilson suggested, "Prussian autocracy . . . could never be our friend," then how could America prepare to ally with Great Britain with its continued control of India, Egypt, and Ireland? The country did not want war, La Follette insisted, and a referendum would prove it by a "more than 10 to one" margin. Ultimately, the fault lay with the administration. From the beginning of the war, the White House had never challenged England's violations of international law as strongly as they had forced Germany to toe the line. "How will history regard this conduct of ours?" he asked. "How will our own people regard it when they come to understand it? We can never justify it."

La Follette wrapped up before seven. Four hours later, the vote was under way. To no one's surprise, Fighting Bob voted against the resolution, as did five of the other eleven "willful men" who had blocked the armed merchant ship legislation, including Stone (of the remaining six, three voted in favor, mostly to go along with the inevitable, and three were no longer in the Senate). No one else joined their side, although Thomas Gore of Oklahoma, whose infamous proposal the previous year tried to restrict American travel, might have voted with them, had he not been too ill to be present.

Wilson received the news shortly after he arrived home from seeing a Jerome Kern musical, *Very Good Eddie*, at the Belasco with Grayson and one of Edith's former in-laws. The House would vote on the same resolution the next day. Less than a dozen representatives, it was expected, would vote against it. Already, pundits were beginning to muse over what to call America's new war, perhaps "The War for Democracy," "War Against Autocracy," or even "The Kaiser's War."

The pacifists refused to give up. The EPF wired a new idea to Wilson suggesting that if war was declared, Congress should contact the Reichstag, emphasizing that conflict could be avoided if the kaiser was deposed and a new democratic government established. Every avenue to peace, no matter how remote, had to be pursued, the very philosophy Addams had championed since the war began. It was not surprising that her presence among the peace forces was so deeply missed that week. "I cannot tell you how glad we are that you are going to be here soon," Eleanor Karsten of the WPP wrote to her from Chicago on Thursday. "It will be a very great comfort."

Karsten, like other pacifists, could already see the road ahead would be very difficult for anyone who differed with the majority. The war had not yet begun, but the incidents of intolerance were multiplying exponentially each day. Effigies of La Follette and Stone went up in Washington, complete with yellow paint and a TRAITORS sign (the real La Follette was sent a mock Iron Cross, supposedly a "reward" for his treachery). A Missouri high school teacher who intentionally stomped on a small American flag and then refused to salute a larger Old Glory found himself bound by a group of male and female students and marched through the streets until he had sufficiently repented.

But superpatriotism was one thing, enthusiasm for the war another. Only a small crowd showed up in the House of Representatives galleries

Thursday morning, April 5, to watch the proceedings. By early afternoon, less than a fifth of the House was present on the floor. But signs suggested the opposition might be more substantial than anticipated, perhaps as many as twenty. Frederick Britten, a Republican congressman who had served on the Chicago city council and knew Addams, insisted there was widespread ambivalence. "You ask your friends around here in the House, 'Are you going to vote for this bill?' and they will say, 'Yes, I hate like the devil to vote for it, but I am going to,'" he explained. "The truth is that 90 per cent of your people and mine do not want war, and 75 per cent of the members here do not want it."

At three o'clock, the surprising decision of the House Majority Leader Kitchin to vote no gave additional backbone to those still on the fence. In an emotional speech, some said punctuated by tears, Kitchin, a Bryan apostle, suggested that the United States might have resorted to German "frightfulness" under similar circumstances. "Why can we not, why should we not forego the violation of our rights by Germany and do as we did with Great Britain, do as we did with Mexico, and thus save the universe from being wrapped in the flames of war?"

Following Kitchin's address, sprinkled with "characteristic idioms of the South" such as "you all," rumors surfaced that as many as one hundred representatives might vote against the resolution, an increase from the earlier predictions but still insignificant. Emily Balch was not surprised. As part of the EPF, she had been compiling the attitudes of congressmen all week, many of whom were voting for war for peculiar reasons, among them "patriotism," "Wilson wanted it," and "if we do not . . . we shall be the laughing-stock of the whole world." Others were not prepared to be sacrificial lambs, like the six opposing senators who, wary congressmen were sure, would "go down in history in obloquy." "The fact that stands out," Balch wrote that day, "is that so many Congressmen are ready to vote against their own judgment, against their conscience, and against what they have reason to believe to be the will of their constituents." A secret ballot, many believed, would have changed the situation considerably.

The debate, better described by one reporter as a "speechmaking festival," continued into the evening hours with no signs of ending anytime soon. The hope that business could be wrapped up before Good Friday fell

by the wayside, as a never-ending stream of congressmen, eventually total-
ling more than one hundred, according to reporters present, felt the need
to go on record in one of the most significant moments in American history.
As the speakers droned on, representatives shuffled in and out of the House
chambers, some retiring to cloakrooms while others read newspapers waiting for a vote to be scheduled. A group of pacifists, including Balch, had
been following the proceedings discreetly. Finally, at 2:45 a.m., they
watched as the speeches ended and a formal vote on the resolution
began.

It was the moment Jeannette Rankin dreaded. All day, reporters and
congressmen had badgered her about how she planned to vote. Her brother
and others had continued to pressure her to vote in favor. The first time
the clerk called her name, she did not respond. Nor did she respond when
her name was called again. All heads then swiveled to the back of the
chamber, where she was sitting. After all the votes had been recorded, the
clerk called out the names of all those who had not yet voted. This time,
Rankin stood up and forced herself to speak. "I want to stand by my country," she announced, "but I cannot vote for war. I vote no." A few pacifist
congressmen cheered. Some reporters, happy to reinforce current gender
stereotypes, claimed she then "sobbed, spasmodically, hysterically," while
others merely noted that "tears came to the eyes of Miss Rankin as she
leaned back in her seat."

The entire episode did not sit well with some suffragists, including
Harriot Stanton Blatch. "This is too great a tragedy for the letting loose of
impulsive emotions," she remarked. Carrie Chapman Catt was more sympathetic. She had heard that "Mr. Kitchin's voice was choked with sobs,
but I haven't had any reporters calling me up to ask me whether he was a
disgrace to the sex on that account." Roosevelt agreed. "To be sure, Jeannette Rankin has shown a lack of some things to be desired in a member
of Congress, but have all the male members been so good? I think not."

A few minutes later, it was over. Rankin and 49 others voted against
war; 373 voted in favor (of the remaining 12 votes, 3 were unfilled seats
because of recent deaths/resignations, 2 were too ill to be present, 6 were
counted as "paired" with another member, and Champ Clark did not vote).

About nine hours later, a government clerk named Emma Clapp was asked to carry the resolution to the White House. As part of her job on the Committee of Enrolled Bills at the Senate, she had taken many a bill over to the Executive Mansion. This time, she missed her streetcar, delaying her departure by ten minutes. After catching the next car, she fretted during the ride about losing the white envelope containing the document, although her greater concern was a "bad sore throat." Twenty minutes later, she handed the envelope to Rudolph Forster of the White House secretarial staff.

It was now after one o'clock on Good Friday, April 6. Wilson had taken a walk with the First Lady earlier and was now at lunch. When the document arrived, the President went over to the usher's room. He wanted no cameras to record the signing. Only Edith, Cousin Helen, Forster, Chief Usher Hoover, and Secret Service man Edmund Starling were there to watch Wilson put his name on the document at 1:18 p.m.

Wilson knew he was leading his nation into what was then the bloodiest war in world history, a war whose causes he would never quite understand. National security was never the motivation, as Wilson himself knew that the nation was not seriously in danger, and the actual death toll from U-boats had been minimal. A victorious Germany might pose a threat in the future, but many believed that a battered and bruised Deutschland would be in no condition to menace anyone for years. Still, he saw war as the only option, even if the United States was far from prepared to fight. ("What's the use of declaring war?" asked one congressman. "What can we do to them? Spit in their beer?") Many still doubted an army would ever be sent over to France. Gradually Wilson had drifted to TR's belief that America's very integrity as a nation depended on involvement, as did her ability to shape the peace to prevent future conflicts certain to occur without a new international organization in place. And American democracy, freshly reinvigorated by the progressivism championed by Wilson, TR, and Addams, would show the way to a better world as part of a new internationalism.

Addams could never agree or accept what she called a "pathetic belief in the regenerative results of war" or the soon to be popular belief in America that this would be the "war to end all wars." War, she believed, was the worst possible solution for Wilson, especially when other options such as the neutral conference/continuous mediation might have had a chance to succeed with committed American involvement. That the President remained unwilling to pursue that course was, in her nephew James Weber Linn's words, "the only defeat that she could not forget." "It seemed to me quite obvious," she later wrote, "that the processes of war would destroy more democratic institutions than he could ever rebuild however much he might declare the purpose of war to be the extension of democracy."

Few Americans shared Addams's disillusion in the first excited hours after the declaration of war, when seemingly everyone wanted to do his or her part, even the most famous pacifist in the nation. "I hereby tender my services to the government," William Jennings Bryan wired the President. "Please enroll me as a private whenever I am needed and assign me to any work that I can do until called to the colors." In France, where he had recently completed his training on the Bleriot monoplane, James Norman Hall greeted the news with relief. "I feel like a different man," he wrote a friend. "Now we can openly proclaim our citizenship. Now we can hold up our heads." The French, Hall observed, were "glad, unquestionably glad. But they feel as do all of us here, that we join reluctantly, unwillingly and only because we must." American troops, he believed, should be deployed immediately to France, even if just a "brigade or two. . . . The moral effect . . . would be tremendous."

Roosevelt still held out hope that he would be part of that brigade. He would have to see Wilson in person, whom he missed the week before, but it was a sacrifice he was prepared to make. Three days after war was declared, he left New York for Washington. His initial destination was not the White House but his daughter Alice Longworth's home at 1736 M Street N.W., where the press soon showed up asking questions. Nick Longworth told them nothing, but they sensed something was up.

A few reporters were waiting for Roosevelt the next day, April 10, when he arrived at the White House gates with Alice at noon, the time Tumulty had given him for the appointment. TR noticed the still marching suffragettes with their "big yellow banners," acknowledging them with a friendly doffing of his hat. It had been eight years since he left office, but he recognized many familiar faces at the White House, Forster among them, and an African American messenger named Wilson Jackson who greeted him with "Glad to see you, Mr. Ex-President."

Wilson, back from golf with Edith, soon emerged, and the two men shook hands as if they were the best of friends. "How are you, Mr. President?" asked TR pleasantly. "I am very glad to see you," Wilson replied.

A thirty-minute conversation in the Green Room followed. As a rather obvious supplicant, Roosevelt was on his best behavior. Privately, Wilson likely relished every moment of holding TR's fate in his hands, but he behaved as if the previous three years had never happened. The President did feel the need to rationalize his delay in going to war, explaining that the country was not "awake to the need," but TR brushed it aside. Let's let bygones be bygones, Roosevelt suggested. Your speech was good, but let me and my division help to make it a reality. He even joked that he would "promise not to come back," which Wilson likely found somewhat amusing. The President seemed intrigued by TR's proposal but remained noncommittal. Besides, how would his volunteer division affect conscription, which would soon be on the table? Roosevelt assured him that he had no plans to take draft-eligible men. He also agreed to help in getting the administration's draft bill passed.

Before their talk ended, they discussed what TR would be allowed to say to the press outside. "The President received me with the utmost courtesy and consideration and doubtless in his own due time will come to a decision," Roosevelt told reporters on the White House portico. "I am heart and soul for the proposal of the Administration for universal military training and for universal obligatory military service. Call it conscription or what you will and it won't scare me." TR seemed especially determined not to offend the administration in any way. "If I say anything I shouldn't, be sure to censor it," he instructed Tumulty. "I'm already under orders." He slapped Tumulty on the back good-naturedly while teasing him about adding him to his division. Roosevelt, Tumulty conceded afterward, was a likable fellow.

Even Wilson agreed. "I was, as formerly, charmed by his personality," he told Tumulty. "There is a sweetness about him that is very compelling. You can't resist the man."

The rest of the day was spent at the Longworths seeing anyone who might be able to promote his two current causes: the administration's conscription plan and his own division. Influential Republicans and Democrats of the House and Senate Committees on Military Affairs, representatives of the Council on National Defense, Jusserand, Spring Rice, FDR, and military men were among those summoned, as was Lodge, who was soon basking in TR's praise for his pacifist thumping. The most surprising appearance was War Secretary Newton Baker, who came at the behest of FDR. In one of the upstairs bedrooms, TR repeated the same pitch he had already made in several letters to Baker, who continued to avoid giving a definite answer. Roosevelt doubted it would be Baker's call anyway. He would follow Wilson's wishes to the letter, TR believed. "If Mr. Wilson should agree with me tomorrow, Mr. Baker would be perfectly sure he always agreed with me."

To many who spoke to him that day, Roosevelt seemed changed from his White House years. The "pep and ginger" was still present, but there was also a "deadly earnestness" about him. "It brought his voice to a lower pitch, and his nervous falsetto—as well known as his flashing teeth—was heard only on rare occasions," a reporter observed. But TR was cautiously optimistic. Wilson had not rejected the idea. "His words may mean much; they may mean little," Roosevelt mused. "He has, however, left the door open."

EPILOGUE

If diplomats think that they will be able to create
peace by changing borders of countries and giving
over parts of one country to the other, according to
the results of the war, they are terribly shortsighted
and fatally mistaken.

—Rosika Schwimmer to Woodrow Wilson, 1914

I f Roosevelt now believed the Wilson administration might be inclined
to see things his way, he was mistaken. A few days after Newton Baker
met with TR, the secretary of war expressed in writing what he was
probably unwilling to say to a former president's face. The American troops
eventually sent over to Europe, he explained, should be under the "most
experienced leadership available," a decision driven by military rather than
"sentimental" reasons.

Of course, Roosevelt was not about to accept such logic. He continued
to engage in a lengthy debate with Baker in two more letters, outlining his
combat experience once again, while insisting that his proposed division
could be quickly trained and deployed. Finally, Baker cut off further discussion in a brief but firm note. A few months later, he was shocked to see
that TR had published their entire correspondence dating back to February
in the *Metropolitan*.

While Roosevelt was engaging in his back-and-forth with Baker, his
friends in Congress were doing their best to force the insertion of a "Roosevelt provision" that permitted volunteer units (despite Wilson's discreet
opposition) as part of the draft legislation now under consideration. By
Thursday, May 17, the long disputed bill was on the verge of passage in a

form that would allow Wilson, if he wished, to authorize four divisions of volunteers to be raised.

Earlier that day, Roosevelt's friend John Parker had requested an appointment with the President. Parker, a Democrat turned Bull Mooser who had actively supported Wilson in the recent election, had to be seen, even if the President knew why he was coming. When Parker arrived at the White House at 3:45 p.m., he did not take long before asking Wilson for two things: Roosevelt's division with Leonard Wood at the head and the "privilege of telling you some things that others do not tell you." The President agreed, although he warned Parker that he had already made up his mind that there would be no overseas mission for TR.

Parker did not pull any punches. He mentioned that the scuttlebutt was that Wilson was "extremely jealous of my friend, Theodore Roosevelt" and chided him as an "autocrat" with a tendency to antagonize even members of his own party. And Wilson should remember that he was "simply an American citizen exalted for the time being," a mere "hired man of the people" who would be well advised to "take the people absolutely into your confidence wherever you can do so."

Wilson listened to Parker for nearly ten minutes, his prodigious self-control intact, although the "flash of color in his cheeks" and "glint in his eye" let Parker know he was not happy. He was even more unhappy when Parker dared to say that he "hoped" Wilson "would not play politics."

"Sir, I am not playing politics," the President bristled. "Nothing could be more advantageous than to follow the course that you pursue." The simple fact was that Roosevelt was not qualified. "His experience in military life has been extremely short," Wilson reminded Parker, and TR had "shown intolerance of discipline" while serving last time. This was not a knee-jerk decision, the President explained, but one carefully reached "after conference and consultation with the ablest and best posted men in each of the various branches of the United States Government."

Parker did not divulge the outcome of his meeting to the press, or apparently even to Roosevelt, who immediately wired Wilson the next day requesting permission to raise his divisions shortly before the draft bill was ready for the President's signature. By this point, Wilson had a full explanatory statement on the Roosevelt matter ready to be released to the public along with other information on the new legislation.

"It would be very agreeable to me to pay Mr. Roosevelt this compliment," he explained. "But this is not the time or the occasion for compliment or for any action not calculated to contribute to the immediate success of the war." Instead of citing TR's scant military background, Wilson emphasized practical issues. The Roosevelt division would poach some of the much needed experienced regular army officers needed to train the new draftees. And what the U.S. military "most needed are men of the ages contemplated in the draft provision of the present bill, not men of the age and sort contemplated" in the Roosevelt division.

The next day, he sent a formal telegram to Roosevelt, once again reiterating that "my conclusions were based entirely upon imperative considerations of public policy and not upon personal or private choice."

A bitter TR believed otherwise. It was no secret that Wilson actively (and understandably) disliked Roosevelt and relished killing his dreams of glory once and for all. But less partial observers, especially those in the military, also were opposed (except Wood), believing volunteer units of this kind would undercut the success of the draft. They also wanted no repeat of the insubordination, bloated casualty lists, and occasional recklessness of Roosevelt's performance in the Spanish-American War. General John Pershing, the newly appointed commander of the American Expeditionary Force, believed Roosevelt was in no shape to serve. TR did attract support from Georges Clemenceau, the French prime minister, who publicly expressed enthusiasm for a Roosevelt-led force to be sent over, but Wilson chose to ignore the request. The President could not agree with Democrats such as Senator Gilbert Hitchcock of Nebraska that it would be preferable to have Roosevelt "blundering in Europe where he can be restrained than croaking at home where he might be a demoralizing influence."

Newton Baker would always insist that he, not Wilson, made the final decision, reinforced by the attitudes of the General Staff and other high-ranking officers. As Baker later explained, he simply could not in good conscience "entrust the lives of American soldiers to a man as utterly unqualified as T.R." Nor could he send him abroad "in some minor capacity,"

especially since Roosevelt "would have still felt charged with the responsibility of commander-in-chief."

In the aftermath of the rejection, a devastated TR could do little but
pour fresh invective on the "utterly selfish, treacherous, and vindictive man"
in the White House. "He is exceedingly base," Roosevelt wrote his friend
William Allen White. "His soul is rotten through and through; he hasn't a
thought for the welfare of this country; or for our honor; or for anything
except his own mean personal advancement." But TR knew there was
nothing he could do. "The President has insisted that I should be only a
looker-on—and that's all there is to it."

W ilson's transition to war president proceeded smoother than he originally anticipated. With the draft legislation now in place, millions
of American men between the ages of twenty-one and thirty would register
on June 5, although it would be months before a substantial force could be
sent over to Europe. But ambivalence about the war and the degree of
American commitment continued to persist, at least in the Midwest, according to Ray Stannard Baker, who noted a sense of "We don't like it, but
we're going through with it to the end." Such lukewarm attitudes naturally
concerned the administration, and Wilson had no qualms about signing into
law the Espionage Act, which cracked down on activities and the dissemination of printed materials viewed as undermining the war effort. In the
months that followed, he did little to stop the worst abuses of the legislation
(further strengthened by the Sedition Act in 1918), resulting in widespread
suppression of radical publications and indictments of socialists, members
of the Industrial Workers of the World union, and other left-wing organizations during the course of the war.

The man who had once feared war-fueled intolerance and had kept a
steady hand on the country's emotions for years was now willing to sacrifice
his ideals for what he perceived to be the good of the country, if not the
entire world. His attitudes about pacifists also underwent a disturbing
transformation. "What I am opposed to is not the feeling of the pacifists,
but their stupidity," Wilson declared in a speech to the American Federation of Labor in November 1917. "My heart is with them, but my mind has

a contempt for them. I want peace, but I know how to get it, and they do not."

The President's statement was not especially surprising to Addams. For months, Wilson's colleagues had made it clear they shared none of her views about the war or how it should be waged. Her April trip to Washington after the war declaration to champion the cause of conscientious objectors and testify against the Espionage Act had achieved little and succeeded only in distancing her even further from the mainstream. She tried to articulate her current position in "Patriotism and Pacifists," a speech she gave several times in the late spring and early summer. Pacifists were not "traitors and cowards," she explained, even if she still believed that war "affords no solution for vexed international problems" and "tends to obscure and confuse those faculties which might otherwise find a solution." Nor were pacifists head-in-the-sand isolationists; in fact, America "should lead the nations of the world into a wider life of coordinated political activity" in some "international agency not yet created." But two comments attracted the most attention: Addams's statement that German Americans had "every right to be considered as an important factor in the situation, before war was declared," and her suggestion that the United States should not allow the enemy civilian populations to starve. Once again, her critics saw red, viciously attacking her "pro-German twaddle," "sentimental mush," and "seditious balderdash." "Your actions (traitorous, as I believe them) furnish abundant proof that it is unsafe to allow women too great freedom in National affairs," a Chicago man wrote her.

Already, Addams had learned an important lesson. "During war," she later wrote, "it is impossible for the pacifist to obtain an open hearing." Much of the public, increasingly worked into an unthinking patriotic frenzy as the war progressed, now saw "that woman" as an enemy of the state. Passersby spat on mail extending from the door to the Woman's Peace Party headquarters on Chicago's South Michigan Avenue, while others "befouled" the door "in hideous ways." She even witnessed a federal agent show up at the national WPP annual gathering hoping to uncover signs of sedition, although he soon realized the gathering was harmless.

What troubled her more was a growing sense of her own disconnection

from the rest of the country, even many of her former progressive colleagues, some of whom were encouraged by new wartime policies such as
federal control of the railroads. "I feel as if a few of us were clinging together in a surging sea," Addams wrote a friend. But to resist the tide,
some warned, would permanently destroy her standing in America. Friends
like Julia Grace Wales and David Starr Jordan all jumped ship, as did
Elizabeth Glendower Evans, who now believed the war was justified and
"for the freedom of the world." At times Addams grew frustrated with
those who could not understand her stance. "Miss Addams I think felt this
passiveness in me," Ida Tarbell later wrote. "I couldn't get out and cry,
'Peace, Peace,' on the street corner and she could and must. She suffered
too deeply over it."

The creation of the Food Administration, one of Wilson's war agencies,
gave her a renewed sense of purpose. Headed by Herbert Hoover, fresh
from his relief efforts in Belgium, the new organization pushed and prodded the American public to conserve and produce food for the war effort.
When approached by Hoover to give talks for the Food Administration,
she was happy to comply. And the American public, especially women's
groups, seemed to accept her in that role, even though her pacifist activities
remained unacceptable to much of the country.

Other pacifists weathered the war more successfully. Wilson steered
William Jennings Bryan back onto the stump, where he could do valuable
work addressing troops, raising money for Liberty Bonds, and stressing food
conservation. Bryan's conservation talks also allowed him to make the
case for a cause increasingly near and dear to him: prohibition, which would
become federal law after the war. Henry Ford, meanwhile, loyally backed
the administration, converting his plant into a "huge war factory" while
spouting patriotic platitudes such as "America will fight to the last cent and
the last man that every sort of militarism may be swept from the world."
Ford had so redeemed himself that Wilson even asked him to run for Senate
in 1918 against Truman Newberry, who had served in Roosevelt's cabinet.
Naturally, TR did his best to torpedo the Ford candidacy, reminding the
Michigan voters of the eccentric mogul's detestable pacifist activities and
his son Edsel's draft deferment. Roosevelt breathed a sigh of relief when
Ford was beaten by a few thousand votes.

The prophecy that American entry into the war would quickly bring victory to the Allies proved far from accurate. German submarines sank record amounts of Allied shipping through August 1917, a disturbing trend finally reversed by the long deferred adoption of the convoy system and the participation of American destroyers. Nor did the German grip on their current gains show any sign of loosening, regardless of the 175,000 American troops in France by the end of the year.

By early 1918, James Norman Hall was now part of the American forces, after a transfer from the Lafayette Escadrille. He had already discovered that air combat could be even more dangerous than the brutal trench warfare he experienced as a British tommy. Soon after completing training, Hall had lost control of his craft when he took a German bullet in the left arm. As his plane rapidly descended, he was sure he was done for. Somehow, he managed to turn off the motor and straighten out at almost the last moment and landed his bullet-ridden plane only three hundred meters or so from the German trenches. Two more near death experiences followed: one involving a jammed machine gun and the other a hair-raising descent down a mountaintop that nearly destroyed his plane. After three combat victories, Hall's luck finally ran out in May, when his plane was hit by antiaircraft fire, forcing him to land in German territory where he was taken prisoner for the duration of the war.

"We are like monks in a convent," he complained in a letter home. "We're almost entirely out of touch with the outside world."

Quentin Roosevelt, Roosevelt's youngest son, had also joined the air corps and would shoot down his first German airplane in early July. "I am perfectly delighted," TR boomed to reporters. "I am proud as can be." He was just as proud that Archie, Ted, and Kermit were also serving, although he and Edith worried about their safety. That he could not be with them in the "greatest struggle of the century" deeply depressed him. At times, his frustrations gave way to emotional outbursts in public, such as when he was ready to fight the AFL leader Samuel Gompers on stage for implying a race riot in East St. Louis was partly due to employers "luring colored men from the South" or nearly erupting when a heckler (a *"creature,"* TR labeled him) asked him why he "didn't go over and fight"?

Early in the war, Roosevelt momentarily considered offering his services to Wilson for noncombat work, but ultimately rejected the idea. Lowering himself to "ask to do a big job, a hazardous job, which I could do especially well was one thing; to ask to do a much smaller job, which many other men can do at least as well as I can do, is another thing." And if the President threw him a bone of some kind, TR would be forced to accept a position that might intentionally be "disagreeable or useless." He would also have to put a stop to the one passion that seemed to keep him going: criticizing the administration's delays and missteps in conducting the war. Week after week, he blasted away in the pages of the *Metropolitan* and in a column syndicated by *The Kansas City Star.* Buried beneath the boasting and bluster were a few nuggets of truth: America would have been in a stronger position to make an immediate difference in the war if Wilson had prepared sooner and more aggressively. "We would have made all our blunders and suffered all our delays at a time when they did not count—and the war would have been over now," Roosevelt wrote his son Ted. And he could not help smirk when the President now thundered that "there is . . . but one response possible from us . . . righteous and triumphant force which shall make right the law of the world."

TR's health continued to deteriorate. "I feel like I'm a hundred years old and have never been young," he complained to a friend. He spent a month in the hospital in early 1918 for a near fatal rectal abscess and mastoiditis that left him deaf on the left side. Wilson sent a note of concern to Edith Roosevelt, although he had otherwise maintained his long-standing policy of ignoring any Roosevelt rants. Some observers, like the columnist Arthur Brisbane, thought the President should say something, especially when TR's more inflammatory comments in the midst of war probably "would put in jail some little Socialist editor, and cause his newspaper to be suppressed." But Wilson understood that making a martyr out of TR, increasingly perceived as the leader of the GOP, would not be wise.

The death of Quentin in combat in July created a great deal of public sympathy for Roosevelt. Condolences poured into Sagamore Hill, including one from the President himself. Quentin had died just as his father would have wished, but the pain of the loss was almost unbearable. "There is no use of my writing about Quentin," he remarked in a letter to the novelist Edith Wharton. "I should break down if I tried."

B y the time the news of Quentin's death reached the United States, the war had changed considerably. Tens of thousands of American troops were now marching into France each week, helping to offset German divisions that had been transferred from the Eastern Front after the new Bolshevik regime in Russia withdrew from the war. "Our military situation has deteriorated so rapidly that I no longer believe we can hold our own over the winter," German Field Marshal Prince Rupprecht observed in August. "The Americans are multiplying in a way we never dreamed of."

The end of the war was now in sight. For months, Wilson had been mulling over the final peace settlement, his thinking continuing to evolve considerably from the "Peace without Victory" speech. Pope Benedict's August 1917 peace move, which Addams found promising, did not appeal to him. Rolling the international situation back to 1914, even with future disarmament and arbitration part of the plan, was no longer acceptable. It was now, the President declared, America and her allies' responsibility to "deliver the free peoples of the world from the menace and the actual power of a vast military establishment controlled by an irresponsible government" that intended to "dominate the world."

A few months later, in January 1918, Wilson further outlined his views on the kind of peace he envisioned in the Fourteen Points speech before a joint session of Congress. Many of the points had long been supported by Addams, such as the call for arms reduction, freedom of the seas, "open diplomacy," "impartial adjustment of all colonial claims," and a league of nations. Others dealt with territorial issues. "An evident principle runs through the whole program I have outlined," the President explained. "It is the principle of justice to all peoples and nationalities, and their right to live on equal terms of liberty and safety with one another, whether they be strong or weak."

Both Addams and Schwimmer were enthusiastic about the speech, but Roosevelt was not, especially by early October when the Germans, recognizing the war might soon be lost, offered to open up peace talks based on what TR called the "mischievous" Fourteen Points. Germany must surrender unconditionally, he believed. "Let us clearly show that we do not desire to pose as the umpire between our faithful and loyal friends and our treacherous and brutal enemies, but that we are the stanch friend of our friends and the stanch foe of our enemies." As for any league of nations, he could see little good in it. It might have some value, he wrote Mark Sullivan that fall, "if we treat it as an addition to, and not as a substitute for, preparing our own strength, if we don't attempt too much, and above all if we insist on absolute good faith in both promise & performance."

In the early days of November 1918, the German will to fight collapsed for good. On November 11, the Germans had little choice but to accept an armistice. After more than four years of fighting, the war had come to an end.

Roosevelt was unable to take part in the celebrations throughout America. He had been admitted to the hospital that day for back pain, thought to be related to a rheumatic condition. His doctor continued to promote the charade that there was nothing seriously wrong with him and that his "blood pressure and arteries" were "those of a man of forty," but TR would not be allowed to go home until Christmas Day. As he recuperated, he mused over Wilson's decision to go to France for the peace conference. That the President would face difficulties realizing his vision for the postwar world was certain. "We have not suffered as much and we have not rendered as much service as the leading Allies," Roosevelt insisted. Wilson was getting the seat at the peace table he so dearly wanted, but TR knew the chair would have been considerably larger if the United States had begun the task of developing her military might sooner (had the war lasted even six more months, the presence of a now massive American army on the Western Front would have enormously strengthened Wilson's bargaining position).

House, who had been sent to Europe in October to confer with the Allies, preferred that Wilson stay in Washington and allow him to handle the negotiations. Instead, he would have to settle for one of the positions in the American delegation, which the Colonel believed was not especially strong (one of Wilson's correspondents had even suggested a woman be selected, perhaps Addams). Lansing, whom Wilson and House had labeled "stupid" of late, was going, as was General Tasker Bliss. The bigger issue was the President's decision not to select a Republican of any consequence, especially when bipartisan support in the Senate would be necessary to ratify any treaty. For several months, House and Wilson had batted around various big names. Roosevelt and Taft had been quickly discarded, as had Hughes ("there is no room big enough for Hughes & me to stand in," Wilson griped). The final peace commissioner slot eventually went to Henry White, who had held ambassadorships to Italy and France during TR's presidency.

Wilson, accompanied by Edith, arrived in Paris on December 13, 1918, to a hero's welcome. Since it soon became clear that the Allies were not inclined to begin the peace conference for several weeks, the Wilsons spent much of the interim in England and Italy before heading back to Paris on January 6. That night, as their train crossed over the French border from Italy into Modane, a messenger handed Wilson a note. Roosevelt had died that morning in his sleep of an embolism, according to his doctors. Wilson's uncompromising rival, the man who had been a relentless thorn in his side since 1912, was gone. There would be no presidential duel in 1920.

Wilson followed the proper presidential protocol, sending condolences to the family and even generously rewriting a TR proclamation sent to him by the State Department. Inwardly, he likely felt a sense of vindication. He was in Paris shaping the peace of the world for years to come, while Theodore Roosevelt was now part of history, soon to be as remote as Lincoln and Washington.

Still, his bitterness toward Roosevelt remained strong. The British Prime Minister Lloyd George later recalled that his attempt to acknowledge TR's death elicited an "outburst of acrid detestation" from Wilson. Nor could the President bring himself to admit Roosevelt's considerable contributions. Less than a week after TR's passing, he felt the need to inform Gifford and Amos Pinchot's sister, Antoinette, now the wife of Sir Alan Johnstone, that "he did not consider Theodore Roosevelt a great man." Where then, she asked, was the "great man" to deal with the "great events happening in the world today." "I think Colonel House is such a man," Wilson replied. "He is equal to the task."

Wilson's relationship with House had remained strong. He still believed their minds were in sync and that his adviser was interested only in service and not recognition. When the President left the conference on February 14 for a brief trip home, he asked House to take his place as America's representative on the Council of Ten now hard at work on the treaty. By this time, Wilson had presented the Draft Covenant of the League of Nations, the radical new organization envisioned as a world assembly of nations, each with one vote and an executive council with five permanent members: the United States, the United Kingdom, France, Italy, and Japan. World peace and the protection of members from "external aggression" would be the League's primary goal.

While the President was contending back home with the domestic reaction to the League, especially the growing Republican hostility in the Senate, House kept Wilson's seat warm in Paris. "When the President is away I never hesitate to act and to take as much responsibility as either of the others," the Colonel recorded in his diary. But when Wilson returned in March, he was not happy with House's handiwork in his absence, especially what he perceived as a disturbing willingness to yield too easily to the French perspective. For the first time, Wilson likely had an epiphany that he had kept his "best friend" on too loose a leash, a friend whose ego seemed to be growing larger by the day. From that point, Wilson began to eye House far more warily.

House, meanwhile, privately wished Wilson had stayed home, especially since he could no longer act "on my own initiative as I did when the President was away."

The Council of Ten gave way to a new Council of Four consisting of Wilson and the governmental heads of Great Britain (Lloyd George), France (Georges Clemenceau), and Italy (Vittorio Orlando). Over three months, amid numerous disagreements and arguments, they hammered out a treaty while the League of Nations Covenant was finalized. Meanwhile in Zurich, another conference was under way, the first gathering of the Women's International League for Permanent Peace since the 1915 meeting at The Hague. Just as she had four years earlier, Addams had sailed over on the

Noordam, accompanied by friends and pacifists such as Alice Hamilton, Emily Balch, and Jeannette Rankin, who had recently been defeated in a bid for the Senate. Before the conference began, Addams had spent time in Paris, meeting with House and touring the war-torn areas of France. Alleviating hunger and starvation, especially among the defeated nations' populations, was now of vital importance to her, and she wired Wilson from Zurich imploring that the peace conference take action. "I hope most sincerely that means may be found," the President wrote Addams on May 16, "though the present outlook is extremely unpromising because of infinite practical difficulties."

The same "infinite practical difficulties" had limited his influence in the final version of the treaty now in the hands of the German representatives. Clemenceau and the French, bent on revenge and future security, had proved especially intractable. Wilson was pleased that the League of Nations was part of the treaty, but the harsh terms imposed on Germany— substantial reparations, sole blame for the war, and loss of all her colonies—were far from the "healing peace" he had wished for. Nor were such terms acceptable to Addams and the members of the women's conference, which immediately passed a resolution opposing the peace treaty in its current form. To Addams, only the inclusion of the League of Nations, however imperfect, offered any hope for the future as a substitute for the troublesome "old nationalism" that led to war in the first place.

"Miss Addams, as always, was for accepting even a quarter-loaf, and doing as much with it as could be done," Alice Hamilton later observed. James Norman Hall, now back home in the United States, agreed: "If we don't get a league out of this war, what will it all have been for?"

Representatives of the new German government had no choice but to sign the treaty in the Hall of Mirrors at Versailles on the afternoon of June 28, 1919, exactly five years after the Sarajevo assassination. Wilson, House, and the remainder of the American delegation signed minutes later. Later that evening, Wilson prepared to board a train to Brest, where he and Edith would sail for home. House was at the station, but he now knew the President's feelings toward him had changed, a transformation encouraged by the First Lady and others close to Wilson who had never cared for him. Whether the change was permanent or temporary he did not know. "For the moment," the Colonel admitted, Wilson "is practically out from under my influence." Before the departure, House advised the President to adopt a "conciliatory" attitude in dealing with the Senate, in whose hands the fate of the treaty and the League lay. But Wilson did not seem to agree. "House, I have found one can never get anything in this life that is worthwhile without fighting for it," he remarked. Moments later, Wilson disappeared from House's life forever.

Wilson returned home that summer to an America convulsed with race riots, strikes, and a growing crackdown on radicals of all kinds. But the treaty and the votes needed for ratification in a Republican-controlled Senate (64 if all 96 members were present) occupied most of his thoughts. At least 40 senators were likely to vote in favor, but just as many wanted changes or "reservations" to the treaty and the League of Nations Covenant. Another 8 "irreconcilables" would not accept the agreement in any form, including Roosevelt's 1912 running mate Hiram Johnson, elected to the Senate in 1916, who insisted that TR would have been leading the fight against ratification. More likely, Roosevelt would not have rejected the League outright but would have insisted on multiple exceptions and loopholes, the path that his friend and Wilson nemesis Henry Cabot Lodge championed. For Lodge, article 10 and its stipulation to uphold the "territorial integrity" of League members was especially unacceptable, lest it lead to the deployment of American forces all over the world without congressional authorization.

Wilson, unwilling to make substantial concessions, decided that he would take the League case to the people that September, the same strategy he had pursued for preparedness back in 1916. But this time the speaking tour was far more grueling, with multiple stops scheduled in the West over a three-week period, too many for a man whose health, never strong to begin with, appeared to be worsening. He had battled the flu in Paris and dysentery in Washington, and there were also disturbing signs that he was not at his full powers mentally. Some of his earlier speeches on the tour lacked the trademark Wilson zing, but his performance improved as the tour progressed. In San Diego, he even invoked a 1914 comment by TR that appeared to support "an agreement among the great powers . . . to abide by the decision of a common tribunal" and "to back with force the decision of that common tribunal." "A very worthy utterance," the President told the crowd. "I am glad to align myself with such utterances as those." A few days later, he played the same Roosevelt card again to a crowd in Pueblo, Colorado, before concluding with a dramatic finish. "There is one thing that the American people always rise to and extend their hand to, and that is the truth of justice and of liberty and of peace," he insisted. "We have accepted that truth and we are going to be led by it, and it is going to lead us and through us the world, out into pastures of quietness and peace such as the world never dreamed of before."

But it was not to be. That evening on the train, Wilson experienced near debilitating symptoms of headache, nausea, difficulty breathing, and facial twitching. The decision was made to cut short the tour and head back to Washington immediately. "I just feel as if I am going to pieces," he admitted. His condition worsened on the journey back east. Dr. Grayson, along for the tour, noticed "a curious drag or looseness at the left side of his mouth," a likely sign of a transient ischemic attack or mild stroke. At the White House, Wilson suffered a full-blown stroke on the right side of his brain (impacting the left side of his body) on October 2, further complicated by a subsequent infection. Edith Wilson made sure his condition remained hidden from the American public, although rumors soon surfaced that there was something seriously wrong with the President. She also controlled access to her husband and assumed a number of his responsibilities along with Tumulty and Grayson.

Wilson eventually improved somewhat, but the remainder of his term was marked by periods of erratic decision making and behavior in a man who was no longer competent to serve. The Senate, meanwhile, voted down the League of Nations in November 1919 both with and without Lodge's reservations. A final attempt in March 1920 also failed, thanks to the President's growing rigidity and unwillingness to compromise.

House believed that the League of Nations might have gotten through if Wilson had stepped down as president, perhaps as a resounding tribute to a fallen leader. He thought he could have persuaded Wilson to resign, although it was now clear to him that he was persona non grata. The

Colonel exchanged a few perfunctory letters with his old friend in 1920, but Wilson had no interest in rekindling their relationship. In his currently damaged emotional state, he grew even more suspicious of House, egged on by Edith and Grayson. "I once thought he was too good to be true," Wilson told Grayson. "In Paris I first realized the change that had taken place when he suggested that I turn everything over to him and let him run things. That was my first indication that he was going wrong and had swelled up." The personal loss weighed heavily upon Wilson. "I hope no more of my friends will turn out like House. . . . It darkens my life."

After his second term ended, Wilson spent the last three years of his life with Edith in a house on S Street in Washington, about two miles from the White House, which was occupied by a reactionary Republican, Warren Harding. (Had Roosevelt survived, the GOP might well have chosen someone more ideologically acceptable to TR, if not TR himself.) Like Roosevelt, Wilson found the transition to ex-president difficult. He tried practicing law with Bainbridge Colby, his last secretary of state after he finally rid himself of Lansing, but he still harbored delusional fantasies about presidential runs in 1920 and 1924, even sketching out a possible nomination acceptance speech. But he would not live to see another presidential campaign. On the morning of February 3, 1924, Wilson died at the age of sixty-seven, a victim of the stroke that had destroyed his presidency and his hopes for the postwar world. Vengeful to the end, Edith Wilson made sure that House was not to attend the public funeral service in the capital.

Even without his Wilson connection, the Colonel continued his favorite pastime of meeting and keeping in touch with the leading lights in America and Europe. As historians and writers began to document the Wilson years, House felt the need to address criticisms of his role in the administration and at Versailles. With House's assistance, the Yale historian Charles Seymour completed a four-volume biography, *The Intimate Papers of Colonel House*, which included generous selections from his letters and diary, which he finally ended for good in 1926. (Edith, who jealously guarded her husband's complex legacy until her death in 1961, refused House permission to print Wilson's letters.) The Colonel remained puzzled over his break with Wilson, unable or unwilling to take even the slightest responsibility for the split. With the election of Franklin Delano Roosevelt in 1932 and a new Democratic administration in Washington, House would get another chance to bask in the glow of presidential power. FDR was not a Wilson clone ("This one is genuinely fond of people and shows it," House remarked), but he was happy to cultivate House's support and politely listen to his advice on occasion until the Colonel's death in 1938.

After the war, James Norman Hall moved to Tahiti, both to resume his writing career and to escape the hurly-burly of modern life. His occasional visits back home convinced him that he could no longer live in the increasingly industrialized America of the 1920s. He steadily cranked out books, many cowritten with Charles Nordhoff, another American pilot, throughout the decade, none of which caught the public's fancy. It was not until Hall and Nordhoff decided to write a novel based on the book Hall saw in the Paris bookstore in 1916 that they finally hit pay dirt. *Mutiny on the Bounty*, published in 1932, became a bestseller and an Oscar-winning Hollywood smash three years later. Two other volumes in the *Mutiny* trilogy also sold well. Hall had achieved the literary success he always wanted, but he continued to long for an America "a little more like it used to be."

The postwar years were initially difficult for Jane Addams. Public opinion, shaped by the continued intolerance toward radicals in the early 1920s, remained against her. Her ideas about pacifism, newly influenced by Gandhi, whom she tried to see in India, still seemed vaguely threatening, even when expressed by a woman now in her sixties. At the 1924 meeting of the Women's International League of Peace and Freedom (the new name for the International Committee of Women for Permanent Peace), presided over by Addams, the FBI sent an agent to monitor the proceedings and record the speeches. An informant wrote to J. Edgar Hoover in 1926 warning about Addams and "others of her ilk, who are doing their level best . . .

to break down the morale of our citizens and eventually emasculate our national defense." Not surprisingly, she became a favorite target of the likes of the American Legion and other military organizations who now denounced Hull-House as a hotbed of communism and Addams herself as the "most dangerous woman in the country."

The always indomitable Rosika Schwimmer also found America less than hospitable during the Roaring Twenties. After a brief stint serving as ambassador to Switzerland for the new republic of Hungary, ongoing political turmoil in her native land forced her to flee to the United States in 1921. She soon discovered that America had changed a great deal in the five years she had been away. Especially disturbing was a growing wave of anti-Semitism loudly trumpeted by the nationally distributed *Dearborn Independent* that Henry Ford had purchased in 1918. Ford's relatively benign prewar anti-Semitism had evolved into something far more sinister, nudged along by the more rabid Ernest Liebold, the same underling who had once tried to thwart his boss's peace activities. That Schwimmer and her Peace Ship scheme were to blame for Ford's views was now widely believed. Others were certain she was a "German spy and a communist," charges that she successfully fought in a libel case.

It was not surprising that her attempts to become an American citizen proved difficult. Statements such as "I am an uncompromising pacifist, for whom even Jane Addams is not enough of a pacifist," did not help matters. But it was not her activism and atheism that doomed her, but her declared unwillingness to bear arms in the event of war. Her naturalization case eventually reached the Supreme Court in 1929, where the decision to deny her application was affirmed 6–3. "I'm a woman without a country," she told reporters. "Al Capone is all right; he is ready to shoot. But I am dangerous."

To her credit, Addams did not distance herself from Schwimmer. She helped raise money for the Hungarian's legal fight and visited her in 1934 in a Chicago hospital, where Schwimmer complained that her role in the women's peace movement had been intentionally marginalized. But Addams's own reputation was undergoing a rehabilitation. More than a decade of attacks finally began to dissipate by the end of the 1920s, so much so that honors began to fall her way, including selection to *Good Housekeeping*'s list of the twelve "greatest living women" in 1931 and the Nobel Peace Prize that same year (Wilson had won it back in 1920). She turned over her prize money to the Women's International League of Peace and Freedom. "For years I've been asking people for money for peace," she remarked, "so it seemed a little inconsiderate when I got a little money of my own not to give it to peace."

Late in life, Addams had no regrets about her pacifist activities from 1914 to 1917, which she still believed were misunderstood. After Mark Sullivan sent her an advance chapter of his latest volume of *Our Times*, his massive popular history of recent America, she took the time to send him a detailed reply correcting some of his misconceptions about the peace movement. "We of course never imagined that we could bring the war in Europe to an end," she wrote, "but we did hope that a body of neutrals with no diplomatic power of course, sitting continuously, might be able to make suggestions for peace which would shorten the conflict."

Following her death from cancer on May 21, 1935, fifteen months after her beloved Mary's passing, fulsome tributes poured in for the woman who "became the whole world's friend." In twenty years, she had come full circle: from saint to traitor to beloved icon once again.

It has long been recognized that World War I and its aftermath unleashed developments that dramatically shaped the course of the twentieth century. And America's role in this monumental sea change was enormous, even if its military involvement was minimal compared with that of the Allies and Germany.

But what if America had pursued a different path? Certainly, Wilson had options—some viable, others less so—to attempt to shift the country's trajectory away from war. He could have removed a major source of conflict by supporting restrictions on American travel. He could have lined up with the neutrals, as Addams had advocated since 1914, or used the Allies' deep financial dependence on the United States to force the two sides to talk. "I am not sure," Colonel House admitted years later, "that we did not make a greater mistake in not going ahead and calling for a peace conference rather than leaving it to the Allies to be the judges." Wilson also could have pushed harder and earlier for a military buildup, just as TR and House himself supported, one large enough by 1917 to make the Germans think twice about involving America in the war. Even after the unrestricted submarine declaration and the disclosure of the Zimmermann Telegram, Wilson still had it within his power to make a convincing case for continued neutrality, and much of the country, outside of the East Coast, likely would have followed him.

Wilson, of course, believed American involvement was necessary so that a new democratic world order could prevail. But how would history have changed had the United States remained out and the Allies remained unable to defeat Germany? A clear-cut German triumph, many believed then and now, would not only have dramatically shifted the balance of power in Europe, but would also have threatened the future security and interests of the United States. A militaristic nation such as Germany, newly emboldened by victory and a damaged British empire, would be likely to flex its muscles again in the future, perhaps with the aid of Japan.

Without American involvement, there was also the possibility of a less sinister outcome to the Great War, had it continued for another several years. Both sides, weary of the catastrophic losses and sacrifices, might have been finally willing to call a halt to the fighting, resulting in a true "peace without victory." "Without American assistance," Count Johann von Bernstorff later wrote, "the end would have been a draw, with all the advantages foreseen by Mr. Wilson in 1916." Such an outcome, Bernstorff believed, would have maintained "a certain equilibrium in Europe," one likely to make "true democracy possible in our continent," perhaps even undermining the "continuance of our patriarchal military regime" in Germany. Still, an inconclusive war might have created more problems than it solved. It would merely have given both sides a chance to lick their wounds, rebuild their military apparatus, and resume hostilities a few years later, unless a truly viable international organization strongly backed by the United States was in place and prepared to intervene.

When World War I ended, the 1912 presidential campaign seemed like a distant memory to most Americans. They dimly recalled that Roosevelt, Wilson, and Addams had spoken at that time for a new America, one where progressivism in its various forms would shape the course of the United States for years to come.

Neither Wilson nor his Bull Moose opponents Roosevelt and Addams could have anticipated in 1912 that the favorable reform climate would soon begin to fade, not to return for another generation. Instead, an unprecedented global war intervened, a war that would force America to confront questions far more serious than domestic concerns. How should the United States best protect its interests? What are America's responsibilities to other nations and populations around the world? And exactly what did America stand for?

Between the outbreak of hostilities in 1914 and the eventual entry of the United States into the conflict in 1917, Addams, Wilson, and Roosevelt presented their own vision of America's place in the Great War and beyond. As progressives, they believed that intervention, not passivity, was always the proper course to promote positive change. But they could not agree on how best to achieve peace and a new international order. Roosevelt believed America ultimately could achieve little on the global stage without a substantially stronger army and navy. To Addams, such militaristic solutions were archaic and unnecessary. Instead, the United States should cast aside the old diplomacy and work together with other nations to create new institutions and mechanisms to end the current war and prevent future conflicts.

Addams and many other pacifists believed Wilson shared their perspective. But as the war went on, Wilson's aversion to a military buildup began to dissipate. And his decisions seemed to increase, rather than decrease, the likelihood of eventual hostilities with Germany. By 1917, Wilson had come to believe that American involvement in the war, unpleasant as it might be, was necessary for the good of the country and the world. It was a view Addams could never accept.

To their collective credit, Addams, Roosevelt, and Wilson never feared taking unpopular stances, even when it meant being denounced as a coward, warmonger, or traitor. They understood that the stakes for the United States during the Great War were tremendously high, so high that it was crucial that the nation make the "right" decision, even at a cost to each of their own personal ambitions. The ramifications of how America embraced or rejected the responsibility of global power, they recognized, would be felt decades after their own fleeting time in the spotlight. Even more than a century later, the choices made in 1917 continue to cast a long shadow over the United States, if not the world.

ACKNOWLEDGMENTS

Thanks to my agent, Eric Lupfer at Fletcher & Company, who believed in this project in its earliest stages. I am also grateful to my editor, Jake Morrissey at Penguin Random House, whose thoughtful commentary and perceptive suggestions greatly strengthened the manuscript. Thanks as well to my four research assistants: Cyrus Ready-Campbell, Seth LaShier, Dante Laricchia, and Benjamin Goldstein. Seth was especially valuable in tracking down material at the Library of Congress. Finally, a big thank-you to my wife, Michél, who somehow tolerated my long disappearances in my office, lost in the world of World War I America, with patience and love.

A NOTE ON SOURCES

The primary and secondary literature on the World War I era is enormous, far too enormous for one person to absorb and process in their lifetime. For this book, I relied most heavily on the voluminous papers of Addams, Roosevelt, and Wilson for the 1914–1917 period. For additional background, I read at least one (and often multiple) New York, Chicago, and Washington newspaper for each day from August 1914 through April 1917.

The following collections are abbreviated in the citations below:

APP: Amos Pinchot Papers, Library of Congress

DSJP: David Starr Jordan Papers, Hoover Institution Archives

FOP: Foreign Office Papers/Public Record Office, www.nationalarchives .gov.uk

FrPP: Frank Polk Papers, Yale University Manuscripts and Archives

GPP: George Perkins Sr. Papers, Columbia University, Rare Book and Manuscript Library

HD: House diary/Edward Mandell House Papers, Yale University Library Digital Collections

HIP: Harold Ickes Papers, Library of Congress

ITD: Documents of Ida Tarbell, Allegheny College, https://dspace .allegheny.edu/handle/10456/13708

JAP: Jane Addams Papers, microfilm edition

JCOP: John Callan O'Laughlin Papers, Library of Congress

JNHP: James Norman Hall Papers, Grinnell College Libraries, Special Collections

LeWP: Leonard Wood Papers, Library of Congress

LLP: Louis Lochner Papers, microfilm edition

LWP: Lillian Wald Papers, microfilm edition

PLP: Pethick-Lawrence Papers, Trinity College Library, Cambridge, England

PWW: Arthur Link et al., eds., *The Papers of Woodrow Wilson,* 69 vols. (Princeton, N.J.: Princeton University Press, 1966–1993)

RSBP: Ray Stannard Baker Papers, microfilm edition

RSP: Rosika Schwimmer Papers, New York Public Library

RSP-HI: Rosika Schwimmer Papers, Hoover Institution Archives

TRDL: Theodore Roosevelt Digital Library, Dickinson State University

TRP: Theodore Roosevelt Papers, microfilm edition

WAWP: William Allen White Papers, Library of Congress

WJBP: William Jennings Bryan Papers, Library of Congress

WPPP: Woman's Peace Party Papers, microfilm edition

WWP: Woodrow Wilson papers, microfilm edition

WWPL: The Woodrow Wilson Presidential Library and Museum (presidentwilson.org)

Other abbreviations used in endnotes:

EMH: Edward Mandell (Colonel) House

JA: Jane Addams

JNH: James Norman Hall

TR: Theodore Roosevelt

WW: Woodrow Wilson

NOTES

Prologue: The Rough Rider, the Reformer, and the Scholar

1 "This convention": *The Outlook*, August 24, 1912.
1 "quasi-religious": H. L. Mencken, *Prejudices—Second Series* (New York: Alfred A. Knopf, 1920), 123.
1 "men in the press": *The Outlook*, August 17, 1912.
2 "Four-fifths of the whole": *Baltimore Sun*, June 29, 1912.
2 "America's most eminent": *Chicago Examiner*, August 8, 1912.
2 "gracious figure": *The Outlook*, August 17, 1912.
2 "Not even": William Henry Harbaugh, *Power and Responsibility: The Life and Times of Theodore Roosevelt* (New York: Farrar, Straus and Cudahy, 1961), 439.
2 "brief": *New York Herald*, August 8, 1912.
2 "I arise": *Chicago Examiner*, August 8, 1912.
2 "one of the few men": *Chicago Inter Ocean*, August 8, 1912.
3 "I was so excited": *Chicago Tribune*, August 8, 1912.
3 "fine!": *New York Times*, May 29, 1912.
3 "just as radical": Kathleen Dalton, *Theodore Roosevelt: A Strenuous Life* (New York: Alfred A. Knopf, 2002), 382.
3 "sane radical": TR to W. B. Rainsford, December 12, 1914, TRP, reel 357.
3 "A minimum wage": *New York Evening Post*, August 7, 1912.
4 "frankly Socialistic": *New York Times*, August 7, 1912.
4 "Of course": *Chicago Tribune*, August 8, 1912.
4 "I am *not* conservative": John Milton Cooper Jr., *Wilson: A Biography* (New York: Alfred A. Knopf, 2009), 146.
4 "in farm wagons": *New York Times*, August 8, 1912.
5 "Oh, I wish": *New York Times*, August 8, 1912.
5 "have come to": *Speech of Governor Wilson Accepting the Nomination for President of the United States* (Washington, D.C.: GPO, 1912).
5 "Third term": *New York Herald*, August 8, 1912.
5 "double-d'd": Marcet Haldeman-Julius, *Jane Addams as I Knew Her* (Girard, Kans.: Haldeman-Julius Publications, 1936), 14.
6 "in such horrid": Jane Addams, *Twenty Years at Hull-House* (New York: Macmillan, 1962), 3.
6 "curved spine" . . . "ugly": Addams, *Twenty Years*, 6–7.
6 "Mount Holyoke": *Rockford Star*, January 17, 1915, JAP, reel 62.
6 "I was absolutely": Addams, *Twenty Years*, 64.
7 "little Italian": Addams, *Twenty Years*, 110.
7 "They were not to live" . . . "happy dust": Alice Hamilton, *Exploring the Dangerous Trades: The Autobiography of Alice Hamilton, M.D.* (Boston: Little, Brown, 1943), 59–60, 100.
7 "too much": Addams, *Twenty Years*, 57.
7 "went further": JA to Lillian Wald, August 17, 1912, JAP, reel 6.
8 "We are learning": Jane Addams, *Democracy and Social Ethics* (New York: Macmillan, 1905), 6.
8 "Dearest": Louise W. Knight, *Jane Addams: Spirit in Action* (New York: W. W. Norton, 2010), 125.
8 "career": James Weber Linn, *Jane Addams: A Biography* (New York: D. Appleton-Century, 1935), 149.
8 "see the greatest man": Mrs. Philip Snowden, *A Political Pilgrim in Europe* (New York: Cassell, 1921), 77.

8 "the foremost": *Ladies' Home Journal*, March 1908.

9 "weakling" . . . "strenuous": Dalton, *Theodore Roosevelt*, 10, 20.

9 "best man" . . . "combined strength": Theodore Roosevelt, *Theodore Roosevelt: An Autobiography* (New York: Macmillan, 1914), 7.

10 "I had always felt": Roosevelt, *Autobiography*, 222.

11 "Roosevelt, mounted": *Scribner's Magazine*, October 1898.

11 "splendid little": *San Francisco Examiner*, May 8, 1948.

12 "simplified spelling" . . . "The very rich": Dalton, *Theodore Roosevelt*, 299, 318.

13 "best teacher" . . . "own words": Cooper, *Wilson*, 20–21.

13 "Father, I have": Cooper, *Wilson*, 26.

14 "I have no patience": Cooper, *Wilson*, 51.

15 "old longing": Cooper, *Wilson*, 76.

15 "it is not often": Cooper, *Wilson*, 99.

16 "bored": Phyllis Lee Levin, *Edith and Woodrow: The Wilson White House* (New York: Scribner, 2001), 36.

17 "very sane" . . . "perfect trump": Cooper, *Wilson*, 75, 79.

17 "I believed in": David Lawrence, *The True Story of Woodrow Wilson* (New York: George H. Doran, 1924), 343.

17 "I have not": *New York Times*, November 24, 1907.

17 "the most dangerous": Robert Edwards Annin, *Woodrow Wilson: A Character Study* (New York: Dodd, Mead, 1924), 269.

17 "advocated" . . . "able": Harbaugh, *Power and Responsibility*, 446.

18 "would make": Cooper, *Wilson*, 161.

18 "still an amateur": Bainbridge Colby, "Roosevelt: The Story of an Animosity," *Current History*, August 1930, 863.

18 "egotistical" . . . "His egotism": Lawrence, *The True Story of Woodrow Wilson*, 343.

18 "explained" . . . "There can't": *The Survey*, January 18, 1919, 523.

18 "I have such": TR to JA, January 24, 1906, JAP, reel 4.

19 "don't talk to me": Linn, *Jane Addams*, 293–94.

19 "zealous": Roosevelt, *Autobiography*, 167.

19 "She had no": Linn, *Jane Addams*, 272.

19 "something of the old": RSBP, reel 76.

19 "large sad eyes": Snowden, *A Political Pilgrim*, 77.

19 "Well, he": Charles Willis Thompson, *Presidents I've Known and Two Near Presidents* (Indianapolis: Bobbs-Merrill, 1929), 291.

20 "one of the best read": "Notes for Pen and Brush Talk," ITD.

20 "Her mind": "Jane Addams Notes," ITD.

20 "He knew": Theodore Roosevelt Jr., *All in the Family* (New York: G. P. Putnam's Sons, 1929), 172.

20 "mental machine": William Kent to Ray Stannard Baker, May 25, 1925, RSBP, reel 78.

20 "full of fun": Terrell D. Webb, *Washington Wife: Journal of Ellen Maury Slayden from 1897–1919* (New York: Harper & Row, 1962), 315.

20 "thinking machine": PWW, 31:391.

20 "loves a little nonsense": A. G. Gardiner, *The Pillars of Society* (New York, E. P. Dutton, 1916), 253.

21 "One could set": "Conversations with Stockton Axson," February 1925, RSBP, reel 70.

21 "I would as soon": H. H. Kohlsaat, *From McKinley to Harding: Personal Recollections of Our Presidents* (New York: Charles Scribner's Sons, 1923), 224.

21 "no Florence Nightingale": Arthur Gleason to Leila Seward Gleason, May 6, 1906, Arthur Gleason Papers, box 1, Library of Congress.

21 "hard and cruel" . . . "very auntly": Haldeman-Julius, *Jane Addams*, 3, 6.

21 "Even her closest" . . . "following the custom": Linn, *Jane Addams*, 433.

21 "I never saw": "Theodore Roosevelt—Luncheon," ITD.

21 "Life . . . doesn't consist": Gardiner, *The Pillars of Society*, 267.

21 "a voice that": Frederick S. Wood, *Roosevelt as We Knew Him: The Personal Recollections of One Hundred and Fifty of His Friends and Associates* (Philadelphia: John C. Winston, 1927), 299.

21 "undisputed Chief": *New Republic*, January 13, 1917.

21 "When I am": Mark Sullivan to Corinne Robinson, June 4, 1930, Mark Sullivan Papers, box 16, Hoover Institution Archives.

22 "She was very dependent": Hamilton, *Exploring the Dangerous Trades*, 66.

22 "burglars": John A. Garraty, "T.R. on the Telephone," *American Heritage*, December 1957.

22 "social reform measures": JA to TR, November 20, 1912, JAP, reel 7.

22 "Progressive with the brakes": Eric Rauchway, "What a Piece of Work Is a Man," *Reviews in American History* 40 (2012): 294.

23 "mentally deficient children": *Chicago Tribune*, January 16, 1914.

Chapter 1: A More Complicated World

25 "very short-sighted": TR to Emily Tyler Carow, September 1, 1914, in *The Letters of Theodore Roosevelt*, ed. Elting Morison, vol. 7, *The Days of Armageddon, 1909–1914* (Cambridge: Harvard University Press, 1954), 816.

26 "commonplace": *New York Times*, May 31, 1914.

26 "Women as a class": *Philadelphia Inquirer*, August 9, 1914.

26 "No decent man": *Chicago Tribune*, May 28, 1914.

26 "They paint": *New York Herald*, March 11, 1917.

26 "The Man Who Breaks": *Brooklyn Eagle*, October 16, 1914.

27 "an immoral woman": *Chicago Tribune*, August 22, 1914.

27 "In the last ten": *New York Times*, October 12, 1914.

27 "The world is becoming": *PWW*, 30:248.

28 "encirclement" . . . "The future": Martin Gilbert, *The First World War: A Complete History* (New York: Henry Holt, 1994), 7, 19.

28 "War between": *Washington Post*, July 27, 1914.

28 "If England": Donald Richberg, *Tents of the Mighty* (New York: Willett, Clark & Colby, 1930), 63.

29 "an almost": *Philadelphia Inquirer*, August 3, 1914.

29 "All you have": *Chicago Tribune*, August 9, 1914.

29 "demanded a written guarantee": Herbert Hoover, *The Memoirs of Herbert Hoover: Years of Adventure, 1874–1920* (New York: Macmillan, 1951), 147.

29 "People of culture": *Philadelphia Inquirer*, August 17, 1914.

29 "a man of some": *Hartford Courant*, September 15, 1914.

29–30 "Most Americans": *Philadelphia Inquirer*, August 20, 1914.

30 "peasants singing": *Philadelphia Inquirer*, August 23, 1914.

30 "Is it not then": *Philadelphia Inquirer*, August 18, 1914.

30 "We came over": *Baltimore Sun*, August 27, 1914.

31 "Whatever you do": Roy Cushman to JNH, August 8, 1914, JNHP, box 2.

31 "We'll take": James Norman Hall, *Kitchener's Mob* (Boston: Houghton Mifflin, 1916), 4.

31 "There are really": JNH to Roy Cushman, August 19, 1914, JNHP, box 2.

31 "It makes one": JNH to Roy Cushman, August 27, 1914, JNHP, box 2.

31 "The first, most important": *Washington Post*, October 11, 1914.

32 "nervous break down": WW to Mary Allen Hulbert, June 7, 1914, in *PWW*, 30:158.

32 "The doctor says": Ellen Axson Wilson to Jessie Sayre, July 6, 1914, WWPL.

32 "making actual advance": WW to Joseph R. Wilson Jr., July 24, 1914, in *PWW*, 30:302.

32 "The trouble": WW to Joseph R. Wilson Jr., August 6, 1914, in *PWW*, 30:351.

32 "Very deep": TR to WW, August 5, 1914, in *PWW*, 30:351.

32 "but we have": WW to TR, August 6, 1914, in *PWW*, 30:352.

32–33 "take good care" . . . "Is it all" . . . "Oh my God" . . . "I must not": Ray Stannard Baker interview with Cary T. Grayson, February 18–19, 1926, RSBP, reel 76.

33 "just as the world": Ray Stannard Baker, *Woodrow Wilson: Life and Letters*, vol. 4, *President, 1913–1914* (Garden City, N.Y.: Doubleday, Doran, 1931), 477.

33 "held up": Joseph R. Wilson Jr. to Kate Wilson and Alice Wilson, August 11, 1914, in *PWW*, 30:374.

33 "A great man": Cary Grayson to Edith Galt, August 25, 1914, in *PWW*, 31:564.

33 "effusion and gush" . . . "I expect to win": Terrell D. Webb, *Washington Wife: Journal of Ellen Maury Slayden from 1897–1919* (New York: Harper & Row, 1962), 245–47.

34 "I find": EMH to WW, June 3, 1914, in *PWW*, 30:139.

34 "The situation": EMH to WW, May 29, 1914, in *PWW*, 30:109.

34 "I had never": HD, September 26, 1914.

34 "Mr. House is my": John Milton Cooper Jr., *Wilson: A Biography* (New York: Alfred A. Knopf, 2009), 192.

35 "complement of": *Asheville Citizen-Times*, April 1, 1938.

35 "He wants nothing": David Lawrence, *The True Story of Woodrow Wilson* (New York: George H. Doran, 1924), 68.

35 "It is safe": *North American Review*, April 1916, 560.

35 "go around": Ray Stannard Baker interview with Albert S. Burleson, March 17, 1927, RSBP, reel 72.

35 "Assistant President": HD, February 22, 1915.

36 "join hands": *Philip Dru: Administrator* (New York: B. W. Huebsch, 1912), 272–73.

36 "I have a keen": EMH to WW, July 1, 1914, in *PWW*, 30:242.

36 "There may be": EMH to WW, July 31, 1914, in *PWW*, 30:324.

36 "Please let me suggest": EMH to WW, August 1, 1914, in *PWW*, 30:327.

36 "what are we going": Wilson speech of July 4, 1914, in *PWW*, 30:248.

36 "whether the United States": July 27, 1914, press conference, in *PWW*, 30:307.

37 "one of the new generation": *PWW*, 30:236.

37 "while hoping and praying": July 30, 1914, press conference, in *PWW*, 30:318.

37 "It can, at least": WW to EMH, August 5, 1914, in *PWW*, 30:345.

37 "a single word" . . . "Every night": WW to Mary Hulbert, August 23, 1914, in *PWW*, 30:437.

37 "Hard work": Cary Grayson to EMH, August 20, 1914, in HD.

37 "excitement": August 3, 1914, press conference, in *PWW*, 30:331.

37 "exhibit the fine poise": Public statement, August 18, 1914, in *PWW*, 30:393–94.

39 "For two hours": *New York Tribune*, August 31, 1914.

39 "American and other": Walter Hines Page to William Jennings Bryan, September 11, 1914, in *PWW*, 31:26.

39 "trigger-happy": Brian G. H. Ditcham, review of *The Rape of Belgium: The Untold Story of World War I*, by Larry Zuckerman, *H-War* (online), December 2004.

40 "I found him" . . . "He goes even further" . . . "thought the war" . . . "showed me" . . . "looked forward" . . . "he felt like" . . . "of the great": HD, August 30, 1914.

40 "About Germans there has never": Edward S. Martin, *The Diary of a Nation: The War and How We Got into It* (Garden City, N.Y.: Doubleday, Page, 1917), 23.

41 "German baths were good": Martin, *The Diary of a Nation*, 64.

41 "more German than the Kaiser": Elmer Gertz, *Odyssey of a Barbarian: The Biography of George Sylvester Viereck* (Buffalo: Prometheus, 1978), 164.

41 "He has the simplicity" . . . "certain crudity": A. G. Gardiner, *Prophets, Priests and Kings* (London: Alston Rivers, 1908), 128, 130.

41 "temperament best fitted": TR to Walter Strong, December 15, 1916, TRP, reel 386.

41 "three funniest words": Robert Edwards Annin, *Woodrow Wilson: A Character Study* (New York: Dodd, Mead, 1924), 168.

42 "*Love* is the only": *Philadelphia Inquirer*, October 13, 1914.

42 "innocently as": HD, November 8, 1914.

42 "If the President": HD, September 9, 1914.

42 "He said to forgive": HD, September 29, 1914.

42–43 "believes that unless": HD, September 26, 1914.

43 "importance of this": HD, September 28, 1914.

43 "proper sense of proportion": HD, October 22, 1914.

43 "there is nothing": WW to EMH, August 23, 1914, in *PWW*, 30:450.

43 "deadlock in Europe": "Memorandum of Interview with the President, Dec. 14, 1914," in *PWW*, 31:458–59.

43 "training the boys": James E. West to David Starr Jordan, September 4, 1914, DSJP, box 15.

43 "pray for peace": *New York Times*, October 4, 1914.

43 "such a day": *Chicago Tribune*, October 5, 1914.

44 "Christian brotherhood": James P. Martin, "The American Peace Movement and the Progressive Era, 1910–1917" (Ph.D. diss., Rice University, 1975), 25.

44 "sexual and moral pervert": Lawrence F. Abbott, *Impressions of Theodore Roosevelt* (Garden City, N.Y.: Doubleday, Page, 1922), 189.

45 "When a South Italian": Jane Addams, *Twenty Years at Hull-House* (New York: Macmillan, 1962), 307–8.

45 "it had nothing": Mercedes M. Randall, *Improper Bostonian: Emily Greene Balch* (New York: Twayne, 1964), 325.

45 "gilt and lace" . . . "troubles of our": Regene Henriette Spero Silver, "Jane Addams: Peace, Justice, Gender, 1860–1918" (Ph.D. diss., University of Pennsylvania, 1990), 141–42.

45 "We may admire much": Jane Addams, *Newer Ideals of Peace* (New York: Macmillan, 1907), 28, 210–11, 213, 238.

45–46 "Nobody who was not": Alice Hamilton, *Exploring the Dangerous Trades: The Autobiography of Alice Hamilton, M.D.* (Boston: Little, Brown, 1943), 161–62.

46 "was the first": Jane Addams, *The Second Twenty Years at Hull-House* (New York: Macmillan, 1930), 118.

46 "We must wait": Andrew Carnegie to William Jennings Bryan, October 5, 1914, in WJBP, box 30.

46 "Tolstoyan": Lella Secor to Laura Kelley and Lida Hamm, September 4, 1916, in Barbara Moench Florence, *Lella Secor: A Diary in Letters, 1915–1922* (New York: Burt Franklin, 1978), 85–97.

46 "They are weak": *New York Evening Post*, September 21, 1914.

47 "I feel that": *New York Tribune*, August 7, 1914.

47 "If anybody" . . . "[s]tarve the armies": *New York Tribune*, August 13, 1914.

47 "safeguards": *New York Tribune*, August 26, 1914.

47 "A public protest": *New York Tribune*, August 24, 1914.

48 "great slides": *New York Evening Post*, August 25, 1914.

48 "muffled drums": *New York Tribune*, August 7, 1914.

49 "I am filled": *New York Evening Post*, September 21, 1914.

49 "taught the world": *Christian Science Monitor*, June 17, 1914.

49 "My temperament and habit": Jane Addams, *Peace and Bread in Time of War* (New York: Macmillan, 1922), 133.

49 "gathering" . . . "plan of getting": Paul Kellogg to JA, September 11, 1914, JAP, reel 7.

50 "would bring vigor": Paul Kellogg to JA, September 15, 1914, JAP, reel 7.

50 "labor conditions": Paul Kellogg to George Nasmyth, September 24, 1914, JAP, reel 7.

50 "Women, if they" . . . "It is the result": *Boston Post*, September 20, 1914, JAP, reel 62.

50 "Won't that mean friction" . . . "all the old maids": *Kansas City Journal*, October 22, 1914, JAP, reel 62.

50 "lowest divorce rate": *Manchester Leader*, September 18, 1914, JAP, reel 62.

51 "will set us back": *Boston Traveler and Evening Herald*, September 17, 1914, JAP, reel 62.

51 "various woman's": *New York Evening Post*, September 30, 1914.

51 "The affairs": David Starr Jordan to Harvey Jordan, October 24, 1914, DSJP, box 26.

51 "frightful tragedy": TR to Kermit Roosevelt, November 11, 1914, TRDL.

51 "adroitness": TR to Hiram Johnson, January 28, 1913, in Joseph Bucklin Bishop, *Theodore Roosevelt and His Time Shown in His Own Letters* (New York: Charles Scribner's Sons, 1920), 2:351.

52 "all controversial": *New York Times*, May 27, 1914.

52 "college professor" . . . "who knows nothing" . . . "direct demand" . . . "the very grave" . . . "We certainly": Oscar King Davis, *Released for Publication: Some Inside Political History of Theodore Roosevelt and His Times, 1898–1918* (Boston: Houghton Mifflin, 1925), 436–38.

53 "ceaseless campaign" . . . "A very large": TR to John Callan O'Laughlin, August 27, 1914, TRP, reel 384.

53 "bipartisan boss rule": *New York Times*, July 24, 1914.

53 "grape fruit tonic": Unsigned to TR, November 25, 1914, TRP, reel 194.

53 "modern eating": William Flinn to TR, August 10, 1914, TRP, reel 189.

53 "I am an old man": TR to Charles McCarthy, August 24, 1914, TRP, reel 384.

53 "remarkable run": TR to Kermit Roosevelt, December 2, 1914, TRDL.

53 "I am in every fiber": TR to Raymond Robins, August 12, 1914, TRP, reel 384.

53 "You are the Progressive": John Callan O'Laughlin to TR, August 24, 1914, TRP, reel 190.

54 "destruction of the": William Ransom to TR, July 19, 1914, TRP, reel 188.

54 "I do not feel": TR to E. C. Stokes, August 5, 1914, TRP, reel 384.

54 "You are the only": Joseph A. Griffin to TR, August 31, 1914, TRP, reel 190.

54 "The world would welcome": Wm. B. Dulany to TR, August 31, 1914, TRP, reel 190.

54 "great influence": Warren H. Poley to TR, September 4, 1914, TRP, reel 190.

54 "see Mr. Roosevelt": George Jessup to WW, September 27, 1914, TRP, reel 191.

54 "Colonel, please": W. J. Tilghman to TR, August 22, 1914, TRP, reel 190.

54 "set his own price": John Wheeler to John McGrath, August 10, 1914, TRP, reel 189.

54 "on the side": George Viereck to TR, August 5, 1914, TRP, reel 189.

55 "capacity for hard work": Theodore Roosevelt, *Theodore Roosevelt: An Autobiography* (New York: Macmillan, 1914), 23.

55 "they wished" . . . "slaughtered like rats": Arthur von Briesen to TR, August 11, 1914, TRP, reel 189.

55 "Prussianized" . . . "For the last": TR to Arthur Lee, August 22, 1914, in Morison, ed., *Letters of Theodore Roosevelt*, 7:809–11.

55 "impulsiveness": HD, January 1, 1914.

55 "Both roared": H. L. Mencken, *Prejudices—Second Series* (New York: Alfred A. Knopf, 1920), 112.

55 "I do admire" . . . "He knows armies": Davis, *Released for Publication*, 88, 92.

55–56 "curious mixture" . . . "*I ADORE*" . . . "I do not believe": TR to George Otto Trevelyan, October 1, 1911, in Bishop, *Theodore Roosevelt and His Time*, 2:253–54.

56 "entirely unorganized" . . . "did not like me": TR to George Otto Trevelyan, October 1, 1911, in Bishop, *Theodore Roosevelt and His Time*, 2:246.

56 "'16th century' peasants": Arthur Lee to TR, August 13, 1914, TRP, reel 189.

56 "arm steadily": Rudyard Kipling to TR, September 15, 1914, TRP, reel 190.

56 "witnessed the awful": W. P. Pycraft to TR, September 18, 1914, TRP, reel 191.

57 "What is needed": TR to Heinrich Charles, August 21, 1914, TRP, reel 384.

57 "the violation or disregard" . . . "very properly has offered": Theodore Roosevelt, "The Foreign Policy of the United States," *The Outlook*, August 22, 1914, 1012–13.

57 "national life or death": Theodore Roosevelt, "The World War: Its Tragedies and Its Lessons," *The Outlook*, September 23, 1914, 169–73.

57–58 "formulate his policy": Lawrence F. Abbott, "President Wilson, Mr. Roosevelt, and Belgium—a Reply to Ex-Governor Glynn," *The Outlook*, March 29, 1916, 734.

58 "misled" . . . "no obligation": TR to George Williams, October 31, 1916, TRP, reel 215.

58 "An ex-President": TR to Rudyard Kipling, October 3, 1914, TRP, reel 357.

58 "support of the administration": Albert Bushnell Hart to TR, October 1, 1914, TRP, reel 191.

58 "it has been very hard": TR to Cecil Spring Rice, October 3, 1914, in *The Letters of Theodore Roosevelt*, ed. Elting Morison, vol. 8, *The Days of Armageddon, 1914–1919* (Cambridge: Harvard University Press, 1954), 821–22.

58 "The prayers appointed": TR to Morris Jastrow Jr., November 14, 1914, in Morison, ed., *Letters*, 8:842.
58 "blue-rumped ape": TR to Arthur Lee, September 4, 1914, in Morison, ed., *Letters*, 8:817–18.
58 "armed strength": TR to Henry Coonley, September 21, 1914, TRP, reel 384.
58 "revolt against war": *Chicago Tribune*, October 5, 1914.
58 "an arrogant man": Walter Rockhold to TR, October 17, 1914, TRP, reel 192.
58 "The kaleidoscope": TR to Rudyard Kipling, October 3, 1914, TRP, reel 357.

Chapter 2: A War with Which We Have Nothing to Do

59 "I pray God": *Washington Evening Star*, December 16, 1914.
59 "adopt a certain": F. A. McKenzie, *Americans at the Front* (New York: George H. Doran, 1917), 9.
59 "where they will do": R. W. Taylor to TR, November 30, 1914, TRP, reel 194.
59 "for the American Ambulance Hospital": TR to R. W. Taylor, December 12, 1914, TRP, reel 357.
60 "timely features": *New York Sun*, November 15, 1914.
60 "The most desperate": Nathan Haverstock, *Fifty Years at the Front: The Life of War Correspondent Frederick Palmer* (Washington, D.C.: Brassey's, 1996), 170.
60 "flower of the nation": JNH to Roy Cushman, August 19, 1914, JNHP, box 2.
60 "downright London toughs": JNH to Roy Cushman, September 19, 1914, JNHP, box 2.
60 "God pity": *Des Moines Register*, February 15, 1916.
60 "Our beds": JNH to Roy Cushman, October 31, 1914, JNHP, box 2.
60 "love of adventure": JNH to Roy Cushman, December 29, 1914, JNHP, box 2.
60 "pitiful sights": JNH to sister Dorothy, October 16, 1914, JNHP, box 2.
60–61 "If Germany": JNH to Mother, December 25, 1914, JNHP, box 2.
61 "How in Heaven's": JNH to Roy Cushman, November 28, 1914, JNHP, box 2.
61 "The daily list": JNH to Roy Cushman, December 29, 1914, JNHP, box 2.
61 "The roads were littered" . . . "I saw one regiment": William J. Robinson, *My Fourteen Months at the Front: An American Boy's Baptism of Fire* (Boston: Little, Brown, 1916), 19–20, 40–41.
61–62 "For the poor": Alan Seeger, *Letters and Diary of Alan Seeger* (New York: Charles Scribner's Sons, 1917), 29.
62 "terrific and incessant": Henry Beach Needham to TR, November 27, 1914, TRP, reel 216.
62 "any war": TR to Rudyard Kipling, November 4, 1914, in *The Letters of Theodore Roosevelt*, ed. Elting Morison, vol. 8, *The Days of Armageddon, 1914–1919* (Cambridge: Harvard University Press, 1954), 829.
62 "cannot think": Emmeline Pethick-Lawrence to Frederick Pethick-Lawrence, October 31, 1914, PLP.
62 "more obsessed": Emmeline Pethick-Lawrence to Frederick Pethick-Lawrence, October 31–November 1, 1914, PLP.
62 "When suffrage": *Los Angeles Times*, October 27, 1914.
63 "It is for her": *Christian Science Monitor*, November 3, 1914.
63 "full democracy" . . . "the nineteenth century": *New York Times*, October 27, 1914.
63 "sweetly gracious": *Newark Evening News*, October 29, 1914, JAP, reel 62.
63 "half full": Emmeline Pethick-Lawrence to Frederick Pethick-Lawrence, October 29, 1914, PLP.
63 "women of America": *New York Tribune*, October 31, 1914.
63 "I begin to see": Emmeline Pethick-Lawrence to Frederick Pethick-Lawrence, October 31–November 1, 1914, PLP.
63 "democratic control": *Boston Post*, November 9, 1914.
64 "I want the people": *The Outlook*, November 18, 1914.
64 "This is an amazing": Emmeline Pethick-Lawrence to Lady Constance Lytton, November 9, 1914, PLP.
64 "strangely conservative": Emmeline Pethick-Lawrence to Frederick Pethick-Lawrence, November 5, 1914, PLP.
64 "In some ways": Emmeline Pethick-Lawrence to Frederick Pethick-Lawrence, November 18, 1914, PLP.
64 "three-guinea-pig": TR to Agnes Repplier, August 26, 1915, TRP, reel 359.
64 "perpetual noise": Emmeline Pethick-Lawrence to Frederick Pethick-Lawrence, October 31–November 1, 1914, PLP.
64 "ear piercing voices": Emmeline Pethick-Lawrence to Frederick Pethick-Lawrence, November 17, 1914, PLP.
64 "how horribly": Emmeline Pethick-Lawrence to Frederick Pethick-Lawrence, November 23, 1914, PLP.
64 "very kind letters": Emmeline Pethick-Lawrence to Frederick Pethick-Lawrence, November 11, 1914, PLP.
64 "I find Hull-House": Emmeline Pethick-Lawrence to Frederick Pethick-Lawrence, November 23, 1914, PLP.
65 "bright, loose-fitting dresses": Anne Wiltsher, *Most Dangerous Women: Feminist Peace Campaigners of the Great War* (London: Pandora, 1985), 10.

65 "all force and fire": C. Roland Marchand, *The American Peace Movement and Social Reform, 1898–1918* (Princeton, N.J.: Princeton University Press, 1972), 195.

65 "very little place": *Boston Globe*, March 21, 1915.

66 "She talks": "Comment on RS Lectures in USA," RSP, box 58.

66 "comedienne" . . . "alarmist": David S. Patterson, *The Search for Negotiated Peace: Women's Activism and Citizen Diplomacy in World War I* (New York: Routledge, 2008), 29, 31, 348.

66 "send offers": *Christian Science Monitor*, September 8, 1914.

66 "We must not": Wiltsher, *Most Dangerous Women*, 32.

67 "I looked": Rosika Schwimmer to JA, August 17, 1914, JAP, reel 7.

67 "Idiots!!": Patterson, *Search for Negotiated Peace*, 35.

67 "You will find": J. Keir Hardie to Rosika Schwimmer, August 28, 1914, RSP-HI, box 1.

67 "The President is": "The Pacifist Wilson," RSP-HI, box 44.

67 "The President was": *Washington Herald*, September 19, 1914.

67 "may be blocked": Patterson, *Search for Negotiated Peace*, 39.

68 "see the undertaker": Undated fragment, c. 1914, RSP, box 42.

68 "I wonder": Carrie Chapman Catt to Aletta Jacobs, November 13, 1914, in Mineke Bosch and Annemarie Kloosterman, eds., *Politics and Friendship: Letters from the International Woman Suffrage Alliance, 1902–1942* (Columbus: Ohio State University Press, 1990), 48.

68 "group of Hungarian": Patterson, *Search for Negotiated Peace*, 348.

68 "I have signed it": JA to Paul Kellogg, n.d. [September 1914], JAP.

68 "unfortunate temperament": Beth S. Wenger, "Radical Politics in a Reactionary Age: The Unmaking of Rosika Schwimmer, 1914–1930," *Journal of Women's History* 2, no. 2 (1990): 84.

68 "She is embittered": Emmeline Pethick-Lawrence to Frederick Pethick-Lawrence, November 11, 1914, PLP.

68–69 "We are working": *Chicago Tribune*, November 25, 1914.

69 "I have the impression": Rosika Schwimmer to Carrie Chapman Catt, November 29, 1914, Carrie Chapman Catt Papers [microfilm edition], reel 6.

69 "urge mediation": William Jennings Bryan to WW, September 19, 1914, WJBP.

69 "keep the matter": HD, September 28, 1914.

69 "return to the status": Jules Jusserand to French Foreign Ministry, September 8, 1914, in *PWW*, 31:16.

69 "sign of weakness": Reinhard R. Doerries, "Imperial Berlin and Washington: New Light on Germany's Foreign Policy and America's Entry into World War I," *Central European History* 11, no. 1 (1978): 38.

69 "power of public opinion": Count Bernstorff, *My Three Years in America* (London: Skeffington & Son, 1920), 43.

69 "Dollarica": Frederic William Wile, *Men around the Kaiser: The Makers of Modern Germany* (Indianapolis: Bobbs-Merrill, 1914), 176.

70 "real neutrality": WW to James Gerard, October 19, 1914, in *PWW*, 31:181.

70 "A GENTLE": Press release, WWP, reel 320.

70 "new interdependence": *New York Times*, August 9, 1914.

71 "a vassal state": *New York Evening Post*, January 6, 1915.

71 "threw all conventions": Cone Johnson to Ray Stannard Baker, October 15, 1932, RSBP, reel 78.

72 "Madison was compelled": HD, September 30, 1914.

72 "broken in spirit": HD, November 6, 1914.

72 "There is nothing": WW to Mary Hulbert, September 20, 1914, in *PWW*, 31:60.

72 "I fight to keep": WW to Mary Hulbert, October 11, 1914, in *PWW*, 31:141.

72 "visitors and delegations": WW to Mary Hulbert, October 11, 1914, in *PWW*, 31:141.

73 "chief real interest": WW to Mary Hulbert, November 8, 1914, in *PWW*, 31:281.

73 "on pending" . . . "papers to prepare" . . . "so tired": WW to Mary Hulbert, October 11, 1914, in *PWW*, 31:141.

73–74 For the Trotter/Wilson confrontation, see *PWW*, 31:298–308.

74 "I want to run": WW to Nancy Saunders Toy, November 9, 1914, *PWW*, 31:289.

74 "a hideously empty": WW to Mary Hulbert, November 8, 1914, in *PWW*, 31:281.

74 "lady of wit": WW to Mary Hulbert, October 18, 1914, in *PWW*, 31:174.

74 "I long for the time": WW to Mary Hulbert, November 22, 1914, in *PWW*, 31:344.

74 "If I could see": WW to Mary Hulbert, December 6, 1914, in *PWW*, 31:408.

74 "The President is a peculiar": HD, November 14, 1914.

74 "hardening of the arteries": HD, October 20, 1914.

75 "and he could not help": HD, November 14, 1914.

75 "Both old parties": *New York Sun*, October 23, 1914.

75 "as if he were a candidate": Davis, *Released for Publication*, 426.

75 "I use myself up": TR to William Allen White, November 7, 1914, in Morison, ed., *Letters of Theodore Roosevelt*, 8:834–40.

75 "particle of good": TR to Francis Heney, December 22, 1914, TRDL.

76 "young man who has": Fred Lewis to TR, October 20, 1914, TRP, reel 192.

76 "It is a habit": Charlotte Stanley to John McGrath, October 23, 1914, TRP, reel 192.
76 "average American": TR to Meyer Lissner, November 16, 1914, in Morison, ed., *Letters of Theodore Roosevelt*, 8:843–45.
76 "tired of reformers": TR to James R. Garfield, November 9, 1914, TRP, reel 357.
76 "four inches long": TR to Willis Hulings, November 28, 1914, TRP, reel 357.
76 "If men have not": TR to Meyer Lissner, December 11, 1914, TRP, reel 357.
76 "cause is exactly": TR to Archie Roosevelt, November 7, 1914, TRP, reel 385.
76 "there is not an idea": *Daily Princetonian*, October 31, 1914.
77 "wonderful dialectician": TR to William Allen White, November 7, 1914, in Morison, ed., *Letters of Theodore Roosevelt*, 8:834–40.
77 "lunatic fringe": TR to Archie Roosevelt, November 7, 1914, TRP, reel 385.
77 Dough Moose: *Brooklyn Standard Union*, September 13, 1912; "The people of this": Meyer Lissner to TR, December 21, 1914, TRP, reel 195.
77 "damned please": Davis, *Released for Publication*, 442.
77 "private citizen": *New York Sun*, November 16, 1914.
77 "enormous changes": Perkins quoted in William Dudley Foulke to TR, December 26, 1914, TRP, reel 195.
77 "On no spot": *Philadelphia Inquirer*, November 5, 1914.
77 "good long period": EMH to WW, November 9, 1914, in *PWW*, 31:291.
78 "hideous disaster": *New York Times*, September 27, 1914.
78 "good people": *New York Times*, November 1, 1914.
78 "Great military empires": *New York Times*, November 1, 1914.
78 "loquacious": *New York Times*, October 4, 1914.
78 "too timid": *New York Times*, November 1, 1914.
78 "but if I must choose": *New York Times*, October 4, 1914.
78 "last great war": *New York Times*, September 27, 1914.
78 "an agreement": *New York Times*, October 18, 1914.
78 "international police force": *New York Times*, October 4, 1914.
78 "Such a scheme": *New York Times*, October 18, 1914.
78 "not criticizing": *New York Times*, September 27, 1914.
78 "[t]here are plenty": *New York Times*, October 4, 1914.
78–79 "powerful forward" . . . "devil" . . . "destruction of Russia": *New York Times*, October 11, 1914.
79 "tendency to exaggerate": TR to Rudyard Kipling, October 3, 1914, TRP, reel 357.
79 "spiritless and selfish" . . . "But that there should be": *New York Times*, November 8, 1914.
80 "a very genuine respect": TR to Rudyard Kipling, November 4, 1914, in Morison, ed., *Letters of Theodore Roosevelt*, 8:829–31.
80 "our men": D. Arthur Mez to TR, November 15, 1914, TRP, reel 193.
80 "intellectual wrestling" . . . "I know that I am finding": George Sylvester Viereck, *Roosevelt: A Study in Ambivalence* (New York: Jackson Press, 1920), 105–10.
80 "I am happy" . . . "I am really glad": TR to Belle Roosevelt, November 7, 1914, TRDL.
80 "just at the very time": Davis, *Released for Publication*, 442.
80–81 "The dreadful thing": TR to Reginald Rowan Belknap, December 3, 1914, TRDL.
81 "very self-absorbed": TR to Kermit Roosevelt, November 11, 1914, TRDL.
81 "I wish to heavens": TR to F. C. Selous, December 4, 1914, TRP, reel 357.
81 "timid man": TR to Cecil Spring Rice, November 11, 1914, in Morison, ed., *Letters of Theodore Roosevelt*, 8:840–42.
81 "our educated men": TR to Kermit Roosevelt, December 28, 1914, TRDL.
81 "The action of the President": *New York Times*, December 6, 1914.
81 "below the belt": Herbert Croly to Willard Straight, December 10, 1914, Willard Straight Papers (microfilm edition), reel 5.
81 "The very extravagance": WW to Dudley Field Malone, December 9, 1914, in *PWW*, 31:429.
81 "modern tendencies": William Allen White to TR, December 28, 1914, TRP, reel 195.
82 "Socialist propaganda": Henry Bourne Joy to Truman Newberry, December 24, 1914, TRP, reel 195.
82 "one of my most bitter": TR to Truman Newberry, December 31, 1914, TRP, reel 357.
82 "guarantees me": TR to Archie Roosevelt, December 8, 1914, TRDL.
82 "mania": TR to William Allen White, November 7, 1914, in Morison, ed., *Letters of Theodore Roosevelt*, 8:834–40.
82 "there are moments": TR to Kermit Roosevelt, December 2, 1914, TRDL.
82 "She ought never": TR to Kermit Roosevelt, December 28, 1914, TRDL.
82–83 "no longer fit": TR to Belle Roosevelt, November 7, 1914, TRDL.
83 "a division": TR to Edward North Buxton, December 19, 1914, TRDL.
83 "Of all the nations": *New York Times*, November 15, 1914.
83 "I myself have seen": *New York Tribune*, October 31, 1914.
83 "if Germany comes out": TR to William Dudley Foulke, December 12, 1914, TRDL.
83 "Modern wars": *New York Sun*, November 15, 1914.

83–84"A Regular Army": *Army and Navy Register,* October 24, 1914.

84 "one of the most dangerous": Oswald Garrison Villard to WW, December 16, 1914, in *PWW,* 31:475.

84 "intrigue": Diary of Cary Grayson, March 13, 1919, WWPL.

84 "a leading antisuffragist": Terrell D. Webb, *Washington Wife: Journal of Ellen Maury Slayden from 1897–1919* (New York: Harper & Row, 1962), 300.

84–85 "The belief" . . . "Every voter" . . . "the blame": *Boston Globe,* October 17, 1914.

85 "talk about the present war": *New York Times,* December 6, 1914.

85 "We are from 30,000": *Boston Globe,* December 17, 1914.

85 "The question is": *New York Sun,* December 6, 1914.

85 "make the country": HD, November 4, 1914.

85 "large reserve force": HD, November 25, 1914.

85 "The President does not" . . . "shock the country": HD, November 4, 1914.

86 "unholy": *New York Times,* October 16, 1914.

86 "mental exercise": *Boston Globe,* October 20, 1914.

86 "it may be easy": *Boston Globe,* December 8, 1914.

86 "Wouldn't Teddy": David Lawrence, *The True Story of Woodrow Wilson* (New York: George H. Doran, 1924), 83.

86–87 "being prepared" . . . "we shall not alter": Message to Congress, December 8, 1914, in *PWW,* 31:421–24.

87 "rocked with applause": *Boston Globe,* December 9, 1914.

87 "red school houses": George von Lengerke Meyer to TR, November 19, 1914, TRP, reel 194.

87 "are you happy": George von Lengerke Meyer to TR, November 30, 1914, TRP, reel 194.

87 "an elaborate argument": TR to Julian Street, July 8, 1915, in Joseph Bucklin Bishop, *Theodore Roosevelt and His Time Shown in His Own Letters* (New York: Charles Scribner's Sons, 1920), 2:388.

87 "more responsible": TR to William Calder, May 12, 1917, TRP, reel 390.

87 "very worst men": TR to Henry Cabot Lodge, December 8, 1914, in Morison, ed., *Letters of Theodore Roosevelt,* 8:861–62.

87 "Partisan tactics": WW to Nancy Saunders Toy, December 12, 1914, in *PWW,* 31:455.

87 "Bryan yellow crowd": Leonard Wood diary, October 19, 1914, LeWP, box 8.

88 "harm . . . done to": *New York Times,* December 2, 1914.

88 "The enormity" . . . "tax of militarism" . . . "the best prepared": *Chicago Tribune,* December 6, 1914.

88 "foolish": Theodore Roosevelt, "America—on Guard!" *Everybody's Magazine,* January 1915, 120.

88 "entirely peaceful": TR to E. S. Van Zile, January 8, 1915, TRP, reel 357.

88 "Why should" . . . "The war has set suffrage": *Chicago Tribune,* December 6, 1914.

89 "'social workers' and others": JA to Madeline Breckinridge, November 30, 1914, JAP, reel 7.

89 "There is great eagerness": JA to David Starr Jordan, December 8, 1914, JAP, reel 7.

89 "large and ill assorted assemblage": JA to Rosika Schwimmer, December 11, 1914, RSP-HI.

89 "merely because they are eager" . . . "good deal of emotionalism": JA to Carrie Chapman Catt, December 14, 1914, JAP, reel 7.

89 "who do not know each other well": JA to Carrie Chapman Catt, December 21, 1914, JAP, reel 7.

90 "necessity of foreign women" . . . "arrogance": Carrie Chapman Catt to JA, December 29, 1914, JAP, reel 7.

90 "woman's mass meeting": Rosika Schwimmer to Carrie Chapman Catt, November 29, 1914, Carrie Chapman Catt Papers, reel 6.

90 "arbitration committee": *Chicago Tribune,* December 16, 1914.

90 "evidently unstrung": Patterson, *Search for Negotiated Peace,* 45.

90 "I am sorry not to be": JA to Carrie Chapman Catt, December 14, 1914, JAP, reel 7.

90 "little use for women": Carrie Chapman Catt to JA, December 16, 1914, JAP, reel 7.

90 "At the invitation": JA to Lucia Ames Mead, December 28, 1914, JAP, reel 7.

90 "outsiders . . . taking their work": Carrie Chapman Catt to JA, December 29, 1914, JAP, reel 7.

91 "I do not know yet": WW to Nancy Saunders Toy, December 12, 1914, in *PWW,* 31:516.

91 "You were *right* to tell": WW to Mary Hulbert, December 27, 1914, in *PWW,* 31:538.

91 "I would put real": WW to Nancy Saunders Toy, December 12, 1914, in *PWW,* 31:456.

91 "when the cup of sorrow": William Jennings Bryan to WW, December 1, 1914, in *PWW,* 31:379.

91 "wipes" or "wipers": *Washington Post,* December 9, 1914.

91–92 "duty, as the leading" . . . "Surely these Christian": William Jennings Bryan to WW, December 1, 1914, in *PWW,* 31:379.

92 "had a profound": Ray Stannard Baker interview with Lindley Garrison, November 30, 1928, RSBP, reel 75.

92 "If Bryan had been": Grayson diary, March 19, 1919, WWPL.

92 "something must be": Ray Stannard Baker, *Woodrow Wilson: Life and Letters,* vol. 5, *Neutrality, 1914–1915* (New York: Greenwood Press, 1968), 297.

92 "they must not judge": Wood diary, November 9, 1914, LeWP, box 8.

92 "working for peace": HD, December 3, 1914.

92 "President's Ambassador-at-large": HD, January 23, 1915.
93 "If the Kaiser" . . . "knew that the war": HD, December 23, 1914.
93 "a reactionary of the worst sort": HD, September 18, 1914.
93 "oldest son": Margaret Wilson to Jessie Sayre, November 19, 1914, WWPL.
93 "a spoilsman to the core": Diary of Nancy Saunders Toy, January 3, 1915, in *PWW*, 32:10.
93 "We both thought": HD, December 3, 1914.
93 "During the evening": Robinson, *My Fourteen Months*, 36.
94 "There will be nothing": Willa Cather to Ferris Greenslet, December 21, 1914, Willa Cather Archive, (www.cather.unl.edu).

Chapter 3: A Strict Accountability

95 "An accident": *New York Evening Post*, February 23, 1915.
95 "it's useless": *New York Evening Post*, February 27, 1915.
95 "we blasted": John Reed to Jules Jusserand, March 11, 1915, TRP, reel 199.
95–96 "As for our": *New York Evening Post*, February 27, 1915.
96 "ought to be shot": TR to Carl Hovey, March 13, 1915, TRP, reel 358.
96 "loved France": John Reed to Jules Jusserand, March 11, 1915, TRP, reel 199.
96 "can write": TR to Jules Jusserand, March 15, 1915, TRDL.
96 "be shot if he": Carl Hovey to TR, March 12, 1915, TRP, reel 199.
96 "learning the fine art": JNH to Roy Cushman, March 24, 1915, JNHP, box 2.
96 "All the fellows": JNH to Mother, March 15, 1915, JNHP, box 2.
96–97 "small" . . . "a head taller": JNH to Mother and family, March 8, 1915, JNHP, box 2.
97 "If I come safely": JNH to Father, February 18, 1915, JNHP, box 2.
97 "some of the greatest": JNH to George Courtwright Greener, February 20, 1915, JNHP, box 2.
97 "when we used to coast": JNH to Mother and all, January 22, 1915, JNHP, box 2.
97 "a rarity with Englishmen": JNH to Mother and all, March 14, 1915, JNHP, box 2.
97 "hearty American hand clasp": JNH to Mother and family, March 8, 1915, JNHP, box 2.
97 "What a wretchedly" . . . "Thank Heaven": JNH to Roy Cushman, February 7, 1915, JNHP, box 2.
97 "never heard": Diary of Nancy Saunders Toy, January 5, 1915, in *PWW*, 32:21.
98 "these records": *Washington Times*, January 8, 1915.
98 "His fist": Diary of Nancy Saunders Toy, January 5, 1915, in *PWW*, 32:21.
98 "a war more of ammunition": Arthur Lee to TR, March 21, 1915, TRP, reel 199.
98 "I do not think that people": Gerard dispatch, January 24, 1915, in *PWW*, 32:145.
99 "there were five hundred thousand": Gerard dispatch, January 24, 1915, in *PWW*, 32:145.
99 "something like a civil war": Cecil Spring Rice to Edward Grey, February 12, 1915, FOP, FO 800/85.
99 "Our greatest mistake": Count Bernstorff, *My Three Years in America* (London: Skeffington & Son, 1920), 19.
99 "You can have no idea": F. A. Mahan to TR, February 11, 1915, TRP, reel 198.
100 "There is danger": *The Spectator*, January 23, 1915.
100 "Together, England": WW to Mary Hulbert, February 14, 1915, in *PWW*, 32:232.
100 "Both sides are seeing": WW to Nancy Toy, March 7, 1915, in *PWW*, 32:334.
100 "both sides heartily dislike": Henry Cabot Lodge to TR, January 15, 1915, TRP, reel 197.
100 "Do you not think it likely": Jackson Day speech, January 8, 1915, in *PWW*, 32:29–41.
101 "angry" and "cheap": Henry Cabot Lodge to TR, January 15, 1915, TRP, reel 197.
101 "The Republicans are": WW to Nancy Toy, January 31, 1915, in *PWW*, 32:165.
101 "only to keep Bryan out" . . . "Never for a moment": Nancy Toy diary, January 3, 1915, in *PWW*, 32:9–10.
101 "sufficiently handicapped": HD, January 24, 1915.
102 "One hundred million people": *New York Tribune*, January 27, 1915.
102 "every man": *New York Herald*, January 26, 1915.
102 "Isn't it tough": *New York Sun*, December 29, 1914.
102 "federal employment bureau": *New York Herald*, January 27, 1915.
102 "does not realize" . . . "unimaginative, mediocre": HD, January 4, 16, 1915.
103 "Let them talk": *Chicago Tribune*, February 2, 1915.
103 "not afraid": Anna Garlin Spencer to JA, January 18, 1915, JAP, reel 8.
103 "In the crush": *New York American*, January 11, 1915, JAP, reel 62.
103 "women be given": *The Independent*, January 25, 1915.
104 "You have set": *Washington Post*, January 11, 1915.
104 "the most convincing": Madeleine Black to JA, January 21, 1915, JAP, reel 8.
104 "because they have been told" . . . "sacrifice of life": Addams's speech of January 10, 1915, is reprinted in *The Advocate of Peace*, March 1915, 64–65.
104 "somewhat startling": Jane Addams, *Peace and Bread in Time of War* (New York: Macmillan, 1922), 8.

104 "organized opposition": *Chicago Tribune*, January 11, 1915.

105 "Jane Addams presided": Terrell D. Webb, *Washington Wife: Journal of Ellen Maury Slayden from 1897–1919* (New York: Harper & Row, 1962), 256.

105 "want to join": Anna Garlin Spencer to JA, January 18, 1915, JAP, reel 8.

105 "bright little matron": *Cincinnati Commercial Tribune*, April 4, 1915, JAP, reel 62.

105 "A Mere Man": Letter reprinted in *The Musical Leader*, January 28, 1915, JAP, reel 62.

105 "behind my back": Rosika Schwimmer to Mrs. John Jay White, February 16, 1915, JAP, reel 8.

106 "If it would relieve": Rosika Schwimmer to JA, February 16, 1915, JAP, reel 8.

106 "nervous and hysterical": Antoinette Funk to JA, March 29, 1915, JAP, reel 8.

106 "absolutely foolish": Rosika Schwimmer to JA, January 29, 1915, JAP, reel 8.

106 "fundamental to the undertaking": Hetty L. Cunningham to JA, March 1, 1915, JAP, reel 8.

106 "man-killing in Europe": *The Independent*, January 25, 1915.

106 "usual lectures" . . . "plays and festivals": JA to Mrs. Christian Hemmick, February 2, 1915, JAP, reel 8.

106 "not in entire agreement": Henry Haskell to JA, February 19, 1915, JAP, reel 8.

106 "unwilling to be" . . . "in view": James Brown Scott to JA, March 13 [?], 1915, JAP, reel 8.

107 "any peace delegations": Kate Waller Barrett to JA, January 29, 1915, JAP, reel 8.

107 "propaganda": Belle La Follette to Elizabeth Thacher Kent, January 26, 1915, JAP, reel 8.

107 "as near despair": Oscar King Davis, *Released for Publication: Some Inside Political History of Theodore Roosevelt and His Times, 1898–1918* (Boston: Houghton Mifflin, 1925), 445.

107 "merely answering": TR to Belle Roosevelt, January 16, 1915, TRDL.

107 "stout fighters": Arthur Lee to TR, March 21, 1915, TRP, reel 199.

108 "head of a brigade": TR to William Chanler, January 13, 1915, TRDL.

108 "American-American": TR to Mark Sullivan, January 4, 1915, TRP, reel 357.

108 "I don't care a rap": TR to Charles Demport, May 18, 1915, TRP, reel 385.

108 "coolness toward England": J. St. Loe Strachey to TR, February 1, 1915, TRP, reel 198.

108 "a good citizen": TR to George Viereck, March 15, 1915, in *The Letters of Theodore Roosevelt*, ed. Elting Morison, vol. 8, *The Days of Armageddon, 1914–1919* (Cambridge: Harvard University Press, 1954), 910–11.

109 "I never expected to hate": Henry Cabot Lodge to TR, March 1, 1915, TRP, reel 199.

109 "real man": TR to Mark Sullivan, February 19, 1915, TRP, reel 358.

109 "purchase a quarrel": TR to D. Thompson, March 1, 1915, TRP, reel 358.

109 In a lengthy letter to Rublee: TR to Judith Rublee, February 9, 1915, JCOP, box 11; see also *Chicago Tribune*, April 17, 1915.

110 "Jane Addams inspired idiots": TR to Cecil Spring Rice, May 1, 1915, TRP, reel 416.

110 "afraid of her": John Kingsbury to JA, January 17, 1913, JAP, reel 7.

110 "brought about state by state": *PWW*, 32:22.

110 "Suffrage for women": Nancy Toy diary, January 6, 1915, in *PWW*, 32:21.

110 "show him the birth": Thomas Dixon to Joseph Tumulty, May 1, 1915, in *PWW*, 32:142.

110 "on the white panels": *St. Louis Post-Dispatch*, February 19, 1915.

111 "It is like writing" . . . "very unfortunate production": John Milton Cooper Jr., *Woodrow Wilson: A Biography* (New York: Alfred A. Knopf, 2009), 272–73.

111 "devoted" . . . "easily taught": Woodrow Wilson, *A History of the American People*, vol. 9, *Reunion and Rationalization* (New York: Harper & Brothers, 1918), 17, 46.

111–112 "The producer seems" . . . "You can use history": *New York Evening Post*, March 13, 1915, and *Chicago Defender*, March 20, 1915.

112 "unspeakable fellow": WW to Joseph Tumulty, April 24, 1915, in *PWW*, 33:68.

112 "dove of peace": *Washington Evening Star*, February 23, 1915.

112 "ignore the war": *Boston Globe*, March 9, 1915.

112 "Our neutrality": *Boston American*, March 14, 1915, JAP, reel 62.

112 "The more life and treasure": Rudyard Kipling to TR, December 4, 1914, TRP, reel 194.

113 "how utterly unreliable" . . . "was so anxious": HD, January 13, 1915.

114 "You are the only one" . . . "made all sorts": HD, January 13, 1915.

114 "We are both of the same": HD, January 24, 1915.

114 "most trusted friend" . . . "Your unselfish": HD, January 25, 1915.

114 "Your words of affection": EMH to WW, January 26, 1915, in *PWW*, 32:128.

114 "chaperone" . . . "preposterous": *New York Evening World*, January 30, 1915.

114 "His mission": Press conference of February 9, 1915, in *PWW*, 32:200.

115 "It is something": *New York Herald*, February 8, 1915.

115 "To sink": *New York Evening Post*, February 12, 1915.

116 "England wants to starve": *Washington Post*, December 23, 1914.

116 "The submarine has come" . . . "That it is useful": Franklin Roosevelt, "The Future of the Submarine," *North American Review*, October 1915, 508.

116 "man who will do much": *Washington Evening Star*, January 24, 1915.

116 "preposterous": JNH to Roy Cushman, February 7, 1915, JNHP, box 2.

116 "Doubtless some": JNH to Father, February 18, 1915, JNHP, box 2.

116 "it would involve": *New York Tribune*, February 28, 1915.

117 "He is conscious": Franklin Lane to E. W. Scripps, June 1, 1915, in Anne W. Lane and Louise Herrick Wall, eds., *The Letters of Franklin K. Lane, Personal and Political* (Boston: Houghton Mifflin, 1922), 175.

117 "public statement" . . . "boys drawing": Lindley Garrison memorandum [c. February 5, 1915], in *PWW,* 32:193.

117 "strict accountability" . . . "American vessel": *New York Tribune*, February 12, 1915.

118 "deliberate with the United States": *New York Times*, February 19, 1915.

118 "We are liable": William Jennings Bryan to WW, February 15, 1915, in *PWW*, 32:235.

118 "We are now ambling": TR to Albert Fall, February 22, 1915, TRP, reel 358.

118 "professorial views": TR to Edward Grey, January 22, 1915, in Morison, ed., *Letters of Theodore Roosevelt*, 8:876–81.

119 "it would not meet": HD, February 27, 1915.

119 "If this order in council": *Chicago Tribune*, March 22, 1915.

119 "I am very much afraid": John Callan O'Laughlin to A. Briantschanoff, March 6, 1915, JCOP, box 5.

119 "in the most friendly spirit": *New York Times* quoting *The Times* of London, April 6, 1915.

119 "debate with" . . . "We cannot convince": WW to William Jennings Bryan, March 24, 1915, in *PWW,* 32:424–425.

120 "something wrong": TR to Cecil Spring Rice, February 5, 1915, in Morison, ed., *Letters of Theodore Roosevelt*, 8:888–89.

120 "command of the seas": TR to Edward Grey, January 22, 1915, in Morison, ed., *Letters of Theodore Roosevelt*, 8:876–81.

120 "We do what we can": Edward Grey to TR, March 13, 1915, TRP, reel 199.

120 "absolutely trustworthy": HD, January 11, 1915.

120–121 "that the war could be settled": HD, February 11, 1915.

121 "Grey by name": J. St. Loe Strachey to TR, October 13, 1916, TRP, reel 215.

121 "nature, solitude": HD, February 13, 1915.

121 "You cannot go": WW to EMH, February 20, 1915, in *PWW*, 32:265.

121 "looks upon" . . . "keep in as close": EMH to WW, February 21, 23, 1915, in *PWW*, 33:267, 278.

121 "put too much trust": EMH to WW, March 9, 1915, in *PWW*, 32:350.

121 "a man of great force": HD, March 1, 1915.

122 "I think constantly": EMH to WW, March 8, 1915, in *PWW*, 32:341.

122 "tentatively accepted": EMH to WW, March 14, 1915, in *PWW*, 32:374.

122 "Roosevelt's friends": EMH to WW, March 15, 1915, in *PWW*, 32:376.

122 "points of common interest": HD, March 22, 1915.

122 "It seems that every German soldier": EMH to WW, March 26, 1915, in *PWW,* 32:438.

123 "to tentatively look upon": HD, March 19, 1915.

123 "The world is upon": EMH to WW, March 20, 1915, in *PWW*, 32:403.

123 "seems incapable": TR to Stewart Edward White, March 3, 1915, TRP, reel 358.

123 "card index system": *New York Times*, March 7, 1915.

123 "I should be ashamed": TR to Mrs. John C. Graham, March 5, 1915, TRDL.

124 "call for a Peace Army": Margaret Pfannebecker to JA, March 3, 1915, JAP, reel 8.

124 "The country would be infinitely": *Washington Post*, January 27, 1915.

124 "peace society organizer": Willis J. Physioc to TR, March 22, 1915, TRP, reel 199.

124 "shocking" and "unnecessary": *Christian Science Monitor*, March 9, 1915.

124 "To start a project": *New York Sun*, March 6, 1915.

124 "Theodore, the militarist": *Philadelphia Record*, March 11, 1915, JAP, reel 62.

124 "a great sporting event": *Philadelphia Record*, March 7, 1915, JAP, reel 62.

124 "There was one man": *New York Times*, March 12, 1915.

125 "killed by the soldiers": *New York Times*, March 8, 1915.

125 "Come and join": *New York Times*, March 6, 1915.

125 "expert stenographer": Edward Bok to JA, February 16, 1915, JAP, reel 8.

125 "They are simply more vocal": Jane Addams, "As I See Women," *Ladies' Home Journal*, August 1915.

126 "drew down the lids": Marcet Haldeman-Julius, *Jane Addams as I Knew Her* (Girard, Kans.: Haldeman-Julius Publications, 1936), 16.

126 "out of the long past": JA to Lillian Wald, March 26, 1915, JAP, reel 8.

126 "sickened her": Walter I. Trattner, "Julia Grace Wales and the Wisconsin Plan for Peace," *The Wisconsin Magazine of History* 44, no. 3 (1961): 203.

126 "more academically framed sketch": Rosika Schwimmer to Mrs. Ragaz, June 8, 1936, Alice Park Papers, Hoover Institution Archives, box 1.

126–127 "is on fire": George W. Nasmyth to JA, January 15, 1915, JAP, reel 8.

127 "I should welcome": WW to JA, March 8, 1915, JAP, reel 8.

127 "I shall not leave": *New York Morning Telegraph*, April 18, 1915, JAP, reel 63.

127 "trying to organize": Carrie Chapman Catt to JA, January 16, 1915, JAP, reel 8.

127 "was willing to die": Carrie Chapman Catt to Rosika Schwimmer, March 2, 1915, RSP, box 55.
127 "the greatest, most unparalleled": Emmeline Pethick-Lawrence to JA, March 10, 1915, JAP, reel 8.
128 "moral adventure": JA to Ray Stannard Baker, March 26, 1915, JAP, reel 8.
128 "Women who are willing": JA to Lillian Wald, March 26, 1915, JAP, reel 8.
128 "Don't you think": JA to Emily Balch, March 26, 1915, JAP, reel 8.
128 "turning point in my life": David S. Patterson, *The Search for Negotiated Peace: Women's Activism and Citizen Diplomacy in World War I* (New York: Routledge, 2008), 60.
128 "There are times": JA to William I. Hull, April 3, 1915, JAP, reel 8.
128 "no one can predict": JA to Lillian Wald, April 6, 1915, JAP, reel 8.
128 "My only trouble": WW to Nancy Toy, March 7, 1915, in *PWW*, 32:334.
129 "tall . . . dark-haired": *New York Times*, October 10, 1915.
129 "wearing a red": WW to Edith Galt, August 13, 1915, in *PWW*, 34:190.
129 "lived on feminine inspiration": David Lawrence, *The True Story of Woodrow Wilson* (New York: George H. Doran, 1924), 179.
129 "worldly pleasures": *Chicago Tribune*, November 10, 1918.
129 "He is *perfectly* charming": Edith Galt to Annie Bolling, March 23, 1915, in *PWW*, 32:423.
129 "weak lung": *Los Angeles Times*, November 21, 1915.
130 "Russian influenza": *Washington Times*, January 28, 1908.
130 "marry again": "Memorandum of a Talk with Dr. Stockton Axson," August 28, 1931, RSBP, reel 70.
130 "It was murder": *Montreal Gazette*, March 30, 1915.

Chapter 4: A Disgrace to the Women of America

131 "I do wish": *New York Tribune*, May 10, 1915.
131 "Japanese danger": Unknown (signature unreadable) to John Callan O'Laughlin, March 25, 1915, JCOP, box 5.
132 "a wave of patriotism": John Callan O'Laughlin to unknown, April 26, 1915, JCOP, box 5.
132 "insolent" . . . "Lord, how": TR to John Callan O'Laughlin, May 6, 1915, TRP, reel 385.
132 "the view they take": William Jennings Bryan to WW, April 19, 1915, in *PWW*, 33:28.
133 "My throat and nose": William J. Robinson, *My Fourteen Months at the Front: An American Boy's Baptism of Fire* (Boston: Little, Brown, 1916), 140.
133 "I expect to join": JNH to Mother and all, May 2, 1915, JNHP, box 2.
133 "I do not like": WW to William Jennings Bryan, April 3, 1915, in *PWW*, 32:468.
133 "barbarism gone mad" . . . "In the light": *New York Evening Post*, March 30, 1915.
134 "very regrettable": *New York Times*, April 1, 1915.
134 "I am very much worried": William Jennings Bryan to WW, April 6, 1915, in *PWW*, 32:487.
134 "firm demand": Robert Lansing to William Jennings Bryan, April 5, 1915, in *PWW*, 32:483–84.
134 "capable of furnishing": William Jennings Bryan to WW, April 6, 1915, in *PWW*, 33:71.
135 "To insist now": WW to William Jennings Bryan, April 28, 1915, in *PWW*, 33:85.
135 a gathering of the Associated Press: Associated Press speech, April 20, 1915, in *PWW*, 33:37–41.
135 "a stench in the nostrils": TR to W. S. Lawnvill, April 10, 1915, TRP, reel 358.
135 "return at least": TR to W. R. Thayer, April 9, 1915, TRDL.
135–136 "I see by the morning": TR to Joseph Choate, April 21, 1915, TRP, reel 200.
136 "entirely ruthless": TR to Ladislaus Hengelmuller von Hengervar, June 23, 1915, TRDL.
136 "German efficiency": TR to Maurice Egan, May 6, 1915, TRP, reel 385.
136 "position of international drum major": *New York Times*, November 29, 1914.
136 "protested strenuously": TR to Joseph Choate, April 21, 1915, TRP, reel 200.
136 "What is the use": Robert Pellissier, *Letters from a Chasseur à Pied* (privately printed, 1917), 149.
137 "the largest moving picture" . . . "I believe it has": J. Stuart Blackton to TR, April 5, 1915, TRP, reel 200.
138 "army and navy cabal": Oswald Villard to David Starr Jordan, April 15, 1915, DSJP, box 81.
138 "was making a grave mistake": HD, June 14, 1915.
138 "The ignorance of Europe": HD, April 16, 1915.
138 "His mind and mine": HD, April 30, 1915.
138 "Peace talk": April 30, 1915, diary entry in Burton J. Hendrick, *The Life and Letters of Walter H. Page* (Garden City, N.Y.: Doubleday, Page, 1922), 2:414.
139 "fools' errand": JA to David Starr Jordan, April 9, 1915, JAP, reel 8.
139 "arch-feminist": Terrell D. Webb, *Washington Wife: Journal of Ellen Maury Slayden from 1897–1919* (New York: Harper & Row, 1962), 261–62.
139 "has courage": Marcet Haldeman-Julius, *Jane Addams as I Knew Her* (Girard, Kans.: Haldeman-Julius Publications, 1936), 17.
139 "silly women": *Chicago Tribune*, April 17, 1915.
139 "women's conference": *New York Tribune*, April 13, 1915.
139 "We are not so foolish": *New York Sun*, April 9, 1915.

139 "The most we can hope": *New York Tribune*, April 13, 1915.
139 "formulate plans" . . . "Now is the time": *New York Sun*, April 9, 1915.
139 "Colonel Roosevelt and I": *New York Tribune*, April 13, 1915.
140 "cry of a barbarian": *Washington Post*, April 18, 1915.
140 "make no effort": *Literary Digest*, May 1, 1915, 1022–23.
140 "It is hoped": *Springfield Republican*, April 12, 1915, JAP, reel 62.
140 "The general feeling": TR to Kermit Roosevelt, January 27, 1915, TRDL.
140 "It will be a rather": TR to Kermit Roosevelt, May 8, 1915, TRDL.
141 "propped up in bed": TR to Endicott Peabody, April 18, 1915, TRP, reel 358.
141 "has intellect": Robert Emmett O'Connor, "William Barnes, Jr.: A Conservative Encounters the Progressive Era" (Ph.D. diss., SUNY Albany, 1971), 110.
142 "circus day": *New York Herald*, April 22, 1915.
142 "It appeared": *New York Sun*, April 20, 1915.
142 "over a third": New York (State) Appellate Division, *Record in the Matter of William Barnes vs. Theodore Roosevelt*, 1915, 1:199.
142 "Neither rules": *New York Herald*, April 22, 1915.
142 "make him do": *New York Herald*, April 23, 1915.
143 "Instead of telling": *New York Herald*, April 24, 1915.
143 "drove home his points": *Washington Times*, April 29, 1915.
143 "You can't tire me out": *New York Sun*, April 29, 1915.
143 "little sleeping powders": Alexander Lambert to TR, April 22, 1915, TRP, reel 200.
143 "We've made him rewrite": *Boston Transcript*, April 29, 1915.
143 "You have already disposed": Frank Knox to TR, May 3, 1915, TRP, reel 200.
143 "Mr. Bawnes": *Syracuse Herald*, January 6, 1919.
143 "to bleat about peace" . . . "I felt the keenest": TR to Cecil Spring Rice, May 1, 1915, TRP, reel 416.
143 "they are a disgrace": TR to Marchesa Antonio de Viti de Marco, June 1, 1915, TRP, reel 358.
144 "Through the mine" . . . "and I do not see": *New York Evening Globe*, April 13, 1915, JAP, reel 63.
144 "greatest fear": *New York Morning Telegraph*, April 13, 1915, JAP, reel 63.
144 "all sorts": JA to Lillian Wald, April 6, 1915, JAP, reel 8.
144 "those dreadful Hull-House people": Rosika Schwimmer to Lola Maverick Lloyd, September 14, 1915, RSP, box 62.
145 "Indeed, I can't": *New York Tribune*, April 14, 1915.
145 "It will break": *New York Evening Globe*, April 13, 1915, JAP, reel 63.
145 "megaphoning messages" . . . "I don't know whether": *New York Tribune*, April 14, 1915.
146 "How can Dutch people": "Journal of Miss Emily Greene Balch," April 1915, Emily Greene Balch Papers, reel 18.
146 "frivolous, high-heeled, and flirtatious": Madeleine Zabriskie Doty, *Short Rations: An American Woman in Germany, 1915–1916* (New York: Century Company, 1917), 7.
146 "It is so simple": Mary Heaton Vorse to Joe O'Brien, April 1915, Mary Heaton Vorse Papers, Walter Reuther Library, Wayne State University.
146 "working girls": Balch diary, April 14, 1915, Emily Balch Papers, reel 18.
146 "Is war ever justifiable?": Doty, *Short Rations*, 4–5.
147 "The women on the whole": JA to Mary Rozet Smith, April 22, 1915, JAP, reel 8.
147 "Miss Addams is really": Alice Hamilton to Mary Rozet Smith, April 22, 1915, JAP, reel 8.
147 "I like her more": Mary Heaton Vorse to Joe O'Brien, April 1915, Mary Heaton Vorse Papers.
147 "a very heterogeneous group": Mercedes M. Randall, *Improper Bostonian: Emily Greene Balch* (New York: Twayne, 1964), 147–48.
147 "wore her best underclothing" . . . "No one knew": Doty, *Short Rations*, 8.
147–148 "We had a gun" . . . "*Hoch der Kaiser*": Alice Thacher Post, "A Pacifist Journey in War Time," *The Public*, May 21, 1915, 495.
148 "bribed" fisherman: *New York Tribune*, April 30, 1915.
148 "peacettes": Doty, *Short Rations*, 12.
148 "peace babblers": *The Advocate of Peace*, July 1915.
148 "We are perfectly satisfied": *Daily Graphic*, n.d. (c. April 1915?), Archives Unbound database, Gale Primary Sources, https://www.gale.com/primary-sources/archives-unbound.
149 "We are not allowed" . . . "Miss Addams shines": Balch diary, April 1915, Emily Balch Papers, reel 18.
149 "willing to risk anything": *New York Times*, April 27, 1915.
149 "Daughters of the Dove of Peace": Hendrick, *The Life and Letters of Walter H. Page*, 2:13–14.
149 "We dance about": Doty, *Short Rations*, 12.
150 "the wooden shoes": Mary Chamberlain, "The Women at the Hague," *The Survey*, June 5, 1915, 219.
150 "I'm so glad": Doty, *Short Rations*, 15.
150 "big, fine, wholesome": *New York Evening Sun*, May 26, 1915, JAP, reel 63.
150–151 "by a gesture" . . . "Yesterday it seemed": International Women's Committee for Permanent Peace, *Report—International Congress of Women, The Hague—April 28th to May 1st 1915*, 87, 96–97.

151 "searched to the skin": Chamberlain, "The Women at the Hague," 222.

151 "1,000 women stood": *New York Sun*, May 22, 1915, JAP, reel 63.

151 "new type of women": *New York Globe*, May 20, 1915, JAP, reel 63.

151 "silly . . . platitudes" . . . "There must be free speech": *Report—International Congress of Women*, 128–29.

152 "statesmanlike handling": *New York Evening Post*, May 21, 1915.

152 "extraordinary parliamentary skill": Randall, *Improper Bostonian*, 157–58.

152 "pulled the best out": *New York Evening Post*, June 9, 1915.

152 "democratic control": *Report—International Congress of Women*, 38.

152 "shocked the professional pacifists": Rosika Schwimmer to Louis Lochner, March 22, 1915, in *Revolutionary Radicalism: Its History, Purpose and Tactics with an Exposition and Discussion of the Steps Being Taken and Required to Curb It* (Albany: J. B. Lyon, 1920), 1:972–73.

152 "I don't appeal" . . . "Brains—they say": *Report—International Congress of Women*, 173–74.

153 "you can never understand: JA to Mary Rozet Smith, May 9, 1915, JAP, reel 8.

153 "The great achievement": Chamberlain, "Women at the Hague," 219.

153 "any church meeting": Unidentified clipping, May 1915, JAP, reel 63.

153 "which we do not claim": *Christian Science Monitor*, June 7, 1915.

153 "think it 'silly and base'": JA to Mary Rozet Smith, May 6, 1915, JAP, reel 8.

153 "one chance in ten thousand": JA to Mary Rozet Smith, May 9, 1915, JAP, reel 8

153 "waters adjacent to the British Isles": *New York Sun* (and many other papers), May 1, 1915.

154 "John Smith": *New York Evening World*, May 1, 1915.

154 "I'm sentenced": *New York Herald*, May 2, 1915.

154 "highly improper": Robert Lansing to William Jennings Bryan, May 1, 1915, in *PWW*, 33:92–93.

154 "friendly desire": William Jennings Bryan to WW, May 1, 1915, in *PWW*, 33:91.

154 "energetic action": TR to Archie Roosevelt, May 19, 1915, in *The Letters of Theodore Roosevelt*, ed. Elting Morison, vol. 8, *The Days of Armageddon, 1914–1919* (Cambridge: Harvard University Press, 1954), 922–23.

155 "I believe that a sharp": EMH to WW, May 5, 1915, in *PWW*, 33:108.

155 "boil over" . . . "But they respect him": Franklin Lane to EMH, May 5, 1915, in Charles Seymour, *The Intimate Papers of Colonel House* (Boston: Houghton Mifflin, 1926), 1:458–59.

155 "Mrs. Norman Gault[sic]": *New York Herald*, April 15, 1915.

156 "I hope it will give": WW to Edith Galt, April 28, 1915, in *PWW*, 33:87.

156 "loved Southland" . . . "high office": Edith Galt to WW, May 7, 1915, in *PWW*, 33:128.

156 "It had taken possession": WW to Edith Galt, June 4, 1915, in *PWW*, 33:339–40.

156 "really know": John Milton Cooper Jr., *Woodrow Wilson: A Biography* (New York: Alfred A. Knopf, 2009), 283.

156 "What an unspeakable pleasure": Edith Galt to WW, May 4–5, 1915, in *PWW*, 33:109.

157 "It will be my study" . . . "The wonderful woman": WW to Edith Galt, May 6, 1915, in *PWW*, 33:118.

157 "not stopped thinking": WW to Edith Galt, May 5, 1915, in *PWW*, 33:112.

157 "awful conditions": Edith Galt to WW, May 9, 1915, in *PWW*, 33:133.

157 "deep and tender friendship" . . . "All that you have": WW to Edith Galt, May 7, 1915, in *PWW*, 33:126–27.

157 "fifth cousin": *New York Herald*, May 5, 1915.

157 "From 1898": TR to Kermit Roosevelt, May 8, 1915, TRDL.

158 "what you read": David S. Patterson, *The Search for Negotiated Peace: Women's Activism and Citizen Diplomacy in World War I* (New York: Routledge, 2008), 85.

158 "I almost expect such a thing": John Milton Cooper Jr., *Walter Hines Page: The Southerner as American, 1855–1918* (Chapel Hill: University of North Carolina Press, 1977), 306.

158 "The truth of the matter" . . . "a flame of indignation": HD, May 7, 1915.

Chapter 5: Too Proud to Fight

159 "I do not deny": *New York Herald*, June 4, 1915.

159 "dropping of a bomb": *New York Herald*, May 8, 1915.

159 "NONE PERISH": *Washington Evening Star*, May 7, 1915.

159–160 "Do you think": Melville E. Stone, *Fifty Years a Journalist* (Garden City, N.Y.: Doubleday, 1921), 322.

160 "an extraordinarily great detonation": Arthur Link, *Wilson: The Struggle for Neutrality, 1914–1915* (Princeton, N.J.: Princeton University Press, 1960), 371.

160 "greatest crisis": WW to William Allen White, May 24, 1915, in *PWW*, 33:247.

161 "In the awful possibilities": Edith Galt to WW, May 7, 1915, in *PWW*, 33:127.

161 "I have not seen": Henry Lee Higginson to Charles Eliot, May 10, 1915, in Bliss Perry, *Life and Letters of Henry Lee Higginson* (Boston: Atlantic Monthly Press, 1921), 2:474.

161 "Thank Heaven": JNH to Aunt Dizzy, May 10, 1915, JHNP, box 2.

161 "Nobody but": HD, May 12, 1915.

161 "Anglo-American partnership" . . . "English-speaking folk": John Milton Cooper Jr., *Walter Hines Page: The Southerner as American, 1855–1918* (Chapel Hill: University of North Carolina Press, 1977), 266–67.

161 "the freely expressed unofficial feeling": Walter Hines Page to Wilson and Secretary, May 8, 1915, in *PWW*, 33:130.

161 "a failure to act now": HD, May 9, 1915.

162 "demand" . . . "We are being weighed": EMH to WW, May 9, 1915, in *PWW*, 33:134.

162 "I do not know": *New York Herald*, May 8, 1915.

162 "That's murder": Joseph Bucklin Bishop, *Theodore Roosevelt and His Time Shown in His Own Letters* (New York: Charles Scribner's Sons, 1920), 2:376.

162 "represents not merely piracy": *New York Sun*, May 8, 1915.

162 "detailed views": Wheeler Syndicate to John McGrath, May 8, 1915, TRP, reel 200.

162 "take lead in denouncing": John Callan O'Laughlin to TR, May 8, 1915, TRP, reel 200.

162–163 "would likewise justify": Theodore Roosevelt, "Murder on the High Seas," *Metropolitan*, June 1915, 3.

163 "except to express confidence": *Brooklyn Eagle*, May 8, 1915.

163 "It is more important": Bishop, *Theodore Roosevelt and His Time*, 2:376.

163 "hydroaeroplanes": *New York Tribune*, January 31, 1915.

163 "as you do not read" . . . "Germany has a right": William Jennings Bryan to WW, May 9, 1915, in *PWW*, 33:134–35.

163 "The people of this country": *New York Tribune*, May 10, 1915.

164 "a splendid man" and "absolutely safe": *Chicago Tribune*, May 12, 13, 1915.

164 "I am a great admirer" . . . "an unflinching attitude": *New York Times*, May 14, 1915.

164 "nothing can be settled": *Chicago Tribune*, May 12, 1915.

164 "majority": *Brooklyn Eagle*, May 10, 1915.

164 "in the name of God" . . . "it is a human affair": Charles Lee Swem diary, May 10, 1915, in *PWW*, 33:138.

164–165 "It is his problem": *Brooklyn Eagle*, May 11, 1915.

165 "considering very earnestly": Statement of May 8, 1915, in *PWW*, 33:154.

165 "My love for you": WW to Edith Galt, May 9, 1915, in *PWW*, 33:137–38.

166 "wonderful love": Edith Galt to WW, May 10, 1915, in *PWW*, 33:146.

166 "series of pictures": *Philadelphia Inquirer*, May 11, 1915.

166 "I present to you": *Boston Globe*, May 11, 1915.

166–167 "thorough Americans" . . . "being *too proud to fight*": *Philadelphia Inquirer*, May 11, 1915.

167 "I did not know" . . . "I do not know just": WW to Edith Galt, May 11, 1915, in *PWW*, 33:161–62.

167 "mawkish": John Callan O'Laughlin to TR, May 11, 1915, TRP, reel 200.

167 "made me gag": Joseph Bucklin Bishop to TR, May 12, 1915, TRP, reel 200.

167 "milk and water" . . . "I do not believe": *New York Sun*, May 12, 1915.

167 "I dislike Roosevelt intensely": Joseph Bucklin Bishop to TR, May 12, 1915, TRP, reel 200.

167 "Truly Providence": *New York Sun*, May 14, 1915.

168 "truculent and bloodthirsty person": TR to Arthur Lee, June 17, 1915, in *The Letters of Theodore Roosevelt*, ed. Elting Morison, vol. 8, *The Days of Armageddon, 1914–1919* (Cambridge: Harvard University Press, 1954), 935–42.

168 "If he does not stand": TR to John Callan O'Laughlin, May 19, 1915, TRP, reel 385.

168 "I'm too proud to fight": *Binghamton (N.Y.) Press and Leader*, May 13, 1915.

168 "What in the name": JNH to Aunt Dizzy, May 11, 1915, JNHP, box 2.

168 "I saw men skipping rope": *New York Press*, May 25, 1915, JAP, reel 63.

169 "right moment": Anne Wiltsher, *Most Dangerous Women: Feminist Peace Campaigners of the Great War* (London: Pandora, 1985), 107.

169 "What of Belgium?": *The Survey*, September 4, 1915.

169 "I have had a long training": *Christian Science Monitor*, June 7, 1915.

170 "most favorable": JA to Mary Rozet Smith, May 16, 1915, JAP, reel 8.

170 "I cannot see": EMH to WW, May 11, 1915, in *PWW*, 33:158–59.

170 "world was against": John Callan O'Laughlin to TR, May 15, 1915, TRP, reel 200.

170 "You people are not": "Memorandum of Conversations with Former Attorney General Gregory at Houston, Texas, March 14 and 15, 1927," RSBP, reel 76.

169–170 "Mr. Bryan": HD, June 20, 1915.

171 "relinquish the hope": William Jennings Bryan to WW, May 12, 1915, in *PWW*, 33:165–66.

171–172 "lives of non-combatants": *New York Times*, May 14, 1915.

172 "I have an idea": Robert Pellissier, *Letters from a Chasseur à Pied* (privately printed, 1917), 155.

172 "went to dinner": David Lawrence to WW, May 14, 1915, in *PWW*, 33:199–201.

172 "When Miss Addams": *Life*, May 27, 1915.

172 "Wilson should receive applause": John Callan O'Laughlin to TR, May 21, 1915, TRP, reel 200.

173 "I dream that": WW to Edith Galt, May 11, 1915, in *PWW*, 33:161.
173 "I love you": WW to Edith Galt, May 14, 1915, in *PWW*, 33:204.
173 "best little evader": *New York Sun*, May 18, 1915.
173 "I think the proudest minute": Edith Galt to WW, May 17, 1915, in *PWW*, 33:216.
173 "I feel like I was living": Edith Galt to Annie Bolling, May 16, 1915, WWPL.
173 "complete acceptance": WW to Edith Galt, May 21, 1915, in *PWW*, 33:233–34.
173 "You have not yet completely": WW to Edith Galt, May 24, 1915, in *PWW*, 33:248.
173 "interpret by my kisses": WW to Edith Galt, May 21, 1915, in *PWW*, 33:234–35.
174 "Right of free travel": James Lawrence Troisi, "Ambassador Gerard and American-German Relations, 1913–1917" (Ph.D. diss, Syracuse University, 1978), 207.
174 "almost insulting": Walter Görlitz, ed., *The Kaiser and His Court: The Diaries, Note Books, and Letters of Admiral Georg Alexander von Müller, Chief of the Naval Cabinet, 1914–1918* (London: MacDonald, 1961), 79.
174 "They are easily carried": Count Bernstorff, *My Three Years in America* (London: Skeffington & Son, 1920), 15.
174 "not like him at all": *Chicago Tribune*, June 9, 1915.
174 "It seems as though": *New York Evening Post*, May 21, 1915.
174 "march gayly": *New York Times*, July 11, 1915.
175 "Even in the midst": Madeleine Zabriskie Doty, *Short Rations: An American Woman in Germany, 1915–1916* (New York: Century Company, 1917), 39.
175 "If you knew our good" . . . "she was carrying ammunition": Alice Hamilton, "At the War Capitals," *The Survey*, August 7, 1915, 418.
175 "all that does not answer": Emily Balch to Louis Lochner, June 1, 1915, JAP, reel 8.
175 "mysterious, almost superhuman knowledge": Alice Hamilton, "Colonel House and Jane Addams," *New Republic*, May 26, 1926, 9–11.
175 "to which they looked forward": James Gerard, *My Four Years in Germany* (New York: Grosset & Dunlap, 1917), 295.
176 "enormous factories": Hamilton, "At the War Capitals," 419.
176 "like a little brother": Alice Hamilton, *Exploring the Dangerous Trades: The Autobiography of Alice Hamilton, M.D.* (Boston: Little, Brown, 1943), 171.
176 "habit of glancing": Frederic William Wile, *Men around the Kaiser: The Makers of Modern Germany* (Indianapolis: Bobbs-Merrill, 1914), 204.
176 "see only what the employer": Hamilton, *Exploring the Dangerous Trades*, 172.
176 "Of him it can be": Wile, *Men around the Kaiser*, 19.
177 "crush German militarism" . . . "He went on to": David S. Patterson, *The Search for Negotiated Peace: Women's Activism and Citizen Diplomacy in World War I* (New York: Routledge, 2008), 87.
177 "very legalistic mind": TR to Joseph Bucklin Bishop, May 6, 1915, TRP, reel 385.
177 "I am simply unable": TR to Ethel Derby, May 12, 1915, TRDL.
177 "the act of the machine": *New York Herald*, May 20, 1915.
177–178 "This man": *New York Herald*, May 21, 1915.
178 "pale as a ghost": *New York Herald*, May 22, 1915.
178–179 "We find for the defendant": *New York Sun*, May 22, 1915.
179 "I'd like to give you": *New York Herald*, May 22, 1915.
179 "For the Plaintiff": *New York Sun*, May 22, 1915.
179 "I am happy": *Syracuse Journal*, May 22, 1915.
179 "We were all thrilled": Franklin Roosevelt to TR, May 25, 1915, TRP, reel 200.
179 "My interest": TR to Arthur Lee, June 17, 1915, in Morison, ed., *Letters of Theodore Roosevelt*, 8:935–41.
179 "telegraph me immediately": Archie Roosevelt to TR, May 16, 1915, TRP, reel 200.
179 "unless they are kicked": TR to Archie Roosevelt, May 19, 1915, in Morison, ed., *Letters of Theodore Roosevelt*, 8:922–23.
180 "It becomes more and more": WW to EMH, May 18, 1915, in *PWW*, 33:217.
180 "Page does not like": HD, May 19, 1915.
180 "We are dealing with passion": WW to Mary Hulbert, May 23, 1915, in *PWW*, 33:241–43.
181 "Clearly no self-respecting": *New York Times* quoting the *London Daily News*, July 16, 1915.
181 "England is playing": Franklin Lane to John Crawford Burns, May 29, 1915, in Anne W. Lane and Louise Herrick Wall, eds., *The Letters of Franklin K. Lane, Personal and Political* (Boston: Houghton Mifflin, 1922), 173.
181 "We are bound up": EMH to WW, May 25, 1915, in *PWW*, 33:254.
181 "I have concluded": HD, May 30, 1915.
181–182 "has already expressed": *New York Times*, May 31, 1915.
182 "The real test": Editorial reprinted in *Pittsburgh Press*, June 1, 1915.
182 "take up the different" . . . "treat them": William Jennings Bryan to WW, June 2, 1915, in *PWW*, 33:310–11.

182 **"prevent our citizens"** . . . **"the authorities"**: William Jennings Bryan to WW, June 3, 1915, in *PWW,* 33:321–26.

182 **"renewed protest"**: William Jennings Bryan to WW, June 5, 1915, in *PWW,* 33:342–43.

182 **"He is too good"**: Franklin Lane to EMH, May 5, 1915, in Charles Seymour, *The Intimate Papers of Colonel House* (Boston: Houghton Mifflin, 1926), 1:459.

183 **"has been Secretary of State"**: HD, June 24, 1915.

183 **"he was making the biggest mistake"** . . . **"I think I can do"**: Ray Stannard Baker interview with Josephus Daniels, August 8, 1936, RSBP, reel 73.

183 **"The President is wrong"**: Paolo E. Coletta, *William Jennings Bryan,* vol. 2, *Progressive Politician and Moral Statesman, 1909–1915* (Lincoln: University of Nebraska Press, 1969), 343.

183 **"safeguarding of American lives"**: *New York Times,* June 11, 1915.

183 **"carry out the double wish"**: WW to William Jennings Bryan, June 7, 1915, in *PWW,* 33:349.

183 **"policy . . . of words"**: TR to Albert B. Hart, June 1, 1915, in Morison, ed., *Letters of Theodore Roosevelt,* 8:927.

183 **"there is now a chance"** . . . **"who has been your comrade"**: WW to Edith Galt, June 9, 1915, in *PWW,* 33:377–78.

183–184 **"not for a moment"**: WW to Edith Galt, June 11, 1915, in *PWW,* 33:383–84.

184 **"do a lot of mischief"**: WW to Edith Galt, June 9, 1915, in *PWW,* 33:377–78.

184 **"awful creature"**: Edith Galt to WW, June 10, 1915, in *PWW,* 33:381.

184 **"really had decided"**: TR to Owen Wister, June 23, 1915, in Bishop, *Theodore Roosevelt and His Time,* 2:386.

184 **"utterly worthless"**: TR to William Howland, June 17, 1915, TRDL.

184 **"part of his second note"**: *New York Evening Sun,* June 28, 1915, JAP, reel 63.

184 **"I think the crisis"**: June 11, 1915, conversation, Louise Hague/Count Bernstorff, in RG 59, Records kept by Leland Harrison, classified case files/telephone conversations tapped by agents, National Archives and Records Administration, Washington, D.C.

184 **"No stranger man"**: WW to Edith Galt, June 19, 1915, in *PWW,* 33:422.

184 **"He suffers from"**: WW to Edith Galt, June 8, 1915, in *PWW,* 33:366–67.

184 **"his crass government"**: WW to Edith Galt, June 3, 1915, in *PWW,* 33:334.

184 **"did not approve"**: HD, January 27, 1916.

185 **"When the time comes"**: Charles Willis Thompson, *Presidents I've Known and Two Near Presidents* (Indianapolis: Bobbs-Merrill, 1929), 170.

185 **"in a strong position"**: EMH to WW, June 16, 1915, in *PWW,* 33:405–7.

185 **"the side which possesses"**: Martin Gilbert, *The First World War: A Complete History* (New York: Henry Holt, 1994), 173.

185 **"Most of the men"**: JNH to Mother and family, May 21, 1915, JHNP, box 2.

185 **"avoid any intimacy"**: James Norman Hall, *Kitchener's Mob* (Boston: Houghton Mifflin, 1916), 42.

185 **"The great adventure"**: JNH to Roy Cushman, June 15, 1915, JHNP, box 2.

186 **"happy"**: JNH to Mother and family, June 1, 1915, JHNP, box 2.

186 **"the tremendous sadness"**: JNH to Roy Cushman, June 15, 1915, JHNP, box 2.

186 **"horses . . . so thin"**: Jane Addams, Emily G. Balch, and Alice Hamilton, *Women at The Hague: The International Congress of Women and Its Results* (New York: Macmillan, 1915), 37.

186 **"pale, emaciated"**: Hamilton, *Exploring the Dangerous Trades,* 173.

186 **"There was almost no food"**: Marcet Haldeman-Julius, *Jane Addams as I Knew Her* (Girard, Kans.: Haldeman-Julius Publications, 1936), 22.

186 **"What does the United States"**: Transcript of Henry Street meeting, September 27, 1915, LWP, reel 103.

186 **"It perhaps seems to you"**: Addams, Balch, and Hamilton, *Women at The Hague,* 96.

186 **"Foolish"**: *New York Times,* July 11, 1915.

186 **"At last the door"**: Addams, Balch, and Hamilton, *Women at The Hague,* 96.

186 **"tall, broad-shouldered"**: Hamilton, *Exploring the Dangerous Trades,* 173.

187 **"getting nothing out"**: Patterson, *Search for Negotiated Peace,* 88.

187 **"would not be unreasonable"**: Mercedes M. Randall, *Improper Bostonian: Emily Greene Balch* (New York: Twayne, 1964), 174.

187 **"I only trail along"**: Alice Hamilton to Louise de Koven Bowen, May 16, 1915, in Barbara Sicherman, *Alice Hamilton: A Life In Letters* (Cambridge: Harvard University Press, 1984), 192.

187 **"Hungarian aristocrats"**: Hamilton, *Exploring the Dangerous Trades,* 173.

187 **"timid"**: Paul Kellogg to Louis Lochner, July 21, 1915, LLP, reel 50.

187 **"Our hotel could serve"**: Addams, Balch, and Hamilton, *Women at The Hague,* 45.

187 **"within a short time"**: *New York Tribune,* May 23, 1915.

187 **"suicide of civilized Europe"**: Terry Philpot, "World War I's Pope Benedict XV and the Pursuit of Peace," *National Catholic Reporter,* July 19, 2014 (online).

187–188 **"long-sleeved"** . . . **"very ugly"**: Hamilton, *Exploring the Dangerous Trades,* 175–76.

188 **"ghoulish collection"**: Addams, Balch, and Hamilton, *Women at The Hague,* 49.

188 **"We naturally did not try"**: *New York Times,* June 24, 1915.

188 "destroy Germany": Randall, *Improper Bostonian*, 176.
189 "surely been interesting": JA to Mary Rozet Smith, June 18, 1915, JAP, reel 8.
189 "very exigent cables" . . . "It will really be": JA to Rosika Schwimmer, June 26, 1915, JAP, reel 8.
189 "exactly the same outlook": Bertrand Russell to Lucy Donnelly Martin, July 13, 1915, JAP, reel 8.
189 "I have spoken more freely": Edward Grey to Eric Drummond, June 20, 1915, FOP, FO 800/95.
190 "Never again must women": Addams, Balch, and Hamilton, *Women at The Hague*, 109.
190 "with the greatest interest": WW to Judith Rublee, June 2, 1915, in *PWW*, 33:314.
190 "the only Power": *New York Evening Post*, July 7, 1915.
190 "Much as I love": Edith Galt to WW, June 18, 1915, in *PWW*, 33:421.
190 "Lord and Master": Edith Galt to WW, June 10, 1915, in *PWW*, 33:381.
190 "I believe I enjoy": Edith Galt to WW, June 18, 1915, in *PWW*, 33:421.
190 "flat and lacking": Edith Galt to WW, June 3, 1915, in *PWW*, 33:335.
191 "I will be glad": Edith Galt to WW, June 18, 1915, in *PWW*, 33:421.
191 "I am complete in you": WW to Edith Galt, June 21, 1915, in *PWW*, 33:433.
191 "man with not too many ideas": EMH to WW, June 16, 1915, in *PWW*, 33:409.
191 "keep him busy" . . . "will be barred": HD, June 14, 1915.
191 "was the sort of man": Baker interview with Daniels.
192 "He greeted me with warmth" . . . "I feel that his health": HD, June 24, 1915.
192 "most of the Progressives": TR to O. K. Davis, June 23, 1915, TRDL.
192 "I must just as well": TR to Arthur Lee, June 17, 1915, in Morison, ed., *Letters of Theodore Roosevelt*, 8:935–41.
192 "Much like a very": TR to Mrs. Thomas Hitchcock, May 29, 1915, TRP, reel 358.
193 "smashing me": TR to Raymond Robins, June 3, 1915, in Morison, ed., *Letters of Theodore Roosevelt*, 8:927–35.
193 "I believe the President": HD, June 18, 1915.

Chapter 6: "I Didn't Raise My Boy to Be a Soldier"

194 "I see that it will naturally": Edward Grey to EMH, July 14, 1915, in *PWW*, 33:145.
194–195 "R. Pearce" . . . "felt as far downtown" . . . "very well dressed": *Washington Times*, July 3, 1915; *Washington Evening Star*, July 3, 1915.
195 "his great influence" . . . "I wanted him to be": *New York Herald*, July 5, 1915.
195 "in a perfect hell": *New York Sun*, July 4, 1915.
195 "acted at the direction": *Washington Times*, July 3, 1915.
195 "not influenced by any": *New York Sun*, July 4, 1915; Frank Holt to WW, December 8, 1914, WWP, reel 325.
196 "The purchases of war munitions": William McAdoo to WW, August 21, 1915, in *PWW*, 34: 275.
196 "continual praise": TR to Owen Wister, June 23, 1915, in Joseph Bucklin Bishop, *Theodore Roosevelt and His Time Shown in His Own Letters* (New York: Charles Scribner's Sons, 1920), 2:386.
196 "The people are following you": Samuel H. Thompson to WW, July 3, 1915, in *PWW*, 33:473.
196 "I'm glad you're going": *New York Sun*, June 26, 1915.
196 "I promise with all my heart": "A Pledge," June 29, 1915, in *PWW*, 33:458.
197 "I think I shall have": WW to Edith Galt, June 14, 1915, in *PWW*, 33:396.
197 "George Washington's grandson": *Washington Evening Star*, July 11, 1915.
198 "employed by jingoes": *New York Herald*, June 12, 1915.
198 "suggest a means": *New York Tribune*, June 17, 1915.
198 "You are using too much": *New York Herald*, June 18, 1915.
198 "have to arbitrate everything": TR to W. H. Cowles, June 17, 1915, TRDL.
198 "abject pacifist song": *New York Tribune*, July 22, 1915.
198 "would also in their hearts": TR to John McCann, July 10, 1915, TRP, reel 359.
198 "fit to be a mother": *San Diego Sun*, July 27, 1915.
199 "bustling, fatuously-benevolent Jew": TR to Agnes Repplier, August 26, 1915, TRP, reel 359.
199 "have not shown the smallest particle": TR to Henry Green, July 2, 1915, TRP, reel 385.
199 "A great mistake has been made": *New York Evening Post*, July 7, 1915.
199 "How could I": *New York Evening Sun*, July 6, 1915, JAP, reel 63.
199–200 "For months we have seen": *New York Times*, July 6, 1915.
200 "there is evidently need" . . . "a curious confusion": JA to Rosika Schwimmer, July 6, 1915, JAP, reel 8.
200 "back over the frontier": Martin Gilbert, *The First World War: A Complete History* (New York: Henry Holt, 1994), 178.
200 "I was told": *Washington Post*, July 6, 1915.
200 "sad and really terrible" . . . "there is real danger": JNH to Roy Cushman, July 23, 1915, JNHP, box 2.

201 "The chief factor": JNH to Roy Cushman, July 20, 1915, JNHP, box 2.

201 "Three cheers": *Chicago Tribune,* July 10, 1915.

201 "It's good to see": *The Survey,* July 17, 1915.

201 "From the first word": Marcet Haldeman-Julius, *Jane Addams as I Knew Her* (Girard, Kans.: Haldeman-Julius Publications, 1936), 26.

201 "We heard everywhere": *The Survey,* July 17, 1915.

202 "make their men practically drunk" . . . "They have a regular formula": *Advocate of Peace,* August 1915, 197. The phraseology is slightly different in *New York Times,* July 10, 1915.

202 "was no more dangerous": *Chicago Tribune,* July 10, 1915.

202 "negotiation rather than through": Paul Kellogg to JA, September 21, 1915, JAP, reel 8.

202 "Many Americans romanticized": Alice Hamilton, *Exploring the Dangerous Trades: The Autobiography of Alice Hamilton, M.D.* (Boston: Little, Brown, 1943), 180.

202 "complacent and self-satisfied": *New York Times,* July 13, 1915.

203 "joy of combat": *New York Times,* July 14, 1915.

203 "understand how men": *Philadelphia Inquirer,* n.d. [July 1915], JAP, reel 63.

203 "ancient spinster": *Houston Post,* July 12, 1915, JAP, reel 63.

203 "crack-brain old creature": *Indianapolis Times,* July 21, 1915, quoting *Bellingham (Wash.) Herald,* JAP, reel 63.

203 "foolish, garrulous woman": *Louisville Courier-Journal,* July 21, 1915, JAP, reel 63.

203 "badly overrated": *Rochester Herald,* July 19, 1915, JAP, reel 63.

203 "Look into the trenches": *New York Times,* July 30, 1915.

203 "Don't believe": Robert Pellissier, *Letters from a Chasseur à Pied* (privately printed, 1917), 189.

203 "Sergeants and corporals poured whisky": *New York Herald,* July 21, 1915.

203 "had received a half-pint": Pellissier, *Letters from a Chasseur à Pied,* 189.

203 "a prominent official": *New York Times,* August 15, 1915.

204 "foolish" women could not: James Brown Scott to TR, August 18, 1915, TRP, reel 201.

204 "it is uncertain whether": *Woman's Journal,* September 4, 1915, JAP, reel 63.

204 "I had my first experience": Jane Addams, *Peace and Bread in Time of War* (New York: Macmillan, 1922), 134.

204 "Do not throw over": M. Denkert to JA, August 12, 1915, JAP, reel 8.

204 Germany's reply to Wilson's second note: *New York Times,* July 10, 1915.

205 "What I said then": *New York Herald,* July 12, 1915.

205 "I think we might": WW to EMH, July 12, 1915, in *PWW,* 33:492.

205 "invigorated" . . . "outline of the argument": WW to Edith Galt, July 20, 1915, in *PWW,* 33:538–42.

206 "Garrison was an intensely argumentative": Ray Stannard Baker, memo of conversation with WW, May 12, 1916, in *PWW,* 37:33.

206 "schoolmaster": Ray Stannard Baker interview with Lindley Garrison, November 30, 1928, RSBP, reel 75.

206 "solemn, conceited ass": WW to Edith Galt, August 31, 1915, in *PWW,* 34:392.

206 "to a Yes or No": Lindley Garrison memo, July 20, 1915, in *PWW,* 33:536.

206 "He seems to feel": WW to Edith Galt, July 20, 1915, in *PWW,* 33:539–42.

206 "insist on our rights" . . . "limit our trade": Lindley Garrison memo, July 20, 1915, in *PWW,* 33:536.

206 "character and cargo": *New York Times,* July 24, 1915.

206 "consider that" . . . "said very little": Lindley Garrison memo, July 20, 1915, in *PWW,* 33:537.

207 "She has accumulated": EMH to WW, July 17, 1915, in *PWW,* 33:516.

207 "nothing of value": HD, July 19, 1915.

207 "would not resent" . . . "bold stroke": Minutes of Henry Street meeting, July 20, 1915, LWP, reel 103.

208 "the President is not 'for women'": JA to Paul Kellogg, July 27, 1915, JAP, reel 8.

208 "Gentlemen, it is bewildering": *Chicago Tribune,* July 22, 1915.

209 talk with Wilson was "encouraging": JA to Emily Balch, August 3, 1915, JAP, reel 8.

209 "final parting": WW to Edith Galt, July 21–22, 1915, in *PWW,* 34:8.

209 The latest German response: *New York Times,* July 24, 1915.

209 "Utterly impertinent": Reinhard Doerries, *Imperial Challenge: Ambassador Count Bernstorff and German-American Relations, 1908–1917* (Chapel Hill: University of North Carolina Press, 1989), 111.

209 "whose departure for bed" . . . "momentous decision": WW to Edith Galt, July 21–22, 1915, in *PWW,* 34:9.

210 "throw every bit of its power": *Chicago News,* July 22, 1915, JAP, reel 63.

210 "stand behind the president": James P. Martin, "The American Peace Movement and the Progressive Era, 1910–1917" (Ph.D. diss., Rice University, 1975), 188.

210 "what the real duty": WW to Fred Yancey, August 4, 1915, RSBP, reel 69.

210 "I know these good people": David S. Patterson, *The Search for Negotiated Peace: Women's Activism and Citizen Diplomacy in World War I* (New York: Routledge, 2008), 122.

210 "favor a continuance": Robert Lansing to WW, August 18, 1915, in *PWW,* 34:236–37.

211 "I think that he really takes": JA to Emily Balch, August 3, 1915, JAP, reel 8.

211 "had his hand on the pulse": HD, August 16, 1915.

211 "This was a comfort": Emily Balch to JA, August 19, 1915, JAP, reel 8.

211 "conference of neutral nations": WW to Edith Galt, August 18, 1915, in *PWW*, 34:243.

212 "I had the impression": Haldeman-Julius, *Jane Addams*, 17.

212 "determined to commit suicide": WW to Edith Galt, August 8–9, 1915, in *PWW*, 34:140.

212 "Did you notice what its" . . . "had embarked": Charles Willis Thompson, *Presidents I've Known and Two Near Presidents* (Indianapolis: Bobbs-Merrill, 1929), 170.

213 "Men are easily puzzled": TR to Kermit Roosevelt, August 28, 1915, TRDL.

213 "could have aroused": TR to A. V. Baird, September 1, 1915, TRP, reel 359.

213 "a modified Swiss System": EMH to WW, August 8, 1915, in *PWW*, 34:134.

213 "ice cream and cake affair": *New York Herald*, August 9, 1915.

213 "This is a very real thing": Charles Belmont Davis, ed., *Adventures and Letters of Richard Harding Davis* (New York: Charles Scribner's Sons, 1917), 381.

214 "It was a 'get-wise-quick'": *Collier's*, October 9, 1915.

214 "Wood-Roosevelt affair" . . . "taken me": WW to Edith Galt, August 15, 1915, in *PWW*, 34:209.

214 "the trial judge was wrong": *New York Tribune*, July 24, 1915.

214 "bully!": *New York Sun*, August 3, 1915.

215 "Damn the Mollycoddles": *San Francisco Chronicle*, July 21, 1915.

215 "professional pacifists": *Washington Evening Star*, July 22, 1915.

215 "It would not be true": TR to Arthur Lee, August 6, 1915, in *The Letters of Theodore Roosevelt*, ed. Elting Morison, vol. 8, *The Days of Armageddon, 1914–1919* (Cambridge: Harvard University Press, 1954), 960–61.

215 "near-socialist": TR to Reginald Kauffman, August 26, 1915, TRP, reel 359.

215 "great questions": TR to Lawrence Godkin, August 16, 1915, TRDL.

215 "sit tight" . . . "stock was on the": Meyer Lissner to William Allen White, July 29, 1915, TRP, reel 201.

215 "Roosevelt is utterly discredited": EMH to Walter Hines Page, August 4, 1915, in *PWW*, 34:85.

215 "completely under the control": TR to Kermit Roosevelt, August 6, 1915, TRDL.

216 "it is of prime consequence": TR to George Perkins, September 3, 1915, in Morison, ed., *Letters of Theodore Roosevelt*, 8:971–73.

216 "The President has never realized": HD, July 10, 1915.

216 "credible threat of force": Thomas Bruscino, "American Military History: A Look at the Field," *Reviews in American History*, December 2012, 576.

216 "Preparedness is not": *New York Tribune*, July 22, 1915.

216 "the demand for reasonable preparedness": WW to Lindley Garrison, August 19, 1915, in *PWW*, 34:248.

216 "eat his words": TR to Lawrence Godkin, August 16, 1915, TRDL.

217 "I do not think": WW to Oswald Villard, September 7, 1915, in *PWW*, 34:428.

217 "hysteria" and "war mad" behavior: Harold Ickes to Louis Lochner, August 17, 1915, HIP, box 35.

218 "The people will see things": EMH to WW, August 10, 1915, in *PWW*, 34:158.

218 "You of course realize": WW to EMH, July 19, 1915, in *PWW*, 33:526.

219 "cheat our enemy": Galt, August 21, 1915, in *PWW*, 34:284.

219 "I am as restless as any caged": WW to Edith Galt, August 5, 1915, in *PWW*, 34:101.

219 "I do not want you to go": WW to Edith Galt, August 11, 1915, in *PWW*, 34:167–68.

219 "a single kiss": WW to Edith Galt, August 21, 1915, in *PWW*, 34:285.

219 "the glass over a picture": WW to Edith Galt, August 13, 1915, in *PWW*, 34:179.

219 "It seems the President": HD, July 31, 1915.

219 "The capacity of your mind": WW to Edith Galt, August 13, 1915, in *PWW*, 34:190–91.

220 "I don't believe I ever": Edith Galt to WW, August 3, 1915, in *PWW*, 34:78.

220 "big envelope": WW to Edith Galt, August 17, 1915, in *PWW*, 34:231.

220 "If the afternoon mail": Edith Galt to WW, August 13, 1915, in *PWW*, 34:195.

220 "You don't want it all business": WW to Edith Galt, August 15, 1915, in *PWW*, 34:209–10.

220 "common" . . . "was not brought up": WW to Edith Galt, August 28, 1915, in *PWW*, 34:351–52.

220 "I can't help feeling": Edith Galt to WW, August 26, 1915, in *PWW*, 34:338.

220–221 "But you are right" . . . "if only because he loves me": WW to Edith Galt, August 28, 1915, in *PWW*, 34:352–53.

221 "I've just come from kissing": WW to Edith Galt, August 19, 1915, in *PWW*, 34:244.

221 "Here it comes!": *New York Herald*, September 3, 1915.

221 "staggered as though": *New York Sun*, September 3, 1915.

221 "magnificent courage": *New York Sun*, December 4, 1915.

221–222 "If we assume": *Boston Globe*, August 20, 1915.

Chapter 7: A Second Crisis

223 "Our people do not": EMH to WW, August 22, 1915, in *PWW*, 34:299.
223 "tights without" . . . "Coney Island will be kept": *New York Herald*, July 12, 1915.
224 "Convention? What an": *New York Sun*, August 1, 1915.
224 "in a gray sack suit": *Philadelphia Inquirer*, August 21, 1915.
224 "What's all this?": WW to Edith Galt, August 20, 1915, in *PWW*, 34:259.
224 "We were caught": *Washington Herald*, August 21, 1915.
224 "The force of the swirling": *New York Herald*, September 4, 1915.
225 "It is just an act": WW to Edith Galt, August 19, 1915, in *PWW*, 34:258.
225 "worst thing that could possibly": WW to Edith Galt, August 20, 1915, in *PWW*, 34:261.
225 "Outside of the newspapers": Robert Lansing to WW, August 20, 1915, in *PWW*, 34:265.
225 "all the facts": WW to Robert Lansing, August 21, 1915, in *PWW*, 34:271.
225 the "idiot" James Gerard: WW to Edith Galt, September 11, 1915, in *PWW*, 34:454.
225 "the first citizen of the world": EMH to WW, August 22, 1915, in *PWW*, 34:299.
226 "The President has clearly put it": HD, August 22, 1915.
226 "If she does" . . . "sweet counsellor": WW to Edith Galt, August 19, 22, 1915, in *PWW*, 34:257, 290.
226 "sacrifice of American honor": *New York Sun*, August 22, 1915.
227 "comprehensive plans": *Richmond Times-Dispatch*, August 25, 1915.
227 "relieve at once every officer": Frederick Palmer, *Bliss, Peacemaker: The Lives and Letters of General Tasker Howard Bliss* (New York: Dodd, Mead, 1934), 106–7.
227 "impertinent Prussian": WW to Edith Galt, c. August 23, 1915, in *PWW*, 34:296.
227 "I suspect some mere": WW to Edith Galt, August 24, 1915, in *PWW*, 34:304.
227 "I believe the President": HD, August 24, 1915.
227–228 "Theodore, as an ex-President": Hermann Hagedorn, *Leonard Wood* (New York: Harper & Brothers, 1931), 2:163.
228 "That's a very nice dog": *New York Tribune*, August 26, 1915.
229 he reminded his listeners: This account of TR's Plattsburg appearance is based upon the reports in *New York Herald*, *New York Tribune*, *New York Sun*, and *New York Press*, all on August 26, 1915.
230 "It was a mighty poor place": Willard Straight to H. P. Fletcher, September 16, 1915, Willard Straight Papers (microfilm edition), reel 5.
230 "use your influence": *New York Herald*, August 12, 1915.
230 "He was the most indiscreet man": Ray Stannard Baker interview with Lindley Garrison, November 30, 1928, RSBP, reel 75.
230 "issues which excite" . . . "delivered outside": *New York Herald*, August 27, 1915.
230 "I evidently drew blood": TR to Frances Parsons, August 31, 1915, TRDL.
230 "It was worthwhile": TR to Archie Roosevelt, September 2, 1915, in *The Letters of Theodore Roosevelt*, ed. Elting Morison, vol. 8, *The Days of Armageddon, 1914–1919* (Cambridge: Harvard University Press, 1954), 964–66.
230 "eat his words": Edith Galt to WW, August 26, 1915, in *PWW*, 34:337.
230–231 Julian Street journeyed: Julian Street, *The Most Interesting American* (New York: Century Company, 1915).
232 "The best way to vanquish": WW to Edith Galt, August 28, 1915, in *PWW*, 34:353.
232 "I feel like a pilot": WW to Edith Galt, August 26, 1915, in *PWW*, 34:333.
232 "complete satisfaction": *New York Tribune*, August 26, 1915.
232 "attitude of a single": Arthur Link, *Wilson: The Struggle for Neutrality, 1914–1915* (Princeton, N.J.: Princeton University Press, 1960), 571.
233 "liners will not be sunk": J. von Bernstorff to Robert Lansing, September 1, 1915, in *PWW*, 34:400.
233 "one of the greatest": Oscar Straus to WW, September 2, 1915, Oscar Straus Papers, Library of Congress.
233 "This must and should": *New York Herald*, September 3, 1915.
233 "the most ample amends": *New York Tribune*, September 2, 1915.
233 "her submarine campaign": TR to George Perkins, September 3, 1915, in Morison, ed., *Letters of Theodore Roosevelt*, 8:971–73.
233 "our tomfool people": TR to J. William White, September 3, 1915, TRP, reel 359.
234 "Washington gossip" . . . "I am absolutely": WW to Edith Galt, August 26, 1916, in *PWW*, 34:331.
234 "WHO IS THE FIRST LADY": *Washington Herald*, August 29, 1915.
234 "Everything is being watched": Edith Galt to WW, August 29, 1915, in *PWW*, 34:365.
234 "wretched newspaper people": Edith Galt to WW, September 3, 1915, in *PWW*, 34:415.
235 "not like me as well": Edith Galt to WW, September 2, 1915, in *PWW*, 34:406.
235 "precious intimate matters": WW to Edith Galt, September 3, 1915, in *PWW*, 34:414–15.
235 "appear to strangers": Edith Galt to WW, September 6, 1915, in *PWW*, 34:425.
235 "It's illuminating": Mary Hulbert to WW, June 16, 1915, in *PWW*, 33:413.
235–236 "anonymous letter" . . . "must have fallen": HD, September 22, 1915.

236 "deeply ashamed" . . . "A public man": "Outline and Two Drafts of Statements," c. September 20, 1915, in *PWW*, 34:496–97.

236 "awful earthquake": Edith Galt to WW, September 21–22, 1915, in *PWW*, 34:501.

236 "stand by me": Edith Galt to WW, September 19, 1915, in *PWW*, 34:490.

236 "hold the dear hands": WW to Edith Galt, September 21, 1915, in *PWW*, 34:500.

236 "so fine" . . . "superman": Edith Galt to WW, September 21–22, 1915, in *PWW*, 34:502.

236 "We must rebuild": Edith Galt to WW, September 20, 1915, in *PWW*, 34:496.

237 "had been indiscreet" . . . "by the end of the year": HD, September 22, 1915.

237 "wonderful counsellor": WW to Edith Galt, September 23, 1915, in *PWW*, 34:510.

237 "if the President were able": HD, September 24, 1915.

237–238 "He is just as nice": Edith Galt to WW, September 24, 1915, in *PWW*, 34:518–19.

238 "conduct of the British": Robert Lansing to WW, August 30, 1915, in *PWW*, 34:368.

239 "disorganize and hold up": John Bach McMaster, *The United States in the World War* (New York: D. Appleton, 1918), 174.

239 "if Dumba, why not": WW to EMH, September 7, 1915, in *PWW*, 34:426.

239 "diplomatic triumph": HD, August 31, 1915.

239 "this case in no way": J. von Bernstorff to Robert Lansing, September 8, 1915, in *PWW*, 34:436.

239 "obviously disingenuous": WW to Edith Galt, September 10, 1915, in *PWW*, 34:439.

239 "I suppose the *Arabic*": John Callan O'Laughlin to Mabel O'Laughlin, September 10, 1915, JCOP, box 9.

239 "Our situation": Cary Grayson to Altrude Gordon, September 12, 1915, WWPL.

240 "The Secretary of State": WW to Edith Galt, September 13, 1915, in *PWW*, 34:463.

240 "He seemed to be much depressed": Robert Lansing to WW, September 13, 1915, in *PWW*, 34:462.

240 "German bad faith": J. von Bernstorff to T. von Bethmann-Hollweg, September 14, 1915, in Count Bernstorff, *My Three Years in America* (London: Skeffington & Son, 1920), 154.

240 "no passenger vessel": EMH to WW, September 26, 1915, in *PWW*, 34:520.

240 "formal disavowal": WW to EMH, September 20, 1915, in *PWW*, 34:493.

240 "regrets and disavows": J. von Bernstorff to Robert Lansing, October 2, 1915, in *PWW*, 35:13.

241 "There is no question": TR to Kermit Roosevelt, October 1, 1915, TRDL.

241 "'Ave you got yer wills" . . . "picked up an arm": James Norman Hall, *Kitchener's Mob* (Boston: Houghton Mifflin, 1916), 146–71.

242 "We can hardly stand": Mrs. A. W. Hall to JNH, September 30, 1915, JNHP, box 2.

242 "I have lived a century": JNH to Roy Cushman, October 6–7, 1915, JHNP, box 2.

242 "for the future happiness": JNH to Mother, October 9, 1915, JHNP, box 2.

242 "Life is not worth": TR to Horace Plunkett, September 1915, TRP, reel 359.

242 "break down": TR to Leslie Tarlton, August 6, 1915, TRP, reel 359.

242 "good antlers": TR to Franklin Roosevelt, October 7, 1915, TRP, reel 359.

243 "I shall never again make": TR to Kermit Roosevelt, October 1, 1915, TRDL.

243 "gouty old man": TR to Belle Roosevelt, October 24, 1915, TRDL.

243 "What inspiration is this man": John J. Leary Jr., *Talks with T.R.* (Boston: Houghton Mifflin, 1920), 325.

243 "he should have shown": Carrie Chapman Catt to JA, August 15, 1915, JAP, reel 8.

243 "She secretly thinks": Mary Rozet Smith to Emily Balch, c. August 17, 1915, JAP, reel 8.

243 Jane Addams of Europe: *New York Evening Mail*, August 25, 1915, JAP, reel 63.

244 "to have Holland": Emily Balch to JA, July 3, 1915, JAP, reel 8.

244 "This was meddling" . . . "absolutely amoral": Mercedes M. Randall, *Improper Bostonian: Emily Greene Balch* (New York: Twayne, 1964), 199, 382.

244 "any form of atrocity" . . . "deepest sympathy": HD, July 24, September 1, 1915.

244 "such as had visited": Rosika Schwimmer to JA, August 20, 1915, JAP, reel 8.

245 "see these two firebrands": Aletta Jacobs to JA, September 8, 1915, JAP, reel 8.

245 "He was very kind": Aletta Jacobs to JA, September 15, 1915, JAP, reel 8.

245 "it would necessarily depend": WW to Robert Lansing, August 31, 1915, in *PWW*, 34:399.

245 "I loathe the neutrals": Anne Wiltsher, *Most Dangerous Women: Feminist Peace Campaigners of the Great War* (London: Pandora, 1985), 119.

245 "so awfully callous": Louis Lochner to Anna Lloyd, September 22, 1915, JAP, reel 8.

245 "surprised and almost dismayed": Sarah Adams to JA, September 24, 1915, JAP, reel 8.

245 "sane and reasonable": David S. Patterson, *The Search for Negotiated Peace: Women's Activism and Citizen Diplomacy in World War I* (New York: Routledge, 2008), 139.

246 "military peace": Transcript of Henry Street meeting, September 27, 1915, LWP, reel 103.

246 "It is ignoring": Rosika Schwimmer to WW, October 3, 1914, RSP, box 46.

246 "If we are to influence": Transcript of Henry Street meeting, September 27, 1915, LWP, reel 103.

246 "sex strike": *San Francisco Chronicle*, July 20, 1915.

246 "mass demonstrations and rallies": Blanche Wiesen Cook, "Woodrow Wilson and the Antimilitarists, 1914–1917" (Ph.D. diss., Johns Hopkins University, 1970), 123.

246 "do everything in my power": *New York Herald*, August 23, 1915.

247 "habits and conduct": *New York Herald*, January 26, 1915.
247 "sinewy": Julian Street, *Abroad at Home* (New York: Century Company, 1914), 99.
247 "Find out something": Street, *Abroad at Home*, 101.
247 "eat only when hungry": *New York Sun*, July 8, 1915.
247 "poison": *Monroe Journal* (Monroeville, Ala.), September 12, 1916.
247 "employers must be taught": Lewis Maverick diary, December 10, 1915, Hoover Institution Archives, box 1.
247 "I do not think": *New York Evening Post*, January 22, 1915.
247 "I wouldn't give five cents": Street, *Abroad at Home*, 103.
247 "there would be no hospitals": *New York Tribune*, January 25, 1915.
248 "I have prospered much": *New York Herald*, August 23, 1915.
248 "They must learn how": *New York Sun*, September 9, 1915.
248 "uprising of the industrious" . . . "This country ought to thank": *New York Herald*, September 23, 1915.
248 "ideas took no root": WW to Edith Galt, September 22, 1915, in *PWW*, 34:510.
248 "nations would be afraid": *Washington Herald*, September 23, 1915.
248 "I know that anything": *New York Herald*, September 23, 1915.
249 "solicited for funds": Elizabeth P. Dowling to Mrs. Frank R. McMullin, September 14, 1915, JAP, reel 8.
249 "May I take the liberty": Julia Grace Wales to JA, September 30, 1915, JAP, reel 8.

Chapter 8: Preparedness U.S.A.

250 "Our people": TR to Kermit Roosevelt, November 21, 1915, TRDL.
250 "Never was there such a popular": *New York Sun*, August 22, 1915.
250 "The vulgarity of the Chaplin pictures": *New York Tribune*, October 13, 1915.
251 "There is no need to stir up": WW to Thomas Dixon, September 7, 1915, in *PWW*, 34:427.
251 "By George": *New York Herald*, October 27, 1915.
251 "lower Manhattan": *New York Herald*, September 10, 1915.
251 "drunken soldiers": *New York Tribune*, September 10, 1915.
251 "victims of the invaders": *New York Evening World*, September 10, 1915.
252 "thoroughly bad Americans": TR to Richard Gorman, November 24, 1915, in *The Letters of Theodore Roosevelt*, ed. Elting Morison, vol. 8, *The Days of Armageddon, 1914–1919* (Cambridge: Harvard University Press, 1954), 989–91.
252 *The Trumpet Call of the Bull Moose*: *New York Evening Post*, October 2, 1915.
252 "free to be gay": WW to Edith Galt, October 5, 1915, in *PWW*, 35:27.
252 "Is there anything": WW to EMH, September 29, 1915, in *PWW*, 34:537.
252 "There is so much talk": HD, October 1, 1915.
252 "It won't change": Ray Stannard Baker interview with Albert Burleson, March 17, 1927, RSBP, reel 72.
253 "graceful, rather plump figure": *Washington Herald*, October 7, 1915.
253 "fine white teeth": *New York Herald*, October 7, 1915.
253 "her cheerful disposition": *Washington Herald*, October 7, 1915.
253 "I am of no importance": *Washington Evening Star*, October 7, 1915.
253 "Isn't she stunning!": *New York Herald*, October 9, 1915.
253 "Mrs. Galt is very handsome": *New York Tribune*, October 9, 1915.
253 "They whispered and laughed": *Philadelphia Inquirer*, October 10, 1915.
253 "We all thought Wilson": Donald Richberg to TR, November 5, 1915, TRP, reel 202.
253–254 "had built himself up": William Allen White to Mark Sullivan, November 1, 1915, WAWP, box 27.
254 "My wife is dead!": TR to Charles Bull, February 4, 1916, in Morison, ed., *Letters of Theodore Roosevelt*, 8:1014–15.
254 "The cold peace": Mary Hulbert to WW, c. October 11, 1915, in *PWW*, 35:53.
254 "breach of promise suit": HD, December, 18, 1915.
255 "President's indiscretions": HD, November 12, 1915.
255 "There is a deliberate": HD, November 22, 1915.
255 "It would be bad enough": WW to Edith Galt, August 19, 1915, in *PWW*, 34:254.
255 "shown her some of my European": HD, November 4, 1915.
255 "confidential talk" . . . "think aloud to the President": HD, November 30, 1915.
256 "do something decisive": HD, October 8, 1915.
256 "he had never been sure": HD, September 22, 1915.
256 "their cause" was "our cause": HD, November 28, 1915.
257 "absolutely no independence": John Callan O'Laughlin to TR, November 2, 1915, TRP, reel 202.
257 "I now have the matter": HD, October 14, 1915.
257 "altogether right": WW to EMH, October 18, 1915, in *PWW*, 35:80.
257 "it would be necessary": EMH to Edward Grey, October 17, 1915 (draft), in *PWW*, 35:81.

257 "I do not want to make": WW to EMH, October 18, 1915, in *PWW*, 35:80.

257 "practically . . . insure": HD, November 25, 1915.

257 "somewhat disorganized": JNH to Mother, October 9, 1915, JHNP, box 2.

257 "For the past month": JNH to Mother, October 31, 1915, JHNP, box 2.

258 "For of all the uncomfortable": JNH to Mother, October 24, 1915, JHNP, box 2.

258 "Tommy's body": *Boston Globe*, December 9, 1915.

259 "incredible stupidity!": Walter Görlitz, ed., *The Kaiser and His Court: The Diaries, Note Books, and Letters of Admiral Georg Alexander von Müller, Chief of the Naval Cabinet, 1914–1918* (London: MacDonald, 1961), 115.

259 "Britain's Joan of Arc": *New York Herald*, October 23, 1915.

259 "while she lay": *New York Herald*, October 20, 1915.

259 "one more to their list": *New York Sun*, quoting the *Boston Traveler*, October 24, 1915.

259 "Such a deed": TR to Samuel Dutton, November 24, 1915, TRP, reel 385.

259 "Every person, man or woman": *Christian Science Monitor*, October 23, 1915.

259 "the best of the lot": HD, November 28, 1915.

259–260 "A divorce lawyer": William J. Flynn, "Tapped Wires," *Liberty*, June 2, 1928, 19–22.

260 "Nearly every piece": William F. Noble, "A Student's View of the Ford Expedition," *The Mid-West Quarterly*, July 1916, 327–28.

260 "God was on their side" . . . "I and my cousins": HD, January 27, 1916.

260 "would stand no nonsense": James Gerard to Ray Stannard Baker, November 4, 1930, RSBP, reel 75.

260 "German, English": HD, January 27, 1916.

261 "There is not the slightest": John Callan O'Laughlin to TR, November 2, 1915, TRP, reel 202.

261 "The British have gone": HD, November 24, 1915.

261 "The vital points for us": Cecil Spring Rice to Edward Grey, October 24, 1915, FOP, FO 800/85.

261 "fraternize with the opposition": HD, December 15, 1915.

261 "our oil and copper shipments": HD, October 14, 1915.

262 "never felt so much like": G. Beer to Gilbert Parker, February 6, 1916, FOP, FO/196.

262 "He is a queer Sir Cecil": EMH to WW, December 21, 1915.

262 "Some less childish man": WW to EMH, December 24, 1915, in *PWW*, 35:387.

262 "word of thanks": Walter Hines Page to EMH, November 12, 1915, in Burton J. Hendrick, *The Life and Letters of Walter H. Page* (Garden City, N.Y.: Doubleday, Page, 1922), 2:72.

262 "strike the weapon": Edward Grey to EMH, November 11, 1915, in *PWW*, 35:256.

263 "After a year of war": Theodore Roosevelt, "The Duty of the United States to Its Own People," *Metropolitan*, November 1915, 16.

263 "It is really unfair": Edward Grey to Cecil Spring Rice, November 3, 1915, FOP, FO 800/85.

263 "it would be read in England": TR to J. L. Garvin, November 12, 1915, TRDL.

263 "If England has not": Theodore Roosevelt, "The Duty of the United States to Its Own People," *Metropolitan*, November 1915, 16.

263 "the great work": Spring Rice telegram, November 26, 1915, FOP, FO 800/85.

264 "The silly English": TR to Kermit Roosevelt, November 21, 1915, TRDL.

264 "rather jumpy": TR to Maurice Egan, December 7, 1915, TRDL.

264 "The average Englishman": TR to J. St. Loe Strachey, February 22, 1915, in Morison, ed., *Letters of Theodore Roosevelt*, 8:897–903.

264 "great original do nothing": O. P. Williams to JA, October (?) 1915, JAP, reel 9.

264–265 "So many around her": Louis Lochner to David Starr Jordan, October 23, 1915, LLP, reel 50.

265 "states my position": JA to Anita McCormick Blaine, October 26, 1915, JAP, reel 9.

265 "You have taken the wind": Stockton Axton to WW, October 5 [6], 1915, in *PWW*, 35:33–34.

266 "increase the proportion of the hysterical element": *New York Sun*, October 3, 1915.

266 "Every woman needs" . . . "You don't know how lucky": *New York Herald*, September 10, 1915; *New York Evening World*, September 10, 1915.

266 "Many of our suffrage campaigns": *New York Sun*, October 3, 1915.

266 "If my husband opposed" . . . "I am tired": *New York Herald*, October 23, 1915.

266 "They ought to take care": *New York Tribune*, October 17, 1915.

266 "In this reactionary period": Carrie Chapman Catt to JA, November 12, 1915, JAP, reel 9.

266 "unscrupulous power": Jane Addams, "Peace and the Press," *The Independent*, October 11, 1915.

267 "We could only reply": Jane Addams, *Peace and Bread in Time of War* (New York: Macmillan, 1922), 32.

267 a public "manifesto": *New York Times*, October 16, 1915.

267 "White House": Paul Kellogg to Louis Lochner, October 5, 1915, LLP, reel 50.

267–268 "We think the United States": *Chicago Tribune*, October 13, 1915.

268 "Militarism is like that": Louis Lochner, "Should There Be Military Training in the Public Schools," *Advocate of Peace*, November 1915, 249.

268 "we believe in real defense": Jane Addams/WPP Officers to WW, October 29, 1915, JAP, reel 9.

269 "follow a wise and conservative": WW to JA, November 2, 1915, JAP, reel 9.

269 "strengthened my faith": David Starr Jordan to Jessie Jordan, October 26, 1915, DSJP, box 35.

269 "been the main factor": TR to Kermit Roosevelt, October 24, 1915, TRDL.

269 "unless America prepares": TR to Samuel Dutton, November 24, 1915, TRP, reel 385.

269 "the bulk of our people": TR to Kermit Roosevelt, October 15, 1915, TRDL.

269 "Safety First" and "Thank God for Wilson" buttons: James Townsend to TR, November 18, 1915, TRP, reel 202; *Harvard Advocate*, December 8, 1915.

270 "dissemination of pacificist literature": TR to James E. West, November 30, 1915, in Morison, ed., *Letters of Theodore Roosevelt*, 8:992–93.

270 "He recognized that there are": Frederick S. Wood, *Roosevelt as We Knew Him: The Personal Recollections of One Hundred and Fifty of His Friends and Associates* (Philadelphia: John C. Winston, 1927), 395.

270 "fat, rheumatic blind old man": TR to Belle Roosevelt, November 11, 1915, TRDL.

270 "Unless I write very briefly": TR to George Van Horn Mosely, November 17, 1915, in Morison, ed., *Letters of Theodore Roosevelt*, 8:979.

270 "pantalettes": Stacy A. Cordery, *Alice: Alice Roosevelt Longworth, from American Princess to Washington Power Broker* (New York: Viking, 2007), 259.

270 "We sit and read": TR to Belle Roosevelt, October 24, 1915, TRDL.

270 "National Defense Speech": Joseph Tumulty memo, c. October 25, 1915, in *PWW*, 35:107.

270 "selecting gowns": *New York Sun*, November 5, 1915.

271 "Washington housewives": *New York Tribune*, October 27, 1915.

271 "for prudence sake": WW to Edith Galt, November 2, 1915, in *PWW*, 35:160.

271 "I shall hold you in my arms": WW to Edith Galt, November 3, 1915, in *PWW*, 35:164.

271 "Buffet Présidentiel": *New York Herald*, November 5, 1915.

272 "negroes": Wilbur F. Sadler to WW, October 30, 1915, in *PWW*, 35:141.

272 "Does it not conform": For WW's Manhattan Club speach, see *PWW*, 35:167–73; see also *New York Herald*, November 5, 1915.

272 "He said the day he got out": HD, November 5, 1915.

272–273 "I ain't hurted" . . . "What Mr. Wilson proposes": *New York Herald*, November 6, 1915.

273 "as absurd": TR to Henry Wise Wood, November 6, 1915, TRP, reel 359.

273 "Either we need to prepare" . . . "an inefficient rival": *New York Herald*, November 12, 1915.

273 "warn the people": *New York Tribune*, November 9, 1915.

273 "he would class Christ": *Washington Evening Star*, November 10, 1915.

273 "blasphemous falsehood": TR to Albert Joab, November 24, 1915, TRDL.

273 "bewhiskered farmer": *New York Sun*, August 27, 1915.

274 "won its position in the world": *New York Herald*, November 6, 1915.

274 "If, as the militarists assert": *New York Sun*, November 17, 1915.

275 "kept wiping" . . . "No, that is for me": Louis Lochner, memo of meeting, November 12, 1915, in *PWW*, 35:195–99.

275 Wilson seemed more "mellow": Louis Lochner to Julia Wales, November 12, 1915, in *Revolutionary Radicalism: Its History, Purpose and Tactics with an Exposition and Discussion of the Steps Being Taken and Required to Curb It*, vol. 1 (Albany: J. B. Lyon, 1920), 987.

275 "Usually he was difficult" . . . "has no plan": Louis Lochner, "Additional Data Regarding Our Interview," November 12, 1915, in *PWW*, 35:199–200.

275 "the most precious asset": David Starr Jordan to Jessie Jordan, November 19, 1915, DSJP, box 35.

275 "a good Chinese citizen": TR to Fred Cardway, October 16, 1915, TRDL.

276 "On that day": David S. Patterson, *The Search for Negotiated Peace: Women's Activism and Citizen Diplomacy in World War I* (New York: Routledge, 2008), 150–51.

277 "The German-Jewish bankers": Rosika Schwimmer, "The Humanitarianism of Henry Ford," *B'nai B'rith News*, October–November, 1922, 10.

277 "considerable number of Jews": TR to Fraser Metzger, October 30, 1915, TRP, reel 359.

277 "work at the Hague Conference": E. G. Pipp to JA, November 18, 1915, JAP, reel 9.

278 "There is really one word": *Detroit Journal*, November 20, 1915.

278 "gasped": *New York Sun*, November 24, 1915.

278 "assurances that every neutral nation": *Detroit Free Press*, November 22, 1915.

279 "suffrage organizations": *New York Sun*, November 24, 1915.

279 "all the anxious mothers": Telegram draft, November 21, 1915, JAP, reel 9.

279 "positively refused": Lola Maverick Lloyd undated letter/memo recalling events of November 1915, RSP, box 64.

279 "It may be some time": *New York Sun*, November 24, 1915.

Chapter 9: Out of the Trenches by Christmas

280 "I'm willing to spend": *Washington Evening Star*, November 23, 1915.

280 "you can eat all you wish": *Des Moines Register-Sun*, November 21, 1915.

281 "a controversy between themselves": HD, November 21, 1915.

281 "a mechanical genius": HD, November 22, 1915.

281 "agree . . . that something" . . . "But you are": Louis Lochner, *Henry Ford: America's Don Quixote* (New York: International Publishers, 1925), 21.

282 "I beseech you": *New York Times*, November 25, 1915.

282 "It's for me": *The Argosy*, December 8, 1915, in LLP, reel 50.

282 "a better plan" . . . "He's a small man": Lochner, *Henry Ford*, 24–25.

283 "out of the trenches": For various versions of the "out of the trenches" statement, see *New York Sun, New York Tribune*, and *New York Times*, all on November 25, 1915.

283 "I can't tell you": *New York Tribune*, November 25, 1915.

283 "erect the machinery": *New York Sun*, November 25, 1915.

283 "appeal to the men": *New York Times*, November 25, 1915.

283 "longest gun in the world": *New York Herald*, November 25, 1915.

283 "Get people talking": *New York Times*, November 25, 1915.

283 "I'm on the job": *New York Sun*, November 25, 1915.

284 "the people in New York": Jane Addams, *Peace and Bread in Time of War* (New York: Macmillan, 1922), 37.

284 "tiresomely cautious": Lola Maverick Lloyd to Rosika Schwimmer, July 30, 1915, RSP, box 61.

284 "I had already": Addams, *Peace and Bread in Time of War*, 37.

284 "I'll make him go": *New York Tribune*, November 25, 1915.

284 "representative Americans": Henry Ford to David Starr Jordan, November 24, 1915, DSJP, box 20.

285 "Peace Demonstration": David Starr Jordan to Henry Ford, January 3, 1916, DSJP, box 20.

285 "If you see it": Ida Tarbell, *All in the Day's Work: An Autobiography* (New York: Macmillan, 1939), 312–13.

285 "after I sail": *Chicago Herald*, November 29, 1915, JAP, reel 64.

285 "to see what": *New York Sun*, December 4, 1915.

285–286 "Her rooms": Mrs. Philip Snowden, *A Political Pilgrim in Europe* (New York: Cassell, 1921), 46.

286 "I do not sleep": Rosika Schwimmer to JA, November 29, 1915, JAP, reel 9.

286 "passionate exaggerations": Snowden, *A Political Pilgrim in Europe*, 45.

286 "THE ENGLISH ARE FOOLS": See Martin Gilbert, *The First World War: A Complete History* (New York: Henry Holt, 1994), 218–19; *New Republic*, November 6, 1915; *Washington Evening Star*, November 27, 1915.

286 "All I can say": *Baltimore Sun*, November 27, 1915.

286 "exceedingly nice": Rosika Schwimmer to Lola Maverick Lloyd, November 26, 1915, RSP, box 65.

286 "voluble, bitter": Snowden, *A Political Pilgrim in Europe*, 46.

287 "elimination of militarism": Edward Grey to EMH, November 9, 1915, in *PWW*, 35:186.

287 "The British are" . . . "putting our thoughts": HD, November 25 and 28, 1915.

288 "an enterprise without": Carrie Chapman Catt to Harriet Thomas, December 27, 1915, JAP, reel 9.

288 "our best woman and queen": *The Henry Ford Peace Expedition: Short Selections from American Letters* (1916).

289 "reasonable preparedness" . . . "I am afraid": Ben Lindsey to TR, November 27, 1915; TR to Ben Lindsey, December 14, 1915, TRP, reels 202, 359.

289 "He is ignorant": John J. Leary Jr., *Talks with T.R.* (Boston: Houghton Mifflin, 1920), 257.

289 "Almost no one": JA to David Starr Jordan, December 28, 1915, JAP, reel 9.

289–290 "Nobody can spend a cent" . . . "How do you expect": *New York Herald*, December 3, 1915.

290 "Tell people to cry peace": *New York Evening Post*, December 4, 1915.

290 "Three Cheers" . . . "Theodore Roosevelt was on board": *New York Times*, December 5, 1915.

290 "We love you": *The Argosy*, December 6, 1915, in LLP, reel 50.

290–291 "I feel as though": Lochner, *Henry Ford*, 66.

291 "kept distinct": JA to Aletta Jacobs, December 12, 1915, JAP, reel 9.

291 "Must we accept": Aletta Jacobs to JA, December 23, 1915, JAP, reel 9.

291 "Henry dares": *Life*, December 9, 1915.

291 In an hour-long speech: WW's address to Congress of December 7, 1915, is in *PWW*, 35:293–310.

291–292 "She is rather pretty" . . . "I don't see": *New York Tribune*, December 8, 1915.

292 "What a smug thing": TR to R. S. Codman, December 11, 1915, TRP, reel 359.

292 "entirely correct" . . . "What does Mr. Wilson mean": *New York Tribune*, December 8, 1915.

292 "lost his mind": Franklin Lane to John Wigmore, December 8, 1915 in Anne W. Lane and Louise Herrick Wall, eds., *The Letters of Franklin K. Lane, Personal and Political* (Boston: Houghton Mifflin, 1922), 188.

292 "Byzantine logothete": *New York Tribune*, December 8, 1915.

292 "one who accounts" . . . "lawyers and orators": *New York Herald*, December 9, 1915.

293 "The people are realizing": Dwight Heard to TR, November 26, 1915, TRP, reel 202.

293 "Now they say" . . . "benefactor of great wealth": *New York Tribune*, December 22, 1915.

293 "had no political significance": *Washington Herald*, December 19, 1915.

293 "Do They Want Roosevelt": *New York Tribune*, December 11, 1915.

293–294 "his election would do" . . . "a dangerous dog": *New York Tribune*, December 28, 1915.

294 "faker supreme" . . . "Self-seeking": *New York Tribune*, December 22, 24, 1915.

294 "extreme reactionary crowd": Frank Knox to TR, December 17, 1915, TRP, reel 203.
294 "like to see you President": Henry Cabot Lodge to TR, December 2, 1915, TRP, reel 202.
294 "a really vital national crisis": TR to Henry Cabot Lodge, November 27, 1915, in *The Letters of Theodore Roosevelt*, ed. Elting Morison, vol. 8, *The Days of Armageddon, 1914–1919* (Cambridge: Harvard University Press, 1954), 991–92.
294 "some assurance": J. A. H. Hopkins to TR, December 21, 1915, TRP, reel 203.
295 "We hold the balance": Meyer Lissner to Dwight Heard, December 27, 1915, TRP, reel 203.
295 "interesting and important" . . . "important if true": EMH to WW, September 28, 1915; WW to EMH, September 29, 1915, in *PWW*, 34:536–37.
295 the "sane" center: TR to C. F. Amidon, December 30, 1915, TRP, reel 359.
295 "It is a common saying": *New York Sun*, November 18, 1915.
295 "I told Brooks": HD, November 14, 1915.
295 "materially strengthen" . . . "The last time": HD, December 15, 1915.
296 "disarmament": WW to EMH, December 24, 1915, in *PWW*, 35:387–88.
296 "special agent": HD, December 15, 1915.
296 "canvas the prospects": *New York Evening Post*, December 21, 1915.
296 "no idea of doing that": *New York Tribune*, December 22, 1915.
297 "a dozen of" . . . "one of alligator": *Washington Herald*, December 14, 1915.
297 "You will have no need": *New York Herald*, December 15, 1915.
297 "many pieces of needle work": *New York Sun*, December 16, 1915.
297 "What was he whistling?": *Washington Evening Star*, December 18, 1915.
297 Edith's "awful" family: Nell McAdoo to Jesse Sayre, December 4, 1915, WWPL.
297 "colored 'mammy'": *Washington Post*, December 19, 1915.
297 "from the doorway": *Washington Herald*, December 19, 1915.
297 "rich, dark fruit cake": *Washington Evening Star*, December 18, 1915.
298 "splendid photographic": *Washington Evening Star*, December 18, 1915.
298 "I think of her daily": Barbara Kraft, "Some Must Dream: The History of the Ford Peace Expedition and the Neutral Conference for Continuous Mediation" (Ph.D. diss., American University, 1976), 298.
298 "Hope your faith in our mission": Henry Ford to JA, December 21, 1915, JAP, reel 9.
298 "never wavered in my allegiance": JA to Rosika Schwimmer, December 26, 1915, JAP, reel 9.
299 "broken by the apparent failure": *San Francisco Examiner*, December 24, 1915.
299 "pathetically foolish": *Washington Times*, December 25, 1915.
299 "The Big Vital Issue" . . . "a greater favorite": *Washington Evening Star*, December 17, 19, 1915.
300 "Battleship Target Games": *New York Evening World*, November 25, 1915.
300 "Kitty Twinkle": *Washington Evening Star*, December 17, 1915.
300 "liked some of their more simple": TR to Kermit and Belle Roosevelt, December 27, 1915, TRDL.
300 "The negroes put on" . . . "electric lights": *New York Herald*, December 25, 1915.
300 "as important": HD, December 25, 1915.
300 "It is possible": WW to EMH, December 24, 1915, in *PWW*, 35:387.
300 "He clearly places": HD, December 25, 1915.
301 "We refuse to do our": TR to Samuel T. Dutton, November 24, 1915, TRP, reel 385.
301 "isn't possible": Walter Hines Page to Frank Doubleday and Others, Christmas 1915, in Burton J. Hendrick, *The Life and Letters of Walter H. Page* (Garden City, N.Y.: Doubleday, Page, 1922), 2:117.

Chapter 10: A World on Fire

302 "We need to prepare": *Washington Evening Star*, January 15, 1916.
302 "known as 'free thinkers'" . . . "I am guilty": *New York Evening World*, January 18, 1916.
302 "My reports from the west": *Pittsburgh Press*, January 15, 1916.
302 "Women simply": *Boston Globe*, January 17, 1916.
303 "bring the little bundle": John Milton Cooper Jr., *Woodrow Wilson: A Biography* (New York: Alfred A. Knopf, 2009), 68.
303 "happy as children": Edith Wilson to Sallie Bolling, December 19, 1915, in *PWW*, 35:372.
303 "jumped down": *New York Herald*, January 3, 1916.
303 "We have started the people": *New York Sun*, January 3, 1916.
303 "So far as neglectful citizens": *New York Tribune*, January 3, 1916.
304 "I had just finished": *Washington Evening Star*, January 4, 1916.
304 "entirely safe": *New York Herald*, January 11, 1916.
304 "faithful old Susie": Edith Wilson to Altrude Gordon, January 14, 1916, WWPL.
304 "lack of leadership" . . . "if every last Congressman": "A Memorandum by Joseph Patrick Tumulty," January 4, 1916, in *PWW*, 35:424.
305 "no single citizen": *New York Herald*, January 6, 1916.

305 "a nation of cowards" . . . "It is a little strange": R. E. Cropley to Thomas Gore, February 24, 1916; Thomas Gore to R. E. Cropley, February 24, 1916, TRP, reel 206.

305 "it seems to me": James Gerard to EMH, February 23, 1916, in Charles Seymour, The *Intimate Papers of Colonel House* (Boston: Houghton Mifflin, 1926), 2:210.

306 "fire in self-defense": Patrick Devlin, *Too Proud to Fight: Woodrow Wilson's Neutrality* (New York: Oxford University Press, 1975), 417.

306 "They can hardly expect": Cecil Spring Rice to Edward Grey, January 29, 1916, FOP, FO 800/242.

307 "inspired with sentimental": Eustace Percy, "The USA and Our Blockade," January 24, 1916, FOP, FO 800/96.

307 "it would be well": TR to Arthur Lee, February 18, 1916, TRP, reel 385.

307 "posed together": HD, January 19, 1916.

307 "an agreement with the civilized world": EMH to WW, January 11, 1916, in *PWW*, 35:465.

308 "the United States would like": HD, January 11, 1916.

308 "intervention" . . . "big battles": HD, January 14, 1916.

308 "find yourself": EMH to WW, January 16, 1916, in *PWW*, 35:488.

308 "no man had ever": EMH to WW, January 15, 1916, in *PWW*, 35:485.

308 "not nearly as cunning": Devlin, *Too Proud to Fight*, 463.

309 "I believe I have": EMH to WW, January 16, 1916, in *PWW*, 35:488.

309 "We need you": Rosika Schwimmer to JA, January 10, 1916, JAP, reel 9.

309 "She has always been able": Harriet Thomas to Madeleine Doty, December 23, 1915, JAP, reel 9.

310 "war-mad persons": *New York Herald*, January 6, 1916.

310 "Cannot something be done": Alice Jenkins to JA, January 16, 1916, JAP, reel 9.

310 "kindly impulses": William Redfield to William Kent, February 3, 1916, JAP, reel 9.

310 "With all these charming": *Los Angeles Times*, January 12, 1916.

310 "official peace disciple": *Washington Post*, January 12, 1916.

311 "Our people just now": Harold Ickes to TR, December 17, 1915, TRP, reel 203.

311 "the Bull Moose and the Elephant": Franklin Lane to Edward Adams, January 11, 1916, in Anne W. Lane and Louise Herrick Wall, eds., *The Letters of Franklin K. Lane, Personal and Political* (Boston: Houghton Mifflin, 1922), 198.

311 "We are all hopeful": *New York Herald*, January 12, 1916.

311 audiences "went wild": Richard B. B. Chew Jr. to TR, February 9, 1916, TRP, reel 206.

311 "men who a little while ago": Scott Bone to J. C. O'Laughlin, March 13, 1916, JCOP, box 5.

312 "We want a President": Ernest Shillabeer to TR, January 2, 1916, TRP, reel 204.

312 "Sometimes I have felt": TR to Charles Laidlaw Williams, January 13, 1916, TRP, reel 385.

312 "wake up our people": TR to Henry Cabot Lodge, February 4, 1916, TRP, reel 385.

312 far too "brash": William Allen White to Gifford Pinchot, February 10, 1916, WAWP, box 28.

312 "continually dealing": Francis Watson to TR, December 6, 1915, TRP, reel 202.

312 "great world crisis": TR to Wayne MacVeagh, January 29, 1916, in *The Letters of Theodore Roosevelt*, ed. Elting Morison, vol. 8, *The Days of Armageddon, 1914–1919* (Cambridge: Harvard University Press, 1954), 1010–11.

312 When he arrived in Philadelphia: *Philadelphia Evening Ledger*, January 20 and 21, 1916; *New York Sun*, January 21, 1916.

313 "turn to me, but I am absolutely": TR to Dwight Heard, January 11, 1916, TRP, reel 385.

313 "Giants are strong": *New York Times*, March 19, 1916.

313 "every young buck": *New York Sun*, March 21, 1916.

313 "surrounded by a throng": *New York Herald*, February 18, 1916.

313 "the Woman's Section": Terrell D. Webb, *Washington Wife: Journal of Ellen Maury Slayden from 1897–1919* (New York: Harper & Row, 1962), 273.

313 "enlist every able-bodied woman": *Washington Evening Star*, January 22, 1916.

313 "how to obey": Lillian Wald to John Haynes Holmes, February 25, 1916, LWP, reel 103.

314 "It is proposed to tax": *Washington Herald*, January 5, 1916.

314 "small and insufficient increase": TR to Henry Cabot Lodge, January 26, 1916, in Morison, ed., *Letters of Theodore Roosevelt*, 8:1006.

314 "hatred of the North": Ray Stannard Baker interview with Lindley Garrison, November 30, 1928, RSBP, reel 75.

314 In her opening statement: Addams's House testimony of January 13, 1916, can be found in *To Increase the Efficiency of the Military Establishment of the United States: Hearings before the Committee on Military Affairs, House of Representatives, Sixty-fourth Congress, First Session, on the Bill to Increase the Efficiency of the Military Establishment of the United States; Part 1* (Washington, D.C.: GPO, 1916), 201–13.

317 A few hours later, she repeated: Addams's Senate testimony of January 13, 1916, can be found in *Conference on Neutral Nations: Hearing before the Committee on Military Affairs, United States Senate, Sixty-Fourth Congress, First Session, Relating to Conference of Neutral Nations, January 13, 1916* (Washington, D.C.: GPO, 1916).

317 the "world's Messiah": *Boston Herald*, January 18, 1916, quoted in *Woman's Protest against Woman's Suffrage*, February 1916.
317 "Somebody ought to lead": *Minneapolis Journal*, c. January 15, 1916, JAP, reel 64.
318 "About the best thing": Ogden, Utah, newspaper clipping, January 15, 1916, JAP, reel 64.
318 "several tubercular foci" . . . "serum treatment": Harriet Thomas to Aletta Jacobs, January 25, 1916, JAP, reel 9.
318 "Your coming and that": Louis Lochner to JA, January 26, 1916, JAP, reel 9.
318 "friend's trick": Louis Lochner to Alfred Kliefoth, c. January 27, 1916, Ford Peace Plan Papers, box 5, Library of Congress.
319 "poisoned by adverse criticism": Lola Maverick Lloyd to Rosika Schwimmer, March 9, 1916, RSP, box 76.
319 "emphatically out of sympathy": TR to Henry Ford, January 29, 1916, TRDL.
319 "Honest criticism": Henry Ford to TR, February 3, 1916, TRP, reel 205.
319 "go over at length": TR to Henry Ford, February 9, 1916, in Morison, ed., *Letters of Theodore Roosevelt*, 8:1022.
319 "There is no enthusiasm": Joseph Tumulty to WW, January 17, 1916, in *PWW*, 35:492–94.
319 "He will find": *New York Sun*, January 20, 1916.
320 "The labor men": *New York Tribune*, January 28, 1916.
320 "The world is on fire": *PWW*, 36:26–35.
320 "chatted and smiled": *Pittsburgh Daily Post*, January 30, 1916.
320 "although she is a large woman": *Pittsburgh Press*, January 30, 1916.
320 In speeches over the next five days: *Addresses of President Wilson, January 27–February 3, 1916* (Washington, D.C.: GPO, 1916).
321 "Do you mean Bryan": *New York Tribune*, February 4, 1916.
321 "enormous stretch of coast": WW's full St. Louis speech can be found in *PWW*, 36:114–21; quote is from 119–20.
322 "intoxicated by the exuberance": "Memorandum of Conversations with Walter Lippmann—Dec. 9–10, 1927," RSBP, reel 79.
322 "kill the President": Cary Grayson to Altrude Gordon, January 31, 1916, WWPL.
322 "Munich of America" . . . "oatmeal, bacon": *New York Herald*, February 1 and 5, 1916.
322 shouted "yes!": *New York Tribune*, February 4, 1916.
322 "I don't care": *Des Moines Register*, February 2, 1916.
322 "Put it there, Wilson": *St. Louis Post-Dispatch*, February 3, 1916.
322 "Get out of the way": *New York Herald*, February 2, 1916.
322 "I admire your": *Des Moines Register*, February 2, 1916.
322 "He is incomparably stronger": *New York Tribune*, February 4, 1916.
322 "furious shouting": TR to Kermit Roosevelt, February 7, 1916, TRDL.
322 "a most interesting": WW to Richard Olney, February 7, 1916, in *PWW*, 36:138.
323 "He had spent": Walter Görlitz, ed., *The Kaiser and His Court: The Diaries, Note Books, and Letters of Admiral Georg Alexander von Müller, Chief of the Naval Cabinet, 1914– 1918* (London: MacDonald, 1961), 131.
323 "suitable apology": EMH to WW, February 1, 1916, in *PWW*, 36:85.
323 "profound regret": Arthur Link, *Wilson: Confusions and Crises, 1915–1916* (Princeton, N.J.: Princeton University Press, 1964), 94–100.
324 "Time . . . was against us": Görlitz, ed., *The Kaiser and His Court*, 129.
324 "greatly inconvenience England": Bernhard Huldermann, *Albert Ballin* (New York: Cassell, 1922), 248.
324 "alliance with America": Görlitz, ed., *The Kaiser and His Court*, 135.
324 "compulsory enlistment for training": WW to Lindley Garrison, February 9, 1916, in *PWW*, 36:145.
325 "Wilson was damn glad": Baker interview with Garrison.
325 "a miniature edition": *New York Herald*, March 10, 1916.
325 "in sympathy": B. W. Huebsch to Rosika Schwimmer, March 23, 1916, RSP, box 77.
325 "had a deep-seated": Ray Stannard Baker interview with Newton Baker, April 6, 1928, RSBP, box 71.
325 "now on sale by all booksellers": *New York Evening World*, February 11, 1916.
326 "if a man's wife's face": *New York Sun*, February 12, 1916.
326 "help build a battle ship": *New York Tribune*, February 4, 1916.
326 "Grandchildren and battleships" . . . "He looks just": *New York Tribune*, February 12, 1916.
326 "when things political": *New York Herald*, February 12, 1916.
326 "There are only two things": *New York Sun*, February 15, 1916; "madness": Link, *Wilson: Confusions and Crises*, 99.
327 "No one can tell": "Mem. on Woodrow Wilson," ITD.
327 "little schooling": *New York Tribune*, December 8, 1915.

327 "good deal of profanity": J. C. O'Laughlin to Mr. Ambassador, February 19, 1916 (postscript c. February 22), JCOP, box 10.
327 "banged his fist": *Washington Times*, February 24, 1916.
328 "under constant surveillance" . . . "stubborn race": HD, January 28 and 29, 1916.
329 "hell will break loose": EMH to WW, February 3, 1916, in *PWW*, 36:125.
329 "I again told them": HD, February 7, 1916.
329 "necessity of helping": Cambon's memorandum of February 2, 1916, is summarized in *PWW*, 36:126.
329 "congratulated himself": Jules Jusserand to Aristide Briand, March 31, 1916, in *PWW*, 36:390.
330 "more British": HD, February 14, 1916.
330 "Everything the President": HD, February 9, 1916.
330 "House is doing": John Milton Cooper Jr., *Walter Hines Page: The Southerner as American, 1855–1918* (Chapel Hill: University of North Carolina Press, 1977), 327.
330 "beginning of the end": EMH to WW, February 10, 1916, in *PWW*, 36:166.
330 "demand" . . . "we would throw": EMH to WW, February 10, 1916, in *PWW*, 36:167.
330 "a carefully sprung trick!": Cooper Jr., *Walter Hines Page*, 326.
330 "even go so far": HD, February 14, 1916.
330 the House-Grey Memorandum: *PWW*, 36:180.
331 "You and I speak": HD, February 23, 1916.
331 "much of great importance": EMH to WW, February 25, 1916, in *PWW*, 36:217.
331 "He cannot come again": Ross Gregory, "The Superfluous Ambassador: Walter Hines Page's Return to Washington, 1916," *The Historian* 28, no. 3 (1966): 394–95.

Chapter 11: A Test of Strength

332 "biggest mistake of his life": Paolo E. Coletta, *William Jennings Bryan*, vol. 3, *Political Puritan, 1915–1925* (Lincoln: University of Nebraska Press, 1969), 28.
332 "No one seems to think": Edward Krehbiel to Lillian Wald, February 24, 1916, LWP, reel 103.
332 "Counsel of Imperfection": JA to William Hull, January 16, 1916, JAP, reel 9.
333 "The trouble with her": Julia Grace Wales to unknown, February 15, 1916, LLP, reel 50.
333 "true story": Rosika Schwimmer to JA, January 10, 1916, JAP, reel 9.
333 "A ship-load of amateurs": David Starr Jordan to JA, March 13, 1916, JAP, reel 9.
334 "There is no time": JA to Rosika Schwimmer, February 18, 1916, JAP, reel 9.
334 Mary was her "secretary": Jessie Jordan to David Starr Jordan, March 31, 1916, DSJP, box 35.
334 "felt her distance": Marcet Haldeman-Julius, *Jane Addams as I Knew Her* (Girard, Kans.: Haldeman-Julius Publications, 1936),19.
334 "an extreme radical surcharged": *New York Herald*, January 31, 1916.
334 "the most precious asset": David Starr Jordan to Crystal Eastman, March 3, 1916, DSJP, box 19.
335 "Members of both Houses": William Stone to WW, February 24, 1916, in *PWW*, 36:210.
335 "do everything in my power": WW to William Stone, February 24, 1916, in *PWW*, 36:213–14.
335 "stand-up-for-our rights program": Paul Kellogg to JA, March 9, 1916, JAP, reel 9.
336 "A Mayor keeps": *New York Herald*, February 26, 1916.
336 "deliberately misinterpreted": *Washington Post*, February 27, 1916.
336 "attending public discussion": *Boston Globe*, February 27, 1916.
336 "politician to be successful" . . . "one of the boldest": *New York Sun*, March 1, 1916.
337 "playing politics" . . . "compromise resolution": *New York Herald*, March 2, 1916.
337 "Does not the president realize": *Washington Post*, March 2, 1916.
337 "that certain Senators": *New York Herald*, March 3, 1916.
337 "What the President said": *Charlotte Daily Observer*, March 3, 1916.
337 "armed merchant vessel": *Washington Post*, March 4, 1916.
337 "The question is" . . . "To vote against": *Washington Evening Star*, March 7, 1916.
338 "The question was presented": *Washington Evening Star*, March 8, 1916.
339 "Ha!" . . . "All sorts of stories": *New York Herald* and *New York Times*, March 6, 1916.
339 "crazy to hear": Edith Wilson to Altrude Gordon, March 6, 1916, WWPL.
339 "I cannot adequately" . . . "sitting at the head": HD, March 6, 1916.
339 "The life I am leading": HD, March 10, 1916.
340 "irritating publicity and functions": TR to Kermit Roosevelt, February 24, 1916, TRDL.
340 "strewed flowers in his pathway": *New York Times*, March 8, 1916.
340 "not in the least interested": TR's Trinidad statement of March 9, 1916, is reprinted in Executive Committee of the Progressive National Committee, comp., *The Progressive Party: Its Record from January to July, 1916, Including Statements and Speeches of Theodore Roosevelt* (New York: Press of The Mail and Express Job Print, 1916), 11–13.
341 "a reasonable amount of iron": TR to William R. Thayer, March 29, 1916, TRDL.
341 "build up a successful party": Reprinted in *New York Herald*, March 18, 1916.

341 "adviser in chief": *New York Herald*, March 11, 1916.
341 "Hughes has never": J. C. O'Laughlin to James Gerard et al., January 27, 1916, JCOP.
342 "Everything I have said": *New York Tribune*, March 25, 1916.
342 "bandit raid": *New York Herald*, March 30, 1916.
342 "a situation I do not understand": Norman Hapgood, *The Changing Years* (New York: Farrar & Rinehart, 1930), 240.
342 "It would not only destroy": HD, March 17, 1916.
343 "a very sharp, quick explosion": *Supplement to the American Journal of International Law*, October 1916, 266.

Chapter 12: Teetering on the Abyss

345 "These are certainly times": WW to Richard H. Dabney, April 26, 1916, WWPL.
345 "aerial combats": *El Paso Herald*, April 5, 1916.
345 "the great weapon of slaughter": Carl Snyder to TR, April 4, 1916, TRP, reel 207.
345 "young Queen" . . . "imitation fort": *New York Tribune*, May 5, 7, 1916.
345 "I want more girls": *Daily Arkansas Gazette*, May 11, 1916.
345 "commonplace, an everyday affair": *St. Louis Post Dispatch*, May 28, 1916.
346 "if America went to war": *Daily Arkansas Gazette*, May 11, 1916.
346 "illegal and inhuman conduct": Robert Lansing to WW, March 27, 1916, in *PWW*, 36:372.
346 "I am afraid": HD, March 27, 1916.
346 "many particulars to be considered": WW to Robert Lansing, March 30, 1916, in *PWW*, 36:381.
346 "He does not seem to realize" . . . "lead the way out": HD, March 28 and 30, 1916.
347 "as ignorant of his intentions": HD, April 2, 1916.
347 "war will be declared by": Viereck/Rau telephone conversation, April 3, 1916, FrPP, box 38.
347 "would not be without its advantages": EMH to WW, April 3, 1916, in *PWW*, 36:405.
348 "inevitable": HD, April 6, 1916.
348 "of incalculable advantage": Edward Grey to Lord Sanderson, May 19, 1915, FOP, FO 800/111.
348 "preferred talking": HD, April 6, 1916.
349 "think it over" . . . "We would be far safer": TR to George Perkins, April 6, 1916, in *The Letters of Theodore Roosevelt*, ed. Elting Morison, vol. 8, *The Days of Armageddon, 1914–1919* (Cambridge: Harvard University Press, 1954), 1029–31.
349 "When you hit him": Julian Street to TR, May 22, 1916, TRP, reel 209.
350 "I have been scrupulously": TR to Marshall Stimson, May 10, 1916, TRP, reel 360.
350 "hypocritical word-juggler": TR to George Roosevelt, February 1, 1917, TRP, reel 387.
350 "infinitely more astute": TR to Anna Roosevelt Cowles, January 27, 1916, in Morison, ed., *Letters of Theodore Roosevelt*, 8:1007.
350 "have neither courage": TR to Anna Roosevelt Cowles, February 3, 1916, in Morison, ed., *Letters of Theodore Roosevelt*, 8:1011.
350 "dangerous man": Charles Willis Thompson, *Presidents I've Known and Two Near Presidents* (Indianapolis: Bobbs-Merrill, 1929), 206.
350 "unscrupulous cunning": TR to Henry Cabot Lodge, February 4, 1916, TRP, reel 385.
350 "cutest little Machiavelli": Robert Sloss to TR, June 28, 1916, TRP, reel 212.
350 "I have never talked": Ray Stannard Baker, memo of conversation with WW, May 12, 1916, in *PWW*, 37:32–33.
350 "A campaign between": Herbert Croly to Willard Straight, April 6, 1916, Willard Straight Papers, reel 5.
351 "diabetic complications": *Chicago News*, April 6, 1916, JAP, reel 64.
351 "The love and understanding": Marcet Haldeman-Julius, *Jane Addams as I Knew Her* (Girard, Kans.: Haldeman-Julius Publications, 1936), 10.
351 "There are some compensations": JA to Marcet Haldeman, April 11, 1916, JAP, reel 9.
351 "ought to be encouraged": *Addresses of President Wilson, January 27–February 3, 1916* (Washington, D.C.: GPO, 1916), 68.
351 "lunatic fringe": TR to Amos Pinchot, November 3, 1916, in Morison, ed., *Letters of Theodore Roosevelt*, 8:1122.
351 "People are 'seein' things": *The Survey*, April 22, 1916.
352 "to guard your home": *Washington Evening Star*, April 15, 1916.
352 "bludgeon of Oyster Bay": *New York Herald*, April 7, 1916.
352 "You wanted to see": *Des Moines Register*, April 13, 1916.
352 "improvised a bowling match": Wilson meeting with AUAM, May 8, 1916, *PWW*, 36:639.
352 "four times as much space": *St. Louis Post-Dispatch*, April 15, 1916.
352 "It is a mortification": *New York Herald*, May 22, 1916.
352 "socialists and the pacifists": *New York Times*, April 8, 1916.

353 "war vessel": *New York Times*, April 13, 1916.
353 "commission of inquiry": Gottlieb von Jagow to J. von Bernstorff, April 17, 1916, in *PWW*, 36:499.
353 "The German alibi": Editorial was republished in *New York Herald*, April 14, 1916.
353 "severe cold": *New York Herald*, April 11, 1916; "digestive spell": HD, April 11, 1916.
353 "last page" . . . "declared it weak" . . . "He said he did not care": HD, April 11, 1916.
354 "even in wartime": HD, March 30, 1916.
354 "the telephone is very dangerous": Bernstorff/White telephone conversation, April 14, 1916, FrPP, box 38.
354 "The difference between": EMH to WW, June 1, 1916, in *PWW*, 37:135.
354 "a killing load": WW to Rev. John Fox, April 12, 1916, in Ray Stannard Baker, *Woodrow Wilson: Life and Letters*, vol. 6, *Facing War, 1915–1917* (New York: Greenwood Press, 1968), 311.
354 "This country has not the time": Jefferson Day speech, April 13, 1916, *PWW*, 36:475.
354 "merely for herself": D.A.R speech, April 17, 1916, *PWW*, 36:490.
354 "*Er is verrückt*": Klaeissig/Fuehr telephone conversation, April 17, 1916, FrPP, box 38.
355 "What does he ask us": *Washington Evening Star*, April 19, 1916.
355 "only one instance": *Washington Post*, April 19, 1916.
355 "looked tired": *New York Herald*, April 20, 1916.
355 "Imperial German Government": Speech before Congress, April 19, 1916, *PWW*, 36:506–10.
355–356 "We have some complaints" . . . "it would be a crime" . . . "If Germany now does": *New York Herald*, April 20, 1916.
356 "This is neither the time": *Washington Post*, April 22, 1916.
356 "He has done": TR to Henry Cabot Lodge, February 4, 1916, TRP, reel 385.
356 "Roosevelt cussed out": Wood diary, March 31, 1916, LeWP.
357 "had to work with every man": TR to Gustavus Pope, April 12, 1916, TRP, reel 360.
357 "Every time I have gone": Henry L. Stoddard, *It Costs to Be President* (New York: Harper & Brothers, 1938), 171.
357 "psychic astrologer": *New York Herald*, April 21, 1916.
358 "I do not want the work": Stoddard, *It Costs to Be President*, 114.
358 "cannot be elected" . . . "save the party": William Howard Taft to Charles Evans Hughes, April 11 and 12, 1916, in Merlo Pusey, *Charles Evans Hughes* (New York: Macmillan, 1951), 1:318–20.
359 "He is everything": Frank B. Howard to John Palmer Gavit, June 13, 1916, Palmer-Gavit Family Papers, Albany Institute of History and Art.
359 "Mr. Hughes is a very": Oscar King Davis, *Released for Publication: Some Inside Political History of Theodore Roosevelt and His Times, 1898–1918* (Boston: Houghton Mifflin, 1925), 46.
359 "He would rather be Hughes" . . . "I was sure": Pusey, *Charles Evans Hughes*, 1:234, 236.
360 "calm bewhiskered Buddha": Terrell D. Webb, *Washington Wife: Journal of Ellen Maury Slayden from 1897–1919* (New York: Harper & Row, 1962), 279.
360 "I tried hard to prevent": Bernstorff/White telephone conversations, April 21–22, 1916, FrPP, box 38.
361 "The British Government": HD, April 21, 1916.
361 "refused to interrupt" . . . "English submarine": April 22 and 28, 1916, entries, Walter Görlitz, ed., *The Kaiser and His Court: The Diaries, Note Books, and Letters of Admiral Georg Alexander von Müller, Chief of the Naval Cabinet, 1914–1918* (London: MacDonald, 1961), 151, 153.
361 "Under this a submarine": *New York Herald*, April 21, 1916.
362 "His Majesty" . . . "a great mistake": April 30 and May 1, 1916, entries, Görlitz, ed., *Kaiser and His Court*, 153–54.
362 "Do you come like a Roman": James Gerard to Robert Lansing, May 3, 1916, in *PWW*, 36:614–16.
362 "He is not in a position": May 3, 1916, entry, Görlitz, ed., *Kaiser and His Court*, 155.
363 "He spoke with much feeling": HD, May 3, 1916.
363 "harsh tone" . . . "Then it is war": Count Bernstorff, *My Three Years in America* (London: Skeffington & Son, 1920), 215.
363 "B. is here": Olive White/Archibald White telephone conversation, May 5, 1916, FrPP, box 38.
364 "insolent" attitude: Robert Lansing to WW, May 6, 1916, in *PWW*, 36:621.
364 "deliberate method": For the *Sussex* note, see *New York Times*, May 6, 1916.
364 "the 'gold brick' swindle": Robert Lansing to WW, May 6, 1916, in *PWW*, 36:621.
365 "We will settle this": J. C. O'Laughlin to TR, May 5, 1916, JCOP, box 11.
365 "parliamentary control": Louis Lochner, *Henry Ford: America's Don Quixote* (New York: International Publishers, 1925), 149.
365 "a very warm personal regard": Harold Ickes to TR, April 17, 1916, TRP, reel 208.
365 "I know I must be a thorn": JA to Harold Ickes, May 1, 1916, JAP, reel 9.
366 "I'm not afraid of him": *Chicago Tribune*, April 29, 1916.
366 "Glad to meet you": *Chicago Examiner*, April 30, 1916.
366 "tea gown": *Chicago Tribune*, April 30, 1916.
366 "army of conservation": Paul Kellogg to Lillian Wald, February 17, 1916, JAP, reel 9.
366 "fundamentally progressive" party: *New York Herald*, April 17, 1916.

367 "there was such a thing": May 7, 1916, entry in Webb, *Washington Wife*, 277.

367 "They will not permit": *The Survey*, January 15, 1916, 444.

367 "very bright mind": David Starr Jordan to Jessie Jordan, April 3, 1916, DSJP, box 35.

367 "For months the people": *Chicago Tribune*, April 11, 1916.

368 "I just can't think": *New York Sun*, April 23, 1916.

368 "make motor fuel": *New York Herald*, April 22, 1916.

368 "even Wilson is infinitely preferable": J. C. O'Laughlin to James Keeley, April 21, 1916, JCOP, box 7.

368 "have these people come": Blanche Wiesen Cook, "Woodrow Wilson and the Antimilitarists, 1914–1917" (Ph.D. diss., Johns Hopkins University, 1970), 62.

368 "bathed in the typical": Charles Hallinan memo to Committee, May 2, 1916, APP, box 16.

368 Wilson gave a virtuoso performance: A transcript of WW's meeting of May 8, 1916, with the AUAM can be found in *PWW*, 36:634–48.

369 "We-we-we-want peace": *New York Herald*, May 13, 1916.

370 "rubber-heeled shoes" *Brooklyn Eagle*, May 14, 1916; "His pants": *New York Sun*, May 14, 1916.

370 "chair I sat in" . . . "Three cheers": *New York Sun*, May 14, 1916.

371 "all armor plate": *The Survey*, April 1, 1916, 37.

371 "To the Marchers": *New York Tribune*, May 14, 1916.

371 "I have never had anything": Lella Secor to Loretta Secor, May 15, 1916, in Barbara Moench Florence, *Lella Secor: A Diary in Letters, 1915–1922* (New York: Burt Franklin, 1978), 69–74.

371 "most intense distrust" Marshall Stimson to TR, April 21, 1916, TRP, reel 208; "every cent": anonymous to William Hard, April 1916, TRP, reel 208.

372 "too materialistic": Brooks Adams to TR, May 5, 1916, TRP, reel 209.

372 "keeping the peace powder dry": Paul Kellogg to JA, April 5, 1916, JAP, reel 9.

372 "preaching" . . . "I wish I were a man" . . . "I wish I were a millionaire": Rosika Schwimmer to Lola M. Lloyd, May 26, 1916, RSP, box 77.

372 "wickedness, meanness": Rosika Schwimmer to Lola M. Lloyd, May 10, 1916, RSP, box 77.

372 "The injustice" . . . "I get physically weak": Rosika Schwimmer to Lola M. Lloyd, May 26, 1916, RSP, box 77.

373 "uncensored" account: *Fitchburg [Mass.] Sentinel*, May 13, 1916; "One of the best": *Chicago Tribune*, June 25, 1916; "The most vivid": from an ad in *The New York Times*, June 18, 1916.

373 "hum-drum life of peace": JNH to Charles Payne, January 12, 1917, JNHP, box 3.

Chapter 13: Last Stand of the Bull Moose

374 "I now have a considerable": TR to Arthur Lee, June 7, 1916, in *The Letters of Theodore Roosevelt*, ed. Elting Morison, vol. 8, *The Days of Armageddon, 1914–1919* (Cambridge: Harvard University Press, 1954), 1055.

374 "The general situation": Arthur Lee to TR, May 10, 1916, TRP, reel 209.

375 "Germany is like a poker player": *New York Tribune*, May 27, 1916.

375 "Everybody feels there must be": Edward Grey to EMH, April 7, 1916, in *PWW*, 36:511–12.

375 "I see evidences": EMH to WW, May 14, 1916, in *PWW*, 37:42.

375 "What the Allies want": HD, April 30, 1916.

375 "a very sad business": Horace Plunkett to TR, June 28, 1916, TRP, reel 212.

375 "mail over on war-ships": Charles Willis Thompson, *Presidents I've Known and Two Near Presidents* (Indianapolis: Bobbs-Merrill, 1929), 207.

375 "the difference between the offense": TR to Frederick Reiter, May 3, 1916, TRP, reel 360.

376 "altogether indefensible": WW to EMH, May 16, 1916, in *PWW*, 37:57.

376 "embarrassing demands": Walter Hines Page to WW, June 9, 1916, in *PWW*, 37:184.

376 "it would be interpreted" . . . "great scheme": Edward Grey to EMH, May 29, 1916, in *PWW*, 37:132.

376 "French and English": HD, June 23, 1916.

376 "Why should we wait": Joseph Tumulty to WW, May 16, 1916, in *PWW*, 37:58–59.

376 "greatest opportunist": William Howard Taft to Charles Hughes, April 12, 1916, in Merlo Pusey, *Charles Evans Hughes* (New York: Macmillan, 1951), 1:320.

377 "When we turn from moral suasion": *New York Herald*, May 19, 1916.

377 "impracticable": EMH to WW, May 19, 1916, in *PWW*, 37:77.

377 "integrity and sovereignty": Memorandum of May 24, 1916, in *PWW*, 37:102.

377 "thought and purpose": For WW's LEP speech of May 27, 1916, see *PWW*, 37:113–16.

378 "Pacifists and militarists": *New York Times*, May 29, 1916.

378 "consent to an entangling alliance": Memorial Day address, May 30, 1916, in James Brown Scott, ed., *President Wilson's Foreign Policy: Messages, Addresses, Papers* (New York: Oxford University Press, 1918), 200–201.

378 "rest of the world": Wilson speech to National Press Club, May 15, 1916, in *PWW*, 37:48.

378 "the gallery filled": Walter Hines Page to EMH, May 30, 1916, in *PWW*, 37:226.
378 "pick out some expression": EMH to Edward Grey, June 8, 1916, in *PWW*, 37:179.
379 "domestic matters": HD, June 23, 1916.
379 "work I have done": HD, April 22, 1916.
379 "A Man": *Collier's*, April 22, 1916.
379 "I hope the President": HD, April 10, 1916.
379 "about themselves for their own interests": Wilson speech to National Press Club, May 15, 1916, in *PWW*, 37:51.
380 "The status of Mr. House": Jules Jusserand to Aristide Briand, June 1, 1916, in *PWW*, 37:135.
380 "dodges trouble": HD, November 22, 1915; "does not get the best results": HD, June 10, 1916.
380 "helpful" moves: HD, April 6, 1916; "Many Protestants": HD, May 24, 1916; "some of Tumulty's": HD, March 11, 1916.
380 "no place in one country": EMH to WW, May 10, 1916, *PWW*, 37:11; "It lowers my opinion": WW to EMH, May 17, 1916, *PWW*, 37:61.
381 "hallucination that Mr. Wilson": Owen Wister to TR, May 12, 1916, TRP, reel 209.
381 "little wars": TR to Henry Wise Wood, May 27, 1916, TRP, reel 360; "badly armed black men": TR to William Allen White, December 18, 1916, WAWP, box C34.
381 "Mere outside preaching": TR to Anna Roosevelt Cowles, April 27, 1916, TRDL.
382 "not very strong": TR to Kermit Roosevelt, May 9, 1916, TRDL.
382 "He was signing letters": *New York Tribune*, May 7, 1916.
382 "open letter": *Saturday Evening Post*, May 13, 1916.
383 "sordid set of machine masters": TR to Charles Washburn, May 6, 1916, TRP, reel 360.
383 "Some of the republicans": *New York Herald*, June 9, 1916.
383 "If the Progressives would": Charles Sumner Bird to TR, May 29, 1916, TRP, reel 209.
383 "to act so that the Progressives": TR to Charles Bonaparte, May 29, 1916, TRP, reel 385.
383 "social and industrial justice": TR to Dwight Heard, April 17, 1916, TRP, reel 360.
383 "Remember that you owe": Charles Washburn to TR, May 3, 1916, TRP, reel 209.
384 "Roosevelt deals": Baker memo of conversation with Wilson, May 12, 1916, in *PWW*, 37:37.
384 "sane and sincere reformer" . . . "entirely an honest man": Pusey, *Charles Evans Hughes*, 1:173, 243.
384 "He declared that he did not": John J. Leary Jr., *Talks with T.R.* (Boston: Houghton Mifflin, 1920), 62.
384 "powerful, cold": TR to Kermit Roosevelt, January 17, 1916, TRDL.
384 "Baptist hypocrite": *Washington Herald*, May 5, 1916.
385 "In international matters": John A. Garraty, "T.R. on the Telephone," *American Heritage*, December 1957.
385 "There are some of them": Thompson, *Presidents I've Known*, 204.
385 "We MIGHT win": *New York Herald*, May 23, 1916.
385 "full of Eastern scare gas" . . . "need not be studied nor considered" . . . "created artificially" . . . "last resort": Henry Wise Wood to editor of *New York Times*, May 15, 1916.
385–86 "simple childlike nature" . . . "faith of an early Christian": G. D. Pope to TR, May 16, 1916, TRP, reel 209.
386 "Some pacifist" . . . "an animal forever": *Collier's*, June 10, 1916.
386 "We're for you here!": *New York Tribune*, May 20, 1916.
386 speak at the Opera House: For TR's Detroit speech of May 20, 1916, see Executive Committee of the Progressive National Committee, comp., *The Progressive Party: Its Record from January to July, 1916, Including Statements and Speeches of Theodore Roosevelt* (New York: Press of The Mail and Express Job Print, 1916), 32–52.
386 "I've got two sons": *New York Tribune*, May 20, 1916; "if every mother": *Detroit Free Press*, May 20, 1916.
387 "understand the trend": *New York Herald*, May 21, 1916.
387 "to the tune": *Washington Times*, May 28, 1916; "Fine, fine!": *New York Tribune*, May 28, 1916.
387 "we shouldn't permit our sons": *Chicago Tribune*, May 31, 1916; "Teddy Battle Cry": *Chicago Tribune*, May 31, 1916.
388 "visionary plans about world action": For TR's Kansas City and St. Louis speeches of May 30 and 31, 1916, see *The Progressive Party: Its Record*, 53–71; *New York Herald*, June 1, 1916; *New York Tribune*, May 31, 1916.
388 "The plain people": *New York Tribune*, May 31, 1916.
389 "Of course he is wrong": E. W. Rankin to William Allen White, June 21, 1916, WAWP, box C37.
389 "short, stocky and efficient": *Collier's*, June 10, 1916.
390 "Colonel, what train": *New York Sun*, June 5, 1916.
390 "If I were a betting" . . . "rise up and demand": *New York Herald*, June 2, 1916.
390 "bunch of Roosevelt bullfinches": *Chicago Examiner*, June 7, 1916; "You'll make 'em treat us": *New York Tribune*, June 7, 1916; "The Man from Oyster Bay": *Chicago Tribune*, June 7, 1916.
391 "misquoted": John A. Garraty, *Right-Hand Man: The Life of George W. Perkins* (New York: Harper & Brothers, 1960), 335.

391 "representative of all that": *New York Evening World*, August 23, 1912.
391 "Supposing that matters": Garraty, "T.R. on the Telephone."
391 "wonderful fight": Perkins/Roosevelt telephone conversation, June 5, 1916, GPP, box 14.
391 "From his own standpoint": TR to Oliver Bainbridge, June 23, 1916, TRDL.
392 "When Mr. Harding": *Chicago Tribune*, June 8, 1916.
392 "living flag": *New York Herald*, June 8, 1916; "Suffrage Plank": *New York Tribune*, June 8, 1916; "Red men": *Chicago Examiner*, June 8, 1916.
393 "Red bandanna handkerchiefs": *New York Tribune*, June 8, 1916; "began gyrating": *Chicago Herald*, June 8, 1916.
393 "They are right up": Garraty, *Right-Hand Man*, 337.
393 "complete reunion": William Jackson to TR, June 7, 1916, TRP, reel 211; "professional German-Americans": Roosevelt to Jackson, June 8, 1916, in *The Progressive Party: Its Record*, 88–90.
394 "get down on our knees" . . . "The one thing" . . . "never intend" . . . "harmony conference": *New York Sun*, June 9, 1916.
395 "I don't want those burglars": Garraty, *Right-Hand Man*, 341.
395 "Roosevelt's great embarrassment": Dudley Field Malone to WW, June 7, 1916, in *PWW*, 37:167.
395 "T.R. is not patient": *Chicago Tribune*, June 9, 1916.
395 "Why Not, Why Not" . . . "Sit down, Grandma": *New York Herald*, June 10, 1916.
396 "I really feel hopeful": Perkins/Roosevelt telephone conversation of June 9, 1916, GPP, box 14; "We have been playing poker" . . . "There is a very wide difference": Garraty, "T.R. on the Telephone."
396 "It's all a mistake": *Chicago Tribune*, June 10, 1916.
397 "about the cheapest fake": TR to Joseph Bishop, December 22, 1914, TRP, reel 357.
397–398 "all along the line" . . . "desperate calamity" . . . "I know Lodge's": Roosevelt/Perkins, Roosevelt/Butler telephone conversations, June 10, 1916, GPP, box 14.
398 "Next to Penrose": David Starr Jordan to Knight Jordan, August 1, 1916, DSJP, box 38.
398 "No, no!" . . . "There comes a time": *New York Herald*, June 11, 1916.
399 "I hope to God": *Chicago Examiner*, June 11, 1916.
399 "at least stood by": *New York Herald*, June 11, 1916.
399 "Roosevelt is going to refuse": *Chicago Examiner*, June 11, 1916.
399 "grateful for the honor": *New York Sun*, June 11, 1916.
400 "cheerless, depressed, bewildered": *New York Herald*, June 11, 1916; the "least creditable document": *Chicago Examiner*, June 11, 1916.
400 "It was a sad": Bainbridge Colby, "Memorandum for Ray Stannard Baker," 1930, RSBP, reel 72; "Big bronzed men": John Reed, "Roosevelt Sold Them Out," *The Masses*, August 1916.
400 "If ever there was a time": Thomas Robins to TR, June 11, 1916, in Morison, ed., *Letters of Theodore Roosevelt*, 8:1074.

Chapter 14: Summer of Anxiety

401 "The situation is a very puzzling": TR to William Allen White, June 23, 1916, WAWP, box C34.
401 "In the Italian district": *New York Tribune*, July 9, 1916.
402 "dust and dry": *New York Sun*, July 8, 1916; "stable fly": *New York Herald*, July 2, 1916; "magnetic currents": *New York Herald*, July 28, 1916.
402 "surroundings . . . considered ideal": *New York Tribune*, August 13, 1916.
402–403 "guaranteed cure": *New York Herald*, August 16, 1916; "spray rooms": *New York Herald*, September 13, 1916.
403 "The hygienic conditions": *New York Tribune*, July 27, 1916; "it has killed": TR to Richard Derby, August 21, 1916, TRDL; "AMYL-KIJO": W. D. Elger to TR, August 16, 1916, TRP, reel 213.
404 "We haven't even seen Ellen": Margaret Wilson to Jessie Sayre, September 9, 1916, WWPL.
404 "New York Plague": *Manchester Guardian*, August 22, 1916; "No news": Dillwyn Starr to family, September 12, 1916, in *The War Story of Dillwyn Parrish Starr* (New York: G.P. Putnam's Sons, 1917), 80.
404–405 "This war has already": *St. Louis Post-Dispatch*, April 19, 1916; "next war, thirty or forty years": Edward S. Martin, *The Diary of a Nation: The War and How We Got into It* (Garden City, N.Y.: Doubleday, Page, 1917), 246; "Have you seen anything": *New York Tribune*, July 23, 1916.
405 "The loss": JNH to Roy Cushman, September 11, 1916; "accompany various": JNH to George Greener, October 2, 1916, JNHP, box 2; "I'm as happy as a lark": JNH to Roy Cushman, October 16, 1916.
406 "out of politics": *New York Herald*, June 11, 1916.
406 "Theodore—the people": Corinne Roosevelt Robinson, *My Brother Theodore Roosevelt* (New York: Charles Scribner's Sons, 1921), 303.
406 "I would have done my best": TR to E. A. Van Valkenburg, September 5, 1916, in *The Letters of Theodore Roosevelt*, ed. Elting Morison, vol. 8, *The Days of Armageddon, 1914–1919* (Cambridge: Harvard University Press, 1954), 1114.
406–407 "his face would flush": *New York Herald*, June 15, 1916; "I don't want any": John J. Leary Jr., *Talks with T.R.* (Boston: Houghton Mifflin, 1920), 137; "Is he quiet?": *New York Tribune*, June 15, 1916.

407 "white duck trousers": *Washington Times*, June 14, 1916; "walked with a jaunty swing"; *Chicago Tribune*, June 15, 1916.

407 "Be Prepared—If You Care": *Washington Evening Star*, June 14, 1916; "thirteen pretty girls" . . . "ruins of a home": *Washington Times*, June 14, 1916.

408 "disloyalty . . . must be absolutely": For WW's Flag Day speech of June 14, 1916, see *PWW*, 37: 221–25.

408 "No matter what Hughes": EMH to WW, June 15, 1916, in *PWW*, 37:237.

408–409 "But we didn't go to war": *Official Report of the Proceedings of the Democratic National Convention Held in Saint Louis, Missouri June 14, 15 and 16th, 1916*, 23; "What would Teddy": *New York Tribune*, June 15, 1916; "settled our troubles": *Official Report of the Proceedings of the Democratic National Convention*, 23.

409 "one of the most degrading": TR to Anna Roosevelt Cowles, July 23, 1916, TRDL; "The convention went frantic": *Collier's*, July 29, 1916.

409–410 "It was so frightfully cut" . . . "tremendous international young people's movement": Lella Secor to Laura Kelley and Lida Hamm, September 4, 1916, in Barbara Moench Florence, *Lella Secor: A Diary in Letters, 1915–1922* (New York: Burt Franklin, 1978), 87, 89; "It seems funny to see": Lella Secor to Loretta Secor, n.d. [June 1916], in Florence, *Lella Secor*, 75; "peace hacks": Lella Secor to Laura Kelley and Lida Hamm, September 4, 1916, 86.

410 "perhaps more devoted": JA to Lillian Wald, May 18, 1916; "all effort": JA to Emily Balch, August 16, 1916, JAP, reel 9.

410 "She is so sweet": Lella Secor to Laura Kelley and Lida Hamm, September 4, 1916, in Florence, *Lella Secor*, 90; "Rebecca and I": Lella Secor to Loretta Secor, July 1916, in Florence, *Lella Secor*, 81–82.

410 "should close now": TR to Mr. Menard, July 30, 1916, TRP, reel 416.

410 "They told me": JA to Martha French, June 19, 1916, JAP, reel 9.

410–411 "consistent both": Marcet Haldeman-Julius, *Jane Addams as I Knew Her* (Girard, Kans.: Haldeman-Julius Publications, 1936), 21; "She had a compulsion": Haldeman-Julius, *Jane Addams*, 16.

411 "The suffering mothers": Jane Addams, *The Long Road of Woman's Memory* (New York: Macmillan, 1916), 140; "old wives' tale": Addams, *Long Road of Woman's Memory*, 4.

411 "This is the Miss Addams": Ellery Sedgwick to JA, February 23, 1916, JAP, reel 9; "It is the Miss Addams": Ellery Sedgwick to JA, February 29, 1916, JAP, reel 9.

411–412 "Your peace mission": Lucien Price to JA, September 13, 1916, JAP, reel 10; "You have been the greatest influence": Louis Lochner to Jane Addams, July 2, 1916, JAP, reel 9.

412 "all good Progressives": Louise de Koven Bowen to Harold Ickes, June 21, 1916, HIP, box 29.

412 "composed of as sordid": TR to Arthur Lee, August 11, 1916, TRP, reel 385.

412 "The people of America": *Chicago Examiner*, June 9, 1916.

412–413 "Wilson and his party": Owen Wister to TR, June 7, 1916, TRP, reel 211; "knew well": Henry Higginson to TR, June 13, 1916, TRP, reel 211; "no human being": TR to E. A. Van Valkenburg, September 5, 1916, in Morison, ed., *Letters of Theodore Roosevelt*, 8:1114.

413 "You would be accused": J. C. O'Laughlin to TR, June 19, 1916, TRP, reel 211.

413 "worst President": TR to Whitney Warren, July 6, 1916, TRDL; "The trouble with the Progressive Party": TR to William Dudley Foulke, July 27, 1916, TRP, reel 385.

413 "be embodied in the structure": TR to Progressive National Committee, June 22, 1916, Morison, ed., *Letters of Theodore Roosevelt*, 8:1067–74.

414 "unspeakably foolish": TR to Charlotte Stanley, July 18, 1916, TRP, reel 385; "it was not I": TR to William Hill, June 30, 1916, TRDL.

414 "if there is the remotest": J. A. H. Hopkins to George Perkins, April 28, 1916, TRP, reel 201; "I cannot believe" . . . "little, and perhaps": J. A. H. Hopkins to TR, July 11, 1916, TRP, reel 212.

415 labeled a "skunk": John A. Garraty, "T.R. on the Telephone," *American Heritage*, December 1957.

415 "Colonel Roosevelt, welcome!": *New York Herald*, June 29, 1916; "make an aggressive fight": Leary, *Talks with T.R.*, 57.

415 "make me look": TR to John C. Rose, June 16, 1916, TRP, reel 385; "I HAVE KEPT": *Chicago Examiner*, June 8, 1916.

415 "our Balkan Peninsula": Roosevelt/Butler telephone conversation, June 10, 1916, GPP, box 14; "It looks now": EMH to WW, June 19, 1916, in *PWW*, 37:268.

416 "I do not want war": *New York Tribune*, June 25, 1916.

416 "If the administration": TR to John Parker, June 27, 1916, John Parker Papers, box 4, University of Louisiana at Lafayette.

417 "direct conference": Executive Board of Woman's Peace Party to WW, June 27, 1916, in *PWW*, 37:308; "My heart": WW to JA, June 28, 1916, JAP, reel 9.

417 "Mr. President, keep" . . . "The easiest thing": Speech to New York Press Club, June 30, 1916, in *PWW*, 37:333–34; "The people do not": EMH to WW, July 1, 1916, in *PWW*, 37:338.

417 "This man": Leary, *Talks with T.R.*, 109; "I would like to finish": TR to Cecil Spring Rice, July 16, 1916, TRP, reel 416.

418 "I think he has been inspired": Homer Cummings memo, c. August 15, 1916, in *PWW*, 38:37.

418 "super-submarine": *New York Herald*, July 10, 1916; "sent to America": *New York Evening Post*, September 2, 1916, printed a letter that quoted the *Times* of London's theory.

419 "While operating": *New York Herald*, July 10, 1916; "submerging every": *New York Herald*, July 11, 1916; "Germans are fonder": *New York Herald*, July 11, 1916; "it must have been": *New York Times*, July 14, 1916.

419 "coffin": *New York Herald*, July 22, 1916; "the man who is like": *New York Times*, July 14, 1916; "The Preparedness maniacs": Ellen Slayden diary, July 14, 1916, Maury Maverick Sr. Collection, box 2L102, Center for American History, University of Texas at Austin; "great Zeppelin machines": *New York Herald*, July 14, 1916.

419 "nails, cartridges": *Chicago Tribune*, July 23, 1916.

420 "panic-stricken women": *Washington Evening Star*, July 31, 1916; "wrenched off its hinges": *Brooklyn Standard Union*, July 31, 1916.

420–421 "There are men who say": Müller to Kurt von Monbart, July 2, 1916, in Walter Görlitz, ed., *The Kaiser and His Court: The Diaries, Note Books, and Letters of Admiral Georg Alexander von Müller, Chief of the Naval Cabinet, 1914–1918* (London: MacDonald, 1961), 180; "deciphering of": June 30, 1916, entry in Görlitz, ed., *Kaiser and His Court*, 178.

421 "winning at last": David Lloyd George to EMH, July 31, 1916, in HD; "always favored Home Rule": TR to Sydney Brooks, August 25, 1916, TRP, reel 386; "trade secrets": Edward Grey to unknown, July 3, 1916, FOP, FO 800/242; "I am seriously considering": WW to EMH, July 23, 1916, in *PWW*, 37:467.

421–422 "all indications": Cecil Spring Rice telegram, July 24, 1916, FOP, FO 800/86; "heading a league": Cecil Spring Rice to Edward Grey, September 15, 1916, FOP, FO 800/86; "anti-German": Cecil Spring Rice to Edward Grey, September 4, 1916, FOP, FO 800/86.

422 "They are just as much": TR to Robert Sloss, June 7, 1916, TRP, reel 360; "The stress of the situation": HD, June 29, 1916; "all the great powers": EMH to WW, November 17, 1916, in *PWW*, 38:669; "unless the United States": HD, May 24, 1916.

422 "Judged by figures": Cecil Spring Rice to Edward Grey, August 10, 1916, FOP, FO 800/86.

423 "If they are not ready": EMH to WW, July 30, 1916, in *PWW*, 37:502.

423 "objects and causes": Edward Grey to EMH, June 28, 1916, in *PWW*, 37:413.

423 "The only conditions": Eric Drummond to Cecil Spring Rice, July 25, 1916, FOP, FO 800/86; "a make-believe umpire": TR to Lawrence Godkin, August 16, 1915, TRDL.

424 "American apathy": JA to Rosika Schwimmer, August 24, 1916, JAP, reel 9.

424 "I don't believe in war": *Monroe Journal* (Monroe, N.C.), September 12, 1916.

425 "We take our hats off": *Detroit Free Press*, July 11, 1916; "is on to the interests": *New York Herald*, July 11, 1916.

425 "Poor Mr. Ford": JA to Emily Balch, August 23, 1916, JAP, reel 9.

425–426 "independent offspring": Rosika Schwimmer to William Randolph Hearst, August 24, 1916, RSP, box 80; "The way Mr. Ford's": Clara Ford to Rosika Schwimmer, August 12, 1916, RSP, box 80; "incredible brutality" . . . "on the road to insanity": Rosika Schwimmer to JA, August 19, 1916, JAP, reel 9.

426 "I am . . . disgusted": Rosika Schwimmer to Lola Maverick Lloyd, August 21, 1916, RSP, box 80.

426 "Mr. Ford firmly": JA to Rosika Schwimmer, August 22, 1916, JAP, reel 9.

426 "The indignation": Rosika Schwimmer to JA, August 19, 1916, JAP, reel 9.

426–427 "I will search": WW to JA, August 5, 1916, JAP, reel 9; "who can be kept in line": Norman Hapgood to WW, August 14, 1916, in *PWW*, 38:34.

427 "I must admit": WW to Edith Galt, August 29, 1915, in *PWW*, 34:360; "good luck": *St. Louis Globe-Democrat*, September 24, 1916.

427 "I dote on fun": WW to Edith Galt, August 27, 1915, in *PWW*, 34:344–45; "balanced on his head": HD, May 3, 1916.

427–428 "the new Mrs. Wilson": HD, August 27, 1916; capacity to "hate": WW to Edith Galt, August 13, 1915, *PWW*, 34:192; "the trouble with children": Helen Bones to Jessie Sayre, July 9, 1916, in *PWW*, 40:575.

428 "autopeds": *New York Herald*, August 28, 1916; "There is something just": *New York Tribune*, August 20, 1916.

429 "Who's all right?": *New York Tribune*, August 1, 1916.

429 "Don't think much": *New York Herald*, August 2, 1916.

429–430 "A term on the bench": Leary, *Talks with T.R.*, 57; "What the average voter": TR to Charles Evans Hughes, August 11, 1916, in Morison, ed., *Letters of Theodore Roosevelt*, 8:1098.

430 "shockingly superficial": Chester Rowell to TR, August 23, 1916, TRP, reel 213; "Chautauqua lecturer encounters": William Hoster to TR, September 1, 1916, TRP, reel 213; "In political circles": *Washington Herald*, August 23, 1916.

430 "worth six": John Palmer Gavit to Travis Whitney, August 19, 1916, Palmer-Gavit Family Papers, Albany Institute of History and Art.

431 "better adapted": Henry L.Stoddard, *It Costs to Be President* (New York: Harper & Brothers, 1938), 114; "I would thank God": Alexander Moore to TR, August 24, 1916, TRP, reel 213.

431 "out of politics": *New York Herald*, August 18, 1916; "I don't wish": TR to John Bass, August 19, 1916, TRP, reel 385; "Of course he is": L. J. Duncan Clark to TR, August 1, 1916, TRP, reel 213.

432 "They [The Republicans] haven't anything": "Remarks before Members of DNC," December 8, 1915, in *PWW*, 35:314: "the President's internal": J. C. O'Laughlin to James Gerard, August 31, 1916, JCOP, box 7.

432 "I am not fertile": WW to Theodore Wright, June 21, 1916, in Ray Stannard Baker, *Woodrow Wilson: Life and Letters*, vol. 6, *Facing War, 1915–1917* (New York: Greenwood Press, 1968), 264.

432–433 "The great trouble": Amelia Fry interview with Alice Paul, "Conversations with Alice Paul: Woman Suffrage and the Equal Rights Amendment," University of California/calisphere.org; "That killed him": *New York Herald*, August 2, 1916.

433 "common understanding": *Washington Times*, July 4, 1916; "Answer, Mr. President": *Washington Herald*, July 5, 1916.

433 "angler for votes": WW to Ellen Duane Davis, August 5, 1916, in *PWW*, 37:529; "For beauty": *New York Herald*, September 9, 1916.

434 "People do not read": Ray Stannard Baker interview with George Creel, March 23, 1932, RSBP, reel 73.

434 "could get them to parley": EMH to WW, August 19, 1916, in *PWW*, 38:52; "Any offer of mediation": *New York Tribune*, September 14, 1916.

434 "We must make peace" . . . "No chance": August 25, 1916, entry in Görlitz, ed., *Kaiser and His Court*, 197.

435 "I am worried": Reisinger/Albert telephone conversation, August 29, 1916, FrPP, box 38.

435 "shed tears": August 28, 1916, entry in Görlitz, ed., *Kaiser and His Court*, 198.

435 "The opinion is growing": *New York Herald*, August 10, 1916; "business and professional": Minutes of ANCC meeting, July 6, 1916, Lella Secor Florence Papers, Swarthmore College Peace Collection.

436 "conservative wing" . . . "white flannel suit": Lella Secor to Laura Kelley and Lida Hamm, September 4, 1916, in Florence, *Lella Secor*, 85–97; "Their point of view": Transcript of meeting with ANCC, August 30, 1916, in *PWW*, 37:115–17; "he thought it would hamper": Baker memo of conversation with Wilson, May 12, 1916, in *PWW*, 37:37; "I believe that": Transcript of meeting with ANCC, August 30, 1916, in *PWW*, 37:115–17.

436–437 "During the moments" . . . "offend": Lella Secor to Laura Kelley and Lida Hamm, September 4, 1916, in Florence, *Lella Secor*, 85–97; "But it does": Lella Secor to JA, September 9, 1916, JAP, reel 10.

437 "far more belligerent": Lella Secor to Loretta Secor, September 4, 1916, in Florence, *Lella Secor*, 97–98; "fearlessness, courage, independence": Blanche Wiesen Cook, "Woodrow Wilson and the Antimilitarists, 1914–1917" (Ph.D. diss., Johns Hopkins University, 1970), 154; "There is hope": Amos Pinchot to E .A. Hempstead, July 25, 1916, APP, box 16; "a wooden man": Amos Pinchot to Sidney Norman, July 25, 1916, APP, box 16.

437 "Hughes's international reputation": Arthur Lee to TR, July 26, 1916, TRP, reel 212.

437 His first speech: For TR's Lewiston speech, see *New York Herald*, September 1, 1916; *Boston Post*, September 1, 1916.

438 "Walk right up": *New York Sun*, September 9, 1916.

438 "everyone who works": J. C. O'Laughlin to James Gerard, August 31, 1916, JCOP, box 7.

438–439 "summer White House": *New York Tribune*, September 3, 1916; "We have in four years": For WW's acceptance speech of September 2, 1916, see *PWW*, 38:126–39.

439 "fussing about": *New York Tribune*, September 11, 1916.

440 "we have good reason": Charles Evans Hughes to TR, September 15, 1916, TRP, reel 214.

440 "too much of a judge": Cecil Spring Rice telegram, September 21, 1916, FOP, FO 800/86; "no light task": TR to James R. Garfield, September 28, 1916 in Morison, ed., *Letters of Theodore Roosevelt*, 8:1119.

440 "That's music": *New York Herald*, September 14, 1916.

440 "nuts": *New York Sun*, September 24, 1916; Dubbed Omega: *New York Herald*, September 25, 1916.

441 "the record is there": Press conference of September 29, 1916, in *PWW*, 37:287; "For a little while": *Washington Evening Star*, October 1, 1916.

441 "menace" of "Anglo-Saxonism": Jeremiah O'Leary to TR, June 1, 1916, TRP, reel 209; "Your foreign policies": Jeremiah O'Leary to WW, September 29, 1916, in *PWW*, 38:285; "Your telegram received": WW to Jeremiah O'Leary, September 29, 1916, in *PWW*, 38:286; "the best thing so far": EMH to WW, September 30, 1916, in *PWW*, 38:317.

441 "All our foreign policy": For WW's Shadow Lawn speech of September 30, 1916, see *PWW*, 38:301–12.

442 "since he took to writing": *New York Herald*, September 19, 1916.

Chapter 15: An Election and a Peace Move

443 "Everything I believe in": *Collier's*, October 28, 1916.

443 "You are doing the best work": *Chicago Defender*, November 25, 1916.

444 "doubtful states": *Washington Evening Star*, October 28, 1916; "You have grievously": W. E. B. Du Bois to WW, October 10, 1916, in *PWW*, 38:459; "old darkey": "Remarks at a Reception in Cincinnati," October 26, 1916, in *PWW*, 38:524.

444 "wholly unfit": TR to Henry Cabot Lodge, December 4, 1916, in *The Letters of Theodore Roosevelt*, ed. Elting Morison, vol. 8, *The Days of Armageddon, 1914–1919* (Cambridge: Harvard University Press, 1954), 1132.

444 "high falsetto": *Detroit Free Press*, October 1, 1916; "big labor leaders" . . . "argued for preparedness": *New York Tribune*, October 1, 1916.

445 "I would have seized": *Detroit Free Press*, October 1, 1916; "Mr. Wilson is not a bit": Edward S. Martin, *The Diary of a Nation: The War and How We Got into It* (Garden City, N.Y.: Doubleday, Page, 1917), 323.

445 "a fat-headed": Meyer Lissner to TR, September 25, 1916, TRP, reel 214; "You strengthen them": Henry Stoddard to TR, October 3, 1916, TRP, reel 215.

445 "Good!" and "Right!": *New York Herald*, October 4, 1916; "people with shoulders": *New York Sun*, October 4, 1916.

446 "It is very galling": TR to Robert Bass, July 28, 1916, TRP, reel 385.

446 the steerers offered ten cents: *Chicago Tribune*, October 18, 1916.

446 "I think that there never": JA to Paul Kellogg, August 10, 1916, JAP, reel 9; "If we have war": J. C. Anderson to Amos Pinchot, March 20, 1916, APP, box 15.

446–447 "representing eight nationalities": *Chicago Herald*, November 16, 1916, JAP, reel 64; "southerner of the virulent type": Vachel Lindsay to JA, October 15, 1916, JAP, reel 10.

447 "I am a Republican": *San Francisco Chronicle*, September 14, 1916; "I know Hughes": *New York Herald*, September 28, 1916; "grown a mile": Louis Lochner, *Henry Ford: America's Don Quixote* (New York: International Publishers, 1925), 184.

447 "anarchist": *Chicago Tribune*, June 23, 1916; "$5 for every $1": *New York Evening World*, October 5, 1916; "many fine qualities": HD, October 2, 1916.

447–448 "Eight-Hour Wilson": *New York Tribune*, October 5, 1916; "They are making votes": *New York Tribune*, October 6, 1916; "To hear him talk": HD, November 2, 1916.

448 "we wanted to see" . . . "You are a clean shaven": *New York Herald*, October 5, 1916.

448–449 "I cannot deny myself": WW to JA, October 17, 1916, JAP, reel 10; "Shame!": *New York Tribune*, October 20, 1916; "Where's your baby?": *Chicago Tribune*, October 20, 1916; "There was a swift surge": *New York Tribune*, October 20, 1916; "Pitch 'em": *Chicago Examiner*, October 20, 1916.

449 "violent attack": *New York Tribune*, October 20, 1916; "It is strange": *Chicago Tribune*, October 22, 1916.

449–450 "I still believe in suffrage": *San Francisco Examiner*, November 2, 1916; "a party whose policy": *Chicago Tribune*, November 12, 1916.

450 "You can never be quite sure": Anna Howard Shaw to Aletta Jacobs, April 18, 1916, in Mineke Bosch and Annemarie Kloosterman, eds., *Politics and Friendship: Letters from the International Woman Suffrage Alliance, 1902–1942* (Columbus: Ohio State University Press, 1990), 162.

450 "Louisville went wild" . . . "He tells us stories": Corinne Roosevelt Robinson, *My Brother Theodore Roosevelt* (New York: Charles Scribner's Sons, 1921), 310–13.

451 "Instead of carrying": *New York Sun*, October 27, 1916; "Just 103 babies": *New York Tribune*, October 19, 1916.

451 "That's right": *New York Tribune*, October 20, 1916; "What did you do?": *New York Tribune*, October 25, 1916.

451 "You're the best": *New York Sun*, October 27, 1916; "We know you're": *Chicago Tribune*, October 27, 1916; "we're for you, Teddy": *New York Tribune*, October 25, 1916.

451 "is the kind of a man": Arthur Wallace Dunn, *From Harrison to Harding: A Personal Narrative, Covering a Third of a Century 1888–1921* (New York: G.P. Putnam's Sons, 1922), 2:347.

452 "There was nothing incoherent": Donald Richberg, *Tents of the Mighty* (New York: Willett, Clark & Colby, 1930), 77; "Results in Chicago": John J. Leary Jr., *Talks with T.R.* (Boston: Houghton Mifflin, 1920), 63.

453 "Wilson and Peace with Honor?": *New York Herald*, November 4, 1916; "How many men": *New York Evening World*, November 4, 1916.

453 "Why doesn't he name me": *Pittsburgh Press*, November 3, 1916.

453 "articulate voice": Shadow Lawn speech, October 7, 1916, in *PWW*, 38:364; "vocal element" . . . "those who brag": Shadow Lawn speech, October 28, 1916, in *PWW*, 38:551; "Give it to Teddy": *New York Tribune*, October 15, 1916.

453–454 "All I have tried" . . . "Have you ever heard": Cincinnati speeches, October 26, 1916, in *PWW*, 38:540, 531; "confined and provincial": Omaha speech, October 5, 1916, in *PWW*, 38:337–8; "when we can find something": Buffalo speech, November 1, 1916, in *PWW*, 38:588; "when all the rest of the world": Indianapolis speech, October 12, 1916, in *PWW*, 38:418; "saving ourselves": Shadow Lawn speech, October 14, 1916, in *PWW*, 38:437.

454 "Unless the United States": Edward Grey to Theodore Marburg, September 16, 1916, FOP, FO 800/242.

454 "Permit a respectful": *New York Tribune*, October 13, 1916; "Put him out" . . . "Sir, I would have had": *Louisville Courier-Journal*, October 13, 1916.

455 "old Hughes": John Palmer Gavit to Travis Whitney, October 19, 1916, Palmer-Gavit Family Papers, Albany Institute of History and Art; *unofficial spokesmen*: *New York Tribune*, October 17, 1916;

"bearded iceberg": TR to William A. Wadsworth, June 23, 1916 in Morison, ed., *Letters of Theodore Roosevelt*, 8:1078; "fault-finder" . . . "If the Republican party": John Palmer Gavit to Travis Whitney, October 19, 1916.

455 "labor unions drag" . . . "fierce partisan": *New York Tribune*, October 1, 1916; "the coarse crew": *New York Herald*, September 4, 1916; "men of the lowest class": *New York Tribune*, September 4, 1916; "postscript": *New York Herald*, October 31, 1916.

456 "fiendish lies": WW to Sylvester Beach, June 26, 1916, in Ray Stannard Baker, *Wilson: Life and Letters*, vol. 6, *Facing War, 1915–1917* (New York: Greenwood Press, 1968), 286; "petty gossip": Leary, *Talks with T.R.*, 326; "You can't cast": William Allen White, *Woodrow Wilson: The Man, His Times and His Task* (Boston: Houghton Mifflin, 1924), 269.

456 "Misquotations": *Washington Evening Star*, October 28, 1916; "I have such an utter contempt": "Interview with Henry Noble Hall," October 31, 1916, in *PWW*, 38:565; "with the motley crowd": WW to William B. Wilson, October 23, 1916, in *PWW*, 38:513.

457 "not made Wilson fight": Leary, *Talks with T.R.*, 59.

457 His speech at Cooper Union: *New York Herald*, November 4, 1916; *New York Tribune*, November 4, 1916.

458 "rather a good speech": TR to Quentin Roosevelt, November 7, 1916, TRDL.

458 "a matter of intense interest": *Richmond Times-Dispatch*, October 29, 1916; "biggest thinkers in America": *Logansport (Ind.) Pharos-Tribune*, November 6, 1916; "abuses inevitably developed": *Sacramento Star*, November 3, 1916.

459 "this country is progressive": Shadow Lawn speech, September 30, 1916, in *PWW*, 38:305; "intelligent woman": *Kewanee (Ill.) Daily Star Courier*, November 1, 1916.

459 "moneyed class"; HD, November 2, 1916; "Apparently New York had come": *New York Tribune*, November 3, 1916; "We're with you, Woody!": *New York Times*, November 3, 1916; "The President reminds me": HD, November 2, 1916.

460 "infinitely more accurate": EMH to WW, November 4, 1916, in *PWW*, 38:616.

460 "teleautograph stereopticon": *Chicago Tribune*, November 7, 1916; "look toward the Hearst Building": *Chicago Examiner*, November 5, 1916; "steady horizontal beam": *New York Herald*, October 30, 1916.

460 "Princeton yell": *New York Evening Post*, November 7, 1916.

460–461 "careless scratching": *Chicago Tribune*, November 7, 1916; "It was indeed": *New York Times*, November 8, 1916; "half drunk foreigners": Lella Secor to Loretta Secor, November 7, 1916, in Barbara Moench Florence, *Lella Secor: A Diary in Letters, 1915–1922* (New York: Burt Franklin, 1978), 113.

461 "Stop! Don't break": *New York Herald*, November 8, 1916; "so close that it will be": *New York Herald*, November 9, 1916; "We will wait": *New York Herald*, November 8, 1916.

461 "What mode of polished cant": Owen Wister to TR, November 8, 1916, TRP, reel 215; "I wish to express": *New York Herald*, November 8, 1916.

462 "We're not dead yet" . . . something "definite": *New York Tribune*, November 8, 1916.

462 "How's it going, Joe?": *Asbury Park (N.J.) Press*, May 19, 1942.

462 "Bully for you": *New York Sun*, November 9, 1916; "played the best game": *Washington Evening Star*, November 15, 1916.

463 "He kept us out of *sleep*": *New York Tribune*, November 9, 1916; "Wilson Has a Winnin' Way": *New York Sun*, November 9, 1916; "I make this statement": *New York Evening World*, November 8, 1916.

463 "question of the Southern ballot": *New York Herald*, November 30, 1916.

463 "problems . . . even more difficult": WW to Bella Shope, December 5, 1916, WWPL; "strongest man politically": *New York Tribune*, November 10, 1916.

464 "The fact that Wilson": HD, November 23, 1916.

464 "No amount of calls": *New York Herald*, November 13, 1916.

464 "an unequivocal mandate": Jane Addams, *Peace and Bread in Time of War* (New York: Macmillan, 1922), 58; "bound to nothing": *Boston Herald*, November 28, 1916. JAP, reel 64; "carry out the will": Addams, *Peace and Bread*, 58.

465 "They are heavy drinkers": JNH to Charles Payne, January 12, 1917, JNHP, box 3.

466 "something ludicrous": *New York Herald*, October 10, 1916; "Except for destroying": *New York Sun*, October 10, 1916.

466 "non-combatants in open rowboats": *New York Tribune*, October 11, 1916.

466 "The *U-53* has shown us": *New York Sun*, October 15, 1916; "until it stares": *New York Tribune*, October 11, 1916.

467 "loves to play": Diary of Cary Grayson, June 15, 1919, WWPL; "British empire has invested": *New York Tribune*, September 29, 1916.

467 "Clearly a threat": EMH to WW, October 20, 1916, in *PWW*, 38:494.

468 "the only invincible people": Walter Hines Page to WW, May 12, 1916, in *PWW*, 37:28–29; "Here is another damn fool": HD, April 6, 1916.

468 "bath in American opinion": WW to EMH, August 21, 1915, in *PWW*, 34:272; "manikin," a "lawbook-precedent": Ross Gregory, "The Superfluous Ambassador: Walter Hines Page's Return to Washington, 1916," *The Historian* 28, no. 3 (1966): 397; "He is surrounded by": John Milton Cooper Jr.

Walter Hines Page: The Southerner as American, 1855–1918 (Chapel Hill: University of North Carolina Press, 1977), 344.

468 "his point of view": HD, September 19, 1916; "heartily in sympathy": Page notes of meeting with WW, September 23, 1916, in *PWW*, 38:241.

469 "if the Allies wanted": HD, November 15, 1916; "sane Saviour": Cecil Spring Rice to Edward Grey, May 19, 1916, FOP, FO 800/86; "It is safe to say": Horace Plunkett to EMH, November 2, 1916, in *PWW*, 40:31–32; "We think Wilson" . . . "not popular here": Edward Grey to J. St. Loe Strachey, October 9, 1916, FOP, FO 800/111.

469 "creditors of the world": Shadow Lawn speech, November 4, 1916, in *PWW*, 38:613–14.

470 "We have to pay $10,000,000": *New York Tribune*, October 20, 1916; "if things go on": Arthur Link, *Wilson: Campaigns for Progressivism and Peace, 1916–1917* (Princeton, N.J.: Princeton University Press, 1965), 184; "trade war": Patrick Devlin, *Too Proud to Fight: Woodrow Wilson's Neutrality* (New York: Oxford University Press, 1975), 549.

470 "are irritating almost": HD, November 17, 1916.

470 "I prefer a restricted": December 21, 1916, entry in Walter Görlitz, ed., *The Kaiser and His Court: The Diaries, Note Books, and Letters of Admiral Georg Alexander von Müller, Chief of the Naval Cabinet, 1914–1918* (London: MacDonald, 1961), 225.

471 "deep knowledge": James Gerard memo, RSBP, reel 75; "Gerard states that": Wood diary, October 30, 1916, LeWP, box 9.

471 "I do not believe": HD, November 2, 1916.

471 "That is against": Fuehr/Haimhausen telephone conversation, November 21, 1916, FrPP, box 38.

472 "I can only reply": *New York Herald*, November 16, 1916; "entitled to a full equality": *Ladies' Home Journal*, November 1916.

472 "I would like to visit": TR to Arthur Lee, November 10, 1916, in Morison, ed., *Letters of Theodore Roosevelt*, 8:1125.

472 "spend a little": WW to EMH, November 13, 1916, in *PWW*, 38:637.

472–473 "Unless we do this" . . . "an unfriendly act" . . . "deeply disturbed": HD, November 14, 1916.

473 "best friend": HD, November 15, 1916; "his tendency to offend" . . . "must be guided": HD, November 17, 1916.

474 "I have tried": *Collier's*, October 28, 1916.

474 "reprehensible pacifists": Herbert Drake to TR, October 27, 1916, TRP, reel 215; "entrance of America": Norman Angell memorandum, c. November 20, 1916, in *PWW*, 40:12–17.

475 "I have no regrets": Charles Evans Hughes to TR, November 25, 1916, TRP, reel 216.

475 "lasting peace": WW prolegomenon, c. November 25, 1916, in *PWW*, 40:67; "join a league of nations": "A Draft of Peace Note," c. November 25, 1916, in *PWW*, 40:72–74.

475 "not trying to mediate" . . . "same error": HD, November 26, 1916; "one of the most unjustifiable": WW to John Sharp Williams, December 5, 1916, in *PWW*, 40:168; "If you do it now": EMH to WW, November 30, 1916, in *PWW*, 40:111.

476 "full of endearing phrases": *New York Tribune*, November 12, 1916.

477 "faked. . . . I don't want": Field/Bernstorff telephone conversation, November 16, 1916, FrPP, box 39.

477 "he has been slapped": Townsend/Bernstorff telephone conversation, November 23, 1916, FrPP, box 39; "All Want Peace": *New York Times*, November 20, 1916; "It makes the British": Townsend/Bernstorff telephone conversation, November 23, 1916, FrPP, box 39; "each nationality": *Washington Evening Star*, November 30, 1916.

477 "he expected to be": HD, November 26, 1916.

478 "muddy the waters": EMH to WW, December 4, 1916, in *PWW*, 40:137.

478 "conscription a part" . . . "embarrass": Amos Pinchot to WW, August 9, 1916, APP, box 17; "smuggled into the bill": *New York Herald*, September 18, 1916.

479 "They are jailing boys": Amos Pinchot to W. S. Rainsford, July 20, 1916, APP, box 16.

479 "because we believe that women": *New York Tribune*, December 13, 1916.

479 "slenderer than she was": *New York Herald*, December 13, 1916; "extremely handsome": *Washington Post*, December 13, 1916.

480 "Soldiers: In agreement": *Washington Evening Star*, December 12, 1916.

480 "My parents": *New York Herald*, December 13, 1916; "any time": *Chicago Tribune*, December 13, 1916.

480 "the market is terribly": White/Bernstorff telephone conversation, December 12, 1916, FrPP, box 39.

481 "unconquerable strength": *New York Times*, December 13, 1916; "If the Allies refuse": *New York Tribune*, December 17, 1916.

481 "It is all up to London": Townsend/Bernstorff telephone conversation, December 17, 1916, FrPP, box 39; "Mr. Limerick": Haimhausen/Stevens telephone conversation, November 18, 1916, FrPP, box 39.

481 "Mr. President, what will": *New York Herald*, December 6, 1916; "We're going to let down banners": *New York Tribune*, December 10, 1916.

482 "why the Allies": HD, December 3, 1916; "We cannot go back": WW to EMH, December 8, 1916, in *PWW*, 40:189.

482 "for we are a democracy": Lansing diary, December 3, 1916, in *PWW*, 40:311.

482 "probably the only step": Robert Lansing to WW, December 10, 1916, in *PWW*, 40:209; **Wilson understandably "depressed":** HD, December 14, 1916.
483 "Is Wilson to lose": *New York Evening Post*, December 18, 1916.
483 "Things have moved": WW to EMH, December 19, 1916, *PWW*, 40:276.
484 "It may be that peace": *New York Times*, December 21, 1916.
484 "that thought" . . . "I find the President": HD, December 20, 1916; "desire for peace" . . . "the greatest security" . . . "I am convinced": HD, December 14, 1916.
485 "the first hypersensitive reaction": JA to WW, December 20, 1916, JAP, reel 10; "organized politically": Addams, *Peace and Bread*, 52.
485 "it is not for a stranger": J. C. O'Laughlin to TR, December 22, 1916, JCOP, box 11; "I loathe and detest" . . . "The funniest thing": Townsend/Bernstorff telephone conversation, December 22, 1916, FrPP, box 39.
485 "verge of war": *Washington Evening Star*, December 21, 1916.
486 "wildest day": *Chicago Tribune*, December 22, 1916; "The whole atmosphere": WW to Robert Lansing, December 21, 1916, in *PWW*, 40:307.
486 "most terrible thing": *New York Tribune*, December 28, 1916; "Western woman": *New York Herald*, December 15, 1916; "safe and sane": *Englewood Economist* (Chicago), December 20, 1916.
486 "immoral and misleading": *New York Herald*, January 4, 1917.
487 "let anyone bully you": *New York Herald*, December 23, 1916; "The antics": Leary, *Talks with T.R.*, 62.
487 "very happy Christmas": WW to Lucy and Mary Smith, December 27, 1916, in *PWW*, 40:336.

Chapter 16: Peace in Sight

488 "This war is so unprecedented": *New York Tribune*, February 5, 1917.
488–489 "I had not been apprised": *New York Herald*, January 10, 1917; "It is only when women" . . . "He holds his party": *New York Tribune*, January 10, 1917; "most militant move ever": *Washington Herald*, January 10, 1917.
489 "throw them at the President?": *New York Herald*, January 13, 1917; "suffrage idiocy": Helen Bones to Jessie Sayre, January 16, 1917, WWPL.
489 "Ring out old wars": *New York Tribune*, January 1, 1917: "What we desire": *Chicago Tribune*, January 1, 1917.
490 "I won't go": Arthur Link, *Wilson: Campaigns for Progressivism and Peace, 1916–1917* (Princeton, N.J.: Princeton University Press, 1965), 234; **The quick response Berlin sent:** *New York Times*, December 27, 1916; "diplomacy in the open": *New York Evening Post*, December 27, 1916.
490 "'poisoned chalice' peace note": TR to J. St. Loe Strachey, January 1, 1917, in *The Letters of Theodore Roosevelt*, ed. Elting Morison, vol. 8, *The Days of Armageddon, 1914–1919* (Cambridge: Harvard University Press, 1954), 1139; "Such terms": *New York Herald*, January 12, 1917.
491 "They asked for everything": Bernstorff/Eddy telephone conversation, January 11, 1917, FrPP, box 39.
491 "business relations": *New York Herald*, January 30, 1917; "profoundly immoral": *New York Herald*, January 4, 1917.
491 "hard-line interests": David S.Patterson, *The Search for Negotiated Peace: Women's Activism and Citizen Diplomacy in World War I* (New York: Routledge, 2008), 303.
492 "The President could force": Norman Hapgood to EMH, December 30, 1916/January 4, 1917 in *PWW*, 40:497.
492 "conjectural journalism": George Creel, *Rebel at Large: Recollections of Fifty Crowded Years* (New York: G.P. Putnam's Sons, 1947), 234; "may be a real progressive": Harold Ickes to Matthew Hale, January 10, 1917, HIP, box 32.
493 "peace almost at any price": HD, January 2, 1917; "desire for peace is partially due": HD, November 20, 1916.
493 "both Wilson and House": J. von Bernstorff to German Foreign Office, December 29, 1916, in *PWW*, 40:364; "American mediation": Count Bernstorff, *My Three Years in America* (London: Skeffington & Son, 1920), 220.
493 "future security of the world" . . . "It is better to take": HD, January 3, 1917.
494 "his mind is a vacuum" . . . "There will be no war": HD, January 4, 1917; "yellow races": John Milton Cooper Jr., *Woodrow Wilson: A Biography* (New York: Alfred A. Knopf, 2009), 375.
494 "activities": HD, January 3, 1917; "Do you know the 'new way'": HD, March 3, 1917; "the little circle close": HD, January 12, 1917; "I feel very lonely": WW to EMH, January 24, 1917, in *PWW*, 41:4.
495 "The important thing": *Chicago Tribune*, January 6, 1917; "any kind of military service" . . . "an army or navy": *New York Sun*, January 7, 1917.
495–496 "evil genius": Louis Lochner to Lola M. Lloyd, March 6, 1917, LLP, reel 50; "hurried talking": Louis Lochner to Ferdinand Leipnik, January 23, 1917, LLP, reel 50; "troubled look": Lochner to

Members of the Ford Peace Commission, February 14, 1917, LLP, reel 50; "I don't think": Louis Lochner, *Henry Ford: America's Don Quixote* (New York: International Publishers, 1925), 206.

496 "I am afraid": Lillian Holt to JA, January 25, 1917, JAP, reel 10.

496 "war was brought on": HD, January 11, 1917; "willing to submit": EMH to WW, January 15, 1917, in *PWW*, 40:477; "If Bernstorff": EMH to WW, January 18, 1917, in *PWW*, 40:517.

497 "I am afraid": J. von Bernstorff to EMH, January 20, 1917, in *PWW*, 40:517.

497 "constant 'chatter'": *Washington Times*, January 22, 1917; "I enjoyed intensifying": Alice Roosevelt Longworth, *Crowded Hours: Reminiscences of Alice Roosevelt Longworth* (New York: Charles Scribner's Sons, 1933), 242.

497 "staccato, yet well-measured precision": *Washington Herald*, January 23, 1917; The President recounted: "Peace without Victory" speech, in *PWW*, 40:533-39.

498 "great state paper" . . . "thinks he is President": *New York Herald*, January 23, 1917.

498 "peace without conquest": Walter Hines Page to WW, January 20, 1917, in *PWW*, 40:532; "When the war between Spain": *New York Herald* quoting the *London Morning Post*, January 23, 1917.

498-499 "the most powerful expression": Ida Tarbell to JA, January 26, 1917, JAP, reel 10; "Isn't it fine": JA to Louis Lochner, January 23, 1917, JAP, reel 10; "'Justice Without Lynching'": *New York Sun*, January 26, 1917.

499 "this is the time": WW to EMH, January 24, 1917, in *PWW*, 41:3.

500 "We can get a better": J. von Bernstorff to Theobald von Bethmann Hollweg, January 27, 1917, in *Official German Documents Relating to the World War* (New York: Oxford University Press, 1923), 1:303; and *PWW*, 41:52; "think twice": January 29, 1917, entry in Walter Görlitz, ed., *The Kaiser and His Court: The Diaries, Note Books, and Letters of Admiral Georg Alexander von Müller, Chief of the Naval Cabinet, 1914-1918* (London: MacDonald, 1961), 235.

500 von Kemnitz resurrected a scheme: On the origins of the Zimmermann Telegram, see Thomas Boghardt, *The Zimmermann Telegram: Intelligence, Diplomacy, and America's Entry into World War I* (Annapolis. Md.: Naval Institute Press, 2012).

501-502 "I know it is": Lansing memo of February 4, 1917, in *PWW*, 41:119; "barred zones": *New York Herald*, March 1, 1917; "Certainty of War with Germany": Justus D. Doenecke, *Nothing Less than War: A New History of America's Entry into World War I* (Lexington: University Press of Kentucky, 2011), 249; "white civilization" . . . "unless he was convinced": Lansing memo of January 31, 1917, *PWW*, 41:120-21.

502 "sad and depressed": HD, February 1, 1917.

502 "looked haggard": Louis Lochner to JA, February 1, 1917, JAP, reel 10; "may change the whole world" . . . "If it can be done": "Interview with Pres. Wilson," February 1, 1917, LLP, reel 50.

503 "supercrisis": *Washington Evening Star*, February 4, 1917; "I look about": *New York Herald*, February 2, 1917; "if he escapes impeachment": *New York Herald*, February 1, 1917; "promptly assemble our fleet": Straus diary, February 2, 1917, Oscar Straus Papers, Library of Congress, box 24.

504 "for the interest": Lansing memo of February 4, 1917, in *PWW*, 41:123; "he didn't wish to see": Franklin Lane to George Lane, February 9, 1917, in Anne W. Lane and Louise Herrick Wall, eds., *The Letters of Franklin K. Lane, Personal and Political* (Boston: Houghton Mifflin, 1922), 234.

504 "final warning": *New York Sun*, February 3, 1917; "That depends on how": *New York Tribune*, February 3, 1917.

504-505 "we ought to fight" . . . "madmen of Europe": *New York Herald*, February 3, 1917; "beginning of a league of nations": JA to WW, February 3, 1917, JAP, reel 10.

505 "For the first time": *New York Herald*, February 4, 1917; "destroy American ships": "Address to a Joint Session of Congress," February 3, 1917, in *PWW*, 41:111; "He was almost modest": Terrell D. Webb, *Washington Wife: Journal of Ellen Maury Slayden from 1897-1919* (New York: Harper & Row, 1962), 291.

505 "show our virility": *Washington Evening Star*, February 3, 1917; "taken the right stand": JNH to George Greener, February 6, 1917, JNHP, box 3; "I believe in standing": *Chicago Tribune*, February 4, 1917; "show the President": *Chicago Examiner*, February 4, 1917.

506 "German sympathizers": *New York Herald*, February 4, 1917; "But between Germany": *New York Tribune*, February 5, 1917.

506 "It saddens me": HD, February 3, 1917.

506 "I don't care what": *Washington Herald*, February 4, 1917; "rank Social Democrat": *New York Tribune*, February 4, 1917.

507 "Sure thing": *New York Tribune*, February 15, 1917; "demented" young "crank": *New York Herald*, February 15, 1917; "It is quite possible": *New York Evening Post*, February 14, 1917; "Tell him" . . . "something pathetic": HD, February 15, 1917.

508 "war mad": Louis Lochner to JA and David S. Jordan, February 3, 1917, JAP, reel 10; "many . . . disturbed and bewildered": Harriet Thomas to JA, February 5, 1917, JAP, reel 10; "wisdom can devise": JA et al. to WW, February 6, 1917, JAP, reel 10.

508 "intolerant of all": Louis Lochner to Emily Balch, March 1, 1917, LLP, reel 50; "It can move quickly": *Washington Evening Star*, February 12, 1917.

508–509 "declares that we": *New York Evening Post*, February 8, 1917; "universal military training": *New York Tribune*, February 12, 1917.

509 "our best hope": *Washington Evening Star*, February 12, 1917; "makes for delay": JA to Rose D. Forbes, February 14, 1917, JAP, reel 10; "If it is worthwhile": *Chicago Examiner*, January 24, 1917.

509 "what would Germany": *Washington Times*, February 4, 1917; "could be secured" . . . "essential questions": *New York Tribune*, February 8, 1917; "impracticable": Lawrence Sherman to JA, February 13, 1917, JAP reel 10.

510 "throttle the greater evil": Paul Kellogg to JA, February 9, 1917, JAP reel 10; "A miserable crawl": *New York Herald*, February 9, 1917; "She is handsome": Webb, *Washington Wife*, 298; "I never said": *New York Tribune*, February 6, 1917; "hoped that the old": Louis Lochner to Ada M. Clark, February 8, 1917, LLP, reel 50.

510–511 "war weary": István Tisza to Rosika Schwimmer, January 11, 1917, RSP, box 85; "Living in a belligerent": Rosika Schwimmer to Mme. Kolb, February 15, 1917, RSP, box 85.

511 "long lines waiting to enlist": Ida Tarbell to EMH, February 8, 1917, in *PWW*, 41:216; "Why should I join": *Chicago Examiner*, February 8, 1917; "steel, oil and financial magnates": Ray Stannard Baker interview with Josephus Daniels, March 20, 1929, RSBP, reel 73.

511 "within thirty days": *New York Tribune*, February 13, 1917; "songs by German composers" . . . "Does patriotism": *New York Evening Post*, February 9, 1917.

512 "prize fight": *Baltimore Sun*, March 15, 1917.

512 "certain Americans": Robert Lansing to WW, February 12, 1917, in *PWW*, 41:203.

513 "for two years": EMH to WW, February 10, 1917, in *PWW*, 41:190.

513 "We are very well aware": Lillian Wald to WW, February 8, 1917, WWP, reel 320.

513–514 "If we are": Franklin Lane to George Lane, February 9, 1917, in Lane and Wall, eds., *Letters of Franklin K. Lane*, 235; "some historian": *New York Tribune*, February 9, 1917; "physically impossible": *New York Herald*, February 6, 1917; "double target" . . . "any great preparedness": Franklin Lane to George Lane, February 16, 1917, in Lane and Wall, eds., *Letters of Franklin K. Lane*, 236.

514 "entirely indifferent": *New York Tribune*, February 5, 1917.

514 "War or Peace": *Washington Evening Star*, February 12, 1917; "How many people": Fanny Garrison Villard to JA, February 15, 1917, JAP, reel 10.

515 "If we are": *Chicago Tribune*, February 19, 1917; "I think that the best way": WW to Charles Hamlin, February 15, 1917, in *PWW*, 41:233.

515 "American women": *Washington Evening Star*, February 7, 1917; "When the civil war": *Washington Evening Star*, February 20, 1917.

516 "We want bread!": *Washington Evening Star*, February 20, 1917; "worst scene that City Hall" . . . "raiding the cellars": *New York Evening Post*, February 20, 1917; "lead all the women": *New York Tribune*, February 22, 1917; "The Italian family": *New York Herald*, February 23, 1917.

516 German "frightfulness": *New York Herald*, February 7, 1917.

517 "feeling humiliated": Franklin Lane to George Lane, February 20, 1917, in Lane and Wall, eds., *Letters of Franklin K. Lane*, 238; "meant business": TR to Alexander Moore, February 13, 1917, TRP, reel 388; "he has the slightest feeling": TR to Hiram Johnson, February 17, 1917, in Morison, ed., *Letters of Theodore Roosevelt*, 8:1154; "hard on the horse": *New York Tribune*, February 20, 1917.

517–518 "sneak out of going to war": TR to H. C. Lodge, February 20, 1917 in Morison, ed., *Letters of Theodore Roosevelt*, 8:1156; "bull moose in the corner": Longworth, *Crowded Hours*, 245; "I am praying": TR to Mrs. Mary A. Ward, March 2, 1917, TRP, reel 388; "I think I could do": TR to William Allen White, February 17, 1917 in Morison, ed., *Letters of Theodore Roosevelt*, 8:1153; "Please, Teddy": *Philadelphia Inquirer*, February 12, 1917, quoting *Berlin Gazette*.

518 "The great burning question": Roy Cushman to JNH, February 17, 1917, JHNP, box 3; "I don't know": *New York Evening Post*, February 15, 1917; "I can't define it": *New York Evening Post*, February 27, 1917.

518 "the cause of humanity": *New York Tribune*, March 3, 1917.

519 "No present opponent": *New York Evening Post*, February 26, 1917; "large force abroad": Cecil Spring Rice to Foreign Office, February 23, 1917, FOP, FO 800/242.

519–520 "Are we going to put" . . . "armed neutrality": *Washington Evening Star*, February 26, 1917; "serious blunder": *New York Evening Post*, March 10, 1917; "not now contemplating": *Washington Evening Star*, February 26, 1917; "we want to be your reservoir": J. Allen Baker to Arthur Balfour, April 2, 1917 (quoting House's comments of February 23, 1917), FOP, FO 800/211.

520 "I call upon": *New York Evening Post*, February 28, 1917; "wretched bronchitis": JA to Marcet Haldeman-Julius, February 14, 1917, JAP, reel 10.

520–521 "Thank God": *New York Times*, February 12, 1917; "We know no one": Rose D. Forbes to JA, February 12, 1917, JAP, reel 10; "the highest patriotism": JA to WPP members, February 7, 1917, JAP, reel 10; "I hope the friends": *Washington Times*, February 28, 1917.

521–522 "German people" . . . "Your President": *Friends Intelligencer*, March 10, 1917; "**through a crack**" . . . "**contention that the people**" . . . "I found my mind": Jane Addams, *Peace and Bread in Time of War* (New York: Macmillan, 1922), 64–65; "**If you knew**": William Hull to Ray Stannard Baker, October 10, 1935, RSBP, reel 76.

523 "**stir up all the trouble**": EMH to WW, February 26, 1917, in *PWW*, 41:297.

523 "**important war story**" . . . "**act of war**": *New York Herald*, March 1, 1917.

523 "*consent on our part*" . . . "merely wanted to prompt": Boghardt, *Zimmermann Telegram*, 74; "most diabolical plot": *Cedar Rapids Evening Gazette*, March 1, 1917; "reveals a spirit": *Atlanta Constitution*, March 2, 1917.

523 "**What Germany attempts**": *New York Tribune*, March 2, 1917; "**This man**": John J. Leary Jr., *Talks with T.R.* (Boston: Houghton Mifflin, 1920), 328.

524 "**The idea of such**" . . . "**I cannot believe**": *New York Herald*, March 2, 1917; "**thrown up their hands**": *New York Evening Post*, March 6, 1917.

524–525 "**Somehow or other**": Boghardt, *Zimmermann Telegram*, 206; "**idiot**" Kemnitz . . . "**What rubbish**": Boghardt, *Zimmermann Telegram*, 195; "**democratic views**": Bernstorff, *My Three Years*, 346.

525 "**Every Senator**": *New York Tribune*, March 11, 1917.

526 "**a damaged and dishonest hoopskirt**": TR to William Allen White, December 18, 1916, WAWP, box C34; "**grandstand plays**": *New York Evening Post*, March 7, 1917; "**extraordinary and autocratic power**": *New York Evening Post*, March 27, 1917; "**short, energetic body**": Maud Wood Park, *Front Door Lobby* (Boston: Beacon Press, 1960), 25.

527–528 "**I'll not even shake hands**": Thomas Brahany diary, March 4, 1917, in *PWW*, 41:328; "**they'll crucify you**": Belle Case La Follette and Fola La Follette, *Robert M. La Follette, June 14, 1855–June 18, 1925* (New York: Macmillan, 1953), 1:625; "**little group of perverts**": La Follette and La Follette, *Robert M. La Follette*, 1: 629; "**any small group of Senators**": TR to John Richeson, March 21, 1917, in Joseph Bucklin Bishop, *Theodore Roosevelt and His Time Shown in His Own Letters* (New York: Charles Scribner's Sons, 1920), 2:422.

528 "**feeble and timid war**": TR to William Allen White, March 15, 1917, WAWP, box C38; **interchangeable "skunks"**: TR to Kermit Roosevelt, March 1, 1917, TRDL; TR to Hiram Johnson, February 17, 1917 in Morison, ed. *Letters of Theodore Roosevelt*, 8:1154; "**are anxious I should do**": Leonard Wood diary, March 4, 1917, LeWP, box 8.

528–529 "**too much armed**": *New York Tribune*, March 5, 1917; "**I'm not defending**" . . . "**Before the war**" . . . "**Some of us believe**": *New York Tribune*, March 18, 1917.

Chapter 17: The Final Battle

530 "**It seems to me**": David Starr Jordan to William Jennings Bryan, April 1, 1917, WJBP, box 31.

530–531 "**I never like**" . . . "**strike while the iron**": HD, March 4, 1917; "**group of eleven Senators**": *New York Times*, March 5, 1917.

531 "**twelve Iscariots**": Cecil Spring Rice to Foreign Office, March 9, 1917, FOP, FO 800/242; "**de facto war**": *New York Herald*, March 9, 1917.

531–532 "**We stand by**": *Washington Evening Star*, March 4, 1917; "**Will our people**": Terrell D. Webb, *Washington Wife: Journal of Ellen Maury Slayden from 1897–1919* (New York: Harper & Row, 1962), 294; "**The high wind**": *New York Evening Post*, March 5, 1917; "**we may even be drawn**": *New York Times*, March 6, 1917.

532–533 "**so much necessary legislation**": *Washington Herald*, March 10, 1917; "**administration circles**": *New York Herald*, March 10, 1917; "**would not declare war**": Blair Lee to William Jennings Bryan, February 29 [sic], 1917, WJBP, box 31.

533 "**War Sunday**": *New York Tribune*, March 12, 1917; "**I think our ministers**": WW to Joseph Tumulty, c. February 20, 1917, *PWW*, 41:257; "**the swiftest racehorse**": *New York Tribune*, March 12, 1917;.

533–534 "**unready and could do**": Leonard Wood diary, March 11, 1917, LeWP; "**general idiot cry**": TR to H. C. Lodge, March 13, 1917, in *The Letters of Theodore Roosevelt*, ed. Elting Morison, vol. 8, *The Days of Armageddon, 1914–1919* (Cambridge: Harvard University Press, 1954), 1162; "**The people who have**"; TR to H. C. Lodge, March 18, 1917, in Morison, ed., *Letters of Theodore Roosevelt*, 8:1163.

534 "**international idealism**": Emily Balch to WW, March 5, 1917, in *PWW*, 41:340; "**The President has changed**": *New York Evening Post*, March 16, 1917; "**Militarists**": *New York Tribune*, March 4, 1917; "**The discouraging thing**": Louis Lochner to Lola M. Lloyd, March 6, 1917, LLP, reel 50.

534–535 "**anarchists**": *New York Tribune*, March 2, 1917; "**pro-Germanism**": *New York Tribune*, March 13, 1917; "**preaching of disloyal doctrine**": *New York Herald*, March 6, 1917; "**certain eminent social workers**": *Boston Post*, March 2, 1917.

535–536 "**It is not sensible**": John Dewey to Amos Pinchot, March 30, 1917, APP, box 19; "**Nicholas has at last**": *New York Tribune*, March 17, 1917; "**Russia is wonderful**": TR to Frances Parsons, March 19, 1917, TRDL; "**due largely to your influence**": EMH to WW, March 17, 1917, in *PWW*, 41:423; "**The Russian Socialists**": Lola M. Lloyd to Louis Lochner, March 25, 1917, LLP, reel 50.

536 "trying to make my way": *New York Evening Post*, March 14, 1917; the word "scab": *Washington Evening Star*, March 13, 1917.

537 "If Wilson wants war": Reinhard R. Doerries, "Imperial Berlin and Washington: New Light on Germany's Foreign Policy and America's Entry into World War I," *Central European History* 11, no. 1 (1978): 48; "God sent me": *Washington Herald*, March 18, 1917; "bullet proof armor": *Washington Evening Star*, March 20, 1917.

538 "four-inch shell": *New York Tribune*, March 20, 1917.

538 "I felt that it would not": TR to H. C. Lodge, March 22, 1917, in Morison, ed., *Letters of Theodore Roosevelt*, 8:1166; "overt acts of war": *New York Tribune*, March 20, 1917; "raise a division": TR to Newton Baker, March 19, 1917, in Morison, ed., *Letters of Theodore Roosevelt*, 8:1164.

538 "go to war hard": *New York Sun*, March 21, 1917; "he will let you go": Merlo Pusey, *Charles Evans Hughes* (New York: Macmillan, 1951), 1:368; "Mr. Root and Mr. Hughes": *New York Evening Post*, March 23, 1917.

539 "make up for the failure": Russell Coles to TR, April 20, 1917, TRP, reel 229; "I am old": TR to Russell Coles, November 2, 1916, TRP, reel 386; "retired commander in chief": TR to Newton Baker, March 23, 1917, in Morison, ed., *Letters of Theodore Roosevelt*, 8:1166; "most extraordinary documents": WW to Newton Baker, March 27, 1917, in *PWW*, 41:478.

539–540 "would aid the Russian" . . . "out-and-out pacifists": Robert Lansing to EMH, March 19, 1917, in *PWW*, 41:429–30; "inertia": HD, March 19, 1917; "we can no longer": EMH to WW, March 19, 1917, in *PWW*, 41:429.

540 "forget there ever was": William Allen White, *Woodrow Wilson: The Man, His Times and His Task* (Boston: Houghton Mifflin, 1924), 355–56; "people believed he would not": HD, March 25, 1917; "God would hold him": *PWW*, 41:316.

541 "sentiment of America": David Starr Jordan to Jessie Jordan, March 20, 1917, DSJP, box 36; "must decide which": *New York Evening Post*, March 26, 1917; "We're at war": *New York Evening Post*, March 21, 1917.

541–542 "temporize with the German Government" . . . "suffused with tears" . . . "would force us to act": Lansing memo of March 20, 1917 meeting, in *PWW*, 41:441–43; "I do not care": Josephus Daniels diary, March 20, 1917, *PWW*, 41:445; "is not in a working mood": Thomas Brahany diary, March 21, 1917, in *PWW*, 41:449.

542 "every day of deliberation": William Jennings Bryan to JA, February 13, 1917, JAP, reel 10: "she has neglected": *Washington Evening Star*, April 2, 1917; "My hair isn't red": *New York Tribune*, February 25, 1917.

543 "I think I satisfied them": HD, March 25, 1917; "It's great fun": Louis Lochner to Alfred Kliefoth, March 26, 1917, LLP, reel 50.

543 "counter-demonstration": Louis Lochner to Lola M. Lloyd, March 29, 1917, LLP, reel 50; "Wall Street employees": David Starr Jordan to Jessie Jordan, March 25, 1917, DSJP, box 36; "H'ray for Teddy": *New York Times*, March 25, 1917; "our bloodthirsty ex-President": *New York Herald*, March 25, 1917; "ejected and beaten up": David Starr Jordan to Jessie Jordan, March 25, 1917; "Let us all pray": *New York Herald*, March 25, 1917; "A few arrests": *New York Herald*, March 25, 1917.

543–544 "You contemptible": Anonymous to Emergency Anti-War Committee, March 26, 1917, WPPP, reel 10; "used only during riots": *Washington Evening Star*, March 26, 1917; "inoffensive German employed": Josephus Daniels diary, March 30, 1917, in *PWW*, 41:506; "now in a hysterical condition": Isaac Sherwood to Amos Pinchot, March 24, 1917, APP, box 19.

544 "vigorous policy of protection": Amos Pinchot to WW, March 27, 1917, APP, box 19; "lost his nerve": David Starr Jordan to Jessie Jordan, March 25, 1917, DSJP, box 36.

544–545 "ask Congress" . . . "a coarser fiber": HD, March 27, 1917; "between the German people" . . . "neither of them could endure": HD, March 28, 1917.

545 "He jumped up": *New York Herald*, April 4, 1917; "big game of the sea": John J. Leary Jr., *Talks with T.R.* (Boston: Houghton Mifflin, 1920), 170; "It is a good sport": Leary, *Talks with T.R.*, 166.

545–546 "invade the Capital": Form letter by Lella Secor, March 27, 1917, WPPP, reel 11; "This pitifully small sum": *New York Herald*, March 29, 1917; "I don't want my boy": *New York Evening Post*, March 30, 1917; "Please let also": M. S. Shields to EPF, March 29, 1917, EPF Collected Records, 1914–1917, Swarthmore College Peace Collection; "We voted": R. Faria to EPF, March 30, 1917, EPF Collected Records, 1914–1917, Swarthmore College Peace Collection.

547 "even the prospect": David Starr Jordan to Jessie Jordan, March 30, 1917, DSJP, box 36; "it costs $50,000": *Chicago Tribune*, March 31, 1917; "why they had not enlisted": *Washington Evening Star*, March 29, 1917; "The pacifists are robbing us": *New York Herald*, March 30, 1917; "martyred patriot": *New York Evening World*, April 3, 1917.

548 "alleged males": *New York Herald*, March 30, 1917.

548 "I write with difficulty": HD, April 29, 1917; "Many here remain convinced": *New York Tribune*, March 31, 1917; "There are some who advocate": *Tampa Times*, April 2, 1917.

548–549 "THE NAVY NEEDS YOU": *New York Tribune*, March 29, 1917; "A young man": Webb, *Washington Wife*, 298; "peace pilgrims": *New York Sun*, April 1, 1917; "pilgrims of patriotism": *New York Evening Post*, March 31, 1917.

549 "Any one who is a pacifist" . . . "Any one that wants to go": *New York Herald*, April 3, 1917; "You are a damned liar" . . . "return the compliment": *Boston Globe*, April 3, 1917; "He just hauled": *New York Sun*, April 3, 1917; "a fist in pacifist": *New York Herald*, April 4, 1917.

550 "female emotionality": Alice Hamilton, *Exploring the Dangerous Trades: The Autobiography of Alice Hamilton, M.D.* (Boston: Little, Brown, 1943), 200; "cranks" of all kinds: *New York Tribune*, April 4, 1917; "Something I never": *Washington Times*, April 2, 1917.

550–551 "It would be interesting" . . . "signs of nervousness": HD, April 2, 1917.

551 "They have discriminated" . . . "ludicrous cartoons": *Washington Times*, April 2, 1917; "business men, professors": *New York Tribune*, April 2, 1917; "I have known": *Washington Times*, April 3, 1917.

553 "the voice of": *Des Moines Register*, April 3, 1917; "To my mind": Maud Wood Park, *Front Door Lobby* (Boston: Beacon Press, 1960), 74; "visibly nervous . . . his fingers": *New York Evening Post*, April 3, 1917; "a warfare against mankind": "Address to Joint Session of Congress," April 2, 1917, in *PWW*, 41:519–27; "cleared his throat twice sharply": *New York Tribune*, April 3, 1917.

554 "Mr. President, you have expressed": *New York Herald*, April 3, 1917; "visibly nervous and quite pale": Brahany diary, April 2, 1917, in *PWW*, 41:531; "My message to-day": Joseph Tumulty, *Woodrow Wilson as I Knew Him* (Garden City: Doubleday, Page, 1921), 256; "as families are prone": HD, April 2, 1917.

555 "several hundred young men" . . . "There is little hope": *Washington Evening Star*, April 3, 1917; "going into a reactionary war": *Washington Times*, April 3, 1917; "We want war!": *New York Herald*, April 3, 1917; "murderer" . . . "type of character": *New York Sun*, April 5, 1917; "wring their necks": *New York Tribune*, April 3, 1917; "stranger, believed to be German": *New York Sun*, April 3, 1917.

555–556 "Wilson has no true": Fannie Villard to May Wright Sewall, April 4, 1917, May Wright Sewall Papers, www.digitalindy.org, Indianapolis Public Library Digital Collections; "not very original cant": Elsie Charlton to Eleanor Karsten, April 1917, WPPP, reel 9; "Congress has the power": *New York Evening Post*, April 3, 1917.

556–557 "Tell him I'm all alone": *New York Herald*, April 4, 1917; "Tell the President that I'm prepared": *Chicago Examiner*, April 4, 1917; "a great State paper": *New York Herald*, April 4, 1917; "endorsement of what I have": TR to John Belford, April 16, 1917, TRP, reel 389; "raise a division": *New York Herald*, April 4, 1917; "three regiments of regulars": EMH to WW, March 30, 1917, in *PWW*, 41:502; "obsession that he is": John Sharp Williams to WW, April 4, 1917, WWPL; obligated to "consult him": *New York Tribune*, April 5, 1917.

558 "irreverently or disrespectfully": *Washington Times*, April 4, 1917; "Negro uprising": *New York Tribune*, April 4, 1917; "The only way": *New York Tribune*, April 5, 1917.

558 "Many years hence": *New York Evening Post*, April 5, 1917; "a war against all nations": La Follette's speech was reprinted as *Sen. Robert M. La Follette, Sr.'s Senate Speech against U.S. Entry into the World War* (Madison, Wisc.: Progressive Publishing, 1937).

559 "The War for Democracy": *Washington Post*, April 6, 1917; "I cannot tell you how glad": Eleanor Karsten to JA, April 5, 1917, JAP, reel 10; a TRAITORS sign: *Washington Post*, April 6, 1917; a "reward" for his treachery: *Washington Times*, April 6, 1917.

560 "You ask your friends": *Chicago Tribune*, April 6, 1917; "Why can we not": *New York Sun*, April 6, 1917.

560 "characteristic idioms": *Wilmington (Del.) Journal Every Evening*, April 6, 1917; "patriotism": *Congressional Record*, Vol. 55, Pt. 1, March 5–April 24, 1917, 338; "speechmaking festival": *New York Times*, April 6, 1917.

561 "I want to stand": *New York Times*, April 6, 1917; "sobbed, spasmodically": *New York Evening World*, April 6, 1917; "tears came": *Washington Times*, April 6, 1917; "This is too great" . . . "Mr. Kitchin's voice": *New York Tribune*, April 7, 1917; "To be sure": Leary, *Talks with T.R.*, 263–64; "paired" with another member: *Washington Evening Star*, April 6, 1917.

562 "bad sore throat": *New York Evening World*, April 7, 1917; "What's the use": *New York Tribune*, March 22, 1917.

562–563 "pathetic belief": Jane Addams, *Peace and Bread in Time of War* (New York: Macmillan, 1922), 62; "the only defeat": James Weber Linn, *Jane Addams: A Biography* (New York: D. Appleton-Century, 1935), 377; "It seemed to me quite obvious": Addams, *Peace and Bread*, 65.

563 "I hereby tender": William Jennings Bryan to WW, April 6, 1917, in *PWW*, 41:556; "I feel like a different man": JNH to George Greener, April 9, 1917; "glad, unquestionably glad": JNH to Roy Cushman, April 3, 1917, JNHP, box 3; "brigade or two": JNH to George Greener, April 9, 1917.

563–564 "big yellow banners" . . . "Glad to see you": *Washington Times*, April 10, 1917; "How are you": *New York Herald*, April 11, 1917; "awake to the need": TR to J. C. O'Laughlin, April 13, 1917, TRDL;

"promise not to come back": George Creel, *Rebel at Large: Recollections of Fifty Crowded Years* (New York: G.P. Putnam's Sons, 1947), 188.

564–564 "The President received me": *New York Evening World*, April 10, 1917; "If I say anything": *Washington Evening Star*, April 10, 1917; "charmed by his personality": Tumulty, *Woodrow Wilson*, 288; "if Mr. Wilson": Leary, *Talks with T.R.*, 99; "pep and ginger": *Washington Times*, April 11, 1917; "His words may mean": Leary, *Talks with T.R.*, 97.

Epilogue

566 "If diplomats think": Rosika Schwimmer to WW, October 3, 1914, RSP, box 46.

566 "most experienced leadership available": Newton Baker to TR, April 13, 1917, in *The Letters of Theodore Roosevelt*, ed. Elting Morison, vol. 8, *The Days of Armageddon, 1914–1919* (Cambridge: Harvard University Press, 1954), 1175; "Roosevelt provision": Gilbert Hitchcock to WW, May 18, 1917, WWP, reel 336.

567 "the privilege of telling you": For the Parker/Wilson conversation of May 17, 1917, see Parker memo, John Parker Papers, box 4, University of Louisiana at Lafayette.

568 "It would be very agreeable": *New York Sun*, May 19, 1917; "my conclusions were based": WW to TR, May 19, 1917, TRP, reel 234; "blundering in Europe": Gilbert Hitchcock to WW, May 18, 1917, WWP, reel 336.

568–569 "entrust the lives": Ray Stannard Baker interview with Newton Baker, April 6, 1928, RSBP, box 71; "in some minor capacity": Newton Baker to Walter McCaleb, February 28, 1931, Walter McCaleb Papers, box 6, Syracuse University; "He is exceedingly base": TR to William A. White, May 28, 1917, in Morison, ed., *Letters of Theodore Roosevelt*, 8:1199; "The President has insisted": TR to Gifford Pinchot, May 26, 1917, TRDL.

569 "We don't like it": *New York Tribune*, June 17, 1917; "What I am opposed": *New York Tribune*, November 13, 1917.

570 "Patriotism and Pacifists": *City Club Bulletin*, June 18, 1917, 184–90; "pro-German twaddle": undated (c. June 1917) *Cleveland News* clipping, JAP, reel 10; "sentimental mush": *Cleveland Plain Dealer*, June 15, 1917, JAP, reel 64; "seditious balderdash": *St. Paul Pioneer Press*, June 12, 1917, JAP, reel 10; "furnish abundant proof": F. E. Morton to JA, June 12, 1917, JAP, reel 10.

570–571 "During war": Addams, *Peace and Bread*, 111; "that woman": Tarbell, *All in the Day's Work*, 334; "befouled": Addams, *Peace and Bread*, 128; "together in a surging sea": JA to Helena Dudley, April 19, 1917, JAP, reel 10; "for freedom of the world": E. G. Evans to Mrs. Raymond Unwin, September 2, 1917, WPP, reel 11; "Miss Addams I think": "Jane Addams notes," ITD.

571 "huge war factory": *Chattanooga News*, May 27, 1918.

572 "We are like monks": *Boston Post*, November 3, 1918.

572–573 "I am perfectly delighted": *Boston Globe*, July 11, 1918; "greatest struggle of the century": TR to Kermit Roosevelt, May 26, 1917, TRDL; "luring colored men": *New York Sun*, July 7, 1917; "*creature*" . . . "didn't go over": *New York Tribune*, November 2, 1917.

573 "ask to do a big job": TR to A. P. Gardner, June 6, 1917, Theodore Roosevelt correspondence and compositions, Houghton Library; "disagreeable or useless": TR to Eleanor Butler Roosevelt, September 17, 1917, Theodore Roosevelt Jr. Papers, box 8, Library of Congress; "We would have": TR to Theodore Roosevelt Jr., January 6, 1918, in TR Jr. Papers, box 8; "one response possible": *New York Tribune*, April 7, 1918.

573 "I feel like I'm a hundred": Frederick S. Wood, *Roosevelt as We Knew Him; The Personal Recollections of One Hundred and Fifty of His Friends and Associates* (Philadelphia: John C. Winston, 1927), 424; "would put in jail": Arthur Brisbane to WW, December 18, 1917, WWP, reel 336; "There is no use": TR to Edith Wharton, August 15, 1918, in Joseph Bucklin Bishop, *Theodore Roosevelt and His Time Shown in His Own Letters* (New York: Charles Scribner's Sons, 1920), 2:455.

574 "Our military situation": Martin Gilbert, *The First World War: A Complete History* (New York: Henry Holt, 1994), 451–52; "deliver the free peoples": Patrick Devlin, *Too Proud to Fight: Woodrow Wilson's Neutrality* (New York: Oxford University Press, 1975), 684; "open diplomacy": Charles E. Neu, *Colonel House: A Biography of Woodrow Wilson's Silent Partner* (New York: Oxford University Press, 2015), 332–33; "impartial adjustment" . . . "An evident principle": *New York Times*, January 9, 1918.

575 "mischievous" Fourteen Points . . . "Let us clearly show": *Kansas City Times*, October 25, 1918; "if we treat it": TR to Mark Sullivan, November 8, 1918, Mark Sullivan Papers, box 1, Library of Congress.

575 "blood pressure and arteries": *New York Tribune*, November 13, 1918; "We have not suffered": *New York Tribune*, December 4, 1918.

576 "stupid": Neu, *Colonel House*, 362; "there is no room big enough": John Milton Cooper Jr., *Woodrow Wilson: A Biography* (New York: Alfred A. Knopf, 2009), 457.

576 embolism: *New York Tribune*, January 9, 1919; "outburst of acrid detestation": David Lloyd George, *The Truth about the Peace Treaties* (London: Victor Gollancz, 1938), 1:232; "he did not consider": HD, February 16, 1919.

577 "external aggression": *New York Sun*, February 15, 1919; "When the President is away": Neu, *Colonel House*, 402; "on my own initiative": Cooper, *Woodrow Wilson*, 485.

578 "I hope most sincerely": WW to JA, May 16, 1919, JAP, reel 12.

578 "healing peace": Cooper, *Woodrow Wilson*, 452; "old nationalism": *Washington Evening Star*, August 24, 1919; "accepting even a quarter-loaf": Alice Hamilton, *Exploring the Dangerous Trades: The Autobiography of Alice Hamilton, M.D.* (Boston: Little, Brown, 1943), 235; "If we don't get": *Boston Globe*, March 23, 1919.

578–579 "For the moment" . . . "conciliatory": Neu, *Colonel House*, 419, 422.

579–580 "territorial integrity": *New York Times*, March 1, 1919; "an agreement among": *Addresses of President Wilson: Addresses Delivered by President Wilson on His Western Tour September 4 to September 25, 1919* (Washington, D.C.: GPO, 1919), 269; "There is one thing": *Addresses Delivered by President Wilson on His Western Tour*, 370.

580 "I just feel": Diary of Cary Grayson, September 26, 1919, WWPL; "a curious drag": Cooper, *Woodrow Wilson*, 530.

581 "I once thought" . . . "I hope no more": Neu, *Colonel House*, 616.

581 "This one is genuinely fond": Neu, *Colonel House*, 482.

582 "a little more like": *Des Moines Register*, May 28, 1950.

582–583 "others of her ilk": H. A. Jung to J. E. Hoover, May 5, 1926, in Jane Addams FOIA file, www.vault.fbi.gov; "most dangerous woman": *Chicago Tribune*, May 26, 1926.

583 "German spy and a communist": *St. Louis Post-Dispatch*, June 29, 1928; "I am an uncompromising": *Brooklyn Eagle*, June 27, 1929; "I'm a woman without": *Baltimore Evening Sun*, May 29, 1929; "Al Capone is all right": *Dubois (Penn.) Morning Courier*, June 4, 1929.

584 "greatest living women": *St. Louis Post-Dispatch*, March 3, 1931; "For years I've been asking": *Chicago Tribune*, April 17, 1932; "We of course": JA to Mark Sullivan, September 2, 1933, JAP, reel 25; "became the whole world's friend": *San Francisco Examiner*, May 22, 1935.

584–585 "I am not sure": Charles Seymour, *Intimate Papers of Colonel House* (Boston: Houghton Mifflin, 1926), 2:231; "Without American assistance": *Foreign Affairs*, March 15, 1924; "a certain equilibrium": *San Francisco Examiner*, March 4, 1923.

INDEX

Photos and illustrations are represented in *italics*